MASTERPLOTS II

SHORT STORY SERIES
REVISED EDITION

MASTERPLOTS II

SHORT STORY SERIES
REVISED EDITION

Volume 7
Sho–Two

Editor, Revised Edition
CHARLES MAY
California State University, Long Beach

Editor, First Edition
FRANK N. MAGILL

SALEM PRESS
Pasadena, California   Hackensack, New Jersey

Editor in Chief: Dawn P. Dawson

Editorial Director: Christina J. Moose   *Assistant Editor:* Andrea E. Miller
Project Editor: R. Kent Rasmussen   *Research Supervisor:* Jeffry Jensen
Production Editor: Cynthia Beres   *Acquisitions Editor:* Mark Rehn
Copy Editor: Rowena Wildin   *Layout:* Eddie Murillo

Some of the essays in this work originally appeared in *Masterplots II, Short Story Series*, edited by Frank N. Magill (Pasadena, Calif.: Salem Press, Inc., 1986), and in *Masterplots II, Short Story Series Supplement*, edited by Frank N. Magill and Charles E. May (Pasadena, Calif.: Salem Press, Inc., 1996).

∞ The paper used in these volumes conforms to the American National Standard for Permanence of Paper for Printed Library Materials, Z39.48-1992 (R1997).

Library of Congress Cataloging-in-Publication Data
Masterplots II : Short story series / editor Charles May. — Rev. ed.
    p.   cm.
Includes bibliographical references and index.
ISBN 1-58765-140-8 (set : alk. paper) — ISBN 1-58765-147-5 (vol. 7 : alk. paper) —
    1. Fiction—19th century—Stories, plots, etc. 2. Fiction—19th century—History and criticism. 3. Fiction—20th century—Stories, plots, etc. 4. Fiction—20th century—History and criticism. 5. Short story. I. Title: Masterplots 2. II. Title: Masterplots two. III. May, Charles E. (Charles Edward), 1941-
PN3326 .M27 2004
809.3′1—dc22

2003018256

First Printing

TABLE OF CONTENTS

TABLE OF CONTENTS

TABLE OF CONTENTS

MASTERPLOTS II

SHORT STORY SERIES
REVISED EDITION

A SHOWER OF GOLD

Author: Donald Barthelme (1931-1989)
Type of plot: Antistory
Time of plot: The 1960's
Locale: New York City
First published: 1962

Principal characters:
  PETERSON, a sculptor
  MISS ARBOR, a television game-show employee
  JEAN-CLAUDE, the dealer for Peterson's sculptures
  KITCHEN, Peterson's barber and a self-styled philosopher
  THE PRESIDENT, Peterson's buddy

The Story

Desperate for cash, Peterson, a self-declared minor artist whose welded sculptures are not selling, signs on as a contestant for the television game show *Who Am I?* The title of the program is apt, for its producers purport to entertain their audience with probes into the futility, alienation, anonymity, and despair of modern life. Interviewing with Miss Arbor to become a *Who Am I?* contestant, Peterson counters her dedication to absurdity with his own doubts that absurdity even exists. When Miss Arbor asks if he encounters his own existence as gratuitous, he replies that he has an enlarged liver. This exchange confirms Peterson's dilemma: In Miss Arbor's words, Peterson may not be interested in absurdity, but absurdity is interested in Peterson.

As if in punishment for his disbelief, absurd things begin to happen. Peterson visits the gallery where he has consigned his sculptures for sale. His dealer, Jean-Claude, tries to convince him that his works would sell better if they were cut into smaller pieces. Peterson refuses, and the source of his swollen liver is identified as the rage and hatred he feels when he sees that not one of his works is displayed.

Peterson returns to his loft, drinks beer (apparently a second source of his liver complaint), and ponders money and the President. He is running out of money to buy beer for himself and milk for his kitten. Even worse, he feels he may be letting his buddy, the President, down by selling himself to television.

He begins to weld a new sculpture titled *Season's Greetings* from three old auto radiators and a discarded telephone switchboard. Suddenly, the door bursts open and the President rushes in, swinging a sixteen-pound sledge hammer. He sets to work on *Season's Greetings*, breaking it in half. Peterson protests, dejected that his friend, the President, would act against him in such a way. For his trouble, he is bitten on the neck by a Secret Service agent. The President then says, "Your liver is diseased. That's a good sign. You're making progress. You're thinking."

Peterson later discusses his disillusionment with Kitchen, his barber. Kitchen responds with a quote from Blaise Pascal: "The natural misfortune of our mortal and feeble condition is so wretched that when we consider it closely, nothing can console us." Kitchen then warns that *Who Am I?* really does a job on its contestants.

That night, a tall, foreign-looking man armed with a switchblade arrives at Peterson's loft and identifies himself as a cat-piano player. He describes the instrument as a keyboard of eight cats—the octave—encased in a cabinet so that only the cats' heads, tails, and paws protrude. Pulling tails and pressing paws produces various notes from the cats. Peterson's kitten weeps, and the hideous music begins.

The next day, Sherry, Ann, and Louise, three California girls in blue jeans and heavy sweaters, appear at Peterson's loft. They move in over Peterson's protests, and repeat Kitchen's depressing quote from Pascal.

Peterson views all these absurdities as punishment for even thinking about going on *Who Am I?* and begs Miss Arbor to replace him, to no avail. On the program, two other contestants answer questions about their lives and are rebuked by the audience when a polygraph reveals them to be liars and fools. Peterson, unwilling to accept humiliation at the hands of the media, mounts an offensive as his best defense: "I was wrong, Peterson thought, the world is absurd. The absurdity is punishing me for not believing in it. I affirm the absurdity. On the other hand, absurdity is itself absurd." He then speaks to the cameras, adding to the list of absurdities that have nipped at his heels in recent days. Then he asserts: "In this kind of world, absurd if you will, possibilities nevertheless proliferate and escalate around us and there are opportunities for beginning again. . . . My mother was a royal virgin and my father a shower of gold." His declares that his youth was noble and rich, and that such nobility may be recaptured, both by himself and by his viewers, if only they will turn off their television sets, cash in their life insurance policies, and indulge in mindless optimism.

Themes and Meanings

In all of Donald Barthelme's work, the objects of day-to-day existence are charged with meaning. In "A Shower of Gold," Peterson's life is trivialized by television. Peterson attempts to defend himself against the despair of modern life by donning the armor of disbelief in absurdity, only to provoke a frontal attack from an incredibly bizarre series of absurdities—from the President who wields a sledge hammer to the violent stranger who makes music from the anguish of cats.

Peterson, who sees himself as a minor artist both in his sculpture and in his life, embraces his inferior status, but at the same time believes that better things are possible for himself and his television audience. In affirming descent from royalty and the gods, he lays claim to an inheritance of dignity and self-worth that lies waiting if only modern people will acknowledge the absurd and, in so doing, escape its tyranny.

In many of his works, Barthelme blows the whistle on the age of unreason by immersing his readers in what he calls "dreck," the ocean of trivial, pointless things that trap modern people in a sea of psychological emptiness. When Barthelme shows Peterson welding radiators and switchboard together into art, he depicts perhaps humanity's noblest aspiration: to build order out of chaos, to chisel beauty out of the stone of ugliness, to recast the trivial into the consequential.

Peterson is Barthelme's Everyman, so buried under the sensory overload of modern living that be cannot determine where his own insanity ends and the world's insanity begins. In Peterson's world, everything is equally important, so everything is equally trivial. Peterson longs for direction and some sense of priorities. He finds hope only in the reassurance of his heritage, those better times to which all people might return if they would but eschew television and the isolation it spawns. "How can you be alienated without first having been connected?" Peterson asks, as Barthelme asks in "A Shower of Gold."

Style and Technique

Critic Marvin Mudrick has called Barthelme a "comedian turned thinker," and never is Barthelme's cutting humor more sharply focused than when aimed at the weight of intellectual baggage people carry around with them. Consider this exchange:

> "What do you have strong opinions about?" Miss Arbor asked. . . . "I believe," Peterson said, "that the learning ability of mice can be lowered or increased by regulating the amount of serotonin in the brain. I believe that schizophrenics have a high incidence of unusual fingerprints, including lines that make almost complete circles. I believe that the dreamer watches his dream in sleep, by moving his eyes." "That's very interesting!" Miss Arbor cried. "It's all in the *World Almanac*," Peterson replied.

On the more serious side, Barthelme jams into this story all the trash modern life has to offer, from the raw materials of Peterson's sculptures to the bizarre feats of athletic prowess exhibited by the contestants on *Who Am I?* In a world in which presidents show up on one's doorstep bent on destruction and men torture animals in the name of art, where can hope possibly hide?

Barthelme, one the twentieth century's finest experimental writers, weaves humor, satire, and symbolism together into a verbal collage in "A Shower of Gold." He arranges objects, persons, and events in a surreal fashion reminiscent of the flexible clocks and disembodied eyes draped about the barren landscape of a Salvador Dali painting. A gamesman with language, Barthelme believes that words are never accurate mirrors to reflect experience. However, as distorting as they may be of life's true image, he also believes that words are the only tools at hand to reveal and repulse the cultural and personal annihilation threatened by the banality of modern technology, communication, and social order. Therein lies the poignancy of Peterson's impassioned plea to his television audience and of Barthelme's almost editorial closing comment: "Peterson went on and on and although he was, in a sense, lying, in a sense he was not."

Faith Hickman Brynie

SHOWER OF GOLD

Author: Eudora Welty (1909-2001)
Type of plot: Realism
Time of plot: The early twentieth century
Locale: Morgana, Mississippi
First published: 1948

>   *Principal characters:*
>   MRS. FATE RAINEY, "Miss Katie", the narrator
>   SNOWDIE MCLAIN, the wife of King McLain
>   KING MCLAIN, a traveling man

The Story

Mrs. Fate Rainey is talking to an implied listener, a visiting stranger in Morgana, Mississippi. After Snowdie McLain comes for her butter and leaves, Mrs. Rainey begins to tell Snowdie's unusual story. It is the story of how badly King McLain treats his wife and how well she takes it, a private story, though everyone knows it. "But," Mrs. Rainey says, "I could almost bring myself to talk about it—to a passer-by, that will never see her again, or me either." Mrs. Rainey then relates several astonishing incidents from Snowdie's married life.

First, she explains the inexplicable marriage between King McLain, the most desirable man in the area, notorious for the number of children he is supposed to have fathered, and Snowdie Hudson, a teacher and the albino daughter of a respectable family. In Mrs. Rainey's opinion, King has wanted to shock the community, to keep it off balance.

This desire also accounts for King's staying away from Snowdie for long periods. Though he works as a traveling salesperson, he is gone too often and too long. The next astonishing incident occurred after his longest absence to that date. He sent Snowdie a note asking to meet her in Morgan's Woods. Though it is quite difficult to construct an accurate chronology from Mrs. Rainey's account, it appears that Snowdie's twin sons were conceived under the tree where she met King, and that King departed immediately afterward, leaving his hat on the bank of the Big Black River to make it appear that he had drowned. However, it may be that he impregnated Snowdie and left his hat on the river bank at a later date.

Mrs. Rainey's characterization of the town's reactions to these strange events is amusing. It ranges from a kind of wondering, almost admiring acceptance of the inevitable in King's behavior, on the one hand, to a kind of outraged sympathy for poor Snowdie, on the other. Though the women of Morgana should think King a scoundrel, they find him irresistibly attractive. Though they want to pity Snowdie, she seems irrepressibly happy. When Snowdie announces her pregnancy to Mrs. Rainey, she is radiant: "She looked like more than only the news had come over her. It was like a shower of something had struck her, like she'd been caught out in something bright." Snowdie seems to find joy in her life despite King's supposed death. King continues to fascinate the town. No one seems really to believe that he is dead.

The story's second part centers on the most recent astonishing event, the apparent return of King to Morgana on Halloween, when his sons are about eight years old. No one sees his visit except an ancient black man, Plez, whose testimony is impeccable, and King's two sons, who confront him on the front steps of his house, wearing outlandish costumes and roller skates. Plez's account of the antic meeting suggests that it is a sort of exorcism, and the boys report that they have frightened off a "booger." Though no one in town will tell Snowdie the full account, all know it. Mrs. Rainey knows that Snowdie believes that King came that day, and she believes that Snowdie holds it against her that she was there at the time, somehow preventing the desired meeting.

Mrs. Rainey finishes her narration, regretting that her friendship with Snowdie has cooled since that day, and reflecting, "With men like King, your thoughts are bottomless. . . . But I bet my little Jersey calf King tarried long enough to get him a child somewhere." Finally, she expresses amazement at her ability to say such things.

Themes and Meanings

"Shower of Gold" opens *The Golden Apples* (1949), a collection of stories that has much of the unity of a novel. It can be argued that the collection has a kind of lyrical form. Eudora Welty describes the pervading impulse of the collection when she describes her motive for writing as a lyrical impulse "to praise, to love, to call up, to prophesy." Some of the meanings of "Shower of Gold" emerge from examining the allusions to myths.

The title alludes to the story of Zeus's intercourse with Danae, mother of Perseus. According to Ovid, Perseus was "conceived in joy beneath a shower of gold." Snowdie is similar to Danae, whose father did not want her to bear children, in that the people of Morgana see her as fated to remain single because she is an albino. King is like Zeus in his reputation for fornication and, later, for adultery. That their children are twins suggests an allusion to the union of Zeus with Leda, which produced two pairs of twins. By associating King with Zeus and Snowdie with at least two of Zeus's mortal lovers, Welty sets up an opposition that gives meaning to the story and that is elaborated in the other stories of *The Golden Apples*.

To Mrs. Rainey, one of the mysteries of the McLain marriage is that Snowdie is quite happy to be abandoned with only her children. During King's absence, she lives contentedly, "taking joy in her fresh untracked rooms and that dark, quiet, real quiet hall that runs through her house." This happiness arises from the opposition between Snowdie and King. This opposition may be described with the terms "Apollonian" and "Dionysian" as Friedrich Nietzsche uses them in *Die Geburt der Tragödie aus dem Geiste der Musik* (1872; *The Birth of Tragedy out of the Spirit of Music*, 1909).

Snowdie is Apollonian, preferring a quiet, orderly, and stable life. She is willing and happy, on the whole, to live her life in the narrow, intensely rule-governed town of

Morgana, where public opinion rigidly enforces social and sexual morality. King is Dionysian, a wanderer of the fields and of the world, lawless, promiscuous, and fascinating. His principle of being seems to require that he flout rules and upset categories. Snowdie's happiness is a product of her marriage to this wild man. Without his unpredictable returns, the sexual pleasure he provides, and the children he fathers, Snowdie's life would be unbearable, too orderly and fixed. Because of his wildness, she is virtually immune to the oppressive pity of Morgana. The McLain marriage is filled with creative and fulfilling tension, a source of renewal that prevents stagnation.

This pattern of necessary opposition is central to *The Golden Apples*. Characters in the other stories suffer because of imbalances between these opposing forces and, in various ways, seek out the kind of balance that will make their lives seem meaningful and complete. Though the opposition in this story is between a man and a woman, parallel oppositions in other stories take multiple forms, between friends of the same sex, within individual characters, and between Dionysian women and Apollonian men. "Shower of Gold" may be seen to introduce the volume by presenting an example of a balanced opposition against that the central conflicts of the following stories may be judged.

Style and Technique

One of the most interesting aspects of technique in this story is Welty's use of first-person narration. Mrs. Rainey draws the reader directly into the story, requiring that one imagine oneself a stranger passing through town and, somehow, finding oneself in Mrs. Rainey's dairy. Like many of Welty's first-person narrators, Mrs. Rainey is not very careful to remember her listener's ignorance of town affairs. As a consequence, Mr. Rainey repeatedly runs ahead of her story and must go back to fill in details. "Shower of Gold," like "Why I Live at the P.O." and "Petrified Man," requires the reader to make careful and sometimes complex inferences in order to follow the narration successfully. Finally, however, all the pieces are given, even if their order seems idiosyncratic. Welty is a master of this sort of narration, which gives so convincing an illusion of hearing the actual voice of a speaking character. Reading this story is at first like plunging into an alien world, but as the reader rereads and contemplates the narration, that world becomes increasingly familiar, convincing, and rich.

Another effect of this mode of narration is humorous irony. Mrs. Rainey, like Snowdie and most of Morgana, does not understand the story she tells. She tells it precisely because it is beyond her how this marriage can continue to satisfy both parties. She responds to the attractiveness of King and Snowdie, perceives the balance that they achieve, yet cannot understand how it works, because it so clearly offends conventional morality. Mrs. Rainey's perpetual amazement at the McLain marriage provokes laughter and delight.

Terry Heller

A SICK CALL

Author: Morley Callaghan (1903-1990)
Type of plot: Domestic realism
Time of plot: 1932
Locale: An unspecified city in North America
First published: 1932

> *Principal characters:*
> FATHER MACDOWELL, a kind old priest
> ELSA WILLIAMS, a sick parishioner
> JOHN WILLIAMS, her husband
> JANE STANHOPE, Elsa's sister

The Story

Father Macdowell is an old, slightly deaf priest who always has "to hear more confessions than any other priest at the cathedral." His vast tolerance and slight deafness seem to account for his popularity as a confessor, yet his massive size hints at another dimension to his character: He is gentle, but he is also formidable in the exercise of his priestly office.

One day, after hearing confessions for many hours, he is reading in the rectory when the house girl informs him that a woman is waiting to see him about a sick call. The tired, old priest asks hesitantly if he was specifically requested—he was. So he goes to the waiting room.

Miss Jane Stanhope, a fine-looking young woman, is there crying. She explains that her sister Elsa is seriously ill, perhaps dying, and wishes to received the Sacrament of Extreme Unction. In the Roman Catholic Church, this sacrament is administered to those in danger of death and involves the priest's anointing of the sick person with oil blessed by the bishop. Father Macdowell replies that he hopes the situation is not so critical as to call for the last rites of the Church and offers to go with her and hear Elsa's confession. Just before they set out from the rectory, Jane reveals the complication that explains why she was particular about seeing him and no other priest. Her sister's husband, John Williams, is not a Catholic; the couple was married outside the Catholic Church two years ago; John is against religion in general; and the girl's family, except for Jane, has ostracized them. Father Macdowell assures her that all will be well, and they set off.

During the short walk, Jane offers additional information about the situation. The two young people have been exceptionally happy together. Nevertheless, Jane has just come from Elsa, who desperately wants to see a priest but fears that her husband will find out that she asked for one; just before Jane left for the rectory, John threatened violence if a priest were brought in. Father Macdowell radiates confidence and warmth, and proceeds on his mission.

When they knock on the door, John opens it and is fiercely indignant at the sight of a priest with his sister-in-law. He rebukes her for bringing him and stands obviously poised in expectation of a counterattack from the massive old man. Father Macdowell smiles serenely at him, nods his head, complains of the disadvantages of his deafness, and slides by the astonished young man into the hallway.

As Father Macdowell starts down the hall, he asks John to speak louder so that he can hear him. John stops him again and tries to make it clear that he is not wanted there. John still is expecting, even longing for, a direct confrontation, partly to relieve his pent-up anger and pain. However, Father Macdowell once again disarms his rage with a gentle request to see the sick girl. Without waiting for a reply, he sets off down the hall, looking for her. Now John grabs his arm and restrains him physically. Once again, Father Macdowell refuses to meet anger with anger. He tells John that he is very tired and would merely like to sit a moment with the girl and rest. John hesitates to deny so modest a request from such a poignant figure; while he fumbles for a reply, Father Macdowell finds the girl's room. John comes in after him.

Elsa is lying in bed. She avoids making eye contact with her husband and barely speaks to the priest. The little she does say, however, makes it clear that she desires the priest's blessing but fears it because it means expressing sorrow for the sin of marrying outside the Church. In other words, she must express sorrow for placing human affection for John before religious duty.

The conflict of wills between Father Macdowell and John goes on as before, but this time John seems in control. He absolutely refuses to leave the room so that the priest can hear his wife's confession. She weeps, seems resigned to the situation, and asks merely for the priest to pray for her. Father Macdowell, too, seems resigned to the situation. He kneels and prays silently for the girl's recovery. While he prays, he comes to realize that John is even more afraid of losing his wife to the Church than to death. He also realizes that Elsa was willing to give up everything—friends, family, religion—to marry John. He has a glimpse here of their conjugal love and is surprised by its intensity.

Father Macdowell tricks John into leaving the room briefly to get him a drink of water, and in the interlude he hurriedly hears Elsa's confession. John returns just as the priest is giving his blessing at the end. He is stunned to find that his wife needed something beyond his love, protection, and understanding.

Father Macdowell and Jane leave the house. For a moment, he is exultant that he rescued the soul of a girl in such peril. Then he feels some slight qualms about his pious duplicity in dealing with John. Finally, he wonders if he came between John and Elsa in any way: He marvels at the beauty of their staunch love for each other, tries to dismiss this beauty as "pagan," but ends by feeling "inexpressibly sad."

Themes and Meanings

The story provides a convincing dramatization of the moral complexity of life, even for someone as saintly as Father Macdowell. As an elderly priest who is well acquainted with the stratagems by which people seek to excuse wrongdoing, Father

Macdowell would certainly agree with the maxim that the ends do not justify the means. Hence, it is ironic, if somewhat comic, that the priest is forced into a mild deception in order to carry out his mission of mercy.

Thematically more interesting is the story's contrast between priestly and conjugal love. In Father Macdowell's scale of values, love of God is preeminent. Although he does not overlook or despise the temporal world, his eyes are fixed on eternity. There is something both wonderful and frightening about this single-mindedness. He is a kind and tolerant priest. However, he allows nothing to stand in his way when it comes to the dictates of his religion.

Contrasted with his love for God is the love of John and Elsa for each other. There is something both wonderful and frightening about this love as well. It has the power to transform and enrich human life. They, however, have made gods of each other, and this exclusive devotion seems destined for tragedy, given human frailty and limitations. Thus, there is considerable insight into complex human emotions in this story, which at first glance might appear to be no more than an anecdote about an ordinary incident in a priest's life.

Style and Technique

The story is written in Morley Callaghan's usual reportorial style, with succinct character sketches and highly selective physical details, providing the necessary context for dialogue that serves to propel the narrative forward. The third-person narration is coyly noncommittal about the old priest's thoughts and feelings until the very end of the story. Nothing "seemed" to shock Father Macdowell; he walked "as if" his feet hurt; he "didn't seem to hear"; he sighed "as if" he were tired. The prose style is evasive, in a sense, and prepares the reader to accept Father Macdowell as both a sincere priest and as a consummate actor who can adapt himself to different situations.

Callaghan's muted style gives the effect of looking through the narrative directly into unmediated reality. Part of the reason for Callaghan's success in conveying a sense of reality or authenticity in his writing is that he gets the details right when he describes a particular occupation or activity. Father Macdowell is a completely convincing portrait of an old priest, and one of the more memorable clerics in literature.

Michael J. Larsen

THE SICK CHILD

Author: Colette (Sidonie-Gabrielle Colette, 1873-1954)
Type of plot: Psychological
Time of plot: Unspecified
Locale: Paris
First published: "L'Enfant malade," 1942 (English translation, 1950)

Principal characters:
JEAN, a ten-year-old boy stricken with poliomyelitis
MADAME MAMMA, his mother

The Story

The sick child of the title is ten-year-old Jean. His legs are semiparalyzed, and he is extremely weak and emaciated, but pallor has given him an ethereal beauty. From the beginning of the story, the reader is led to expect that he will die. The description of the sickroom suggests a prosperous and cultured background.

The first part of the story establishes a delicate relationship between the sick child and his widowed mother, whom he calls "Madame Mamma." He tries to conceal his pain from her; she tries to conceal her anxiety from him. They both know that they are deceiving each other in their determination to protect each other from the truth.

There is another and more compelling reason—which becomes the central part of the narrative—for Jean to keep his mother distanced from his real thoughts. He is conserving his daytime energy so that at night he can indulge in fantastic journeys of the imagination, which have become the reality of his sickbed existence. To conceal this reality from his mother, he has adopted a slightly mocking approach toward her, which gives him some power over her. His long-drawn-out illness has made him hyperreactive to sensations, with all the senses intermingled: He can hear smells, taste sounds, smell textures. He has become intensely involved with words and uses a secret vocabulary to describe the people and the everyday things around him.

His nighttime journeys are often sparked by his power to animate the everyday objects or sensations within his bedroom. The scent of lavender, sprayed by his mother, becomes a cloud of fragrance on which he can ride through the skylight into the world beyond. He can fly freely and flowingly, above fields and pastures, with complete control over his adventures and over everything within them. He laughs as he flies, although he never laughs in bed. He dreads landing back in bed, for he often bumps himself on the iron frame and wakes up in pain. He denies the pain that he feels, however, when Madame Mamma questions him.

Besides his mother, the most frequent visitor to the sickroom is the maid Angelina, whom he has rechristened "Mandora." He loves Mandora because she radiates a profusion of colors, sounds, and feelings. His least favorite visitor is the doctor, whom he finds patronizing and cold. He regards the children who visit him—his cousin

Charles, with his scratched knees and hobnail boots, and a little girl who talks about her ballet lessons—as tolerable daytime irritations, for he knows that when night falls, he can find true enjoyment by flying away on one of his adventures again.

One night, Jean's voyage ends when he comes down to earth and hears some words that he cannot quite grasp. The reader understands them as "crisis" and "poliomyelitis." Jean hears them in the shape of people's names and conjures up visions of their owners.

In a protracted period of delirium, the boy's fantasies take on a different and more disturbing texture. Inanimate objects, which were previously at his beck and call, begin to defy him. He finds himself in the grip of unfamiliar presences and sensations. He wants to cry out to Madame Mamma, but an invisible wall separates him from her.

As the fever mounts, strange feelings assail his legs, as if they are being assaulted by ants; menacing forces attack him with burning heat and icy cold. A sudden calm and sadness indicates to the reader that Jean is close to death. His hallucinations become increasingly disoriented. Occasionally, consciousness breaks through as he hears, in distorted form, the sound of bedside voices.

Still struggling to take command of the situation, he at last succumbs to tears. He feels the touch of soft flesh and hair and falls asleep with the knowledge that he is nestling on his mother's shoulder. When he awakens, he has regained enough of his old self to greet her with one of his slightly mocking comments.

In a state of blurred consciousness, he politely asks Madame Mamma to scratch his calves as the "ants" are plaguing him again. This indication that he has regained some feelings in his legs causes excitement among the adults at his bedside, but he becomes conscious of a hateful presence among them and tries to use his powers to abolish it. He discovers that it is the doctor and that the doctor's eyes are filled with tears.

The following weeks bring a muddled and lethargic succession of short and long sleeps, sudden awakenings, and small treats of jelly and vanilla milk. As the "ants" become increasingly active and his appetite returns, Jean's powers decrease until he is no longer able to conjure up his cherished visions. Inanimate objects refuse to obey him. He can no longer fly. He has defeated death. He is on the mend and is sleeping well at night, but the nights are without marvels. The final word of the final sentence indicates that, contrary to the reader's expectations, Jean is disappointed.

Themes and Meanings

Colette's sensitive, subtle, and unsentimental perception of childhood, which is evident in her factual stories about her own child, is refined and developed to the farthest limits in "The Sick Child" by her penetration of the mind of a boy brought close to death by poliomyelitis. The delicate borderline that she traces between imagination and reality reflects the boy's own subjectivity in which his nighttime fantasies become his reality, compensating for the daytime torment of confinement and helping him to make some sense of the pain. In more general terms, Colette is examining the gap that she perceives between a child's and an adult's reality.

At first, the deception that mother and child practice on each other seems no more than a form of courtesy. As the narrative unfolds, however, the gap between them is shown to be of more fundamental significance. In a revealing passage expressing his innermost thoughts, Jean ponders over the impossibility of explaining to Madame Mamma that a sick and suffering child can be actually happy: far less unhappy, he reflects, than when he was being pushed about in a wheelchair.

The quality of his happiness (or, more precisely, his lack of unhappiness) is a key to the story's deepest interior observation. Jean's dislike of the doctor is associated with the doctor's patronizing attempt to get him to pass the time by sketching. Jean, although absorbed by reading, which feeds his imagination, has already rejected the idea of drawing; he has found that it demands a daunting revelation of truths he prefers not to reveal or to face. There is a similar train of thought in Colette's story, "The Seamstress," about her nine-year-old daughter; the child's imagination flows freely when she is reading but is channeled into more intimidating areas when social pressures force her to learn to sew.

Jean's disappointment at the end of "The Sick Child" can therefore be understood not simply in terms of his own loss of imaginative power, or in the more generalized terms of the final paragraph that considers "children whom death lets go," but as Colette's bitter protest against the pressures of the adult world that extinguish the free, untrammeled imagination of childhood and alter the quality of childhood perception.

Style and Technique

The story is unfolded in a prose style of exquisite delicacy. In the child's world of imagination, the senses are blended with one another; objects transform themselves into different shapes and textures; fantasy merges with reality. The images take on an even greater plasticity in the nightmare of high fever and in the child's gradual, fluctuating return to consciousness.

The free-ranging, protean dynamic of the fantasy passages contrasts with the more formal style used to describe the actual events in the sickroom and the exchanges between the sick child and Madame Mamma (names are seldom used). Although the narrative is developed mainly through the child's subjective vision, the structure of the story, in which the adult reality of the sickroom keeps entering his consciousness in a blurred and distorted form, enables the reader to understand the progress of the illness much more clearly than Jean himself does, and to visualize the comings and goings in the sickroom. At the same time as being deeply involved in the child's private experiences, one must inevitably identify with the adults' desperate hope for his recovery, a hope that has been made fragile by repeated references to Jean as "the child who was going to die" or "the child promised to death."

By establishing this shifting center of sympathy, Colette is able, at the end, to swing the reader from one reaction to its opposite—first relief that the boy has unexpectedly recovered, then dismay and shock at the finality of the word "disappointed." This unstressed and rather gentle word at the very end of the story commands a reinterpretation of all that has gone before.

Nina Hibbin

THE SIGNAL-MAN

Author: Charles Dickens (1812-1870)
Type of plot: Ghost story
Time of plot: The nineteenth century
Locale: A train track in rural England
First published: 1866

> *Principal characters:*
> THE NARRATOR, a man walking by the railroad tracks
> THE SIGNALMAN, a railroad employee who signals to trains as
> they pass by.

The Story

"The Signal-Man" describes an eerie encounter between two men, the anonymous narrator of the story and a railway signalman. The signalman confides to the narrator that he has seen some disturbing sights that he believes are ghostly apparitions. The story reflects the narrator's initial skepticism, which turns to horrified belief at the conclusion.

The story opens as the narrator is taking a walk in the country. He sees a signalman by the train track at the bottom of a steep cutting. He calls to the signalman, makes his way down a zigzag path to the track, and converses with him. The signalman is strangely fearful of the man, revealing that the man's greeting reminded him of a disturbing supernatural apparition he has seen—and heard—at the mouth of a nearby tunnel. The narrator wonders briefly if the signalman himself is a spirit because of his strange manner.

The signalman invites the narrator to return and meet him at his signal box on the following night. At that time, the signalman tells his visitor more about the apparition. It took the form of a man who appeared in front of the tunnel waving desperately and crying, "Look out! Look out!" The signalman telegraphed warnings to other stations along the line but to no avail. Six hours later, a terrible train accident occurred. On another day, the figure reappeared and assumed an attitude of extreme grief. A few hours later, a woman died on one of the trains going by the signalman's post. The signalman is tortured by his inability to make any life-saving use of these supernatural warnings. The signalman's visitor considers with deep anxiety how he might help the man but can think of nothing efficacious.

Not long after this conversation, one evening when out walking, the narrator also sees the apparition at the mouth of the tunnel, standing with his arm over his eyes and desperately waving a warning with the other arm. Running to the signal box, the narrator learns that the signalman was run over and killed by a train that morning. One of the men working by the railway tells the narrator that the signalman was standing with his back to the oncoming train. Like the ghostly apparition the narrator saw that evening, this man covered his eyes to avoid seeing the signalman destroyed while continuing to wave his arm in warning.

Themes and Meanings

In "The Signal-Man," Dickens makes supernatural beings interact with real people in realistic situations to express concerns about human interconnectedness. His better-known story *A Christmas Carol* (1843) employs the same strategy. Unlike *A Christmas Carol*, however, "The Signal-Man" is a pessimistic story with a sad ending.

In "The Signal-Man," a ghostly apparition either warns or belatedly informs a helpless watcher of fatal tragedies. In nineteenth century fiction, the railway was often used to symbolize anxiety about technological progress obliterating traditional ways of life and supplanting intimate social connections with impersonal technological systems. This anxiety is evident in "The Signal-Man" as tragedies occur despite of the carefully constructed means established to ensure safety: telegraph signals, red lights, flags, and bells. Dickens emphasizes the signalman's careful attention to his duty in his faithful adherence to routine and his constant watchfulness. Nevertheless, even when they are conscientiously deployed, technological communications can be ineffectual in preventing the deaths taking place on the railway. The train seems to have an untamed power of its own, impervious to the stratagems of the people who invented it.

Loneliness and social isolation are also prominent features of "The Signal-Man." The empty countryside and the steep zigzag pathway that separates the narrator from the signalman in the story's beginning emphasize the sense of isolation. Neither man is given a name. Each wonders whether the other is a ghost rather than a human being. Although there are systems in place for communicating by telegraph, there are no people nearby with whom to share the fear and the worry—other than through this chance encounter between the protagonists. In contrast to the characters' anonymity and ontological vagueness, the rushing train has an undeniable physical presence and energy. Humanity has been reduced to isolated, ineffectual, doubtfully real figures in a barren landscape in which only the train has power.

The supernatural apparitions are eerie but not dangerous. They do not threaten the human characters, but their ineffectual desperation and grief are deeply unsettling. They seem to be symbolic of human caring and empathy, an empathy that is tragically disconnected from any real power to do good. They seem to show that although the power and means to provide help and comfort are cut off, the desire to be humanly interconnected and to prevent tragedy and suffering is still strong.

Style and Technique

The opening of "The Signal-Man" is striking in its modernistic evocation of existential isolation. The first sentence is a cry: "Halloa! Below there!" Instead of identifying the speaker, the text goes on to describe the reaction of an unidentified man who hears the voice but cannot determine its origin. By withholding the identities of both the first speaker and the listener (the narrator and the signalman), Dickens creates a feeling of dislocation and uncertainty that effectively communicates his theme of loneliness and human powerlessness. The narrator's and the signalman's brief suspicion that each may be a spirit rather than a human contributes to the eerie and mysterious mood.

In contrast to these characters' uncertain entrance into the story, the train makes its narrative entrance with brutal vitality. Before the narrator and the signalman can make physical contact, the air vibrates with "violent pulsation," and the train passes by in an "oncoming rush" that nearly pulls the narrator into its wake. The contrasting presentation of human characters and train underscore Dickens's theme of technology's dehumanizing power.

The steep incline that the narrator must traverse to meet with the signalman, the zigzag path, and the foreshortened perspectives evoked in the opening scene create a feeling of vertiginous insecurity. This mood is further emphasized by the description of the signalman's station: a solitary post just outside a gloomy dark tunnel next to a dripping wall of "jagged stone" that blocks out the sky and the sunlight.

The story unfolds mainly in dialogue that is terse and urgent, creating a feeling of inexorable momentum toward a dreadful end. Beyond the initial description of the gloomy location, there is very little attempt to build atmosphere through description. The narration has a quality of reportorial objectivity that builds the reader's acceptance of the importance of the ghostly apparitions. Although the narrator at first wonders whether the signalman is prey to nervous indispositions that give rise to imaginary visions, he discovers from his own experience at the end of the story that the ghosts have a reality independent of any individual imagination. The narrator's attitudinal transformation from skepticism to horrified belief persuades the reader to gradually enter into the story's spell.

The ghosts, most often appearing in the form of a man covering his eyes with one arm and waving desperately with the other, are the story's most striking visual images. Their anonymous desperation and ineffectual passion portray the tragedy of technology destroying human agency and connection. By introducing ghostly elements into a realistic setting, Dickens transforms the modern technological landscape into a gothic setting in which horrible tragedies evade human control. This combination of elements unifies two forms of anxiety: the ancient fear of the supernatural and the modern fear of impersonal, implacable, heartless technology.

Constance Vidor

THE SIGNING

Author: Stephen Dixon (1936-   )
Type of plot: Impressionistic
Time of plot: Unspecified; possibly the 1970's
Locale: A large city in the United States
First published: 1974

>   *Principal characters:*
>   THE NARRATOR
>   LASLO, a hospital security guard
>   A BUS DRIVER
>   A DOCTOR

The Story

The unnamed narrator resolutely refuses to abide by any and all of the bureaucratic and legal rules that apply on the death of a relative, in this instance the death of his wife. After his wife dies, he kisses her hands and leaves the hospital room. A nurse runs after him as he walks down the hall. When she asks what he wants done with his wife's body, the widower suggests that they burn it or give it to science. The horrified nurse states that he will draw up the proper legal papers, but that this will take some time. The narrator says he does not have time and rushes out of the hospital and onto a bus. Laslo, a hospital security guard (the only character in the four-page story who has a name), is ordered to follow the bereaved husband onto the bus, even though he does not clearly understand what is transpiring. All the parties involved are hyperconsciously aware of what is and is not part of their jobs—that is, the legal obligations of their employment. The bureaucrats back at the hospital are only concerned with not being sued by the beleaguered husband and with disposing of the body.

As the doctors shift their duties to Laslo, Laslo tries to make the bus driver responsible for handing the narrator over to his authority. The bus driver clearly understands the heart of the legal dilemma: "In or out friend, but unless you can come up with some official authority to stop this bus, I got to finish my run." A conversation ensues between Laslo and the hospital officials on a two-way radio as he attempts to explain what is taking place on the bus. His two-way radio is the intermediary between the bureaucrats back at the hospital and the heartbroken husband as they attempt to arrange an alternate location where he can sign the proper release forms so that the doctors may use parts of the dead woman's body to help others continue living.

The narrator is so adamant about detaching himself from his dead wife that he begins to discard all of his personal belongings that she gave him or with which she is associated. First he throws his wristwatch out the window, then he disposes of his jacket, shirt, tie, pants, shoes and socks, so that he is left almost naked. He would have discarded his underwear, but he remembered that he had bought them the day before and his wife never had a chance to see or touch them.

The narrator finally speaks into the two-way radio to the doctors at the hospital and explains that he and his beloved wife spent too many years in this city, on these streets and bridges, perhaps even on the bus they are presently riding. He tries to uproot the seat on which they are sitting, until finally Laslo handcuffs him. The semi-hysterical man smashes his head through the window of the bus in a desperate attempt to blot out the horror of memory and consciousness. He ends up back at the same hospital and in the same examining room where his wife was treated before being transferred to a semi-private room. He refuses to sign the papers that give the hospital the right to use his wife's organs for transplants, because he does not want to risk bumping into her and somehow recognizing them in another person. The doctor in charge finally takes his writing hand and guides it until he has signed the papers.

Themes and Meanings

This short but highly intense story contains several of the common themes around which Stephen Dixon has built a highly respected literary reputation. The enemies in this story are the bureaucratic systems that function beyond human and humane control. The unnamed narrator first appears as an emotionally disturbed person because he wants immediate closure to his obligations as a married man after his beloved wife dies. He demands such radical closure, however, because he cannot bear the consciousness that death forces him to confront or the memory of his happy years with his wife. His grief is so desperate and potentially overwhelming, he attempts suicide near the story's conclusion. The death of his beloved has canceled out any residual meaning that mechanistic, bureaucratic systems need to operate and maintain an orderly society. The system that needs to continue functioning in this story is one that must dispose of dead bodies in an efficient and legal manner and tries to utilize their organs to keep people alive. What is absent in this kind of system is any consideration of the depth of the grief and loss of the widower and the existential emptiness that threatens to overcome him. The hospital sustains life through a system that lacks the capacity to philosophize over the meaning of life or the significance of love. The emotionally detached bureaucratic system forces the narrator to confront two of life's most profoundly disturbing facts: the horror of consciousness and the inability to escape the memory of the past. It is to Stephen Dixon's credit as an artist that he can treat, with redeeming but sardonic wit, the same themes that Jean-Paul Sartre and Albert Camus dramatized so bleakly in some of the darkest books of the twentieth century.

Style and Technique

The narrator is both comic and pathetic in his attempts to escape the obligations of mechanistic systems. Dixon intermittently places comic voices in the middle of potentially tragic scenes. After the narrator throws his watch out the window, the man behind him on the bus asks: "Why don't you just pass it on back here?" Earlier, the narrator himself acts as a ventriloquist in trying to get the bus driver to continue the trip, claiming that "your slowpokey driving and intermittent dawdling has already made me ten minutes late." Just as the narrator is deciding to get rid of his socks, Laslo attempts to get him to stop: "'Leave them on,' Laslo says, 'They look good and I like brown.'" Although the scene in which the narrator begins to throw his clothing out of the bus window is comic, it is also heartrending because the grieving husband cannot bear to touch anything that reminds him of his beloved wife.

The most compelling technique used in this disturbing story is that Dixon begins it at the end. Few writers bother to think about the bureaucratic system that takes place after the beloved is dead, when the narrator declares he is alone and leaves the hospital. Dixon's postmodernist imagination always probes into what is absent—what other writers overlook. His technique generates the action in the story, which consists of a man's desperate attempts at closure.

As often happens in Dixon's stories, the protagonist is trapped in a bureaucratic system that, when resisted, produces even more complications and predicaments. Because he refuses to sign a legal document, he precipitates a series of quasi-slapstick actions that end in his forced signature; he is completely denied his freedom to the one thing that makes him unique: his own name. Dixon begins and concludes the story with the central issue—a man's signature, that which gives him his legal and philosophical identity. It is the final tragedy of the story that he loses not only his wife but also his identity and his dignity.

Patrick Meanor

SIGNS AND SYMBOLS

Author: Vladimir Nabokov (1899-1977)
Type of plot: Psychological
Time of plot: Unspecified; probably the late 1940's
Locale: Boston
First published: 1948

> *Principal characters:*
> AN ELDERLY COUPLE, Russian immigrants living in Boston
> THEIR TEENAGE SON, who is institutionalized

The Story

An elderly, poor Russian émigré couple intend to pay a birthday visit to their son. He is institutionalized in a sanitarium, diagnosed as afflicted with referential mania. It is an incurable disease in which the patient imagines that everything that happens around him is a veiled reference to his personality and existence. He is certain that phenomenal nature shadows him wherever he may be, that trees can divine and discuss his inmost thoughts, that coats in store windows want to lynch him—in short, that he must be on his guard every minute of his life. The boy's most recent suicide attempt was brilliantly inventive, as he sought to "tear a hole in his world and escape."

On the parents' way to the sanitarium, the machinery of existence seems to malfunction: The subway loses its electric current between stations; their bus is late and is crammed with noisy schoolchildren; they are pelted by pouring rain as they walk the last stretch of the way. On their arrival, they are informed that because their son has again attempted suicide, their visit might unduly agitate him, so they do not see him.

While awaiting their bus on their way home, they observe a tiny, half-dead baby bird twitching helplessly in a rain puddle; it is doomed to die through no fault of its own. On the bus, they are silent with worry and defeat; the wife notices her husband's hands twitching, like the bird's body, on the handle of his umbrella.

At home, after a somber supper and after her husband has gone to bed, the wife pulls the blinds down to block out the rain and examines the family photo album, filled with the faces of mostly suffering or dead relatives. One cousin has become a famous chess player (an oblique reference to Luzhin, the protagonist of Vladimir Nabokov's 1929 novel, *The Luzhin Defense*, who commits suicide). She follows photos of her son's degeneration from moody toddler, to insomnia from the age of six, to his fear of wallpaper and pictures at the age of eight, to his special schooling by ten years old and, soon afterward, his disconnection with the outside world.

In the story's last section, the time is past midnight and the husband staggers into the living room, sleepless and in pain, to join his wife. The couple decide, bravely, to remove their son from the hospital and care for him at home, each intending to give up part of the night to watch him in his bedroom. Then the phone rings: a wrong number.

When it rings a second time, the wife carefully explains to the same caller how she must have misdialed. The husband and wife sit down to their midnight tea. Their son's unopened birthday present shares the table with their cups. The phone rings for the third time; the story ends. Its signs and symbols suggest, in all likelihood, that this last call is from the sanitarium to announce that their son has finally succeeded in escaping this world.

Themes and Meanings

Displaced persons and madmen recur in Nabokov's fiction, with these people finding no joy in his universe. The central thematic question this story asks is whether one is necessarily demented to conclude that nature and society are hostile to humankind. Although the son is certifiably deluded, the real world presented by the narrator and observed by the parents is fully consistent with the boy's vision of it. These parents have made great sacrifices for their son; they have poignant memories of his disturbed childhood and are now willing to care for the hopeless boy in their cramped, two-room apartment. However, all creatures and phenomena in this story—humans, birds, flowers—are linked to one another in an ineluctable chain of suffering. The parents have been forced to leave their homeland, where the husband had been a successful businessman, and are now totally dependent on his seldom-seen brother, whom they call "the Prince." The wife recalls endless waves of pain that, for reasons unknowable, she and her husband have had to endure. She remembers her Aunt Rosa who endured bankruptcies, train accidents, and cancerous growths only to be murdered by the Germans. The boy, the bird, the aunt, and the parents all testify to a universe of inexorable and implacable powers that snuff out the lights of life, imagination, creativity, justice, and happiness.

Style and Technique

The beauty and power of this story, which may be Nabokov's best, is conveyed through scrupulously refined and repetitive images, details, and motifs. These are intricately designed and fashioned so that reading the text is also an experience of working through an interlocking network of signs and symbols.

The dominant point of view is the wife's, who is fully aware that she presents "a naked white countenance to the fault-finding light of spring days." Her and her husband's experiences are uniformly hostile: the stalled subway train, his brown-spotted (cancerous?) hands, the boy's acne-blotched face, the half-dead bird, her concept of people as comparable to beautiful weeds who "helplessly have to watch the shadow of [the farmer's] simian swoop leave mangled flowers in its wake, as the monstrous darkness approaches." This darkness destroys her aunt's, her son's, and the couple's lives.

The story constructs an elaborate referential system to pit the realm of creative imagination against the threatening pattern of realistic experience. Nabokov uses incidental details to form an active synergy of designation. Thus, Aunt Rosa's world is destroyed, as the baby bird's is: brutally, irrationally, fatally. The boy avoids squirrels as he does people. When six years old, he draws birds with human hands and feet, reminding the reader of the dying bird's spasms and the husband's twitching hands. Slowly, detail by detail, the trappings of life accumulate, only to be annihilated.

Thus, from the intricate and circuitous structure of "Signs and Symbols," Nabokov goes on to incandescent, imaginative compositions that establish mirror-image relationships between the physical, tangible world and the shadowy, shaped, invented world.

Artistically, "Signs and Symbols" is nearly flawless: It is intricately patterned, densely textured, and remarkably intense in tone and feeling. For once, Nabokov the literary jeweler cuts more deeply than his usual surfaces, forsaking gamesmanship and mirror-play and other gambits of verbal artifice to enter the frightening woods of inassuageable, tragic grief.

Gerhard Brand

SILENCE

Author: Carlos Bulosan (1911-1956)
Type of plot: Social realism
Time of plot: Unspecified
Locale: Unspecified
First published: 1979

> *Principal characters:*
> AN UNNAMED MAN, the protagonist
> A FEMALE COLLEGE STUDENT

The Story

A man living in an unnamed town has rented a series of rooms, first near a park, then near a bakery, and finally, "in desperation," in a roominghouse adjacent to a college. His moves, each to a different section of town, are motivated by loneliness. The park was filled with young people enthusiastically playing games, but he had no part in their delight. The workers in the bakery building treated him as though he were not there. Now he only looks at the college campus from his window; he has not spoken to anyone in the five years that he has been in town.

The man works long hours every day to combat his isolation, but his evenings are almost unbearable for him. He paces slowly, looking at old pictures on the wall, lies sleeplessly in bed thinking of the past, or simply sits in a wooden chair, staring blankly at the walls. He has conversed with nearly all the objects in his room, even the walls.

One Sunday morning he notices the green curtains on his window and is surprised that it has taken him so long to discover them. As he looks out this window and spots a girl sitting on the college lawn, reading a book, he experiences a catharsis. After an hour the girl leaves, and the man dashes to a nearby store to buy white curtains, to match the color of her sweater. The next afternoon, after he hurries home from work, he sees the girl in her place on the college lawn and is shocked because she is now wearing a red sweater and a black skirt. A similar scenario is repeated each day for six months, during which time the man matches the colors of the girl's skirt and sweater until his room becomes a riot of color. When the girl does not appear during the two weeks at Christmas break and occasionally thereafter, the man is so let down that he does not go to work.

One day a friend visits. The man considers sharing his source of joy with his friend, but, feeling jealous, decides not to. Never again does he receive a visitor. After adding two heavy locks to his door, he turns out his light and peers out his window. Spring comes and then summer, with its heat, ripening fruits, full-leafed trees, and warm wind from the sea. In mid-June the girl leaves, never to return. A year passes. The man stops working and his curtains fade and become soiled.

Themes and Meanings

The theme of human alienation from both the natural environment and the social environment is common in modern literature; however, for any reader conversant with the life of Carlos Bulosan this does not reduce his story's expressive quality. Although Bulosan's never-specified "he" character is Everyman, the man's universality does not detract from the realization that the story is an outpouring of Bulosan's own depression, even despair. A member of a several-decade-long wave of immigration from the Philippines, Bulosan lived in the United States from 1930 to his death in 1956, but never took up American citizenship. His personal alienation and even brutalization are depicted graphically in his quasiautobiographical *America Is in the Heart* (1946). His feelings of loneliness so touchingly presented in "Silence" are also articulated in the selection of his letters entitled *The Sound of Falling Light* (1960), edited by Delores Feria, and biographies by Susan Evangelista and P. C. Morantte.

"Silence" is unusual for a Bulosan piece in that it expresses no discernible social protest. Because of the prevalence of social protest themes in his writings and because of his brief stint as a labor leader in the early 1950's, most of the critical commentaries on Bulosan's works have been Marxist. A Marxist reading of "Silence," however, would be difficult to sustain. Several details in the story indicate that its protagonist is not affluent (for example, his carpet is "threadbare"), but he has enough money to purchase new curtains every day for six months, and there is no hint of want—for example, he is never hungry. The man is certainly not representative of the downtrodden masses: He has no encounters with police, bosses, social arrangements, or government, and there is no hint of class struggle. The one socially significant allusion in the story is entirely positive: "He had rented a little room near a park where young men and women of many races were always shouting in excited voices over their games." Here there is no segregation, no oppression, no disharmony.

"Silence" is, in fact, virtually classic literary existentialism, except that its environment is never hostile—it is merely indifferent, at worst. However, even the seeming indifference is brought on as much by the protagonist's withdrawal as it is by the lack of responsiveness of his surroundings. As an apparently childless adult, how can he expect to share in the glee of children playing in a park? He stands in the street as the bakery workers pass him but he does not greet them. He peers from his room at the college lawn but does not even cross the street to stroll through it, much less make any conversational overtures. One wonders how he manages never to say anything because he goes to work every day. Why does he talk to the walls and his clock and caress a chair when inanimate objects have no capacity to respond? At the end, he goes out of his way to isolate himself by installing extra locks on his door and never inviting his friend for a return visit. "Silence" is about a man who is allowing—if not actively willing—his life to drain away.

Style and Technique

Bulosan creates an atmosphere of utter dreariness by using a flat, almost monotonous prose style. His third-person point of view enhances the sense of detachment that his protagonist experiences. The most conspicuous technique in the story is its lack of specific names, dates, places—in short, any concrete references. This keeps the reader at arm's length from the narrative, thereby helping the reader to experience feelings of exclusion similar to those of the protagonist. Bulosan is so careful about the indefiniteness of his story that he does not refer to specific devices, clothing styles, vehicles, events, or other objects or contrivances that might enable a reader to localize either a time setting or a place for the story.

There is room for doubt about the protagonist's soundness of mind, although the third-person narrative stance militates against suspecting the reliability of the plot happenings. Why does the protagonist withdraw into a shell when doing so is obviously painful to him? At times one may detect inconsistencies, as in the oxymoronic expression "watching his shoes move and gleam in the glare of the faint light." However inclined a reader may be to see the plot as revealing the unraveling of a mind, the coherence of the symbolism works against a deconstructionist reading of the story. The "young men and women of many races" mentioned in the first part of the opening paragraph are neatly paralleled by the different colors of curtains that the narrator later buys. Both represent life, vitality, fecundity and are subtly linked by the "little voices" (the children's) mentioned in paragraph four, which urge the protagonist to look out again at the girl on the college lawn. The statement in paragraph nine that "she had become a part of his whole existence" explains why he buys curtains to match her sweaters and skirts: Doing so symbolically brings her into his world. The tragedy—as he finds out to his cost—is that the world cannot be brought into the self; the self must go into the world.

The progression of the seasons reflects the human life cycle of growth to maturity and is an indication that if one does not mate when the time is right (in spring or summer), one suffers the spiritual death of aloneness. The sight of the girl causes within him "a flood of sunlight." However, the protagonist fails to act on the cue that external nature provides him in the spring: "The students walked on the pathways in groups and in twos, reading books and looking at the spring sun. Their heads glowed softly in the sunlight, their young mouths opened wide to admit some of it into their beings." All the protagonist need do is admit some sunlight into his being, but he never does. He leaves for work in half-darkness, he returns at night, he remains sequestered in his room; at story's end, when he leans out the window and weeps bitterly, it is again night.

L. M. Grow

THE SILENCE OF THE LLANO

Author: Rudolfo A. Anaya (1937-   )
Type of plot: Regional, Magical Realism
Time of plot: The early twentieth century
Locale: The prairie of northeastern New Mexico
First published: 1982

> Principal characters:
> RAFAEL, a rancher near the village of Las Animas, New Mexico
> RITA, his wife
> RITA, his daughter
> DOÑA RUFINA, an old midwife and healer

The Story

The story opens with the people of the small adobe village of Las Animas discussing the state of Rafael, a young rancher in the llano, the desolate plains country of northeastern New Mexico. The llano is nearly empty of people, and the villagers of Las Animas claim its silences can steal a man's soul. This has happened to Rafael.

Rafael's life on the llano has been a rough one. When he is fifteen, his parents die while traveling to town in a blizzard. Left alone to fend for the livestock, the young man loses half of his cattle to vicious winter storms.

In the spring, Rafael travels to Las Animas and tells the priest his parents have died. The villagers and other ranchers gather for a funeral mass, and then all go on with their lives except for Rita, a young woman who became orphaned as a child and has grown up behind the church. She falls in love with Rafael, and they marry. The two are very happy in their isolated existence on Rafael's ranch. He tends the livestock and improves the adobe house while Rita plants a garden and revives the neglected peach trees. Soon Rita becomes pregnant, and the young couple look forward to starting a family in their prairie paradise.

However, Rita's pregnancy is troubled, and in December, when the baby is due, she begins to bleed and feels unnatural tensions in her body. She tells Rafael to get Doña Rufina, the midwife and folk healer who lives in Las Animas. The old crone helps Rita give birth, but the healer is powerless to stop the hemorrhaging.

Rita dies, and Rafael, bitter over his beloved wife's death, will have nothing to do with his new daughter. Doña Rufina stays at the ranch and raises the daughter, also named Rita, and loves her as if she were her own child. Meanwhile, Rafael says few words to either Rita or Doña Rufina, preferring the silence of the llano where he can brood over his feelings of emptiness.

After seven years, Doña Rufina dies, and Rafael continues to avoid Rita, who raises herself. She becomes a child of nature, adding to her rudimentary Spanish the language of the animals because they are the only creatures with whom she speaks. Meanwhile, she matures into an attractive woman, innocent and lovely.

Around this time, some hunters drive by the ranch, and after slaying a deer, they pound on Rafael's door, demanding to meet his virgin daughter. Rafael refuses them entry, but a few weeks later, he is out mending fences and becomes uneasy when he sees a dust devil formed by an automobile heading for the ranch. Quitting work early, he returns to find Rita has been raped, the blood of her lost virginity an echo of the blood of her birth. In a plea for help and understanding, Rita calls Rafael by name for the first time.

Unfortunately, the shock and fear of the situation overwhelm Rafael, and he flees the ranch, as he did the day his wife died. That night he sleeps in the tool shed, and in the morning, he sees an apparition of his wife at the woodpile, for his daughter, by calling his name, has torn open the wound of his beloved's death. Trying to outrun the manifestation, he rides off again, only to be pursued by the vision of a woman riding a whirlwind. Back at the adobe house, he stands on the hill and watches his daughter bathe in the watering tank. The memory of his wife performing the same action pours through him, and he rides to his daughter. Using Rita's name for the first time, he gently bids her to plant a garden next to her mother's grave by the peach trees. At last, he has acknowledged his daughter and reopened his heart to the world's beauty.

Themes and Meanings

As with his classic novel *Bless Me Ultima* (1972), Rudolfo A. Anaya explores in "The Silence of the Llano" the relationship between place, culture, and the Latino individual in the New Mexico of the early to mid-twentieth century. Anaya's fascination for this time and region has two origins. First, this is the landscape of his childhood, for Anaya grew up in the desolate prairie lands near Santa Rosa, New Mexico. Second, this is the era when this region began to lose its uniqueness because of the transformations caused by technology and the modern world. It is significant that Rita's rapist arrives by automobile, a harbinger of twentieth century change and its dangers.

At the story's opening, Anaya establishes the twin forces of land and culture. He writes how the llano's oppressive vastness creates a silence that steals human souls. To escape this silence, the ranchers go to town just to hear the old men gossip in front of Las Animas's general store. They also go there for the healing of the soul through the priest and the healing of the body through *las curanderas*, or folk healers, like Doña Rufina.

Thus the dual influences of the rugged land and the rural, Catholic-Spanish civilization shape the young rancher Rafael, as they did most Hispanic men and women of mid-twentieth century northern New Mexico. Early on, Rafael learns the tough lesson of the llano's cruelty when his parents die in a blizzard and he loses half his herd. However, Rita breaks through his resultant stoicism, and for a brief time, the couple live in a pastoral Eden. However, Anaya knows that the llano breaks such paradises quickly, and with Rita's death, Rafael retreats into a private world devoid of human contact. Out of bitterness and blame, he even severs any connection with his own daughter.

Ironically, it is another tragic moment that breaks through Rafael's shell. His daughter's rape shocks him into seeing his wife's spirit, and this experience heals his wounded heart and allows him to return to his true nature as a caring and loving man, as symbolized in the new garden he will dig for his daughter.

Finally, it is important to note that Anaya also believes that the llano can be a place of nurturing and beauty. During his brief marriage, Rafael becomes drunk on the spring air and revels in the glories of the prairie's night sky. His wife coaxes a gemlike green garden and peach trees lush with blossoms from the dry soil. Rita, the daughter, while growing up on her own, learns the language of the animals and the ways of nature.

Thus the llano shapes its inhabitants into a people who possess a deep spirit, strong emotions, and a rich culture. They become great through their struggles with the land and life, and Rafael, by transcending his tragedies to return to his love of land and family, also attains that greatness.

Style and Technique

In "The Silence of the Llano," Anaya portrays a unique American region and its people through a powerful use of setting and character. His sharply drawn descriptions of the New Mexican plains and foothills create a powerful impression, forming a landscape that is in essence another main character. Anaya's human characters are just as finely described as the landscape, and the combination forms a classic sense of place.

Anaya also makes frequent use of motifs and symbols. A number of key images echo throughout the story. For example, there is a hillside on which Rafael stops to watch with pride his young wife at work. This is also the place where he pauses to study the ominously silent ranch just before he discovers the rape. The blood of that rape reminds the reader of the blood of Rita's birth, just as the stars that gave Rafael joy when his wife was alive give him a sense of aloneness when she is dead.

Drawing on the wondrous myths and legends of the Hispanic Southwest, Anaya creates symbols for "The Silence of the Llano" that further the story's meaning as well as help create a sense of place. For example, in New Mexican culture, the owl is a bird of ill omens and death, and the coyote is a trickster who brings chaos and unwanted change. In a foreshadowing of the dark events to come, Rafael hears owls and coyotes after his wife arrives at the ranch, and his daughter hears them several nights before she is raped.

This use of regional mythology evokes the Magical Realism of Gabriel García Márquez, Isabel Allende, and other Latin American authors. In Magical Realism, the fantastic and the mundane often operate side by side, and this is certainly the case in "The Silence of the Llano." When Doña Rufino is dying, she perceives the feminine figure of death riding across the plains on a wooden cart, and Rafael sees a woman riding a whirlwind using lightning as a whip. Indeed, it is through this magic that Rafael reconnects with his loving heart.

John Nizalowski

SILENT PASSENGERS

Author: Larry Woiwode (1941-   )
Type of plot: Domestic realism
Time of plot: The late twentieth century
Locale: A ranch in an unnamed high-plains state in the United States
First published: 1993

> *Principal characters:*
> STEINER, a forty-five-year-old business executive
> JEN, his wife
> JAMES, their nine-year-old son
> THEIR TWIN SEVEN-YEAR-OLD DAUGHTERS
> BILLY ARCHER, owner of the horse that injures James
> A VIETNAMESE EMERGENCY ROOM PHYSICIAN
> A PEDIATRIC NURSE

The Story

"Silent Passengers" is the deceptively simple story of the gradual and initially uncertain recovery of a young boy from an accident, as seen through the eyes of his father. Steiner is the middle-aged owner of a silicon-chip company on the coast (which coast is never specified). His distant ranch appears to be something between an avocation and a hobby; at any rate, he is not very adept at handling the necessary chores. Just before the accident, he is desultorily attempting to get a tractor to work, a task a neighbor eventually accomplishes. Regardless of how he may appear in his company, he does not seem to be a very forceful figure in this environment; his son James makes a mild joke about Steiner's impotent repetition of the word "but" when confronted by a plumber's refusal to come quickly to repair a broken bathroom. Steiner's character is also deftly indicated in his motivation for the bathroom's repair: He wants his place to appear as comfortable as possible, not for his family, but for the visit of a skillful colleague from the east coast.

Steiner has another deficiency that is alluded to only once in the text, the shadow of which seems to haunt him as he anxiously watches over his injured son. Steiner has a drinking problem and has just drunk two beers while repairing the tractor when he allows James to visit a neighbor's ranch, where the accident occurs. The guilt that Steiner feels for indulging himself and which is partially inspired by the reproach he sees in James's eyes for his drinking, hovers like a shadow behind the text. Even though Steiner does not allow his wife, Jen, to feel any guilt for allowing James to be injured and he does not consciously admit to any blame himself, Steiner's fervid anxiety over his son's condition, which seems to be little more than the powerless anguish that any parent feels over an injured, helpless child, is exacerbated by his sense of guilt over bringing his son to a place where such an accident was possible and his tepid though real resumption of drinking.

James's slow but deliberate recovery is aided by two kind health care workers: the doctor who immediately tends him in the emergency room and the pediatric nurse who helps him through a mild crisis during his early hospital stay. However, it is his parents who are most instrumental in James's essential healing. When James is fading during a mild crisis, it is Steiner's calling of his name that causes his heart rate to recover. When a pediatrician cautions Steiner and his wife not to expect too much, it is Jen's cradling of her son in her arms that evokes James's physical reaction of trying to return his mother's embrace, which signals the beginning of his long recovery.

The climax of the story occurs on the family's return to the ranch, when James, still unable to speak and walking awkwardly, approaches some of the family's quarter horses. Steiner, understandably, fears a recurrence of the accident, but James's instinctive, innocent trust in the essential nature of the creatures who had injured him marks the real beginning of his full recovery (which is briefly related in the final paragraph of the story). The healing for Steiner, James, and their whole family is incarnate in that moment of acceptance when the wind of the high plains causes their hair to rise, "silent in the wind," and the ranch, which had before seemed a rich man's toy, takes on a new beneficial, even salvific, aspect.

Themes and Meanings

"Silent Passengers" deals with every parent's nightmare: the despairing feeling, wrenching and numbing at the same time, that comes from watching over a stricken child. Every emotion that accompanies this dark vigil is delineated, from remorse and guilt and anger to the final cautious glimmerings of hope. The story's title emerges from these feelings—Steiner and Jen are "silent passengers," helpless and separate, in James's recovery. Steiner is enough of an everyman to make his reactions universal, and even though Jen is described totally from the exterior, her inherent and automatic maternalism makes her an everywoman.

However, the story also treats characteristic Larry Woiwode concerns, the family being chief among them. From the novel *Beyond the Bedroom Wall: A Family Album* (1975) to his memoir *What I Think I Did: A Season of Survival in Two Acts* (2000), Woiwode's chief subject has been the family and the fluctuating relationships that make up its dynamics. In "Silent Passengers," the never-ending concern of parents for their children is treated. As Steiner moves through the storm of emotions that embroil him after the accident, and as he watches James's slow and halting recovery, he becomes ever more aware of James as a person, a singular, unique, and irreplaceable creature. Steiner remembers, for instance, that James was always good at forgiveness and ready to forgive him—a trait that parents often do not recognize in their children, forgetting that forgiveness is a two-way street. James also had the ability to cheer Steiner up. The fact that family members all too easily take one another for granted until moments of crisis and possible separation is gently but forcibly reinforced here.

The setting of the story is also characteristic of Woiwode, the high-plains ranch as the home and center of the Steiners' lives. Although Steiner does not seem sufficiently serious about the opportunities that such an environment can afford, at least his motivation for establishing a home there—to spend more time with his children—is worthy and perhaps even efficacious in James's recovery.

One other concern of Woiwode's, his deep religious sense, is hinted at in the conclusion to this story. The moment Steiner keeps remembering in the future, the moment when his family's hair is blown "straight up" by the wind as James, Jen, and the twins turn to him from the horses, is the final epiphany of the story. The wind could just be an element of nature, but it also could be a sign of the Spirit (a word whose derivation means, among other things, wind) in their lives. Love, that of Steiner and Jen, has called James back to them, and James's love binds them together in this moment.

Style and Technique

The narrative does not unfold in chronological order, which in this case heightens the suspense. It begins with the family's first return to the ranch from the hospital with James, and the accident and its aftermath are related in flashbacks. As the story moves on the parallel tracks of the return to the ranch and the accident and its aftermath, each track illuminates the other.

The intense focus of the story is revealed in the characters' names, or rather the lack of some of them. The reader is never told Steiner's first name, which establishes a certain distance between the reader and the character and probably prevents a too close, and in this case uncomfortable, intimacy. It also invites speculations on the meaning of his last name; Steiner is stonelike (unemotional, unfeeling) in his pre-accident life but becomes more rocklike (dependable) in his reactions during and after the accident.

Similarly, the reader never learns the twins' individual names; they are thrust to the edges of the story, only noticeable in their inspiration for the motivation of Billy Archer, the neighbor whose horse injures James, to invite the children to his ranch, or for their reactions to James's actions. However, Woiwode's eye for character, typically deft and careful, is charitable in the best sense of the word in his depictions of the emergency room doctor and the pediatric nurse, who are capable of making a personal connection to James and his parents despite the omnipresence of such implicit tragedies in their own professional lives.

The traditional technique of the concluding epiphany is used here in its normal literary sense of a key moment of insight, often left to the main character (as well as the reader) to interpret. The vision of a family frozen and suspended against the stark beauty of nature, rescued, perhaps momentarily, from imminent danger and the threat of death, remains before Steiner as his son returns to normality. He—and the reader—must ponder its meaning. It is also an epiphany in the religious sense of the word, a presentation, a showing forth, of the invisible and spiritual and eternal against the impermanent and heartbreaking mundane world.

William Laskowski

SILENT SNOW, SECRET SNOW

Author: Conrad Aiken (1889-1973)
Type of plot: Psychological
Time of plot: About 1920
Locale: An unspecified American town
First published: 1932

Principal characters:
PAUL HASELMAN, the protagonist, a young boy who suffers from "daydreams"
MR. HASELMAN
MRS. HASELMAN
MISS BUELL, Paul's teacher
THE DOCTOR
DEIDRE, one of Paul's classmates

The Story

In "Silent Snow, Secret Snow," Conrad Aiken describes the increasing emotional isolation of a boy, Paul, who prefers his imaginative world of silence and retreat to the real world of parents and teachers. Aiken limits his third-person point of view to Paul, through whose eyes readers view corruption and authority, as well as serenity, peace, and perhaps insanity.

The story begins with Paul in the classroom of Miss Buell, the geography teacher, who instructs her students in the different regions of the globe. As she conducts her class, Paul muses about his secret, the world of snow that is slowly replacing the real world. Every day, Paul senses that the snow, which exists only in his own mind, is getting deeper. As the snow deepens, Paul has more difficulty hearing the mail carrier's steps, which he believes are muffled by the snow: The first day, he first hears the mail carrier's step six houses away; the next day, five houses away; eventually, he will not hear the carrier's step at all. Although he realizes that his daydreaming distresses his concerned parents, who seek physical reasons for his preoccupation, he treasures his secret world and fears to reveal his secret to them. Miss Buell also senses Paul's inattention, but she seems more concerned with humiliating him than with helping him. When she asks Paul a question, he does manage to answer correctly, but only with a large amount of effort.

On his "timeless" walk home from school, Paul sees through the "accompaniment, or counterpoint, of snow" a series of items of "mere externality" (internal matters are more important to Paul). As he approaches his street, he anticipates seeing the snow and reviews its progress, suddenly realizing with disappointment that in fact he had not heard the mail carrier's steps that morning until he knocked at his family's door. He wonders, "Was it all going to happen, at the end, so suddenly?"

That evening, the doctor arrives and gives Paul a physical examination to determine the cause of his problem. After Paul reads a passage from Sophocles, the doctor concludes that there is nothing wrong with his eyes and that the cause is "something else." When he asks about Paul's worries, Paul becomes evasive and retreats into his snow world, where he receives reassuring promises from the "voice" of the snow. The doctor continues to probe, and Paul's parents become impatient with him when he will admit only that he thinks about the snow. When he refuses to divulge more information, his father, who has grown increasingly exasperated, uses his "punishment" voice. At this point, Paul escapes by running upstairs to his room, where the snow engulfs the furnishings and speaks to him of peace, remoteness, cold, and white darkness. When his mother suddenly enters the room, he sees her as a hostile presence that threatens his world. He cries out, "Mother! Mother! Go away! I hate you." Those words solve everything, for the snow resumes its speech about peace, cold, remoteness, and, finally, sleep.

Themes and Meanings

Aiken's "Silent Snow, Secret Snow," like Willa Cather's "Paul's Case," concerns a boy's emotional and psychological estrangement from the real world. Although some critics have seen the retreat to the snow world as representative of a death wish, it seems more to represent schizophrenic detachment into a fantasy world. Psychological criticism of the story is almost inevitable because Aiken himself was much influenced by Sigmund Freud, whose theory of the Oedipal complex seems related to the conflict between Paul and his father. (The passage Paul reads for his eye test is from Sophocles' *Oidipous epi Kolōnōi* (401 B.C.E.; *Oedipus at Colonus*, 1729) Psychological readings are further encouraged by events in Aiken's life: As an eleven-year-old, he had seen his father kill his mother and then commit suicide.

The story, however, is more than a clinical case study of a person who is suffering from a psychological disorder. Aiken's background is literary as well as psychological, and his story relies heavily on the theme of "two different worlds," a theme that is reinforced through imagery of geography and exploring. Paul tries to lead a double life (a "public life" and the "life that was secret") in two worlds, but he also is aware of the necessity of keeping a balance between those worlds. His mother expresses her concern about his living in another world, and when he realizes the depth of the snow on the sixth day, he understands that the "audible compass of the world" is thereby narrowed as the snow world supplants it. As the story progresses, Paul loses his balance (on the homeward walk he notices the egg-shaped stones that are mortared "in the very act of balance") and falls, albeit willingly, into the snow world, which he has been determined to explore: "He had to explore this new world which had been opened to him."

In fact, Aiken's story abounds with references to explorers: Robert Edwin Peary, Robert Falcon Scott, Sir Ernest Henry Shackleton, Christopher Columbus, and Henry Hudson. These references are instructive: Scott reached the South Pole but perished on the return trip; Hudson searched for the Northwest Passage to the Orient, a region as exotic as the snow world, but Paul observes that Hudson was disappointed. Explorations of the new worlds may seem promising and exciting, but those journeys also end in disappointment, death, or dead ends. The inner geography is mirrored by the geography lesson being taught by Miss Buell, who first talks about the equator and then about the North Pole, the "land of perpetual snow."

Paul's exploration becomes in part 2 a kind of odyssey, a journey homeward, not necessarily to his parent's home (he asks himself, "Homeward?"), but to another home. The journey to the snow world that is completed when the "bare black floor was like a little raft tossed in waves of snow" actually starts in the classroom, where Paul is also adrift. Like a captain at sea, he charts his course by the stars, in this case the "constellation of freckles" on the back of his classmate Deidre's neck. In effect, Deidre serves as a guide, a reference point by which he can calculate his position. When class is over, he follows her in rising from his seat.

Style and Technique

Aiken's story relies on both literary and psychological symbolism. By forcing the reader to adopt Paul's point of view, Aiken encourages his audience to identify with the boy, who seems locked in conflict with his father in a classical Oedipal situation. Paul mentions his conflict with his father and mother, but he only speaks of talking with his mother. When the examination (the "inquisition" as seen by Paul) occurs, Paul hears his father's soft and cold voice of "silken warning"; later, Paul hears the "resonant and cruel" punishment voice. In fact, Paul cannot meet his father's gaze, for he sees only his father's brown slippers, which come closer and closer.

Not only does the reader adopt Paul's perspective (the examination is an "inquisition" and a "cross-examination," both of which imply Paul as persecuted victim), but also the reader shares Paul's thoughts as Aiken moves from third-person limited point of view to an even more intimate stream-of-consciousness narration. As a result, Paul's interpretation of the events seems so convincing that a concerned mother's visit becomes an invasion by an "alien," that a cruel "I hate you!" becomes an exorcising phrase. (The references to "exorcism" and "inquisition" suggest that Paul's world has become a religion for him.)

Aiken's style also involves the use of imagery that suggests corruption and the failure of relationships. As he walks home, Paul notices "items of mere externality" that comment ironically on his internal state: a dirty newspaper touting an ointment for eczema, a physical corruption; "lost twigs descended from their parent trees," surely a reference to his own relationship to his father; a piece of gravel on the "lip of a sewer," balanced like Paul between two states; "a fragment of eggshell," which suggests birth and a divided personality; and a gateway with balanced egg-shaped stones, thereby connoting an entrance to another world while referring again to birth and potential development.

Perhaps because of his relationship with his father, Paul also pauses at the empty birdhouse, which obliquely relates to his own home. That the mere details are meant to represent the real world seems obvious because Aiken uses large-scale terms with small objects: There is a "continent of brown mud" and a "delta" near the gutter. What Paul sees is a microcosm of the macrocosm, the real world.

Compared to this world of "the usual, the ordinary," Paul's snow world is understandably appealing, because it is a combination of "ethereal loveliness" and terrifying beauty. Aiken observes that no fairy story Paul had ever read could compare to it, and, ironically, when the snow speaks, it is in terms of a fairy tale, which can also be beautiful and terrifying (and many deal with failed family relationships): "I will tell you a better story than Little Kay of the Skates or the Snow Ghost." In the familiar guise of a fairy tale, the snow draws Paul into a story of a flower becoming a seed. Rather than stressing growth and development, the story describes regression and withdrawal from the real world.

Thomas L. Erskine

A SILVER DISH

Author: Saul Bellow (1915-   )
Type of plot: Psychological
Time of plot: The mid-twentieth century
Locale: Chicago
First published: 1978

> *Principal characters:*
> WOODY SELBST, a businessman
> MORRIS SELBST, his deceased father
> MRS. SKOGLUND, a wealthy widow

The Story

After his father's death, Woody Selbst feels a yawning emptiness in his life. At the age of sixty, he is deeply disturbed by questions about the meanings of life and death. In his period of mourning, he recalls a trip to the White Nile, where he had seen a buffalo calf being seized by a crocodile while the parent buffalo looked on without understanding what was happening. Their brute grief now helps him to cope with his own.

As Woody reflects on his own life, his father's, and their unusual relationship, the story reveals the contours of Woody's imagination and the travails of his experiences. His present life is full of cares, for he supports his invalid mother and two insane sisters, one of whom he has committed to a mental institution; a wife, from whom he has been separated for fifteen years; a mistress; and, now, his father's widow, Halina, and her son, who plays the organ at games in the stadium. Despite the number of dependents whom he has accumulated, Woody lives alone, working as a tile contractor.

As a youth, Woody grew up fast, and his spirit has remained independent; at the funeral parlor, he insisted on dressing the corpse for burial, and at the funeral, he rolled up his sleeves and shoveled the dirt himself. There is no harm in Woody, yet his self-respect has not allowed him to live entirely within the law and has led him, over the course of his life, into theft, smuggling, procuring, and adultery. Still, he is moved by honesty, he hates faking, and he has always held in his heart both a belief in love and "a secret certainty that the goal set for this earth was that it should be filled with good, saturated with it."

Woody's memories and reflections probe these elements of his personality. His parents exerted very different influences on him. His mother had been converted to Christianity by Aunt Rebecca's husband, the Reverend Dr. Kovner, himself a converted Jew, whose ministry was financed by a wealthy widow, Mrs. Skoglund. Kovner imparted his fervor to Woody and "taught him to lift up his eyes, gave him his higher life." After the boy accepted Jesus as his personal redeemer, he was paid fifty cents to stand up in churches and give his testimony.

Though not a very devout Jew, Morris Selbst was increasingly alienated from his converted family. He considered Kovner a fool and resented the way his wife and daughters were being turned into "welfare personalities" who would lose their "individual outlines." Standing for "real life and free instincts, against religion and hypocrisy," he tried to rescue his son from their religion and hypochondria. Under their influence, he believed, Woody would not "even understand what life is. Because they don't know—those silly Christers."

Morris was an earthy, common, thick, physical man, "like a horseman from Central Asia, a bandit from China." He had fallen in love with a refined English girl in Liverpool, in whose cellar he had slept, having been abandoned at the age of twelve by his family of Polish Jews on their way to America. Then, at sixteen, he scabbed his way onto a ship during a seaman's strike and brought Woody's mother with him to Brooklyn. Settling eventually in Chicago, he pursued horses, cards, billiards, and women, always living life in "his own vital, picturesque, original way."

Woody remembers one spring afternoon when his father deserted the family and took off with a married woman, Halina Bujak, who worked in his shop. "From now on you're the man of the house," Morris told his fourteen-year-old son before asking him for money to buy gasoline.

Woody's central memory involves the time his father stole a silver dish and the two came to blows over the theft. They had braved a blizzard to come to Mrs. Skoglund's home in Evanston to ask for fifty dollars, which Morris said he needed to keep his business going. While the old lady and her servant withdrew to pray over the matter, Morris shocked his son by picking the lock on a cabinet, taking out a silver dish, and stuffing it into his trousers. Woody begged him to put it back, but he would not, so Woody wrestled his father to the floor, receiving several blows to the face, enough to rattle his teeth, before the ladies returned.

They left with the silver dish and a check for fifty dollars. Later, after the theft had been discovered and Morris had fallen under suspicion, Woody stoutly maintained his father's innocence, on pain of being expelled from the seminary where Mrs. Skoglund had been paying his tuition.

Father and son debated the episode "in various moods and from various elevations and perspectives for forty years and more, as their intimacy changed, developed, matured." After the funeral, Woody reflects on how his father, with a silver dish, had defeated his mother's influence and "carried him back to his side of the line, blood of his blood."

Indeed, when Woody became a man, he chose to live his life imaginatively, expensively, as his self-willed father might. On vacations, he traveled to such places as Mexico, Uganda, Istanbul, Delphi, Burma, and Jerusalem. In Japan, he saw the temple gardens, the holy places, and "the dirtiest strip show on earth." In Addis Ababa, he lured an Ethiopian beauty from the street into his shower. He taught American obscenities to a black woman in Kenya.

The story ends with Woody's memory of his father's death. The old man was writhing in his hospital bed, trying to rip out the intravenous needles. Woody astonished the nurses by climbing into bed with his father to soothe and still him. While he held him in his arms, he felt his father's body growing colder and colder as life left it.

Themes and Meanings

Written at a time when Americans, young and old, were perplexed by "the generation gap," this story explores relationships between the generations of a quintessentially American family. Like many characters in ancient and modern literature, Woody finds the search for his identity inextricably tangled with his genealogical roots. From his parents, he inherits seemingly incompatible impulses toward sincerity and mischief, instinct and refinement, recklessness and responsibility. Woody is "leading a double life," the narrator says, "sacred and profane."

Coming to terms with his own identity is, therefore, largely a matter of reaching an understanding of his father's vices, an understanding that goes beyond the righteous scorn or kind forgiveness of his mother and her circle. The episode involving the silver dish brings Woody's emotional conflicts into sharpest relief; he gathers from it a comprehension not only of his father's energetic though immoral imagination but also of his female relatives' insipid religiosity. His immediate reaction to the theft was like theirs, but ultimately he sided with his father against them.

Perhaps the most intriguing insight in this study of generations is the way the author has made the father more immature than the son. Morris's impulsiveness, his puerile sinning, and his financial irresponsibility often seem more juvenile than Woody's foibles: Consider the irony of a son physically punishing his father for stealing; imagine a fourteen-year-old boy financing his own father's desertion. Often the child plays father to the man.

For all the individuality with which these two characters are drawn, they assume mythic dimensions inasmuch as they stand for two of the nation's most interesting generations, those that made the 1920's roar and the 1960's soar. An immigrant, Morris is a typical burly, passionate, broad-shouldered Chicagoan who survived the Great Depression. He wants his son to be "like himself, an American." By the time his father dies, Woody has grown "fleshy and big, like a figure for the victory of American materialism." With his Lincoln Continental, his tile business, and his foreign vacations, Woody typifies mid-century generations of Americans who brought seeds planted by indigent immigrants to fruition. Born a Jew, converted to Christianity, and finally lapsed into agnosticism, Woody embodies the dynamic religious mélange of American culture. The tensions and anxieties he suffers from the competing claims of these traditions are those of the nation as a whole.

Style and Technique

Although this story belongs to the tradition of American realism, its technique should be distinguished from the more external, hard-boiled objectivity of realists such as Ernest Hemingway. This story is more concerned with revealing the inward thoughts and feelings of its characters than to present them in a succession of dramatic incidents. Characters' reactions to events are as important as the events themselves.

The story is based on Woody's memories and mental reflections, but it does not plunge the reader into a stream of consciousness. Thoughts and actions are presented objectively rather than subjectively, through the words of a narrator who refers to Woody in the third person. Such narratorial objectivity may blunt the lyricism of Woody's plaint, though it absolves him of much of the onus of self-pleading.

Convincing characterizations are achieved through ingenious selection of revelatory detail, such as Morris's theory of breast cancer, the image of Mrs. Skoglund's servant wiping the doorknobs with rubbing alcohol after guests had left, or the mention of Woody's wife still not being able to shop for herself though she had lived alone for fifteen years.

The style is, for the most part, casual and plain. The diction is generally less crude than that of most men such as Morris and Woody, but dialogue is rendered naturally, without obtrusive literary elevation.

The sound of bells is perhaps the most delicately drawn image in the story. Woody believes that their "vibrations and the banging did something for him—cleansed his insides, purified his blood." Connected as they are with churches, bells recall the religious agony at the center of Woody's life. They also symbolize the honesty that Woody and his father valued so highly, for, as the narrator says, "A bell was a one-way throat, had only one thing to tell you and simply told it." Woody's soul is perhaps best described by the narrator's epithet, "bell-battered."

John L. McLean

THE SILVER MINE

Author: Selma Lagerlöf (1858-1940)
Type of plot: Didactic
Time of plot: 1788
Locale: Dalecarlia, Sweden
First published: "Silvergruvan," 1908 (English translation, 1910)

> *Principal characters:*
> KING GUSTAF III OF SWEDEN
> PARSON OF DALECARLIA
> MINERALOGIST
> OLAF and
> ERIC SVARD, soldiers
> ISRAEL PER PERSSON, a peasant
> STEN STENSSON, an innkeeper who discovers (with the parson,
> the Svards, and Persson) the silver mountain

The Story

As a result of King Gustaf's demands that it go faster, his coach, traveling on a poor rural road of Dalecarlia, breaks down. The king's will is thus proved limited, unable to control objective reality. While his coach is being repaired, the king visits a church, where he beholds what he takes to be "the finest lot of folk he had ever seen . . . with intelligent and earnest faces." He is prompted to appeal for their help in his war against the Russians and Danes, but the peasants shift the burden of a response to their pastor. In the vestry, a rugged and rough peasant greets the king, who, again judging on the basis of outward appearance, snubs the peasant (who is in fact the pastor). Instead of immediately identifying himself, the peasant-pastor provokes the king to reveal his elitist bias, his contemptuous attitude, to the peasantry.

The peasant explains to the king that the pastor may be able to procure money for the king by narrating the story of how the parson, together with four hunters from the parish, stumbled on a hidden silver mine and how these "dignified and excellent men" were corrupted by the prospect of so much wealth. Confronted with the ensuing moral degeneration of the parishioners, the parson resolves that he will not reveal to anyone the whereabouts of the silver and that if the people persist in their evil ways, he will leave them.

Given the parson's tested virtue of self-abnegation, the king doubts if he could convince him to reveal the secret treasure. The peasant (whose alternate identity as parson the king fails to discern) makes an exception if the silver were used to save the Fatherland. This subordination of the peasantry's welfare to the nation triggers a sudden illumination in the king, who changes his haughty stance and now acclaims the evasive congregation as "a beautiful sight" totally gratifying for Sweden's king. The pastor's practice of not exalting himself above his flock quickens "all that was noble and great within" the king.

The reader senses at this point that the king has already intuited the pastor behind the poor peasant's unassuming but astute "disguise." Despite the danger besetting the kingdom, the king formulates the moral decision that "the kingdom is better served with men than with money."

When the king is asked by a peasant outside the church whether the pastor gave their collective response, the king replies yes. No doubt the community's trust in their pastor, based on an actualized egalitarian principle, contrasts with their suspicion of the king, whose army, riddled with traitors, signifies the king's morally questionable rule. This episode of moral instruction through a didactic recollection of a past incident suggests the need for a democratic mutuality of concern and the abolition of class distinctions if justice and compassion are to prevail.

Themes and Meanings

It is clear that the salient thematic issue involves the blindness of the king (monarchical authority) to the plight of his subjects; the injustice of a hierarchical, feudal system based on private ownership of property (land, in particular) that fosters violent competition; and the priority of the spiritual good of the community over the claims of the wealth-seeking individual. On the surface, it is easy to reduce such a complex web of thematic motifs to the simplistic idea that money, or speculation of property, corrupts; that wealth is the root of all evil. If one reflects further, however, one can see that it is on the problematic relation between the king and the parson, who represents the peasantry or common people, that the text focuses. Although the prospect of owning the silver ruins the people, the parson believes that it can do good in the service of the country.

When the king inquires if the pastor is ready to be responsible for surrendering that wealth to the Fatherland no matter what happens to the parishioners, he says that he is, and that the fate of his flock "can rest in God's hand." This demonstrates the pastor's independence of mind, his strong faith, and his loyalty to the welfare of the nation. He is therefore selfless both as peasant and as pastor in relation to a larger good to which, he believes, even the king should submit. This value the king confirms when he decides to preserve the integrity of the peasants: "Inasmuch as you have labored and starved a lifetime to make this people such as you would have it, you may keep it as it is."

Connected with this paternalistic care for the spiritual health of the peasants is the king's conservative attitude that these subjects should not disturb the status quo or rebel against the present social arrangement. The silver mine betokens disruption and subversion of the existing class system. The fratricide committed by Olaf Svard (recounted in the parson's story told to the king) and the promise Svard exacts from the parson before he is hanged (that nothing of the mine be given to his children) proves this unsettling effect of the possibility of access to power through wealth.

The fact that the peasantry delegate their right of representation to the pastor may argue for their conservatism, their habit of allowing others to speak and make decisions for them. Because of his poverty and honesty, however, the pastor demonstrates the unifying and stabilizing practice of democracy: He refuses to make his wisdom dominate his flock. He subordinates himself to his parishioners. In contrast, the king maintains his aristocratic distance up to the end, refusing even to acknowledge openly his mistake in not recognizing the pastor underneath the peasant, even though he affirms the superior value of such "men" over money. The king reconfirms the pastor's role of "spiritual adviser" in this validation of unflinching self-denial of which the pastor is the model.

Where, then, is the criticism of hierarchy? It appears in the pastor's decision not to reveal himself to the king and simply deal with him as a peasant, forcing the king to regard him seriously for what he has to say. The king not only ignores the peasants but also despises them. By expressing his criticism of the pastor as "a bit arbitrary" and authoritarian because he "wants to be the only one to counsel and rule in this parish," preaching "a pure and clear gospel," the peasant detaches himself from his assigned role as pastor and indirectly voices the protest of the dispossessed subjects and plebeians against indifferent rule. The king's patronizing approval of the pastor as portrayed by the peasant sanctions the fact of class division: "'Then, at all events, he has led and managed in the best possible way.' He didn't like it that the peasant complained of one who was placed above him. 'To me it appears as though good habits and old-time simplicity were the rule here.'" "Good habits" and "simplicity" imply submission to an unjust social order. It is only through this ruse, an example of peasant cunning, that the peasant succeeds in bringing the king to listen to him and realize that the dominated class has something that equals if not transcends the honor and aristocratic learning of the privileged nobility.

However, this project of the narrator-peasant to engage in dialogue with the king and teach him a lesson is accomplished at the expense of maintaining the peasants' poverty as their only resource, the sole guarantee of their virtue. So long as the king represents the Fatherland, his right to rule is not questioned—but then the peasants in the beginning do not really recognize him. In effect, the king has not earned the right to exercise kingly authority, and he remains powerless at the end, even though he may have gained insight into the humanity of his peasant subjects. His rule remains arbitrary; the "silver" quality of the people remains hidden, unexplored and untapped. The egalitarian peace and communal wholeness of such rural retreat, with nature and religion blended together, will endure despite intrusions of arbitrary power and the seductions of the individualistic, war-ridden world.

Style and Technique

The structure of the narrative comprises three parts: the breakdown of the king's coach caused in part by the poor country roads, the king's speech to the Sunday worshipers in which he tells a lie, and the king's reception of the pastor's narrative of the silver and its lesson. Employing a third-person point of view moving from the king to the pastor, the narrative progresses from description of the king's accident, over which he has no control, to his enforced listening to the parson's narrative of the accidental finding of the mountain and the subsequent ordeal of the people. This progression suggests the influence of inscrutable fate, of a providential force that guides human destiny.

The two principal protagonists dramatize the disparity and conflict between the peasantry and the monarchy. They conform to the conventional view that attributes taciturn cunning and prudential calculation to the oppressed peasantry, and paternalistic if arbitrary nobility to the king. Here, however, such feudal obligation is amiss: The peasants never expect a visit from the king. The king's remark to the parson's disclosure of the people's plight captures the king's indifference: "'Human beings here would certainly be no better than others if this world's temptations came closer to them,'" said the parson. "'But there's no fear of anything of the sort happening,' said the King with a shrug."

The narrator's characterization of the pastor is a subtle embodiment of the fundamental moral problem of how an oppressed class can make its voice heard. The whole point of the story-within-a-story framework, which contains the people's answer to the king's appeal, becomes clear: Fiction, the imagination that imbues the storyteller with a magical power, enables him to project the exemplary role of the pastor whose mind and actions coalesce in a way that condemns the king's duplicity. That framework traps the king in the tangle of suspense, even though at the end the king redeems himself by generously acknowledging the intrinsic worth of his dominated subjects.

Selma Lagerlöf concentrates on delineating a few gestures and remarks loaded with meaning, relying on actions that imply considered moral thought and judgment. The parson's story suggests that a selfless will can prevent fate and social norms from destroying humans; it delivers a whole philosophy, a utopian vision of community, exceeding the utilitarian demand of the king. By incorporating the parson's sacrifice into the routine event of a king's unexpected stopover, Lagerlöf suggests that an unjust society can be saved and renewed by mobilizing the spiritual strength and shrewdness of the peasantry.

E. San Juan, Jr.

SILVER WATER

Author: Amy Bloom (1953-   )
Type of plot: Realism
Time of plot: The 1980's
Locale: Connecticut
First published: 1991

> *Principal characters:*
> VIOLET, the narrator
> ROSE, her mentally ill sister
> DAVID, her father, a psychiatrist
> GALEN, her mother, a musician
> DR. THORNE, Rose's therapist

The Story

Written by a psychotherapist, "Silver Water" dares to be funny about a very serious subject, the mental illness of a family member. The story is told in the first person by Violet, the sister of the mentally ill Rose, and begins with an anecdote about the sisters being taken to see the opera *La Traviata* when Violet was twelve and Rose was fourteen. After the opera, in the parking lot, Rose says, "Check this out" and opens her mouth and sings with what Violet describes as a voice like mountain water in a silver pitcher. Violet relates this incident to all of Rose's therapists, wanting them to know that before she started aimlessly singing commercials and fast-food jingles, there had been Puccini and Mozart and hymns so sweet "you expected Jesus to come down off his cross and clap." Violet wants everyone to understand that before Rose became psychotic and gained so much weight that she had to wear maternity tops and sweatpants, she was the prettiest girl in Arrandale Elementary School.

Rose had her initial psychotic break, first recognized by her mother, Galen, and sadly acknowledged by her psychiatrist father, David, when she was fifteen. Violet describes the family therapists they take Rose to see and how the family hates them. The worst therapist they take Rose to see refers to her in the third person even though she is present, a fact that Violet points out and with which the entire family agrees. The best family therapist they meet is Dr. Thorne, a three-hundred-pound Texan whom Rose loves and calls Big Nut. After meeting Dr. Thorne, Rose starts taking her medication, loses fifty pounds, and begins singing at an African American church down the street from the halfway house in which she stays. As time passes, Violet goes to college and Rose manages to cope well; though she hears voices that urge her to do "bad things," usually Dr. Thorne can bring her back again.

However, after five years of seeing Rose, Dr. Thorne dies. Rose stops taking her medication and gets thrown out of the halfway house for pitching someone down the stairs. The family tries various means to help Rose. At one point, her mother promises her that she can drive the new family car if she will take her medication. While the family waits for Rose's new insurance to take effect, she gets worse, breaking the furniture and keeping the family up all night. At one point she begins banging her head against the floor, until Violet, who is home from her job teaching English, stops her by throwing herself on the kitchen floor, becoming the spot against which Rose was banging her head. Violet goes to Rose's room the next morning and, finding her semiconscious from an overdose of pills, allows her to die in her arms. At the funeral, Violet remembers Rose at age fifteen singing with a voice like "silver water" in the parking lot after the opera.

Themes and Meanings

"Silver Water," which won a National Magazine Award when it was first published, is the best-known story, as well as one of three stories about Violet's family, in Amy Bloom's first collection of stories, *Come to Me*. The book was enthusiastically received because Bloom, a practicing psychotherapist, was able to make the reader sympathetic to such sensitive and taboo subjects as mental illness, voyeurism, and incest. Although "Silver Water" has been praised as an "unflinching look" at how mental illness can both destroy and unite a family, the story is absolutely unsentimental, using instead the comic point of view of Violet, the sister of the mentally disturbed Rose.

The key to the story's thematic significance is Bloom's treatment of Rose and her family's means of coping with her mental illness. Although Rose has psychotic breaks and engages in inappropriate behavior, she is intelligent, talented, and witty. Also, although the family is clearly distressed by her illness, they laugh at her behavior and mock the family therapists they take her to see. For example, at one such session, when Rose begins massaging her breasts, her usual "opening salvo" for new therapists, the family laughs. When the therapist, in all seriousness, asks why everyone thinks Rose's inappropriate behavior is funny, Rose burps loudly, and the family laughs again. When the therapist continually refers to Rose in the third person, Rose calls him Ferret Face and the family laughs again. When they leave, Violet says that Rose was still nuts, but at least they had had a little fun. This comic approach holds the family together.

What Bloom does in "Silver Water" is merge the serious medical condition of mental illness with the common notion of referring to any bizarre, comic behavior as "crazy." In fact, when Rose begins acting strangely at age fifteen, her mother tells her father, who is a psychiatrist, that Rose is "going off," that she is "going crazy." Although such terminology for mentally ill people is often considered insensitive, Bloom accepts the fact that in spite of the fact that often the behavior of the mentally ill is frightening, it is also sometimes quite funny.

Rose and the family love Dr. Thorne precisely because he, like them, maintains a comic approach to Rose's illness. For example, when Rose goes through a phase of wanting to have sex with everyone, he tells her that he just cannot make love to every beautiful woman he meets. When Thorne, a Texan who weighs three hundred pounds, dies of an aneurysm, Rose, confronted with seriousness once again, stops taking her medication and gets steadily worse. At this point in the story, as Rose becomes more and more uncontrollable, her behavior is not funny any more, but rather self-destructive. Consequently, Violet's allowing her to die after taking an overdose of pills is seen as an act of love for one who has been completely transformed and is beyond hope of recovery.

Style and Technique

Style is everything in "Silver Water." The plot is minimal, and the theme of the pain and difficulty a family experiences when a family member suffers mental illness is obvious. However, neither plot nor theme constitutes the appeal of the story. Rather it is the clever, brittle, witty tone of Violet, the narrator, that gives the story its energy and charm. For example, when Rose begins singing in the choir of an African American church, Violet describes her as "bigger, blonder, and pinker than any two white women could be." She describes Dr. Thorne's funeral as like a Lourdes for the mentally ill. People were shaking so badly from years of taking medication, she says, that they fell out of the pews. Both the crazy people and the not-so-crazy huddled together in the church like "puppies at the pound." Although the actuality of what Violet describes here is certainly not funny, the way she describes it is calculated to make the reader laugh.

However, it is not only the comic point of view that makes the story work, but also the tenderness and love that Violet simultaneously expresses toward her sister, both at the beginning when she describes that moment when Rose sings in the parking lot, her voice crystalline and bright, and at the end, when she cradles Rose in her arms and sits with her until she dies of an overdose.

The perspective that Bloom brings to mental illness in this story would perhaps sound brittle and uncaring except for the fact that Violet and, indeed, her whole family have earned the right to take a comic approach to Rose's mental illness. Furthermore, because Bloom is a psychotherapist, she also convinces the reader that she has earned the right to take a less than serious approach. The tone of the story gives the reader permission to laugh at what is at once both terribly sad and also very funny. That Bloom does this with such cleverness may be too facile to some readers, but nevertheless, the success of her book *Come to Me*, which was nominated for the National Book Award and sold very well, seems to suggest that she has given readers permission to respond to the mystery of mental illness with kind amusement.

Charles E. May

A SIMPLE HEART

Author: Gustave Flaubert (1821-1880)
Type of plot: Psychological
Time of plot: The nineteenth century
Locale: The French province of Normandy, in and around Pont-l'Eveque, Trouville, and Honfleur
First published: "Un Cœur simple," 1877 (English translation, 1903)

> *Principal characters:*
> FÉLICITÉ BARETTE, the protagonist and "simple heart" of the title, an orphaned farmgirl who spends her life as a domestic in Pont-l'Eveque
> MME AUBAIN, her widowed employer
> PAUL AUBAIN and
> VIRGINIE AUBAIN, Mme Aubain's children, ages seven and four, respectively, at Félicitié's arrival in the household
> VICTOR LEROUX, Félicité's nephew

The Story

"A Simple Heart" embraces in only a few pages the story of an entire life, that of a woman born into the most unfortunate and narrowest of circumstances, a woman who lives within the narrowest frame of reference. The story is divided into five distinct sections. The first gives an overview of the Aubain household and the daily routine of Félicité Barette. For fifty years, the surrounding world sees her as a possession of Mme Aubain, a paragon of domestics: frugal, hardworking, unchanging. She seems an automaton, a wooden woman. The human being behind the mask is seen in the subsequent parts of the story.

Félicité, an orphan reared haphazardly as a barnyard laborer, exposed to want and abuse, is without personal attractions or affections. She is courted briefly by a brusque young farmer who is looking for an establishment and safety from the draft. When he marries a wealthy, older widow, Félicité spends one night in the fields, weeping, then gives notice and leaves her farm for the small town of Pont-l'Eveque. In front of the inn there, she meets the young Mme Aubain, a widow in reduced circumstances, and is engaged as a domestic after a brief conversation, because she is full of such goodwill and makes so few demands, although she is very ignorant. Félicité's early involvement with the Aubain household centers on her affection for the children of her employer. She also orients herself within a weekly round of visits from a set circle of acquaintances of Madame and occasional idyllic visits to the Aubain property in the countryside. On one such visit, Félicité saves the family from a charging bull, bravely holding it at bay until all escape. She ignores her newfound reputation for heroism. A more far-reaching concern is Virginie Aubain's resulting nervous invalidism, treated by ocean baths at Trouville. There Félicité is reunited with a long-lost sister and meets her young nephew Victor, another child for her to love. This second part of her story ends with the breaking of the Aubain family circle as Paul is sent away to school

Virginie is now sent to catechism lessons, in preparation for her first Communion, and Félicité is introduced to the world of religious faith, which she accepts, despite her years, in a childlike manner. She trembles in sympathy with each step of Virginie's initiation into the Church, feeling more of a thrill as the beloved child accepts the Host than when she herself goes to Communion. However, Virginie, in her turn, must go away to school, and Félicité is desolate. She and Mme Aubain lead parallel but nonintersecting affectionate lives. Madame can attempt to fill the void with letters, but the illiterate Félicité invites her nephew Victor and lavishes her love on him. As he grows older, he becomes a sailor, bringing her small gifts from his first short voyages. His first long voyage takes him to Havana. Félicité, with her childlike vision of the world, cannot comprehend the distances involved, does not understand when shown a map, and imagines a world of cigars and cartoon blacks. Virginie Aubain's worsening illness obscures Félicité's anxieties over Victor. When he dies of fever and poor doctoring in Havana, her grief is enormous, but she stifles its expression and continues her round of work. Virginie's death at the convent school prostrates her mother. It is the servant who must care for the little body, praying over her darling and wishing for a miracle, Félicité who must care for and groom the little grave. In time, Mme Aubain recognizes this silent anguish, and her acceptance of Félicité's grief in one moment of sympathy binds the servant to her with a devotion that is quasi-religious.

The fourth part of the story is dominated by Loulou, a parrot that is swept into the domestic backwater of the Aubain household by faraway political events. Bright in color, quaint in his actions, he fascinates Félicité and fills her life with affection again. The details of his life absorb her. When he escapes, briefly, she devotes such fervor to searching for him that she catches a severe chill, suffers from angina, and eventually loses her hearing. The parrot's shrill voice becomes her only link to the world of sound, but in 1837 he dies, during a severe cold spell. On Mme Aubain's suggestion, Félicité sends Loulou to Le Havre to be stuffed. On his return, he becomes her idol, placed in her small room along with all the religious and personal relics of her life. Here, with the passage of time and her increasing isolation from the world, the parrot comes to represent the Holy Spirit. She sleepwalks through life, rousing only to preparations for the yearly celebration of the Feast of Corpus Christi. The even tenor of the years in broken by three events: Paul Aubain marries, the old family lawyer kills himself amid shameful circumstances, and Mme Aubain, disheartened by both events, sickens and dies. Félicité is deprived all at once of her reasons for living; she remains in the Aubain home, maintained in her attic room by a legacy from Mme Aubain, but Paul sells the other contents of the home and leaves it empty, up for rent or sale. Life is narrowed to the smallest scope possible, and many years pass with no change in externals, except that the house grows more and more dilapidated. One damp, cold winter, Félicité coughs blood, and around Easter, she develops pneumonia.

The final movement of "A Simple Heart" brings the death and transfiguration of

Félicité, lying blind, deaf, and cared for out of charity by a kind neighbor. The temporary altar used for display of the Host during the procession of Corpus Christi has been built in the Aubain courtyard, and Félicité has sent her only treasure, Loulou, to adorn it. She creates the procession, the gay sights and sounds in her mind as she lies dying, the typical small-town personalities amid the excitement and flowers of the summer festival. When the neighbor climbs up and peeks out Félicité's attic window, Loulou is seen, a brilliant blue patch amid the surrounding profusions of flowers, laces, and personal treasures given to enrich the altar. Félicité smells the incense rising to her room, and in communion with the festival below, slips gently out of life into a Heaven whose opening skies reveal a gigantic parrot hovering in welcome.

Themes and Meanings

Gustave Flaubert uses the story of Félicité to study the transcendence of the qualities of love, courage, and faith in a life firmly anchored in the most tragic, sordid, and limited circumstances. Félicité has no pretensions to beauty or intellect, and every aspect of her life has its burden of sorrow. She has glimpses of the tragically barren nature of her life in general, forever a servant, her loves lost to death or betrayal. However, her own capacity to love and serve beautifies and transforms this life. It is impossible to discuss Félicité without reference to the strong Christian framework given by the writer, both through Félicité's faith and through her embodiment of an ethic expressed in the Gospels. She is a loving, suffering servant, feeding the hungry, caring for the dying, ever humble and childlike in her faith.

The parrot, Loulou, invested by Félicité with qualities of a religious image, embodies the paradox of Félicité's faith. There is much that is comical and grotesque in the old servant's love for the gaudy bird. However, there is much that is also an element of purest mysticism, which transforms Loulou into a fully satisfying symbol of the divine in Félicité's life, the power of the Holy Spirit, imperfectly understood yet leading the soul to transcendence. The reader shares Félicité's deathbed vision and trusts its clarity as the heavens open before her.

It has been suggested that Flaubert based the characters and plot of this story on autobiographical elements. Félicité corresponds to Julie, a faithful servant in his mother's house; Mme Aubain resembles the author's mother; geographical names and descriptions are those of Flaubert's youth; and some specific incidents of the plot, such as the death of Virginie Aubain, parallel events in the life of the author's family. Such biographical details, however, are not essential to an understanding of "A Simple Heart" and, in fact, may detract from the impact of the story. By the power of art, deeply felt, intimately personal material is generalized and transformed, and the transfiguration of the simple Félicité parallels the reweaving of Flaubert's story into hers.

Style and Technique

An omniscient, third-person narrator leads the reader into the world of Félicité and the Aubain family, laying out the vignettes of daily life that finally combine to form a portrait complete in all particulars. Great care is taken to produce an impression of point-to-point congruence with reality, as if one is reading a biography. Thus, many dates are explicit; the reader learns that M. Aubain died in 1809, that Victor Leroux sailed for Havana in 1818, and that Loulou died in 1837. However, although these dates are scattered throughout the story, they serve as points of reference for an orderly narration and do not overpower it. The tone of "A Simple Heart" is always steady, unemotional, even in dealing with the most touching of scenes. Dialogue is the ordinary, simple expression that predominates. The author's eye is avid for the homely detail; he exhibits Félicité as she eats her meals, slowly and deliberately, picking up the crumbs of her bread with a moist fingertip, Félicité cherishing little Virginie's moth-eaten hat as a holy relic, Félicité wearing a traditional Norman headdress whose wings mimic those of the parrot Loulou.

Flaubert's description of Félicité is framed by his evocation of her whole milieu, with pithy descriptions of typical characters such as the family lawyer, an aged veteran of the Terror of 1793, and Mme Aubain's daughter-in-law. The reader sees the Norman countryside, breathes the sea air with Virginie, attends catechism class in the country church, and joins the procession on the feast of Corpus Christi. Flaubert is known as a great stylist, forever dedicated to the search for *le mot juste*, the right word. Here, this famous search produced clear and pungent images, compact yet satisfying, which continue to bring readers into the world of Félicité Barette.

Anne W. Sienkewicz

THE SIN-EATER

Author: Margaret Atwood (1939-   )
Type of plot: Psychological
Time of plot: The 1970's
Locale: A North American city
First published: 1977

> *Principal characters:*
> JOSEPH, a psychiatrist who has just died
> THE UNNAMED NARRATOR, his female patient

The Story

The title of this story refers to a Welsh tradition in which a "sin-eater" was a person who sat up with the body of someone who died and ate a meal in the presence of the deceased in order to transfer the dead person's sins to himself or herself so that the soul of the dead could go to heaven. This symbolism is the focus of this tale about a modern psychiatrist who dies unexpectedly, leaving several former wives and many female patients feeling betrayed.

When the narrator first hears about the psychiatrist's death, she—like his other women—is horrified, yet also angry with him for having risked his life by pruning a tree, from which he fell to his death. There is a hint that the psychiatrist may have planned his death in order to punish the women who relied on him, forcing him to assume a strength of character that he did not have. His relationship with the narrator was more than professional, but less than intimate. Her sense of his betrayal infects her memories of their therapy sessions and leads her to reexamine her notions of reality and strength. As she tries to find meaning in Joseph's death, if not in his life, she recreates discussions that always led to his problems, needs, or fears. It is in this context that the story of "The Sin-Eater" is told.

Joseph, the dead psychiatrist, believed himself to be the sin-eater of his generation, absorbing all the problems, fears, and sins of his patients. However, as the story progresses, it becomes increasingly clear that his sessions were more therapeutic for him than for the women with whom he surrounded himself. He was a sad, insecure, and immature man who used women to massage his ego and make him feel important.

When the narrator attends Joseph's memorial service, she discovers that she has more in common with his former wives than with his other patients, whom she calls "crazies." Her past conversations with him now make more sense to her as she realizes that she never really needed him. She recognizes that he was a weak man who needed these women, manipulated them, and devoured their hearts and souls, rather than their sins.

The narrator dreams of meeting Joseph at an airplane terminal, where he offers her cookies, which she recognizes as his sins. At first they seem too much for her, but her fears are overcome by her instinct that her strength will support her in accepting his sins. She now knows that she can cope with life without him.

Themes and Meanings

Margaret Atwood frequently approaches the issue of selfhood in terms of a search for identity and in terms of violations of the self, as well as the dualities of life. In this story, she portrays the male psychiatrist superficially; he was clearly a person who hated women, as well as a weakling who made himself feel strong by surrounding himself with women with low self-esteem who loved and respected him because of his appearance of strength and character. The story's narrator, on the other hand, is revealed as a person with flaws, but also with great gifts.

"The Sin-Eater" explores the differences between appearance and reality. Eventually, the narrator achieves an epiphany in her attempts to strip away the superficial appearance of her psychiatrist and thereby discover the truth of both his identity and her own. The psychiatrist appeared to be strong but was in reality very weak. He assumed the role of protective parent while he was really living as a self-centered child. These contradictions ultimately led to his finest deceit—pretending to be the "sin-eater" for his women patients and former wives. Ultimately, the narrator's dream reveals her to be the true martyr.

Because Joseph smothered his women with pretended love and fatherly concern, his death, painful as it is for them to accept, ironically frees them to live more realistic and honest lives for the first time. The reader follows the narrator's movement from shocked disbelief to anger and a sense of betrayal, through fear and nostalgia, and finally to acceptance and self-respect. The reader becomes so much a part of her psyche that her dream is relatively easy to interpret.

In her dream, the narrator envisions the waiting room to heaven (or hell) as an airplane terminal in which everyone is rushing to their destiny. She sees Joseph and his blue hand as signifying death. She is supposed to devour some party cookies decorated with moons and stars. The man who tries to attract her attention has his mouth sewed shut, and the narrator recognizes him as a boy whom Joseph never forgave for destroying his flowers. His presence shows the narrator how important it is that she devour what Joseph calls his sins so that he will no longer be haunted by his selfish behavior.

The cold blue of Joseph's hand reveals that he is dead in the dream, even while his normal banter to the narrator reminds her of their former relationship. When he offers her cookies, they repel her: "They look too rich," meaning that there are too many for her to swallow. Joseph's smile, however, promises her acceptance, if not salvation. As she begins to eat the cookies, their decorative stars grow bigger and bigger until she is consumed by the universe. This dream symbolizes her ability to accept the truth about Joseph and her willingness to be the sin-eater for the sin-eater.

This story suggests that the role of victim or martyr is an individual choice, not a predetermined destiny. The narrator thinks that absorbing all of her psychiatrist's sins will be too much for her tiny soul until her dream convinces her of her own inner strength and she comes to respect herself and believe that she can survive alone.

Style and Technique

The title of "The Sin-Eater" establishes from the story's start the symbolic importance of those who sacrifice themselves for others' sins, and the story opens with a remembered conversation between the narrator and her psychiatrist. At first, readers are as shocked and disturbed by images of eating in the presence of a corpse as the narrator is. That this person is also symbolically devouring the dead person's sins is even more morbid.

The narrator's journey toward self-identity emerges in a series of remembered conversations between her and Joseph that are clearly and precisely portrayed with vivid details. As she searches for meaning, her self-addressed questions reveal a pattern. In every instance, her attempts to get treatment, support, or understanding from Joseph led to his interrupting her in order to catalog his own problems with women and their lack of understanding, as well as his fatigue and the resentment that he directed at his demanding patients.

As the narrator compares Joseph's self-image and view of his life to the realities of his life that are revealed by the comments of his former wives and patients, she recognizes that his life was a sham. This leads to her dream, which brilliantly symbolizes the nature of their relationship. She emerges strong, independent, and courageous, no longer needing a father figure to protect her.

By showing all Joseph's former wives and patients in one room, Atwood reinforces the shock of recognition that hits the narrator—a moment of insight that reveals to her the absurdity and the lie of Joseph's life and self-image. That alone is not enough, however. She must also come to grips with the fears that led her to seek psychiatric help in the first place. This is where the symbolism of the sin-eater becomes crucial to understanding Atwood's theme. The sin-eater legend suggests that a person becomes a sin-eater not by desire, but by urgent necessity, just as one becomes a prophet. This duty was so horrible, so repugnant, that only those desperate for money or food would choose to undertake it. Other people feared sin-eaters because they thought their sins would rub off on them, but they also respected them for their courage and devotion to duty.

The narrator's dream combines symbols to imply a certain meaning, yet Atwood is careful not to explain its images. This forces the reader to undertake the same journey of self-discovery as the narrator does—without fear, but with some hope. Her journey ends as the reader's begins.

Linda L. Labin

SINGING DINAH'S SONG

Author: Frank London Brown (1927-1962)
Type of plot: Psychological
Time of plot: The 1950's
Locale: A factory in a northern U.S. city
First published: 1963

> *Principal characters:*
> THE NARRATOR, a punch-press operator in a factory
> DADDY-O (JAMES), his friend and fellow worker
> CHARLIE WICOWYCZ, his shop foreman
> MR. GROBBER, the plant boss

The Story

Framed by the songs of Dinah Washington, this story falls into four parts. As it opens, the narrator recalls his work as a punch-press operator at Electronic Masters Incorporated, a company that molds sheet steel into frames for radio and television speakers. The work is demanding, the pay minimal, the heat maximal, the foremen constantly pushing workers to go faster, and the machines intolerably noisy. The work is almost more than he can bear: "I get to thinking about all that noise that that big ugly punch press makes, and me sweating, scuffing, trying to make my rates, and man I get eeevil."

Two things keep him going—his love of Dinah Washington's music that he hears over the cacophony of the shop, and his admiration for his fellow-worker, Daddy-o, who enjoys Dinah even more than he does. Daddy-o is known by a nickname because his real name, James, is not mythical enough. He is tall, strong, and dark-skinned, and he has a powerful voice. "Actually, sometimes Daddy-o scares you." He is the model against whom other men judge themselves.

On the fateful day of the second part, Daddy-o's behavior is unaccountably strange. He arrives three hours late, dressed in his best suit, shirt, tie, shoes, and hat, and he stands smoking under the giant "No Smoking" sign. He struts over to his punch press with an odd and jaunty glint in his eye. This is strange enough, but when he does the unthinkable and tries to stick his hand into the back of the machine, where all the electrical switches are, everyone stops to watch. Charlie Wicowycz, the foreman, and Mr. Grobber, the boss, try to lead Daddy-o away from the machine. At this, Daddy-o looks at each worker in turn, smiles, and makes a gesture of possession, his arms and legs spread in front of the machine: "Ain't nobody getting this machine. I own this machine, baby. This is mine. Ten years! On this machine. Baby, this belongs to me."

The third part reveals how the company deals with Daddy-o's illness and his claims of ownership. Although the sympathetic narrator tries to call Daddy-o's wife, the boss and foreman use the routine method of dealing with a troublemaker: They call the police. For all his strength and ten years of labor, Daddy-o is worn out and therefore expendable. When a big, mean-looking police officer with icewater eyes starts to bludgeon Daddy-o, the narrator again intervenes by leading him to the paddy wagon. Daddy-o walks out reluctantly. When he stops to look back at his machine, the officer clubs him, and he falls into the wagon. "I swear I could have cried," the narrator recalls.

The narrator is reminiscing again as the story concludes. He looks at Daddy-o's machine. It does not seem right without his friend. At first he is proud of how fine a worker Daddy-o was and how sharp he looked today. Then he realizes that his own situation is not much different. "I got to think about my machine. . . . Seemed funny to think it wasn't really mine. It sure seemed like mine." Like Daddy-o, he sings to keep from crying, singing Dinah's song "Blow Top Blues"—a song about a person driven insane by the pace of urban life.

Themes and Meanings

Best known for his journalism and his novels, *Trumbull Park* (1959) and the posthumous *The Myth Maker* (1969), Frank London Brown sets most of his fiction in working-class Chicago during the era of the Civil Rights movement. His usual setting is an area of work or home where blacks and whites must meet and engage one another. His first novel, for example, is named for a well-known housing development and recounts the racial violence of the late 1950's, when the real-life Brown family were among the first African Americans to take up residence there. In his fictional account, all blacks are subjected to a massive campaign to drive them out: anonymous threats, screaming mobs, bombs thrown through windows. The police are at best callous and indifferent. Ugly, smelly, clanging paddy wagons are ever present, carrying the blacks past the mobs to work, markets, and schools, even to hospitals to bear their children. However, the overarching element of the book is noise—raucous, unyielding noise. A white person is almost always screaming, usually obscenely; bricks shatter windows; firebombs set apartments ablaze; and fire trucks and police cars sound their bells and sirens constantly. Noise and tension feed each other. To relieve the tension, the main character, an airplane factory worker, draws on his favorite music, especially the songs "We Shall Not Be Moved" and "Every Day I Have the Blues."

These same elements are all present in "Singing Dinah's Song," but in a slightly different mix. Rather than race, the emphasis here is on class, on how little laborers have to call their own. Like the main characters of Brown's novel, Daddy-o has long been a figure of heroic strength and self-restraint. In his sorrows, he is like Billie Holiday. In his defense of workers' rights, he is like Samuel Gompers and John L. Lewis. In his sacrifice, standing cruciform in front of his machine, he is like Jesus. He believes that ten years of labor have given him possession of a small part of the factory. The narrator and everyone else know, however, that he owns nothing. Like slave owners, capitalists own everything, their workers nothing. For his labor, Daddy-o receives a neurosis, a concussion, and a jail term.

However, Daddy-o represents only half of the story. The narrator is equally important in assessing how much a man can withstand and how much he possesses. He is no hero. Like Ralph Ellison's "Invisible Man," he does not possess even his own name. However, he represents the small people, the average people who are Brown's readers. Faced with the institutional violence of capitalism and the law, he is helpless. He cannot help Daddy-o physically or financially. He cannot even keep Charlie from calling the dreaded police. He cannot get through to Daddy-o's wife. He cannot prevent the police from hurting Daddy-o or taking him away. He certainly cannot legally possess the machine that he calls his own. The lesson, inescapable even to him, is that he will not be able to prevent the same tragedy from befalling himself—and, by implication, everyone.

Style and Technique

Although brief, "Singing Dinah's Song" is dense with implication and allusion. After Billie Holiday, Dinah Washington was the most prominent blues vocalist of the 1950's. Her recordings were a staple of black jukeboxes in all northern cities, as Aretha Franklin would be a decade later. Like Brown, she grew up in Chicago and died young. Like Daddy-o, she sought to mold the cacophony of urban existence into rhythms of the soul. Like both of them, she saw life as a contest between noise and melody. Like them, she celebrated the spiritual heroism of the black working class. Throughout the decade, she sang poignant songs of frustrated dreams and unrequited love that mixed high-pitched, gospel-inspired intensity with tender, languorous understatement. Such was the bittersweet effect that Brown wished to translate into his writing. As Daddy-o says, "Ain't that broad mellow?"

The narrator retains the colloquial phrasing when he admits, "I was so shook when my buddy Daddy-o did his number the other day. I mean his natural number." Such common language is the vehicle for common themes—the basic human needs of jobs and dignity—that is frequently found in the work of Chicago writers. All use nicknames to give their characters a larger, mythic significance. If Daddy-o must break, must do "his natural number," then all mere mortals must soon follow. In *Poems from Prison* (1968), Etheridge Knight pays tribute to Brown with a poem on Dinah Washington and the memorable "Hardrock Returns to Prison from the Hospital for the Criminal Insane." Hardrock is a Daddy-o in prison gear who goes wild, is sent away for electroshock, and comes back without a mind.

John Sekora

THE SINGING MAN

Author: Fielding Dawson (1930-   )
Type of plot: Vignette
Time of plot: The 1960's
Locale: New York City
First published: 1973

> *Principal characters:*
> THE SINGING MAN, a delivery person
> THE NARRATOR

The Story

The anonymous narrator describes a local celebrity of sorts who regularly visits his east-side neighborhood: a large black man who pushes a hand truck and makes various kinds of deliveries. What distinguishes him from the others who make deliveries is that he sings loudly and attracts considerable attention: "The man who sings is the object of a lot of response and the victim of a million silent and spoken jokes, but there is no stopping him, because he really loves to sing." Although the black and Latino men admire him, and even envy his complete lack of self-consciousness, they also seem embarrassed by him because he may appear to be an old-fashioned stereotype to people of other races. However, this huge, singing figure seems to disturb white businesspeople because they think he is embarrassing members of his own race.

As the narrator studies the varied responses to this embarrassing but evocative figure, he notices other elements that intensify crowd reactions. To make matters worse, the singing man often forgets the words to the songs that he bellows out and occasionally even loses the thread of the melody—a situation that requires him to improvise melodies of his own. Blacks and Latinos think that white businesspeople regard the singing man as an extension of them, because he also is black, as if the white businesspeople expect them all to burst into song. In short, this figure initiates what the narrator calls a "street game."

Making the situation even more tense are the types of songs that the singing man loves to perform. These include songs like "Old Man River," from a former age that no one except hardened bigots, sentimental cynics, and irrelevant sleepwalkers want to recall. Even with these songs, the singing man often forgets the words, leaving his multicultural audience torn between wanting to help him remember and wishing that he would forget such politically incorrect songs. Through all this, the man appears unshaken by anything. The effect of "Old Man River" on the neighborhood is that it creates a "silence like a suddenly emptied city, crystallizes, and forms a *hard edge*."

The singing man saves his greatest song for his exit from this racially mixed area on Park Avenue South and Union Square. His "song of songs" is the Irish folk classic "Danny Boy." His eyes shine, his shoulders move, and he tosses his head and sings.

On an afternoon just before Christmas, the narrator sees the singing man walking by the subway entrance at Union Square. Vapor emerges from the man's lips as they form the words to "Danny Boy." He is aware of nothing but his song. The narrator has his last view of the man as his voice rises and breaks in the second octave. Though the narrator loses sight of him, he continues to hear him sing.

Themes and Meanings

The theme of this artful vignette is similar to that in many of Fielding Dawson's stories: It is a portrait of the artist. Dawson finds art and artists everywhere, but especially in his own neighborhood in the Union Square and Gramercy Park areas of New York City. However, Dawson does not just write about the theme of the artist; he delves into the very creative processes that artists practice. This vignette delineates that process in several compelling ways. The narrator, who is obviously an artist or writer himself, views this scene within what he calls "the street game," or what Dawson calls in another story "the theater of the streets." In this scenario, an unnamed singing man becomes "The Singing Man"; that is, he becomes before the eyes of the reader a mythic figure—the bard. Ancient bards were teachers, examples, and spokespeople for their people. An ancient bard, like this figure, was in contact with higher forms of divinity—in this case Orpheus, the god of song. The power of the bard was, and is in this story, to transform the consciousness of his listeners into richer and more profound aesthetic and spiritual experiences, experiences that might release them from their narrow and provincial mindsets and permit them to become aware of—even if only momentarily—their common humanity. This is exactly what Dawson's figure accomplishes even in the middle of a culturally diverse neighborhood. The song of the bard crystallizes that area for a brief moment, and the narrator notes the process in spite of the singing man's forgetfulness or the "political incorrectness" of his limited repertoire. Only art can transcend these difficult and complex boundaries by the purity of its song.

Also taking place in this narrative is a demonstration of how the narrator actually creates a riveting scene out of the chaos of everyday life. This vignette delineates the process of creativity as it transforms out of virtually nothing something deeply moving.

Style and Technique

Dawson employs a number of linguistic and painterlike methods in this highly compelling portrait. One critic identifies subject matter with method in this piece and calls it "a process parable." Because Dawson comes out of both a literary and an artistic tradition that refuses to separate form from content, that designation seems apt. Because there is no plot in this sketch, certain recurring motifs give form and structure to the seeming chaos of everyday life. As the narrator repeats over and over the words "the singing man," eventually those repetitions formulate themselves into the emergence of "the Singing Man"—a mythic figure that goes back to the days of the ancient bards. Dawson is demonstrating the process of how that operation takes place, and has always taken place wherever figures such as this appear. The actual black delivery person certainly is unaware of his mythic function, but that is the point of the story. These events and characters take place continuously, but only those attuned to their resonating presence note them and record their spiritual significance.

The other word that recurs repeatedly is "again." It is this continuous process of the resurfacing of the bard that occurs again and again. A sensitively attuned artist or writer would detect these mythic occurrences and figures every day, and this is what Dawson documents in this short but powerful vignette. The dense complexity of the syntax also mirrors the quickly changing movement of the attentions of both the narrator and the multicultural inhabitants of this particular neighborhood. That syntax also exhibits the patterns of perceptions that are instantaneously exchanged within and among the group.

Dawson has demonstrated at least three distinct processes in this piece: how an anonymous figure becomes a mythic one, how the Singing Man's Orphic power unifies a diverse group of people, and how such a "story" actually is created before the eyes of the reader. It is a virtuoso piece of complex writing that few contemporary writers would even attempt to duplicate.

Patrick Meanor

THE SIRE DE MALÉTROIT'S DOOR

Author: Robert Louis Stevenson (1850-1894)
Type of plot: Adventure
Time of plot: 1429
Locale: France
First published: 1882

> *Principal characters:*
> DENIS DE BEAULIEU, the protagonist
> BLANCHE, the niece and ward of Sire de Malétroit
> ALAIN, SIRE DE MALÉTROIT, Blanche's uncle

The Story

Denis de Beaulieu, a young cavalier, is precocious in the arts of chivalry and war. Not yet twenty-two years old, he has already killed a man in battle and is confident as he goes about his affairs. One dark, unsettled September night in 1429, Denis finds himself alone in a territory jointly occupied by Burgundian and English troops. Although he is there under safe conduct, that means little in the brutal realities of the Hundred Years' War. His situation is perilous and, after visiting a friend, he becomes lost in the unfamiliar surroundings on his return to his inn. The streets are narrow and pitch dark; he is filled with claustrophobic terror and fears being assaulted as he tries to find his way back to the security of his lodgings.

In the silent darkness of his ominous journey, Denis comes on an impressive house of some great family, ornamented by pinnacles and turrets with a chapel projecting from the main structure. The door is sheltered within a deep porch and overhung by two gargoyles. The house reminds Denis of his own house at Bourges. As he seeks to retrace his steps, he encounters a party of men-at-arms who would think nothing of killing him and leaving him where he falls. Discovered by the drunken soldiers, Denis beats a frantic retreat, taking refuge within the porch of the great house that he has just left, ready to defend himself to the death. As he draws his sword and leans against the great door, it opens before his weight and he enters as if rescued by Providence. No sooner is he within the great house than the door closes of its own accord, leaving him in absolute darkness. Saved from the marauding soldiers, Denis now faces a new fear: being trapped within a strange house.

Following a thin shaft of light up a staircase, Denis finds himself in a large apartment. Directly facing him as he enters the strongly lighted room, seated on a high chair beside the chimney, is the Sire de Malétroit, who resembles a bull, goat, or domestic boar rather than a human being. His beautiful white hair hangs straight around his head, like a saint's. His hands appear untouched by age and are at once fleshy and delicate; his tapered, sensual fingers are like those of one of Leonardo da Vinci's women. All the while, the Sire de Malétroit sits patiently on his chair like the statue of a god, contemplating Denis. In a musical murmur, he invites Denis to enter, saying he has been expecting him all evening. Having never seen the master of the house, Denis is bewildered and insists there is some mistake. When Malétroit continues to speak to Denis as an expected visitor, the young man thinks he is dealing with a lunatic. His confusion is heightened by a hurried sound of voices praying behind a wall hanging directly opposite him. When Malétroit refers to Denis as his dear nephew, the young man momentarily loses control, calling the old man a liar and threatening to force his way out of the house with his sword. Denis is told that if he tries to escape, he will be bound hand and foot by the sire's armed retainers.

At this point, the wall hanging covering the chapel door is lifted, and Denis, escorted by Malétroit and a tall priest, beholds a young girl attired in bridal finery kneeling in front of the altar, and he begins to realize his desperate situation. Malétroit explains that his family honor has been compromised by a young man who has been secretly courting his niece, standing near her daily in the church and writing her letters. He set a trap for this man in the ingenious contrivance of the door. Now that Denis has fallen into the trap, Malétroit thinks that he is the guilty party, whom he will force to marry his niece and restore the family honor. Even if Denis is not the man, however, he now shares the family's disgraceful secret; if Malétroit cannot wipe away the dishonor, at least he can stop the scandal by forcing the marriage. He gives Denis two hours to agree to marry Blanche or be hanged, and he leaves the two alone in the chapel for the allotted time.

Denis and Blanche spend this time together talking about love, honor, shame, marriage under duress, the uncertainty of life, and the transience of reputation. Their feelings for each other change several times, until they terminate in mutual trust, love, and respect. Denis will marry Blanche, not to redeem her honor, and she will marry him, not to save his life—they will marry because they truly love each other. At the end of the two hours, Malétroit enters the chapel, observes the two embracing and kissing, and wishes his new nephew a good morning.

Themes and Meanings

This story is primarily one of adventure and atmosphere, made particularly fascinating by the character of the Sire de Malétroit, as memorable a grotesque as any created by Edgar Allan Poe. There is also the underlying idea that one's ultimate destiny may be determined by unforeseen circumstances. Denis's visit to a friend ultimately ends in his engagement to Blanche, a person whom he never met previously. An individual as strong and self-willed as Denis de Beaulieu may become a victim of fate as easily as the hapless Blanche. In another sense, however, character is fate, for if Denis and Blanche do not fall in love in the two hours allotted to them by Malétroit, Denis will be hanged, becoming another forgotten casualty of the Hundred Years' War. In the opening paragraph, Robert Louis Stevenson writes that Denis's decision to visit a friend was unwise and that he "would have done better to remain beside the fire or go decently to bed." These words appear hard to reconcile with the true love that Denis develops for Blanche. Perhaps more to the point of the story's theme are the words that Malétroit speaks to Denis: "Two hours of life are always two hours. A great many things may turn up in even as little a while as that."

Style and Technique

The grotesquerie of Alain, Sire de Malétroit, the gothic setting, and the bizarre circumstances of the story all demand a high level of verisimilitude. Stevenson provides this in at least two ways: the omniscient point of view and the accumulation of descriptive details. The objective narration by the all-knowing author gives a sense that an actual event that took place in September, 1429, is being reported. Stevenson's style includes few similes and metaphors, as if he fears they may interfere with the reader's direct perception of what is going on. To create a feel for the Middle Ages, which Stevenson also masterfully accomplishes in another short story, "A Lodging for the Night," the author embellishes his narrative with such terms as "bartizan," "embrasure," "weir," "buttresses," "salle," "damoiseau," and "messire." The Christian names of Denis, Alain, and Blanche, as well as the place names of Chateau Landon and Bourges, also contribute to the medieval ambience.

The description in this story, particularly of physical setting, is so filled with sensory detail as to be almost photographic in its vividness. Denis's fearful journey through the dark passageways is vivified by such phrases as the "touch of cold window bars," "denser darkness" which threatens "an ambuscade or a chasm in the pathway," and the "strange and bewildering appearances" of the houses where the darkness was not as absolute. In the final moments of the story, the cock crows, heralding the dawn, and the daylight arising from the east grows "incandescent and [casts] up that red-hot cannon ball, the rising sun." It is at this moment of dawn that Denis and Blanche, now lovers, give their full consent to each other. If the symbolism is somewhat obtrusive, it is also effective in this strange tale of medieval romance.

Robert G. Blake

THE SISTERS

Author: James Joyce (1882-1941)
Type of plot: Domestic realism
Time of plot: 1895
Locale: Dublin, Ireland
First published: 1904

> *Principal characters:*
> THE NARRATOR, an adult recalling a childhood experience
> THE BOY'S AUNT
> ELIZA FLYNN, the sister of Father Flynn
> NANNIE FLYNN, the sister of Father Flynn

The Story

In this opening story from James Joyce's *Dubliners* (1914), the unnamed narrator is an adult recalling his first direct experience with death when he was a boy in Dublin in 1895. He tells of passing on several evenings the house in which a retired old priest, who was his mentor, lay dying. Then, when the boy, who lives with his aunt and uncle, comes down to dinner one night, he hears them and a neighbor talking about the priest, who has just died.

Old Cotter, the neighbor, says that "there was something queer . . . something uncanny about him" and refers to the priest as "one of those . . . peculiar cases." The uncle recalls that Father Flynn taught the boy "a great deal . . . and they say he had a great wish for him." However, the "wish," or respect, that the priest had for the boy does not impress old Cotter and the family, for they are anti-intellectual and indifferent to education. The uncle even disparagingly refers to his nephew as "that Rosicrucian" and agrees with Cotter that youngsters should focus on physical activities.

During their conversation, the adults talk about the boy as if he were not present, though they closely observe him. Knowing this, the boy continues eating "as if the news had not interested [him]." Actually, he becomes increasingly upset by the comments and crams his mouth with porridge to keep from venting his anger.

The next morning, he goes to the New Britain Street house where the priest lived with his two sisters above a drapery shop, and the bouquet and card on the door confirm for him the fact that his old friend indeed has died; therefore, he does not want to knock. Wandering about Dublin in the wake of this decision, he remarks to himself that neither he nor the day "seemed in a mourning mood" and that he felt "a sensation of freedom as if . . . freed from something by his death." Though he does not comprehend what is happening, he is, for the first time, seeing that the world at large is unaffected by one person's death and that life goes on. In other words, the death of his mentor—or surrogate parent—is a major event in his progress toward maturity. As he continues to walk through sunny Dublin (the narrator mentions the sun twice in this context, as if emphasizing the indifference of the world to Father Flynn's death), the boy remembers what the priest had taught him, including "stories about the catacombs and about Napoleon Bonaparte, and . . . the meaning of the different ceremonies of the Mass and of the different vestments worn by the priest."

That evening, accompanied by his aunt, he visits "the house of mourning," climbing a narrow staircase "towards the open door of the dead-room," which he hesitates to enter until one of the priest's old sisters beckons to him repeatedly. There Father Flynn is lying, "solemn and copious, vested as for the altar, his large hands loosely retaining a chalice." When the three kneel at the foot of the bed to pray, the boy cannot "because the old woman's mutterings distracted [him]." At this point, about two-thirds through the story, the focus shifts to Nannie and Eliza, the priest's old sisters.

Nannie leads the guests to the sitting room, where she serves wine and crackers, and then sits on a sofa and falls asleep, having fulfilled her duties as hostess and having introduced the boy to the mysteries of the "dead-room" and welcomed him into the fraternity of adults with the sherry. Gently prodded by the boy's aunt, Eliza (sitting "in state" in her late brother's armchair) tells about Father Flynn's last days. Among other things, she recalls noticing "something queer coming over him latterly" and mentions that she would "find him with his breviary fallen to the floor, lying back in the chair and his mouth open." Then Eliza gets to more substantive matters, which in the aggregate clarify the veiled comment ("something queer . . . something uncanny . . . peculiar . . . ") that old Cotter made about Father Flynn.

Eliza begins by saying, "The duties of the priesthood was too much for him. And then his life was, you might say, crossed." His problem started, she says, when he broke the chalice. Others said that it was "the boy's fault," that is, the carelessness of the acolyte who assisted the priest at the altar, and the people made light of the incident, because the chalice "contained nothing," the wine already having been transubstantiated into Christ's body and blood. According to Eliza, however, the incident "affected his mind," and "he began to mope by himself, talking to no one and wandering about by himself."

The crucial incident, which presumably led to Father Flynn being relieved of his duties and retired, occurred one night when he was needed to make a call, perhaps on a dying parishioner. "They looked high up and low down," Eliza tells the boy and his aunt, and finally tried the locked chapel. There two priests and the clerk found him alone in his dark confessional "wide awake and laughing-like softly to himself." Clearly, "there was something gone wrong with him." Eliza has the last word, for the story concludes with this statement.

Themes and Meanings

The first three of the fifteen stories that compose the collection *Dubliners* deal with youngsters and are initiation works, narrative pieces about different aspects of the rite of passage, the progress from childhood to adulthood. Because it is the opening story in the book, "The Sisters" has the youngest hero, and it shows him confronting directly for the first time the reality of death. The story also develops the archetypal motif of the search for a father. The boy, apparently an orphan (he lives with an aunt and uncle), finds in the priest a substitute father, a kindly man who teaches him about many things, nurturing his intellect and preparing him for the future; yet Father Flynn himself is an imperfect, eventually demented, man—and priest—who is unable to face his own faults and inadequacies and ends up going mad in his own confessional.

The third theme is that of paralysis, which Joyce introduces in the first paragraph, when the boy, gazing up at the dying priest's window, says "paralysis" to himself, a word that "had always sounded strangely in [his ears]," like "gnomon in the Euclid" and "simony in the Catechism." Linked as it is with the other two words, "paralysis" refers to more than the priest's physical imperfection, which is the result of the debilitating stroke he has suffered; it also calls to mind his spiritual and social imperfections. Further, Joyce's introduction of the paralysis motif in the first paragraph of this opening story also signals its general significance for the entire volume.

In a 1904 letter, Joyce speaks of writing a group of stories: "I call the series Dubliners to betray the soul of that . . . paralysis which many consider a city." Indeed, the fourteen stories that follow "The Sisters" introduce characters from many walks of life who are frustrated with their lives but unable to effect change. Personally, socially, and vocationally or professionally, these Dubliners—young as well as old—are paralyzed, ineffectual failures. The story, then, can be interpreted as the first of Joyce's fifteen visions of Dublin, the capital of Ireland, which he left for good on October 8, 1904, to live the remainder of his life on the Continent.

Style and Technique

Despite the obvious symbolism, Joyce's style in this story and elsewhere in *Dubliners* is straightforward and realistic (some have even said naturalistic), and it has been compared to that of Anton Chekhov, Guy de Maupassant, and Emile Zola. Any such indebtedness notwithstanding, Joyce conceived of "The Sisters" (like the rest of *Dubliners*) as an "epiphany," a story in which a character experiences a "sudden spiritual manifestation." In this story, the boy gains enlightenment, learning the truth about Father Flynn; significantly, at the very moment of the revelation, when Eliza pauses for a bit, the boy rises, goes to the altar-like table where Nannie has laid out the refreshments, and tastes his sherry, a conscious ceremonial gesture in the concluding act of this particular rite of passage.

Eliza is the third medium through which Joyce develops Father Flynn's character in the story. First there is the narrator, who recalls his experiences when a boy with the priest; second, there is the dialogue between Cotter and the boy's uncle, who raise questions and speak negatively about Father Flynn. The sympathetic attitude of the boy, called into question by the mutterings of the neighbor and uncle, finally is placed in the proper perspective by Eliza's testimony.

Gerald H. Strauss

THE SKY IS GRAY

Author: Ernest J. Gaines (1933-   )
Type of plot: Realism
Time of plot: World War II
Locale: Bayonne, Louisiana
First published: 1963

> *Principal characters:*
> JAMES, the narrator, an eight-year-old black boy
> OCTAVIA, James's mother
> ROSE MARY, his aunt
> MONSIEUR BAYONNE, a black folk doctor
> HELENA and
> ALNEST, an old white couple who keep a store in Bayonne
> A STUDENT, a young black man

The Story

As the narrative opens, James and his mother, Octavia, are waiting by the roadside for the bus that will carry them to Bayonne. The weather is cold, and James knows that his mother will be worried that her family lacks wood to keep them warm until her return. She worries about other things as well, especially when James is not there to assume the man's role in her absence. James is instinctively drawn to his mother and feels the urge to put his arm around her, but he restrains himself, knowing that she regards such a display of affection as weakness and "crybaby stuff."

James has been silently suffering for some time with a toothache, about which he told no one because he knew that there was no money for the dentist. James's aunt first became aware that he was in pain, but he swore her to secrecy. She did send for Monsieur Bayonne, a folk healer, to treat the tooth, but his remedies were ineffective. The pain became so unbearable that it could no longer be kept secret from James's mother, so now they are on their way to have it removed. They have money "enough to get there and get back. Dollar and a half to have it pulled," and fifty cents left over to buy a "little piece of salt meat."

As they prepare for the day, James recalls the time before his father went off to the war, when things were better for the family. He also recalls when his mother made him kill two redbirds caught in the traps that he and his brother set for owls and blackbirds. James did not want to kill the redbirds, but his mother killed the first one and then demanded that he kill the other. He refused, and she beat him until he gave in. Afterward, as they ate the tiny morsels, James felt the pride the others had in him for providing even this small meal. He later understood that his mother's stern discipline was preparing him in case he had to carry on in her stead.

The ride to town on a Jim Crow bus is uneventful except for James's self-conscious flirtation with a small girl, which amuses the other passengers. Alighting in Bayonne,

James becomes aware of the penetrating cold, which seems more intense than at home. They make their way to the dentist's office, where James listens to an exchange between a preacher who believes it best not to try to understand suffering, and a young, educated black man who insists that people should "question everything. Every stripe, every star, every word spoken. Everything." These two exchange views on religion, which the young man rejects. Growing angry and frustrated at the young man's calm rejection of Christian complacency, the preacher finally strikes him twice in the face. The young man merely sits down and reads as the preacher bolts out the door. Later, the young man has a similar exchange with a woman to whom he says, "Words mean nothing. Action is the only thing. Doing, that's the only thing." James observes these scenes without comment, but clearly he is impressed by the contrast in values and attitudes between the old and new generations of black southerners. He thinks, "When I grow up I want be just like him. I want clothes like that and I want keep a book with me too."

The nurse announces that the dentist will see no more patients until after one o'clock, and that all those waiting must leave and return then. Having no place to go to escape the bitter cold, James and his mother walk, window-shopping. When James's eyes are drawn to a café where white people are eating, his mother insists that he keep his eyes to the front. After walking the length of Bayonne and back, they enter a hardware store, where James has a chance to get warm while his mother pretends to examine ax handles. Soon after returning to the street, James is cold again. Hunger gnaws at him. The courthouse clock shows a quarter to twelve—another hour and a quarter before they can return to the warmth of the dentist's office. It has now begun to sleet.

After desperately trying to get into the closed dentist's office to escape the weather, James's mother heads for the black section of town. They go to a warm café, where, because she feels obligated to spend something, Octavia orders milk and cookies for James and coffee for herself. She eats nothing. A man at the bar puts a coin in the juke box and asks Octavia to dance. The episode ends with Octavia pulling a knife on the pimp. She and James return to the cold street.

As Octavia and James again walk toward the dentist's they encounter an elderly white woman who asks if they have eaten. Octavia proudly answers that they "just finish," but the woman insists that they come into her store anyway. Her husband inquires from the back, where their living quarters are and whether she has found them yet, so the reader knows that she was on the street awaiting James and Octavia. Later she explains that she saw the two of them pass earlier, and waited for them to return. She tells them she has warm food on the stove; then, when Octavia seems ready to leave, she quickly adds that it is not free: she asks James to put her garbage out in return for the food. When James actually carries the can out to the street, it is so light that he is sure it is empty. Afterward he is allowed to wash up, and a meal is served him and his mother. Their hostess calls the dentist and arranges for James to see him as soon as the office opens.

As James and his mother leave, Octavia turns and asks the lady if she has salt meat, which she does. When Octavia asks for "two bits worth," Helena cuts off much too large a chunk. Asserting her fierce pride, Octavia refuses to accept this charity and turns to go. Only when Helena cuts off about half the chunk of meat does she accept it. On the street again, James turns his collar up against the sleet. His mother tells him to put it down again. "'You not a bum,' she says, 'you a man.'"

Themes and Meanings

"The Sky Is Gray" takes as its major theme the issue of black pride in the face of intolerable conditions of poverty. James and his family are reduced to poverty, ironically, by his father's service in the army. In the face of these hardships, James has been forced to sacrifice his childhood to the harsh realities of survival in a hostile, unforgiving world. The episode in which he is forced to kill the redbirds in order for the family to eat powerfully dramatizes the extent to which his mother must force him to overcome his own natural feelings for the sake of the family's need. As James comes to realize, there is no room for softness or gentleness in their world. What superficially appears to be cruelty on Octavia's part is her way of preparing him for a hard future.

Despite the grinding poverty of their lives, Octavia retains her pride and instills it in her son. James, like any child, cannot fully understand why his mother insists on paying her way when charity is offered, but the reader is aware that she is developing in him a sense of pride and character that will enable him to rise above his environment. Intuitively, he wants to be like the educated young black man he saw in the dentist's office, but he can become so only if he develops a sense of manhood based on self-reliance, self-respect, and pride. Octavia gives him that opportunity, even though her methods are hard. When, at the end of the story, she tells him that he is a man, she is refusing to allow him to be less.

Another theme of the story has to do with the kindness of Helena, whose generosity transcends the color line. As the young man says, it is by action rather than words that people should be measured. Even in the segregated South, simple human kindness can and does exist. After the callous disregard of the dentist and other whites in the story, Helena offers James an object lesson that people should be judged by what they do, not by who they are. Though this theme is never stated overtly, it is implicit throughout.

A last important meaning is the sense of a changing South implied by the conversation between the young black man and the preacher in the dentist's office. While the older man speaks of acceptance of suffering injustice as the duty of Christians, the young man represents a rising generation that will eventually throw off the shackles of segregation. Though James is still too young to understand these arguments, he is being reared to become one of that generation.

Style and Technique

Ernest J. Gaines is a master of the dialect of his home region of southern Louisiana, and he uses this skill to good advantage in "The Sky Is Gray." His use of the point of view and language of an eight-year-old boy, who narrates the story in his own words, is also an important stylistic device. The conversation between the preacher and the student that occurs in the dentist's office, for example, is presented without comment on the boy's part, because James lacks the intellectual capacity to analyze or even fully understand the significance of all that he sees and experiences. Abstractions such as the question of God's existence are beyond his intellectual range, so he simply repeats the dialogue as he heard it. Thus, the narrative is straightforward and simple; Gaines's themes and meanings are implicit rather than explicit, shown rather than told.

The effective integration of language, theme, and narrative voice makes this story an excellent example of the literary realism for which Gaines is justly respected by critics and reviewers.

William E. Grant

SLAUGHTERHOUSE

Author: Greg Sarris (1952-   )
Type of plot: Psychological
Time of plot: The 1980's
Locale: The western United States
First published: 1991

> *Principal characters:*
> FRANKIE, the fourteen-year-old narrator
> BUSTER COPAZ, the leader of his gang
> CAROLINE COPAZ, Buster's cousin and Frankie's idealized
>   girlfriend
> OLD JULIA, Frankie's friendless aunt

The Story

Frankie, the fourteen-year-old narrator, has a Portuguese father and a Native American mother. They all live amid a chaos of poverty with his father's brother Angelo, various Indian relatives, and several other children. Frankie, who describes himself as too old for his mother to tend and too young to get a job, spends his time hanging out with a racially mixed group of teenagers from the rundown community. They are not vicious boys, only bored adolescents who fill their lives with idle talk about girls and an obsessive interest in the seedy adult world that surrounds them.

Worried about his sexual powers, Frankie fantasizes about Caroline, an American Indian girl who has recently moved into a shabby neighborhood called the Hole. He thinks that she might become his first sexual conquest, but the prospect of negotiating such an encounter scares him. Moreover, his genuinely tender feelings for Caroline clash with his pressing sexual need and cause him great confusion. He desires both a virgin and a sexual dynamo, and he does not know how to resolve this dilemma.

The local slaughterhouse often looms up in the boys' imagination because it has a mysterious aura as a holy site of animal sacrifice and accumulating myth. It is more than that, however. It stands on Santa Rosa Avenue, a neighborhood where people keep chickens and cows in their yards and where small houses lurk behind abandoned refrigerators and other appliances. At night, two nefarious local denizens, Smoke and Indian Princess Sally Did, sell girls in the slaughterhouse. This commercial enterprise constantly occupies the sex-haunted imaginations of the coalition members—Buster Copaz and Mickey Toms (Indians, like Frankie), Victor James (African American), and the "angel-face" Navarro twins, Jesus and Ignacio.

The slaughterhouse has a companion barn, used to store hay for the horses on death row, which becomes an observation post for the curious boys as they snoop on Smoke and Sally Did. One day when the conspirators are in the barn, eagerly examining a girlie magazine they haven stolen from Sally Did's Cadillac, they draw straws to see who will sneak into the slaughterhouse that night to spy on the patrons. Frankie draws the short straw.

Apprehensive about this frightening commitment to his gang, Frankie spends the day seeking distraction. He visits an aunt, Old Julia, who laughs gleefully at his efforts to tidy up her yard. Later he calls on Caroline at her bedraggled home, where he comes under the amused eye of a neighbor, old man Toms. Walking under the cypress trees with Caroline, Frankie tries to convince her of his sincerity, but his sexual overtures prompt her cutting rejection that he is "just like all the rest." Caroline runs home, leaving Frankie angry and confused.

Frankie then goes home to the domestic confusion that reigns among his extended family. His father sits with Uncle Angelo at the kitchen table, where they console themselves with beer, while his mother, her hair festooned with pink plastic curlers, pushes beans around in a pot. Grandma and Old Uncle are by the stove, and noisy children contribute to the general disorder. After his belly is full of beans, Frankie faces up to his appointment at the slaughterhouse as his only chance to salvage a day filled with defeat.

The slaughterhouse is menacing at night, with the screams of dying horses and the smell of their rubbery guts weighing heavily on Frankie's lively imagination. What he observes there, however, is innocuous and banal. Smoke, Sally, and "the girls" promenade around a makeshift arena made up of cardboard boxes stacked on three sides and Sally's gold Cadillac on the fourth. Sally and an orange-haired black girl are leading another girl in a dark shawl in some kind of ceremony accompanied by music from a big transistor radio. The girl wears a tight red dress and wobbles as if she is drunk. Behind her lipstick and "done up" hair, Frankie recognizes Caroline as the apparent initiate.

Frankie gropes his way out of the slaughterhouse to the waiting coalition, where the admiring boys are disappointed by his deflating report of "just some people dancing around." They muster a poker face, though, and head for the park to find "some chicks," staying tough to the end. For Frankie, however, the experience spells the end of whatever scrap of youthful idealism his soul has retained.

Themes and Meanings

Greg Sarris's "Slaughterhouse" exemplifies the archetypal initiation theme, the story of a young person's loss of innocence and induction into adulthood. Frankie's hunger for sexual knowledge signifies his physical maturation and contends against his feelings for Caroline, whose own loss of innocence appears in her contemptuous remark to Frankie that her mother was right and that he is just like all the others. Her disillusioning experience with Frankie probably contributes to her abandoning herself to the ritual ministrations of Smoke and Sally Did in the slaughterhouse, the event that concludes Frankie's difficult day and smothers his hopes in nihilism.

"Slaughterhouse" presents a modern retelling of Nathaniel Hawthorne's symbolic tale "Young Goodman Brown," in which a young, good man leaves his wife, Faith, at home and ventures into the woods at night on a mysterious mission. Soon he meets a stranger, obviously the devil, who leads him to a chapel-like forest clearing, where a black mass is being conducted to induct a young woman into the worship of Satan. The woman is Goodman's own Faith. Thus, when he cries out at the end, "My Faith is gone," the moral is clear. "Slaughterhouse" ends similarly, with Frankie looking up, "and there was nothing in the sky."

A related but lesser theme emerges in the sketch of the boys who bond together in a gang like cubs in a pack. Faced with the perennial challenges of adolescence—sex, identity, and finding a place for themselves—they effect worldliness and lean on one another for support in an intimidating world. Within such groups, one boy usually masters his own insecurities, puts on a brave face, and stands out as the leader. Within Frankie's gang, that role falls to Buster Copaz.

The boys strut around in a setting of civic distress. The slaughterhouse, a tattered capitol, dominates this empire of disfranchised exiles living on the outer fringes of town. The prostitute Sally Did drives a gold Cadillac, a depressing symbol of what upward mobility means on Santa Rosa Avenue. Frankie's home life reveals poverty among the six-packs, but Caroline's situation defines absolute squalor. She lives in the Hole, "two lines of brown army barracks" in the most depressed area of South Park. Given the attention that it receives, the setting becomes an important narrative element in "Slaughterhouse," conveying by implication a great amount of information about the struggling adolescents who are forced to fend for themselves.

Style and Technique

As Frankie tells his story in his own words, he chatters on and on about sex, family, the gang, and all their concerns. His is generally a beguiling voice, open and frank about his fears and uncertainties; it suggests a shrewd mind in control. His mind is not sophisticated or especially educated, but it is observant, and thus the language of the story works well in carrying the main theme of a young person's journey to discovery.

The two old people whom Frankie meets during his long afternoon of waiting serve as a kind of chorus. Old Julia and old man Toms say little as they watch Frankie go about his round of time-filling activities, but they reveal their amusement at the folly of youth through their laughter. Precisely what strikes Old Julia as so funny remains unclear, but the adults' role as tolerant spectators of adolescent problems is clear.

To confine the events of the story to one day, Sarris resorts to a flashback in Frankie's mind to review his relationship with Caroline. This device allows the touching picture of the two young people playing husband and wife and mocking the banal dialogue of middle-class domestic life. They also play at being Romeo and Juliet, with convincing comic effect. The wholesome appeal of Frankie and Caroline in these scenes emphasizes both the inescapable struggle between the flesh and the spirit that so bedevils Frankie, and the final fall into knowledge of the two innocents.

Frank Day

SLEEP

Author: Larry Brown (1951-   )
Type of plot: Domestic realism
Time of plot: The late twentieth century
Locale: Inside a house
First published: 1990

> *Principal characters:*
> LOUIS, the narrator, an elderly married man
> HIS WIFE, a psychologically disturbed woman

The Story

Louis is reflecting on how cold it is outside his bed and how he does not want to get up. His wife has awakened him on this night, as she does every night, telling him that she hears noises downstairs, that he must investigate to make sure no one else is in the house, to ensure all is safe and sound. He pretends to be asleep for as long as he can, hoping that his wife will give up on trying to wake him. He knows she will not give up, that she does not sleep at nights. She sleeps only in short naps during the daytime, and even then she moans, twists, and shakes her head no. These nightmares and the nightly vigils have been in play for many years before the night in which this story takes place.

Louis has his flashlight on the nightstand. When his wife begins cursing him and the cursing becomes so severe that his ears hurt from it, he finally jolts out of bed, takes the flashlight, and goes downstairs to look for the nothing that he knows is there.

In the midst of his trying to sleep and then his getting up and going downstairs, he thinks frequently of the food that he would like to eat for breakfast. He names eggs and bacon, a leftover steak, coffee and orange juice, pancakes, and so forth. When he peers into the kitchen, he considers again the possibility of making himself coffee and sitting up with it and smoking a few cigarettes, but he knows that it is the wrong time of night for doing that.

He thinks on and off about places he has been where he was cold, such as a ranch in Montana where he spent time with an army buddy. It was in the winter, and when they went out to feed the cows, they sometimes found a calf frozen to the ground. He remembers a moment in a snowstorm in Kansas when he drove his car off the road into a ditch and instead of getting out, he stayed in the car for nine hours with the heater running, until the car finally ran out of gas. Louis contrasts the warm feel of his pajamas against the memory of such extremely cold weather. He thinks of a similarly cold experience in North Carolina with the frigid, icy wind blowing off the ocean and penetrating his clothes, freezing his own feet into blocks, and he feels the warmth between his toes under the blanket, wishing he could stay under the covers and thinking that if his place were reversed with his wife's, he would not wake her up and make her do the things that she makes him do.

When he returns to the bed after banging doors downstairs, so that his wife can hear him and know that he has checked every possible place, his wife is in a nearly conscious dream state. She says, "Mama had three kittens," and she says no more. This makes no sense to Louis, but he considers himself lucky that she does not continue with the story. Louis sits on the edge of the bed and listens to the intense, overpowering silence of the house and then gets into bed. He moves toward his wife, although he does not know why. The story closes with Louis thinking of himself as a young man in Alaska, the snow and the sled dogs, and the polar bears that were fishing for seals. He wonders how they can live in the cold water, but decides they just get used to it.

Themes and Meanings

Larry Brown's central theme in this story relates to the futility of human existence. As a way of easing his wife's burden and thereby easing his own burden, Louis makes a nightly check of the house. Sometimes this happens more than once a night. Louis is not particularly angry about it but wishes that he did not have to do it, wishes that his wife did not need that of him. This is much like the fatalistic existential human experience, where people continue to live and go about normal activity as if everything were fine, when they actually have the helpless feeling that there is no meaning in life and little reason to go on.

Louis keeps thinking of how nice it would be to eat some good, hot food. It is the wrong time for breakfast, unfortunately, and this is a reminder of the limitations and restrictions constantly faced in life. Louis does not lash out against the greater structure of the universe, which implies that it is the wrong time for breakfast or to sit up and drink coffee; instead, he goes about the business he was assigned and he kills time until he can continue sleeping, as is his proper function in this late hour.

He does not argue against his wife when she hears imaginary voices, because he knows that she does not sleep well. He has seen her sleeping for many years and he knows it is a tortured sleep, a painful and terrible time for her. Considering that, and that he loves her, he makes her feel as comfortable as he can by going downstairs and looking around.

The coldness that Louis keeps feeling is his temporary problem, his current and most tangible reason to be against the idea of these nightly vigils. The implication is that if the cold were not bothering Louis, there would be a story much the same with something else causing the problem, like wind, or summer heat, or even streetlights. The coldness is not what is wrong as much as it indicates a dilemma that is larger and more unwieldly. By referring to the cold and remembering all the cold places he has been, Louis is asking an age-old question that is central to much of religion and philosophy: Why is there pain in the world and why must he take part in it? While walking about the house, he thinks of all those cold places and the suffering he has endured, and he does not get any closer to answering the question. He determines that it must be his fate to suffer, and he must get used to it as the polar bears do. Somehow, by being used to the cold and the suffering, a person is able to conquer it. By expecting troubles and suffering, a person circumvents at least part of the drama and tragedy that is inherent to the human experience.

Style and Technique

This story is written lightly and without the incredibly dark or foreboding tone that might accompany a story of this nature. Although it is not as humorous as much of Brown's writing, it has an undertone of the absurdity of life; it brings into focus the ideas that people often do things they do not want to do, and they do things when they have no idea why. Nor is it noticeably Mississippian, as his work normally is. The presence of a microwave oven indicates at least the latter part of the twentieth century, but the juxtaposition of a person feeling warmth against coldness could be from anywhere and at any time.

The story is written in the first-person, conversational present tense. Louis is thinking to himself rather than telling a story to anyone in particular. The style is brief and easy to follow. By using commonplace items and well-known places, and presenting the main problem of the unpleasant coldness outside the bed versus the gentle warmth under the blankets, the author makes this story accessible and implies much more than is actually said. The text itself is only a few pages, very short even for a short story.

Most of the action occurs inside Louis's head. His wife appears only as Louis sees her and thinks about her. The reader does not learn her name or anything about her except that she causes periodic discomfort to Louis. By knowing what Louis is thinking, rather than watching him act out his life tangibly, Brown brings his character's deeper sense of personality to life easily and effectively.

As Louis seems fairly old, the most likely symbols here will tie warmth to life and coldness to death. More than that, this story is an honest and unflinching view of the human experience that does not apologize for bending toward the dark side.

Beaird Glover

THE SLIDE AREA

Author: Gavin Lambert (1924-   )
Type of plot: Social realism
Time of plot: The 1950's
Locale: Los Angeles
First published: 1959

> *Principal characters:*
> THE NARRATOR, a screenwriter
> ZEENA NELSON, the owner of a secondhand furniture store
> HENRIETTA "HANK" NELSON, her sister, a murder victim
> SISTER HERTHA, a nurse at St. Judith's Hospital
> COUNTESS OSTERBERG-STEBLECHI, a wealthy eccentric

The Story

The nameless narrator spends a late afternoon and night in the early summer drifting around the Los Angeles area. He is writing a film script without enthusiasm when he would rather be working "on the novel I am hoping to write and pretend is already under way." He leaves his office and wanders through the decaying sets on the back lot, then drives his battered 1947 Chevrolet to the ocean while meditating on the bizarre essence of Los Angeles: "not a city, but a series of suburban approaches to a city that never materializes." At the Pacific Palisades, he notices the omnipresent, ominous warning signs: DRIVE CAREFULLY; SLIDE AREA; BEWARE OF ROCKS. He watches as three elderly picnickers are rescued, apparently uninjured, from a huge pile of mud and stones.

In a Santa Monica bar, the narrator meets his friend Zeena Nelson, who is drunk and distraught because her sister, Henrietta, nicknamed "Hank," has been shot and the nuns at St. Judith's Hospital will not tell her about the woman's condition. He calls the hospital, and Sister Hertha informs him that Henrietta Nelson is dead. He leaves Zeena roaming the beach in a daze. Sister Hertha later telephones to ask him to come there to take away Zeena, who refuses to leave the hospital. The nun explains that Hank was shot in the head by an unidentified man whom she brought home.

The narrator remembers how he met Zeena and Hank at their secondhand furniture store and occasionally ran into them thereafter in bars or on the beach: "This is how everybody met them. This is how I am with Zeena today, by accident." He retrieves Zeena from the hospital and drives to her house in a seedy Venice neighborhood.

Themes and Meanings

Gavin Lambert has written extensively about films and Hollywood as the founder of *Sequence*, former editor of *Sight and Sound*, and author of *On Cukor* (1972) and *The Making of "Gone with the Wind"* (1973). He has written or co-written such screenplays as *Bitter Victory* (1957), *Sons and Lovers* (1960), and *I Never Promised You a Rose Garden* (1977). The themes of "The Slide Area" are also examined in other stories in *The Slide Area: Scenes of Hollywood Life* (1959), his 1963 novel *Inside Daisy Clover*, and his screenplay for the 1965 film version of the latter. Lambert's Hollywood fiction is in the tradition of such British examinations of the Los Angeles scene as the novels *Prater Violet* (1945) by Christopher Isherwood and *The Loved One* (1948) by Evelyn Waugh, as well as Paul Mayersberg's nonfiction *Hollywood: The Haunted House* (1967).

The protagonist of "The Slide Area" is less the narrator than Los Angeles itself, which Lambert sees as representative of the United States, a metaphor for the aimlessness of twentieth century life. Los Angeles lacks any definite identity because it is constantly in a state of flux, is "a comfortable unfinished desert" in which "between where you are and where you are going to be is a no-man's land." The crumbling cliffs of the Pacific Palisades perfectly embody the way in which chaos always lurks beneath the insubstantial surface. The narrator sees Los Angeles as having "nothing at all to do with living. It is a bright winking mirage in the desert; you are afraid to look away in case it has vanished when you look back." The narrator describes how a development site is built over where a prehistoric animal has recently been excavated, as if to ask whether all the history since this creature roamed the earth has led illogically to this.

Lambert comments frequently in "The Slide Area" on the nature of reality. On the back lot, the narrator considers the replica of a residential street to have "as much and perhaps more reality than the real thing." It is difficult to distinguish the real from the unreal, for the real world persists in imitating the world of film. Indeed, this phony world can almost be seen as superior because the artificial canvas sky is bluer than the real one and spotlights are always standing by "to reinforce the sun."

Leaving the film sets does not lessen the narrator's sense of unreality; there is always something "almost supernatural" in the air, sometimes described by Los Angeles television weather forecasters as "neurotic." The physical and psychological spheres become inseparable. This lack of distinction is appropriate, according to the narrator, because "In America, illusion and reality are still often the same thing. The dream is the achievement, the achievement is the dream." With so little grasp on reality, even time becomes irrelevant. The narrator does not tear off the calendar leaves in his office: "Let time stand still or move back, it doesn't matter."

Lambert's themes are most effectively conveyed when the narrator goes to a drugstore and finds Countess Osterberg-Steblechi surveying the paperback crime novels. She is interested in *The Case of the Black-Eyed Blonde* but will not buy it because at thirty-five cents it is too expensive. The widow of a wealthy European banker, her chauffeur-driven Rolls Royce awaiting her, the countess claims that she is "heartrendingly poor." Swollen like a balloon, her dyed-red hair looking like a wig, she personifies the decadence and decay that Lambert associates with the United States.

Style and Technique

"The Slide Area" is almost an essay about Los Angeles, the United States, the state of civilization, and the nature of reality, with Lambert's thematic points illustrated by brief scenes involving his characters. The story is arranged as a series of snapshots of the people and places the narrator encounters, with his impressions of them as they relate to his view of the world. As is appropriate for a Hollywood story by a film critic and screenwriter, the style is cinematic: a series of seemingly random images that come clearly into focus with the Zeena scenes at the end. The film it most closely resembles and seems most influenced by is *Sunset Boulevard*, Billy Wilder's cynical 1950 vision of death and despair in Hollywood.

Lambert's cinematic style can be seen in the close-ups that he presents of his characters' faces to capture their emptiness. The countess's face "looks like the moon after an explosion, the features are blasted fragments." Zeena "has once been beautiful, but now her face has something ruined about it, as if she's been waiting too long, in vain, for the telephone to ring."

Michael Adams

A SMALL, GOOD THING

Author: Raymond Carver (1938-1988)
Type of plot: Realism
Time of plot: The late twentieth century
Locale: A town in the United States
First published: 1983

> *Principal characters:*
> HOWARD WEISS, a young executive
> ANN, his wife
> SCOTTY, their son
> A BAKER, unnamed

The Story

Ann Weiss is not pleased with the baker from whom she orders her son Scotty's eighth birthday cake. Though the baker is of an age to have children, and even grand-children, he takes no interest in her son's birthday and seems to have no time for small talk. The transaction is direct and impersonal, and Ann leaves the bakery vaguely dis-gruntled by the man's coldness.

Two days later, on his birthday, Scotty and a friend are walking to school when Scotty is hit by a car and knocked to the pavement. The driver of the car stops, but drives on when Scotty gets up, shaken but apparently unharmed. Scotty returns home, lies down on the sofa, and loses consciousness. Alarmed because she cannot rouse him, Ann telephones her husband, Howard, who telephones an ambulance.

At the hospital, Howard and Ann are assured by their physician, Dr. Francis, that nothing serious seems to be wrong with Scotty. He is only in a deep sleep, not in a coma, and will soon awaken. That evening, while they await tests results, Howard goes home to bathe and change clothes. After he has reached the house, the phone rings, and the caller tells Howard that he has an unclaimed birthday cake. Impatient and con-fused, Howard denies any knowledge of a cake and hangs up, only to be disturbed by a second call a few minutes later. This time, the caller says nothing, then hangs up.

Back at the hospital, Howard discovers that Scotty, still unconscious, is being fed intravenously. Ann is anxious about his not waking up. Howard suggests that Ann go home for a while and tells her about the phone calls, but she refuses to leave Scotty. When Dr. Francis comes in on late-night rounds, Howard and Ann demand to know why Scotty has not yet awakened. The doctor assures them that Scotty is suffering from a hairline fracture of the skull and a mild concussion, but that he seems to be out of any real danger and should soon wake up. He is merely asleep, not in a coma. Later that night, another doctor, a radiologist, comes into the room and announces that a brain scan will be performed on Scotty. The increasingly anxious parents accompany their son downstairs to radiology and return with him to his room at dawn.

Scotty does not awaken the next day, despite Dr. Francis's assurances that he will do so. The exhausted Howard and Ann maintain their vigil in the hospital room. When Dr. Francis makes his second visit of the day, he expresses his bewilderment that Scotty has not awakened and this time calls the condition a coma. After the doctor leaves, Howard convinces Ann to go home to rest and feed the dog. No sooner has she arrived home, however, than the phone rings; the caller mentions Scotty's name and hangs up. Terrified, Ann calls the hospital and receives assurances from Howard that their son's condition has not changed.

Early the next morning (it is now Wednesday), after Ann has returned to the hospital, Howard tells her that the doctors have decided to operate on Scotty. However, even as they are discussing the proposed surgery, Scotty opens his eyes, gazes blankly at his parents, suffers a spasm, and dies. Dr. Francis later attributes the death to a "hidden occlusion" and expresses sympathy. Dazed, Howard and Ann return home, and the phone rings yet again. Ann curses the caller and bursts into tears. Another call, this one late at night, prompts Ann to make the connection she has so far missed: The baker, angry about the unclaimed cake, has been making the calls.

The couple drive to the shopping center bakery to confront the baker. Though it is past midnight, he is still at work, and Ann pounds on the door to get his attention. When he opens the door, Ann pushes past him, identifies herself, and accuses him of making the calls. She angrily explains that her son is dead. Moved and ashamed, the baker asks them to sit down. He talks about the frustrations of his work, the disappointments of his life; he asks their forgiveness. He serves them coffee, cinnamon rolls, and fresh bread, explaining that, "Eating is a small, good thing in a time like this." Relaxed and contemplative, the three sit eating and talking until the break of day.

Themes and Meanings

Like many of Raymond Carver's stories, "A Small, Good Thing" is about bad things happening to good people and about how suddenly and irrevocably luck can change. Howard and Ann Weiss have done all the things expected of an upwardly mobile, middle-class couple; nothing has prepared them for a calamity of the magnitude of an only child's death, and both are at a loss about how to deal with it. As his son lies unconscious after the accident, Howard reflects on the remarkable good luck that has characterized his life thus far: His education and his marriage have gone without a hitch, and neither tragedy nor disgrace has touched his family. Still, he realizes that there are forces "that could cripple or bring down a man if the luck went bad, if things suddenly turned."

During their son's stay in the hospital, both Howard and Ann find themselves wishing that things were back to normal—as though wishing could make it so. At one point, Ann longs for "a place where she would find Scotty waiting for her when she stepped out of the car, ready to say Mom and let her gather him in her arms."

There is every reason to believe, however, that Howard and Ann will survive the devastation of Scotty's death, and the story's most positive moments deal with the heightened sympathy for other human beings that often comes with personal tragedy. In a hospital waiting room, Ann meets a black family, one of whose members, Franklin, is being operated on after a knife fight. She becomes almost mystically bound to them through mutual suffering, telling them her story and listening to theirs. Scotty's death brings out the good side of the mostly unsympathetic Dr. Francis, as well: After the boy dies, the physician seems to Ann "full of some goodness she didn't understand." Howard and Ann become closer to each other through shared misfortune, and both become more magnanimous human beings. The story's final image—the grief-stricken parents and the childless baker awaiting the morning's light together—is clearly an affirmative one, illustrating as it does what the poet William Wordsworth called "the soothing thoughts that spring out of human suffering."

Style and Technique

Carver's clear, uncluttered syntax; short, simple sentences; and judicious use of repetition make comparisons with Ernest Hemingway inevitable. With Hemingway, Carver clearly represents the realist tradition in fiction, and the stories collected in *What We Talk About When We Talk About Love* (1981), *Will You Please Be Quiet, Please?* (1976), and *Cathedral* (1983, the collection in which "A Small, Good Thing" appears) established him as one of that tradition's foremost American practitioners.

The profundity of such stories as "A Small, Good Thing" resides in what lies beneath the uncomplicated surface of Carver's prose: complex and universal emotions with which even the most casual reader must instantly identify. In his quest for the right word that will trigger this sympathetic response, Carver does for twentieth century America what Flaubert did for France a century earlier: He exposes and records the emotional nuances, the tensions and the trials, of a troubled middle class.

J. D. Daubs

THE SMALLEST WOMAN IN THE WORLD

Author: Clarice Lispector (1925-1977)
Type of plot: Psychological
Time of plot: The twentieth century
Locale: Central Congo and a large metropolis
First published: "A menor mulher do mundo," 1960 (English translation, 1972)

> *Principal characters:*
> LITTLE FLOWER, the smallest woman in the world
> MARCEL PRETRE, an explorer, hunter, and man of the world

The Story

The action plot of the story is quite simple. An explorer, Marcel Pretre, while on an excursion into equatorial Africa, comes across a tribe of extraordinarily small pygmies living in the forest. These pygmies tell him of an even smaller race of pygmies living deeper within the jungle. He travels even deeper into the heart of the luxuriant tropical forest and there discovers the smallest race of pygmies in the world. Among these minute creatures, he discovers "the smallest of the smallest pygmies in the world," a tiny woman no more than forty-five centimeters (twenty-six and one-half inches) tall. She is mature; indeed, she is conspicuously pregnant, and she is quite black. She does not attempt to speak, and the reader learns that the tribe, the Likoualas, has only a very limited language and that its members communicate primarily by gestures.

The explorer is awed by this unique creature, considering her the rarest and most extraordinary creature on the earth because of her diminutive size. He takes photographs of her, prepares a description, and sends the photograph and article on to a newspaper, which publishes the life-size photograph, together with the article, in its Sunday supplement.

As readers of the Sunday newspaper see the photograph, they react in different ways, and these reactions and the comments they make are explored in the story as the next part of the narrative. The scene then shifts back to the jungle, where the explorer and the tiny woman are regarding each other while he continues to gather data about her. He has named her Little Flower, and he gazes at her in wonder. Little Flower, herself, is feeling warm, safe, and happy, and within her arises spontaneously a feeling of love for the explorer. However, the author notes that she loves Marcel Pretre in the same appreciative, admiring manner that she loves his ring and his boots.

Little Flower smiles at Marcel, and he responds by returning her smile. However, he is not sure at all what she is smiling about or what response he is indicating with his own smile. Marcel's awareness of Little Flower's emotion, and some perception of his own feeling, increases. He becomes embarrassed by these feelings, and to reestablish his self-control he returns to taking notes very intently. This moment of awareness and self-discovery that Little Flower, the uncivilized, natural creature, has forced on him reveals his own inner depths and so frightens him that he rejects the revelation and returns to the mechanical routine of gathering data and taking notes about her. He rejects the emotions that Little Flower reveals and his own emotions as well, because he is unable to handle and respond to the spontaneous and unabashed natural emotions that his mannerly existence suppresses.

As a final note, rather like the "moral" at the end of a fable by Aesop, the scene shifts again to the metropolis, where an old woman reading about the tiny woman in the Sunday supplement responds with platitudes, commenting that "it just goes to show," meaning that unlikely things are indeed possible. "God," she adds, "knows what He's about."

Themes and Meanings

The reader is left to ponder what God, Little Flower, Marcel Pretre, and the author are about. Clearly, the significance of the story does not lie in the story line. The action is so minimal as to qualify it for the designation "antistory." However, this lack of action is typical of the stories of Clarice Lispector and does not constitute an oversight or flaw in the construction of the narrative. She has a purpose to her writing that is far more important to her than recounting the adventures of fictional characters: The story exists as a vehicle through which to demonstrate her philosophical convictions.

Lispector, a thoroughgoing existentialist, explores in her stories the pain of ambiguity experienced by her fictional characters. Trivial moments generate confrontations with self-discovery that are wrenchingly sad, revealing to the characters their weakness in fearing freedom and the absurdity of human existence. The very triviality of the event, coupled with its profound impact, lends a grotesque incongruity to the moment and generates a flash of insight into the existentialist ambiguity of the human condition, which has been labeled the Absurd.

Marcel Pretre, explorer, hunter, and man of the world, moves from civilized, conventional surroundings into the equatorial jungle. This journey takes him into a setting of lush, rampant vegetation, where the jungle, the humidity, and the heat suggest the pervasive force of nature as one explores more and more deeply within the uncivilized jungle, and symbolically within the human personality. However, Pretre ignores the lush presence of the untamed jungle as he probes deeper and deeper. When, in the deepest interior of the jungle, he discovers the ultimate human creature, the smallest woman in the world, Pretre feels awed almost to the point of giddiness at actually confronting nature's rarest product, a truly unique creation. Nature has derived this ultimate creature from a succession of smaller and smaller pygmies. Pretre has a sense that he has "arrived at the end of the line." He is enchanted by her rarity, charmed by her strangeness, and attracted to her as "a woman such as the delights of the most exquisite dream had never equaled."

Little Flower is the totally natural person, one who has never suffered the anguish of having to make choices and impose restrictions. She lives wholly in concord with her impulses and emotions, and she cares not at all for the acceptance or the indifference of humanity because she scarcely comprehends the existence of the rest of the world. When Marcel sends her picture and description to the newspaper for publication in the Sunday supplement, he treats her as a curiosity for the amusement of the bored weekend reader. He describes her as "black as a monkey," and the picture he sends makes her look much like a dog. The identification with animal characteristics emphasizes the identification of Little Flower with nature, as well as her difference from the civilized people reading the paper. Her differences evoke in certain readers of the newspaper article a recognition of the uniqueness of each person, and the consequent alienation of every person from others. Readers are forced into moments of insight that strip away the conventional amenities and force them to recognize their own character and the implications of their own condition within the scope of civilized humanity.

The comment of the old woman at the end of the story gains force as one realizes that the author is suggesting that God (or Nature) knows what He is about in forcing people from time to time to acknowledge their natural feelings. Failure to acknowledge and fulfill these impulses and emotions represents a choice to restrict and thwart one's own personality, leading to a loss of touch with one's own self and a failure, because of weakness and fear, to achieve one's full potential.

Style and Technique

The author employs limited physical description but detailed omniscience when she explores the thoughts and feelings of the characters in the story. She describes the characters sometimes from the internal perspective of their thoughts and feelings, and at other times simply by describing their behavior, letting the reader determine the implications.

Lispector uses humor as a contrast to the overarching themes of failure and isolation that inform the story. An example of her humor occurs in the scene in which Little Flower scratches herself "where one never scratches," while the explorer is regarding her with awestruck adoration, and he modestly averts his gaze.

The author uses symbolism constantly. The jungle, the animal references, the newspaper supplement, the explorer and his long search leading to his discovery, his helmet, his notes, the treetop home, and the name Little Flower are all conspicuous symbols in this story. Lispector's intense exploration of the emotional moments of crisis and discovery, and the contrast of this intensity with the surface calm of the action, give the story a special focus on the inner conflict of the characters. None of the characters is particularly well developed. They are all, except for Little Flower, intended to represent deep psychological complexities, and the author forces recognition of their ambiguities and the meaning, or meaninglessness, of their existence.

Betty G. Gawthrop

THE SMELL OF DEATH AND FLOWERS

Author: Nadine Gordimer (1923-   )
Type of plot: Psychological
Time of plot: The early 1950's
Locale: Johannesburg, South Africa
First published: 1956

> *Principal characters:*
> JOYCE McCOY, a pretty young white woman, the main
>   protagonist
> JESSICA MALHERBE, a white antiapartheid political activist
> EDDIE NTWALA, a black man who attends the multiracial party
> DEREK ROSS, the host of the multiracial party
> RAJATI, Jessica Malherbe's Indian husband
> MATT SHABALALA, a black participant in the act of civil
>   disobedience
> MALCOLM BARKER, Joyce McCoy's brother-in-law

The Story

The story is told by an omniscient narrator in the third person. Although the narrator occasionally looks inside the mind of another character, the story is told chiefly from the point of view of the female protagonist, Joyce McCoy.

Joyce McCoy, a pretty and somewhat shallow young white woman of twenty-two, returns to South Africa from England, where she has lived for five years. As the story begins, Joyce, accompanied by her brother-in-law Malcolm Barker, is attending a party in Johannesburg. Because members of all races are present, this social affair is most unusual for South Africa. There, Joyce dances with a black man, Eddie Ntwala; this is the first time in her life that she has ever done such a thing.

A fateful step is taken by Joyce at the very beginning of the story, when she catches sight of Jessica Malherbe. Jessica is a white antiapartheid activist who has rebelled against her traditional Afrikaner family background by both her political choices and by her choice of an Indian, Rajati, for a husband. As the party finally draws to a close, Joyce, on the spur of the moment, asks for permission to take part in an act of civil disobedience planned by Jessica: a protest march, by a group composed of members of all of South Africa's races, into the segregated African section of the town; such a march is illegal under the South African apartheid system.

Joyce's initial request, made at the party, gets no reply; she gains Jessica's reluctant permission to join the march only after visiting her on separate occasions in the days following the party. When Joyce does go to Jessica's apartment on the day of the protest, to gather with the other marchers, she feels a strong sense of panic, which she overcomes with difficulty; only after having overcome this panicky sensation is she able to get into the car with the other demonstrators. Once the demonstrators have marched into the African section, Joyce is, like all the other demonstrators, placed under arrest for having violated the rules of apartheid.

Themes and Meanings

The main theme of the story is the possibility of a radical leap from political apathy to wholehearted involvement in a just cause. At the beginning of the story, the protagonist is a pretty but shallow woman; at the end of the story, she has been arrested for an act of civil disobedience and has come to feel the righteousness of the blacks' fight against apartheid, and to make their cause her own. Such a conversion to political activism is, for Joyce, not a matter of intellectual ratiocination; nobody tries to convince her to join the demonstration. Instead, the struggle takes place almost entirely within Joyce's emotions.

The first milestone in Joyce's move toward emotional involvement in the black cause is her dance with a black man at the multiracial party. As Joyce dances with Eddie Ntwala, the author looks inside Joyce's mind, showing both the protagonist's anxious queries to herself about what she is feeling and her relief that she still feels "nothing." Here, in this moment of introspection, the reader sees the beginning of the struggle for Joyce's soul between apathy and commitment. The second milestone is Joyce's inner struggle with her emotions at Jessica's apartment, a struggle that leads to her final decision to keep her earlier promise to take part in the demonstration.

The third and final milestone occurs just after her arrest, when the police are taking down the names of the demonstrators. By this time, the author relates, Joyce no longer feels "nothing"; instead, she feels what the black onlookers are feeling at the sight of her, a young white woman, being arrested. For Joyce, a genuine sense of solidarity with the oppressed has finally triumphed over her earlier indifference to the larger world; she now knows how the blacks feel when they are oppressed by white authority.

In "The Smell of Death and Flowers," Nadine Gordimer strongly suggests that the motives for undertaking acts of political courage are not always purely idealistic ones. Taking part in an antigovernment demonstration, although indeed dangerous, can be a means whereby an individual can, through involvement in the camaraderie of political activism, break out of personal isolation and a crippling inability to feel anything strongly; such a dangerous act thus provides psychological benefits to the participant.

Although she evidently has faith in South African whites' ability to travel down the road to multiracial political activism by achieving genuine empathy with the plight of the blacks, Gordimer has no illusion that the path to fellow feeling with the victims of oppression is an easy one to tread. In her narration of the gathering of the protesters for the march into the African location, Gordimer points out that Matt Shabalala, the black participant, knows that he is taking far greater risks than Joyce— for he, a married man, is endangering his future hopes for employment, thereby placing his entire livelihood at risk. Joyce, Gordimer pointedly notes, thinks that she, in her excited anticipation of what will happen, is feeling exactly what Shabalala is feeling, but she is not. Even here, then, in the midst of the common struggle, Gordimer shows that there is a gap in empathy between the races that only shared experiences can close.

Style and Technique

Gordimer relies heavily on imagery to illuminate certain aspects of Joyce McCoy's character. When Gordimer first introduces Joyce, she compares her to a pink, cold porcelain vase, compares Joyce's face to the type of face found in a Marie Laurencin painting, and describes Joyce's prettiness as "two-dimensional." When Joyce conducts her banal, almost incoherent conversation with her black dancing partner, the author describes her voice as "small" and "flat." The reader's impression of Joyce's superficiality is further reinforced by her initial remarks concerning Jessica Malherbe: an observation of how "nice" the antiapartheid activist looks, and of how good that woman's perfume is. The author again mentions how Jessica looks, using Joyce's original words, when Joyce first puts the question to Jessica about joining the demonstration; the author thereby implies that the original sensory impression is still uppermost in Joyce's mind. When Joyce first puts the question to Jessica, Joyce's face is described as "blank" and "exquisite," and her manner of making the request is compared to that of someone requesting an invitation to a dinner party. With such techniques, the author gives a vivid picture of a young woman who is all pretty surface and has no intellectual depth.

In charting Joyce's road to political commitment, Gordimer plays again and again on olfactory imagery. Twice in the story, Joyce becomes aware of the smell of death and flowers, identified with the odor of incense. The first time that this aroma comes into Joyce's consciousness is when she is at the multiracial party. In a flashback, Joyce suddenly remembers having noticed this particular smell years earlier, when she had been shopping at an Indian shop in Johannesburg and had been followed by a mysterious stranger who tried to molest her. In the same flashback, Joyce suddenly remembers the same smell of death and flowers as having pervaded the funeral of her English grandfather. The second time that Joyce becomes aware of the smell is during her difficult struggle, while at Jessica's apartment on the day of the march, to suppress her own anxieties about taking part in the planned antigovernment demonstration.

The author uses this aromatic imagery to symbolize the influence exerted on Joyce's decision-making processes by psychic elements of which the protagonist is hardly aware. The imagery of smell looms in Joyce's consciousness whenever she faces something new or shocking or when she is contemplating a leap into the unknown, a decision from which there is no turning back. The smell is to some extent associated with Joyce's deeply buried anxieties about miscegenation. Thus, she first becomes aware of the smell when she learns, at the party, that Jessica has an Indian husband; her mind then flashes back to when that mysterious man of vaguely Indian appearance had tried to molest her. The smell returns to Joyce's consciousness on the day of the march, in Jessica's apartment, at precisely the moment when Joyce meets Jessica's husband.

The smell of incense, of death and flowers, is also associated with the code of good manners inherited from Joyce's family background and, by extension, from the English mother country. At the funeral for her grandfather, Joyce had first noticed this smell. The smell returns to her consciousness during the crucial inner struggle in Jessica's apartment, when Joyce decides that good manners require her to take part in the demonstration as she had promised. The smell of death and flowers thus represents not only the lifeless code of formal politeness inherited from England but also the possibility of new life (flowers) arising from this inherited tradition: a symbol of resurrection as well as of death.

Paul D. Mageli

THE SMILES OF KONARAK

Author: George Dennison (1925-1987)
Type of plot: Realism
Time of plot: The 1960's
Locale: New York City
First published: 1979

> *Principal characters:*
> TAGGART, who is a playwright, poet, and reviewer
> KARLA, Taggart's lover
> EVERETT WILDER, an aging neighborhood activist

The Story

At the beginning of this story, set in New York during the early 1960's, a time of beatnik literature and social consciousness among intellectuals, a writer, Taggart, meets Karla at a party given in honor of Taggart's latest play. Its success is a gauge of Taggart's ripening as a writer in his thirties. Blessed with inherited money, he has spent years developing his craft without the bind of an ordinary job. Although Taggart's destiny of success is apparent, that of his casual but intimate acquaintance Karla is less clear. She has known much frustration in her few years since taking degrees in teaching and social work. These conventional paths to careers merely exposed her to the miseries of working amid bureaucratic agencies that defeated Karla's intention to solve society's many problems. She quit her teaching job and, early in the story, resigns her position as a social worker.

After their first night together, Karla asks Taggart's advice. He has no solution for her problem, knowing already through other friends' experiences the pitfalls of the "helping fields." Characteristic of Taggart, however, he argues the sublime negativity of such occupations, urging Karla to temper her passionate need for instant and permanent effects with a dose of detached realism. Karla's spirit will not be so appeased. Prostitution, she imagines, will be the answer, allowing her to minister to human needs and earn a living. Taggart is shocked at her idealism, if not her impulsive obliviousness, and when her work leads to a painful disillusionment, unspecified in the story, he feels bitterly righteous. She ignored his counseling, which she had sought during their first night together.

Although Karla's dreams of "the right job" are dispelled, Taggart's self-esteem as a writer is challenged, not by any personal failure to create literature but by Karla's irreverence for the beatnik poetry writing and readings he values and through meeting Luis Fontana, a young Puerto Rican gang leader with literary aspirations. Luis is charged with possession of narcotics and receives a three-year sentence. In prison he is murdered, a crime the officials feebly attempt to rig as a suicide. After promises of further investigation, the Luis issue dies nearly as swiftly as did the boy himself. Luis,

Taggart senses, was the real-life embodiment of the human energies—assertiveness, pride, intelligence—which Taggart imaginatively ascribes to his literary characters, who, precisely because they are imaginary, are privileged, enjoying immunity from the fate that befalls Luis. That Luis as a playwright lacked the skills to embody the experience of "life on the edge" in the violent city puts Taggart's own unique gifts in an ironic light, as he writes successfully of things of which he is not truly part.

Nevertheless, Taggart does feel the reality of such harshness abrading the human soul. Karla feels it as well, and her intention has been to lessen its force. She accepts the leadership of a reading clinic organized by Taggart's friend Everett, an aging political activist who has spent a lifetime adjusting his politics to reality. Taggart's stance toward the harshness, while sharing in the actual clinic work and reuniting with Karla in the process, is through his art: "How mysterious it was that artistic form should absorb and recreate the spirit!" Despite the sadness, the grimness of things, the artist exists, and if not triumphant, then mysteriously persistent. The story's final scene has Taggart suddenly remembering that he is scheduled to read at the Eiffel, a community center for Beat poets. Karla assures him that they will read to themselves if he does not show, but impelled by his difficult-to-explain connection to the brotherhood, Taggart heads for the center, Karla at his side, and "every ten steps or so he broke into a trot, and she would shrug and smile and run beside him."

Themes and Meanings

The story's title alludes to a central theme. Midway through the story, Taggart has a nostalgic reverie featuring his wife Naomi, from whom he is now divorced. She was extremely beautiful. She appears clearly in his sad reflections, smiling at him while the present Karla sleeps beside him. He has a vision of photographs that once fascinated him, pictures of "sculptured orgiasts" from the Indian Temple of Konarak, abode of the sun god. In their erotic abandonment the figures smile smiles that, in Taggart's perception, "were not images of private bliss, but presupposed a community of trust, perhaps even a community of love." Taggart, citizen of New York City, where Puerto Ricans, blacks, Italians, Slavs, Mexicans, and Jews make a disharmonious cultural hash, senses that the orgiasts' smiles are utopian, their orgy "a visionary hope of trust." The seemingly perfect fit of Taggart's relationship with Naomi was only seeming. Still, Taggart is assailed by the vision of her beauty, her smile, and her ravishing appeal; the memory of those first hours with Naomi endures despite the disharmony and disappointment that followed.

George Dennison suggests that the dream of compatibility is truer than the acknowledged incompatibility, whether among New York's many races or between a man and a woman. He injects Karla into Taggart's life as an antidote to disillusionment, for Karla, a Texas girl with a southerner's ingenuous frankness, is not a native of the community of the disillusioned. Her continuing love, her calling up from the street to Taggart's apartment ("'Heyyyy, TAAA-gart!' He had never before been hailed like this in the vast city of New York"), enacts for Dennison the possibility that the smiling figures ideally represent. Karla may not perfectly complement Taggart or agree with him on every point, but she is with him in an unprecedented communion, creating for the moment something of the harmony that the photos of the orgiasts so attractively advertise: "The small voice rang up confidently out of the vastness, and he began to smile and feel buoyant."

Style and Technique

"The Smiles of Konarak," published in 1979, details a period nearly twenty years before the date of publication. The first sentence reads: "Early in the nineteen sixties a group of New York poets built a diminutive theater in a Lower East Side settlement house and proceeded to produce their own plays." The focus narrows rapidly to one playwright, Taggart, but the ambience of the early 1960's is itself a considerable presence in the story. Billie Holiday records play during the dance at Taggart's celebration; Beat poets drink cappuccinos and compose lines of poetry "by the laws of chance."

Dennison seems intent on that time when the hopes that sustained the revolutionary 1960's, era of free and brotherly love, were at their freshest. What has happened since that time, "history," has neither fulfilled those hopes nor definitively discredited them.

To enhance the historical feeling, Dennison leaves his characters in states of limbo, neither granting their dreams nor arguing their impotence. The success of Taggart, an isolated and definitely fortuitous fact—he is lucky enough to have a share of genius—is juxtaposed to Karla's frustrations, and those of other characters, such as the political activist Everett and his friend Luis Fontana. The characters with the greatest enthusiasm for changing the world are frustrated, while the more detached Taggart earns nothing but praise for his writing. The plot contains no development to a climax, but is composed through a series of dramatized scenes that collectively form a sense of culmination. Dennison's style seeks gently to embody the spectacle of life free of literary comment. One example of this is the closing scene, when Taggart and Karla attend an outdoor play in a park. Of all plays to perform, the company has picked William Shakespeare's *Coriolanus* (1607-1608): "Had ever Shakespeare such an audience as this!? . . . Their speech was a babble of contending phrases." Life is more a spectacle than literature. The comings and goings of Ukrainians, Poles, Puerto Ricans, and one particularly belligerent black woman, "with red hair and dully gleaming sores on her legs," who stands on stage before the play shaking her fist at the audience, are, Taggart admits, more interesting than the performance of the "real" actors.

Through the story's re-creation of an era, the reader feels both the distance of the past and its still-forceful presence, much as Taggart experiences the still-living smiles of his long gone wife, Naomi.

Bruce Wiebe

THE SMOKER

Author: David Schickler (1969-   )
Type of plot: Realism, psychological
Time of plot: The late twentieth century
Locale: New York City
First published: 2000

> *Principal characters:*
> DOUGLAS KERCHEK, a thirty-one-year-old high school English
>   teacher
> NICOLE BONNER, a nineteen-year-old student
> SAMSON BONNER, Nicole's father
> PAULETTE BONNER, Nicole's mother
> CHIAPAS, an apprentice barber

The Story

"The Smoker" is told in the third person through the consciousness of Douglas Kerchek, a teacher of high school English. He has a Ph.D. in English from Harvard and lives alone. The title refers to a recurring event, the Friday Night Smokers hosted by the Society of Gentlemen club in Kerchek's hometown, Allentown, Pennsylvania. As a high school senior, he had often been invited to box at the smokers.

The two main characters are Kerchek and Nicole Bonner, a student at St. Agnes High School at Broadway and West Ninety-seventh. The story opens with Kerchek musing over a note Nicole has appended to her essay on William Shakespeare's *Othello, the Moor of Venice* (1604) describing her late night reading in bed (a novel a night), her disdain for Hunter S. Thompson, and her family's habit of sharing a brandy before bedtime. Kerchek is taken aback by the intimacy of Nicole's observations and by her personal, nearly impertinent, question about how he had bruised his ankle. He has written a keenly observed and detailed letter strongly supporting Nicole's application for admission to Princeton. Nicole is not only a year older than his other AP English students, she is brilliant as well and, in Kerchek's eyes, "dangerously alluring."

As a solitary well-built man, good-looking with a dash of gray at the temples, Kerchek knows he is a figure of interest among the young women at St. Agnes School. He is not attracted to his female colleagues so he does not date any of them. Kerchek walks the five blocks from school to his noisy apartment building where he lives alone, finding as usual the lobby outside his apartment filled with Chicano men drinking and playing high-stakes poker. They call him "Uno" because he may stop to have one beer with them, but only one beer. In his apartment, he has a sandwich and begins his paper grading only to be interrupted by a phone call from Nicole, who has copied his phone number from the principal's Rolodex. He spends ten minutes on the phone with Nicole, tongue-tied as a teenager contributing, little to the conversation. The next morning, still irritated with himself for his inept conversation, he puts on a "smart coat and tie" and gives a pop quiz on vocabulary and titles. Nicole responds by writing verbatim from memory the first few pages of Herman Melville's *Moby Dick: Or, The Whale* (1851).

Three weeks later on a rainy Tuesday, Nicole seeks Kerchek out from the faculty lounge to say that she has been accepted to Princeton and to invite him to a thank-you dinner with her parents at their place in the Preemption apartment building at West Eighty-second and Riverside. Slightly stunned, Kerchek accepts, gets a fresh but inept haircut from Chiapas, and shows up for the Thursday dinner. Nicole, dressed in an exquisite black silk evening gown as black as her hair, and her parents, Simon and Paulette, welcome him to their penthouse. The situation is jovially confrontational, putting Kercheck off balance as he is challenged to "teach them something." Samson challenges Kercheck further "to test his mettle" before announcing that he and Paulette wish to arrange a marriage between Kercheck and Nicole. Later Nicole and Kercheck are shown into Samson's study, where they are alone together for the first time in their new roles. Nicole tells Kerchek that she knows "what the world is like" and how long people can go in New York City without finding someone and that she understands loneliness even if she is only nineteen. Kercheck, the more romantic of the two, wants to know if Nicole is in love with him. Nicole, the practical one, is fully prepared to fall in love with him "as of the first week in June" when the prom and graduation are behind her. He orders her to make a fist and hit him as hard as she can. She does, showing them both what lies in their future.

Themes and Meanings

"The Smoker" first appeared in *The New Yorker* and then in David Schickler's first book, *Kissing in Manhattan* (2001). In this story, the principal theme is loneliness in the big city. It is not good for a person to be alone, and the best match may be one based on intellectual attraction. However, being single, intelligent, and alone in New York City poses a problem to be solved. One solution appears to be suggested by the name of Nicole Bonner's apartment house, The Preemption. A preemption is the right to acquire something before anyone else. Hence, the Bonners propose to arrange a marriage between Kerchek and Nicole and thereby directly acquire a well-credentialed husband for their daughter without running the "risks" of the "open market" in Princeton, which Nicole will attend, or the city of New York. Kerchek, although from a hardscrabble Pennsylvania town, is a Harvard Ph.D., intelligent, employed, good-looking, and physically fit. The Bonners, Samson and Paulette, appear to have acquired money in some way but little or no culture, only the veneer of sipped brandy and a huge heirloom collection of unread but leather-bound books that cover a wall of the main room in the Bonner apartment. They have one daughter, Nicole, who is both bright and beautiful, not to mention remarkably self-assured. The Bonners test Kerchek by various means, including repeated punches to the shoulder and verbal assaults, to see whether he measures up.

Schickler cleverly—and ironically—exploits the comic possibilities of the single man teaching in an all-girls parochial school. Furthermore he exaggerates the games, purposes, and devices of the usual "courtship audition dinner," thereby creating a comic examination of the serious social and cultural issue of finding a suitable mate. The meanings of the story may be seen most clearly revealed toward the end of the evening and the end of the story, where Schickler implicitly contrasts Nicole's (and her parents') practical approach to the serious matter of finding a suitable mate in the wilderness of Manhattan with all the romantic notions of falling in love in New York City. For one thing, the Bonners assure Kerchek that theirs is just such an arranged marriage. For another, all three of them see in Kerchek a lonely but very eligible man, well-educated and good at his profession but one who is, as Nicole says directly, "just killing time."

Style and Technique

Comic inversion, allusion, action, and dialogue are four technical devices that Schickler deploys consistently and deftly to give the story its quirky comic tone. From the first sentence, Schickler weaves a deft and seamless tapestry of allusions to novels, plays, and games that develop the theme of sexual attraction with interesting and sometimes fateful if not fatal consequences. Like Shakespeare's comedies dealing with the sexual pursuit, this story is high comedy, not tragedy. However, Schickler's allusions to Shakespeare's *Othello, the Moor of Venice* and *King Lear* (1605-1606), Kerchek's remembered high school boxing career, Nicole's Cleopatra haircut, Samson's suggestive name, and Chiapas's inept cutting of Kerchek's hair all suggest that the wrong marriage can result in tragedy and the "right one" in an examination of issues of power and subversion.

Throughout the story, the writing is taut and economical, marked with witty functional dialogue that develops character and moves the plot. Schickler tracks Nicole's aggressive yet subtle pursuit of Kerchek and reveals Kerchek's vulnerability to the campaign through a series of short scenes alternated with descriptions of his physical appearance, his solitary life, his attention to the details of teaching, and his own substantial intellect. Schickler balances Kerchek's scholarly, bookish nature with functional allusions to his boxing background and his habit of jogging and working out.

Schickler packs his story with details of settings both exterior and interior that not only suggest their literal functions as classroom, chapel, and contrasting apartment buildings but also advance the plot and reveal the themes by their work as symbols. Kerchek's world at the beginning of the story is a comfortable loop that links his classroom and his apartment. Nicole Bonner disturbs that world just as Eve "disturbed" Eden, as Cleopatra disturbed Rome's Egyptian campaign. When Kerchek gets "the boxing feeling" in his stomach, he knows that he must fight or flee. Schickler shows that he has been preempted from doing either.

Theodore C. Humphrey

THE SNAKE

Author: John Steinbeck (1902-1968)
Type of plot: Naturalistic
Time of plot: The early 1930's
Locale: Monterey, California
First published: 1936

> *Principal characters:*
> DR. PHILLIPS, a marine biologist
> AN UNNAMED WOMAN

The Story

Dr. Phillips, a marine biologist, enters his cramped laboratory on what is now Cannery Row in Monterey, California. White rats run about in their cages. Captive cats used in laboratory experiments meow, hungry for milk. A cage full of snakes, which seem to recognize Phillips, pull in their tongues.

Phillips lights his fire, sets a kettle of water on the stove, and drops his dinner, a can of beans, into it. He goes into his Spartan bedroom, removes his boots, and returns to the other room, where he empties a sack of starfish on the dissecting table, preparatory to beginning an experiment with them. He then takes a bottle of milk and heads for the cat pen. Before he feeds the cats, he removes one, strokes it, then puts it into a sealed box attached to a gas jet, which he turns on. As the cat inside struggles softly, he feeds the others.

As Phillips sets up his starfish experiment, he hears soft footfalls on the stairs, then a sharp knocking on his door. Opening it, he finds a tall, lean woman, straight black hair close to her head, dressed in a dark suit. Her eyes glitter in the light. Protesting that he is busy and in the middle of an experiment that must be carefully timed, Phillips tries to put her off, but she finally persuades him to admit her. Phillips explains his experiment to her and asks if she wishes to look through his microscope at part of it. She declines.

During a ten-minute lull between the timed stages of his experiment, Phillips takes the dead cat from the box in which it has been gassed and secures it on a cradle. After deftly cutting into one of its arteries, he pumps embalming fluid into it.

When Phillips finally has time to talk with the woman, she asks him whether he has a male rattlesnake. Phillips has one that he knows is male because he has seen it copulating. The woman offers him five dollars for the snake but wants him to keep the reptile in captivity for her. She then asks him to feed her snake a rat, for which she pays him. Reluctantly, Phillips puts the rattlesnake into a separate cage, then snares a live rat to drop into the snake's cage. The woman stands and watches as the doomed rat preens. The rattlesnake advances toward it, snaps it up in its unhinged jaw, and begins to swallow the struggling animal. Finally, only a bit of the rat's tail can be seen.

Phillips notices that as the snake approaches the rat, swaying back and forth, the woman also sways. He cannot stand to watch the snake consume the rat, nor can he look at the woman, fearing that if she is also moving her mouth, he will become sick. He returns to his experiments that, because they have been neglected for so long, are ruined and must be discarded. The woman leaves but tells Phillips that she will return and that he should feed her snake rats, for which she promises to pay him.

For several weeks, Phillips expects the woman to return, but she never does. Sometimes he thinks that he sees her in town, but on closer observation, always finds that he is wrong.

Themes and Meanings

"The Snake" is fraught with psychosexual meaning that can be interpreted in Freudian ways but that is best looked at from a Jungian standpoint. John Steinbeck contends that he has told this story exactly as it actually happened in his friend Ed Ricketts's Cannery Row laboratory and denies knowing what—if anything—it means. Other people in Monterey also witnessed the event, and, although their basic memories of it are similar, they have differing memories of its details.

It is known that as this story was incubating in Steinbeck's mind, he and Ricketts had several conversations about Jungian psychology with Joseph Campbell, one of the theory's foremost proponents. It is also known that Steinbeck had read Carl Jung and was reasonably well versed in Jungian psychology. From a Jungian point of view, the woman in the story is a psychological archetype who represents repressed forces within Dr. Phillips. Steinbeck connects her with the sea. As she enters the laboratory, the sounds that she and the sea make are virtually indistinguishable sighs. The woman may be seen as representing Jung's collective unconscious.

As Steinbeck presents her, the woman herself is snakelike. Tall, lean, dressed in black, she sways like the snake seeking its prey; as the rattlesnake pounces on the rat and begins to consume it, the woman's jaws move. From a Freudian perspective the snake becomes a phallic symbol; from a Jungian perspective it becomes an androgynous symbol, just as Phillips's starfish are androgynous—a fact that his experiment of uniting the sperm and ova of single starfish in his watch glasses emphasizes. The snake represents the male (phallic) in that it emits venom, but, as Steinbeck portrays it, it also represents the female (vaginal) by swallowing the white rat whole.

Phillips and the woman stand in sharp contrast to each other. The woman buys a rattlesnake from Phillips purely for the personal satisfaction of seeing it eat a live rat. As a scientist, Phillips has no qualms about sacrificing a cat in an experiment, so long as there is a reason; however, he deplores the unnecessary sacrifice of any form of life. The woman's actions, therefore, appall him.

This story, the first in which Steinbeck's friend, Ed Ricketts, is depicted, has to do with elemental, primordial forces. Phillips's (Ricketts's) laboratory is close to the tidal pools from which all sorts of life spring. The pools are just below his floor, watered by the ocean whose waves lap in within a few feet of the scientist. There is an Edenic quality about the laboratory, and, just as Eve brought temptation into the Garden of Eden, so did the unnamed woman disturb the ascetic equilibrium of Phillips's workplace.

Phillips can deal psychologically with rattlesnakes capturing and consuming rats in the natural state, just as Steinbeck does in *The Red Pony* (1938), in which vultures converge on the lifeless carcass of a pony and dip their voracious beaks into the dead animal's eyes. He has no difficulty either with having Lenny smother small, furry animals in *Of Mice and Men* (1937). Steinbeck customarily deals with human life in animal terms. He views humans as part of the broad animal kingdom, seeing human behavior reflected in the behavior of other animals.

In Jungian terms, snakes embody the murky world of human instincts. Snakes are used to express sudden, surprising flashes of the unconscious mind. In this story, with its snake and its "snake-woman," the snake-woman seems to emerge from the primordial tidal pool near the laboratory. When she arrives, Phillips cannot distinguish between her sighs and those of the sea. When she leaves, her footfalls are imperceptible, presumably because she is returning to the primordial pool from which she first—at least symbolically—emerged.

Style and Technique

This early story astounded Steinbeck's agent as well as the publishers to whom he sent it—all of whom considered it too bizarre to print. He finally published it in a local newspaper, the *Monterey Beacon*, in 1936, but it did not receive widespread national distribution until appearing in Steinbeck's collection *The Long Valley* in 1938.

The microcosm that Steinbeck creates in the laboratory is, in some ways, misleading. The laboratory is small, its two rooms furnished only with what is needed. However, being situated above the tidal pool, it has a taproot to the whole of creation. Steinbeck's use of setting could not be more effective than it is in this story, which, according to various witnesses, actually took place in Ed Ricketts's laboratory, where Steinbeck spent a great deal of time.

The woman in this compressed story appears at the laboratory from the street outside; however, as the story develops, Steinbeck raises subtle doubts about where she actually comes from. By the time she departs, the question of her origin hovers. The woman, having attained a highly symbolic stature, becomes a quite mystical memory.

Steinbeck skillfully juxtaposes the mythic world (the woman) and the scientific world (Dr. Phillips), the ideal against the real, the fanciful against the factual. However, the woman, as the representative of the mythic world, deals cavalierly with life, for which Phillips has a respectful reverence.

By using only two characters in this story, Steinbeck sets up effectively the philosophical dichotomies that emerge from it. He reinforces the mythic quality of the snake-woman by having her say that she will return and then having her disappear forever.

R. Baird Shuman

THE SNAKE CHARMER

Author: Varlam Shalamov (1907-1982)
Type of plot: Social realism
Time of plot: The mid-1930's to the mid-1950's
Locale: A forced-labor camp in the Kolyma region of northeastern Siberia
First published: "Zaklinatel zmei," 1978 (English translation, 1980)

> *Principal characters:*
> THE NARRATOR, a political prisoner in a work camp
> PLATONOV, a fellow political prisoner, a former screenwriter
> FEDYA, a criminal

The Story

Two political prisoners are sitting on a fallen tree during a work break. One of them, a former screenwriter named Platonov, is telling the narrator the story of his "second life," his life in the camps. It turns out that Platonov has spent a year at the Jankhar mine, a place notorious even by the standards of Kolyma, a region of northeastern Siberia.

Platonov explains, however, that only the first few months were bad. The only political prisoner—therefore the only educated one—among common criminals, he survived the year at Jankhar by telling the stories of Alexandre Dumas, *perè*, Arthur Conan Doyle, and H. G. Wells, and in return was fed, clothed, and protected by the thieves. He assumes that the narrator has also made use of this, the one advantage of the literate prisoner. The narrator has never been a "novelist," however, and suggests that "novel-telling" is the lowest form of humiliation. At the same time, he does not find fault with Platonov and says only that a starving man can be forgiven much.

Platonov plans, if he lives long enough, to write a story about his own storytelling career, and he has even thought of a title, "The Snake Charmer." However, he dies too soon—three weeks after this conversation, he collapses while breaking rock and dies as so many have died, of hunger, weakness, and heart failure. The narrator, who liked Platonov for his curiosity and lively interest in the world outside, decides to tell the snake charmer's story.

The snake charmer's story begins as Platonov finishes his first, exhausting day at Jankhar. He waits for the roll to be called and while waiting reflects on the fact that the end of the working day is not really the end, that they all must return their tools, fall in for yet another roll call, march five kilometers to gather firewood, then haul the logs back to camp. No vehicles are used for hauling wood, and the horses are too ill and weak to leave the stable—which leads Platonov to thoughts about human endurance and human instinct, the instinct (not will) that makes even a dying man cling tenaciously to life. Man, he thinks, is tougher than any animal.

When he finally gets to the barracks, he sees that not everyone has worked that day. A group is perched on the top bunks, watching a card game. Platonov barely has time to sit down on the edge of a bunk when one of the toughs addresses him as a generic "Ivan Ivanovich." When Platonov answers that that is not his name, he is shoved over to the chief thug, threatened, and then slugged in the face. The thug, Fedya, orders him to sleep by the slop bucket, the foulest spot in the barracks.

Platonov knows that these thugs are not joking—he has already seen two thieves strangled to settle scores. He does as he is told, but Fedya is bored and restless; Fedya wants his feet scratched but is not satisfied with the way the young thief Mashka does it. He rouses Platonov again with orders to carry out the bucket and stoke the stove.

Most of the prisoners are asleep by this time, but Fedya wants a story. The thieves roust Platonov out one more time and almost ingratiatingly ask him if he can "tell novels." Platonov considers, doubts racing through his mind over the bargain he is about to make—and agrees. Fedya immediately brightens, gives him some bread and a cigarette, and asks him his name. Platonov offers a selection, then begins the tale chosen by Fedya. It is dawn by the time he finishes the first part. Fedya is delighted and lets Platonov sleep in the best bunks with the thieves.

When the prisoners are leaving the barracks the next morning, a big country boy gives Platonov a vicious shove and curses him. However, all it takes is one word from another prisoner, and the big one apologizes, asking Platonov not to tell Fedya what has happened. Platonov promises not to tell.

Themes and Meanings

An ordinary political prisoner in the forced-labor camps of Kolyma might survive cold, hunger, and disease; he might survive overwork and lack of sleep; he might survive brutal beatings by the camp guards. However, even if he lived through all these things, he might not make it through the encounter with one group of his fellow prisoners—the common criminals, or *urkas*. Thieves, murderers, and rapists in the outside world, they exercise their talents in the camps as well.

The *urka* subculture—and here that term is frighteningly literal—dates back to brigand gangs of the seventeenth century and has lived on through revolution and social upheaval. Often bizarrely and profusely tattooed, maimed, and scarred, speaking their own argot, rewarding and punishing according to their own code, the *urkas* have seemed barely human to many a new arrival in the camps. However, their position is a privileged one. They receive better food, warmer clothing, lighter work—and steal or extort whatever they cannot get "legally." Anything a political owns is fair game. The *urkas* live in an uneasy truce—not alliance—with the camp administration, not only because the administration fears them, not only because their absolute amorality terrifies the other prisoners, but also because they are useful in enforcing official policy. They are one more means of breaking the politicals' spirit. The *urkas* are told that though they might be guilty, erring, prodigal sons and daughters of the Soviet motherland, they are nevertheless still part of the family, not yet the lowest of the low. The politicals, however, are total outcasts, traitors, filth. An urka can thus rob, brutalize, or even murder a political with virtual impunity—he is actually helping the administration do its job.

However, there is one *urka* custom that has saved many a "friar," or intellectual. The *urkas* love hearing novels, preferably adventure tales or mysteries, and preferably as close to the original as possible. For a lump of bread, some soup, a blanket, and immunity from beatings, an educated prisoner can play Scheherazade to the criminal court, telling and retelling Dumas's *Le Comte de Monte-Cristo* (1844-1845; *The Count of Monte-Cristo*, 1846), Victor Hugo's *Les Misérables* (1862; English translation, 1862), and other stories.

Hence, Platonov's dilemma: Are the compromises that make physical survival possible always the same ones that make moral survival impossible? This is the central question of the story, and this is what races through Platonov's mind before he gives Fedya his answer. He toys with the idea that perhaps even here he can be useful, can educate, can enlighten in the noble old tradition of the Russian intelligentsia. However, both he and the reader realize immediately that these are the terms of Platonov's old life, not his new one. He will be saving only himself, and some other unfortunate will be the butt of jokes, curses, and abuse. Is "novel-telling," then, really any more noble than carrying out the slop bucket? Or is it the moral equivalent of scratching a thug's feet?

Platonov does not answer the question for himself or for the reader, but he makes his choice and tells his tale. His final words do not resolve the ambivalence, but they do speak in his favor, just as the narrator's introduction did. Platonov is now safe, albeit temporarily and precariously, and high enough in the hierarchy to exercise some tiny bit of power himself. He can, with a word, arrange for someone else to be beaten, but he chooses not to.

Style and Technique

One of the chief sources of irony in all of Varlam Shalamov's stories is his narrative method itself—horrific events recited in calm, undramatic fashion, an objective account of murderous absurdity. In "The Snake Charmer," he adds a more explicitly moral dimension to that irony by prefacing Platonov's story with a conversation between Platonov and the narrator, and by letting the narrator inform the reader of Platonov's death. When Platonov tells the narrator that he wants to write a story about his "novelist" days, he automatically begins his sentence with a camp formula, a cautionary charm. If he lives, he will write the story. While the narrator agrees that Platonov's title is a good one, he reminds him that the main thing is to survive to write it. Platonov, the "novelist," dies before he can write anything down, and the narrator, who has avoided becoming just such an entertainer, is left to tell his story, the story of a man who did what he himself refused to do.

Thus the reader already knows this narrator's point of view and his attitude toward Platonov and his choice. Platonov's doubts and waverings are filtered through the mind of a man who would not have done what he did. However, Shalamov himself refuses to turn that irony into either self-righteousness or sarcasm. His narrator has his own storytelling code, and he does not betray it, but tells the truth.

Jane Ann Miller

THE SNIPER

Author: Liam O'Flaherty (1896-1984)
Type of plot: Adventure
Time of plot: The early 1920's
Locale: Dublin, Ireland
First published: 1923

> *Principal characters:*
> A SNIPER, a Republican
> ANOTHER SNIPER, a Free Stater
> A MAN IN AN ARMORED CAR
> AN OLD WOMAN

The Story

"The Sniper" relates an encounter in downtown Dublin, near the O'Connell Bridge, between a sniper for the Republicans and a sniper for the Free Staters. Guns roar in the distance as the Republican sniper lies on a rooftop. He is a young boy. "His face was that of a student—thin and ascetic, but his eyes had the cold gleam of a fanatic . . . the eyes of a man who is used to look at death."

It is a June evening, and the sniper, who has had nothing to eat since morning, hungrily wolfs down a sandwich and takes a short drink from the flask of whiskey he carries in his pocket. He desperately wants a cigarette and finally risks showing his position by igniting a match and lighting one. Instantly, a bullet hits the wall near him. He takes two puffs of the cigarette and snuffs it. He raises himself to look over the parapet, but another bullet whizzes by his head, and he flattens himself against the roof.

An armored car crosses O'Connell Bridge and stops just below the sniper's position. An old woman with a tattered shawl around her head comes out of a side street to talk with a man in the turret of the armored car. The sniper wants to shoot at the armored car, but he knows that his bullets will not penetrate its fortified exterior. The old woman points in the direction of the sniper, who now realizes that she is an informer. When the man inside opens the turret to talk with her, the sniper shoots, and the man slumps over lifeless. The woman hurries toward the side street, but the sniper shoots again. The old woman shrieks and falls into the gutter. The car speeds away, the man in the turret still slumped there. More shooting is heard, and the sniper knows that it is coming from the roof across the way. He has been hit in his right arm, in which he has lost all feeling.

The sniper takes out his knife and uses it to rip open his shirt. He sees that a bullet has gone into his arm but has not emerged from the other side. He takes out his field-dressing kit, breaks off the top of the iodine bottle that he pulls from it, and pours the dark liquid into his wound. Then he applies the bandages from his kit, using his teeth to tie the knot.

The sniper knows that he must get off the roof by morning or else the enemy sniper will kill him. He realizes that the sniper on the roof across the way is watching him every minute and will not let him get away. Taking his rifle, which is useless to him because his wounded arm makes it impossible for him to fire it, he puts his army cap on the muzzle and raises it slightly above the parapet. A shot rings out and the cap falls to the earth far below. The sniper lets his left arm hang lifelessly over the parapet, holding his rifle in it. Then he lets the rifle fall and rolls over.

The opposing sniper, assuming that his enemy is dead, relaxes his vigilance and stands up on the roof. The Republican sniper aims his revolver at his opponent and fires. The enemy sniper reels over the parapet in his death agony, then falls to the earth. The Republican sniper is suddenly revolted by what he sees and by what he has done. "His teeth chattered. He began to gibber to himself, cursing the war, cursing himself, cursing everybody." He drains his whiskey flask in one draft.

The sniper leaves the roof. When he gets to the street, his curiosity overcomes him and forces him to steal over to see whom he has shot. He attracts machine-gun fire as he goes toward the dead sniper, but he is not hit. He flings himself down beside the body of the man he has killed, then turns it over. He finds himself staring into his own brother's face.

Themes and Meanings

"The Sniper" emphasizes one of the greatest ironies of civil war: Brother is pitted against brother. In this story, Liam O'Flaherty deals with a strife that has divided Ireland for more than sixty years and still shows few signs of moderating. The Republican sniper in the story is young, and his youth is emphasized. However, under conditions of war, this youth is growing up fast, probably too fast. He has the look of a fanatic, and he is forced to develop the cunning of a seasoned warrior. If he fails to develop that cunning, he will not live.

In the course of two hours, the young sniper kills three people, one his own brother—who, ironically, is poised to kill him if he is given the opportunity. The Republican sniper outwits the Free Stater into being careless, and this carelessness costs the Free Stater his life.

In a sense, carelessness also costs the man in the turret of the armored car his life. He should not have responded to the old woman who came to give him information. Had he not exposed his head, he could not have been killed, because the car's armor would have protected him. In a moment of relaxed security, he makes himself vulnerable and loses his life. In the next instant, the sniper kills an old woman.

O'Flaherty demonstrates the impersonality of war: One shoots the Enemy, not people. When the sniper is doing his killing, it is the Enemy at whom he is firing. The Enemy, however, becomes a person when the protagonist sees the opposing sniper's body fall to the ground. He is sickened at the thought of what he has done, and one can only speculate on the implications for him of discovering, ultimately, that it is his own brother he has killed.

O'Flaherty is saying that soldiers grow up fast or not at all. There is no question that the sniper does what he has to do, and at the beginning, there is a great adventure in what he is doing. The adventure, however, depends on anonymity. No one in this story has a name, and everyone, even, to an extent, the protagonist, is seen from a distance. Once one is killing people, the whole impact of what war is about crowds in on the killer.

Although one perhaps cannot go so far as to call "The Sniper" a pacifist tract, certainly it depicts several of the worst horrors of war. It shows that war makes life seem cheap. It shows that war also hardens the hearts of those who participate in it. In the end, the story shows the absurdity and futility of fighting against individual human beings.

Both snipers in this story are pawns of forces larger than themselves, and these forces split families, shatter loyalties, and pervert the very causes that they purport to be fighting to preserve. The first irony is that men will kill other men. The second and greater irony in the O'Flaherty story is that in this case the two men are of the same parents.

Style and Technique

Fear and tension pervade "The Sniper." O'Flaherty, making full use of his tight unity of place, builds tension steadily and systematically in several ways. The reader is told that one can hear the thunder of ammunition exploding in the distance. In the immediate milieu that the author creates, bullets whiz by and every simple act, such as lighting a cigarette, must be weighed carefully for its potential danger. The sniper is essentially a schoolboy caught up in a situation over which he must gain control. If he fails, he dies.

O'Flaherty creates a feeling of tension by his skillful use of short, clipped sentences and simple, direct vocabulary. As the tension is built, each sentence reveals only one bare fact:

> The turret opened. A man's head and shoulders appeared, looking towards the sniper. The sniper raised his rifle and fired. The head fell heavily on the turret wall. The woman darted toward the side street. The sniper fired again. The woman whirled around and fell with a shriek into the gutter.

The beat of these sentences is like the beating of one's heart. To read a paragraph so tightly controlled and structured as this one is to have one's breath taken away.

O'Flaherty, because he has to emphasize how totally on his own the young sniper is, cannot have dialogue in this story. The sniper must be on the roof alone. The omniscient observer must tell everything that happens without being intrusive. O'Flaherty thus keeps a tight rein on a story that is highly dramatic but whose dramatic impact must be made through understatement.

R. Baird Shuman

THE SNIPER

Author: Alan Sillitoe (1928-   )
Type of plot: Psychological
Time of plot: 1914-1918 and 1964
Locale: Nottingham, England, and Gommecourt, France
First published: 1981

> *Principal characters:*
> NEVILL, a farm laborer, a sergeant in World War I, and a mechanic
> AMY, his wife
> A FANCYMAN, Amy's lover

The Story

The patrons at The Radford Arms pub are astonished to see an old man suddenly leap on one of the tables and begin to dance. Everyone looks at the man's feet, expecting him to fall down. Some continue to find the performance amusing, but others start to ignore him, more interested in consuming their last drinks because it is near closing time. The man still hops around and, at the same time in a sort of singsong voice, talks about a murder he committed a half century ago. The dancer, crushed by guilt and fear, wants to confess publicly, now that his life is near its end. Few people are listening, however, and those who listen hear nothing that makes much sense. Had they been able to figure out what the old man was saying, they would have heard how he killed his wife's lover in 1914.

The story is told in flashback. Nevill, suspecting that his spouse is unfaithful, lies in wait for her in the woods, where he believes she and her fancyman will have their rendezvous. From his hiding place, he watches Amy follow her lover into the shelter of the trees. Nevill waits while the two make love, considering that it might be best to go home, but his compulsion for retribution is strong. When her passion is spent, Nevill's wife leaves to return home, but her lover remains behind to smoke a cigarette. Nevill stalks him and batters his neck with the butt of a shotgun, giving him the coup de grace, when he is on the ground, by smashing his temple. Nevill then hides the body.

Before Nevill leaves the wood, he kills a rabbit and sells the dead animal at a local bar; he then drinks a beer with the proceeds and listens to some other patrons talk about the war. Nevill thinks that they do not know what life is all about. The next day, he returns to the woods and buries the body, making sure that he disguises the grave with dead twigs and rotting leaves. Afterward, he goes down to the recruiting office and enlists, believing "that the army would be as good a place to hide as any." Amy is so distraught at the prospect of her husband's departure that for a moment Nevill regrets having joined the army, but he puts this out of his mind.

He leaves to fight in France, but the memory of the murder follows him. Ironically, his fear that he might be apprehended at any moment contributes to his proficiency as a soldier, "for he did not live from day to day like most of the platoon. . . . [H]e existed by the minute because every one contained the possibility of him being taken off and hanged." He becomes a lance corporal and, because of his superior marksmanship, is made a sniper, a job that obliges him to remain concealed, quietly scanning the enemy lines for quarry, "letting his body into complete repose so as to make no move," picking off those careless enough to show their heads around a parapet in an unguarded moment. He remains like this throughout the day, trying to remain undetected. After nightfall, a new sniper's post will be built, and tomorrow he will "be in a different position and, corked face invisible, could start all over again." The memory of his past continues to haunt him. Each morning, when he awakes, he realizes that he has not yet been "taken up" for the one he has killed in Nottingham. Sometimes he sees the murdered man's likeness in the opposite trenches.

Nevill's sniping days come to an end through a fluke. He is behind the lines with his company at the communal bathhouse, where the water is only a few degrees above freezing. The men are complaining bitterly about the icy spray, but Nevill makes light of this and begins to shout, "It's too hot! It's scalding me to death. Turn it off! I'm broiled alive. Put some cold in, for Christ's sake." The men begin laughing, and the tension breaks. Nevill has no idea what prompted him to act as he did, but his captain admires his performance, thinking that this is a man who can control men through firmness and display of wit. The captain promotes Nevill to sergeant.

Becoming a noncommissioned officer makes Nevill's life more dangerous. Now he will fight with his platoon in the front ranks in the forthcoming big assault. When the day arrives, Nevill tries to give his men courage, walking along the trench asking them if they have drunk their allotment of rum. Before they go over the top, Nevill's lieutenant tells him that he is wanted at Battalion Headquarters. The reason, unknown to the lieutenant and Nevill, is to ask Nevill why he applied for so many ration allotments the previous week, but Nevill automatically assumes that this is his long-awaited summons to be arrested for the murder he committed in Nottingham, and he begs the lieutenant to allow him to participate in the attack with his men. He says he will go to Battalion Headquarters afterward. The lieutenant agrees.

The attack is a debacle. Most of the platoon is cut to pieces, the survivors dispersed all over the battlefield. Nevill finds himself isolated in a shell-hole with a man called Jack Clifford. In trying to knock out a German machine-gun nest that has them pinned down, Clifford is mortally wounded. With the bullets and shrapnel flying overhead, Nevill tells the blood-soaked Clifford about how he murdered his wife's lover. "It's on'y one you killed, sarge. Don't much matter," says the dying man. Nevill tries to carry Clifford to safety, "thinking that as long as he hung on to him he need never consider the hangman again." He manages to bring him in, but he is not rewarded for his bravery, because the wounded man is already dead.

Nevill is demobilized in 1919, and he returns to Nottingham to find Amy, who welcomes him back. During the war, Amy has been a munitions worker, filling shells in a factory at Chilwell. She wrote him letters in which she said that she loved him and would always love him. She told him that she was having a baby. However, Nevill realized that the child could hardly be his. Nevertheless, when he returns, he pretends to be the child's father. Amy and Nevill have two sons of their own. Nevill is never brave enough to tell her what he told Jack Clifford in that shell-hole in France. He senses that if he does, it would mean the end of their relationship.

Now, years later and nearly eighty, Nevill tries to tell the strangers at The Radford Arms pub. Even those who hear his words refuse to believe him and think that he is senile. Several good souls drive him back home to his wife. He does not live long after that. Amy finds him dead one morning, sitting fully dressed by the fireplace. Some of his neighbors, who come to the funeral, are not surprised. They have heard about his dancing on the table and assume that after that, the end could not have been far away.

Themes and Meanings

Nevill, like many of Alan Sillitoe's heroes, is an outsider, but his alienation is in large part self-imposed. Although he comes from the lower classes (in a society where "lower class" means no class), social problems are only incidental to this story. Nevill's crime, the quintessential antisocial act, does not flow from the class struggle, nor from feelings of rage against economic exploitation or political oppression, nor is it conditioned by any societal code of honor. Even among the lower classes in England in 1914, it was not considered particularly good form for a husband to punish a sexual transgression with death. Unless intended as an act of independence against a sort of sexual exploitation, the deed might be considered part of a desire to preserve one's territory against a poacher. Nevill fully realizes what he is doing: "Now that he knew for certain, there seemed no point in pursuing them, for he could call the tune any time he liked." However, he believes that he is compelled to bring the affair to an end, as if by coming this far retreat would be unconscionable, "the deliberate putting forward on the grass of one foot after another was as if he advanced on a magnetised track impossible to sidestep."

In the army, he is directed by no such emotion. He becomes a cold, methodical hit man, accepting his sniper job as a normal part of a day's work. He is proud of his professionalism, each of his kills being proof of his expertise, his cleverness, and his self-discipline. He feels less concern about exterminating Germans than about those rabbits he had shot in order to buy a few drinks. His country's laws, which prohibit murder on the small scale, now condone and bless it on the grand scale. Thus, Nevill's routine slaughter, directed against strangers, becomes more horrific than his *crime passionnel* and is all the more chilling for its abstraction. The war provides a means for Nevill to remove the memory of the man he killed in Nottingham. "In pushing aside the image of the hangman coming to get him across no-man's-land . . . he had only to punctuate his counting of the minutes by a careful shot at some flicker on the opposite sandbags." Nevill, however, finds it impossible to free himself socially and psychologically.

The deed directs his life to greater dependence, conformity, and regulation. Haunted by fear of discovery, he seeks escape in the most restricted of societies. After the army, his attempt at catharsis unsuccessful, he returns home and decides to lead a life of complete domesticity, remaining with the woman who was impregnated by the man he had slain. His nightmare continues, as does his search for relief, finally culminating in a desperate attempt to achieve resolution in an absurd dance on the table in a pub, an act of liberation manque. Here is a hero whose desire is not for the transformation of society, but for peace of mind.

Style and Technique

Though Sillitoe was born a decade after the end of the Great War, his descriptions of the effects of trench warfare on the lives of the participants make one recall the poems of Siegfried Sassoon:

> Shells of shrapnel balls exploded above their heads. They stopped silently, or rolled against the soil as if thrown by an invisible hand. Or they were hidden in a wreath of smoke and never seen again. The wire was like a wall. The guns had cut only one gap so they were like a football crowd trying to get off the field through a narrow gate on which machine guns were trained.

Sillitoe relies on such compelling passages to keep the reader moving through his story.

He also sustains interest through the skillful interaction of nature with the mind of his character. Consider the way in which he sets up the murder itself, a murder that the reader has already been informed has taken place. Nevill's bloody thoughts blend with the locale in which they will be translated into action. All living things and natural phenomena seem to be one with the character's primitive determination to seek justice: "A breeze which carried the smell of grass made him hungry." "The last of the sun flushed white and pink against his eyes." "A platoon of starlings scoured back and forth on a patch of grass to leave no worm's hiding place unturned." "The odour of fungus and running water on clean pebbles was sharpened by the cool of the evening."

Sillitoe creates grand suspense by his use of the flashback. The beginning of the story reveals exactly enough about the protagonist to compel interest. (The narrative hook of an octogenarian dancing on a table is by itself intriguing and inventive.) What motivates his activity? Why, after half a century, does the old man want to speak his peace? Nevill is not Sillitoe's usual proletarian hero, who attempts to fight external forces beyond his control. Nevill's struggle is within himself, and Sillitoe seems to convey that he, too, is seeking to find answers to the same questions that he poses. Sillitoe has learned that the less a character is made to appear a victim of society, the less he becomes a stereotype, and the more compelling and interesting he can be as an individual. Nevill, despite all one is told about his actions, still remains distant and aloof. Sillitoe allows the reader to share his anxieties but keeps his distance, surrounding him with an imagery of pessimism and gloom.

Wm. Laird Kleine-Ahlbrandt

SNOW

Author: Alice Adams (1926-1999)
Type of plot: Domestic realism
Time of plot: An April day during the 1970's
Locale: California's Sierra Nevada Mountains
First published: 1979

> *Principal characters:*
> GRAHAM, a successful San Francisco architect who is divorced
> CAROL, his new girlfriend, a florist
> SUSANNAH, his adult daughter
> ROSE, Susannah's friend and lover

The Story

Graham has brought three women together for a weekend skiing trip and is feeling apprehensive about having done so. He is not certain what he feels for his new girlfriend, Carol; he worries that he has spent his life misunderstanding his daughter, Susannah; and he is not sure that he really wants to meet Susannah's lover, Rose. The athletic Graham easily strides ahead of the group, not realizing that each of the women who follows is privately dealing with apprehensions of her own. Carol worries that Graham might be interested in her only because she is beautiful, Susannah is painfully aware of how overweight she must appear in Carol's presence, and awkward Rose seems terrified of everything.

Just when they need cheering up, Graham happens on a lovely open glade, the perfect place for lunch. He has thoughtfully packed a buffet of fried chicken and wine, and the group basks in brilliant sunshine, good food, and the enjoyment of friendly small talk. They feel forgiving of one another's faults and are greatly refreshed when they pack to leave.

Not far down the trail, however, each person is again struck with misgivings of a different sort. Graham worries that he might not have been a good father to Susannah; Carol has a headache from the wine and feels lonely; Susannah is worried about Rose's fragile health and about how difficult she herself has been toward her father; and Rose feels helpless, weak, and miserably cold. When they return to their rented house in Alpine Meadows, they are all greatly relieved to take off their skis and get into their baths.

After resting, Graham goes to the kitchen to prepare a hearty dinner. The three women at first converse amiably in the living room. The gentle voices turn strident, though, as each woman, in anger, confesses a painful secret from her past that she did not intend to reveal. Although they strive to be strong and not to elicit pity from one another, their automatic sympathy forges a bond, and Graham feels a new understanding and tenderness for each woman.

After Graham's good dinner and a short time relaxing in front of the fire, the two couples retire to their separate bedrooms. A storm arises during the night, which abruptly awakens Rose and terrifies her. As soon as she gains her bearings and discovers Susannah lying in bed next to her, she is comforted and relieved.

Themes and Meanings

First published in *The New Yorker*, "Snow" appeared again as the opening piece of nineteen stories in Alice Adams's second collection, *To See You Again* (1982). "Snow" is considered to be a classic of the short-story genre; work by its author has appeared for twelve consecutive years in *Prize Stories: The O. Henry Awards*.

As with much of her earlier writing, Adams uses the familiar terrain of California for her setting in this story. She writes about well-educated, upper-middle-class women in transit and transition who are feeling their way to independence as well as to a satisfying primary relationship. Her women are largely private people who like to figure things out for themselves, but who have a hard time of it and are not willing to compromise their moral codes. Perhaps carrying the burden of unpleasant childhood memories, they are perceptive but a bit world-weary. They seem shy, yet they hunger for fulfillment and validation, which usually comes about through a change that they had not anticipated.

Although there is a decided focus on women in Adams's stories, it is not accurate to label her as solely a feminist writer. In "Snow," Adams breaks some gender-based stereotypes but reinforces others. Susannah and Rose are comfortable and open with their lesbianism, and Carol owns and runs a florist business, but Graham nevertheless functions as the caretaker and provider for these women. He enjoys his financial success and psychological dominance, but he seems generous with both. He arranged the weekend, brought people together who did not know each other before, prepared and carried the lunch, and plans and hosts the dinner. For each woman, his respect and approval is important. They value themselves, in part, to the extent that they see Graham valuing them. Still, the women outnumber Graham by three to one; they are more self-revealing and even seem more capable of giving and receiving love than he is. Vulnerability is presented as a positive virtue for these women; if one gets hurt along the way, that is part of taking charge of one's own life.

As the initial story in a collection entitled *To See You Again*, it is appropriate that "Snow" works to fulfill the expectations of meeting, desire, and approval suggested by the book's title. Carol and Rose both meet two of the other characters for the first time; Graham and Susannah, the biological family, meet again, uneasily at first, after being apart, and each meets the other's new love interest. All four characters desire to get along.

It is appropriate that Adams selected "Snow" as her story title, for that is the literal and symbolic locus of the tale. During the course of the story, all the characters dig below that cool, white, protective facade that they first present to one another to reveal the warmth and vulnerability of their inner selves. Graham, who begins the story and who seems to be the most self-assured, and Rose, who ends the story and who seems the least self-assured, also are given names with symbolism in Adams's work. "Graham" is the middle name of Jessie Graham Flower, the schoolgirl novelist to whom Adams makes reference in a number of her works. "Rose" also appears in the title of an important, earlier Adams short story, "Roses, Rhododendrons," which describes an insecure girl growing up to discover terrible emotions hidden beneath surface appearances.

Style and Technique

The narrative line of Adams's story is relatively simple and contained, smooth and symmetrically balanced in both development and resolution. There is little exposition and little need for any. Conflicts rooted in relational issues are presented, then resolved. Other issues then arise on a deeper level and are worked through by the time that everyone retires for the night.

The point of view that Adams uses, however, is more complicated. Her characters do not speak to one another during much of the story. They are alone on the trail, skiing single-file, each in turn rehearsing private worries through internal dialogue. Adams allots roughly equal time to all four characters, and each one is sympathetically presented. Their conversations occur when they gather over a meal, enabling them in a direct way to resolve nagging issues that had been silently plaguing them. In both the picnic setting in the glade and at the rented cabin over supper, food and drink provide the opportunity for securing emotional well-being.

For the most part, the characters discover that their fears are groundless because they are all well-meaning people who desire to get along with one another. While not all their private fears are completely played out in subsequent conversation, enough headway is made so that all can at least get a good night's sleep. The exception is Rose, about whom less information is given than for the other characters, and who has the lowest self-esteem. Still, when the storm awakens her, she takes comfort in the proximity of Susannah's familiar back, and the reader is left with the impression that even the most troubled individual can be psychologically redeemed through human companionship.

Adams's style is direct and economical. She may not reveal all readers wish to know about any individual character, but her condensations and distillations allow readers to intuit those vital connections between situation and character that reveal the complexities of modern life. Little happens, yet much is revealed. Critics have compared her spare, clear language with that of Ernest Hemingway, her focus on private emotions with that of John Cheever, and her elegance and poignancy with that found in F. Scott Fitzgerald.

Jill B. Gidmark

SNOW

Author: Ann Beattie (1947-   )
Type of plot: Neorealist
Time of plot: The late 1970's or early 1980's
Locale: The countryside in an East Coast state
First published: 1983

> *Principal characters:*
> THE NARRATOR, an unnamed woman
> HER FORMER LOVER
> ALLEN and
> HIS UNNAMED WIFE, her former neighbors

The Story

The unnamed narrator relates her story as if she is speaking to her former lover about the time they shared together. She recalls details and events from the winter that they lived in the country, providing information in short vignettes, much as if she were paging through an old photo album, occasionally pausing to describe the scenes it contains. She recalls a chipmunk that once entered the house on a load of firewood and ran for the door, and she remembers when they first moved furniture into the house and accidentally scraped a wall, revealing old layers of wallpaper hung by former inhabitants. She remembers the day of the big snow, when her lover went out and shoveled, and unable to find a hat, wore a bath towel that she helped him to twist on his head like a turban. She recalls the visits of friends who told amazing stories of marvelous good luck before their fire. She also remembers the snow, wonderful and silent, beautiful like an enormous field of Queen Anne's lace.

The narrator divides her attention among memories of that winter, her realization that her lover's vision of the same events differs from her own, and her account of her return to the place of their happiness when the winter is passed, their relationship ended, and their friend and former neighbor Allen has recently died. She sits with Allen's wife next door to where she once lived, and they watch the rain outside fill up the black plastic pool cover and spill over onto the concrete that surrounds it.

She surmises that the story all comes down to the barest outlines: love found and love lost, with the love in this case symbolized by snow.

Themes and Meanings

Despite her reputation for focusing on the angst of the individual and failed relationships, Ann Beattie's most frequent themes are intimacy and friendship, companionship in marriage or love affairs, love as a powerful element of the psyche and of memory, and the impact of human beings on one another. Although Beattie's work has often been criticized for its coldness or lack of emotion, her stories are actually very intense, with powerful emotions held just under the surface. Communication and intimacy are major themes. In "Snow," there is a "he said/she said" approach, in which the narrator recounts her own memories about the place in the country and the time spent together there, and then acknowledges that the man's account of the same times and events would differ from her own. Where she sees the marvelous and the vivid, the remarkable, quirky, and miraculous, he would see only the ordinary, the explicable, and the mundane.

One of the main themes of "Snow" is thus of things being turned upside down, of not being what they seemed. A sense of glory, intimacy, and perfection is coupled throughout with a message of ill-fatedness and separation.

Style and Technique

Beattie's style is often compared to those of Raymond Carver, Ernest Hemingway, J. D. Salinger, and F. Scott Fitzgerald. She resembles these writers in having the skill to represent the consciousness of a generation (in her case, Americans who came of age in the 1960's) and of a certain milieu (the middle class, educated, and urbane). The sparseness of her style connects her to the postmodernist movement in literature, and her neorealist focus on the inner psyches of her characters and the morass of human relationships links her to social realism.

Like the characters of the authors to whom she has been compared, Beattie's characters come from a lost generation. Usually well provided for materially, they have private lives in which intimacy is often difficult or in which they feel cut off from others. The angst of Beattie's characters is conveyed in a minimalist style in which the writing is tight and intricate and images are highly evocative or symbolic.

Beattie's finely crafted stories are as significant for what is left out as for what is expressed on the page. Accounts are studded with silences and spaces in time and detail, in which much is left unsaid or unexplained. In "Snow," for example, readers do not know the characters' names or ages, or the specific place or time in which they live. In other Beattie stories, characters sometimes relate in such an intimate manner that they communicate motivation and understanding without any explicit outward statement.

The flat, sometimes monotonal, controlled style or voice Beattie uses functions to give acute tension to her stories. Her narrators or protagonists, like the one in "Snow," are often people barely maintaining control or emotional and psychological balance in situations that threaten chaos, wherein tragedy has struck, or in which things that once were harmonious have fallen apart. They are like people in shock, suffering not from a lack of feeling, but from too much feeling. Beattie uses a hard-boiled style in which very subjective, sometimes painful or disturbing events are conveyed in a seemingly objective and dispassionate fashion, evoking an emotional reaction from the reader that is suppressed in the stories' protagonists.

"Snow" is sparse, evocative, and dense with meaning, like a haiku. Everything is distilled down to the most essential images, to memories of the moments and turning points that capture the essence of a situation and that encapsulate the meaning of the individual life. The details of how the couple met, what their problems were, or how they parted are left out. Readers know nothing of the relationship of the neighbors, or the circumstances of Allen's death. As Beattie has her female narrator's absent lover say in relation to the art of storytelling, "Any life will seem dramatic if you omit mention of most of it." Such is the case with Beattie's own technique. She makes this explicit in "Snow," wherein she writes through her narrator's voice that "this is a story, told the way you say stories should be told. . . . People forget years and remember moments. Seconds and symbols are left to sum things up."

In Beattie stories intimacy is conveyed in part through a deadpan kind of humor, the ridiculous moment shared. Such symbols or moments in "Snow" include the chipmunk out of its natural context in the house and the towel worn like a turban. The latter is a Beattie trademark device: a man and woman so close that they cross-dress and are willing to appear in a silly fashion before each other; he wears her blouse or her too-short sweatpants, or here, in "Snow," has her show him how to twirl a towel around his hair, then proceeds to wear it outdoors. The memory of this interchangeability, this melding of identity and the overflow of the private into the public, makes the loss of the relationship all the more poignant.

Beattie uses a series of other symbols in the story. Accumulated experience and repressed secrets—garish realities that underlie the seemingly sunny surface of the relationship—are represented in the layers of wallpaper that the couple discover and then cover over with their own layer of yellow paint. The warm glow of the fireplace where friends gather is contrasted with the ice outside, and the snow insulates the couple in the house.

Beattie frequently sets stories in a wintery context (the 1984 story "In the White Night" and the 1976 novel *Chilly Scenes of Winter* are examples), and the word that gives "Snow" its title is the controlling symbol of the story. Superficially it conveys the frozen, numbed nature of the narrator who is coping with the death of her relationship and of her friend. Ultimately, however, it is a word for love. The snow is overwhelmingly positive in the story. It is stunning and exquisite. It is beatific in its whiteness and purity, and it transforms the world, bringing heaven to earth. The snow, the marvelous winter, is also the context for the couple's togetherness, and memory of it crystallizes for the narrator the meaning of their entire time together. It envelops them in its wonder, and it blankets and harbors them in their house. The meager crocuses of the sad and rainy spring that replace it cannot compete with its grandeur.

The shroudlike swimming pool cover is one of the last symbols Beattie presents in the story. It is evocative not only of Allen's death and the neglect and abandonment that death has meant for his widow, but also of the narrator's own loss. The rain that they watch together is like the two women's unstated, unrecorded tears of mourning. It is dismal and, like the crocuses, a poor substitute for the remembered wonders of the snow. The final image is of a snowplow that scrapes away at the roads, which Beattie compares to coronary bypass surgery, again uniting the snow and the heart.

Barbara J. Bair

SNOW

Author: Ted Hughes (1930-1998)
Type of plot: Psychological
Time of plot: The early to mid-twentieth century
Locale: The Arctic
First published: 1960

Principal character:
THE NARRATOR, the amnesiac survivor of an airplane crash

The Story

The narrator thinks he has survived for five months after an airplane crash in an Arctic blizzard, but he does not know for sure. The facts the survivor circles around are these: He is on the planet Earth; chance has destroyed his memory, which his dreams are beginning to reconstruct; he has been walking through a steady blizzard for five months; he has walked enough miles to have crossed the Atlantic Ocean; he is not walking in a straight line and may be making an error by walking in a circle; his mind is not his friend, although it is also his support and defense; and his need to survive is a sacred truth more important than the facts, which devour him when he relaxes his mental fixedness.

When he considers his chances for survival, he concludes that the facts of his existence fit so well together he could almost believe in Divine Providence. For example, he may have fallen through a snow cloud when the plane crashed; he may have awakened in an ammonia atmosphere; he may have had another sort of body; he may have had meaningless dreams instead of the ones that give him evidence of a previous existence; he may have had inadequate clothing; or he may have been without his battered old chair and mysterious harness so perfectly fitted for him to sleep. He admits that these facts should cause him to rejoice, but instead they burden him with a purposeful desire to survive.

From the evidence of his dreams, from the surprising amount of energy he has after five months without eating, and from his strong feelings about his fiancé, he concludes that he must be young, probably twenty-seven years old. The process of this reasoning, however, turns in on itself, because it convinces him of the flimsiness of the evidence on which he is staking everything. It is entirely possible that he is imagining the external world just because he wishes it were true. He concludes that he is in no position to be sure about anything, so a feeling of futility grips him.

If facts cannot support his existence, only faith can stave off the futility. Its contours develop from a central reality: Without energy, he will die, and only a mind of faith will sustain his energy. He must keep his mind firmly fixed on reasonable hopes, he must push out the paralyzing thoughts, he must trust the wind—which is the law of his existence—always keeping his face to it and being resigned to its guidance. By refusing to be in awe of the empty universal storm, by looking pointedly into it, by repeating over and over "courageous and calm," by thus fixing his mind, he can endure.

He is so sure of this method of survival that he makes up a dangerous game. The wooden chair is his only proof of a world that exists outside the raging snowstorm; therefore, he lets go of it and steps into the snow until he can barely discern it as a shadow through the silent, gray blizzard. The rules of his game say that he must not lose control as he reaches the chair again, but he often sobs and kisses it, calling the snowflakes that fall on it by human names. Even so, he believes that he can keep this harmless, mad game under control as long as he walks along, keeping his mind firm and the chair strapped to his back. All he must do is endure.

Themes and Meanings

Ted Hughes first published "Snow" in a British short-story collection in 1960, when he was married to Sylvia Plath, an American poet. Seven years later, it was reprinted in *Wodwo*, the first volume of poetry that Hughes assembled after Plath's 1963 suicide. In introducing *Wodwo*, Hughes said that its stories might be read as notes to the poetry, or as chapters of a "single adventure" that the poems amplify and comment on. One plausible explanation for the single adventure of *Wodwo*, consistent with the whole of Hughes's work, is participation in the Asian pattern of release, destruction, and reintegration. Hughes places the stories, of which "Snow" is the most extreme in examining the breakdown of Western rationality, between uncompromising poems exploring the querulousness of God, the brutishness of nature, and the devastation of warfare.

"Snow" reveals Western cultural thought as bankrupt and humans as free only when they withdraw from failed cultural beliefs, awakening instead by Eastern meditation to a more essential energy necessary for survival. The survivor of the plane crash rehearses his facts over and over, listing them in almost scientific form, repeating the thought experiment to check its veracity. He argues from the particular, for which he has evidence, to the general, the existence of a world outside the raging snowstorm. In the process, he discovers that what seems like brutal honesty is really only wishful thinking. He knows that if he depends on his wishes, he surely will die. The rational survivor stands for all modern peoples because the scientific worldview that has produced airplanes, chairs, and warm clothing is the logical outgrowth of a centuries-old way of thinking, entangled with Christianity itself. The evidences for providential care that the survivor recites bear strong resemblance to the evidences for the existence of God of Western philosophers and theologians.

These thoughts, which seem so carefully formulated, which seem so wonderful in the things they have produced, will, in reality, cause his death as well as the death of Western culture. The thoughts are as deadly as the snowstorm itself; they are lethal as they enter his mind, trying to "make that burrowing plunge down the spinal cord." If he relaxes, they cover him as "pouring silent grey" builds up an "incalculable pressure, too gradual to detect." Judeo-Christian Western rationality has produced a civilization that is killing its members, sometimes literally in war, other times spiritually in emptiness, by self-deluded reliance on the things it has made and the way it has made them.

How then to survive in such a deadly world? Hughes's answer seems to be that people must die to Western rationalism and its products and awaken to primitive or Eastern myths. Concentration and meditation will husband the survival energy deep within them by keeping their minds firmly fixed inward, not outward. The survivor meditates by repeating the words "courageous and calm," much as Buddhists repeat "O jewel of the lotus." This self-control even allows him to attempt a dangerous separation from the only physical object that confirms his existence and guarantees his relative safety. "Snow," its focus on the necessary death to cultural lies, only prefigures the rebirth of the Eastern cycle more apparent in a few of the final poems of *Wodwo*. The reader does not know how long the survivor will continue to live, only that he is still alive at the end of the story. To defy Western thought with Eastern energy is still a dangerous adventure of suffering.

Style and Technique

Hughes was named poet laureate of England in 1984. The vast bulk of his work is poetry, although he has written many critical essays, stories, and radio scripts, as well as works for children. In interviews with Ekbert Faas, Hughes commented on his poetic style. He believed that art should spring from "an immersion into the innermost core of the mind." Meditation and concentration techniques practiced by Eastern religions aid in this artistic process. "Snow" is not only a probable result of this style; it also reveals the style at work in the innermost core of the survivor's mind as he attempts to fix his mind, concentrate, and "repeat that, repeat it like the Buddhists with their 'O jewel of the lotus.' Repeat it till it repeats itself in my very heart, till every heartbeat drives it through my whole body."

The poet should also, Hughes believed, imaginatively enter his subject with all of his senses: "touch it, smell it, listen to it, turn [himself] into it" so that the images, rhythms, and words all "jump to life as you read them." Even though the reader is inside the mind of the survivor, "Snow" is not abstract, but primarily concrete, visual, audible, and sensual, with simple, direct nouns, verbs, and occasional descriptors. When he is far from his chair, the narrator recalls, "Then my heart begins to thump unnaturally, because I seem to make out a dimness, a shadow that wavers deep in the grey turmoil, vanishes and darkens, rises and falls." This achieves what Hughes says he aimed at in a later volume of verse, "a super-simple and a super-ugly language that would in a way shed everything except what [the survivor] wanted to say." No word is wasted in these simple sentences, yet every image resonates at physical and metaphysical levels. The chair predicates the universe. The energy necessary for survival pulses with poetic rhythm and repetition from the words of this powerful short story.

Barbara J. Hampton

THE SNOW-STORM

Author: Leo Tolstoy (1828-1910)
Type of plot: Realism
Time of plot: The 1850's
Locale: The Russian Caucasus
First published: "Metel," 1856 (English translation, 1889)

> *Principal characters:*
> THE UNNAMED NARRATOR
> ALYESHKA, the narrator's manservant
> SLEDGE DRIVERS

The Story

The unnamed narrator of the story (probably meant to be Leo Tolstoy himself) and his manservant Alyeshka start on an evening trip by sledge from Novocherkassk in the Caucasus to a destination in central Russia. As they ride, a winter storm begins, and soon the road becomes covered with heavy, thick snow. The narrator becomes concerned about getting lost and queries his driver about their chances of making it safely to the next post station. The driver is somewhat vague and fatalistic concerning the rest of the journey, suggesting that they may or may not get through. The narrator has little confidence in the driver, who seems inexperienced and sullen.

A few minutes later, the driver stops the sledge, gets down, and starts searching for the road that they have lost. Disturbed by this situation, the narrator orders the phlegmatic driver to turn back, giving the horses their head to seek out the post station from which they started out. To add to the anxiety, the driver tells a story of some recent travelers who got lost and froze to death in a similar storm.

Soon they hear the bells of three mail-express sledges coming toward them and going in the opposite direction. The narrator orders his driver to turn around and follow the fresh tracks of the mail sledges. The tracks and road markers quickly disappear in the drifting snow. The narrator himself now gets out of the sledge to look for the road, but soon loses sight of even the sledge. After finding his driver and sledge, a decision is again made to turn back and return to the station from which they started out.

Again they hear the bells of the mail express, which is now returning to their original starting point, having delivered the mail and changed horses. The narrator's driver suggests that they follow them back. As the narrator's driver tries to turn around, his shafts hit the horses tied to the back of the third mail *troyka*, making them break their straps, bolt, and run. The post driver goes off in search of the runaway horses while the narrator follows the first two sledges at full gallop. In better spirits now that he has somebody to follow, the narrator's driver converses with his passenger affably, telling about his life and family circumstances.

Soon they run across a caravan of wagons, led by a mare without help from the driver, who is sleeping. They almost lose sight of the mail sledges, and the driver wants to turn around again, but they go on.

The old driver who went to get the runaway horses returns with all three and loses little time in reprimanding the narrator's driver, whose inexperience created the problem in the first place.

The narrator begins to daydream, losing himself in the monotonous and desolate snowstorm and musing lyrically about the snow and wind: "Memories and fancies followed one another with increased rapidity in my imagination." The narrator conjures up stream-of-consciousness images of his youth: the old family butler on their baronial estate, summers in the country, fishing, languid July afternoons, and finally a peasant drowning in their pond and nobody being able to help.

The narrator's driver announces that his horses are too tired to go on, and he proposes that the narrator and his servant go with the post sledges. The baggage is transferred, and the narrator is glad to get into the warm, snug sledge. Inside, two old men are telling stories to pass the time. They give very short, blunt answers to the narrator's suggestion that they all might freeze to death if the horses give out: "To be sure, we may." After driving a while longer, the men in the sledge begin arguing about whether what they see on the horizon is an encampment. The narrator becomes sleepy and thinks that he is freezing to death. He has hallucinations about what it must be like to freeze to death, dozing and waking alternately.

The narrator wakes in the morning to find that the snow has stopped and he has arrived at a post station. He treats all the men to a glass of vodka and, having received fresh horses, continues on the next leg of his journey.

Themes and Meanings

"The Snow-Storm" is based on an actual event from Tolstoy's life. While traveling in the Caucasus in 1854, Tolstoy became lost and had to spend the night in a snowstorm. He gives a fictional account of his ordeal in the present story two years later.

"The Snow-Storm" is Tolstoy's Russian version of the classical mythic theme of exile and travel. The story is very topical and specific in regard to time and place. Nevertheless, the narrator, whose experiences the story describes, can be seen as a kind of universal hero or Everyman. The journey thus becomes life; the snowstorm, life's unpredictable mortal dangers that must be faced. Tolstoy goes on to elaborate the conceit on a symbolic level. The powerful snowstorm begins suddenly and without warning. It is a force of nature against which a human being, alone or in congregation, becomes vulnerable. It is sheer good fortune that permits one person to survive while another perishes. This is why Tolstoy has the characters in the story exhibit a kind of Oriental fatalism toward the snowstorm and the danger it represents. Like so many implacable, impersonal misfortunes to which human beings are subject, the snowstorm renders philosophy and religion, as well as human strength and cunning, useless at a moment of great peril.

Russian snowstorms have a special place in Tolstoy's writings. They are frequently used by Tolstoy as a symbol of the elemental, powerful, and uncontrollable force of nature. Unlike his Romantic precursors, however, Tolstoy does not imbue the storm with any sentimental or poetic significance. His approach is realistic, almost scientific. The snowstorm is for Tolstoy but another meteorological phenomenon, characteristic of Russia and other places with similar winter seasons. The accuracy and descriptive power of the young Tolstoy are noteworthy and typical for his whole literary career.

Style and Technique

The story is told in the first person by an unnamed narrator, who probably represents Tolstoy himself. "The Snow-Storm" contains little suspense and almost no adventure. Nothing extraordinary happens—a man gets lost while sleighing in a snowstorm and finds his way to shelter with the help of some mail-express drivers. The main point of interest in the story is the narrator's psychological contemplation of things around him: his driver, the horses' behavior, the storm, the night, and himself.

The language of the story is neutral, unmarked, and stylistically classical. The one literary device characteristic to Tolstoy in the story is the narrator's ability to associate images from the reality around him to his dreams as he alternately dozes and wakes up during the long night of travel.

Although there are no real sociological complications between the nobleman narrator and the serf drivers, there is a hint of distrust between the representatives of two different classes.

R. E. Richardson

THE SNOWS OF KILIMANJARO

Author: Ernest Hemingway (1899-1961)
Type of plot: Psychological
Time of plot: The late 1920's or early 1930's
Locale: Tanganyika near the Kenya border, close to Mount Kilimanjaro
First published: 1936

> *Principal characters:*
> HARRY WALDEN, an American writer
> HELEN, his rich American wife

The Story

As the story opens, the speaker, later identified as Harry, is proclaiming that something is painless. It soon reveals that Harry and his wife, Helen, are encamped somewhere near Mount Kilimanjaro, which, at nearly twenty thousand feet, is Africa's highest mountain. An epigraph at the beginning of the story, before the action is under way, describes the snow-capped mountain, mentioning that the name for its western summit is translated from the local Masai language as the House of God.

Extensive dialogue at the beginning of the story reveals that the speakers, husband and wife, have a combative relationship. Harry has ceased to be in love with Helen, although she adores him. In Harry's dialogue, one quickly detects a deep-seated underlying anger and a contempt for not just Helen but all women. Indeed, Harry feels and expresses guilt about the deterioration of his relationship with his wife, who has quite willingly put her considerable fortune at Harry's disposal. The rub is that the comfortable life that Helen has provided seems to have robbed Harry of the motivation he needs to write. Harry and Helen have left their superficial rich friends behind in Paris, where they are pursuing their inconsequential lives. Harry toys with idea of writing about the idle rich, viewing himself as a sort of spy in their territory.

It is soon revealed that Harry is on his deathbed, suffering from gangrene that is moving rapidly from his lower legs to other parts of his body. He and Helen, along with their African servant, Molo, are stranded in this remote part of Tanganyika because an inept driver failed to check the oil in their truck, causing it to burn out a bearing and become inoperable. Their only hope now is that a plane will land on their compound and fly Harry to a medical facility.

Harry has gangrene because he ignored a thorn prick to his knee some days earlier. As his wound festered and became swollen, he treated it with a mild solution of carbolic acid, which proved to be too little too late. The gangrene kept one step ahead of Harry's attempts to thwart its progress.

Throughout the story, Harry vacillates between consciousness and unconsciousness. His conscious periods become shorter and shorter. Unconsciousness reveries of his past fill his mind and reveal a great deal about his past. The passages during the unconscious state are printed in italics except for the one very near the end in which Harry hallucinates about the plane coming to rescue him.

As it turns out, Harry's illusion of the plane is just that: an illusion. In the end, Helen has Harry's cot carried into their tent. Before long, she tries to rouse him but cannot. She becomes aware that his breathing has stopped, just as a hyena, a carnivore that feeds on dead animals, howls outside their tent.

Themes and Meanings

An underlying theme in "The Snows of Kilimanjaro" concerns the inroads that wealth can make on talent. Harry was once regarded as a promising author, a part of the expatriate movement that flourished in Paris following World War I. Hemingway, very much a part of this literary group, uses this story to articulate a great many of his own fears and feelings regarding his problems. The story has strong autobiographical elements, although the facts of Hemingway's existence that it often suggests are not intended to be taken as accurate autobiographical accounts of his life.

Harry's friends once relished reading what he was writing. After his marriage to Helen, he moved into a different echelon of society and was thrown into the company of rich people who were more comfortable with him when he did not work. It is from these people he hopes to escape when he and Helen go to Africa for what he considers his own rehabilitation. Therefore, their trip is a basic one devoid of the luxuries they could easily command.

Throughout the story, Helen, seemingly in a state of denial about Harry's medical condition, struggles to keep his attitude positive. In doing so, Hemingway creates a character whose optimistic sentiments strike Harry as the platitudes of a fool. Her sanguine sentiments are counterbalanced by Harry's cynical outlook, with the result that they quarrel frequently. Helen wants to strengthen Harry with broth, which, in rare acquiescence, he drinks. In a moment of guilt over how badly he treats Helen, he uncharacteristically tells her that the broth tastes good.

However, what Harry really wants is his whiskey soda. He asks for it several times and sometimes gets it, but always the request and its occasional fulfillment are accompanied by Helen's refrain, "It's not good for you." Helen's concern for her husband is genuine. She is a mother figure, as Hemingway's wives often were. Harry (Hemingway) both wants and needs a mother but also greatly resents his wife's playing this role. The strains of the Harry-Helen conflict increase with every nurturing move that Helen makes.

Style and Technique

"The Snows of Kilimanjaro" is told in the third person and is rich with dialogue. In the italicized portions, which represent Harry's mental meanderings during his frequent periods of unconsciousness, the reader encounters a man who has wandered around Europe, has slept with a great variety of women, and has used other people shamelessly.

Always, however, there is a nagging conscience in Harry that is closely related to the overall sense of loneliness that his exploits cannot eradicate. This underlying guilt is much a part of the Harry-Helen interaction in "The Snows of Kilimanjaro." It reveals a decency in Harry that on careful consideration eclipses his cynicism and self-serving behavior.

Hemingway is a master of visual imagery. In this story, for example, he writes, "Behind the house were fields and behind the fields was the timber. A line of lombardy poplars ran from the house to the dock. Other poplars ran along the point. A road went up to the hills along the edge of the timber and along that road he picked blackberries." Readers gain a remarkable sense of place through such image-invoking descriptions.

Near Kilimanjaro's western summit lie the frozen remains of a leopard. Why it was at that altitude remains a mystery, but the leopard, though seldom mentioned, becomes a symbol for readers to interpret. In "The Art of the Short Story," he calls the leopard part of the metaphysics of "The Snows of Kilimanjaro."

Hemingway suggests Harry's impending death by introducing hovering vultures and a howling hyena into the story, all attracted by the smell of Harry's rotting flesh. He also connects Harry's rotting flesh to poetry—"rot and poetry, rotten poetry."

This story is remarkable in the way it packs so many of the details of Hemingway's life—sex, relationships with women, aesthetic outlook, ethical orientation—into a text of less than thirty pages. The writing is spare and muscular. It makes its points with little fanfare but with memorable clarity.

When Helen asks Harry if he loves her, his answer is that he does not think so, that he never has. This answer evokes memories of Hemingway's story "Soldier's Home," in which there is a similar bit of dialogue between the mother and her son Harold, a soldier returned from the war. In both instances, the male character feels obliged to dash a woman's expectation of an answer that is begged by her question. Above all, Hemingway sought honesty and truth in his writing and demanded nothing less of his fictional characters.

Harry's final reverie is not italicized as are the rest of his unconscious imaginings. In this one, a plane appears overhead, flown by a pilot identified as Compton. It is guided onto a small landing strip by the smoke from smudge pots the servants have ignited.

The plane can accommodate just one passenger, so if Harry is to get medical attention, Helen must remain behind. Harry is loaded onto the plane, which the pilot has said must make a refueling stop in Atrusha. However, once the craft is airborne, the pilot aims it in another direction, flying over the starkly white Mount Kilimanjaro.

In this reverie, Harry sheds himself of Helen, who cannot go along because of the plane's limited capacity, but he approaches the land of the frozen leopard. This ending is reminiscent of the ironic conclusion of Ambrose Bierce's "An Occurrence at Owl Creek Bridge," which perhaps influenced it. That story ends with the protagonist awakening from a happy dream to find that he is being hanged.

R. Baird Shuman

SO MUCH WATER SO CLOSE TO HOME

Author: Raymond Carver (1938-1988)
Type of plot: Psychological
Time of plot: The 1970's
Locale: Western Washington
First published: 1977

> *Principal characters:*
> CLAIRE, the narrator
> STUART, her husband
> GORDON JOHNSON,
> MEL DORN, and
> VERN WILLIAMS, Stuart's fishing companions

The Story

Four buddies—Stuart, the husband of the narrator, Claire; Gordon Johnson; Mel Dorn; and Vern Williams—encounter more "wilderness" than they bargain for on a backcountry fishing trip along the Naches River in western Washington. Carrying camping and fishing gear, food, playing cards, and whiskey, they hike five miles to where they want to fish. Before they finish setting up their camp, Mel finds the nude body of a young woman wedged in branches in the river. One of the men suggests that they start back immediately, but the others want to stay because they are tired, the distance is great, and it is getting dark.

Late that night they tether the woman's body by the wrist to keep it from drifting off. Through the next day and night, they drink, fish, play cards, and clean their cooking utensils in the river near the woman's body. On the second morning, they again fish and drink, finally leaving to hike out. On their way home, Stuart calls the sheriff and they wait for the authorities to arrive.

Most of the story occurs after Stuart returns home. Claire recounts his arrival late that same night after she is already asleep. She finds him in the kitchen drinking beer. Stuart seems upset, but he tells her nothing about his trip; instead, he has silent sex with his wife.

The next morning, after abusive phone calls begin, Stuart finally tells Claire the story that she recounts for the reader. Claire's narrative outlines the deterioration in her relationship with Stuart and her anger at his involvement in such a sordid event— which she learns involved rape and mutilation. She grows angry and suspicious because the men stayed by the river for two days and did nothing about the dead woman.

Over the next two days, Claire cannot stop thinking about the dead woman. On her way to the woman's funeral, a nameless man in a pickup follows and intimidates her. At the funeral Claire learns that a local man was arrested for the murder, and she returns home uneasy, clearly uncomfortable about Stuart's role in these events. Despite her unspoken misgivings, Claire does not tell Stuart where she went or what she has heard. Despite her misgivings, Claire urges Stuart to make love to her quickly before their son comes back in the house.

Themes and Meanings

An eerie quality pervades the narrative of "So Much Water So Close to Home," principally because Raymond Carver implies so much and leaves so much unsaid that one cannot help wondering what the "real" story might be. It is clear that the four fishermen react unfeelingly to the dead woman they find. It remains ambiguous, however, as to what role, if any, one or all of them may have played in her death. Carver makes this uncertainty clear when he allows Claire to remain unsatisfied with the explanation that a local boy acted alone in murdering the woman. Her doubts force not only her, but also the reader, to question just how much she really knows about her husband and their relationship.

By sending the men away from civilization on a backwoods trip, Carver removes them from the constraints and censure of their community. Their failure to question or even express uneasiness about remaining at the river so near the dead woman they tether to a tree emphasizes this point. Later, however, when Stuart begins receiving hateful telephone calls about the events at the river, he loses his temper, indicating that something is indeed wrong, even though Carver never clarifies what Stuart's or the other men's involvement is. Did Stuart or the other men have sex with the dead woman? Did they mutilate her at some point? Did they themselves murder her? By having Claire react to the arrest of the local boy by suspecting that killers have accomplices, Carver forces the reader to remain open to these possibilities.

The violence in "So Much Water So Close to Home" is not limited to the one dead woman: Claire, or any other woman, might just as easily be a similar target. Carver never mentions the dead woman's name; her anonymity symbolizes the vulnerability of all women to random male violence. Carver reinforces this point by including the scene in which an unidentified man in a green pickup truck follows Claire as she drives along the Naches River to the murdered woman's funeral. Not only does this man follow Claire, but after passing her, he returns to where she pulls off the road, invading her privacy by insisting that she open her car window and door. Although she refuses, the potential for physical danger and sexual violence is clear.

By concluding the story with the furtive and hasty coupling of Stuart and Claire, Carver ends on a note of ambiguity. Claire's urging Stuart to make love can thus be read as a desperate attempt on her part to obliterate her doubts about his innocence and reestablish the earlier equilibrium of their marriage and family.

Style and Technique

The spareness of Carver's writing style helps to underscore the ambiguity of "So Much Water So Close to Home." Not only does it allow him to omit incriminating details, it also keeps the "truth" from readers, forcing them to question the veracity of Stuart's account. There remains a strong implication that more has gone on at the river campsite than readers are privileged to know, yet the text itself refuses to provide the concrete evidence that exonerates, or condemns, the fishermen.

Carver's story points toward the guilt of the fishermen in several ways, although it is never clear how much guilt they may share in the woman's death. Did they kill her, or only violate her dignity after death by not acting in a timely manner? Alternatively, might they have mutilated and sexually violated her dead body? The fact that something is eating away at Stuart is clear because he needs reassurance that his wife believes him; he seeks this reaffirmation in his silent sexual grapplings with her on the night he returns home, in an affectionate note that he leaves for her the next day, and in his excessive anger at her mildly probing questions on their picnic.

A conversation that would answer readers' questions and assuage Claire's doubts never occurs. Instead, Stuart grows angry when Claire asks him why he went on the fishing trip. Not only does this exchange leave many questions unanswered, but it is also Carver's way of letting readers know that Stuart has a dark side and a nasty temper. That Claire already knows of Stuart's potential for violence is clear, because she drops her thread of conversation. In creating such a dynamic, Carver causes the reader to wonder whether Stuart is not displaying his previously violent side.

These incidents also allow doubt to grow in Claire's mind, something Carver makes clear in conclusion of the picnic, from which Stuart and Claire return home in silence. As Stuart pretends to concentrate on the highway ahead, Claire observes that he repeatedly looks into the rearview mirror. If he is not implicated in something, she wonders, why is he checking to see if someone is behind him?

Carver is a master at creating an uncomfortable, often menacing atmosphere; his reliance on a first-person narrator and his sparse use of details contribute greatly to this effect. The conclusion of "So Much Water So Close to Home" is especially effective for exactly these reasons. The reader wants to know the "truth" not only about Stuart, but also about the other fishermen: Did they or did they not do something to that young woman?

Melissa E. Barth

SO ON HE FARES

Author: George Moore (1852-1933)
Type of plot: Social realism
Time of plot: The 1900's
Locale: Near Shannon, Ireland
First published: 1903

Principal characters:
ULICK BURKE, the ten-year-old protagonist
HIS MOTHER

The Story

Ten-year-old Ulick Burke, who lives in a cottage near a canal in Ireland, dreams of running down to the water to watch the boats passing, but his mother strictly forbids him to leave their garden. He remembers a time when he walked with his father along a towpath; his father stopped to talk with lockkeepers and promised one day to take Ulick on one of the barges that go to Shannon to meet ships coming up from the sea. Now Ulick is alone, because his father, a soldier, is away from home, and his mother will not let him play with the children who pass by on the other side of the garden gate.

Ulick takes refuge in his dreams, imagining that his father has gone off to war on a barge. He wonders what it would be like to hide on a barge that might take him to the battlefield where he could meet his father walking about with a gun on his shoulder. However, Ulick finds such dreams to be poor stuff, especially since his mother keeps him at home. He is expected to remain aloof, like his mother, who has named their home "Hill Cottage" and has had the name painted on the garden gate. It is the only cottage in the parish that has a name.

Ulick's dreams center on the idea of running away, although he is afraid that his mother will follow him and bring him back home. So desperate is this shy, attractive boy that he considers burning down the cottage. Instead, his excruciating loneliness is relieved by a big boy who asks Ulick to give him gooseberries from the garden. Eager for companionship and hating the idea that the older boy might make fun of him, Ulick gathers the gooseberries and they become friends.

Soon Ulick finds himself in the company of the bigger boy's friends, with whom he engages in mild adventures, such as overturning rocks in a brook and stabbing eels with a fork. Ulick is entranced and happy until his mother catches him at play. When he covers his face with his hands to protect himself from his mother's slaps, she puts a live bee down his back, and he runs away screaming in pain from the stings.

After relieving himself by rolling in a ditch covered with leaves, Ulick crosses a meadow and sees a barge coming through a lock. He runs along the canal, following the boat and thinking how much he hates his mother. He calls to the bargeman, wanting the man to take him aboard. Then he plunges into the water, determined to reach the barge. He sinks in the water, rising once to see a green light and the barge's rudder moving. After losing consciousness, he awakens to find himself on the barge.

Sensing the bargeman's willingness to take him home, Ulick pretends to have run away from Shannon, which he learns is seventy miles from his cottage. The bargeman agrees to take him "home," and later Ulick slips away as they approach Shannon. He spends the night in a haystack and is discovered by a woman who is as kind to him as his mother is cruel. She is a lone widow who takes the attractive Ulick, with his bright blue eyes and soft curls, as her adopted son. Three years later the widow dies, and Ulick, now thirteen, sets out on a wild, rough life. His escape from Hill Cottage now seems like a tale heard in infancy.

Some years later, after Ulick has sailed the coast of Ireland and explored most of its harbors, he decides to revisit Hill Cottage. He is amazed to find a boy just like himself, whose mother has forbidden him to come down to the canal. The boy's name is Ulick Burke. Ulick accompanies his namesake to the cottage and finds that indeed his mother, who has changed little, has had another son, and that his father is again away from home. Although his mother offers him a bed for the night, she reiterates that he was a wicked child. She thought that he had drowned in the canal because his cap was found in the bulrushes. After telling the younger Ulick some tales of the sea, Ulick leaves the cottage and boards the barge, filled with bitterness over his childhood but determined to make his way in the world. Only children, he thinks, throw themselves in the water because their mothers do not love them.

Themes and Meanings

Like "Home Sickness," another story appearing in George Moore's *An Untilled Field* (1903), "So On He Fares" centers on a protagonist caught between two worlds— in this case, between home and the adventurous world just beyond his garden gate, between the confines of his mother's discipline and his exciting dreams. Ulick's mother wants him to know no other place beyond his garden gate. It literally becomes the barrier between him and everything else that he might experience. She is not merely protecting him from the canal, from the possibility of drowning, or from being misled by children and strangers; she is deliberately harnessing him to her will. She has shut out the rest of the world—the world represented by his father's soldiering. Ulick's father is always "away." His mother is always home.

That Ulick's mother is the only local resident to give her cottage a name and to put that name on her gate symbolizes her isolation and haughtiness. She has made Ulick shy of others, and it takes every bit of resentment that he has to make him run away from home. If he is not cowed by his mother's harsh words and physical violence (she slaps him often), it is because of his imagination, his ability to conceive of other worlds and to realize that he will grow only by reaching for them.

Ulick's imagination is emphasized when he is aboard the barge, running away from home. There he cunningly makes up the story about running away from Shannon. As the barge approaches his "home," he pretends to identify his cottage only to say that he has been mistaken, thus prolonging his journey away from his mother.

When the adult Ulick returns to Hill Cottage, the wisdom of his decision to leave home is confirmed. His hostile mother has no imagination whatsoever, no ability to identify with the injured boy. Her new son has been treated better—she does not hit him—but like the older Ulick once was, he is shy and subdued, wanting to know about the world and to hear Ulick's stories, just as the older Ulick once wanted to hear about adventures from his father. However, Ulick must take his younger brother into the garden in order to tell him the stories, because he senses that his mother does not like to hear his voice. His only choice is to go on, to "fare," for home represents the inhibition of all his desires.

Style and Technique

Like other Moore stories, "So On He Fares" is notable for its economical style, which is at once descriptive and symbolic. At the beginning of the story, for example, the narrator describes Ulick watching how the "boats rose up in the locks, how the gate opened and let the boats free." Ulick himself wants to rise up; he wants to open his garden gate so that he can be free. Not surprisingly, in the same moment that Ulick watches the boats, he thinks of his father, who has gone away to war on one of the barges. Ulick associates the idea of being free with leaving home. He is buoyed by the vision of boats rising to the surface, like his own soaring imagination. Moreover, the initial image of the canal foreshadows Ulick's own plunge into the water, in which he sinks, only to rise and to be brought aboard by the bargeman. Ulick goes through a kind of symbolic death in order to be reborn. He risks his life in order really to live.

The symbolism of the boats is deftly handled. It becomes a part of the story's theme even as it functions naturally as part of Ulick's experience. Indeed, plot, theme, and symbolism seem naturally integrated—as they are in the story's title. "So On He Fares" captures Ulick's need to be on the move, for standing still, staying at home, means a kind of death.

After Ulick makes his disappointing visit home, he again leaves on a barge. From its deck he sees the evening sky "opened calm and benedictive." He is out in the world again, and the very journey is a kind of blessing, enabling him to pass ruins, castles, and churches—the fixed record of history in the landscape—against which he can move and fare on. The story's closing sentences, like the opening ones, describe what Ulick feels, but they are also symbolic, a metaphor for the meaning of his life.

Carl Rollyson

A SOLDIER'S EMBRACE

Author: Nadine Gordimer (1923-   )
Type of plot: Social realism
Time of plot: The twentieth century
Locale: An unnamed African country
First published: 1980

> *Principal characters:*
> THE LAWYER, a white liberal displaced by the revolution
> SHE, his wife, the central consciousness in the story
> CHIPANDE, their African friend, recently returned from political exile
> FATHER MULUMBUA, also a friend, a black priest sympathetic to the revolution
> MUCHANGA, their black servant

The Story

The very fact that the woman and her lawyer husband are not given names in this story is significant, for although they are the central characters, they are anonymous colonials whose lives must change, even though they are liberals sympathetic to the local freedom fighters, now that native Africans have taken over this unnamed African country. This story, like many others by Nadine Gordimer, a South African writer, is about the changing world of African society, a world always at tension between the often silent world of the blacks and the increasingly dislodged world of the white colonials. Dislodgement is indeed what "A Soldier's Embrace" is about.

The story begins with the event of the embrace itself, an experience of the lawyer's wife confronting two celebrants of the cease-fire, one white, one black. In an abruptly frozen moment, she kisses them both on the cheek, and as the story progresses and the revolutionaries take more and more control of the city, she remembers that embrace in an obsessively symbolic way—the convergence of the two soldiers with her own confused self symbolizing the dilemma in which she and her well-meaning, liberal husband are caught. She kisses one on the left cheek and one on the right cheek as if they were two sides of one face, and this Janus image of the two faces of African society is the central one that dominates the story.

The two-faced nature of the story centers on the gradually mounting sense of fear and alienation that the couple feel in a world in which they once felt at home. Three Africans who were once friends and whose attitudes change with the revolution add to this feeling of isolation. First, there is Father Mulumbua, a priest from the slums who has gone to prison in the past for shouting freedom slogans; the couple are proud of their friendship with Mulumbua. Now he feels uncomfortable in their home and says little. Then there is Chipande, who has come in out of the bush after being forced to leave by the old white regime. Now with a job in the new order, he comes to visit but is also uncomfortable, restless, and curt. Finally, there is Muchanga, an old servant, who, although they keep him on because they believe that he will not survive alone, causes them to feel somehow guilty.

Gradually, the lawyer loses clients as more and more of the white colonials move across the border; reluctantly he realizes that there is no longer a place for him in this country that he has called his home, for he knows that he will be at risk in the university and will be unwanted as a consultant in the new government. The story comes to an inevitable climax when the lawyer and his wife realize that they must go, and the lawyer accepts a position in the neighboring country. At this point, Chipande, the young friend whom they have known for years, comes, with tears in his eyes, to beg them to stay. At the story's close, the wife sets up Muchanga with a hawker's license and a handcart, realizing that he cannot survive. As she waves good-bye to him, she does not know what to say, for the right words, whatever they were, she feels are left behind forever.

Themes and Meanings

"A Soldier's Embrace" has a curious sense of reflecting the same kind of ambiguous relationship between blacks and whites in Africa with the arrival of independence that must have been experienced by blacks and whites in some areas of the American South after the Civil War. The white couple are liberals and proud of it, taking special pride in welcoming into their home the radical black priest and befriending the poor black Chipande; they also feel a paternalistic attitude toward the servant Muchanga. What the story seems to emphasize is the double face of black-white relations, in which even as the white couple are innocent of a conscious prejudicial attitude toward the blacks, they inevitably seem to manifest such a prejudice. Regardless of what they do, they seem somehow to feel their superiority to the blacks. Even when they exhibit their liberal values, they are too self-conscious of their liberal gestures. This is not to make them particularly culpable, but rather to expose the difficult ambiguity of the white attitude toward the black people in Africa. The lawyer and his wife are not named because they represent the white liberal relationship with blacks in Africa that seems somehow inescapable.

There is no reason that the lawyer and his wife should leave the country except the simple fact that they are white, for they have supported the revolution in belief throughout. Gradually, however, they begin to feel more and more uncomfortable, which suggests that they felt comfortable before only because, even though they never expressed the desire for domination, they were in the dominant position. It is easy to feel liberal toward someone different when one is in a position of power over the other—not so easy when the tables are turned. The subtle revelation that the turning of the tables manifests is what this story is really about.

Style and Technique

The method of the story is typical of many of Gordimer's short stories; it is lean and spare, like the stories of her early modernist precursors, Anton Chekhov and Katherine Mansfield. The story communicates by implication rather than by direct statement. It begins with the embrace that gives it its title and then develops that minor but symbolically dramatic encounter into a metaphor that obsesses the lawyer's wife, but that she herself does not really understand. Throughout the story, the image of her face between the white face and the black face of the two soldiers continually recurs to her, standing for the inescapable dilemma of the white person in Africa.

The point of view of the story is that of an unidentified omniscient narrator, but it sticks closely to the perspective of the lawyer's wife. One curious element of the story is that although the lawyer seems the central liberal white caught in the revolution of black freedom fighting, it is actually his wife who serves as the reflector of the growing discomfort that the couple feel in their home.

The structure of "A Soldier's Embrace" moves back and forth between the personal experiences of the wife, beginning with the embrace and ending with her attitude toward her servant, and the more general problems of the lawyer trying to hold on to his place. These shifts are treated in an abrupt, elliptical fashion by Gordimer; the two faces of the story itself—one personal and one political—are separated by blank spaces in the text. Finally, the technique of the story is gradually to develop the embrace—the white soldier and the black soldier, with the white liberal woman caught in between—into a metaphor of the subtle ambiguity of the Janus-faced reality of black-white relations in modern Africa. It is an ambiguity that is never resolved, for at the end of the story the haughty Chipande comes and begs them to stay with tears in his eyes, like a truant child asking his parents to forgive him and not to leave. Thus, from Gordimer's point of view, moving from childlike dependence to equal friendship is a difficult transition to make. The fact that the wife does not know what to say to her old servant Muchanga means she knew what to say before only because of his role as a servant. Now that is he not, that relationship is left behind, and she truly does have nothing to say. Only with the overthrow of white supremacy does even the white liberal realize how complex his or her relationship with blacks in their own country has been.

Nadine Gordimer had always been a staunch champion of the short-story form, claiming that it is a genre better equipped to capture the nature of human reality than the novel. Basically, Gordimer believes that the coherence of tone necessary to hold a novel together is false to what can really be grasped of human reality, whereas short-story writers practice the art of the present moment, the epiphanic realization that comes sometimes abruptly and sometimes gradually and is good only for that moment. "A Soldier's Embrace" is a good example of Gordimer's view of what the short story does best—reflect an ambiguous state of things that cannot be captured either by the prolonged coherence of tone of the novel or by the conceptual straightforward statement of the essay, but which can be realized indirectly by subtle suggestion.

Charles E. May

SOLDIER'S HOME

Author: Ernest Hemingway (1899-1961)
Type of plot: Psychological
Time of plot: The 1920's
Locale: A small town in Oklahoma
First published: 1925

> Principal characters:
> HAROLD KREBS, a former U.S. Marine who served in World
>   War I
> MRS. KREBS, his mother

The Story

The title of this story suggests a familiar American landmark and symbol: The soldier's home, a place for retired military to live and relive their war experiences. In this tale, however, the soldier's home is neither a haven for former soldiers nor an environment for reminiscing. It is the place to which Harold Krebs, a U.S. Marine who fought in World War I, returns to be alone and to face the lies that he and others utter about the war.

When Krebs returns to his hometown in Oklahoma, after having fought in various European arenas, he discovers that he has changed but that nothing in the town has changed. This dramatic difference between the returnee and those who stayed home sets up the basic conflict in the story: the dishonesty that is demanded for survival. It is demonstrated most clearly in the retelling of war stories, for the townspeople do not want to hear the truth about the atrocities of battle, preferring, instead, lies about the heroics of war. Krebs finds himself telling these lies because dishonesty is the path of least resistance, even though it causes a "nausea in regard to experience that is the result of untruth or exaggeration."

Alienated from his family and the local people, Krebs spends his days aimlessly, sleeping late, reading, practicing the clarinet, and playing pool. He makes no effort to relate seriously with anyone, including women, because he does not want the complications or consequences of relationships. He is home, but it is no soldier's home to which he has returned.

The climax of the story occurs during a conversation between Krebs and his mother. Initiating a discussion with her son about religion and a job—predictable maternal and midwestern topics—Mrs. Krebs leads Harold to tell still another lie. She asks him, "Don't you love your mother, dear boy?" Harold responds with total honesty, "I don't love anybody," causing Mrs. Krebs to cry and revealing her inability and unwillingness to hear the truth. Nauseated by his next statement but believing that it is the only way to stop her crying, he lies and tells her that he did not mean what he said;

he was merely angry at something. Mrs. Krebs reasserts her maternal role, reminding her son that she held him next to her heart when he was a tiny baby, reducing Krebs to the juvenile lie: "I know, Mummy. . . . I'll try and be a good boy for you." Mother and son then kneel together, and Mrs. Krebs prays for Harold.

After this emotional lie, Harold Krebs decides to leave the Oklahoma town, go to Kansas City for a job, and live his life simply and smoothly. The former Marine leaves his home.

Themes and Meanings

One of the story's central concerns might be described by a term that was once fashionable: "the generation gap." In "Soldier's Home," the gap is more like a chasm that separates the ex-Marine from the townspeople. Krebs returns from the war, changed by his experiences, but the local citizenry are exactly what they were before the war—sure of themselves and their values. To stay in the town, to survive this time warp, Krebs must compromise his integrity; he must lie if he is to live among people who do not want to hear the truth.

Krebs represents the transformation brought about by World War I, and in this sense his metamorphosis reflects America's changed face. Before the war, the conventional values of Krebs's hometown had been, for the most part, America's values. After World War I, however, those values were challenged, and the war's returnees were among the chief challengers. In "Soldier's Home," the conflict is between challenger and challenged—the tension between Americans moving into the modern world and Americans protecting Victorian values.

Style and Technique

Ernest Hemingway's understated, detached style is suited to this story of a soldier whose reaction to his environment is itself understatement and detachment. The author's narrative technique, sentence structure, dialogue, lack of symbolism and imagery—all these strategies create a successful marriage between form and content in "Soldier's Home."

Told in the journalistic style of a third-person narrator, the story appears to be a simple, objective, disinterested report of Harold Krebs's return from the war. The first paragraph sets up this expectation of objectivity when the narrator describes a photograph of Krebs and his fraternity brothers in college. What the reader notes, however, are the details that this journalistic narrator chooses to include. Stating, for example, that it was a Methodist college and that all the men in the picture were "wearing exactly the same height and style collar," the narrator is pointing to the conformist mentality of prewar, midwestern America.

The sentence structure is also suited to the message of restraint, of the famous Hemingway code of "grace under pressure." In both the narrator's explanations and the dialogue itself, the clipped sentences imply a control, a sense of holding on and holding in. Thus, a series of sentences might use the same syntactical structure: "He did not want to get into the intrigue and the politics. He did not want to have to do any courting. He did not want to tell any more lies." Brief, simple, and repetitious, this series of "he did not wants" catalogs the ways in which Harold Krebs intends to remain uninvolved, detached, and restrained.

Absent from "Soldier's Home" is imagery that might add an inappropriate complexity to the story. This tale is about one man's efforts to recover a simplicity he once knew; the style of the story, lean and unadorned, reinforces Krebs's struggle to regain the honesty he had known in the war when he had felt "cool and clear inside himself . . . when he had done the one thing, the only thing for a man to do, easily and naturally." Regarding words, sentences, and images in "Soldier's Home," less is definitely more.

Marjorie Smelstor

SOLO ON THE DRUMS

Author: Ann Petry (1908-1997)
Type of plot: Psychological
Time of plot: The 1940's
Locale: New York City
First published: 1947

> *Principal character:*
> KID JONES, a drummer and orchestra leader

The Story

As Kid Jones approaches the Randlert Theater at the corner of Broadway and Forty-second Street, he pauses for a moment and looks up at the marquee where his name is emblazoned in lights below the name of his orchestra. He feels a sense of pride as people rushing past one another on the crowded New York City street stop, look up for a minute, and smile, recognizing his name. This is what he has always wanted, but his moment of triumph is immediately overshadowed by the memory of something that happened as he was about to leave for work that morning—an occurrence that brought his world crashing down around him. The dissolution of his world was accomplished with two simple words, "I'm leaving," uttered almost casually by the woman he loves as she told him that she has fallen in love with someone else.

When the show is about to start, the house lights go down and the orchestra members take their places on stage. As they begin to play, Kid Jones is intensely aware of his surroundings—the light-flooded stage, the smoothness of the music, the disembodied heads of the audience. As he strikes his drums lightly, the spotlight focuses on the trumpeter, who begins his solo, and Jones observes, with pleasure, how perfectly his drums accompany the trumpet. As the music of the trumpet grows louder, his thoughts begin to drift, and he begins to slip slowly from the world of reality. Finally, he can no longer perceive the music as music; the sound of the trumpet becomes the voice of his wife repeating again and again, "I'm leaving, I'm leaving, the guy who plays the piano. I'm in love with him and I'm leaving now today."

As the trumpet solo ends and the spotlight focuses on Jones, he returns to the present and begins his solo on the drums. As he plays, another spotlight picks up the piano player. At the sight of his rival, the Marquis of Brund, Jones becomes infuriated, and his fury is expressed in a savage attack on the drums. The sound is so intense, so jarring, that it startles the other orchestra members, but Jones takes no notice of the heads that turn in his direction as his drums leap with all the fury in him. In his imagination, he is fighting with the Marquis of Brund. He is choking him, sticking a knife in his ribs, and slitting the throat of the man who has stolen his wife.

Then Jones becomes one with his drums, and the theater again begins to fade. He is transported back into the past, this time into his ancestral past, where the great African chieftains wreaked terrible vengeance on their enemies. Then he moves forward to a more recent past, recalling long-buried incidents of his childhood—a childhood spent with a mother who hated him because he reminded her of his father, a man who seduced and deserted her. He remembers the many women he has used and discarded and, finally, the woman he loves who has discarded him.

So engrossed is Kid Jones in his music and his reveries that he is oblivious to the applause that greets the end of his performance; it is only when another member of the orchestra kicks him on the foot that he returns to the present. He stares for a long moment at the Marquis of Brund; then, slowly and deliberately, he bows, again and again.

Themes and Meanings

The theme of Ann Petry's "Solo on the Drums" may be summarized in the aphorism about music having charms "to soothe the savage breast." Stated another way, the story speaks to the cathartic power of music in the lives of people, especially African Americans. From the ritual music of Africa, to the folk songs and spirituals of the slave plantations, to twentieth century blues songs, music has provided a vehicle through which African Americans have gained release from their pain and suffering without resorting to physical violence.

It is apparent almost from the beginning of this story that Kid Jones is experiencing deep emotional stress, compounded by having to share the stage night after night with his romantic rival. Through his music, however, he can vent all the rage inside of him: rage at the Marquis of Brund for stealing his wife, rage at his mother for despising him, rage at his wife for deserting him. As he plays, it seems to him that the music comes "not from the drums but from deep within himself; it was a sound that was being wrenched out of him—a violent, raging, roaring sound." He thinks, "This is the story of my life, this is the story of my hate, this is all there is to me." This raging, roaring sound is the sound of catharsis, the purging of his emotions, and when it is over, he is spent. Through his music, Jones is not only cleansed of hatred, past and present, but also is forced to face some of the harsher realities of his life. Now, the healing can begin.

In "Solo on the Drums," Petry also shows that music can provide a means of escape from the world of reality. This is exemplified in the character of the protagonist, but it is also apparent in the reactions of the audience. As the rhythmic beat of the drums reaches out into the audience, it seems to create a mesmerizing effect. One man sitting near the front of the theater is entranced; he shivers and jerks his head to the rhythm, completely oblivious to his surroundings. A sailor sits with his arms around his girl, and when her hat falls off, neither of them moves; they are transfixed. A boy who has sneaked in by a side entrance and slipped unnoticed into an aisle seat sits motionless, his mouth wide open as he clutches his cap tightly against his chest. Each of these individuals, for a time at least, has managed to escape into a world where the worries and cares of daily living do not exist.

Style and Technique

Petry's style has been described as "rich and crisp, alive and alight on the page . . . charged with sense and pleasure." It has also been said that her style always supports her main intent. Both of these statements may be applied quite accurately to "Solo on the Drums." An example of the degree to which Petry fuses style and meaning is her making her protagonist a drummer, for the drum has always been the most important single instrument in the creation of African and African American music. Traditionally, in African societies, the drum was used as much for communication as for entertainment. Thus, while Jones plays the drums for the entertainment of his audience, some of his reveries reveal the more pragmatic use of the drum. At one point in the narrative, Jones imagines himself the drummer in an African village; as such, he is responsible for keeping the people informed of important events. He is "sending out the news. Grandma died. . . . The man across the big water is sleeping with the Chief's daughter. . . . The war goes well with the men."

Throughout this brief story, there are references to the communicative power of the drums. Sometimes this is done quite directly, as when Kid Jones, deep in reverie, thinks that the drums are talking about his life. Often, however, it is merely implied through Petry's use of language. The drums are often spoken of in terms generally reserved for human beings. At one time, they are said to respond with a whisper; at another time, they talk to the piano; at yet another time, they answer the horn. In both overt and more subtle ways, Petry skillfully interweaves thought and style in "Solo on the Drums."

Gladys J. Washington

SOME LIKE THEM COLD

Author: Ring Lardner (1885-1933)
Type of plot: Wit and humor
Time of plot: About 1920
Locale: Chicago and New York City
First published: 1921

Principal characters:
CHARLES F. LEWIS, an aspiring songwriter in New York City
MABELLE GILLESPIE, a "working girl" in Chicago

The Story

Though "Some Like Them Cold" is told in an unorthodox way, its plot is quite simple. Charles Lewis and Mabelle Gillespie meet by chance in the Lasalle Street train station in Chicago. Charles is about to travel to New York City in order to pursue his fortune as a songwriter. Mabelle is waiting for her sister to arrive for a visit. Charles and Mabelle converse until Charles's train arrives. Before leaving, Charles makes a bet with Mabelle that he will write to her from New York. This he does. Mabelle writes back, and the two carry on their flirtation by means of the United States Postal Service.

At first all goes well. Charles masks his loneliness and uncertainty in New York City by describing his adventures to Mabelle. These adventures fall into two categories: first, the quest for success in the songwriting business, and second, resistance against sexual temptation. Repeatedly, Charles resists the advances of overly aggressive, "painted" women. At the same time, though he teases and flatters Mabelle, he is careful not to cast doubt on her virtue. Mabelle is quite sensitive on this issue. She refers to herself as a "bad" girl for speaking to Charles without a "proper introduction," and she assures Charles that she is not in the habit of doing such a thing. Definitely viewing her own aspirations as secondary to Charles's grandiose ambitions, she passes over most of her own trials and tribulations as a single working girl in Chicago. Instead, through the eyes of her sister and friends, she provides a self-portrait for Charles's inspection.

A "great home girl," Mibs (as her friends call her) is "a great talker," has a humorous nature, likes a good book, and loves to bathe. She goes out to dance or see a show only occasionally. In sum, Mabelle presents herself as modest, sociable, and wholesome. She also expresses boundless confidence in Charles's songwriting ability and repeatedly assures him of his ultimate success.

During the exchange of the first few letters, Charles and Mabelle seem to be pleasant, perhaps slightly silly young people carrying on an ambiguous but harmless flirtation. There is a steady diet of flattery and ego stroking on both sides, with Mabelle in particular providing the moral support needed for Charles to fight "the battle of Broadway." In addition, Mabelle has mentioned a fantasy about some "rich New Yorker" who might bring her there to live. However, exactly what the outcome of the relationship between Charles and Mabelle will be is not clear.

Within a few weeks, that is no longer true. Charles's interest in Mabelle is plainly waning as he makes some personal connections in New York City and begins to fall into the rhythm of the town. More specifically, Charles meets a lyricist named Paul Sears, with whom he begins to collaborate. He does send Mabelle the lyrics from their first song together, "When They're Like You."

> Some like them hot, some like them cold.
> Some like them when they're not too darn old.
> Some like them fat, some like them lean.
> Some like them only at sweet sixteen.
> Some like them dark, some like them light.
> Some like them in the park, late at night.
> Some like them fickle, some like them true,
> But the time I like them is when they're like you.

Although the lyric might not seem particularly impressive to the reader, Mabelle is "thrilled to death over the song." The tide has turned, however, and Charles no longer needs Mabelle's encouragement. Whereas Charles described New York City as dirty and hot at the outset of the story, he now calls it a "great town" and seems willing to burn his bridge back to Chicago. He has found a new home, and because of this Mabelle is shunted to the periphery of his life. Soon Charles's letters become sketchy and much less attentive to Mabelle. "Dear Girlie" becomes "Dear Miss Gillespie." (In return, "Dear Mr. Man" becomes "Dear Mr. Lewis.")

The end comes when Charles, rather insensitively, announces that he has become engaged to Paul Sears's sister Betsy, whom he has described as being "ice cold" (thus the story's title). Though Betsy enjoys the nightlife and is just about everything else that Charles has said he does not like, he seems completely infatuated. Charles offers to keep up his correspondence with Mabelle. Mabelle refuses his offer, however, citing a jealous "man friend." She closes her last letter by congratulating Charles and wondering exactly how Betsy is going to "run wild" on the sixty-dollar salary that he will be earning as a musician in Atlantic City. With this, the story comes to an end less than two months after it began.

Themes and Meanings

Ring Lardner is known primarily as a humorist, and humor has provided an important avenue for American self-expression. Mark Twain is perhaps the best example of this. Humor has enabled Americans to poke fun at themselves in a way that is often quite revealing but not as threatening as other forms of social criticism. "Some Like Them Cold" is a humorous story, particularly in its portrayal of the linguistic and behavioral foibles of its characters and their culture. However, this humor cloaks serious themes.

Indeed, the story's resolution is sad rather than amusing. This is understandable because the story is a study of profound disappointment. Mabelle has thrown herself into conversation and then correspondence with a romantic stranger who might offer a way out of her unfulfilling existence, but she ends up only with a fantasy "man friend" and the specter of becoming an old maid. Charles fails to achieve success as a songwriter and at the story's close has been reduced to the grind and insecurity of being a professional musician. In addition, one gets the definite idea that his marriage will offer little in the way of consolation if, indeed, it even lasts very long. Thus, the story begins with high hopes but ends with the defeat of both main characters.

A number of other pessimistic themes also emerge from the story. Self-delusion and, correspondingly, the absence of self-knowledge pave the way for the disappointments suffered by Charles and Mabelle, as does the fickleness of infatuation. All these things taken together add up to an expose of American manners and morals in the early twentieth century. One might also interpret the story in the light of feminist concerns, paying special attention to the lyrics of "When They're Like You."

However, the story is not completely gloomy. Neither Charles nor Mabelle is necessarily down for the count. One senses that both of the main characters are resilient enough to bounce back, though probably not into each other's arms. These ships have passed in the night and are not likely to renew their encounter.

Style and Technique

The core of Lardner's style and the source of much of his humor lies in his mastery of various American dialects. More specifically, Lardner's characters, most of whom reside in the lower reaches of the middle class or below, use ordinary language rather than the idealized speech of much literature. This usually means that they slaughter grammar, diction, and all else that is sacred in language. However, Lardner's characters also speak colorfully, employing delightful slang expressions and revealing the soul of American society. In this, Charles Lewis and Mabelle Gillespie are no exception. What is different about "Some Like Them Cold" is the fact that the entire story is told through letters. This allows Lardner to have a field day with his characters' spelling, particularly that of Charles, who ends his first letter to Mabelle as follows: "In the mean wile girlie au reservoir and don't do nothing I would not do." (Mabelle seems to be slightly more literate.)

In Lardner's work, the language employed is not primarily an instrument for moving the story along. It is itself the story, providing a window not only into Lardner's characters but also into American society and into the very depths of human nature.

Ira Smolensky

SOME OF US HAD BEEN THREATENING
OUR FRIEND COLBY

Author: Donald Barthelme (1931-1989)
Type of plot: Absurdist
Time of plot: About 1973
Locale: The United States
First published: 1973

> *Principal characters:*
> COLBY WILLIAMS, the protagonist, who has committed an
> unspecified crime
> HIS FRIENDS, who have decided to punish him

The Story

The story concerns the punishment of Colby Williams by his friends. Colby, it seems, has "gone too far"—when, how, and at what, the reader is not told. He readily admits that he has done this, claiming, however, that "going too far . . . was something everybody did sometimes." His friends, an anonymous, all-male group, are unswayed by his reasoning and remain firm in their benevolent conviction that as his "dear friends" they have an obligation to punish him for his transgression by hanging him.

The hanging itself will be the climax of a gala social affair, and the bulk of the story centers on the arrangements that have to be made. Luckily, Colby's friends are a cosmopolitan, multitalented group. They count among their ranks a conductor, an architect, people knowledgeable about printing and about the history of executions, environmental activists, and the owner of a car-and-truck rental business. Everyone's talents are called on and everyone's opinions are consulted, even Colby's. The group is committed to bringing off the affair with éclat, and much of their discussion turns on setting the correctly festive tone for the event and making sure the day will be a success.

Colby shows his tendency to "go too far" when, graciously consulted about his preference for music for the occasion, he suggests Charles Ives's Fourth Symphony, a gargantuan work that would "put [the friends] way over the music budget." Disagreement about this choice threatens to disrupt the arrangements until Colby is sternly admonished to "be reasonable" and "think of something a little less exacting." Once the question of the music is solved, the friends discuss the appearance and wording of the invitations. They dismiss some slight qualms about the illegality of the proceedings by claiming that "we had a perfect moral right [to hang Colby] because he was our friend, belonged to us in various important senses, and he had after all gone too far." Referring to the hanging ambiguously as "An Event Involving Mr. Colby Williams," they determine, will help them to evade unwelcome attention from the law. They decide to serve drinks and magnanimously assure Colby that he can drink, too, before the finale.

The mechanics of the hanging are a more complicated matter, but the friends pool their knowledge to overcome their lack of experience with such things. In a debate between building a gibbet or using a tree, they choose a tree for reasons of ease, economy, and most important, aesthetics—this will be a "June hanging," and the full-leafed tree will "add a kind of 'natural' feeling." Aesthetic and environmental considerations lead the friends to dismiss the idea of a hangman or a firing squad (the latter is Colby's suggestion, his last attempt at "going too far," prudently rejected by Howard as an "ego trip" and as "unnecessary theatrics"). Instead, they decide, the guest of honor will jump off a large rubber ball considerably painted a deep green to blend in with the surroundings. For the noose, rope is selected over wire, for although the latter would be "more efficient," it "would injure the tree."

The friends' scrupulous planning pays off, for at the end the reader is told that "everything went off very smoothly." Not only is the event a social success ("a 'bang-up' production right down to the wire"), but also, perhaps most important, it succeeds in its punitive aim, for "nobody has ever gone too far again."

Themes and Meanings

Meaning is closely allied to style in this story's mock-serious, deadpan consideration of a clearly absurd situation. The friends are a tightly knit group whose strong allegiance to one another and willingness to substitute their own law for the law of the land recall the *esprit de corps* and modus operandi of the Ku Klux Klan, the Mafia, the Central Intelligence Agency, and other organizations engaged in covert activities. Less ominously, this group is reminiscent of such all-male fraternal organizations as the Masons and the Shriners, which use costumes, codes, and procedures known only to their initiates; college fraternities with their hazing rituals; and less formal clubs that nevertheless impose behavioral norms on their members.

The apparent reasonableness with which this group claims the right to chastise their "dear friend" and fellow member is undercut by the gruesomeness and extremity of their chosen method. In short, they make friendship the rationale for murder. The group is fully aware that they are taking the law into their own hands, but rather than finding this a deterrent to action, like many a vigilante group they proceed regardless, taking precautions only to avoid calling undue attention to themselves.

Published in the wake of the Watergate revelations and the controversial nomination of William E. Colby to be promoted from deputy director of the CIA to its head, the story can be read as a commentary on the extralegal operation of such secret organizations. Exactly how such groups "go too far" Donald Barthelme leaves the reader to imagine. In such a reading, however, Colby would be seen as an operative who botched a mission or whose indiscretion threatened to blow the group's cover; the group takes action against him of necessity to protect itself.

While such topical parallels are suggested by the story, they do not account for the friends' show of spirit and commitment to making the affair a success, and a semi-public one at that, since others will be invited to join the festivities. However, just as killing is an extreme form of discipline, the loving planning lavished on this "June hanging" is equally exaggerated. In detailing how the event is planned, Barthelme satirizes such clubby virtues as devotion and sacrifice for the good of the group and love for each of "the boys." Friendship entails obligations, and every character in the story, Colby included, willingly surrenders his autonomy to the group. Colby himself, after a brief defense, accedes to the notion that he should be disciplined. Basically a good team player despite his previous indiscretion, he cheerfully puts his fate into his friends' hands and participates with them in planning his end. His reward for such selflessness: proof of his friends' esteem and a convivial drink with them before his demise. For their part, his friends sacrifice many hours to serious discussion and careful planning. As a further token of their devotion to the group, they both put themselves to considerable expense and donate their respective professional services to make the event a success, thus upholding the reputation of their organization while showing their loyalty to a fellow member. They take the responsibility of membership in this group very seriously—it is a valued privilege—and are glad that the ritual hanging has the desired admonitory effect on the behavior of their members so that the future of their organization will be secure.

Style and Technique

The story includes many traditional elements of a fable: simple, straightforward narration; one-dimensional characters; uncomplicated, black-and-white logic; and a morally satisfying, didactic ending. However, unlike classic fables, which teach useful lessons, in this story the gap between the extreme action (hanging) and the vague offense it purports to correct (going "too far") makes it difficult to take the lesson literally, or even, it would seem, seriously.

Colby is told to "be reasonable," to conform to the commonsense norm of his friends. Reasonableness does indeed seem to be one of the group's leading traits, as is seen in their even-tempered discussion of the numerous practical arrangements for the hanging, with its democratic weighing of pros and cons. However, reason in the service of brutality is reason debased. While they may be reasonable about some matters, for example in providing a tent in case of rain, they are notably unreasonable about others, as when concern for protecting a tree ironically obscures concern for human life. The friends appear to be logical as well as reasonable, moving directly from cause to effect ("And now he'd gone too far, so we decided to hang him"). Their logic, however, is as perverted as their reasoning. After all, they never consider any form of punishment less extreme than murder. The speciousness of this logic originates in the subtle capacity of language as they use it to disguise the nature of reality; hence their self-deluding wit, as when Colby jokes about his friends being "a little Draconian." In the hands of this group, both language and logic are distorted, as if in illustration of George Orwell's famous dictum that "if thought corrupts language, language can corrupt thought."

The alliance of pseudologic and clever wordplay produces an artificial matter-of-factness of tone, a jocose, tongue-in-cheek collusion between readers and the future murderers that invites the reader to play along with the absurd notion of this hanging as social ritual, as wedding/graduation party/Bar Mitzvah. Rather than feel repulsion or moral outrage at the impending killing, readers find themselves worrying about the affair along with Howard, Victor, Hugh, and the others, sympathetically identifying with their concerns about unpredictable weather, transporting guests, and exceeding the budget.

The reader shares Paul's distaste for having Colby jump off a chair ("that would look . . . extremely tacky—some old kitchen chair sitting out there under our beautiful tree") and approves Tomas's considered judgment that instead Colby should stand on a large rubber ball that "would afford a sufficient 'drop' and would also roll out of the way if [he] suddenly changed his mind after jumping off." After the party, the reader rejoices with the hosts that "it didn't rain, the event was well attended, and we didn't run out of Scotch, or anything." Thus caught up in the group's practical concerns narrated in a flat, unemotional manner, the reader is lulled into forgetting the viciousness of their act of "friendship." Ordinariness of tone and focus on the mundane mask the grotesque; the reader responds uncritically by finding it palatable and involving.

It is a sly maneuver on Barthelme's part that he winds up placing the reader in the position of Colby's friends. Just as their distorted, inside-out "reason" carries them inexorably from one decision to the next, their humor and mock logic obscure rational thinking and overcome moral faculties so that the reader, too, tolerates and enjoys the perpetration of a legally indefensible, morally repugnant act. In fact, more than merely identifying with the characters in the story, Barthelme suggests, readers actually mimic them, for in much the same way they are gulled by the reasoning and behavior of Colby's friends, they passively accept and comply with the actions of a government that also on occasion tends to "go too far." The fable thus operates on more than one level. Literally, it may be absurd, a game, an entertainment, but despite the dislike of the present age for moral teaching, it also speaks to a particular condition of the world. At the end, the fable presents the moral learned by Colby's surviving friends, but since Barthelme has inveigled his readers into recognizing that they share the friends' capacity for easy self-delusion, it offers a lesson to everyone.

Nancy Sorkin

SOME SAY THE WORLD

Author: Susan Perabo (1969-   )
Type of plot: Domestic realism
Time of plot: The 1990's
Locale: Suburban United States
First published: 1995

> *Principal characters:*
> THE DAUGHTER, an eighteen-year-old who has long been
>   institutionalized for emotional and mental problems
> MR. ARNETTE, her compassionate stepfather
> HER MOTHER, a self-centered woman

The Story

"Some Say the World" is told by a first-person participant narrator, an eighteen-year-old girl. During her adolescence, the narrator committed several antisocial acts as a result of her destructive pyromania and has been hospitalized frequently and subjected to intense medication, yet her voice seems authoritative. Her telling of her family history, coupled with the interchanges with her stepfather, Mr. Arnette, lead readers to affirm the narrator's perspective. The narration and dialogue evoke a compassionate response toward the troubled teenager and her stepfather while revealing the self-serving indifference of the young woman's mother.

The action of the story is straightforward, with the daughter simply relating some of her troubled past experiences, mostly concerning her fascination with fire, while she passes the time playing board games with her mother's current husband, Mr. Arnette. She and her stepfather realize the dubious nature of the third member of this blended family, and their shared knowledge creates a bond between them. Her mother regularly cheats on Mr. Arnette with her biological father, so both the stepfather and the daughter suffer from loneliness, abandonment, and unfulfilled desire. The time they spend together not only bonds them as fellow sufferers but also allows them the opportunity to decide that they must act by leaving their situation.

The daughter's parents have been divorced thirteen years, but they routinely meet for sexual liaisons at a nearby hotel. The girl, though, has not seen her father since the divorce. Her mother lies to her and Mr. Arnette concerning her activities, trying to hide her involvement with her former husband. The girl and her stepfather eventually become upset by the mother's behavior, so one night they decide to follow her to the hotel in which the liaisons occur. They peek through a window, and see the undeniable truth of their situation. This revelation provides the impetus for them to leave home for good.

As the daughter and Mr. Arnette get to know each other by playing board games, they reveal their loneliness and desires. Mr. Arnette admits that he married the daughter's mother for "company" and that he misses his own children, whom he rarely sees.

He tries to re-create the feeling of a good memory with his children by taking his step-daughter to the local carnival, but she is too anxiety-ridden to get out of the car. Her inability or refusal to accompany Mr. Arnette at the carnival prompts him to question her about the value of her pills and to challenge her to get out of the house more.

This confrontation, along with the other conversations between the girl and her stepfather, encourages the daughter to start living on her own terms. She decides to quit taking her medication, and once she does this, she seems more alive and able to experience feelings. She spends a day looking at pictures of her biological father in a photo album, gaining for the first time some understanding of his life. She regains her appetite. She is able to fry bacon without being consumed by the destructive appeal of fire. She is also able to accompany Mr. Arnette to the carnival, where together they ride a Ferris wheel and celebrate the temporary good feelings of being suspended from the reality of their painful memories and current situations. By this time, they have also become aware of their tender feelings for each other. They decide to run away together to Canada.

Themes and Meanings

The story is about the power of desire and the response to loneliness that result from selfishness. The daughter is the victim of her parents' divorce and of her mother's inattentiveness, lies, and neglect. Mr. Arnette is also a man whose desires have been squelched, a lonely victim of an unfortunate domestic situation.

Fire is used as a primary motif in the story. The emotionally wounded daughter responds to her domestic context by destructive acts of pyromania that get her institutionalized. The motif of fire is further used to suggest the growing potential passion between her and Mr. Arnette. The daughter says that fire "is yours for one glorious moment . . . but wait one moment too long, get caught up in its beauty, and it has grown beyond your control. And it is that moment that I live for . . . when the flame rose above my head: not from fear, but from ecstasy." Additionally, the fire motif connects to the allusion to Robert Frost's poem "Fire and Ice" in which the question of the world's doom is compared to the vicious emotional capacity of human behavior: "Some say the world will end in fire,/ Some say in ice." Frost's poem suggests that desire (fire) can be destructive and could cause the world to end, but rather than meeting with a physical end, the world might become a place not worth living in because of the pain of neglect and human indifference (ice).

The allusion to the poem reveals the narrator's growing understanding of her own unfulfilled desires. For her and Mr. Arnette, loneliness is intricately linked to fire. For the daughter, fire has always been destructive, but perhaps a new positive use of fire, of passion, will become available to her. For Mr. Arnette, his fire has been squelched by the deceit of his wife, and again, perhaps a new possibility exists with his step-daughter as the two of them decide to leave, carrying their feelings for each other with them.

Another theme in the story is the suspension of the material world. A separation between the material and nonmaterial becomes evident when the stepfather and the daughter sit in the Ferris wheel high above the earth. The narrator fears this act is dangerous, but Mr. Arnette responds, "We're safer up here than anywhere else in the world." His statement indicates that the material world is a place of danger, heartache, and unfulfilled desire as opposed to the nonmaterial realm, and even a temporary suspension of the material world allows for good feelings of acceptance and companionship to emerge. The mother's (and apparently the biological father's) inability to understand the essential human needs of acceptance and companionship (as essential as fire and water) underscores the author's themes.

Style and Technique

Susan Perabo describes one week, Monday to Monday, in the characters' lives to demonstrate their routines, which establish the basis for the change in two of the characters. The story is also roughly divided into two halves, the first part showing the daughter heavily sedated and the second part showing her off her medications. The author parallels these two parts with the perspectives of the characters. In the first part, the daughter and stepfather seem trapped and disillusioned. In the second part, they are active and willing to change their situation. The two parts of the story suggest a movement from disorder to order, from a sedated fugue to a clearer perspective illustrated by their suspension above the material world as they sit atop the Ferris wheel trying to exorcise their pain. The author's allusion to Frost's poem, in addition to providing the story title, intensifies the serious nature of the characters' anxiety. Their worlds are disordered and precariously close to ending because of the animosity of misguided human desire.

The story moves along primarily via the dialogue of the characters, although the participant narrator also provides readers with sufficient background information to establish the anxiety of her situation. The story does not follow a conventional plot. There is much more emphasis on characterization and revelatory dialogue, but the story does move toward resolution of the immediate conflicted situation. The resolution, however, is ambiguous. Readers are led to believe the daughter and Mr. Arnette will indeed act by leaving for Canada, but questions remain about the nature of their relationship. Is it only an ecstatic fire of the moment, a fire that will burn out of control? The suspension above the material world on the Ferris wheel is pronounced safe by Mr. Arnette, but their position is temporary; they must eventually come back down to earth. What will be the reality of their experience once the safe but temporary suspension has run its course? Readers celebrate the courage of the characters who act and remove themselves from a deceitful and painful situation, but questions about their ability to maintain a healthy equilibrium in the future remain. Perabo's use of a troubled first-person participant narrative voice skillfully intensifies the ambiguity.

Kenneth Hada

SOMEBODY UP THERE LIKES ME

Author: Ralph Lombreglia (1951-   )
Type of plot: Science fiction
Time of plot: April 12-13, 1999
Locale: San Jose and Palo Alto, California
First published: 1994

> *Principal characters:*
> DANTE ALLEGRO ANNUNZIATA, the narrator
> SNOOKIE LEE LUDLOW, his wife
> MARY BETH, his boss at College of the Mind
> BOYCE P. HOODINGTON, his friend and leader of a project to
>   simulate human consciousness with a computer

The Story

"Somebody Up There Likes Me" is told in the first person from the point of view of the main character, Dante Allegro Annunziata. Most of the action in the story revolves around Dante's reception of and response to e-mail. The primary emphasis is given to the movement of text in Internet communication.

The story opens with Dante receiving four e-mails, the first from his distant wife, Snookie Lee Ludlow, and three from his boss, Mary Beth. He reads Snookie Lee's message, then explains that his wife has left him to pursue a doctorate in women's studies in San Antonio, Texas, 1,500 miles away. He relates his last e-mail to his wife and decides to put off opening the three e-mails from Mary Beth. Dante then describes how he met Snookie Lee at a poetry slam as a student and how they both moved to San Jose when he was offered a professorship at the College of the Mind. He recounts his difficulty with Mary Beth, who is out to get him, and his dislike of being separated from Snookie Lee.

A new e-mail from Dante's friend Boyce P. Hoodington invites him to dinner, and he accepts. On Dante's arrival, Boyce confides that his computer project has been downsized and that he has been terminated. While checking his e-mail, Dante receives a message from Snookie Lee, in which she reveals her nervousness about her upcoming oral exams. She also criticizes higher education as shallow and oppressive because it forces her to regurgitate theories in which she does not truly believe, and she refers to academics, including Dante, as apes.

Over dinner Boyce explains to Dante his new project to build a computer that reflects the knowledge of all the good humanity has achieved. However, first, he needs a new computer. After dinner, Boyce and Dante make their way to see Mickey, a computer quality tester and dealer from whom Boyce has arranged to purchase the finest, most innovative computer available, a Revelation 2000. Mickey shows them a Revelation 2000 and makes Dante try it out. When accessing his e-mail, Dante reads the messages from Mary Beth. The final message affirms that his contract will not be renewed. Both Boyce and Dante decide to buy Revelation 2000 computers, with which they will start their new venture together—building a complete simulation of the mind of humanity, as employees of the independent financier Brubaker, who operates outside the corporate and educational mainstream.

At a bank cash machine, Dante checks his e-mail again and finds a conciliatory e-mail from Snookie Lee. She has failed her oral exams by refusing to respond to the questions and is flying back to Dante that night. He withdraws three thousand dollars for the purchase of a Revelation 2000 and dashes off to buy it and eagerly meet his wife.

Themes and Meanings

Ralph Lombreglia's "Somebody Up There Likes Me" deals primarily with the preservation of authenticity and creativity in an institution-driven and technologically advanced world. Lombreglia's main characters, Dante and Snookie Lee, are both graduates of institutions of higher learning, where they were creative beings. They first meet at a poetry slam and later meet again at a bookstore poetry reading. After becoming a couple and finishing their degrees, they move to San Jose, where Dante begins his teaching career at the College of the Mind.

Dante is an innovative professor who uses computers in the classroom and whose students love him, which ironically causes the institution, epitomized by his chairperson, Mary Beth, to believe he is not academically rigorous in his teaching. Lombreglia juxtaposes a creative, authentic, successful teacher and an oppressive, antiquated educational institution whose leaders adhere to tradition so devotedly as to be unable to accept or reward genuinely creative intelligence. Dante comments on his belief that Mary Beth is out to get him.

The problems at the college create a rift between Dante and Snookie Lee. While she endures the boredom of being an academic's spouse, he suffers the stresses of dealing with abusive supervision. The distance Dante's frustrating employment situation creates between the couple results in their separation and Snookie Lee's decision to pursue a doctorate of her own. However, Snookie Lee realizes that her doctorate will require a mastery of regurgitated theories in which she does not believe, and she deliberately fails her oral exams, returning to San Jose and Dante. At the same time, Dante is being fired from the College of the Mind. These two creative, authentic people are freed from the academic institutions that have stifled their creativity and their love and thus are able to rediscover the happiness of love outside an institution-driven world.

Lombreglia conveys this same theme through Boyce, the highly creative and innovative computer developer and leader of a project to simulate human consciousness with a computer. After Boyce has developed computers with consciousness and communicative abilities, his corporate employer trivializes computer creativity by assigning Boyce the task of designing a computer with lips. Ironically, Boyce's success results in his being fired and his project's being sold to British buyers for a huge corporate profit. Lombreglia illustrates free-market capitalism's oppression of the creative and their achievements in Boyce's being able to realize truly authentic creative freedom only through his alignment with Brubaker, a radical financier outside traditional corporate and educational institutions. With Brubaker's help, Dante and Boyce plan to design the electronic mind of humanity, to capture and record the good humanity has achieved. Lombreglia's point in this story is that such authentic achievement and genuine human love can be sustained only outside the powerful, oppressive institutions of the contemporary world.

Style and Technique

Lombreglia's humorous and yet profound story is stylistically and technically creative in its own right, an implicit exemplification of the story's theme. Irony is central to the message that creativity and authenticity and love are to be found not in the academic and corporate institutions popularly thought to harbor them but also in almost any other place. Indeed, ironically, creativity and love thrive on the disreputable fringes of modern life, in the poetry slams in Boston's bowels, in basement bookstores, in the cluttered shops of outcast computer quality testers such as Mickey, and at the antiquated computers at which Dante creates the innovative messages that help bring Snookie Lee home to him. That Dante's success as a teacher causes him to be fired and that Boyce's success as a computer innovator generates the same ironic fate underscore the reversed expectations. The point is that true originality and skill are exiled from contemporary institutions, which are ultimately devoted to perpetuating a self-serving status quo and not devoted to originality, progress, or happiness.

Lombreglia's use of religiously symbolic names and titles also contributes to the ironic message and adds resonance to the story. The obvious divinity reference of the title "Somebody Up There Likes Me," the Revelation 2000 name for the most advanced computer, and the title of Boyce's wife's proposed book involving modern man's soul suggest the profundity of the story's theme, a struggle between the destructive and instructive, between love and indifference, between creativity and dehumanizing modern life, and even between good and evil. It is also important that the Revelation 2000 can be found only outside the institutions of earthly, secular achievement, universities and corporations.

Literary allusions add to the theme of the story. For example, the fictional Dante's search for Snookie Lee, the modern Beatrice, among multilayered modern evils echoes the historical Dante's *La divina commedia* (c. 1320; *The Divine Comedy*, 1802). Also, Snookie Lee's refusal to answer her orals is described as doing a "Bartleby," a reference to Herman Melville's "Bartleby the Scrivener" (1853), in which a scrivener named Bartleby rebels against the tedium of the modern workplace by saying "I would prefer not to" in response to requests to perform various tasks.

In addition, computers are personified throughout the story, surviving misuse, abuse, and trivialization and reflecting human creativity and achievement. In the grand scheme of somebody up there, they actively help Dante to recover his Beatrice, his love, and happiness, the ultimates of human existence.

John L. Grigsby

SOMETHING OUT THERE

Author: Nadine Gordimer (1923-   )
Type of plot: Social realism
Time of plot: The 1980's
Locale: Johannesburg, South Africa, and its suburbs
First published: 1984

> *Principal characters:*
> JOY, a young white revolutionary
> CHARLES, her former lover, also a revolutionary
> VUSI, a black revolutionary
> EDDIE, a black revolutionary
> MRS. NAAS (HESTER) KLOPPER, the wife of an affluent white real
> estate agent

The Story

A strange, apelike creature is terrorizing the affluent white suburbs of Johannesburg, South Africa. It strikes at night, killing and maiming pets and frightening the many citizens who have seen it. Only young Stanley Dobrow has tried to photograph it, but the photograph turned out badly, revealing only some movement in the treetops. The bizarre happenings occasion much speculation and many letters to the editors of the white newspapers. It is a novel news story and a welcome one, providing as it does relief from the usual depressing fare: labor strikes, student riots, and international sanctions against the white-controlled South African government. To the white citizens of Johannesburg, the ape story seems to be something more immediately applicable to their own lives than does the racial conflict that is dividing their country.

One such citizen is Mrs. Naas (Hester) Klopper, the wife of a prosperous real estate agent, a fastidious woman proud of her fine house and of her skill at maintaining it. When her husband unexpectedly brings home a prospective client and his wife, Mrs. Klopper is ready with tea and sweetbreads to offer them. Charles and Joy Rosser seem shy, but quite pleasant: Mrs. Rosser is expecting their first child, and the couple are interested in the old Kleynhans place, a secluded farm that has stood empty for three years. Later, Naas Klopper shows them the place, and they take it on the condition that they can rent it with the option to buy. Though it seems unorthodox to him, Klopper is impressed with their offer of six months' advance rent, and he agrees to their terms.

The Rossers are not, however, the ordinary young newlyweds they appear to be. Unknown to the Kloppers, and to the rest of the white community, the couple (they are not married, nor are they any longer lovers) have rented the Kleynhans place as a base from which to plan a revolutionary operation against the government. With the help of Vusi and Eddie, black revolutionaries posing as farm laborers, they set about transforming an abandoned shed into an ammunition warehouse and making other preparations for their strike. All four of them are careful to maintain appearances, observing by day the traditional social conventions between white masters and their black servants. Inside the house, however, and under cover of night, they live as equals, coping as best they can with the boredom and restlessness that come from confinement.

Meanwhile, the ape continues its raids on the northern suburbs of Johannesburg, and sightings of it continue to cause anxiety and speculation. Some say that the creature is a baboon; others insist that it is a chimpanzee. At various times, it is spotted by a group of doctors on a golf course, a pair of lovers trysting in a secluded cottage, a black servant in an affluent white household, and a young white police officer's wife (she does not actually see the animal, but it steals a leg of venison that her husband has hung in the kitchen window). Citizens protest that it should be trapped, even killed; the SPCA protests such moves. Still, the sightings remain brief and momentary, with no witness getting a good enough look at the creature to say precisely what it is.

Life goes on at the Kleynhans place. Charles rounds up "necessities" (their word for munitions); Vusi, the older and more experienced of the blacks, instructs Eddie in the use and maintenance of weapons. The four talk politics, analyze the media, read, and wait. Eddie takes a secret trip into the city; Vusi fashions a makeshift saxophone from scrap metal. A complication arises when the black man who had worked for the late Mr. Kleynhans arrives to ask after his mealie patch, which he had planted before his old boss's death. Vusi and Eddie manage to placate him by telling him that they will tend the patch, and he goes away. His visit, however, combined with Eddie's ill-advised trip to the city, creates nervousness and a certain amount of friction among the four revolutionaries as the date of their operation approaches. The tension is finally broken by Eddie and Joy, who begin to dance together one evening to the music of Eddie's tape player. Vusi joins in on his saxophone, and Charles watches them contentedly.

Soon, according to plan, Vusi and Eddie leave the Kleynhans place and move to a rural cave, where they undertake the final stages of their mission. Charles and Joy are visited by the black farmhand, who wonders what has become of the two blacks. Uncertain about what to do, Joy tells him that he may tend the mealie patch himself; her decision makes Charles uneasy, but both of them realize that they will soon be gone. Not long afterward, a massive power failure cripples the city, the result of the bombing of a power station. The Kloppers and the farmhand are questioned about Charles and Joy, who have by now disappeared. The police uncover the facts about the Rossers (which is not their real name) but are unable to apprehend either them or Vusi. Only Eddie is caught, and he is killed by the police as he tries to escape into Swaziland.

The ape, too, is killed, wounded in the arm by a white householder and later found dead. It turns out to have been a common baboon, gone berserk for some unknown reason. Its death is not covered extensively by the newspapers because public interest has been usurped by the attack on the power station.

Themes and Meanings

"Something Out There" is, above all else, a harsh indictment of the South African government's policy of apartheid, under which the races were rigidly segregated and Africans were forced to live in slumlike black "homelands," made to carry identification papers at all times, and subjected to various other indignities. This story explores the tensions of apartheid at the personal, everyday level; the government policy is viewed here, as in much of Nadine Gordimer's work, as a direct result of individual will.

While Vusi and Eddie and their white supporters are treated sympathetically, the white suburbanites are often the subject of bitter satire. Representative of this group is Mrs. Naas Klopper, a woman so taken with the comfortable lifestyle that her husband's prosperity affords her that she has for years neglected her own given name, always referring to herself as "Mrs." An essentially well-meaning woman, she is nevertheless bigoted and shortsighted in the extreme, offering to find the Rossers a new black "boy" to replace the one who had worked for Mr. Kleynhans and taking a generally maternal attitude toward the young white couple. She is a woman unable to connect the political and the personal, incapable of appreciating either the inhumanity of apartheid or her own role in its maintenance. On a symbolic level, her share of responsibility for the violence threatening her society is brought home to her near the end of the story: While searching the Kleynhans place, the police discover that a cookie box in which Charles and Joy have stored munitions is the very box that Mrs. Klopper brought them earlier, filled with her own homemade sweetbreads. It is characteristic, however, of Mrs. Klopper and her kind that this irony escapes her.

This inability to connect also characterizes the whites who figure in the parallel story of the ape attacks. Concerned with the creature only insofar as it threatens their own lives and homes ("so long as it attacked other people's cats and dogs, frightened other people's maids—that was other people's affair," says the narrator), they are unable to band together to find a solution to their common problem. Thus, the ape becomes an appropriately ominous symbol of apartheid itself, "something out there" that serves to expose the amorality of an entire nation.

Style and Technique

This long short story is double-plotted; that is, it is actually two stories that enhance and comment on each other. While the story of the events at the Kleynhans place receives the most attention, it is frequently interrupted by abrupt and often darkly comic sections devoted to the ape attacks. Only gradually does it become clear that the two plots are related in that they both illuminate, albeit in very different ways, the cancerous intolerance at the core of South African society.

The characters of Charles, Eddie, Vusi, and especially Joy are fully rounded, replete with complex motivations and very human shortcomings. The white suburbanites of the ape sections, on the other hand, are frequently stereotypes, monsters of egotism and self-absorption whose personalities are exposed rather than developed. Through her manipulation of these interlocking plots, Gordimer manages to mimic in her fiction what she sees the South African government doing in fact: treating one segment of society as a community of responsible, dignified individuals, the other segment as a simpleminded, inflammatory, and potentially dangerous rabble.

J. D. Daubs

SOMNAMBULISM

Author: Charles Brockden Brown (1771-1810)
Type of plot: Mystery and detective, psychological
Time of plot: The late eighteenth or early nineteenth century
Locale: The forest of Norwood, somewhere in the eastern United States
First published: 1805

> *Principal characters:*
> ALTHORPE, a young man
> CONSTANTIA DAVIS, his beloved, who is engaged to another
> MR. DAVIS, Constantia's father
> NICK HANDYSIDE, a physically and mentally disabled young man
> who likes to scare travelers

The Story

The story begins with an extract from *The Vienna Gazette* that tells the story of a European murder that parallels the one in "Somnambulism" in every detail. When the narrative begins, the narrator and protagonist, a young man later identified as Althorpe, tells of a dinner party at his family's home. His guest, Mr. Davis, receives an urgent letter calling him away. Though it is late at night, Davis resolves to leave immediately, and his daughter Constantia insists on going with him.

Althorpe becomes agitated at the suggestion. He is in love with Constantia; she esteems him but is betrothed to another. He warns Mr. Davis and Constantia not to ride out that night and not to go near a particular oak tree, without saying why the tree is dangerous. Mr. Davis brushes aside Althorpe's warnings, partly from the urgency of his errand but also largely from his suspicion that Althorpe's intimations of danger are merely smokescreens for his affections, of which Constantia's father does not approve.

Unable to persuade Constantia and her father to delay their trip until morning, Althorpe offers to accompany them as guide. Althorpe's insistence and his inability to explain any rational basis for his fears confirm Davis in his decision to leave immediately and without Althorpe. Davis, along with Althorpe's uncle, finally convinces Althorpe to stay behind. After Davis and his daughter leave, Althorpe is even more agitated. He cannot sleep and sits up thinking about the ill-fated journey. His thoughts keep returning to the mysterious oak. Finally falling asleep in his chair, Althorpe dreams that he is unable to prevent an assassin from murdering Constantia but that he pursues the murderer, penetrates his disguise, and shoots him. The next morning word comes from the local doctor that Constantia has been fatally shot.

From a number of subsequent sources, Althorpe reconstructs the story of the previous night. Davis and his daughter see a figure at the oak, and Davis is convinced the figure is Althorpe. Before they can make a positive identification, the figure disappears, only to reappear farther down the road and vanish again. At this point Constantia and her father are stopped by a stranger who warns them to watch out for a local character, Nick Handyside. Nick, the stranger explains, is the retarded son of a local farmer. Nick's face is deformed, and he loves to wander the roadside at night, scaring travelers. The stranger explains that Nick is harmless.

Suddenly they hear a scream, and the horse bolts. The carriage dashes against the oak and is shattered to pieces. The servant chases after the frightened horse, leaving Davis and his daughter alone in the dark. Davis pursues the horse, too, then realizes he had better stay with his daughter. Turning back, he sees and hears a pistol shot and rushes to Constantia, finding her unconscious and bleeding. Davis takes her to the house of a nearby physician, where she dies the following morning.

Themes and Meanings

In the character of Constantia Davis, Charles Brockden Brown presents another of the strong women for which his fiction was famous. His first book, *Alcuin* (1798), was a feminist dialogue following Mary Wollstonecraft's arguments for equality of the sexes. Many critics have maintained that Brown abandoned his feminist leanings in his later fiction, though this story shows that Brown's ideal of strong and able women was still alive in 1805. Constantia objects to Althorpe's overprotective concern for her. Later she scorns her father's apprehension over the mysterious figure in the dark, observing that if he attacked them, it would be one against two, in their favor. Very few writers in 1805 would allow mere numbers to carry more value than gender in a fight or present a young woman as bolder in a pinch than her father.

The second theme common in Brown's fiction and manifest in this story is the motif of the double. Brown's protagonists are often found to have surprising symbolic or circumstantial connections with other characters who at first seem totally alien, and Althorpe is no exception. Althorpe is initially measured against his rival, Constantia's fiancé, though he never appears in the story. More significantly, Althorpe seems mysteriously linked with the local prankster, Nick Handyside. The mysterious figure seen at the oak is assumed by the local farmer to be Nick, but Davis is sure it is Althorpe. The stranger on the road tells Constantia and her father that Nick knows the dark woods intimately, yet earlier Althorpe had told them that he himself knew the woods as well as his own chamber. Althorpe's affinity to Nick Handyside is an early clue to his unconscious role in Constantia's murder.

Related to the theme of the double are Brown's philosophical doubts about the limits of self-knowledge. As narrator, Althorpe gives readers a glimpse of his metal process, and instead of the rational, linear picture of human reason that might be expected from a writer of Brown's generation, there is a jumble of contradictions and rationalizations. In one paragraph, Althorpe very reasonably argues for the propriety of his pursuing Constantia's affections despite her betrothal to another man. In the very next paragraph, he inexplicably reverses himself, praising his rival. This flip-flopping continues for several paragraphs with no resolution.

Brown's critique of reason, in the character of Althorpe, produces the power of imagination as reason's rival. Even before he dreams of it, Althorpe imagines in great visual detail the journey of Mr. Davis and his daughter. His overwhelming powers of imagination are not altogether positive in effect; Althorpe likens his mental processes to superstition and, in another unconscious connection to Nick Handyside, pronounces his apprehensions of the fearful unknown inferior to those of "idiots and children."

Style and Technique

Brown's most striking technical accomplishment in "Somnambulism" is his narrative mode, which experiments with unreliable narrator and interior monologue decades before such techniques were supposed to have been invented. Brown's first-person narrative in this story includes a lengthy and inconclusive detailed decision-making process, in which the narrator, Althorpe, alternately decides for and against pursuing Constantia's affections. The name "Constantia" serves as an ironic contrast to Althorpe's *in*constant thought pattern. Althorpe's inconstant thought is reinforced stylistically in alternations between direct and indirect discourse in the dialogue. Because the first-person format means that all dialogue is ultimately reported by the narrator, Althorpe, direct quotations often merge with indirect. Other characters' references to themselves sometimes say "I" and sometimes "he," though both ultimately derive from Althorpe. Conversely, interior monologues—Althorpe's mental conversation with himself—at times are almost as argumentative and discursive as real conversation, with Althorpe often arguing with himself.

Brown's presentation of a man oblivious to his own deepest thoughts and feelings is ahead of his time not only in narrative technique but also in terms of psychological understanding. In characters such as Althorpe, Brown explored in great detail what Sigmund Freud a century later would call the unconscious. Brown was not doing so in a vacuum, however; many of his friends, such as Benjamin Rush and Elihu Hubbard Smith, were physicians and pioneers in psychology. Nevertheless, no fiction writers in Europe or the United States were recording the phenomenon in the short story quite the way Brown did in "Somnambulism." Althorpe is mortally afraid of the oak in the forest of Norwood yet cannot provide a reason for the fear. However, when Davis and Constantia find out about a very real and concrete danger in the person of Nick Handyside, they marvel that Althorpe never mentioned him.

Finally, the stylistic element most significant to the story may be its very form, the fragment. "Somnambulism" is subtitled "A Fragment" and may in fact have been a portion of a novel Brown never completed. However, its fragmentary state as published in the *Monthly Magazine* in 1805 is functional. Because Althorpe, as unreliable narrator, is incapable of recognizing his own role in the death of Constantia, the reader must piece together the clues to make the story complete. Some of the clues are given in the narrative—Davis's recognition of Althorpe at the oak tree, for example—but the clincher is the parallel story affixed to the story at the beginning, a newspaper account of a similar murder that occurred in Europe. By connecting the newspaper account with Althorpe's fragmentary narrative, the reader can easily conclude that Althorpe himself murdered his own beloved unconsciously, while walking in his sleep.

John R. Holmes

SON OF THE WOLFMAN

Author: Michael Chabon (1963-   )
Type of plot: Domestic realism, psychological
Time of plot: 1995-1996
Locale: Los Angeles
First published: 1998

> *Principal characters:*
> CARA GLANZMAN, a casting agent
> RICHARD CASE, her husband, a television cameraman
> DOROTHY PENDLETON, a midwife

The Story

"Son of the Wolfman" focuses on how the consequences of a rape affect the marriage of Cara Glanzman and Richard Case. The story looks at both characters equally, treating them objectively yet compassionately, focusing more on the confusion of their inner lives than on their actions.

Cara and Richard are both thirty-four and have been together twelve years. Cara's failure to become pregnant, despite trying most of the methods known to medical science, has placed a great burden on the last five years of their marriage. Cara begins looking into getting a divorce on the day the Reservoir Rapist attacks her while she jogs around Lake Hollywood. The day before he is arrested, she learns she is pregnant. She decides to have an abortion but, without consulting Richard, changes her mind at the last minute.

The marriage becomes increasingly strained as the pregnancy progresses, with a silent Richard tending to Cara's needs merely out of a sense of duty. Never asking about her decision, he sulks most of the time. He refuses to understand why Cara wants a midwife and feels intimidated by Dorothy Pendleton, who seems constantly to be judging him.

Dorothy sees bringing Richard to see his obligations as a father—even after she learns the biological truth—as part of her job. She does everything she can to entice him into participating in the preparations for the delivery of the child he hates. When Dorothy intuitively guesses that the baby will be a boy, Richard calls it Wolfman Junior because it is the son of a monster.

Cara is determined that the birth not be induced because the pregnancy began as something over which she had no control and she does not want it to end that way. When the baby's due date passes, Dorothy suggests that Cara's having sexual intercourse with her husband will initiate the birth, but Richard has moved out, never returning from an assignment in Seattle. Cara feels sorry that Richard has moved in with the older brother he has never liked. Answering her plea for help, Richard comes to her in the middle of the night and agrees to renew their intimacy.

When Cara's contractions begin, Richard rushes her to the nearest hospital. After Dorothy arrives, she and a physician's assistant force Richard to stay with Cara. He gradually becomes caught up in the event and, remembering he is a cameraman, buys a disposable camera from a vending machine to photograph the infant's arrival. The story ends with the three seemingly united as a family.

Themes and Meanings

Like much of Michael Chabon's fiction, "Son of the Wolfman" demonstrates the difficulty middle-class Americans have expressing their feelings or understanding those of the people for whom they supposedly care. As with stories such as "House Hunting" and "That Was Me," Chabon is especially adept at delineating failing relationships.

When Richard is unusually quiet following the rape, Cara persuades herself that her husband has been struck dumb by grief, especially because he has never been able to express this emotion. When she asks how he feels about her impending abortion, he merely shrugs. Richard bottles up his pain over the attack on his wife and her decision to have a rapist's child. He is both angry and embarrassed that a rapist has achieved what he has failed to do, and he implicitly questions his manhood. Without articulating it, he almost envies the rapist, an acclaimed athlete and coach. Richard resembles many other Chabon characters, almost always men, who struggle greatly with matters of maturity, sexuality, and parenthood.

The inability to communicate clearly is another of Chabon's typical concerns. He sympathizes with Richard's refusal to try to understand Cara's decision and comfort her during this time of emotional and physical turmoil yet sees his inaction and his aloofness as childish. Chabon's protagonists are usually very self-aware, and Richard anguishes over his fear of talking to Cara about their dilemma, his sense of disgust with her, his guilt over never telling her that he really did not want to have children, and his anger over Cara's not even noticing how lost he is. Emotionally isolated, he has no one with whom he can discuss this ordeal, as his friends abandoned him because of his gloominess.

Cara's emotional state stands in strong contrast to Richard's sense of being lost. Once she decides to go ahead with the pregnancy—for reasons she never explains, even to herself—she experiences a sense of elation and convinces herself that the organism growing inside her is entirely of her making. Like the protagonists of Chabon's *The Mysteries of Pittsburgh* (1988), *Wonder Boys* (1995), and *The Amazing Adventures of Kavalier and Clay* (2000), Cara tries to make the best of things when forces over which she has no control disrupt the relative order of her existence.

Cara's delayed delivery leads to Richard overcoming some of his fears and becoming at least the symbolic father of their child. While the ending of the story seems predictable, sentimental, and unlikely on the surface, it works because Chabon has created such believable, recognizably human characters and presented them without condescension or self-pity. He never romanticizes his characters' anguish.

Style and Technique

"Son of the Wolfman" appears in Chabon's collection *Werewolves in Their Youth* (1999), in which several stories have a gothic subtext and feature werewolf imagery. When Cara's baby is overdue, she has a nightmare about a hairy, stooped creature that she recognizes, even in her dream, as representing her rapist. Her son is born with a faint down covering his shoulders and back. Such devices establish some emotional distance from the characters and their desperate situation. Chabon employs the mythology of popular culture in this story and elsewhere to walk a fine line between the ironic and the heartbreaking, though finally his methods are more traditionally realistic than postmodern.

Chabon creates his setting with just a few broad strokes and without resorting to detailed descriptions. He provides just enough information about Los Angeles and the Hollywood milieu to create the necessary verisimilitude, using only a few show-business references. For example, Cara and Richard once had as a neighbor a palmist who claimed to have warned Bob Crane to change his wicked ways. Because this once successful television actor was a victim of murder, the reference is fitting in a story about how one violent act can radically change lives.

Cara and Richard essentially live in a world of make-believe whose superficiality is challenged by the rapist's act. Richard's need for the comforting cocoon of this world is shown by his fleeing to the job in Seattle to avoid his marital responsibilities and by his need to photograph the birth. Having a camera in his hands provides a degree of control missing from his life since the rape threw everything into chaos.

In both short fiction and novels, Chabon's greatest strength is perhaps his finely drawn characters. Cara and Richard's actions are always logical if occasionally infuriating. Even the members of the supporting cast are well drawn. Dorothy exists primarily as a plot device to spur Richard to action, yet she is also a well-rounded character, a woman who has seen just about everything but has not allowed her experiences to make her cynical. Her refusal to patronize the couple stands out; her humanity is a constant.

Most of all, however, Chabon is a consummate yet subtle stylist. He writes in a deceptively simple, often witty, metaphorical style that rarely calls attention to itself. He is a poet of middle-class failure, loss, despair, and redemption. As his moving portrait of Richard illustrates, no one writes more perceptively about the American manchild. While stories such as "Son of the Wolfman" may remind some of the writings of Raymond Carver, John Cheever, or John Updike, Chabon's blending of style, theme, and characterization is distinctively his own.

Michael Adams

SONNY'S BLUES

Author: James Baldwin (1924-1987)
Type of plot: Social realism
Time of plot: The 1940's and 1950's
Locale: Harlem and Greenwich Village, New York
First published: 1958

> *Principal characters:*
> THE NARRATOR, an unnamed high school math teacher
> SONNY, his younger brother, a jazz pianist

The Story

The narrator, a teacher in Harlem, has escaped the ghetto, creating a stable and secure life for himself despite the destructive pressures that he sees destroying so many young blacks. He sees African American adolescents discovering the limits placed on them by a racist society at the very moment when they are discovering their abilities. He tells the story of his relationship with his younger brother, Sonny. That relationship has moved through phases of separation and return. After their parents' deaths, he tried and failed to be a father to Sonny. For a while, he believed that Sonny had succumbed to the destructive influences of Harlem life. Finally, however, they achieved a reconciliation in which the narrator came to understand the value and the importance of Sonny's need to be a jazz pianist.

The story opens with a crisis in their relationship. The narrator reads in the newspaper that Sonny was taken into custody in a drug raid. He learns that Sonny is addicted to heroin and that he will be sent to a treatment facility to be "cured." Unable to believe that his gentle and quiet brother could have so abused himself, the narrator cannot reopen communication with Sonny until a second crisis occurs, the death of his daughter from polio. When Sonny is released, the narrator brings him to live with his family.

The middle section of the story is a flashback. The narrator remembers his last talk with his mother, in which she made him promise to "be there" for Sonny. Home on leave from the army, he has seen little of Sonny, who is then is school. His mother tells him about the death of his uncle, a story she had kept from him until this moment. His uncle, much loved by his father, was killed in a hit-and-run accident by a group of drunken whites who miscalculated in an attempt to frighten the young man. The pain, sorrow, and rage this event aroused colored his father's whole life, especially his relationship with Sonny, who reminded him of his brother. She tells the narrator this story partly in order to illustrate that there is no safety from suffering in their world. The narrator cannot protect Sonny from the world any more than his father could protect his own brother. Such suffering is a manifestation of the general chaos of life out of which people struggle to create some order and meaning. Though suffering cannot be avoided, one can struggle against it, and one can support others in their struggles.

From this conversation, the narrator brings the story forward through his marriage and return to the army; Sonny's announcement at their mother's funeral that he intends to be a jazz pianist; Sonny's attempt to live with the narrator's wife's family, teaching himself piano while the narrator is away at war; the failure of this arrangement; Sonny's term in the navy; and, after the war, a final break between the brothers because of the narrator's inability to accept Sonny's way of life. The narrator then explains the suffering he and his wife felt at the death of their daughter, suffering that made him want to write to Sonny at the treatment center and that finally began to make him appreciate the importance of having someone to talk to, a source of comfort in suffering.

In the final third of the story, the narrator and Sonny come to an understanding that seems to reconcile them. The narrator is very worried that Sonny will return to heroin. Sonny invites the narrator to hear him play piano with a group in a Greenwich Village club. When the narrator accepts this invitation, Sonny tries to explain why he took heroin. Heroin is a way to try not to suffer, a way to take control of inner chaos and to find shelter from outer suffering. Though he knows that ultimately heroin cannot work, he also knows that he may try it again. He implies that with someone to listen to him, he may succeed in dealing with "the storm inside" by means of his music:

> You walk these streets, black and funky and cold, and there's not really a living ass to talk to, and there's nothing shaking, and there's no way of getting it out, that storm inside. You can't talk it and you can't make love with it, and when you finally try to get with it and play it, you realize nobody's listening. So you've got to listen. You got to find a way to listen.

At the nightclub, the narrator understands what Sonny means when he finally hears him play. He sees that Sonny's music is an authentic response to life. He sees that one who creates music "is dealing with the roar rising from the void and imposing order on it as it hits the air." He understands that his brother's music is an attempt to renew the old human story: "For while the tale of how we suffer, and how we are delighted, and how we may triumph is never new, it always must be heard. There isn't any other tale to tell, it's the only light we've got in all this darkness." Having witnessed Sonny's struggle to play "his blues," the narrator recognizes that those blues are humankind's blues, that Sonny's music gives the narrator and all people a way of finding meaning in their pains and joys. This perception enables the narrator to accept his brother, the life he has chosen, and the risks he must incur.

Themes and Meanings

As the narrator feels united with his brother and, by implication, with all humankind in shared sorrows, he reflects, "And I was yet aware that this was only a moment, that the world waited outside, as hungry as a tiger, and that trouble stretched above us, longer than the sky." This opposition between moments of meaning in loving community and the terrifying, troubled, and apparently meaningless outside world pervades the story in theme and in technique.

The opposition appears in multiple guises. It appears in the housing project where the narrator lives, an attempt to impose order on the old dangerous neighborhood that fails when the project is transformed into merely a new version of the old dangerous neighborhood. The opposition is reflected in his memories of childhood, of being secure in families, not having yet to deal with the horrors of the world, and yet being aware even as a child, that with each passing moment, he came closer to having to live unprotected in the dark, chaotic world. It appears in the story of the death of his uncle: On a warm, beautiful night when the brothers were walking, enjoying each other's company, a wild car suddenly swooped over a hill, to destroy a beloved brother. For African Americans in the middle of the twentieth century, racism is another of the dark forces of destruction and meaninglessness that must be endured. Beauty, joy, triumph, security, suffering, and sorrow are all creations of community, especially of family and familylike groups. They are temporary havens from the world's trouble, and they are also the meanings of human life.

The narrator and Sonny have found alternative ways of making meaning and order. The narrator makes a literal family and a conventional career, as his father did. Sonny becomes an artist, one who expresses for himself and his community and to himself and his community the passions that unite them. By expressing these passions, giving them order in articulation and making them meaningful, he also makes and sustains a kind of family, a community of shared moments of meaning.

James Baldwin often deals with these themes in his fiction and other prose, especially with the problems of the black artist or intellectual trying to find or create a sustaining community.

Style and Technique

Baldwin emphasizes the theme of opposition between the chaotic world and the human need for community with a series of opposing images, especially darkness and light. The narrator repeatedly associates light with the desire to articulate or give form to the needs and passions that arise out of inner darkness. He also opposes light as an idea of order to darkness in the world, the chaos that adults endure, but of which they normally cannot speak to children.

The opposition of light and darkness is often paired with the opposition of inside and outside. Sonny's problem as an artist is that inside himself he feels intensely the storm of human passion; to feel whole and free, he must bring this storm outside by gaining artistic control over it, by articulating it for some listener. Inside is also the location of the family, the place of order that is opposed to outside, the dark and predatory world.

These and other opposing images help to articulate Baldwin's themes of opposition between the meaningless world and the meaning-creating community. The artist, by giving voice to the inner chaos of needs and passions, unites humankind in the face of the outer chaos of random and continuous suffering. The artist helps to create a circle of light in the midst of surrounding darkness.

Terry Heller

SOPHISTICATION

Author: Sherwood Anderson (1876-1941)
Type of plot: Psychological
Time of plot: The late 1890's
Locale: Winesburg, Ohio
First published: 1919

> *Principal characters:*
> GEORGE WILLARD, a young man on the threshold of adulthood
> HELEN WHITE, the banker's daughter

The Story

On a warm autumn evening in Winesburg, Ohio, throngs of county fair-goers laugh and shout, but a young man in his late teens or early twenties walks through the streets silent and withdrawn. He is George Willard, who has made up his mind to leave this small town and find a newspaper job in a big city, where life will not pass him by.

As he walks down Main Street, he is sad and angry, but does not know why. The omniscient narrator, who speaks from the attitude of an older, wiser man (who at times can only guess at what women are feeling), describes the moment when a young man becomes aware for the first time of his small place in the universe and of his approaching death. He calls this moment and this awareness "sophistication" and makes it clear that this kind of sophistication brings underlying sadness. George Willard is experiencing his first adult feelings.

As George the new adult walks along in his sorrow and loneliness, he thinks of his sweetheart, Helen White. A banker's daughter, she is the same age as George but attends college in Cleveland. She dresses well, goes to the theater, and is expected to marry a man from her own social class. On this day, however, she is tired of her social class and its expectations. She has spent the day with a young instructor from her college—this is the reason for George's anger—taking in the county fair and sitting with him on the porch, listening to him talk about himself. Helen is bored with his talk. She too feels newly grown-up and fears that no one has noticed. In her sorrow and loneliness, she longs for George Willard.

For a time it appears that the conflicts within George and Helen, as well as their immaturity in handling them, will keep the two from what they most want. George wants to be with Helen, but he is jealous of the instructor from Cleveland and too proud and angry to make the first move. Helen would prefer George to the instructor, but she enjoys the looks that she receives from friends at the fair as she sits beside the well-dressed stranger. Her mother has confided to the instructor that "there is no one here to associate with a girl of Helen's breeding."

Finally, George summons his courage and strides up to Helen's gate just as she slips out hoping desperately to see him. They walk along the streets, then sit together in the empty grandstand at the fairgrounds, but they find they do not know what to say to each other. They hold hands and kiss a little but mostly they hold each other silently and struggle to understand their own thoughts and feelings. For each of them, the company of the other is comforting, for reasons that neither can explain.

Without discussing it, they both find at the same time that they are ready to head back. Still without speaking, they stand and walk into the dark fields. For a moment as they near town they become children again, laughing and chasing each other down a hill. However, it ends abruptly, and they walk the rest of the way home in dignified silence. Somehow, the narrator explains, "they had both got from their silent evening together the thing needed."

Themes and Meanings

The penultimate story of Sherwood Anderson's *Winesburg, Ohio* (1919), "Sophistication" is one of the collection's few stories that was not published separately before the book appeared. The central figure in the book is George Willard, who encounters, one by one, the various incomplete and lonely people of the town whom Anderson calls "grotesques." Throughout these stories, George Willard is something of a constant; he seems young, healthy, and whole, and this is why the others are drawn to him to tell their stories.

As "Sophistication" opens, George is walking alone through crowds of laughing, excited people. In this initial image, Anderson presents his central theme, the lesson that George must learn: that the essential human condition is to be alone, and lonely. Throughout the rest of *Winesburg, Ohio*, George encounters one lonely figure after another, listening to them tell of their aloneness. George himself is often alone; he is not close to his parents, he seems to have no intimate friends his own age, and he feels different from everyone else. However, until this evening of the fair, he has never minded, never felt lonely.

At first he does not know what he is feeling. He is angry about Helen's being with the instructor instead of him, but he is unwilling to go to her house himself. He is eager to get out into the wide world, but he is beginning to realize that he will be just a speck in it. As he charges through town with his new, grown-up thoughts, he only wants someone to understand him.

He turns to Helen, who has a similar need. She, too, is feeling mature and alone and uncertain, and she wants to be with George so that he will see and understand the change in her. The yearning, Anderson shows, is a common enough one. Throughout George's life, lonely people have presented themselves to him, hoping that he would understand, but he does not.

This is what George and Helen learn on their walk. Significantly, they must walk out of town, away from the influences of their youth, to learn it. Although both feel the same loneliness, and although they are reaching for each other out of that loneliness, in the end they cannot fill that void for each other. Words are clearly insufficient, for they do not speak to each other at all. Passion is not what they seek, and their kissing is brief and unfulfilling. Instead, they sit together silently, holding each other and thinking private thoughts.

People are alone and lonely all their lives. The best one can hope for—and the thing that George and Helen share for this evening—is someone with whom to share one's loneliness. Once they come to understand this, they are ready to return to town, to get on with their adult lives.

Style and Technique

Because Anderson's work focuses on internal conflict and internal resolution, one would expect his writing to give more attention to internal than external matters in general. Even so, many critics have found it surprising that Anderson's sparse style offers so little in the way of descriptive details about location and setting.

The first sentence of "Sophistication" begins "It was early evening of a day in the late fall." The day of the week and the date are unspecified, as are the names of the berries that once grew in the dry fields, or of the stores that the people pass as they walk down Main Street. The implication is that for these people, one day is much like another, a field is a field, a store is a store. They do not notice details about their surroundings, and Anderson wants the reader to ignore them as well. What matters is what George—Anderson's Everyman—is thinking as he walks through Anytown, U.S.A.

George and the narrator do notice the most minute action and detail about the people in the town, however. The narrator describes the stickiness of sleeping children's fingers and the shining faces of young boys with their first sweethearts, but aside from a few dry leaves and interchangeable trees, there are no descriptions of nature. There is much noise, supplied by crying or shouting children, or fiddlers tuning their instruments, or horns blaring, but there are no birds singing or dogs barking. It is almost as though all these players were actors on a stage with no set.

Anderson is almost stubborn in his refusal to describe locations, even when moving around is the central action. All readers know about George and Helen's travels on that long-ago summer night is that they stopped "by a fence near a field of young corn." However, this walk is an important memory for both of them. Their walk this fall evening seems to cover considerable ground—they leave town, cross fields, climb and descend Waterworks Hill, and sit at the fairgrounds. However, these places form only the vaguest pictures in the reader's mind. By providing as few details about the terrain as possible, Anderson keeps the reader's attention focused entirely on the internal struggles of George and Helen.

Cynthia A. Bily

SORROW-ACRE

Author: Isak Dinesen (Baroness Karen Blixen-Finecke, 1885-1962)
Type of plot: Fable
Time of plot: About 1775
Locale: A Danish manor
First published: 1942

>   *Principal characters:*
>   ADAM, a young Danish nobleman returning to his ancestral home
>   after nine years in England
>   HIS UNCLE, the old lord of the manor
>   THE LORD'S YOUNG WIFE, Adam's step-aunt
>   GOSKE PIIL, a serf accused of setting fire to one of the lord's
>   barns
>   ANNE-MARIE, Goske's widowed mother

The Story

"Sorrow-Acre" opens with a leisurely description of the Danish landscape, and it is clear that the setting is to be as strong a character in this folktale as any of the humans populating its stage.

It is the end of the eighteenth century, and at the opening of the story, everything is still in its time-honored place, from manor house through the church to the peasant huts in the village. The winds of change are beginning to blow, however (the serfs will be freed here in 1887), and enlightened ideas from England and the Continent are just beginning to be heard in this semifeudal land.

Adam has been serving in the Danish legation to the court of King George, but now he has returned to his ancestral home "to make his peace with it." In his long absence, his sickly cousin and the heir to this estate has died, leaving Adam, for the moment, as the heir himself: The old lord has now married his son's betrothed, and he hopes to perpetuate his line with another son. During the day of the action of "Sorrow-Acre," Adam spends most of his time in the company of his young step-aunt, and the indication is that he himself will marry her after his uncle's death.

Early in the morning after his arrival, Adam is strolling the grounds and meets his uncle, who, in Adam's childhood, was a second father to him. The uncle is up early, even for this first day of the harvest, but, as he explains, "a matter of life and death" is being acted out that day. It seems that a young peasant has been accused of setting fire to one of the lord's barns. His guilt is not clear, for those who have accused him have reasons to be envious. Anne-Marie, the boy's mother, has intervened, however, and the lord has struck a bargain with her: If Anne-Marie can mow a field of rye by herself, her son will be freed.

When Adam returns that afternoon to the field where his uncle has remained all day, all other work has ceased, and the other peasants are following Anne-Marie in her slow and painful progress. Adam sees that she is close to death, and he urges his uncle to end this "tragic and cruel tale," but the old lord, who believes in the retributive justice of the old order and argues that "tragedy is the privilege of man, his highest privilege," refuses. "I gave Anne-Marie my word," he says simply. In anger, Adam says that he must leave the estate: "I shall go to America, to the new world."

At this very moment, when Adam has apparently given up any opportunity for reconciliation with his homeland, a strange pity takes hold of him. He sees his uncle as a tyrant close to death himself, a man who has lost his only son (as Anne-Marie is killing herself to save hers) and whose own semifeudal world is breaking up. Adam's "forgiveness" of his uncle leads to a "sudden conception of the unity of the universe" and "a surrender to fate and to the will of life." Adam tells his uncle that he will stay, and a clap of thunder sounds: "The landscape had spoken." Adam has been reconciled to his homeland; he now has a "feeling of belonging to this land and soil."

Adam returns to the manor house and does not witness the final act of this tragedy. Several minutes before sunset, Anne-Marie finishes the field, the old lord frees her son, and she dies in her son's arms. The story closes, as it has opened, with a sense of place:

> In the place where the woman had died the old lord later on had a stone set up, with a sickle engraved on it. The peasants on the land then named the rye field "Sorrow-Acre." By this name it was known a long time after the story of the woman and her son had itself been forgotten.

Themes and Meanings

"Sorrow-Acre" is based on a Danish folktale, and, like that older, didactic form, it carries overt lessons. Isak Dinesen has deepened the story's mystery and thereby made its meaning more ambiguous.

At the center of "Sorrow-Acre" is a debate, both real and dramatic, between two ways of life, the past and the present. The old lord is like a god in this aristocratic world, while Adam represents a newer, more liberal view and "the great new ideas of the age: of nature, of the right and freedom of man, of justice and beauty." Adam's view, surprisingly, does not prevail, and it is the uncle who is left at the end watching the close of this tragedy. Adam actually gains his reconciliation with the land by accepting his uncle's sense of justice and order. Eventually, the reader suspects, he may inherit this manor; for now, the old lord is still firmly in control. The reader's sympathy has similarly shifted from an easy identification with the modern ideas of Adam to a recognition of the essential harmony and unity of this almost medieval world.

However, nothing in Dinesen's work is ever so simple. A series of overlapping parallels deepens the mystery and tragedy of the story. Anne-Marie is toiling to save her son, which is exactly what the old lord was unable to do for his own. Ironically, Goske

Piil was his son's only playmate; now he is being accused of setting the fire by a wheelwright who suspects him "with his young wife" (as the reader suspects Adam with the young wife of the lord). Finally, Anne-Marie had another "child and did away with it." These overlapping parallels—actually triangles reminiscent of medieval religious paintings—deepen the structure of the story and reveal the complex web of human life.

This meaning is further complicated by the religious symbolism of the story. Adam is the "new man" returning to Eden, perhaps with the original sin of enlightened knowledge with him. His innocence, however, is no match for the justice of the old gods such as his uncle. Similarly, Anne-Marie is a Christ figure in her superhuman task of freeing her son (and humankind—the serfs will one day be freed) from the justice of the old order. Her effort lives on in the name of the field, "Sorrow-Acre," which is also a reminder of the agony and anguish of human life.

What Dinesen has done, in following out the fateful lines of human interaction and playing with their religious connotations, is make the meaning of the story ambiguous and complex. At the beginning, the reader naturally condemns the cruel notion of justice in this semifeudal society; by the end, the reader's sympathy has shifted and, as Adam senses, the order and harmony of this world seem to be acted out in the tragedy of Anne-Marie. It is not so easy, Dinesen is saying, to pass judgment on the past.

Style and Technique

Like the story's meaning, the form of "Sorrow-Acre" reveals its folktale origins but takes on the complexity of modern fiction. The story is divided into four parts. The opening section is a leisurely description of the Danish landscape and an exposition of all the elements of this medieval world. In the second part, Adam and his uncle meet and begin their debate. Part 3 is a romantic reprieve, a description of the lovely young mistress of the manor as she awakens alone and observes the fertility of this spring morning. The main action of the story takes place in the last part, where the two men argue, are reconciled, and then part, and where Anne-Marie's tragedy is played out.

If the pace of the story is almost stately, the descriptions are rich and passionate. Dinesen lingers over these figures in her landscape and, like some writing god herself, paints all the characters (including the setting) with equal fullness. The shift in the reader's loyalty, from an identification with Adam at the beginning to a recognition of the rightness of the lord's justice at the end, is carried off without calling attention to itself; even Dinesen's religious symbolism seems natural and unobtrusive in the unified fabric of her story.

Style, in short, helps to enhance the power and poignancy of "Sorrow-Acre." By the end of the story, most readers will agree with Adam: "For to die for the one you loved was an effort too sweet for words." Dinesen's words are exactly what make this story one of her most beautiful, as most critics agree—and as this passage on the last page amply illustrates:

At the sound of his voice she lifted her face to him. A faint, bland shadow of surprise ran over it, but still she gave no sign of having heard what he said, so that the people round them began to wonder if the exhaustion had turned her deaf. But after a moment she slowly and waveringly raised her hand, fumbling in the air as she aimed at his face, and with her fingers touched his cheek. The cheek was wet with tears, so that at the contact her fingertips lightly stuck to it, and she seemed unable to overcome the infinitely slight resistance, or to withdraw her hand. For a minute the two looked each other in the face. Then, softly and lingeringly, like a sheaf of corn that falls to the ground, she sank forward onto the boy's shoulder, and he closed his arms round her.

Like few other writers, Dinesen captures a moment of human tragedy and beauty in words.

David Peck

A SORROWFUL WOMAN

Author: Gail Godwin (1937-   )
Type of plot: Fable
Time of plot: The mid-twentieth century
Locale: Unspecified
First published: 1971

> *Principal characters:*
> A WOMAN, a young wife and mother who withdraws from her
>   family
> HER HUSBAND
> HER THREE-YEAR-OLD SON
> A BABY-SITTER

The Story

One winter evening a young wife and mother is sickened by the sight of her husband and child. The next day she looks at them and starts crying and retching. Her husband puts her to bed and gives her some sleeping medicine, letting her sleep through the following day. The next day she tries to resume her duties, but her young son, playing like a tiger, scratches her. At the sight of her blood, she locks herself in her room and calls her husband, who brings in a baby-sitter. Several nights later, she hits the child and throws herself on the floor, saying she is sorry. Realizing that his wife is sick, the husband hires a live-in baby-sitter.

The hired girl is highly energetic. She takes care of the child and household, jokes and dances, plays chess with the husband, and does the woman's hair. Meanwhile, the woman withdraws from family life, sitting in the big room in her old school sweater, reading novels. The husband renews their courtship and asks her out to dinner. Things seem to get better, until one afternoon when the girl brings the child to see his mother, and the child hands the mother a grasshopper that spits brown juice on her. The mother is distressed and tells the husband that the girl upsets her, so the girl is fired.

The husband rearranges his schedule so that he can fix the meals, take care of the household, and take the child to nursery school. The mother stocks her room with food and cigarettes and withdraws further from the family. Finally, she decides that she cannot even see them anymore and communicates with them through notes left under her door. Her husband continues to be understanding as she spends her time sitting in her room, brushing her hair.

One day she comes down from her room and bakes her family a loaf of bread. When she reads their notes of gratitude, she feels pressed into a corner. She suddenly starts working busily, cooking a sumptuous meal, doing laundry, creating paintings and stories, and writing love sonnets. Overjoyed, the husband flings back her door only to find her dead. The story ends with the child asking to eat the turkey dinner his mother has cooked.

Themes and Meanings

Gail Godwin is a feminist author who explores the trials and ordeals of modern women. In *Dream Children* (1976), a collection of her early short stories, she examines the lives of women who are disappointed, betrayed, and lost, women who are desperately trying to escape their unfulfilled lives. "A Sorrowful Woman," which comes from this collection, creates an ironic fable about a woman who can no longer accept her role as wife and mother, the role that patriarchal myths have defined as the proper role for women. Feminists have pointed out how women are trapped by a feminine mystique that holds them up as perfect nurturers and caretakers. To rebel against such a role was once diagnosed as a sickness. This trap or mystique is what the story's protagonist is fighting against, but she sees no alternatives, nor can she define or clearly express her problem. The sorrowful woman represents a type of woman who was not meant to be defined as a wife and mother and who finds herself trapped with no options. The fable maintains its sense of universality. The woman's problem is not created by a husband who is demanding and restrictive; the husband is all too understanding, and the child adjusts well to his separation from the mother. Their acceptance, however, only seems to put more pressure on her to conform to her role.

The remedies proposed to solve the woman's problems are all counterproductive. First, she seeks rest and reprieve from her duties, but a temporary respite is not the solution. Her problem is not overwork; it is the inability to accept her position. Even having a sitter come in to assume her duties does not relieve her from contending with her husband and child. Although she is eventually relieved of their physical presence, their written communications still hem her in.

Her life of withdrawal is equally unproductive. She puts on her old school sweater and escapes into novels, idling away her days and taking sleeping medicine to get her through the night. She seems to have no options open to her but withdrawal. Nevertheless, her withdrawal goes beyond the simple psychological problem of depression. Because the story gives no psychological reason for her withdrawal, it is clear that she cannot tolerate the role that has been given her, nor can she find herself in any other role. Her final attempt to return to her duties kills her, for she is trying to live out a role she can no longer sustain.

Gail Godwin tries to capture the confusion of modern women trapped in worlds they cannot control. "A Sorrowful Woman" is a simple parable that shows how a woman with narrow options unsuccessfully tries to escape her condition through withdrawal and isolation. It has many affinities with a classic piece of feminist fiction, Charlotte Perkins Gilman's "The Yellow Wall-Paper." In both stories, women try to escape the restrictions of family life. Both are upset and cannot see their children. The husbands in both stories seem to act in the best interest of their wives but only drive the wives into further isolation. The heroine in "The Yellow Wall-Paper" escapes into fantasy and madness; the woman in "A Sorrowful Woman" retrenches and works herself to death, exhausting her energies in trying to fit a role that does not suit her.

Style and Technique

The story is told in the form of an ironic fable. It begins with the simple fairy-tale opening: "Once upon a time there was a wife and mother one too many times." This opening introduces both the tone and the theme of the story. The fablelike tone is maintained in the author's terse style. The sentences are short and simple, and the overall tone is matter-of-fact and objective, adding to the irony of the situation. The nameless characters take on a universal or fablelike quality, and the immediate time and locale of the story are undisclosed. The understanding and self-sacrificing husband is "durable, receptive and gentle," a fairy-tale prince who is unable to save his wife. The child is a "tender and golden three," almost angelic. Even the young girl who is hired to take care of the child is described as perfect. The characters have an unreal quality as though they represent types, not real people. They set up the model of a perfect family, a model that the woman cannot accept.

The woman, who is suffering from depression, is described as a "cloistered queen" or a "young virgin in a tower." These fairy-tale images are also symbols of entrapment, for the virgin in the tower is often imprisoned, powerless, and waiting to be rescued. Other images of doom appear in the story. The woman focuses on the child's gray eyes and the husband's gray shirt. The playful child turns into a tiger whose "sharp little claws" rip the woman's flesh. As the wife looks out the window, she sees images of failure and violence: a boy repeatedly falling off of his new bike, a dog chasing a squirrel, and a woman foraging in garbage. All these images are subtle and underplayed, so the story never becomes gothic or moves into the thought patterns of a disturbed character. The story ends on a note of irony: As the exhausted woman lies dead, the child asks to eat the turkey dinner she has fixed.

Like such classic short stories as Herman Melville's "Bartleby the Scrivener" and Edgar Allan Poe's "The Fall of the House of Usher," "A Sorrowful Woman" is based on the gradual and inexplicable withdrawal of the main character from everyday life. The story also follows a seasonal pattern. It begins in winter, a time of death and withdrawal, and ends in spring, a time of renewal. The renewal is ironic, however, as the woman's attempts to return to family life lead to her death.

Paul Rosefeldt

SOUND OF A DRUNKEN DRUMMER

Author: H. W. Blattner (Hedwig W. Bried, 1916-   )
Type of plot: Domestic realism
Time of plot: Unspecified; apparently the 1950's or early 1960's
Locale: San Francisco, California
First published: 1962

> *Principal characters:*
> ELISE LYNCH, a beautiful, twenty-seven-year-old alcoholic
> RICHARD WRIGHTHILL, a wealthy businessman
> ROB, Elise's dearest companion, a German shepherd

The Story

Elise is speeding through San Francisco, alternately rambling on to Rob and sing-ing along with the radio. Rob, her trusted confidant and one true friend, is a German shepherd. Elise is bright, a college graduate with at least a smattering of foreign-language ability, but promiscuous, cynical, and self-deprecating. Her conversations with Rob reveal her childhood in a financially secure but disordered family with a phi-landering father. Her self-identity and self-contempt tie into her sexual abilities. She became sexually active in her teens and was briefly married in high school; she attrib-utes the fact that she got a college degree to having slept with one of her professors.

Elise is a classic beauty: golden hair, intensely blue eyes, perfect features, a lithe body, and flawless skin. Although she is twenty-seven years old, she looks like she is barely out of her teens. Men of all types find her irresistible, and she has made her way in life for some time as a mistress. Her current "owner," as she thinks of the men who support her, is Richard Wrighthill, a middle-aged married man with the resources to give her an expensive apartment, a maid, furs, and a new Cadillac convertible. Richard met her at the home of her former benefactor, Wimberley, a middle-aged man dying of cancer. Struck by her exquisite beauty, Richard immediately decided that he was in love. Wimberley, worried about what would happen to Elise when he died, suggested to her that it would be in her best interest to become Richard's mistress.

Richard convinced himself that Elise was as good and sweet as she was angelic-looking, although her constant drinking and apparent drug use—alluded to briefly—should not have been a secret. When they first discussed the possibility of her becom-ing his mistress, Richard effusively declared his love, while Elise alternated between coarse flippancy and a businessperson's regard for financial details. The next day she left Wim's home and moved into the elegant apartment that Richard leased in antici-pation of her consent.

Richard visited for only a few hours in the evenings, leaving Elise with a great deal of spare time to fill. Often she stayed up all night, drinking, going to wild parties at her neighbor Toni's, and driving drunkenly through town with Rob at her side. Existing mainly on vodka, coffee, and cigarettes, she began rapidly deteriorating—physically and emotionally.

After their arrangement had continued for several months, Richard confronted Elise about her association with Toni—whom he considered to be a bad influence—and Elise's drinking. When he said he had hoped that if he gave her enough rope she would straighten herself out, Elise—who had already attempted suicide at least once—snapped, "Richard, you're quite right. People like me should never be given any rope, they think it's to hang themselves with." Unmoved, Richard—who drank relatively little—accused Elise of being on the road to alcoholism, but she defiantly claimed she was already there. Richard's insistence that he would help her if she got into treatment meant nothing to Elise, who believed that his only motivation for wanting her to take better care of herself was to maintain her as a first-rate sexual partner.

After Elise convinced Richard that they should go out for dinner, he refused to let her order a cocktail, insisting that she concentrate on the meal he ordered for her. Her ravaged system, however, could not handle the rich food, so she rushed to the women's room to vomit. Convinced that Elise went to the bar to sneak a drink, Richard became coldly angry and drove her home in silence. When she tried to tease him out of his irate mood, while continuing to drink heavily, Richard's tone and attitude changed. He called her to him and violated her sexually with such ferocity that she was left bleeding and shaken.

Now that Richard has left, Elise dresses and drives off into the night with Rob, again drunkenly attempting suicide.

Themes and Meanings

The brief mention of Elise's relatives early in the story describes a severely dysfunctional family. She refers to her mother's being in a "constant state of two-mindedness, like having two heads," because of her father's infidelities. In contrast to Elise's sister, a conventional wife, mother, and member of the Junior League, Elise has become the black sheep of the family—following her father's example in her behavior, but splitting herself off from her feelings like her mother. Although in the 1960's, when the story was first published, child molestation and incest were closeted subjects, it is hard to read this story decades later without identifying them as a subtext.

H. W. Blattner's Elise is a strongly drawn character, overshadowing the other players in her life's drama. She is a tragic figure, cut off from her family, without any friends, contemptuous of the men who support her, and descending into drug- and alcohol-induced madness. Although she refers to herself several times as being well versed in sexual techniques, her sexual proficiency is never mentioned by any of the male characters, all of whom seem to be magnetized merely by her beauty. When Richard expresses dissatisfaction with her behavior, he refers to the fact that she will ruin her health and beauty; nevertheless, she believes he is only concerned that she may not be able to keep performing sexually.

There is no indication that Richard ever treated Elise cruelly before the final scene. At one point in Elise's musings, she reveals that Richard makes few sexual demands on her, having "his age and health in addition to his dignity to think about." Later, discussing Richard with a man whom she brings home from one of Toni's parties, she describes him as being mature, responsible, and a rescuer—"more daddy than sugar, actually." When asked if Richard loves her and is kind to her, she simply replies that he has never hit her, as one of the previous men had done. From the beginning, Richard refused to admit what Elise was really like; when they discussed her becoming his mistress and she bluntly referred to it as shacking up, he gallantly insisted that she spoke coarsely only because she was scared. By the story's climax, however, the delusions Richard has tried to maintain about Elise's inner beauty and goodness are blasted away, and he finally feels the same contempt for her that she feels for herself.

Rob, although a dog, is a true character in the story: He is the one creature in whom Elise can confide and on whom she can rely, the one creature who loves and trusts her unconditionally, and the only male whom Elise trusts and respects. Rob also represents to Elise a healthy, guilt-free attitude toward sex, in contrast to her crass, cynical approach to it and the shame and embarrassment that she believes most people feel about it.

Style and Technique

Anthologized in *Fifty Best American Stories, 1915-1965*, "Sound of a Drunken Drummer" is notable for its use of language and makes especially effective use of a limited omniscient point of view. Blattner captures the discordant rhythms of a frenzied mind warped by alcohol and sedatives. Rather than describing Elise's pain, Blattner makes her readers feel it. Confronting the jumbled, tangled, alcoholic reveries careening through Elise's head, the reader has the feeling of being inside a tortured, unsettled mind. The descriptions of Elise's passing out while driving and while walking Rob in the park create a vivid picture of a disoriented mind verging on total loss of control. The story's sequence of events is hard to untangle on first reading, putting the reader in a position similar to that of an alcoholic unable to keep the days and events straight.

Because of the point of view the author chose, Richard is a less clearly defined character than Elise. Seeing him only when he is with Elise, the reader must guess as to how much his concern for her deterioration is motivated by true caring and how much by the crass motives that she ascribes to him. This technique serves to reinforce for the reader Elise's insular disconnection from other people. Although there are many references to its San Francisco setting, the story's themes of sexual control and alcoholism are universal, transcending both location and time.

Irene Struthers Rush

THE SOUTH

Author: Jorge Luis Borges (1899-1986)
Type of plot: Magical Realism
Time of plot: 1939
Locale: Buenos Aires and the southern plains of Argentina
First published: "El Sur," 1944 (English translation, 1962)

> *Principal characters:*
> JUAN DAHLMANN, the secretary of a municipal library in Buenos
> Aires
> THREE YOUNG RUFFIANS
> AN OLD GAUCHO

The Story

Juan Dahlmann works in a library in Buenos Aires. Like many Argentines, he is of mixed heritage. His paternal grandfather was a German minister who emigrated to Argentina in 1871. His maternal grandfather was a famous Argentine military man who suffered a violent death at the hands of Indians on the frontier. In spite of Dahlmann's bookish lifestyle, he prefers to think of himself as more closely linked to his military-hero grandfather, "his ancestor of romantic death." Because of this, Dahlmann keeps some souvenirs that remind him of the more heroic side of his heritage. One of these is a run-down ranch in the South that belonged to his mother's family. Dahlmann is an absentee landowner, however, as his work at the library keeps him in the city.

Dahlmann's life changes dramatically on a February evening in 1939. Eager to examine a rare edition of *Alf layla walayla* (fifteenth century; *The Arabian Nights' Entertainments*, 1706-1708), which he has just obtained, Dahlmann elects not to wait for the elevator in his apartment building but instead rushes up the dark stairs, where he accidentally runs into the edge of an open door. The injury to his head is such that he is forced to spend several feverish days at home in bed. When he does not improve, he is taken to a sanatorium, where he endures a battery of neurological tests. Sometime later, the doctors reveal to him that "he had been on the point of death from septicemia." After several months in the sanatorium, he is told that he should go to his ranch in the South to convalesce.

Dahlmann sets out for the ranch, acutely aware that he who travels to the South "enters a more ancient and sterner world." Once on the train, he attempts to read his still-untouched copy of *The Arabian Nights' Entertainments*, but now, free of the sanatorium, he finds himself distracted by the "joy of life" and pays little attention to the book. He instead gazes out the window at the passing countryside. Though able to recognize much of what he watches go by, he is not intimately familiar with anything in this part of the country, for his firsthand knowledge of the region is "quite inferior to his nostalgic and literary knowledge." As the train moves deeper into the South, Dahlmann dozes.

Because of a ticket mix-up, Dahlmann is forced to disembark at a stop short of his destination. While waiting for further transportation to arrive, he decides to eat in the local general store. There he is harassed by three young ruffians. Though he does his best to ignore them, he is finally forced to acknowledge their taunts. He confronts them. One of them pulls a knife and challenges Dahlmann to a fight outside. When the store owner points out that Dahlmann is unarmed, an old gaucho, "a summary and cipher of the South," throws Dahlmann a dagger, which lands at his feet. Although he knows that he is no match for his opponent, Dahlmann picks up the weapon and, in so doing, accepts the challenge. He views his impending death as "a liberation, a joy, and a festive occasion," for were it between dying a violent and heroic death in the South and dying in the sanatorium, it is the more romantic death that "he would have chosen or dreamt." The story ends as Dahlmann, holding a knife that will probably be of little use to him, goes out to fight.

Themes and Meanings

This story focuses on several significant concerns in the fiction of Jorge Luis Borges. One of these is the Argentine concept of "the South." The southern region of Argentina has both a history and a reputation similar to those of the western region of the United States; the term "the South" carries virtually the same connotations for Argentines as the term "the Old West" does for Americans. Virtually every aspect of the region, from its landscape to its colorful characters to its code of honor, has been romanticized in music, literature, and film. As is the case of the American West, much of the truth about the Argentine South has been replaced by myth. At the same time, much of what is no longer true about the South is still held to be true by many Argentineans. It is the romantic, mythical vision of the region and of those who inhabit it that Dahlmann clings to while living in Buenos Aires. It is also that vision that draws this library employee to the region and compels him to stand up courageously to his aggressors, something he probably would not do under similar circumstances in the city.

Of more profound thematic interest in "The South" is the concept of "real" reality versus "imagined" reality. It is necessary to describe reality as either "real" or "imagined" in the world of Borges's fiction, for the author not only utilizes two types of reality but also deliberately makes little or no effort to distinguish between them. For example, "The South" can be read in two ways. A straightforward reading shows that Dahlmann indeed travels to the South, where he is about to meet a violent death at the hands of a challenger. Another reading, however, implies that Dahlmann never makes the trip at all but, in fact, dies in the sanatorium. This alternative reading suggests that Dahlmann's heroic death is only an illusion, a fever-induced dream, an imagined fulfillment (perhaps even at the point of his death in the sanatorium) of what he would like to have happen in real life. Here, as in other stories, Borges suggests that whether reality is "real" or only "imagined" does not matter; what does matter is the perception of that reality by the person or persons involved. Therefore, whether Dahlmann's heroic demise actually occurs or is merely self-delusion is of no real consequence to Dahlmann himself. In either case, he is allowed to die a death in keeping with the romantic image in which he likes to view himself.

Style and Technique

The technical strength of "The South" lies in the deliberately inserted elements that suggest more than one interpretation of the events presented in the text. The story contains several subtly presented clues that imply that Dahlmann's trip to the South is a product of his feverish delirium. All these clues are found in the second half of the story, which depicts Dahlmann's actions after his supposed release from the sanatorium. For example, when Dahlmann pets a black cat while waiting for the train, he thinks his contact with the cat is "an illusion." Once on the train, he feels as if he were "two men at the same time," one of these free to travel, the other still "locked up" in the sanatorium. The train ride itself is unconventional, as it appears to be a trip "into the past and not merely south." Later, Dahlmann thinks that he recognizes the owner of the general store, but he then realizes that the man simply bears a remarkable resemblance to an orderly at the sanatorium. When the ruffians begin to taunt Dahlmann, he is surprised to learn that the store owner already knows his name, even though Dahlmann has never entered the store in his life. Additionally, the gaucho who tosses Dahlmann the dagger is not a gaucho typical of the 1930's but one whose appearance is more in line with the protagonist's own romantic vision of the region. Finally, there are the words of the narrator as Dahlmann prepares to fight: "He felt that if he had been able to choose, then, or to dream his death, this would have been the death he would have chosen or dreamt." This statement is skillfully worded so as to leave open the possibility of both the "imagined" reality and the "real" reality.

These and other clues that Borges places in the story do not provide definitive evidence that what happens to Dahlmann once he appears to leave the sanatorium occurs only in the protagonist's imagination. They do indeed imply that such may be the case, but they stop short of fully supporting one version of the story and fully eliminating the possibility of the other. This lack of definitiveness is in no way an error, however. It is all perfectly Borgesian, totally in keeping with Borges's view of reality. Owing to the author's subtle clues, the story can be viewed as neither completely realistic nor completely fantastic. To support fully one version of the story would mean denying the existence of the other, thereby ignoring the author's suggestions about the nature of reality itself, for in Borges's fictional world anything is possible.

"The South" is a masterfully written narrative that can be appreciated both as a piece of realistic fiction and as an intriguingly subtle mixture of realism and illusion. It is a work that, because of its double-edged reality, adds another dimension to the term "Magical Realism."

Keith H. Brower

THE SOUTHERN THRUWAY

Author: Julio Cortázar (1914-1984)
Type of plot: Fantasy
Time of plot: About 1966
Locale: The main highway connecting southern France with Paris
First published: "La autopista del sur," 1966 (English translation, 1973)

Principal characters:

AN ENGINEER, who is in a Peugeot 404

A YOUNG WOMAN, who is in a Dauphine

TWO NUNS, who are in a 2CV

A PALE MAN, who is driving a Caravelle and who commits
    suicide

A COUPLE and

A LITTLE GIRL, who are in a Peugeot 203

TWO BOYS, who are in a Simca

TWO MEN and

A BOY, who are in 4 Taunus

AN ELDERLY COUPLE, who are in an ID Citroen

A FARM COUPLE, who are in an Ariane

A SOLDIER and

HIS YOUNG WIFE, who are in a Volkswagen

A TRAVELING SALESPERSON, who is in a DKW

AN OLDER WOMAN, who is in a Beaulieu

A FAT MAN, who is driving a Floride and who deserts

AN AMERICAN TOURIST, who is in a DeSoto

BLACK-MARKET DEALERS, who are in a Ford Mercury and a
    Porsche

The Story

"The Southern Thruway" begins with a traffic jam on the main highway back to Paris from southern France, on a summer Sunday afternoon. It seems to be a perfectly ordinary occurrence as cars slow to a crawl, stop, and start up again. The drivers and passengers look irritably at their watches and begin to exchange comments with those in neighboring cars. As the traffic inches along in increasingly infrequent moves forward, the same group of cars stays together and their occupants gradually become acquainted. Although written in the third person, the story focuses on the experiences and thoughts of an engineer in a Peugeot 404.

Rumors circulate as to the cause of the traffic jam:

No one doubted that a serious accident had taken place in the area, which could be the only explanation for such an incredible delay. And with that, the government, taxes, road conditions, one topic after another, three yards, another commonplace, five yards, a sententious phrase or a restrained curse.

The drivers stay in or near their cars, sweltering in the sun, waiting for the police to dissolve the bottleneck, impatient to move along and get to Paris. The cars continue to move ahead as a group, their drivers chatting to pass the time as they suffer "the dejection of again going from first to neutral, brake, hand brake, stop, and the same thing time and time again."

By the time night falls, the new rumors brought by "strangers" to their group seem remote and unbelievable. The group share food and drink; surreptitiously, they relieve themselves by the roadside. Time begins to blur; "there was so little to do that the hours began to blend together, becoming one in the memory."

The next day, they advance a few yards and continue to hope that the road will soon be clear. Again a stranger brings them hopeful news, but then they realize the "the stranger had taken advantage of the group's happiness to ask for and get an orange," and they become wary and more conscious of their cohesiveness as a group. The cars beyond their primitive commune are also forming themselves into survival units. Those in the group pool their food and water, choose a leader, and send out exploratory parties to seek supplies and information.

The members of the group adapt to their situation. Thefts of communal supplies are punished, care for the children and the ailing is arranged, and even a suicide (the strained man in the Caravelle) is taken in stride and the body sealed into the Caravelle's trunk with glue and Scotch tape. Days go by and the weather turns cold. Inexplicably, the farmers who live near the highway are hostile. They beat and threaten anyone who trespasses, and they refuse to sell food. "It was enough to step out of the thruway's boundaries for stones to come raining in from somewhere. In the middle of the night, someone threw a sickle that hit the top of the DKW and fell beside the Dauphine."

As winter sets in, new ingenuities are necessary. A Ford Mercury and a Porsche sell supplies, at a price, and people make warm clothes out of seat covers, fear for the lives of their car batteries, and huddle together. They help one another through times of desperation and illness. A doctor trudges through the snow to visit the sick. There is happiness in survival, in the security of repeated routines, and in the discreet alliances managed by many of them, including the engineer and the girl in the Dauphine.

With the coming of mild spring days, more sociable relationships with neighbors are restored. Human rhythms accord with the changing seasons: The girl in the Dauphine tells the engineer she is pregnant, and the old lady in the ID dies. Suddenly, "when nobody expected it anymore," traffic begins to move again, slowly at first and then faster. Yearning for Paris—for hot water and clean sheets and white wine— the drivers advance eagerly, but when the engineer looks over into the next lane, the Dauphine is no longer beside him. Trapped in the flow of various traffic lanes, the members of the commune are separated. The group is irrevocably dispersed as the cars move faster and faster, and the engineer realizes sadly that "the everyday meetings would never take place again, the few rituals, and war councils in Taunus's car, Dauphine's caresses in the quiet of night, the children's laughter as they played with their little cars, the nun's face as she said her rosary." The engineer tries to stop and find his friends, but it is impossible as the cars go racing along. He cannot believe that the simple communal joys are left behind as they rush along "at fifty-five miles an hour toward the lights that kept growing, not knowing why all this hurry, why this mad race in the night among unknown cars, where no one knew anything about the others, where everyone looked straight ahead, only ahead."

Themes and Meanings

Julio Cortázar bases his story on an experience common to everyone, a traffic jam, and on a common response: an impatient, exasperated "I feel as though I've been here for days." Well, speculates Cortázar, what if it were days, what if the figure of speech became literally true? The traffic jam becomes an emergency situation that brings out the best in everyone (leadership qualities, compassion, generosity, fairness) as the group collectively fights for survival. Stripped of possessions, of acquired social status and influence, of all the qualities and barriers that would normally isolate them from one another, the denizens of the freeway form close bonds with their companions. There is real satisfaction in contributing to the primitive tribal society where each member of the group has a function and is essential, where each member is cared for and recognized. Twentieth century technology is reduced to a collection of metal boxes and radios that cease to convey any message relevant to their actual situation. The individuals discover resilience and dormant primitive skills within themselves and take pleasure in this meaningful connection with their ancestral heritage. Positive human values are revealed when these superficial overlayers of materialism, technology, and the rush of contemporary life are stripped away. These are twentieth century men and women, and when traffic does move they must inevitably go with it, however regretful they may feel. The metaphors of the river (or highway) of life and the medieval dance of death (of which one is explicitly reminded by the sickle, symbol of death) are ones of inexorable progression; once cars enter the thruway they must move along to their destinations.

Style and Technique

The narrative device of the enclosure (placing the characters in a confining situation that isolates them) serves a variety of functions. The behavior of the characters as they interact with one another may be more easily observed in a situation in which there are minimal outside influences, ensured in "The Southern Thruway" by the hostility of the neighboring cars and farmers. The group is a microcosm of society in general; as in a medieval religious drama, also meant to symbolize the world, the characters include children, youths (the boys in the Simca), and old people, as well as representatives of the Church (the nuns), the military (the soldier), business (the traveling salesperson), professions (the engineer, the doctor), and farmers. It includes all aspects of the human life cycle, from conception (Dauphine's child) to death, both natural and suicidal. The situation encompasses summer and winter, hope and despair.

The technique of identifying individuals only by the names of their cars depersonalizes them and emphasizes their function in the microcosm. It recalls the origin of surnames, when people were called John the Tailor or Paul the Shoemaker. Thus, it is a part of the transition to a primitive communal world of basic need fulfillment where the inessential is stripped away, and "the girl in the Dauphine" becomes simply Dauphine. It is also appropriate to the highway world where driver and car are referred to as one unit ("Watch out for that Ford up there"), where identity is defined by the car. It is also a reminder of the depersonalization of the twentieth century world where individuals are labeled by their social security, registration, or hospital admission numbers.

The sentence rhythms are adapted to the events of the story. While the cars are still moving along, the long sentences flow along, broken by series of jerky clauses as the cars begin to stop and start. As the traffic speeds up at the end, again long breathless sentences hurtle the reader through the night toward Paris.

The traffic jam symbolizes the breakdown of twentieth century technology and the consequent rediscovery of age-old human instincts and values. With warmth and humor, the story presents an optimistic view of basic human nature. It contrasts twentieth century impersonality and hurry with a primitive tribal society and reflects on the differences, returning to the contemporary world in the end.

Mary G. Berg

SPECK'S IDEA

Author: Mavis Gallant (1922-   )
Type of plot: Social realism
Time of plot: The 1970's
Locale: Paris
First published: 1979

> *Principal characters:*
> SANDOR SPECK, a Parisian art dealer
> LYDIA CRUCHE, the widow of painter Hubert Cruche
> SENATOR ANTOINE BELLEFEUILLE, an art collector who owns a
>   collection of Cruche paintings
> SIGNOR VIGORELLI, a rival art dealer from Milan

The Story

As the story opens, Sandor Speck is locking up his art gallery in the Faubourg Saint-Germain neighborhood of Paris. He contemplates his respectable and conservative neighborhood and reflects on the melancholy rainy evening. Speck sits down to his solitary, simple dinner in a neighborhood restaurant and takes out his yellow pad and pencils. He begins to plan his May-June show. Paris art critics are hinting that the time has come, but for what? Speck believes he has the answer, a French painter, who lived from about 1864 to 1949, mostly forgotten, someone whom Speck can reintroduce to the art world. Speck is at work writing the artist's biography and a commentary on his work, envisioning the show. He is stuck, however, on the identity of the artist for his show.

Speck moves on to his meeting of the Masons. At the lodge, he rubs shoulders with the bankers, ambassadors, and politicians who are wealthy potential art buyers. On the sidewalk outside, he overhears Senator Antoine Bellefeuille speaking about the beautiful wife of the artist Hubert Cruche. Speck remembers that the wealthy senator has a house full of the paintings of Cruche. There is the answer to Speck's quest. Cruche overlaps to an astonishing degree with the painter in the yellow notebook and is just the sort of respectable, minor Parisian artist for whom Speck is looking.

Speck has a knack with artists' widows; he is tactful, courtly, and a good listener. A week later, Speck is sitting in the home of Lydia Cruche. He proposes a major Cruche retrospective, "just an idea of mine." He needs the widow's cooperation, for she is the owner of a studio full of her deceased husband's paintings.

Lydia proves difficult and elusive. She is willing to let Speck see the paintings, but she will not let him have them for the show. She reveals that she belongs to an obscure sect, the Japhethites, and believes that there is a commandment forbidding graven images. Speck is crushed. Business and the economy are in a decline. He badly wants and needs this show. He has already spoken to Senator Bellefeuille, who has shown Speck his personal collection of Cruches and agreed to sign the catalogue notes that Speck has ghostwritten, lending the prestige and status of his name and connections to the show.

Lydia Cruche appears to change her mind, and Speck goes back to her villa in the suburbs with paperwork in his briefcase, ready to negotiate an agreement with her. He finds a guest in her house, Signor Vigorelli of Milan. Lydia is now cordial and cooperative, helpful with details for the catalogue. However, Speck is crushed while driving home from the widow's house. He hears Signor Vigorelli on the car radio, discussing the rediscovery of Hubert Cruche!

Speck makes a U-turn, crashes his car into a tree, and begins to walk back to Lydia Cruche's house. She calmly admits that Signor Vigorelli, with her cooperation, is organizing a big Cruche show in Milan in March. Speck protests in dismay: Cruche is his idea. He insists that he must have the show first. Utterly defeated, he trudges to the bus stop to make his way home.

In another sudden reversal, Lydia appears at the bus stop and offers to let Speck be the first to hold a show. Milan is better for money, she says, but we are not talking about money, are we? Speck is confused but recovers quickly. Lydia has a talent for money, he realizes, and he is no match for her. His mind clears, "a yellow notebook fluttered and lay open at a new page." The show will likely go to Milan in the autumn now, he thinks. He begins to write a new note for his exhibit catalogue. Cruche will travel with Speck's blessing. He will sign this note himself. Cruche will cross borders and so will Sandor Speck.

Themes and Meanings

The primary theme of "Speck's Idea" is the effect of World War II on European history. Even though the story takes place more than twenty-five years after the war's end, its emphasis is on the fact that the war and its aftermath have left politics and views of history changed forever. The influence and ideas of fascism are present throughout the story and in the society within which Speck moves. Speck's wife, leaving him, hurls the label "fascist" out the window of the taxi. Later on, Speck shouts "fascist" at Lydia Cruche from the window of a bus.

Speck ponders history; he desires to understand it. He reflects "there was right and right. . . . Nowadays the Paris intelligentsia drew new lines across the past, separating coarse collaborators from fine-drawn intellectual Fascists." The Resistance is no longer chic. Speck himself is clearly seduced by the stability and respectability of conservatism. However, he is infinitely adaptable, regretting that his intellect tends to wander toward imagination, even metaphysics. Throughout the story, Speck changes his plans as needed. In fact, a remarkable aspect of the story is the opening premise that Speck is writing history to fit his own needs. He creates the artist's biography, then he finds an artist who fits the needed profile. However, he does not expect to sign his program notes. Speck will write history, but he will let a conservative and safe politician take credit for his work. Speck cares more about security than he does about asserting his identity.

Conservatism and fascism are connected with money and commerce throughout the story. Speck calls Lydia a fascist at the moment when he realizes that she is not a helpless, pathetic widow after all. In fact, she has a way with money; she has bested him in a business transaction. Money and business are more important than art to this art dealer. As he meditates on the changing definition of fascism, he considers the dreary economy and the declining art market. "His feeling for art stopped short of love; it had to." His attitude toward art is cool, efficient, and professional.

The story does end on a somewhat hopeful note, however, after implying that there is at least a bit of the fascist in each of the main characters. Lydia Cruche has a change of heart. "'Milan is ten times better for money than Paris,' she said. 'If that's what we're talking about. But of course we aren't.'" Speck begins to rewrite his notes once again, but this time he will sign them himself. In a moment of clarity, Speck takes credit for his idea, which now begins to transcend narrow-minded conservatism as the story ends with an image of crossing borders.

Style and Technique

Mavis Gallant's use of setting expresses the respectable conservatism of Speck's world. The Faubourg Saint-Germain neighborhood of Paris is described as a quarter marked by decaying aristocratic elegance. The gallery's only commercial neighbors are a restaurant that caters to lower-echelon civil servants and a bookstore "painted royal blue, a conservative color he found reassuring." Unfortunately this bourgeois respectability is cold; the antiquated heating system is useless, and Speck's gallery is bitterly cold. The image of the bookstore becomes increasingly menacing as Speck's hopes for his idea fade, and he ponders the changing meanings of fascism. What had once seemed calmly respectable takes on an aspect of violence.

An image of evening sadness follows Speck through the low points in his fortunes. As the story opens, Speck is groping for the idea that will carry him to financial security and respectability. He feels a "faint, floating sadness." "In his experience, love affairs and marriages perished between seven and eight o-clock, the hour of rain and no taxis." Later, when Speck has the idea of a Cruche retrospective, the rain has stopped. At another low point, when Speck reflects on the depressing economy and the changing attitude toward fascism, it is once again between seven and eight. At the moment when he hurls the label "fascist" at Lydia Cruche, he is standing at a bus stop on a cold, rainy evening. However, in the final image of the story, Speck has overcome the evening sadness. "He smiled at the bright, wet streets of Paris as he and Cruche, together, triumphantly crossed the Alps."

Gallant is noted for her meticulous use of language and precise details that allow space for complicated social nuances, a feature of "Speck's Idea." The story is long, thirty-eight pages, and the plot meanders, contributing to the mood of disorientation, confusion, and constant change that characterizes Speck's wandering fortunes. Although the style is realistic, the story demands a certain commitment of attention. It is as complicated as a miniature novel.

Susan Butterworth

THE SPINOZA OF MARKET STREET

Author: Isaac Bashevis Singer (1904-1991)
Type of plot: Psychological
Time of plot: 1914
Locale: Warsaw
First published: "Der Spinozist," 1944 (English translation, 1961)

> *Principal characters:*
> DR. NAHUM FISCHELSON, a doctor of philosophy
> BLACK DOBBE, a spinster

The Story

Dr. Nahum Fischelson is a Jewish intellectual who has studied in Switzerland and has achieved some fame as a commentator on the works of Benedict de Spinoza, the seventeenth century Dutch philosopher. As the story opens, Fischelson is a poor old man with a stomach ailment that the doctors cannot diagnose. He lives on an annuity of five hundred marks provided by the Jewish community of Berlin. In an attic room overlooking Market Street in Warsaw, he pursues his study of Spinoza's *Ethics*, brooding on the great philosopher's ideas about the divine laws of reason and about the infinite extension of God. He views the stars through his telescope, seeing in them examples of Spinoza's insight and vision, while below him in the street humankind, blind to Spinoza's sense of ethical propriety, pursues its finite passions.

The chaotic crowd on Market Street is composed of shopkeepers, peddlers, thieves, prostitutes, thugs, police officers, and drunks. Across the street, Jewish boys are toiling over books in the study house. Fischelson is remote from them all, having become more and more isolated over the years. When he first returned from Zurich as a doctor of philosophy, much was made of him in his community. He became the head librarian of the Warsaw synagogue and more than one rich girl was offered to him for marriage. He would not marry, however, preferring to remain as free as his idol Spinoza, and he lost his job as librarian because his ideas clashed with those of the rabbi. He supported himself as a tutor in Hebrew and German, but then he became sick and had to give it up. He no longer goes to the café as he had, for intellectual stimulation and the company of his peers. The Revolution of 1905, moreover, brought such chaos to the society with which he was familiar that it further isolated him. Ideas and even language have changed for the worse, as far as he is concerned, and the crowd-pleasing philosophy of the time infuriates him, despite Spinoza's warning against emotions.

Then World War I starts, and fear is added to Fischelson's illness. Military convoys pass through Market Street, and his subsidy from Berlin is abruptly cut off. He returns to the café he once frequented, but no one there is familiar to him. He seeks out the rabbi of the synagogue where he was head librarian, but the rabbi and his wife have left, ostensibly on vacation. He considers suicide, but he remembers that Spinoza equates it with madness. Thinking that the world has gone mad, he takes to his bed, convinced that his own end is near. He has a confusing dream then about being ill as a boy, being kept away from a Catholic procession passing by his childhood house, and about the end of the world.

At this point, Black Dobbe, an ugly spinster who lives next door to him in the attic, enters his room to get him to read a letter to her from her cousin, a shoemaker who emigrated to New York. Black Dobbe used to peddle bread in the street, but she quarreled with the baker and now sells cracked eggs there. She was engaged three times; each time, though, the engagement was broken. The two boys she was going to marry backed out, and the rich old man to whom she was engaged turned out to be married. She has a low opinion of men—not simply because of her bad luck with them, but because she knows how the underworld on Market Street treats women, sometimes kidnapping them to be prostitutes in foreign countries, a fate she herself once escaped.

At first thinking that Fischelson is dead, Black Dobbe throws a glass of water in his face when she discovers that he is not. She undresses him and makes his bed, then cooks soup for him and cleans his room, which she finds already tidy. That evening she cooks for him again and, though briefly imagining that he might be in league with evil powers, asks him if he has converted from Judaism. He says no.

Fischelson's health takes a turn for the better. Black Dobbe continues to visit him and cook for him. She keeps him up to date on the progress of the war, and he, having told her about his own background, questions her about hers. This is the first time that anyone has ever done this to her. When Fischelson asks her if she believes in God, she says that she does not know. He says that he himself does, and that God's presence is not restricted to the synagogue. Black Dobbe then shows him the trousseau she has collected and carefully preserved.

A short time later, Fischelson and Black Dobbe, much to the amusement of the neighbors who attend the ceremony in the rabbi's chambers, are married. That night, despite his prior warning to Black Dobbe that he is an old man in ill health, Fischelson makes love to her with the feeling and vigor of a young man. Afterward, while she sleeps, he looks at the stars out his window as he did at the beginning of the story, and as he concentrates on the aspect of heat, diversity, and change in Spinoza's divinely determined universe, he asks the spirit of the great philosopher to forgive him for giving in to the world of passion—this source, it seems, of joy and health.

Themes and Meanings

At the heart of this story is the conflict between the world of ideas and the world of passion, between the rational and the irrational, the ideal and the actual, the mind and the body, eternity and time. Fischelson and Black Dobbe dramatize both sides of this equation—Fischelson the intellectual side, and Black Dobbe the physical and emotional. Isaac Bashevis Singer painstakingly shows that each side needs the other, especially that the mental requires its opposite for survival. Fischelson's problem is that he has isolated himself in the ideal through his all but idolatrous devotion to Spinoza, and in so doing—in not paying attention to the other side of his humanity—he has become ill. The story makes a point of showing that his illness has no physical source; that is, his commitment to the mind has caused it, for the doctors whom Fischelson consults cannot attribute his chronic indigestion and stomach pains to anything more concrete than a nervous disorder. Fischelson emphasizes the general over the specific, thereby neglecting many of his needs as a specific human being, and it is this emphasis that provides the context for his impending death. He decides that he is dying, not because of something he has done as an individual but because the Great War has started. His logic is that if destruction has come in general, then his own life is finished. In short, he sees survival in general, not personal, terms.

Black Dobbe, on the other hand, has not had the luxury of looking at life and survival as Fischelson does. She is not supported by a subsidy as he is, and without the support of a man or the backing of a family, it has been particularly difficult for her to make her way in the world as a woman. She has had to rely on the nonintellectual virtues of thrift, courage, and persistence, and on her practical knowledge of how life in the gutter operates, to stay alive. Fischelson can afford to die because death for him is an escape from the chaos of a life from which he has long been traveling away. Black Dobbe cannot afford to die, for life is all that she has.

What Black Dobbe has done is to bring life itself to Fischelson—not life from the point of view of Spinoza's God, but life as it is lived by God's tumultuous creatures. The marriage of Fischelson and Black Dobbe, absurd as it may seem at first, is no more absurd than life itself, which is paradoxical, confusing, and difficult. Moreover, the marriage of these two characters is the story's way of suggesting that human contact, passion, and love define human life at its best.

Style and Technique

One of the major devices of *The Spinoza of Market Street* is the placement of the main characters in a way that dramatizes their condition. Fischelson lives in a room high above the street, cut off from its turmoil, and Black Dobbe lives in a room cut off from sunlight. Fischelson lives between the sky and the earth, descending to the latter only once a week to buy his food, preferring to look at the former through his telescope. The light of vision, of intellectual insight, comes through his window, as it were. Black Dobbe has no window, no intellectual light, and she spends most of her time down in the street, struggling to make a living, her feet firmly on the earth. Fischelson's room, however, is the more important of the two rooms in the end, for it does more than embody isolation. It helps to highlight the fact that man is neither a beast (as the events in the street below seem to assume) nor divine (as the events in the night sky seem to suggest to the mind), but in between. Fischelson's room is where the two extremes meet, bringing new life to the philosopher and a sense of value and meaning to the ignorant peddler. Viewed as a stage, Fischelson's room is where the two components of human destiny—the need to eat and feel and the need to envision life's meaning—play out their importance to each other.

Mark McCloskey

SPIRIT WOMAN

Author: Paula Gunn Allen (1939-   )
Type of plot: Fantasy
Time of plot: The 1970's to 1980's
Locale: San Francisco
First published: 1983

> *Principal characters:*
> EPHANIE, a Native American woman living in San Francisco
> THE SPIRIT WOMAN, a vision who appears to her

The Story

Ephanie, a woman of unspecified age and circumstance, is a Native American living in San Francisco. One morning, she is awakened by the presence of a shadowy form, cloaked in a swirl of vapor, at the foot of her bed. The form slowly assumes the shape of a woman, small, with "something of bird, a hawk perhaps, about her." Her eyes have a strange gleam, and her clothes and appearance are those of a traditional southwestern Pueblo Indian woman. Her hair is cut traditionally, falling in a straight line from crown to jaw, forming perfect square corners on either side, with straight bangs cut at the eyebrows, in the ancient arrangement that signifies the arms of the galaxy, "the Spider." She wears a finely woven shawl, embroidered with spider symbols, and buckskin leggings wrapped around her calves. The woman announces that she has come to tell a story, one that Ephanie has long wanted to hear.

Knowing that this is no mortal visitor but a spirit woman, Ephanie raises herself in her bed and performs the traditional ritual of greeting, the sign of the sunrise, by taking a pinch of corn pollen between her fingers and thumb and opening them as though to free the pollen.

The spirit woman begins to speak, chanting the creation story of the Keres people. Old Spider Woman—known also as Sussistinaku, Thinking Woman, because she creates by thinking things into existence—is the creator of the world. First she creates two sisters to help her, and she structures her creation in the pattern she brings with her from the center of the galaxy, a pattern of corners, turnings, and multidimensional arrangings that "is the sign and the order of the power that informs this life and leads back to Shipap," the home of Iyatiku (Corn Woman), the goddess who governs the spiritual affairs of the Keres people.

Next, the spirit woman explains the relationships and natures of the Keres deities. After Sussistinaku created her two sisters, Uretsete and Naotsete, Uretsete was known as the father, Utset, because Naotsete had become pregnant and had a child. Uretsete is the woman who was known as father, the Sun, and Naotsete is the Woman of the Sun. Iyatiku is another name for Uretsete, and "The One was the unity, the source, Shipap, where Naiya ['our dear mother'] Iyatiku lived."

In the patterns of the spirit woman's stories, Ephanie finds something that she has long sought, a truth and a meaning, an imperative to shape her life in the ancient manner. In addition to explaining the origin and nature of the universe to Ephanie, the spirit woman gives her a prophecy. She explains that the time of ending is coming to Indians, but tells her not to weep, because this is as it should be. In the Keres story of the origin of humankind, humans evolved through a series of four underground worlds before emerging on the earth's surface in this, the fifth world. The spirit people will now leave this world and go on to another place, the sixth world.

The spirit woman explains that there is another earth, almost like this one, but with a new way of looking at reality that is more valid, more real, more vital than the old way. She says that she is in that other world, where there is also a San Francisco, but a different version of the place than the one Ephanie inhabits. She invites Ephanie to visit her in her city. She is confident Ephanie will like it there, and will be surprised to see that there is no death—life and being are the only truth.

Long ago, the people knew death was not possible because they could actually see the person make the transition, leaving the flesh behind, like seeing a person strip off clothes. Then Old Coyote, the Keres trickster figure, said there would be death: Instead of seeing the whole transformation in its entirety, people would see only the body, first alive, then still. The spirit woman tells Ephanie that she must jump and fall into the new world just like Anciena, the sky woman of Iroquois myth, who fell through a hole in the sky and began the human race on earth. With this, the spirit woman seems to dissolve, and Ephanie sleeps and dreams.

Prompted by the spirit woman's visit, Ephanie dreams of women who lived long ago, who knew magic, directed people on their true life paths, and healed them. These were the women of the Spider Medicine Society, "the double women, the women who never married, who held power like the Clanuncle, like the power of the priests, the medicine men. Who were not mothers, but who were sisters, born of the same mind, the same spirit. They called each other sister." Ephanie's room begins to fill with shapes, which turn into women who sing and dance in the ancient way. Ephanie picks a heavily embroidered shawl from the bottom of her bed, wraps it around her shoulders, and joins the dance.

Themes and Meanings

Although "Spirit Woman" constitutes the conclusion of Paula Gunn Allen's novel *The Woman Who Owned the Shadows* (1983), its self-contained unity justifies its separate treatment as a short story. In it, Allen develops her own idiosyncratic interpretation of traditional Keres myths, especially those dealing with creation and death. Through the character of Ephanie, Allen demonstrates the need for a return to the principles, if not the exact rituals, that patterned ancient Native American life. Although most of her myths come from her own Keres people, she imagines these principles as being pervasive throughout pre-Columbian North America.

Most notable among these principles is that of matriarchy. Allen has argued that traditional Indian cultures across the continent were originally gynocentric and matrilineal. The Keres creation story told by the spirit woman to Ephanie pictures Thinking Woman as the first creator, and sees her two sisters (Uretsete and Naotsete) as containing within themselves both male (Utset/the Sun) and female (Naotsete/the Woman of the Sun) natures, making the male a derivative of, and secondary to, the female.

A second theme is the idea that the essential relationship for any woman to achieve is not that of wife or mother but that of sister. It is through her discovery of her sisterhood with the women of the Spider Medicine Society and her participation in their ritual dance that Ephanie finds the true meaning and purpose of her existence. The story concludes with the words of the song, "I am walking—Alive . . . I am Entering—Not alone," indicating that Ephanie has found true life and meaning in the company of women.

Style and Technique

Allen is of mixed Keres, Sioux, and Lebanese heritage, and was brought up at the Keres pueblo of Laguna in New Mexico. Allen's fiction derives not only from Keres beliefs and myths, but also frequently, as in "Spirit Woman," incorporates into the plot materials from the oral tradition, such as the creation story and the explanation of Coyote's responsibility for the entry of death into human experience. The story's structure is that first the myth is presented, followed by Allen's interpretation and the application of that interpretation to the life and situation of the story's main characters.

The physical action of the story is minimal: waking, a gesture of greeting, a dream, a final physical and spiritual waking. The sentences tend to be short and fragmentary, the diction simple and straightforward, but the content is influenced heavily by surrealistic techniques, as when Ephanie's room "filled with shadows. And the shadows became shapes. And the shapes became women singing. . . . With her shawl wrapped around her shoulders in the way of the women since time immemorial . . . she joined the dance. She heard the singing. She entered the song."

Dennis Hoilman

SPLIT CHERRY TREE

Author: Jesse Stuart (1907-1984)
Type of plot: Coming of age
Time of plot: The 1930's
Locale: Rural Kentucky
First published: 1939

> *Principal characters:*
> DAVE SEXTON, the narrator, a high school student in rural
>   Kentucky
> LUSTER (PA) SEXTON, his father, a feisty backwoods Kentucky
>   farmer
> PROFESSOR HERBERT, his principal

The Story

The title of the story identifies the incident that animates the action of this masterful piece of short fiction. Dave Sexton, together with five of his classmates, climbs a neighbor's cherry tree to capture a lizard while on a field trip with his high school biology class. The tree is broken and the six boys must pay for the damage. Unfortunately, Dave Sexton is unable to come up with his dollar. The principal, Professor Herbert, contributes the money for Dave but makes him stay after school to work off the debt. It is at this point that the story begins.

Dave would rather take a whipping than stay after school, because he must help his father with the farm chores. Professor Herbert, however, believes that Dave is too big to be punished in this fashion. When Dave gets home two hours late, Luster Sexton, Dave's father, is furious with his son, as well as with the high school principal, modern education, and society in general. Luster vows to go to school with Dave and put a stop to such foolishness as "bug larnin'." He declares, "A bullet will make a hole in a schoolteacher same as it will anybody else." Before Luster leaves with his son the next morning, he straps on his gun and holster.

Naturally, Luster causes a commotion in the school with his rustic ways and his revolver. He confronts the principal and, after placing his gun on the seat beside him, demands an explanation. Professor Herbert is taken aback and then explains that he had no other choice than to punish Dave in the way he did. He also tells Luster that education has changed since the days when he attended school. When Herbert offers to show Luster what really goes on in high school, he accepts, accompanying the principal on an extended tour for the whole day, and eventually showing up in his son's biology class, where he sees germs under a microscope for the first time.

In the end, Luster understands that the world has changed considerably from the time when he was a boy, and that there is a need to learn more than "readin', writin', and cipherin'.'" When Professor Herbert excuses Dave from the two hours of work yet remaining from him to pay his debt, Luster will not hear of it. So changed is his attitude that he volunteers to help his son sweep the school, insisting now that Dave get all the education he can.

Themes and Meanings

This story demonstrates Jesse Stuart's concern with both the education of and the difficulty of life for rural Americans, especially those out of the mainstream of cultural change. While the story seems on the surface to be about Dave Sexton, it is really the story of Dave's father, Luster: the inappropriateness of his untutored response to the modern world, his anger caused by ignorance, and his willingness to change when given the opportunity to see the facts for himself. Stuart sympathizes, and would have the reader sympathize, too, with those who hold on to ways of life that are no longer quite appropriate—especially if their roughshod ways are redeemed by virtues that tend to be undervalued in more recent times. Luster represents country folk in general. He is ignorant and stubborn, but he is not unreasonable and uncompromising. He finally comes to recognize the value and the importance—indeed, the necessity—of the kind of education his son is receiving, especially Dave's more detailed knowledge of the natural world. The isolation of rural life quickly makes social knowledge obsolete, but it nevertheless keeps those who lead this life in contact with the more elemental knowledge of life and death, of honesty and virtue.

Dave represents young people in rural society. He lives in two worlds at the same time: the outdated world of his parents and the more current world of his school environment and friends. His struggle, the tension of his character, is to keep these two worlds together, functioning harmoniously. That he is willing to do so, that he makes such an effort to lead both lives successfully, is a sure sign of Stuart's optimism and his faith in the young.

In one sense, Stuart's "Split Cherry Tree" is an example of a recurring fictional pattern, the coming-of-age story. Frequently in this pattern, adolescents must solve problems of sexuality or identity in order to become fully functioning adults, though other problems of adulthood are common in this form. For example, many of Ernest Hemingway's young characters learn to deal with the existence of evil. Stuart's variation on the coming-of-age theme requires Dave to solve the dilemma of the old versus the new, the home and the world. In resolving this conflict, Dave becomes ready to assume a more mature place in both his family and society.

Above all, Stuart is concerned with the lives of those about whom he writes. In literary terms, this concern makes him a writer who emphasizes character above either plot or theme, though in this story all three elements are superbly coordinated, a major reason why "Split Cherry Tree" is one of Stuart's best.

Style and Technique

Although the coming-of-age theme is important in understanding the meaning of this story, it is Stuart's handling of character that has made "Split Cherry Tree" one of the classics of the American short-story form. Luster, for example, is finely delineated. For the story to be successful, the reader must see him as a man who is fully capable of carrying out the violence that his threats against Professor Herbert promise. Without that element in his personality, the reader would know far too early that the story is going to have a happy ending, and the drama of the tale would be lost. At the same time, Luster cannot appear so violent and unregenerate that he becomes an out-and-out villain, for this would completely destroy Stuart's theme and ruin his aim of developing sympathy for rural people. Stuart strikes this subtle balance in Luster Sexton's character with a masterful handling of details. Most essential, he imbues Luster with a strong sense of justice and fair play, and this characteristic is evident in Luster's early tirade against the school and its principal.

By building in this trait from the beginning, Stuart prepares the reader unconsciously to see the positive side of Luster's character, which will gain much more prominence in the ending. Luster's character is further enhanced by his love of the natural world. The only thing that he cannot finally forgive about the new school is its killing and dissecting of black snakes. When Professor Herbert offers to chloroform and dissect a snake to show Luster that germs are to be found everywhere, Luster urges him not to, explaining that he does not allow people to kill them on his farm. Dave, the narrator, notices that "the students look at Pa. They seem to like him better after he said that."

Without this sort of careful preparation for the reversal of the reader's attitude toward Luster in the closing part of the work, "Split Cherry Tree" would have the kind of trick ending that mars the work of lesser writers, the kind of endings that feature prominently in some of the weaker stories of O. Henry.

Customarily, the short-story form does not allow writers the freedom to tell stories in which a change of character (or a different interpretation of character by the reader) is featured so prominently. That sort of narrative is usually the province of the novel, which, because of its greater length, can show a gradual change of personality over time. It is a mark of Stuart's mastery of technique that he is able to encapsulate a trait of the longer form and use it with success in a short story.

The character of Dave is also finely drawn. As stated earlier, he lives simultaneously in both the contemporary world and the outdated world of his parents. Were he completely to reject the values of his family—more specifically, to rebel against his father's country ways and attitudes—the story would not be able to carry its meanings and themes. Instead, Stuart places Dave at the fulcrum of both value systems. Dave is embarrassed that his father goes to school with him, but he is not mortified at his father's presence in the high school. Dave enjoys a wider social sphere than his parents.

While Dave seems to enjoy learning as well, especially learning about nature, he does not reject the farming life that nurtured and formed him. On the other hand, he is not solely the child of his parents; the modern world has a strong appeal for him, and he wants to participate in it as fully as he wants to maintain his contact with the hearth and the hollows of his native Kentucky. In the end, his father's acceptance of the school and its modern ideas is a victory for Dave, for it allows him to live a richer, more complete life—sharing the love of his family and enjoying the fruits of the contemporary world as well.

Stuart took an incident he had heard about when he himself served as the principal of a rural Kentucky school and transformed it, through his genius in creating character, into a struggle between the old and the new, the familiar and the exciting. In doing so, Stuart used the short-story technique he had mastered so well, pinpoint characterization, to create a tale in a style that was distinctively his own—masterfully orchestrated, spare of ornamentation, and tightly focused on the lives and tribulations of rural Americans, a group he knew and loved.

Charles Hackenberry

SPOTTED HORSES

Author: William Faulkner (1897-1962)
Type of plot: Realism
Time of plot: The early twentieth century
Locale: Mississippi
First published: 1931

> *Principal characters:*
> FLEM SNOPES, the owner of the horses and one of the principal
> personages in the town of Frenchman's Bend
> BUCK HIPPS, his partner
> HENRY ARMSTID, an unlucky purchaser of one of the horses
> ECK SNOPES, the cousin to Flem and another purchaser of a horse
> VERNON TULL, who is injured by one of the runaway horses

The Story

Flem Snopes returns to Frenchman's Bend after an absence of many months in Texas, accompanied by Buck Hipps and a string of wild spotted horses. The horses are confined in a lot next to the town hotel and put up for auction. On the day of the auction, people from the farms and surrounding countryside gather around the lot but at first are generally reluctant to bid on the animals, which have several times shown that they are unbroken and frankly dangerous. Hipps taunts the audience to no avail but finally succeeds in getting the auction going by giving Eck Snopes one horse for free if Eck will agree to purchase another for five dollars. At this moment, Henry Armstid arrives and demands to be allowed the same terms as Eck, but ends up bidding five dollars for another of the wild animals. Mrs. Armstid begs Hipps not to take her husband's money because it is the last five dollars they possess.

The auction proceeds until all the horses are spoken for and Hipps has collected all the money. When Mrs. Armstid renews her plea, Hipps tells her that she should apply to Mr. Snopes on the following day for the money. In the meantime, the new owners of the horses have gathered to put ropes around the necks of their latest purchases, but the lot gate is left open, and the horses escape and go running through the town and on into the countryside. One of Eck's horses encounters the Tulls crossing a bridge and causes Vernon Tull to fall off his wagon and receive serious, though not fatal, injuries. The rest of the horses, with the exception of the one that Eck purchased (which is upended and breaks its neck), escape, and no one is able to retrieve either his horse or his money. Mrs. Armstid applies to Flem Snopes for the five dollars promised her by Hipps, but Snopes assures her that he never owned the horses and that he does not have her money—although the story is generally disbelieved by everyone in the town.

Ultimately, court suits are brought against Flem and against Eck for reckless endangerment and for damages suffered as a result of the horses' having gotten loose.

None of the suits is successful, however, since ownership of the horses is denied by Flem (with another cousin's corroborating testimony), and the judge rules that since the horse that did the damage to the Tulls was given to Eck and his possession of it was never established (since he never actually was in control of it), in the eyes of the law, Eck technically never owned the horse and thus could not be held liable for any damage inflicted by the animal. The story comes to an end with the adjournment of the court and the judge in exasperation, but with Flem presumably having received the profits from the sale of the horses—although, as another Faulkner character, V. K. Ratliff, might have said, "That ain't been proved yet neither."

Themes and Meanings

"Spotted Horses" is among a series of short stories that William Faulkner wrote from the late 1920's to the end of the 1930's and that would subsequently become part of his trilogy of novels about the rise and fall of Flem Snopes and the general infestation of the country by the Snopes family. First published in 1931 in *Scribner's Monthly*, it was later incorporated in the fourth section of *The Hamlet* (1940), entitled "The Peasants." By itself, the story is a riotous comic portrayal of a shady horse deal, but positioned near the end of *The Hamlet* at the point at which Flem is about to complete his takeover of Frenchman's Bend before moving on to the town of Jefferson, it assumes ominous overtones that are only weakly apparent in Flem's ruthless treatment of Mrs. Armstid.

The horses themselves are several times referred to as "that Texas disease," and it is the image of plague sweeping over the countryside that dominates this and other of the stories in the Snopes saga. Faulkner himself once compared the arrival of the Snopeses to a plague of locusts, and it is clear that he himself viewed the rise of Flem Snopes to a position of power with something like the alarm evinced by V. K. Ratliff, the itinerant sewing machine sales representative who opposes Flem throughout the three volumes in which he figures. The story of the wild horses, symbolizing the unleashing of chaos on the world of the novel, resonates with the earlier comic episode in the novel, related by Ratliff, in which Ab Snopes (Flem's father) is bested in a horse trade by the incomparable Pat Stamper, a legendary trader never known to have been defeated in a deal for anything that walks on four legs. The signal difference between the two episodes, however, lies in the intent of Ab merely to redeem the honor of the land by besting Stamper in a trade, in comparison to Flem's wish simply to acquire as much money as he can as quickly and efficiently as possible.

The two different stories thus illustrate two different historical and socioeconomic periods in the world of the novel: a precapitalist moment of barter economy, as opposed to the properly capitalist world of the cash nexus. The career of Flem Snopes is Faulkner's most telling version of the emergence of the petty bourgeois class that came to dominate the South in the wake of Reconstruction and the transformation of the southern economy from an agrarian-based to a partially industrialized one. Faulkner's great theme, the betrayal of the natural virtues of the land for the sake of financial gain, is depicted here in its most naked form. The abandonment of the moral

economy of the precapitalist world is something that Faulkner consistently condemned, and Flem Snopes is merely the most infamous incarnation of a character-
type that Faulkner frequently realized: the ruthless entrepreneur.

Style and Technique

Faulkner's prose is legendary for its complexity and its violation of the ordinary
constraints of syntax. In addition, as has often been remarked, Faulkner captures the
idiom of the southern rural poor with great acuteness, reproducing not only their diction and pronunciation but also the very rhythms of their speech.

"Spotted Horses" is unusual among most of the other episodes in *The Hamlet* for
not featuring V. K. Ratliff, the archetypal raconteur who figures prominently in early
sections and who is generally on hand to attempt to prevent Flem's doing grave harm
to the community. His steadfast refusal to intervene in this episode, even on behalf of
the Armstids, differentiates this section from the others thematically, as the episode is
distinct technically for its placing Ratliff largely to the side of the action. One can surmise that this relative absence of Ratliff from the action suggests something about the
stage in the plot that has been attained at this point. It is plausible to read here the beginning of the end, in this novel at least, for any principled attempt to stop the onward
march of the Snopeses into the country. The next and final episode in *The Hamlet* involves Ratliff's being easily bilked by Flem into purchasing a worthless piece of property and thereby providing Flem with his entrée into the town of Jefferson. Thus, the
temporary disappearance of Ratliff from the foreground of the narrative would seem
the preliminary to the ultimate triumph of Flem over the community of Frenchman's
Bend.

The story itself harks back to a long tradition of tall tales and Western humor, of
which Mark Twain is probably the most representative and famous figure. The hyperbole in Faulkner's descriptions of the horses derives from this tradition, as does the
general tone of comic excess. Faulkner's humor, like that of Twain, is scarcely innocent, and the inordinate violence that the story depicts is allowed full scope when the
reader finds himself roaring over the antics of the horses and the incapacity of the
men to tame them. This tone is continued in the next novel in the Snopes trilogy, *The
Town* (1957), but the humor becomes increasingly difficult to sustain. One might say
that *The Hamlet* marks a terminus of sorts for Faulkner (although the spirit of this
novel would briefly be revived in his final novel, *The Reivers*, 1962), in that he would
never quite be able to summon up the comic genius that *The Hamlet*, and in particular "Spotted Horses," exhibits in abundance. As an example of this characteristic Faulk-
nerian comedy, "Spotted Horses" is probably without peer in the Faulkner canon.

Michael Sprinker

SPRING VICTORY

Author: Jesse Stuart (1907-1984)
Type of plot: Psychological
Time of plot: 1918
Locale: Rural Kentucky
First published: 1942

> *Principal characters:*
> THE BOY, the central character and narrator, ten years old
> SAL, his mother
> MICK, his father

The Story

During the dead of winter in 1918, a rural farm family faces starvation. After a summer in which the crops failed, the father is sick in bed with a protracted case of the flu, and the four children are all very young, by modern standards, to be of much help. It is left to the narrator's mother to find a path through the dilemma.

Her solution is to resume a craft she learned as a girl, basket weaving, and to enlist the older children in the enterprise. The unnamed narrator, who is ten years old, supplies the raw materials for his mother. Through bitter cold he trudges to a nearby bluff to cut white oak saplings so that they can later be cut, quartered, and splintered to serve as basket-making materials. In addition to his new responsibilities in the basket-making venture, which include taking the finished products to the closest town and selling them, the boy labors on the farm from early morning until night. Much of the description of the story centers on the details of his chores: milking the cow, feeding the stock, and tending the fires. One of his major responsibilities on the farm is cutting, hauling, and splitting firewood, a task with which his mother helps him in the early and middle parts of the tale—but which she leaves entirely to him in the final section of the story.

By any standards, the young boy's lot is a difficult one, but he accepts all of his responsibilities without complaint and carries out each one with surprising success. He relishes the tasks that would customarily be a man's work, and he especially likes selling the baskets that his mother makes each day to his neighbors and the townsfolk. One of the boy's most mature accomplishments is negotiating the purchase of fodder and corn, which will keep the stock alive until the pasture grass returns in the spring. In all things, the lad follows his mother's instructions precisely, selling the baskets for the price she establishes and buying the food that they need to see them through the difficult winter. Through the mother's careful planning, they are even able to put a small sum aside. The father's illness lingers, but all the children do what they can to reduce their mother's household burdens so that she can continue to increase her production of the wares that are sold to provide the food they sorely need. Both the mother and the children develop a sense of pride in their self-reliance, and she cheers her family by reminding them often that even as the snow deepens on the ground, the violets are budding underneath.

Through much of the story, the reader waits for the tragedy that will shatter the stoic bliss of the brave little family. When the narrator's mother sends him to fetch the doctor, it seems as if the ax has finally fallen, and that they will be overwhelmed by nature, snow, and cold, as is the family in Nathaniel Hawthorne's tale "The Ambitious Guest," a narrative that bears comparison to both "Spring Victory" and a similar Jesse Stuart story, "Dark Winter."

The story's surprise ending is that the doctor has been summoned, not to treat the ailing father, but to deliver the mother's baby. Spring finally returns, the father gets well, and their close scrape with disaster draws the family even closer together.

Themes and Meanings

Stuart's paean to rural courage and human love extols the somewhat opposing virtues of self-reliance and family unity. The individual members of the family, from the resourceful mother to the newborn child, can survive only by uniting their efforts against the forces that threaten them, which in this story take the form of a violent winter and the sickness that incapacitates the father. The central character, the ten-year-old son, does whatever is required of him, and he does it without complaint or opposition of any kind. His concerns center on the well-being of his parents, the illness of his father, and the possible threat to his mother's health through overwork as she makes the baskets that temporarily earn the living for all of them. So, too, does his mother focus her thoughts on the survival of her husband and children, the good of the whole, paying as little attention as does her son to her own comfort and convenience. Only by striving to ensure the survival of the whole family can the members do their utmost to provide for their own continuance, though this is not the level on which the family lives its life during this time of trial.

Their efforts are concerted and expended through an unstated love of one another, a love that has existed before the opening of the story and one that will continue, the ending reassures the reader, throughout the life of each family member. Few short stories in American literature reverberate with such a positive view of human ties and affection, and few celebrate quite so wholeheartedly what have come to be considered traditional American values.

Above all, this tale of a poor farming family expresses a deep optimism about the possibilities of life, the peace and solace to be found in fortitude, and the benefits of a cheerful stoicism. One should take life as it comes, the story teaches, and do the best one can with what one has. Love one another and everything will be all right.

Style and Technique

Short-story writers or novelists undertake few challenges as difficult as telling their tale by using an immature narrator. Entrusting the boy to tell the story related in "Spring Victory" was a venture full of pitfalls for Stuart, and his ability to sidestep so many of them is one mark of his accomplishments as a writer of short fiction. The primary problem of this device is that the narrator cannot seem more mature than his years allow, yet he or she must be capable of giving the insights that the writer wants to convey—about the people in the story, about the interpretation of their actions, and about life in general. A story concocted by a real child is full of childishness, but readers of serious fiction expect a story to be coordinated and meaningful. Satisfying the expectations of readers while giving the illusion that the story is actually being told by a child creates a situation in which the believability of the action, let alone the believability of the narrator's character, is constantly in danger of rupture.

Through a careful manipulation of the narrator's language, through his tone of voice as well as through what he merely implies, Stuart makes both the action of the story and the character of the young narrator seem real. The narrator's terseness shows a child not yet very proficient in his use of language, yet his observations are keen and vivid nevertheless. Stuart balances the boy's personality, which at times is almost too good to be true, with his ignorance of life. It comes as a shock to the narrator that the doctor has been summoned to assist his mother with the birth of a child. His sister is surprised to learn that the boy never noticed that his mother was pregnant, yet the reader understands the limitations of inexperience better than she, and such details bring the boy alive and compensate for those times when the reader would have been lazy or complaining if he or she had been asked to do the narrator's chores or suffer his privations.

One need only try to imagine the story told by the mother or the father (or by an omniscient narrator) to see the harvest that Stuart reaped by putting the words in the mouth of the boy. What Stuart learned about life, about love, and about family from his experience of the grueling winter of 1918 was apparent to even a child, and it was the kind of lesson that would stay with him through adolescence, through the time when he would learn his native tongue well enough to tell others what he found valuable enough, many years later, to turn into literary art.

Charles Hackenberry

SPUNK

Author: Zora Neale Hurston (1891-1960)
Type of plot: Sketch
Time of plot: The 1920's
Locale: Florida
First published: 1925

Principal characters:
SPUNK BANKS, a giant of a man who loves Lena Kanty
LENA KANTY, a pretty woman
JOE KANTY, her timid husband
WALTER THOMAS and
ELIJAH MOSLEY, gossipy townsmen

The Story

In a small town in central Florida that is populated exclusively by African Americans, Walter Thomas and Elijah Mosley are sitting on the porch of a store. They notice that Lena Kanty has disappeared into the nearby palmetto bushes with Spunk Banks, who is not her husband.

Unconcerned about town gossip, Spunk and Lena continue down their brazen path, oblivious to the fact that Joe Kanty, Lena's beleaguered husband, has entered the store. Walter and Elijah, who function like a Greek chorus, mock the shy husband and warn him that he is about to be cuckolded. Joe is fully aware of the implications of Spunk and Lena's behavior; he knows that the men at the store have seen her, and he knows they know he knows. Joe pulls out a razor and claims that Spunk has gone too far.

After Joe leaves in search of Lena and Spunk, Walter and Elijah reflect on their role in this family drama. Walter criticizes Elijah for mocking Joe and taunting him to action. Elijah defends himself by saying it is not decent for a man to accept such behavior. Walter then points out Spunk's physical superiority and prowess as a fighter: Spunk is the only man in the village brave enough to ride the circle saw at the sawmill. If Spunk and Joe were to tangle, Joe would not fare well.

Lena's role in this triangle is obvious to all the observers, except Joe. She is in love with Spunk and wants to leave her husband for him. Spunk claims her for his own. The issue is settled definitively when Joe, after following the couple into the palmetto bushes, is killed by Spunk in self-defense.

Spunk and Lena do not live happily ever after, even though the main barrier to their happiness has been eliminated. In another one of their gossip sessions, Elijah asserts that Joe has returned as a ghost to haunt Spunk. The incident had occurred just as Spunk and Lena were preparing for bed. Elijah says that a big, black bobcat had walked around the house howling. When Spunk grabbed his gun, the bobcat stood still, looking at him and howling. Spunk realizes that it is not a bobcat, but Joe.

The townsmen believe in the story about the ghost without question. It causes them to reflect on the relative bravery of the two men. Walter concludes that Joe was the braver, because even though he was frightened of Spunk and knew he had a gun, he still pursued him. Spunk, on the other hand, a natural-born fighter, was scared of nothing. In Walter and Elijah's estimation, it was nothing for Spunk to fight when he was never scared.

A few days later, the ghost appears for the second time. Once again, the story is told from the townsmen's perspective. The men were at work in the sawmill when Spunk inexplicably slipped and fell into the circle saw. As he was dying, the men reached him and heard his last words: "It was Joe, 'Lige . . . the dirty sneak shoved me." Elijah concludes: "If spirits kin fight, there's a powerful tussle goin' on somewhere ovah Jordan 'cause Ah b'leeve Joe's ready for Spunk an' ain't skeered any more."

At Spunk's wake, all the townspeople have gathered to pay their respects to Lena, who is lamenting her loss. Even Joe's father has come. Significantly, old Jeff Kanty, "who a few hours before would have been afraid to come within ten feet of him, stood leering triumphantly down on the fallen giant as if his fingers had been the teeth of steel that laid him low." As they are eating at the wake, the other mourners speculate on who will be Lena's next lover.

Themes and Meanings

Zora Neale Hurston's fiction centers on the people, events, and customs of her hometown, Eatonville, Florida—which is distinguished for being the first incorporated African American township in the United States. Author Alice Walker strongly praises Hurston for the "racial health" that Hurston exhibits in her work and "for exposing not simply an adequate culture, but a superior one." Hurston believed that the greatest cultural wealth of the continent could be mined in towns of the black South, such as Eatonville. There, one could show how the "Negro farthest down" was "the god-maker, the creator of everything that lasts."

These beliefs explain why Hurston became an anthropologist and sought to preserve the Eatonville folktales, anecdotes, and beliefs in her book, *Mules and Men* (1935). In her fiction, however, Hurston portrays the townfolk in a much more realistic manner. Joe's bravery in going after the much larger man is undercut by the fact that he attacks Spunk from behind. Walter's compassion toward the Kantys is undercut by Elijah's mean-spirited, nosy, loud-mouthed behavior. Elijah slaps his leg gleefully when he sees Spunk and Lena head for the bushes in the beginning of the story. Later, through his taunts and teasing, he all but pushes Joe to seek revenge, knowing that Joe is the much weaker opponent.

The townspeople fare no better. From the porch of the store, they view the whole incident as a form of entertainment. When they see Joe head into the bushes after Spunk, they laugh boisterously behind his back. At the end of the story, their attitude does not change even as Spunk lies in front of them at the wake: "The women ate heartily of the funeral baked meats and wondered who would be Lena's next. The men whispered coarse conjectures between guzzles of whiskey."

Hurston pleased no one by portraying the townfolk in this manner. The people of Eatonville were angered at her when they recognized themselves in her stories; she did little to disguise their identities and used their real names. Other famous black writers, such as Richard Wright and Ralph Ellison, did not like Hurston's minstrel-like characters. Hurston knew that she had not made herself popular by what she had written. Her autobiography, *Dust Tracks on a Road* (1942), states: "I sensed early, that the Negro race was not one band of heavenly love. There was stress and strain inside as well as out. Being black was not enough. It took more than a community of skin color to make your love come down on you."

Style and Technique

In *Dust Tracks on a Road*, Hurston relates her mother's dying moments:

> As I crowded in, they lifted up the bed and turned it around so that Mama's eyes would face east. I thought that she looked to me as the head of the bed reversed. Her mouth was slightly open, but her breathing took up so much of her strength that she could not talk. But she looked at me, or so I felt, to speak for her. She depended on me for a voice.

Hurston fulfilled this destiny in her stories and novels; the African American voice is the first thing that a reader notices when reading Hurston's work. In her article "Characteristics of Negro Expression" (1934), Hurston describes African Americans' urge to adorn language and lists their linguistic techniques, such as metaphors and similes ("mule blood—black molasses"); double descriptives ("low-down"); verbal nouns ("funeralize"); and nouns from verbs ("he won't stand straightening"). She disproves the notion that the black idiom is spoken by people of inferior intellect and sensibility. Instead, she asserts that their skill at embellishing the English language is the result of their belief that there can never be enough beauty, let alone too much.

The outcome of "Spunk" turns on the townspeople's ability to manipulate Joe Kanty through their verbal dexterity. When Elijah first spots Spunk and Lena saunter-ing off to be alone, he cries out for all to hear: "Theah they go, big as life an' brassy as tacks." His judgment shapes the villagers' perception of the situation. He reinforces his message by using colorful language. He tells the other men that Spunk is not afraid of anything on "God's green footstool"; that by strutting around with another man's wife, Spunk does not "give a kitty." Joe, on the other hand, is "a rabbit-foot colored man." When it is Spunk's turn to be frightened of the bobcat, he gets so "nervoused up" that he cannot shoot. By first introducing the story of the bobcat and making the others—perhaps even Spunk himself—believe in it, Elijah helps to move the story to its grim conclusion.

Anna Lillios

SREDNI VASHTAR

Author: Saki (Hector Hugh Munro, 1870-1916)
Type of plot: Horror
Time of plot: The early 1900's
Locale: England
First published: 1911

Principal characters:
CONRADIN, a very imaginative, sick ten-year-old boy
MRS. DE ROPP, his cousin and guardian

The Story

Conradin, a ten-year-old boy whom the doctor has given less than five years to live, is antagonized by his cousin and guardian, Mrs. De Ropp, who seems to take delight in thwarting him under the guise of taking care of him. Conradin finds escape in his vivid imagination and in an unused toolshed, in which he keeps two pets—a Houdan hen, on which he lavishes affection, and a ferret, which he fears and comes to venerate as a god.

Conradin names the ferret Sredni Vashtar and worships the beast as his god, bringing it flowers in season and celebrating festivals on special occasions, such as when his cousin suffers from a toothache. When his cousin notices him spending too much time in the shed, she discovers the Houdan hen and sells it. She is surprised when Conradin fails to show any emotion at the news, but Conradin changes his usual worshiping ritual. Instead of chanting Sredni Vashtar's praises, he asks an unnamed boon of his god. Every day he repeats his request for the one wish from the ferret. Mrs. De Ropp, noticing his frequent visits to the toolshed, concludes that he must have something hidden there, which she assumes to be guinea pigs. She ransacks his room until she finds the key to the cage and goes out to the shed.

As she goes to the shed, Conradin watches her and imagines her triumph over him and his subsequent declining health under her oppressive care. He does not see her emerge from the shed for a long time, however, and he begins to hope, chanting to Sredni Vashtar. Finally, he notices the ferret coming out of the shed with dark, wet stains around its mouth and throat.

The maid announces tea and asks Conradin where his cousin is. He tells her that Mrs. De Ropp has gone to the shed, and the maid goes to announce tea to her. Conradin calmly butters his toast, relishing every moment as he hears the scream of the maid and the loud sobs and talk of the kitchen help, followed by the footsteps of someone carrying a heavy burden. Then he hears the kitchen help discussing who will tell the young boy the news as he takes another piece of toast to butter.

Themes and Meanings

This short, macabre story is chilling in its portrayal of the fiendish young boy. Saki takes the boy's point of view toward the annoying, officious cousin, who, the boy believes, delights in tormenting him. The boy lives almost entirely in his imagination. The real world is that which is ruled by adults such as his cousin, who are most disagreeable to him. In this aspect, Conradin seems to be a perfectly normal child at odds with the demands of the cruel outside world. What sets Conradin apart from other children is his almost pathological escape from reality and his achieving his revenge through the agency of the wild animal. What is usually only imaginary to a child is carried to fruition, and the child relishes it.

Conradin's veneration of the ferret comes to take up more and more of his waking hours after his cousin has sold his beloved hen. It becomes an obsession with him, and the reader finally comes to understand that he prays that the beast will kill his cousin. When the ferret actually kills the cousin, the most shocking thing is the boy's nonchalant, almost happy acceptance of the event. It is the boy's reaction to the killing that takes the story out of the realm of reality.

Although Conradin's condition is unusual in that he has been diagnosed as having a short time to live, he could, to an extent, be perceived as a typical boy escaping in his imagination from the cold world. Even his adoration of the ferret seems to differ only in degree from what could be considered normal. Sometimes normal children imagine killing their adult antagonists, and in this case, it could be considered accidental that his cousin is killed (although Conradin makes no effort to warn her, he fully expects her to emerge from the shed victorious, as she usually does when in conflict with him). However, the realization that his prayers have been answered and his cold, calm acceptance of the accomplished fact are shocking.

In a sense, then, the story can be seen as a child's fantasy of getting even with the nonunderstanding world of adults. It is a kind of wish fulfillment of which many children dream. The horror is that Saki presents it as a reality, and the boy as fully enjoying the event.

Style and Technique

All of Saki's short stories are very short and to the point, and "Sredni Vashtar" is no exception. Many of his stories are also as macabre as this one. What distinguishes Saki's stories is his ability to capture the feelings and attitudes of children toward their elders. That he was reared by two aunts, one of whom acted sadistically toward children, is probably what motivated Saki to fill so many of his stories with young children and sadistic elder guardians. His purpose is usually achieved by a quasi-objective narrative stance, in which the narrator interprets events from the point of view of the young protagonist but pretends to relate events objectively, as in this story.

The narrator at the beginning depicts the situation as Conradin views it. To him, Mrs. De Ropp represents "those three-fifths of the world that are necessary and disagreeable and real," while "the other two-fifths, in perpetual antagonism to the foregoing, were summed up in himself and his imagination." The fruit trees in the "dull cheerless garden" are described as being "jealously apart from his plucking, as though they were rare specimens of their kind blooming in an arid waste." It is an adult narrating the perceptions of a child.

Mrs. De Ropp becomes for the boy the epitome of all that is respectable, and thus the antithesis of all that he holds dear. When she has sold his beloved hen, he refuses to let her see how deeply he feels the loss, but he is described as hating the world as represented chiefly by Mrs. De Ropp. His antipathy takes the form of his devoting his energies to praying more fervently to his animal god.

Saki cleverly omits mentioning the subject of Conradin's supplication to Sredni Vashtar, and while the cousin is in the toolshed to get rid of the ferret, the narrator describes Conradin's imagining his cruel cousin's final triumph over him by extirpating the one creature he so venerates. Then, as Saki obliquely informs the reader of the demise of the hated guardian, his description of Conradin calmly eating and enjoying his butter and toast heightens the reader's sense of shock.

Roger Geimer

STALKING

Author: Joyce Carol Oates (1938-   )
Type of plot: Psychological
Time of plot: The early 1970's
Locale: Apparently a U.S. suburb
First published: 1972

> *Principal characters:*
> GRETCHEN, the thirteen-year-old protagonist
> THE INVISIBLE ADVERSARY, the taunting figure that she follows

The Story

On a cold, gritty November day, Gretchen follows the Invisible Adversary through muddy fields and past vacant buildings to a shopping mall, then to a Big Boy restaurant, and, finally, to her own suburban home. It is a landscape littered with the debris of a burgeoning middle America, with its developing tract home subdivisions, detouring traffic, gas stations, banks, restaurants, and stores. The realistic portrayal of the landscape is infused with the sensibility of a young teenager who is so detached from her surroundings and other people that she displays an utter disregard for the consequences of her actions.

Gretchen has hours for her game of stalking on this Saturday afternoon, and her sheer plodding determination is menacing in its relentlessness. In contrast to the Invisible Adversary, who has "long spiky legs brisk as colts' legs," Gretchen "is dressed for the hunt, her solid legs crammed into old blue jeans, her big, square, strong feet jammed into white leather boots that cost her mother forty dollars not long ago, but are now scuffed and filthy with mud. Hopeless to get them clean again, Gretchen doesn't give a damn." Her face, too, is strong, yet neutral and detached. More than just teenage angst, Gretchen's impassivity seems to reflect a deeper discontent and the possibility for destruction.

As the Adversary taunts her, Gretchen follows him through a field to a new gas station that has not opened in the six months that her family has lived in the town. The new building now has broken windows, and snakelike tar has been smeared on the white wall. Cars move past her as they detour because of construction on storm sewer pipes. She remembers the Adversary, and after jumping over a concrete ditch stained with rust-colored water, she contemplates a closed bank before entering the Buckingham Mall. She always seems to notice her surroundings, especially the geometric shapes of signs and the vacancy of buildings, with an aloof impartiality. She barely acknowledges the few people who enter her consciousness. Instead, she plods along, following the Adversary with quiet excitement and with a cunning, patient attitude.

Once inside the mall's drugstore, as a salesgirl's attention is diverted by another customer, Gretchen shoplifts a tube of light pink lipstick. Despite the Adversary's finger-

wagging admonishment, she steals a package from a cardboard barrel without knowing or caring what it is. With the Adversary trotting ahead of her, Gretchen calmly enters another store. In the bathroom, she smears the lipstick onto the mirror and then
tosses the tube, shoplifted toothpaste, toilet paper, and a cloth towel down the toilet
until it clogs. Gretchen's next act of quiet destruction occurs when a boy bumps her
into a trash can; she methodically spills its contents. After a ritual stop in Sampson
Furniture, she enters Dodi's Boutique where she takes several dresses into a dressing
room. She steps on a white wool dress, smearing mud on it, and breaks the zipper on
another.

With the same methodical pursuit of the Adversary, she next enters a department
store. She catches a glimpse of her mother on an escalator. Gretchen's mother does
not see her, and Gretchen makes no effort to make contact with her mother. This stalking is just between the Adversary and the girl. Gretchen eats at a Big Boy restaurant
while the Adversary waits outside. After eating, she follows the Adversary to the
highway. She waits and then sees the Adversary dart out in front of a car. She follows
the staggering and bleeding Adversary to an upper-middle-class neighborhood, gig-
gling that he walks like a drunken man. He leads her to a large colonial house, and she
is entranced at the blood spots the Adversary has left in the foyer. Her boots leave a
trail of mud in her empty house; her mother must still be shopping, and her father is
out of town. Gretchen settles down on the goatskin sofa to watch a rerun of a "Shotgun
Steve" show. Chillingly, with the stalking game at an impasse, Gretchen decides, "If
the Adversary comes crawling behind her, groaning in pain, weeping, she won't even
bother to glance at him."

Themes and Meanings

Joyce Carol Oates has stated in a *Chicago Tribune Book World* article that a single
dominant theme runs throughout her work: "I am concerned with only one thing: the
moral and social conditions of my generation." During the course of her prolific career, Oates has often taken the ordinary conditions of day-to-day living, and, while
presenting the realism of that world, she has also shown the terrifying conditions that
lurk just below consciousness. Gretchen is a character who plays an imaginary stalking game, but her game with the Invisible Adversary becomes hauntingly nightmarish
because of the utter lack of empathy and emotion that she feels toward others.
Gretchen herself becomes almost a mechanical animal as she stalks her prey.

In Scripture, Satan is often referred to as the Adversary, which is no doubt alluded
to in this story with the Adversary's taunting and influence to maliciousness. Here, the
Invisible Adversary is also Gretchen's psychological projection of her own need to
feel something in a gritty suburban world filled with "a jumbled, bulldozed field of
mud," "no sidewalks," "gigantic concrete pipes," "geometric areas," and "artificial
hills." It is not the Adversary but Gretchen who enacts the petty theft, destroys property, and leaves a trail of mud with her scuffed and expensive boots. The plodding and
insistent stalking is menacing in its utter disregard for the broken trail it leaves behind.
Gretchen's undefined malaise and anger are very possibly only the prelude for future

and more damaging devastation, and this is what suggests the underlying terror in the story.

For Gretchen, the world is devoid of any human contact; even her mother does not see her in the department store. Gretchen's reaction to other people—if she notices them at all—is one of physical violence. In gym class, she runs heavily, sometimes bumping into other girls, even hurting them. When a boy in a group at the mall bumps into her, she does not look at them, but coldly and angrily knocks the trash can over onto the sidewalk. Although many critics have commented on the violence that is inherent in so many of Oates's stories, Oates herself does not graphically display the violent acts in her work. In "Stalking," the Adversary is hit by a car and then described as stumbling home. It is Gretchen's initial reaction to this event—the feeling of satisfaction bordering on pleasure—and her ultimate lack of compassion for the Adversary that is so chilling. The Adversary is, after all, her own creation, and her renunciation of this embodiment of her disturbed psychological state leaves her even more empty of human emotion.

Style and Technique

Although Oates has tried many techniques in various genres during her prolific career, she stated in an interview that she has "done a good deal of experimentation with very short stories—'miniature narratives,' I call them. I would like some day to assemble them into a book. They are, in a sense, 'minimalist'; in another sense a species of prose poetry." "Stalking" is barely more than eight pages long, yet the realistic depiction of the suburban wasteland—striking because of its exactness of detail and haunting familiarity—is only the facade for the disturbing psychological repercussions to this environment as they are demonstrated through the character of Gretchen.

Gretchen is an adolescent from an upper-middle-class family, yet she spends her November Saturday in a bizarre game of stalking the demon: her own *Doppelgänger*, her other self. She is a product of the American Dream, and she is also heir to the liabilities that can turn that dream into a nightmare. With her characteristic use of italicized thoughts and feelings, Oates, as always, demonstrates a great fidelity to the American condition, both as it is described realistically and as it is portrayed through those thoughts and feelings that lurk below consciousness. It is the image of the muddy boots that leave their footprints throughout the story with no sidewalks that remains: "Entranced, she follows the splashes of blood into the hall, to the stairs . . . forgets her own boots, which are muddy . . . but she doesn't feel like going back to wipe her feet. The hell with it."

Laurie Lisa

THE STAR

Author: Arthur C. Clarke (1917-   )
Type of plot: Science fiction
Time of plot: The twenty-sixth century
Locale: Aboard an exploratory spacecraft
First published: 1955

> *Principal character:*
> THE NARRATOR, a Jesuit priest and astrophysicist

The Story

The unnamed narrator, a Jesuit priest, is the astrophysicist on an exploratory scientific spacecraft. He is constantly reminded of this duality by his shipmates and by the very decorations and features of his room. The Jesuit speaks throughout the story to an unnamed "you" who is often unknown, sometimes himself, at times St. Ignatius Loyola (founder of the Jesuits), and finally, God. The narrator's several brief asides show his distress over something the ship has discovered.

The ship has come to the Phoenix Nebula, the remains of a star that became a supernova, to try to reconstruct the events that led up to the catastrophe and, if possible, to learn its cause. Expecting to find only the burned star, the ship makes a much more exciting, and ultimately poignant, discovery. The last planet of the star's system survived the burning, and an artifact is sending out a beacon from its surface. Although untrained for this unexpected archaeological work, the crew enthusiastically sets out to discover what secrets and treasures have been waiting through the centuries for discovery and rescue.

A monolithic marker leads the men to the hopes of the race doomed by the supernova, a civilization that knew it was about to die and had made a last bid for immortality. The artifact contains artwork, recordings, and written works, including keys for their translation. It also contains photographs of beautiful cities and happy children playing on beaches under the then-quiet sun. Although the vanished people most likely left only their best, as the narrator acknowledges they had a right to do, their remains show the men from Earth a civilization that could reach neighboring planets, that possessed beauty and culture, but that ran out of time and was destroyed on the brink of interstellar travel, which might have allowed some of its people to survive. To add to the sorrow the men feel, the race looks humanlike, inviting even more empathy.

The men, who teased their astrophysicist on the journey to the nebula about his religious beliefs, ask him how such destruction can be reconciled with God's mercy. The Jesuit tries to accept this questioning and answer it, but cannot. He wonders if even St. Ignatius could have reconciled this situation, although he recognizes that God has no need to justify his actions to humankind. When, as the ship's astrophysicist, he makes his calculations, he finds something that severely tests his own deep faith. He calculates the date of the supernova and when its light reached the Earth.

The reason for the narrator's doubt and seeming despair becomes clear in the final line of the story. Every day stars go nova and every day races die, but this tragedy has a horrific irony for the theologian: "What was the need to give these people to the fire, that the symbol of their passing might shine above Bethlehem?"

Themes and Meanings

The issues in "The Star" relate to the concept of theodicy, which is an attempt to answer the question of the problem of evil that is summed up by three statements: God is good, God is omnipotent or omniscient, and there is evil. The last statement is the easiest to prove and is usually accepted as a given. If God is good, but not omnipotent, he wants to stop evil, but cannot. If God is omnipotent, but not good, he could stop evil, but does not choose to do so. The Judeo-Christian ethic, however, sees God as both good and omnipotent, so some other answer for the existence of evil is necessary. One theodicy is that God has no need to justify himself to humanity; that humanity's free will causes evil is another. Most religious people accept a theodicy that allows them to reconcile their faith in God with the tragic events of everyday life.

The unnamed narrator of "The Star" claims to have reached a point at which his faith is shaken. The nova's date will not be ignored by either his shipmates or his fellow scientists back on Earth, nor can he himself ignore it. He recognizes God's mystery, but can no longer accept it on faith; he has been driven to question all that he had believed.

One may speculate, however, that the Jesuit has not thoroughly lost his faith because the last lines of the story are a plea, almost a prayer, to the God he has tried to claim he no longer accepts. A test of faith may not be the same thing as a loss of faith, and the man, by clinging to his previous dependence on God, may yet save and salvage his understanding of God's mysteries. The reader is free to speculate whether or not the Jesuit—like the biblical Job who first received the answer that God did not need to justify himself—will be reconciled, or can be.

Style and Technique

Arthur C. Clarke's "The Star" won a Hugo Award for best short story of the year. First published in *Infinity Science Fiction*, it has been widely anthologized since then. Many of Clarke's stories have religious themes or elements.

"The Star" makes ample use of symbols. It opens with a description of the juxtaposition of the Jesuit's crucifix with the astrophysicist's computer. The dichotomies of the narrator's life are thus immediately apparent. The narrator's picture of St. Ignatius, the founder of the Jesuit order, which historically has been dedicated to education—bringing light—is juxtaposed with the tracings from his spectrophotometer, which measures another kind of light. The two concepts of light and enlightenment have come together. The narrator even wonders what the pictured man would have made of the pictured tracings.

Another important symbol in the work is the phoenix. The Phoenix Nebula is the supernova the ship has come to study. In mythology, the phoenix is a bird that dies and is reborn out of the ashes of its pyre. The phoenix has been used as a symbol for Jesus and for Christianity because it seems to die but, rather than remaining ashes, it rises from the dead to live again. This is the hope that Christians have for themselves and a major part of the belief they have in Jesus as the Christ. One might argue that out of the funeral pyre of this lost race came the birth of the new race of Christians on Earth, although the Jesuit narrator does not seem able to see this hopeful interpretation of the nebula's catastrophe.

One of Clarke's strengths as a writer of short fiction is his ability to write single-sentence concluding paragraphs that make the reader rethink an entire story. Clarke has used this type of surprise twist ending in other stories, notably "Rescue Party." In "The Star," this final line tells the reader that the light of this nebula was the star seen above Bethlehem, signaling the birth of Jesus. Until this moment, it is the death of this lovely race that seems to drive the priest's despair, despite the answers he seeks to prepare for the questions of others. The clash of his two positions finds a climax in the discovery that he, as an astrophysicist, makes about the date of the nebula and what he, as a priest, knows about that historical date on Earth.

Susan Jaye Dauer

STAR FOOD

Author: Ethan Canin (1960-   )
Type of plot: Psychological
Time of plot: Probably the late twentieth century
Locale: Arcade, California
First published: 1986

> *Principal characters:*
> DADE, the eighteen-year-old narrator
> HIS MOTHER
> HIS FATHER
> A SHOPLIFTER

The Story

Dade, the sensitive young narrator, recalls how he disappointed both of his parents for the first time the summer that he turned eighteen. Perhaps he has disappointed himself too, for throughout the story he slowly realizes that he does not know what direction his life should take. Dade has been told by his father that if he does not take his work seriously, he will end up poor. The father—who owns the grocery store of the title—is a practical man who works hard, runs a clean, thriving business, and maintains good relationships with the community. When he proposed marriage to Dade's mother, he probably saw right to the end of his life, Dade thinks.

Dade works in the store and is sometimes industrious, but often he spends his time daydreaming on the store's roof. He disappoints his father by not being earnest enough about his work in the store. Instead he gazes at clouds, stars, and the sky for hours, trying to make the discovery his mother has always thought he would make. She reminds him that he will someday inherit the store, yet she encourages him to think and dream because she is sure he will someday become a person of limited fame. It is her theory that men like Leonardo da Vinci and Thomas Edison simply stared at regular objects until they saw new things.

Dade initially goes to the roof to clean the large, incandescent star that sits atop the store to advertise its presence. He sometimes stays there for hours to think about the clouds and their shapes. He has studied the names and properties of clouds and gives precise, detailed descriptions. Sometimes his father joins him on the roof. When Dade looks off the roof to the ground, he gazes west to the affluent parts of town where sparkling swimming pools may be seen among the trees and where the girls who drive their own convertibles to high school live. His father, however, forces him to look in the other direction to the neighborhoods populated by rusted old cars and men who sit on curbs all day. Dade, he says, will become one of these men if he does not take business more seriously. However, because Dade is so young, both parents want to give him some space to find himself and his own direction.

A shoplifter forces matters to a crisis. Dade has apprehended shoplifting children on several occasions. One day, however, a middle-aged woman in a gray plaid dress walks out of the store with a cut-rate loaf of rye bread. Dade feels powerless to act under her stare. Later she steals pineapple juice. The thief somehow inspires his pity. His mother explains that he must feel sorry for her. Understanding the son's sensitive nature and reluctance, the father hires a guard. One day on the roof, Dade sees some Air Force jets in the sky. His response to them makes him feel he has seen a sign. Dade tells his dad he is ready to catch the shoplifter, and soon he does. While they are waiting for the father to come to the back room to deal with the shoplifter, Dade changes his mind and allows her to escape, as his mother had sometimes done with children before. In shame or guilt, Dade leaves too, walking with the woman for a while. They do not speak to each other. Later that night as he walks, he realizes that he has disappointed his father and his mother and that he feels alone in the world, like the shoplifter. Moreover, he still has no definite ideas about what direction his life should take.

Themes and Meanings

The primary theme of Ethan Canin's story rests in the conflict between the practical spirit that wants to accomplish concrete and worthwhile things and the tendency for creativity, insight, and romantic dreaming. These two opposing spirits are personified by Dade's businessman father and his hopeful, romantic mother. Their hopes for Dade and his future are played out on the roof and in the store. Down in the store he works hard at the checkout counter and in the stockroom, but sometimes he neglects his work, even when his father needs him, in order to gaze at stars and clouds, which are food for his thoughts. He is an extremely introspective eighteen-year-old, but his musings never seem to come to much. He has no definite goals of his own. Unlike many boys his age, he does not fantasize about cars, girls, sports, or even escaping from his town or his family. He does not think about the drudgery or rewards of running a business, nor mention any friends or pastimes.

As a thoughtful young man, he recognizes his indecisiveness. The family often goes to the movies on Friday evenings. Dade's self-awareness is reflected in his comments about the films:

> I liked the movies because I imagined myself doing everything the heroes did—deciding to invade at daybreak, swimming half the night against the seaward current—but whenever we left the theater I was disappointed. From the front row, life seemed like a clear set of decisions, but on the street afterward, I realized that the world existed all around me and I didn't know what I wanted. The quiet of evening and the ordinariness of human voices startled me.

In an interview published in *Contemporary Authors*, Canin admits that he closely identifies with the character Dade. He thinks the tension between the romantic and practical views of the world creates a driving force that he sees in himself. It is these forces that propel Dade first one way and then the other. Finally, he realizes that he will not make the kind of discoveries his mother is hoping for, and he will also not feel the zeal for stock work and business that his father wishes he did. At one point, Dade shouts to the highway and the cars, "Tell me what I want." He waits expectantly, but no answer comes. At the story's end, he still has not decided where he thinks he should be directing his efforts. Perhaps by realizing that he cannot satisfy either of his parents and recognizing that each person is essentially alone, he has made a start in finding his own direction.

Style and Technique

The story is narrated in the first person by Dade. The style is deceptively simple, and the language is perfectly appropriate to the thoughts of a young person. Introspection and subdued emotion dominate the tone of the story. There is little conversation; much of the story consists of Dade's reflections. One of the characteristics of the story is its use of abundant detail and precise description. Canin has a wonderful sense of the particulars that make up a scene, shown when he describes the layout of the store, the produce, and the characters. Dade's description of his father illustrates the author's skill in description: "He was a short man with direct habits and an understanding of how to get along in the world, and he believed that God rewarded only two things, courtesy and hard work." The description goes on for several more sentences, but readers can get a clear picture of the father from just this one deft sentence.

Another example of Canin's style is illustrated in Dade's comparison of the sky to the sea: "When I looked closely [the sky] was a sea with waves and shifting colors, wind seams and denials of distance, and after a while I learned to look at it so that it entered my eye whole. It was blue liquid. I spent hours looking into its pale wash, looking for things, though I didn't know what." This sort of controlled extended metaphor is not unusual. Shorter lively comparisons such as "my thoughts piled into one another" and "apricot-size balls of hail" abound. This carefully crafted story employs a consistent narrative voice and vivid imagery appropriate to a sensitive, observant young man.

To symbolize the conflict between the parents' views and the son's inner thoughts as well, Canin uses the grocery store ceiling. The father invents a grid system for easy location of foods, which he paints on the ceiling. A few days later, the mother pastes up fluorescent stars among the grid squares, accurately showing constellations even though they could not be seen because of the bright store lights. It seems useless, but the idea appeals to her nevertheless.

Toni J. Morris

STATE OF ENGLAND

Author: Martin Amis (1949-   )
Type of plot: Social realism
Time of plot: The mid-1990's
Locale: London and environs
First published: 1996

> *Principal characters:*
> BIG MAL, a burly nightclub bouncer and bodyguard
> SHEILAGH, his wife
> JET, their nine-year-old son
> FAT LOL, Big Mal's friend and accomplice
> LINZI (SHINSALA), Big Mal's aging Indian mistress

The Story

The central action of "State of England" takes place on the grounds of a private school not far from London. Big Mal is first seen talking on a mobile phone to his wife, from whom he is separated. He and his wife, Sheilagh, are both at the school for a sports day; their son Jet is to run in several races. Big Mal's face is disfigured by a horrible cut, which he received when he and his friend Fat Lol fought with some people in a central London parking lot the night before.

Big Mal's marriage is in trouble, and he is short of money. He married his son's mother just the previous year, but five months ago, he left his wife and son to move in with Linzi across the street. Big Mal and Linzi (whose real name is "Shinsala") spend much of their time watching Indian pornographic films.

Big Mal is unhappy. Not long ago, he lived in Los Angeles for a few years. Although he liked the city, he found he could not make it there on his own. He knows he is an uneducated, lower-class thug and that his associates are, if anything, even more illiterate and pitiful. He reflects on what it is to be a nightclub bouncer: A bouncer mainly keeps people out; if you have to bounce too many people, that means you have been a bad bouncer. By that test, he has been only moderately good at his trade. At the sports day, he is embarrassed by his own appearance.

Although Big Mal is not virtuous, he knows what virtue is. His parents represent some kind of ideal because they stayed married, and Big Mal feels guilty about leaving his wife. He loves his son. He worries about him and tries hard to help him and please him. He takes Jet to films, coaches him on running the race, and somehow finds money to pay Jet's very high tuition. He tells Jet he will eat a burger, even though even the word "burger" makes him sick. The only thing he will not do, although Jet begs him to, is enter the fathers' race.

Big Mal wants his son to be exceptional but realizes that he is not. Jet's academic performance is very poor, and he comes in last in his first race. The one way in which his son stands out among the other boys, Big Mal eventually realizes, is that his skin is whiter.

Toward the end of the story, Martin Amis reveals what happened the previous night. Big Mal had asked Fat Lol to include him in some petty money-making scheme. The scheme consisted of going to a multistoried parking structure in central London and placing boots on the tires of cars that were parked the least bit irregularly. The idea was that car owners would pay them 70 pounds to remove the boots rather than go through what they assume would be a time-consuming procedure to settle their tickets. After installing several boots, they were assaulted by a horde of people returning for their cars—assaulted and beaten badly.

However, things begin to look up for Big Mal. Jet finishes respectably in his last race, and his wife seems to want to take him back. Although that reunion is not assured, Big Mal makes the ultimate effort: He is last seen running with great pain in the fathers' race.

Themes and Meanings

The title of this story indicates that it belongs to a recognizable group of narratives, ones that deal broadly with the "state of England" rather than narrowly with the lives of a few individuals, such as George Eliot's *Middlemarch* (1871-1872) and Margaret Drabble's *The Radiant Way* (1987). To call a short story "State of England" is a bold move by Amis, one that asks readers to understand not just the degradation, pathos, and dark comedy of Big Mal's story but also what the story says about England in the 1990's.

Big Mal recognizes that things have changed since he was a boy. Unlike Fat Lol, who is slovenly, gluttonous, and on the dole, and his wife, Yvonne, who looks like a bank robber, Big Mal has moved on. He has worked as a bouncer in high-class clubs. He has worked in California for a big-time mobster. He has moved out of the East End neighborhood where he and Fat Lol were born. He eats with more restraint than Fat Lol (especially since he became very sick on an airplane after gorging himself on hamburgers). Big Mal dresses well enough and uses a mobile phone.

He knows that the changes are part of a larger pattern. In the England of the 1990's, class, age, race, gender, and even accent and education are not supposed to matter. Everyone is supposed to be equal. At the school Jet attends, there appears to be racial equality: For example, the other families are Japanese and Pakistani.

Everyone is equal—or is supposed to be. However, Big Mal knows, and this is Amis's central theme, that people in England are not treated equally. Big Mal feels inferior because he can hardly read and because his English is bad (his mistress Linzi speaks even worse English than he does, almost as bad as Fat Lol's). He feels like a pariah at the sports day. The ultimate demonstration that the class system still survives is when he and Fat Lol are beaten in the parking lot. Their attackers are upper-class evening-clothes-clad men and women returning from the opera. Big Mal is stunned: It seems that the revolution is being started by the upper classes.

The class system in England still exists. Big Mal's problem is how to adjust to that fact now that he has left the class into which he was born. This story suggests that it is difficult, but people like Big Mal will keep on trying.

Amis once remarked in an interview that Big Mal's story was like his own (Amis left London for New York), and this suggests another way to read this story: Big Mal is an Everyman who tries to adjust to the profusion of ethnic and racial groups in the global village. The perhaps unrealistic lineup of nationalities at Jet's school may point to this more allegorical reading.

Style and Technique

Readers of this story immediately realize they are not in the usual world of polite English narratives. The characters here are from the lowest levels of society, their speech is often illiterate and usually obscene, and their actions are violent. Although Amis's style is brilliantly effective, it is not what many readers expect from a British novelist. His style is hip and colloquial and filled with sentence fragments. It is extraordinarily energetic, even frantic. To use a term employed by British critics, Amis's style is not British or American, but "Mid-Atlantic." It is worth noting that this story was first published in *The New Yorker.*

The narrative of the story of the sports day moves forward in a logical progression, but it does not read smoothly because it is broken into seven short sections, and living in Big Mal's mind leads to many somewhat confusing flashbacks. One important question is not answered until a flashback in section six. However, although the ending leaves readers uncertain about what the future holds for any of the characters, "State of England" ultimately holds together.

One thing that gives the story cohesion is its serious themes. These themes are expressed in many ways, through numerous techniques, including symbolism. Many items that function normally in the story also resonate symbolically. Big Mal's facial wound parallels the wound in his heart. The mobile phones that are everywhere suggest the mobility of society. The fathers' race at the end is an obvious version of a symbol to be found everywhere: the literal race suggests the race to get ahead in the competitive world of the 1990's.

What gives force to Amis's story is also its range. Although the people in it are for the most part disgusting, Big Mal's efforts are touching, especially as he tries to help his son. Also, Amis creates humor, as in his story's inflated, self-important title. Big Mal's mini-essay on what the profession of bouncer involves is eye-opening and hilarious. So is the fate of Fat Lol, who must sell his mobile phone (thus giving up his social mobility) because his own car has been booted.

George Soule

THE STATION-MASTER

Author: Alexander Pushkin (1799-1837)
Type of plot: Satire
Time of plot: The 1830's
Locale: A country station and St. Petersburg
First published: "Stantsionnyi smotritel'," 1831 (English translation, 1875)

> *Principal characters:*
> SAMSON VYRIN, the station-master
> DUNYA, his daughter
> MINSKY, an officer
> THE NARRATOR, a traveler

The Story

After an irrelevant introduction about station-masters in general, the narrator tells about one in particular. Samson Vyrin, a widower, is the harried station-master at a remote location visited by the narrator. The operation runs smoothly because his beautiful fourteen-year-old daughter, Dunya, knows how to calm irritated customers, organize the business of the station, and keep her father on an even keel.

The weary narrator presents his papers to the station-master, who copies them in a log book, a bureaucratic necessity in czarist Russia. As the narrator looks around the station during this process, he notes the presence of paintings on the wall depicting the tale of the prodigal son. The first painting portrays the leave-taking of the son, the second his dissolute behavior as he wastes his inheritance, the third his subsequent poverty and tending of swine, and the fourth the joyous reception of the son by the father as the boy returns to the paternal home. As the station-master completes the recording of the orders, Dunya enters the room with a samovar; the three sit down for a chat and tea. The narrator is very impressed by Dunya and, when he is ready to leave, he asks for a kiss. The narrator remembers this kiss even to this day.

A few years later, the narrator is again in the area and stops at the same station. The paintings depicting the parable of the prodigal son are still on the wall, but the station is unkempt and the master has aged. After a few preliminary remarks, Samson tells the narrator what has happened since their last meeting.

A young officer, a certain Minsky, stopped at the station and fell in love with Dunya. In order to prolong his visit, he feigned an illness and Dunya served as his nurse. When Minsky had apparently recovered and was ready to leave, he offered to drive Dunya to church; Dunya was reluctant, but her father, who liked the young officer, persuaded her to accept the ride. When Dunya did not return later in the morning, Samson went to the church and discovered that Dunya had not been there. Going on to the next station, his fear was confirmed; his daughter had run away with Minsky, according to the master of that station. Samson returned home and fell ill.

When he had recovered, Samson decided to travel to St. Petersburg and try to rescue his daughter from a life of shame. The station-master was sure that the officer meant only to use his daughter and then discard her, thus forcing her to become a prostitute in the large city. He found Minsky and implored him to return his daughter; the officer, however, replied that he and Dunya were in love, what was done was done, and, having handed the old man a sum of money, pushed him out into the street.

In a state of despair, Samson walked around St. Petersburg in a daze and accidentally discovered Minsky's coach before a house. Correctly surmising that his daughter lived there, he told a maid that he had a message for her mistress, brushed past her, and found his daughter in a beautifully appointed room. Dunya was sitting next to Minsky, looking at him tenderly and winding her fingers through his hair. When she saw her father, Dunya fainted and Minsky expelled Samson from the house. The old man returned to his station, took to drink, and wallowed in self-pity. He concludes his story by telling the narrator that he has not heard from Dunya, but he is sure that she has wound up like other women in her position: poor and discarded, living off the streets. He had punctuated this sad tale with frequent sobbing and glasses of rum. The narrator leaves the station, but he has been deeply touched by the story.

Many years later, the narrator is again in the vicinity of the station. He discovers that the station is closed and that Samson has died of drinking. He also learns that the master's grave was visited by a beautiful lady with three children, a nurse, and a dog. The lady arrived in a beautiful carriage, cried over the old man's grave, and tipped the little boy who told her of her father's death. Dunya had finally come home.

Themes and Meanings

Alexander Pushkin's attitude toward religion was skeptical, to say the least; among his writings are works that would be considered blasphemous or irreverent by any standard. In this story, the author uses two New Testament parables—those of the prodigal son and the good shepherd—as contrasts to the reality of the station-master's life.

On his first visit, the narrator sees the four pictures depicting the tale of the prodigal son and recalls the story behind each picture. On his second visit, the narrator again notes the presence of the pictures, thus reminding the reader of the parable. Dunya's experiences and character are quite different from those of the errant son; while the latter is a fool who contributes nothing to his father's work and desires only to spend his inheritance in riotous living, Dunya is the mainstay of her father's station and goes to St. Petersburg reluctantly. The son is depicted with loose women, while Dunya maintains a monogamous relationship with the man she loves. When the son runs out of money, his friends abandon him; he is forced to live with pigs and to eat their food. Dunya, on the other hand, is not abandoned, but rather lives comfortably with a man who loves her very deeply.

The big difference between Pushkin's story and the parable is the delusion of the father, perhaps caused by his viewing of the pictures every day and presuming that reality will parallel what he has read in the Scriptures. Samson persists in believing that his daughter will come to the same end as the prodigal son. He does not wait for his daughter to come home, but seeks her out. When his attempts are unsuccessful, he returns home and drinks himself to death. Dunya does return home, but in finery and with children, not seeking forgiveness and not degraded. The prodigal son realized that he had been foolish and sought to rectify his errors; Dunya has always been independent and has always known what to do under any circumstances. She has not been foolish. Dunya's father, not Dunya, has fallen into ruin. Even on her return to the village, she is in control of her children and tells the young boy that she does not need a guide to the cemetery. She is not the lost person that her father imagines, but rather an assertive young woman in control of her life.

Is this tale, then, a polemic with the parable of the prodigal son, an attack on filial piety and religion? It may only be the use of a tale familiar to all Russian readers of the time in order to make other points, such as the complexity of life or the danger of simply transferring one's reading to reality without thought. On the other hand, given Pushkin's attitude toward religion, it may well have been an attempt on his part to demonstrate the shortcomings of biblical morality.

Samson refers to his daughter as the "lost sheep" and seeks her, just as the good shepherd sought the one lost sheep in the New Testament parable. Samson, however, is unsuccessful, and Pushkin seems to ridicule the efforts of the old man. The officer, who on one occasion is contrasted to a wolf by the station-master (before the flight to St. Petersburg), lures the lost sheep away, while the shepherd returns home empty-handed. Moreover, the reader knows that Samson's effort is ill-advised and not the praiseworthy search of the shepherd; the "lost sheep" is better off with the wolf than with her father at the station.

Despite the religious symbolism, it is possible that Pushkin was attempting to scuttle a literary myth, not religion. The author wrote this story as Romanticism was giving way to realism as the predominant literary influence. One of the typical plots of sentimental novels was the doomed love of social unequals, usually a noble male and peasant female. In this story Pushkin portrays such a situation, but with a completely different ending; the love is enduring. The use of religious symbolism may have been only to buttress his point that established dogma—in this case, literary—had to give way to alternative positions.

Style and Technique

Pushkin stands as an example of the transition from Romanticism to realism; his poetry, especially his early verse, is usually viewed as part of Romanticism, while his prose is seen as the beginning of Russian realism. In this story, Pushkin employs the precision and economy of words that serve as ingredients of realism, but he also begins with a windy introduction that is completely irrelevant to the story. Perhaps Pushkin wanted to demonstrate the two styles within one story in order to point out the great difference between them and to show the superiority of a precise style, telling a story quickly, over a list of irrelevancies.

Philip Maloney

STEADY GOING UP

Author: Maya Angelou (Marguerite Johnson, 1928-   )
Type of plot: Social realism
Time of plot: The late 1950's or early 1960's
Locale: A bus traveling from Memphis, Tennessee, to Cincinnati, Ohio
First published: 1972

> *Principal characters:*
> ROBERT (BUDDY), a twenty-two-year-old African American man
>   traveling north on a bus
> AN ELDERLY WOMAN, who befriends him
> ABE and
> SLIM, two drunken white passengers
> THE BUS DRIVER

The Story

Robert, a young African American man, is having trouble sleeping on the bus taking him north, from Memphis, Tennessee, to Ohio, as it moves through the rain. He is tired and worries about his sister, who, he has recently learned, is ill in Cincinnati.

As he dozes, preoccupied with his concern for his sister's welfare, he recalls their history together. After his parents died when he was fifteen, he had reared his sister himself. Apprenticing at an auto repair shop trained him to become an excellent mechanic. Meanwhile he cared for his sister and supported her when she reached college age and chose to pursue a career in nursing. Robert also has a fiancé, Barbara, who has helped him see the importance of his sister's career choice and of the pride that will come to the family when Baby Sister enters the caring profession and is in a position to help those like their own parents, who died before their time.

Giving up on finding a comfortable resting position, Robert rises from his seat to move forward on the bus but stops when an elderly woman—the only other black passenger—speaks to him. Taking a maternal interest in him, the woman cautions him that two white men (later identified as Abe and Slim) who are drinking were discussing him as he slept. Following the woman's advice, Robert returns to the back of the bus rather than risk confrontation.

When the bus stops, Robert must go to the restroom, so he exits the bus, even though the drunken white men also disembark. He is in the "colored" restroom when Abe and Slim burst in and trap him. Accusing him of going north to pursue white women, they threaten him, making lewd references to his genitals. Robert acts quickly. He knees one man in the groin, seizes a bottle, and hits the other over the head with it. After disguising the blood covering the front of his shirt with a coat belonging to one of the men, he leaves the restroom and bumps into the bus driver, who is looking for his missing passengers. As Robert boards the bus, the woman waiting inside expresses her relief to see him again. The bus continues its journey to Cincinnati, leaving the secret of the missing men in the restroom.

Themes and Meanings

The major theme of "Steady Going Up" is the vulnerability of innocent black men to white violence. Maya Angelou wrote the story out of the consciousness that African American women feel toward the endangerment that black men face, suggesting what the men might do to bolster and protect their manhood. Angelou draws implicitly on a long history of white violence against black men, false accusations that black men lust after white women, and the white stereotyping of black sexuality. In having her young African American protagonist persevere and conquer the white racists who seek to harm him, she reverses the pattern of victimization inherent in decades of lynchings and racial violence.

The story is written in the African American reform tradition of uplift, with the title a version of the motto of the black women's movement, Lifting As We Climb, meaning that each individual black person's achievements and contributions help to lift the race as a whole and aid other African Americans in seizing opportunities historically denied to them.

Style and Technique

Angelou re-creates stereotypes that are emblematic of different segments of the black and white populations. Robert is a good, responsible, caring young man who has been "steady going up." Since the death of his parents he has taken responsibility for the family by learning a trade, making himself a master mechanic, and rearing his younger sister. In looking after her interests, he has assumed the role of a father figure and best friend (as Buddy, her nickname for him, connotes). He has been a kind of guardian angel for her, helping her to attend nursing school and heading north to get her when he hears that she is ill.

Robert is a fine man physically as well as a person of good moral character. His tall physique makes it hard for him to get comfortable on the cramped seats of the bus, and when the elderly woman speaks to him, he is polite and deferential to her in response. The woman, meanwhile, also represents an important social type in the black community. She is the respected elder, what sociologists have called an "other mother," in reference to women who care for all the children in their neighborhoods as if they were their own, and who look out for the welfare of young black people even if they are strangers, offering advice and wisdom. Her religious faith, part of the paradigm of the respected elder, is represented in the Bible that she has on her lap. Her warning to Robert about the white men is based on a cognizance of what can happen to young black men at the hands of white racists. The two vile white men embody white southern lower-class male racism—what the elderly black woman terms trash coming from trash.

Angelou creates a tension that grows throughout the story between Robert's goodness (manifested in his selfless concern for his sister, his polite respect for the elderly woman, and his love for his fiancé) and the ominous presence of the two drunken white men, who eye Robert and move closer to his seat as they drink liquor while the bus travels north. This tension builds to the scene when the bus stops. The tension, which develops out of the reader's fear for Robert and the physical harm that may come to him, is heightened by the use of claustrophobic imagery. Robert's body does not fit into the seats; he cannot move to more commodious seating in the front of the bus because of the white men, so he spends much of his time cramped into a semifetal position. Even outside the confines of the bus he is trapped within the narrow and filthy walls of the "colored-only" restroom that he must use when the white men corner him. The turning point of the story, and the release of tension, comes with Robert's victory over his would-be oppressors and his success in regaining his seat on the bus with his bloody shirt undetected. Ironically, it is the segregated institutions created by whites that protect Robert because the bus driver does not think to look for the missing white men in the nonwhite restroom.

Robert's success against his attackers is more than a personal triumph. It is classic in its dimensions—a David and Goliath story, or a dragonslayer tale in which the good and common hero turns the tables and prevails over forces that seek to destroy him. It also has a political moral as a reversal of the historical pattern of white violence directed at black men. The relief in tension comes when Robert proves himself able to avert disaster, defend himself, and continue on his intended journey to Cincinnati to help his sister. His ability to free himself from the restroom and reenter the bus is by extension his ability to continue through his own volition and capabilities on the "upward" journey of his life. Robert has been steady going up: He has been steadfast and hardworking as he has matured to young adulthood, determined to make a better life for himself and his sister. He proves steady going up north, as well, handling the life-threatening incident with the white racists well. He thus symbolizes a new generation of black people in the United States, coming of age in the era when Jim Crow rules began to fall and a call for rights and dignified self-protection replaced older systems of deference toward whites and victimization of blacks at the hands of whites. Robert represents a whole generation of black men and women steadily rising up.

Barbara J. Bair

THE STEPPE
The Story of a Journey

Author: Anton Chekhov (1860-1904)
Type of plot: Lyric
Time of plot: The 1870's
Locale: Southern Russia
First published: "Step: Istoriya odnoi poezdki," 1888 (English translation, 1915)

Principal characters:
YEGORUSHKA KNYAZEV, the protagonist, a fatherless nine-year-old boy
IVAN KUZMICHOV, a provincial wool merchant and the boy's uncle
FATHER CHRISTOPHER, a Russian Orthodox priest
PANTELEY, the elderly, ailing peasant in charge of the train of carts
YEMELYAN, one of the carters, formerly a choir singer
DYMOV, a handsome, boisterous, and sometimes malicious carter, about thirty
MOSES, a poor Jewish innkeeper
SOLOMON, his half-demented brother
VARLAMOV, a provincial tycoon

The Story

Southern Russia is covered by a vast, prairie-like grassland, "the steppe." Anton Chekhov's story recounts the experiences of the young hero, Yegorushka, during his journey of several weeks across the steppe to the great city of Kiev. His uncle, Kuzmichov, and a family friend, Father Christopher, are accompanying a cart train of sheep wool being taken to market. They are also charged with taking Yegorushka and arranging for his lodging and schooling in Kiev. It is the boy's first time away from his mother, the widow of a civil-service clerk.

The two men, in high spirits, set out early one July morning. Yegorushka is in tears as the dilapidated carriage leaves the familiar town and cemetery where his father and grandmother lie. The men chide the crybaby and discuss the questionable merits of further education, but soon fall silent, subdued by the monotony of the limitless steppe. Yegorushka's feeling of desolation and loneliness deepens.

That evening the party briefly stops at an isolated inn to inquire about their wagon train, which has preceded them, and about the powerful Varlamov, with whom they have business. They are effusively greeted by Moses, the obsequiously affable Jewish innkeeper. While the two friends talk, Moses takes Yegorushka into his squalid quarters, where the boy meets the obese wife and several sickly children.

Overcome at the plight of the orphan, the wife, after an intense discussion in Yiddish, gives Yegorushka a honeycake, a treat the family can ill afford. The boy returns to find the men talking with the half-mad Solomon. The bizarrely ill-clothed brother, as rudely arrogant as Moses is fawning, points out that as a poor Jew, he is doubly damned. Had he great wealth, however, even Varlamov would fawn on him. Their rest over, the party sets out again and soon overtakes the wagon train. Finding all well, they transfer Yegorushka to one of the wool carts and to the care of the head wagoner, old Panteley, while they, in search of Varlamov, will travel separately and meet in Kiev.

Yegorushka awakes in the morning to find himself high atop the last of the twenty carts in the train. A commotion soon brings the spread-out carters together. One, Dymov, has brutally killed a harmless grass snake. The older men are troubled by the needless violence and talk of Dymov's character. When the wagon stops at a well, Dymov, noticing the boy, jokingly accuses Panteley of having given birth to a baby boy overnight. Offended, Yegorushka takes a strong dislike to the laughing carter. This dislike intensifies some days later when Dymov attempts to dunk the boy while the younger men are happily swimming and net-fishing in a river.

The wagons again move out in the cool dusk, and Yegorushka stares at the stars, troubled by feelings of his own insignificance and isolation. He thinks of death. At a rest halt the men gather around the campfire and tell stories prompted by the roadside graves of travelers killed by brigands. These gruesome tales are interrupted by the arrival of a stranger, a hunter. He, too, has a story. After years of unsuccessful courtship, he has married the girl of his dreams. He is ecstatically happy. His account has a strangely depressing effect on the others. When Yegorushka awakes at dawn, he sees the men talking with the much-sought Varlamov, whose impatient figure radiates power and authority.

That night, the weather is oppressively close. The men are tired and ill-tempered, and Dymov picks a quarrel with the inoffensive Yemelyan. Yegorushka rushes to Yemelyan's defense and is derisively brushed aside by Dymov. "Hit him, hit him!" screams Yegorushka, before running away. After eating, Dymov gruffly apologizes to both Yemelyan and Yegorushka, inviting the boy to hit him. The long-threatened storm finally breaks. The constant lightning and thunderclaps terrify the shivering boy, who unsuccessfully tries to hide. Under way again the next day, Yegorushka feverishly dozes and fitfully dreams of his recent experiences. In the late afternoon they at last arrive in Kiev, where he is reunited with his uncle and Father Christopher, who are elated at the successful sale and impatient with Yegorushka's sullen, semidelirious state.

Yegorushka awakens in the morning recovered and refreshed, but surprised not to see sodden wool bales under him. After breakfast a grumbling Kuzmichov takes the boy in search of his new lodgings. Advance arrangements have not been made, but it is hoped that an old friend of Yegorushka's mother will lodge the boy. At length, the widow is found, and with the departure of Kuzmichov and Father Christopher, "Yegorushka felt his entire stock of experiences had vanished with them like smoke.

He sank exhaustedly on a bench, greeting the advent of his new and unknown life with bitter tears. What kind of life would it be?"

Themes and Meanings

The major theme of this story is Yegorushka's awakening to the complex and often harsh world beyond childhood. The boundless steppe is Chekhov's metaphor for life, and Yegorushka's journey through a portion of it is an important stage in his growing up. If Chekhov's steppe is life, it must have the same features: vast, incomprehensible, sometimes frightening, sometimes beautiful, often monotonous, and, most of all, desolate. Loneliness and isolation are the abiding essence of the steppe. The immensity of the landscape, the vastness of the sky, the infinite remoteness of the stars, all contribute to humanity's sense of its own insignificance, the despair and horror, the solitariness that awaits in the grave. Yegorushka is unable to establish rapport with any of his companions. Closely akin to the isolation theme is that of death. Although the boy cannot yet encompass the possibility of his own death, the subject is ever-present. Yegorushka encounters evil for the first time in the quarrelsome and combative Dymov. Even more frighteningly, he recognizes his own powerlessness in its presence. Dymov haunts his fevered dreams.

Yegorushka's education is social as well as moral, for he meets a wide variety of types ranging from the pathetic, disfigured, former singer Yemelyan to the ruthless, almost legendary provincial tycoon, Varlamov. The theme of social prejudice is also evoked in the encounter with the family of the Jewish innkeeper, especially the obsessed brother Solomon.

At journey's end, Yegorushka has had many new experiences. He remains a nine-year-old, but one who has painfully surmounted his first rite of passage. A new stage of his journey, his school years in Kiev, lies before him. He looks forward to them with anxiety, for the school of the steppe has taught him something of the nature of life.

Style and Technique

"The Steppe," like many Chekhov works, has little action or plot. It consists of a series of small, seemingly independent episodes linked by Yegorushka. Taken together, they portray a formative stage in his short life. The story is framed by Yegorushka's departure from home and his arrival in Kiev some weeks later, although only the opening and closing days of the journey are related.

Chekhov's third-person narrative technique is simple. After each of the formative episodes, Yegorushka tries to understand what has happened. Sometimes, he listens as others discuss the event; at other times, he reflects on his own; on still other occasions, the narrator's voice enters and (rather clumsily) "editorializes." "The Steppe" is narrated from two points of view: that of the omniscient author and that of the naïve, nine-year-old Yegorushka. Working on his first long, serious prose piece, Chekhov was not always successful in his effort to distinguish between the two viewpoints.

Chekhov is primarily an artist of mood and atmosphere rather than a social commentator. The story's main vehicle for the poetic evocation of mood is the steppe itself, which is its lyrical heroine, a protagonist no less important than Yegorushka. As the carts lumber on under the stars, the narrator is entranced by the beauty of the steppe:

> In this triumph of beauty, in this exuberance of happiness, you feel a tenseness and an agonized regret, as if the steppe knew how lonely she is, how her wealth and inspiration are lost to the world—vainly, unsung, unneeded, and . . . you hear her anguished, hopeless cry for a bard, a poet of her own.

In Chekhov, the great Russian steppe found its bard.

D. Barton Johnson

A STICK OF GREEN CANDY

Author: Jane Bowles (1917-1973)
Type of plot: Social realism
Time of plot: The mid-1950's
Locale: A town in the United States
First published: 1957

> *Principal characters:*
> MARY, the chief protagonist, a young girl
> FRANKLIN, a slightly younger boy
> MARY'S FATHER
> FRANKLIN'S MOTHER

The Story

Mary is a young girl, apparently about eleven years old, who undergoes a small, gentle rite of passage that forces her to take notice of the world of other children and adults. At the beginning of the story, she is a confirmed loner who stays away from other children, preferring to play in her own domain—a clay pit located a mile outside town. By the story's end, her seclusion sustains her less satisfactorily, and its security appears illusive.

Mary is a "scrupulously clean child" with "well-arranged curls"; her predominant characteristic, made immediately apparent in the story, is that she would like reality to be similarly orderly. She plays alone, because she perceives other children, whose games are noisy and hectic, to be a threat to the world of her imagination. That world is sustained by the clay pit, which Mary imagines is the barracks for a troop of soldiers that she commands. The military life suits her, for just as she cannot bear uncleanliness, she is a stickler for routine.

A mishap disrupts her routine, however, and leads her toward a series of experiences that will submit the world of her clay pit to the influence of the wider world beyond it. While playing in the pit, she slips, gets mud on her coat, and decides that she must wait until dark to go home. She thinks it necessary to concoct for her troops an explanation of why she has remained longer than usual, and tells them that she has decided to give them extra training to make them into a crack "mountain-goat fighting" unit. Despite this ready explanation, the unexpected mishap has worked cracks in her make-believe world. She is certain that her troops will accept her explanation, but she has difficulty accepting the deceit herself.

Other changes in her occur. She experiences new sensations: As night falls, she begins to feel uneasy, like an intruder in her own domain. She skulks home along the darkest streets to hide her dirty coat, somewhat ashamed and apprehensive about the possibility of a reprimand.

At home, her father does reprimand her and tells her to play at the playground like all the other children. The next day, Mary nevertheless returns to her clay pit, jubilant at feeling, for the first time, undaunted by her father's authority. She prepares her men for battle with the children on the playground. When her father drives by without stopping to chastise her again, she is perplexed to find her jubilation somewhat deflated.

A boy, Franklin, appears. He has come from the house above the clay pit. He is both similar to, and clearly different from, Mary. He is fastidious in a worldly sense—he looks "prudently" up and down the street as he crosses to the pit—but he is indifferent to smearing his coat with clay as he slides into the pit. Because Mary has not seen Franklin before, she scoffs dubiously at him when he says that he lives in the house. When he abruptly returns to the house, she follows him, her curiosity engaged by her righteous indignation at finding that she cannot command in him the same respect she does in her troops.

The state of the house, which is being repainted, challenges Mary's appetite for orderliness at the same time that Franklin's indifference to her challenges her egocentricity. The room into which she follows Franklin is so cluttered with furniture that she is forced to squeeze between two bureaus, "pinching her flesh painfully"—the challenge has an intrusive, tangible dimension. Oddly, however, the house also contrasts favorably with her clay pit in some respects. She sits in a chair "deeper and softer" than any she has experienced. With these and several other touches of detail, Jane Bowles suggests that the attraction Mary finds in isolating herself from the world beyond the clay pit is being questioned and subverted.

With the appearance of Franklin's mother, this process quickens. She, like the bureaus, inadvertently demands Mary's attention. The room is so cramped that the mother's knees constantly touch Mary's as she addresses her in an adult, albeit immature and gossipy, fashion. She tells Mary, for example, that she would rather have had a girl than a boy; that would have permitted her to discuss her favorite topic—furnishings. Ironically, she also reveals that Franklin, who has led Mary out of her isolation, is himself a loner: "He sits in a lot and don't go out and contact at all."

The chat, in which neither Mary nor Franklin do any of the talking, is interrupted when the mother tells Franklin to fetch a tea box filled with candy. The social encounter ends when Mary selects a stick of green candy and abruptly leaves. While she continues to harbor an immature hostility toward other people, she also experiences subtle positive results from the encounter with Franklin and his mother. Her perspective on the area surrounding the clay pit has previously been from down in the pit, which she always approached from below; now, she commands a wider panorama from her position uphill from the pit: "She had never experienced the need to look at things from a distance before, nor had she felt the relief that it can bring."

The next day, she returns to the pit, but her make-believe world is now seriously jeopardized. She forgets for the first time to summon her men to order with a bugle call before addressing them. She cannot convince herself of the reality of her barracks.

It is only at this point, when Mary has begun to lose some of her imaginative independence and to incorporate some of the socialization that her father has tried to dictate to her, that her father appears, apparently to reprimand her again.

Themes and Meanings

Mary grows up to a certain extent in the course of the story's action, which takes place over three days. In a sense, however, the story also presents an example of the regrettable erosion of the child's ability to be sustained by imagination. Reality impinges on Mary's imagined world, and once that influence has begun, its course cannot be reversed. At the end of the story, Mary finds how fragile is imagination, because the mere act of trying consciously to shore up her make-believe world erodes it further. She searches about to find a reason why her troops cannot practice their mountain-goat fighting on the steps up to Franklin's house, but "the reason was not going to come to her. She had begun to cheat now, and she knew it would never come."

Rather than suggest merely that this kind of erosion of imagination is a wholly negative thing, Bowles also suggests that it is a necessary compromise with the world that other people inhabit. Not to accept that fact, she suggests, is a failing. This view is made clear in her characterization of Mary, who, while she is scrupulously fair and almost egalitarian in dealing with her troops, is also petulant when dealing with Franklin. Similarly, while she is self-assured in her clay pit, she is uncomfortable in the presence of Franklin's mother. While any variance from the habitual is a threat to her narrowly construed picture of the world, every challenge to her make-believe world has a subtle maturing, socializing influence on her.

That Bowles considers this process of compromise to have its costs is clear in such things as her characterization of Franklin's mother as a gossipy and ill-finished adult who could hardly be considered a compelling model for Mary. This view is reinforced by the triumphant tone Bowles ejects into sentences that describe how satisfying Mary's egocentricity can be: "She was rapidly perfecting a psychological mechanism which enabled her to forget, for long stretches of time, that her parents existed."

Style and Technique

Bowles repeatedly uses physical details and descriptions of settings to suggest personality traits and to flesh out themes. At the opening of the story, for example, she pays close attention to the geometry of the clay pit in which Mary plays. From the pit, Mary can see the "curved" highway, the steep "angle" of the hill in which the pit is dug, the "square" house above, whose steps lead to the curb, "dividing the steep lawn in two." The geometrical imagery describes the way Mary construes her surroundings to suit her needs—as tidy and regular. She has no patience with having to confront the geometry of the hill on its own terms; she finds it "tedious" to have to climb up a set of steep steps to follow Franklin. Once inside Franklin's house, she becomes anxious because the spaces there are cramped and dark, intimidating her so that she "looked around frantically for a wider artery."

A common feature of all of Bowles's writing is an arch, understated humor. That element is apparent here in her choice of a military make-believe world for Mary; such a fascination seems somewhat unusual for a young girl. The subtlety of Bowles's humor appears in such things as the description of the way that Mary walks home from her clay pit in her dirty coat: "She walked along slowly, scuffing her heels, her face wearing the expression of a person surfeited with food." Bowles does not say that Mary is pouting, but it is apparent from this sentence that that is what she is doing. The playground Mary dislikes intensely is called the Kinsey Memorial Grounds—the somber touch in the name supports humorously Mary's perception that it describes a place where the fantasy that sustains her is likely to be buried under the squealing of children who play with little apparent design or imagination.

If Bowles's humor is lightly sketched, so, too, is her theme. It finds its focus not in any token heavily laden with symbolism, but in a simple stick of green candy, an unlikely centerpiece of a rite of passage, but one that is in keeping with the changes Mary experiences.

Peter Monaghan

THE STONE BOY

Author: Gina Berriault (1926-1999)
Type of plot: Psychological
Time of plot: The 1950's
Locale: A farm near a rural community in the United States
First published: 1957

Principal characters:
ARNOLD CURWING, a nine-year-old boy who accidentally kills
his brother
EUGIE CURWING, his fifteen-year-old brother
MR. CURWING, his father
MRS. CURWING, his mother
NORA CURWING, his sister

The Story

"The Stone Boy" is a story about a nine-year-old boy who accidentally kills his older brother as they are on their way to the garden to pick peas. The fact of the accidental killing of Eugie, however, is not the major question posed by the characters in this story. Rather, the question involves why Arnold, after having accidentally killed his brother, does not return home immediately to call for help from his parents but instead spends an hour in the garden, picking peas. Arnold's father and mother and his Uncle Andy are unable to understand what kept Arnold in the garden while his brother lay dead. Arnold, himself, has no answer. All he can say is that the purpose of his trip to the garden in the first place was to pick peas, and the peas had to be picked while it was still cool, before the sun came up. The sheriff comes to the conclusion that the shooting was indeed an accident, that there was no malice intended, and that Arnold is either dim-witted or completely rational but unfeeling, like many criminals.

Under the circumstances, Arnold's father can think of nothing to do but take the gun away from the boy; Uncle Andy accepts the sheriff's explanation to the extent of making ironic and mean comments about Arnold's behavior to the farm people, who call on the Curwings to express their sympathy. Arnold's mother can hardly bear to look at her son, and his sister, Nora, ignores his presence.

If the sheriff is correct in his explanation of Arnold's behavior, then Arnold is, indeed, a stone boy, unable to weep at a tragic accident, uncaring, and perhaps even cruel. On the other hand, one could argue that the boy is only nine, that his remaining in the garden to pick peas was the result of a trauma brought on by a sense of responsibility for the death of a brother who was his favorite companion. In this instance, a reader could question the motivation of the parents, relatives, and friends, who offer Arnold no solace or comfort in a time of intense need. Perhaps the author is demonstrating that "stone" parents create "stone" boys.

Answers to all these questions concerning the motivation of the characters must be found in the details of the story because the point of view Gina Berriault uses restricts the reader to Arnold's consciousness, and Arnold does not know why he behaves as he does. Moreover, since the plot is epiphanic, beginning *in medias res* without exposition and concluding without resolution, the author provides no explanation. In addition, the epiphanic ending of the story is even more puzzling than the unanswered questions concerning motivation. At the end of the story, Arnold's mother attempts to make some human contact with her son, but Arnold rejects her:

> "What'd you want?" she asked humbly.
> "I didn't want nothing," he said flatly.
> Then he went out of the door and down the back steps, his legs trembling from the fright his answer gave him.

This kind of epiphany at the end of the story throws a reader back to the beginning of the story to seek clarification and meaning.

Themes and Meanings

In "The Stone Boy," the roles of the various members of the family assume important dimensions. The father, clearly the stereotypical masculine presence, takes care of those activities outside the house. Mother and daughter are shown only tending to household tasks. Eugie, almost a man, has begun to assume many of the responsibilities of the father. Arnold's ties are still more to his mother, though he envies Eugie and unknowingly attempts to assert dominance. Arnold's attachment to his mother, his continuing need for her, and his subconscious desire to relate to her are as much a motivating factor as is Arnold's need to assert dominance. That Arnold feels a special sympathy for his mother is made evident by his knowledge of her intense discomfort as she tends to the canning in the kitchen where the heat from the wood stove would be almost unbearable. Sometimes, the reader is told, Arnold would come from out of the shade where he was playing and make himself as uncomfortable as his mother was in the kitchen by standing in the sun until the sweat ran down his body. The fear caused by Arnold's desire to emulate his father and older brother, while the nine-year-old is still too young to assume the role, causes Arnold to seek out his mother, especially so that he might express his fear and his hostility and receive from her solace and understanding.

The apparent need of a son to assume the role of patriarch, even if it means revolting against the father (or killing him as in Sophocles' *Oidipous Tyrannos*, c. 429 B.C.E.; *Oedipus Tyrannus*, 1715), is a dominant theme in Western culture. Indeed, the patriarchal model of the culture, in which rule is passed from father to son who becomes father, sometimes creates a situation in which a son may want to rule before his time or in which a father may want to keep his son away from power. Such maneuverings among fathers and sons usually result in some kind of violent behavior.

It is not likely that Berriault is saying that Arnold deliberately killed his brother. However, the complex of events seems to suggest that the accident was accompanied by alternating feelings of submission and dominance. If this suggestion is true, then Arnold would subconsciously understand the reason for the accident and would assume a guilt too great for him to bear. These feelings of guilt, traumatizing the boy, would account for his strange behavior and the strange behavior of family and neighbors. Because they are unable to understand Arnold's needs, family and neighbors reject him in a cruel way, thus inflicting on him the punishment he believes that he deserves. After taking the step, after assuming the desired role, Arnold knows that he cannot go back. He is man enough to wrap around him a robe of pride to protect himself, but still boy enough to be frightened by the position he has unnaturally assumed.

Style and Technique

In "The Stone Boy," Berriault creates symbols within the context of the story to direct readers toward a meaning that is not apparent on the surface. For example, nowhere in the story does the author say that the roles assumed by members of the family are stereotypically patriarchal, resulting in the reenactment of old patterns of behavior, in which sons and fathers sometimes engage in violent actions to keep each other and "their" women in their "rightful" places, as the places are defined by the dominant culture. By creating patterns made up of various telling details in the story, however, the author points readers toward this kind of reading, which gives surface action a meaning far beyond itself and invests characters with motivations deeply embedded in their subconscious.

It is possible for the reader to ignore the elements of symbolic structure and to accept surface content as all there is. Such reading of a symbolic story will cause the reader to miss important, complex, and universal relationships. More depth of interpretation ensures understanding of concepts continually present, linking the past and possibly the future.

Mary Rohrberger

THE STORM

Author: Kate Chopin (1851-1904)
Type of plot: Domestic realism
Time of plot: 1898
Locale: Louisiana
First published: written 1898; published 1969

> *Principal characters:*
> BOBINÔT, an Acadian planter
> CALIXTA, his wife
> BIBI, his four-year-old son
> ALCÉE LABALLIÈRE, a rich Acadian planter and Calixta's former
> lover
> CLARISSE, Alcée's wife

The Story

While Bobinôt and his son, Bibi, are shopping at Friedheimer's store, the air becomes still. Dark clouds roll in from the west, and thunder rumbles in the distance. Father and son decide to wait inside until the storm passes instead of trying to reach home. When Bibi suggests that Calixta may be frightened to be alone, Bobinôt reassures him that she will be all right.

The approaching storm does not, in fact, worry her. She merely closes the doors and windows and then goes to gather the clothes hanging outside. As she steps onto the porch, she sees Alcée Laballière ride through the gate to seek shelter from the rain.

From "At the 'Cadian Ball," to which "The Storm" is a sequel, the reader knows that six years earlier Calixta and Alcée had gone to Assumption together in a fit of passion, and the following year they were about to have another romantic rendezvous in New Orleans when Clarisse intervened. In love with Alcée and suspecting his intentions, Clarisse had proposed marriage. He agreed, and Calixta had then yielded to Bobinôt's suit.

Despite the passage of time and their marriages, Calixta and Alcée's passion for each other has not abated. As they stand at a window, lightning strikes a chinaberry tree. Calixta, startled, staggers backward into Alcée's arms; this physical contact arouses "all the old-time infatuation and desire for her flesh." Alcée asks, "Do you remember—in Assumption, Calixta?" She does indeed. There they had kissed repeatedly; now, as the storm rages, they make passionate love. When the storm subsides, they know that they must separate, at least temporarily.

Bobinôt and Bibi walk home, pausing at the well outside to clean themselves as well as they can before entering the house. Calixta is a fastidious housekeeper, and they fear the reception they will receive after trudging home in the mud. Bobinôt is ready with apologies and explanations, but he needs none. Calixta is overjoyed to see her family and delighted with the can of shrimps that Bobinôt has brought her.

Alcée is as happy as Calixta. His wife has gone to Biloxi, Mississippi, for a vacation, and he writes her "a loving letter, full of tender solicitude" that night, telling her to stay as long as she wants. He says that he misses her, but he puts her pleasure above his own.

Clarisse is happy, too, when she receives the letter. She loves her husband, but the vacation is her first taste of freedom since her marriage. She intends to accept Alcée's offer to stay in Biloxi longer before returning home.

Themes and Meanings

When Kate Chopin prepared the collection "A Vocation and a Voice" for publication (the collection was, ultimately, not published), she excluded "The Storm" because she recognized it as too explicit and advanced for the period. Her description of passionate lovemaking would have been bad enough, but her endorsement of the adultery would have scandalized her readers.

Chopin depicts sex as liberating and enjoyable. Indeed, for Calixta, adultery with Alcée is more satisfying than sex with her husband; it is with Alcée that "her firm, elastic flesh knew for the first time its birthright." Lovemaking with Alcée touches "depths . . . that had never yet been reached."

Nor does this adultery end in tragedy—quite the reverse. Calixta, who would normally be upset with her husband and child for bringing dirt into the house, welcomes them warmly. She is truly happy to be reunited with her family. Because her physical needs have been met, she can share her newfound joy with others.

Alcée's marriage also benefits. He may be telling Clarisse to stay in Biloxi so he can pursue his affair with Calixta—though there is no evidence in the story that the two continue their liaison—but his letter is nevertheless filled with love and regard for his wife and children. Like Calixta, he is physically satisfied and so can be emotionally generous.

Clarisse eagerly snatches at Alcée's offer. For her, as, apparently, for Calixta, marriage is confining. Calixta escapes by having sex with Alcée; Clarisse escapes by forgoing "intimate conjugal life" with him for a while. She will return to her husband, just as Calixta will remain with Bobinôt, yet this innocent adultery has given everyone a breath of freedom, cleansing them as a summer storm freshens and purifies the air.

Chopin's characters here do not rebel against the institution of marriage; they object only to being confined by traditional roles. Given the freedom to satisfy their physical or spiritual needs, they are content with their spouses. In fact, for marriage to succeed, Chopin argues, such freedom is crucial. Far from threatening marriage, this liberty is its only means of salvation.

Style and Technique

The storm is the story's central metaphor, representing the passion of Calixta and Alcée. By linking the two, Chopin indicates that the lovers' feelings are natural and therefore not subject to moral censure. She reinforces this idea through other imagery drawn from nature, likening Alcée to the sun and Calixta to a lily and a pomegranate. Not only do these images come from nature, but they also derive from the biblical book The Song of Songs, giving a kind of religious sanction to the lovers' union.

The storm is not only natural but also powerful, like the passions it symbolizes. While Calixta and Alcée make love, the thunder crashes and the elements roar; the passing of the storm indicates their physical exhaustion. While these passions, like the storm, are strong, they are not destructive. The storm does little damage, and when it passes the sun emerges, "turning the glistening green world into a palace of gems." The rain leaves the world a happier and more beautiful place, just as the lovers part with joy in their hearts. Alcée leaves with a smile, and Calixta answers him with laughter.

Chopin uses language to indicate that this joy derives from the lovers' equality. He is like the sun and she is a "white flame." She cushions but also clasps him, being both active and passive. His heart beats "like a hammer upon her" while she "strokes his shoulders." They "swoon together at the very borderland of life's mystery." In this union of true love there is neither master nor mastered—simply two partners who share desire and fulfillment. For Chopin, that is the only proper relationship between the sexes, the only one likely to bring happiness within marriage, or outside it.

Joseph Rosenblum

A STORY

Author: Dylan Thomas (1914-1953)
Type of plot: Social realism
Time of plot: The early twentieth century
Locale: Wales
First published: 1953

> *Principal characters:*
> THE NARRATOR, a boy on the threshhold of adolescence
> MR. THOMAS, his uncle
> SARAH THOMAS, his aunt
> BENJAMIN FRANKLYN,
> MR. WEAZLEY,
> NOAH BOWEN,
> ENOCH DAVIES,
> WILL SENTRY, and
> O. JONES, his uncle's mates

The Story

In an attempt to provide a momentary respite from the rigors of work and the limits of domesticity, a group of men in West Wales go on an annual outing. It has as its ostensible destination the town of Porthcawl, but it is actually designed to stop at every inviting public house along the way. During the course of the year, a fund is gradually accumulated sufficient to purchase twenty cases of pale ale to supplement the fare of the local pubs and to hire a sightseeing bus for transportation. The story is told from the perspective of a young boy with a poet's flair for descriptive language and a fascination with the eccentricities of the men he accompanies. Because the boy lives in relatively meager circumstances with his uncle's family in a small house adjoining their tiny shop, his range of social circumstances is limited to the intricate detail of the shop, his observations of the peculiarities of his uncle's friends, and the energetically inventive stretch of his imagination. He first hears of the event when he reads an advertisement for sheep-dip, "which was all there was to read."

Because he spends so much time with his relatives, he has created an image of them that gives them a dimension beyond the mundane facts of their lives. His uncle is described as a huge old buffalo bursting the bounds of the little house; his aunt is reduced to a tiny mouselike creature. When his uncle's friends gather to plan their yearly outing, the boy turns his enthusiasm for local mythmaking toward their individualistic turns of speech, rendering their banter as the declarations of men with a singular capability, each exhibiting a skill appreciated and encouraged by the others, and each with a local history that includes some memorable feat from past excursions. There are certain conventions that have become a part of the preparation for the trip, including a temporary tiff in which the boy's aunt, Sarah Thomas, withdraws to her mother's house for the weekend. The uncle's decision to include the boy is a change in the routine, although not without some historical precedent, greeted predictably with good-natured, characteristic complaints before the men subside into tacit acceptance and find other things about which to disagree.

The tour bus leaves the village on a beautiful August morning, making a brief return to collect old O. Jones who, typically, has missed the bus. With impeccable timing, the men arrive at the first public house just as it opens. The boy is instructed to guard the bus against thieves—a preposterous notion—and occupies himself by wistfully looking at the cows while the men carouse in the bar, feeling a familiar sense of isolation ("on the lonely road, the lost, unwanted boy, and the lake-eyed cows") that is at the root of his poetic portraiture. When the men emerge, they are already becoming garrulous and boisterous, a mode of behavior that is compounded by further stops at a series of such exotically named pubs as the Twll in the Wall, the Sour Grapes, the Shepherd's Arms, and the Bells of Aberdovey. The boy remains an observer as the procession continues; he records the men's joyous exclamations, which reveal them in the spirit of freedom that is the goal of their journey. At the close of the day, he describes them as "thirty wild, wet, pickled, splashing men."

At the last stop, a stranger tries to impress everyone with spurious boasts, only to be devastatingly exposed through the rapier wit of Enoch Davies, evidence of the bountiful effects of the entire enterprise. As the bus heads home through the moonlight, the men continue their idiosyncratic behavior with hilarious persistence. Mr. Weazley demands they stop for another drink, while Jones begins to cook supper on his portable stove. Because all the pubs are closed, the party stops and Jones sets up a makeshift kitchen in a field. While he prepares a classic Welsh meal of sausage and mash, his contribution to the gathering, the men drink and sing, their dull cares banished momentarily. The wonderful mood of celebration and ease is evoked in an image of serenity as the boy recalls that he drifted to sleep, feeling safe against his uncle's large waistcoat. For a moment, separated from the obligations of their lives and wives, the company of men has come in contact with eternity.

Themes and Meanings

Dylan Thomas developed "A Story" as a presentation for Welsh television during the last year of his life. Like his well-known poem "Fern Hill," it recalls a joyous time in his youth from the perspective of his mature years. By re-creating the sensory excitement, the almost delicious loneliness, and the feeling of a cosmos of infinite possibilities waiting to be explored, Thomas reaches back to a time in his life prior to the onset of the disappointments that plagued his adult years. Whereas "Fern Hill" depends on a vision of the natural world as a source of wonder and delight, "A Story" is closer to *Under Milk Wood* (1954), his drama about the singular characters of the small Welsh town of Laugharne, which also presents a view of the adult world from a relatively innocent observer who is astonished and highly amused by the antics and odd speech of grownups. There are a number of images of an inspiring landscape, but most of the details are designed to convey the moods of the characters and the atmosphere of the shop, bus, and pubs where the action occurs.

The narrator's introduction to the mysterious world of men is presented as a readjustment of self-perception. At first, the boy's uncle is described in terms of his daunting size and physical presence, while his aunt is depicted as a quaint mouse-figure. There is a distinct separation between the boy and his family because they are rendered in surreal terms. The shop is less a place of commerce than a magical child's realm, with hiding places, strange creatures, and no responsibilities. The uncle's decision to include the boy on the outing is a recognition that he is on the edge of adolescence, and his gradual involvement in the company of men is presented as a part of a ritual that is rooted in ancient customs and folk traditions.

The men know their roles, but have room for verbal improvisation; the sentimentality that tends to weaken *Under Milk Wood* is replaced by an acerbic wit and an eye for human foibles. The tremendous enthusiasm for drink and song that marks the narrative, however, keeps the story within the child's inclination for delight. The men themselves are liberated by everything so that they may momentarily frolic again as the boys they once were. As in a child's dream, time itself seems to stop as food, drink, wit, and friendship transform the scene to "the end of the world in the west of Wales"—a charmed landscape akin to the countryside of "Fern Hill" and "Poem in October" (1946) to which Thomas always longed to return.

Style and Technique

The love of language and the mastery of craft that inform Thomas's finest poems are the source of the stylistic strength that gives "A Story" its unique narrative voice. According to poet and critic Donald Hall, Thomas was "the maddest of word-mad young poets," and his descriptions of the locations and characters of "A Story" are developed from the same long chains of adjectives that mark his poetry. The boy's uncle, in particular, is a figure of imposing dimensions, "a steaming hulk of an uncle, his braces straining like hawsers, crammed behind the counter of the tiny shop at the front of the house, and breathing like a brass band; or guzzling and blustery in the kitchen over his gutsy supper, too big for everything except the great black boats of his boots." Like a line from "Poem in October," the continual employment of qualifying and advancing terms, words recoiling off other words, gives the story its flavor. The mind of the boy is merged with the mind of the mature writer through the use of poetic language that expresses an outlook as well as a skill.

The pleasing peculiarities of the men on the outing are presented through Thomas's deft utilization of vernacular speech, itself poetic in its qualities and features. The story is an homage to the people Thomas lived among in Wales, and the rhythms of his writing may be seen as emerging from the patterns and flow of the conversations he heard in pubs and shops. The dry, laconic humor and the verbal exuberance of the men effectively convey the boozy amiability that Thomas treasured.

Leon Lewis

A STORY BY MAUPASSANT

Author: Frank O'Connor (Michael Francis O'Donovan, 1903-1966)
Type of plot: Psychological
Time of plot: The 1950's
Locale: A provincial town in County Cork, Ireland
First published: 1945

> *Principal characters:*
> TED MAGNER, the narrator and best friend of Terry Coughlan
> TERRY COUGHLAN, the childhood friend of Magner, a teacher in
>   the monks' school
> TESS COUGHLAN, Terry's sister, the childhood friend of Magner
> PA HOURIGAN, a local police officer
> DONNELAN, a friend of Magner

The Story

Having grown up in a small, provincial town in Ireland, the narrator, Ted Magner, states that he has been best friends with Terry Coughlan since they were children. Terry has always been well-spoken and likes classical music and languages. "Whatever he took up, he mastered," says Magner of his friend. Magner remembers the friendly arguments that they had when they were young. "Maybe you don't remember the sort of arguments you had when you were young," the narrator fondly tells his readers, knowing that they do. The argument that he recalls, however, is the one he had with Terry about writers. Magner lists Guy de Maupassant as one of the greatest writers. Terry disagrees, however, saying that there is nothing "noble" about Maupassant's stories; rather, they are slick, coarse, and commonplace.

As they reach young manhood, the two friends drift away from close contact with each other, but Magner continues to be fond of Terry. Terry takes a job teaching in the monks' school, and Magner gets a job elsewhere, beginning to associate with a different crowd, people such as Donnelan, of whom Terry does not approve. Magner tells the reader that Terry slowly grows disillusioned by the behavior of the monks at the school and is discouraged by a form of cheating that the monks condone, allowing one boy to take a state examination using another boy's name. Magner later learns from Donnelan that Terry has begun to drink. His first reaction is, "A sparrow would have about the same consumption of liquor." Magner sees Terry drunk about six months later, however, and realizes that Terry drinks constantly, keeping his drinking a secret from his family and from his sister, Tess. Magner understands why Terry is so secretive: "You might almost say he was drinking unknown to himself. Other people could be drunkards but not he." He wonders whether he should confront Terry about his drinking but realizes that he cannot because "you couldn't talk like that to a man of his kind." He also comments that Terry is drinking himself to death.

When Terry is forty years old, his mother dies. That same year he visits Paris in the summer for the first time. At first, Magner hopes that Terry will begin to straighten out, but later he realizes that "it was worse he was getting."

Finally, Magner is surprised one day several years later to be visited by Pa Hourigan, a local police officer, who asks Magner to speak to Terry about his disreputable life. Magner, who thinks Hourigan is referring to Terry's drunkenness, is amazed to learn that Hourigan is concerned about Terry's consorting with prostitutes: "low, loose, abandoned women," says Hourigan. The police officer, who is worried about Terry's soul, asks Magner to intervene, saying, "Do what you can for his soul, Mr. Magner. As for his body, I wouldn't like to answer." Magner comments about Terry in Latin, "Lilies that fester smell far worse than weeds."

Magner goes to Terry's house to confront him, speaking for a while with Terry and Tess. It reminds him of their old days together, until Tess leaves them alone. After a short time, Magner stands up to leave, realizing that he cannot discuss this situation with Terry: "There was something there you couldn't do violence to," Magner reasons. As he is leaving, Magner looks at Terry's bookcase, commenting, "I see you have a lot of Maupassant at last."

Somehow this remark cuts through the silence and reserve between the childhood friends, and Terry begins speaking honestly of his consorting with prostitutes and his drunkenness. He reveals that when he was first in Paris he took a prostitute to her room and discovered that she had her baby with her. After their transaction, the woman fell asleep; Terry remarks, "It's many years now since I've been able to sleep like that." This remark captures very well the kind of life in which Terry finds himself a prisoner. He continues to talk of the incident with this prostitute—one of many since then—because he remembers that after she awoke, they had a conversation about Maupassant. This conversation reminded Terry of his schoolboy arguments with Magner. Terry says that "it's only when you see what life can do to you" that one can appreciate Maupassant's stories.

Terry reads Magner's thoughts that this was indeed a strange conversation for a French prostitute and "a drunken waster" from the Irish countryside. Magner says sadly, "A man like you should have a wife and children." However, clearly this is not to be, and Magner ends the story with the observation, "And life was pretty nearly through with Terry Coughlan."

Themes and Meanings

In this story, Frank O'Connor is basically concerned with presenting a wasted life. He is especially concerned that despite a promising, bright, idealistic beginning, a person such as Terry Coughlan can allow something inside himself to die. The tragedy is that Terry, once interested in the nobility of human life and thought, can have reached the point where he is drinking himself to death. O'Connor shows clearly the horror of what life can do to certain individuals. The young Parisienne has entered into prostitution in order to earn a living; Terry Coughlan consorts with the lowest prostitutes rather than marry a good woman and rear a family.

A second tragedy that accompanies Terry's disintegration as a person is that Ted Magner is forced to witness the downfall of his best friend. Magner is helpless; there is nothing he can do to turn Terry around. Magner realizes this inability a number of times in the story when he seriously considers confronting Terry about his life situation. People such as Terry "stand or fall by something inside themselves," and no one else can help them, no matter how much they may wish to.

Style and Technique

O'Connor demonstrates his mastery of technique in several ways in this story. He makes special use of his first-person narrator, Ted Magner, to present the decay of Terry Coughlan from a highly personal perspective. Readers are not disinterested viewers of Terry's decay because of the way in which Magner tells the story. In addition, O'Connor makes effective use of colloquial Irish speech. Moreover, O'Connor displays the Irish sense of humor that one expects to find in his stories, having fun with such characters as Donnelan and with Pa Hourigan, who has a special respect for "education." The speech helps to convey the sense of warmth that exists in the personal relations in a small town where everyone knows everyone else and where it is particularly difficult to keep secrets, even those that one would like to keep in the dark.

The use of Maupassant in the story becomes an effective device in helping to organize the story and in presenting characterization and theme. First, the friends disagree about Maupassant—his coarseness and commonplaceness—at the story's beginning. Then, the last two pages conclude the discussion that started probably thirty years before. Both know that Maupassant would end Terry's story with Terry's death, and the narrator says that "life was pretty nearly through with Terry Coughlan" in the concluding sentence. In addition to organizing the story, the Maupassant material is appropriate to Terry because Terry's decay is typical of Maupassant's subject matter. It is moreover only in witnessing the hardships of life, the way life often does not follow one's plans or wishes, that Terry comes to appreciate Maupassant as a writer. Maupassant, according to Terry, may not deal with the noble, but then life itself often presents much that is ignoble.

A. Bruce Dean

THE STORY OF AN HOUR

Author: Kate Chopin (1851-1904)
Type of plot: Psychological
Time of plot: 1894
Locale: Natchitoches Parish, Louisiana
First published: 1894

Principal characters:
LOUISE MALLARD, the protagonist, a beautiful young woman
BRENTLEY MALLARD, her husband
JOSEPHINE, Mrs. Mallard's sister
MR. RICHARDS, a newspaperman, Brentley Mallard's close
friend

The Story

Because Louise Mallard suffers from a heart condition, her sister Josephine gently and carefully gives her the news of her husband's death. Mr. Richards, a close friend of her husband, Brentley Mallard, and the first to learn of the tragic railroad accident that claimed Mallard's life, has accompanied Josephine to help soften what they know will be a cruel blow.

Louise falls, sobbing, into her sister's arms, then retreats upstairs to her room. Josephine, who begs Louise to let her in, would be shocked if she knew what thoughts were racing through her sister's mind. Louise has loved her husband, who has in turn loved her and treated her kindly, but she is not crushed by his death, nor do her reflections make her sick.

Indeed, although she initially hesitates to admit to herself that she is not distressed, she begins to repeat one word: "free." Her life is her own again; no longer will she have to yield to her husband's wishes. Only yesterday she had regarded life as tedious and feared longevity. Now she yearns for long life.

Finally, she yields to her sister's repeated pleas to unlock her bedroom door. Louise embraces her sister, and together they go downstairs to rejoin Richards. As they reach the bottom of the stairs, Brentley comes through the door, unaware of the accident that supposedly has claimed his life. Richards tries to move between him and his wife to shield her from the shock, but he is too late; she has already seen Brentley. She screams and falls down dead. The doctors who examine her afterward say that her weak heart could not bear the sudden joy.

Themes and Meanings

Louise Mallard is Kate Chopin's strongest example of the self-assertive woman—so strong an example, in fact, that Richard Watson Gilder refused to publish the story in *The Century* because he regarded it as immoral. *Vogue*, which finally published it after the success of Chopin's *Bayou Folk* (1894), had initially rejected it for the same reason.

Mrs. Mallard certainly is a woman ahead of her time, for by the standards of the 1890's she should be happy. Her husband loves her and treats her well; she herself acknowledges that he "had never looked save with love upon her." Nor does she dislike Brentley.

However loving Brentley is, though, nothing can compensate Louise for the freedom that she has lost by marrying. Her face "bespoke repression"; no matter how kind Brentley has been, he has still imposed his will on his wife. Hence, Brentley's death is not tragic to her because it gives her own life back to her.

She therefore emerges from her room "like a goddess of Victory," with "a feverish triumph in her eyes." She has won back her freedom. Though Chopin does not specify how Louise will use that liberty, in "Lilacs," the next story she wrote, Mme Farival takes lovers, and Edna Pontellier in *The Awakening* (1899) also seeks sexual gratification outside marriage. Perhaps Louise, too, who resembles these women in her self-reliance, will seek sensual fulfillment.

Edna Pontellier also searches for her true vocation, which she believes is something other and more than mere wife and mother. Chopin regarded contemporary society as degrading to women, who were allotted limited roles in a male-dominated world. Just as the death of her husband sets Louise's body free, so, too, does it free her spirit to find happiness in any way that she wishes.

Her husband's return shatters her hopes. She is again a mere wife, subservient. This sudden reversal, the destruction of her dreams, kills her. Still, she is spared the living death of a stifling relationship, and before she thought her husband was dead she had dreaded a long life. The story's ending is therefore ironic but not tragic because Louise does escape marriage in the only way now open to her.

Style and Technique

Nature imagery underlines the plot and meaning. Although authors typically associate death with autumn and winter, Brentley's supposed death occurs in the spring. The trees are "all aquiver" with new life. Rain has fallen, purifying the air, and now the clouds are parting to show "patches of blue sky." This scene mirrors Louise's situation. The death of Brentley marks the end of the winter of her discontent; her soul can awake from its torpor. She can realize the full potential of her life, so she, like the trees, feels aquiver with life. The clouds again represent her married life, which cast shadows on her happiness, but now the horizon of her life is clearing. As she contemplates her future, she imagines "spring days and summer days" only, not autumn or winter days, because she links herself to the seasons of rebirth and ripening.

In contrast to the world of nature is the cloistered, confining house, symbol of domesticity. In her own room she looks through an open window, another symbol of her freedom. The window does not intervene between her and nature and allows her the scope of infinite vision. She herself locks and unlocks the door to her room, admitting or excluding whomever she wants. She has what Virginia Woolf stressed as so important, a room of her own. However, it is only a temporary, and finally an inadequate, refuge. She leaves it, as she must, to rejoin her sister and Richards; in unlocking her door she paradoxically consigns herself to the prison of her house. Nowhere else in the house is there even a glimpse of nature, and, in contrast to the open window, the front door is locked; only Brentley has the key. He can come and go as he pleases, but she remains trapped within.

Related to this contrast of nature and house is the imagery of up and down. Louise's room is upstairs, and from there she looks at the tops of trees and hears the songs of birds on the roof. Her freedom is thus literally elevating. Her leaving this refuge and going down the stairs foreshadows her loss of freedom. She descends from the heaven of solitude to the hell of marriage again, where she encounters her husband. Now death is her only salvation. Instead of soaring freely like the birds, she can escape only by sinking still lower, into the grave.

Joseph Rosenblum

THE STORY OF MY DOVECOT

Author: Isaac Babel (1894-1940)
Type of plot: Psychological
Time of plot: 1905
Locale: Nikolaev (near Odessa)
First published: "Istoriia moei golubiatni," 1925 (English translation, 1926)

Principal characters:
THE NARRATOR, the unnamed protagonist
MOTHER and
FATHER, the narrator's parents
SHOYL BABEL, the narrator's granduncle, killed during the
pogrom of October 20, 1905
MAKARENKO, an anti-Semitic cripple who strikes the narrator
KHARITON EFRUSSI, a wealthy Jew, the enemy of the Babel
family
KARAVAYEV and
PYATNITSKY, two Russian teachers who are friendly toward the
boy

The Story

"The Story of My Dovecot" describes the effect of the notorious pogrom of October 20, 1905, on the Babel family and particularly on the author himself as a boy of eleven. It is one of Isaac Babel's most autobiographical stories. Nevertheless, the author changes a number of crucial details, including even his age, to yield greater drama. The story is thus clearly a work of fiction, yet the author rightly maintains the verisimilitude of autobiography for its powerful effect on the reader.

The situation of the boy, as the story opens, is precisely delineated: His father will build him a dovecot and buy him three pigeons for it if he gets top marks in the Russian language and arithmetic exams. He needs the very highest scores, because the quota system will admit only two Jewish boys from his form into the preparatory class. If he is accepted into the higher school, his father, with his "pauper pride," will enjoy vicarious success. The pressures on the boy, all ultimately a result of Russian anti-Semitism at every level in the society, are sufficient to keep him in a state of permanent, anxious daydream and reverie.

The boy fails to make the quota because the wealthy Jew Khariton Efrussi, a wheat exporter, bribes the school authorities to admit his own son instead of Babel. Such betrayal by a fellow Jew is unbearable (Babel senior wants to bribe two longshoremen to beat up Efrussi)—but, again, Russian anti-Semitism is the root cause.

In the following year, young Babel succeeds in his aim, befriended by a Russian teacher, Karavayev, who gives him the A+ grade he actually earns, and by Assistant

Curator Pyatnitsky, for whom the boy, in a kind of exalted trance, recites from the works of Alexander Pushkin. After the examination, Pyatnitsky makes a point of protecting young Babel from some menacing Russian schoolboys. These two Russian humanitarians are important exceptions to the widespread anti-Semitism.

The "pauper's ball" that follows the boy's admission into the first class offers insight into the ways that the Babel family copes with life. While Father is delirious with victory (prematurely, as always), Mother is in despair, unable to see the future except as disaster. The reader learns that Grandfather had been a rabbi, was "thrown out for blasphemy," and is now starting to go insane. One uncle had died in a house of ill-fame; another is crazy. Granduncle Shoyl is full of wonderful, lying stories about his past; he now sells fish at the market. All dance and sing while young Babel pictures himself as David having defeated Goliath: "the Russian boys with their fat cheeks" as well as the sons of Jewish parvenus.

At last, the day comes to visit the market and buy pigeons from Ivan Nikodimych. The young lad's joy is destroyed, however, when he hears that Shoyl is perhaps dead. The pogrom, which has grown out of celebrations following the Constitutional Manifesto of October 17, has begun. While police officers look the other way, hordes of Russian scum, many poorer even than Jews, loot Jewish homes and businesses. (The Russian government connived in such pogroms, which sometimes led to the injuring and killing of hundreds of Jews, because they took people's minds away from revolution.)

Young Babel approaches his friend Makarenko, a cripple in a wheelchair, to ask about Shoyl. Makarenko, however, is in a fit of rage because he and his wife are unable to steal all the things that they believe they deserve to have. Doubly angered because the boy has nothing more valuable than pigeons, he smashes the boy on the head with one of the birds. The boy lies on the ground in a daze, with pigeon entrails running down his face.

In the moment of violence, as he overhears Makarenko's wife remark, "Their spawn must be wiped out," young Babel comes to a deep understanding of life. The author as narrator writes that he walked home, "weeping bitterly, full and happily as I never wept again in all my life." A certain genius is required to find the word "happily" here; it denotes that the boy will no longer live in a state of illusion—and that he knows it. In his new awareness, he is able to accept the shocking and ignominious death of Shoyl, who, as he died, had cursed his killers thoroughly—"a wonderful damning and blasting it was."

Themes and Meanings

The most important theme in the story is that of overcoming illusion. Not only the boy but also his entire family avoid facing reality. While it is largely anti-Semitism that leads them to this condition, it is also anti-Semitism in its most vicious form that shocks the boy out of his illusions. The narrator recalls what it was like for him as he lay on the ground with "tender pigeon guts" sliding down over his forehead: "I closed my solitary unstopped-up eye so as not to see the world that spread out before me.

This world was tiny and it was awful. A stone lay just before my eyes, a little stone so chipped as to resemble the face of an old woman with a large jaw." The detail here is so precise that one is convinced that the author experienced it exactly so—and that it was then permanently etched in his memory. These minute details impel the reader to enter the boy's consciousness.

Still lying on the ground, "in his new overcoat," the boy hears hoofbeats in the distance—the pogrom: "Somewhere far way Woe rode across [the trampled earth] on a grezt steed." He becomes aware of the very dirt beneath his nose: "The earth smelled of raw depths, of the tomb, of flowers. I smelled its smell and started crying, unafraid."

All this description evokes in the reader a perception equal to that of the boy. It has the character of an awakening, a revelation—an epiphany. It includes the disturbing realization that violence and death are necessary to produce true understanding. For the boy, the experience becomes also a rite of passage, parallel to Bar Mitzvah. On that day, he became a man.

The pogrom takes on an unreal aspect as Babel describes Russians (and Ukrainians) happily looting and smashing or carrying aloft in processions icons, the Cross, a portrait of the czar. There is almost an invitation here to see the point of view of those others. However, the key to Babel's true attitude lies in his treatment of Makarenko, whom the boy had actually looked on as a friend. The illusion of that friendship is the first illusion the boy loses, as the cripple turns on him like a snake. Although the reader might feel some slight inclination to pity the man bound to a wheelchair, Babel removes that inclination when he has Makarenko say, lamenting his inability to obtain all the booty he wants, "God's picked on me, I reckon." What he means is that God has picked on him to suffer. There might even be something noble in it—a supposition confirmed by Makarenko's next utterance: "I'm a son of man, I reckon." The phrase "son of man" is Jesus's usual manner of referring to Himself in the Gospels. The vicious Makarenko is thus transformed by Babel into a grotesque Christ-figure, and anti-Semitism is revealed for what it is: an attribute of the Christian religion.

Babel dedicated this story to the writer Maxim Gorky. It was Gorky who published Babel's first stories in 1916.

Style and Technique

The most important stylistic feature of "The Story of My Dovecot" is the epiphany described in detail above. This is a device often used by Babel but never more successfully than in this particular story. At its best, the literary epiphany brings into focus all of the main elements of the story in which it appears. It becomes a "showing forth."

Interestingly, Babel echoes the major epiphany of this story with a minor one that acts as an ode to the joy of a young Russian peasant as he smashes the house of a Jew: "Sighing, he smiled all around with the amiable grin of drunkenness, sweat, and spiritual power. The whole street was filled with a splitting, a snapping, the song of flying wood." This epiphany truly reflects the happiness of the peasant, but it is ironic to such a degree that it qualifies as black humor. There is irony also in the fact that the peasant is smashing the house of Khariton Efrussi, thus acting as the instrument of the Babel family's desired vengeance on the hated parvenu. Such a linking of early and late elements in the story lends artistic unity to the work.

Surprisingly, this story contains much humor, required both for emotional relief and as a device for maintaining detachment in the narrating author. An example of such humor is the remark, "Like all Jews I was short, weakly, and had headaches from studying." The exaggeration qualifies as self-deprecating Jewish humor. However, there is also truth in it; many Jews really were short and weak, owing to poverty and poor diet—the consequence of anti-Semitism.

Babel employs a number of effective images that are relatively low-key, not so "or-namental" as in most of his other stories of the early 1920's. An example is his de-scription of the Russian Pyatnitsky, as he walks down a corridor, hemmed in by the shadowy walls, and "moving between them as a barge moves through a deep canal." This positive image of a good Russian is needed in the story—as is the dedication to Gorky—but it cannot make up for the anti-Semitism that is shown in the story to be ubiquitous.

Donald M. Fiene

THE STORY OF SERAPION

Author: E. T. A. Hoffmann (1776-1822)
Type of plot: Gothic
Time of plot: The early nineteenth century
Locale: Germany
First published: "Die Serapionsbrüder," 1819-1821 (English translation, 1886)

> *Principal characters:*
> THE STORYTELLER, an amateur psychologist
> PRIEST SERAPION, a hermit who escaped from a lunatic asylum

The Story

Lost in a thick forest somewhere in the South of Germany, the storyteller happens on a long-bearded hermit, from whom he asks directions to the nearby village of B——. He is puzzled by the reply, though, for the hermit refers to the forest as a desert and recommends that he follow a friend to Alexandria, which is in Egypt, not Germany.

From a traveler on the road he later learns that the odd fellow is known to the villagers as Priest Serapion, a kindly gentleman who is "not quite right in his head." Dr. S—— provides more background, explaining that the hermit, once one of the most brilliant men in the town of M——, was about to be sent on a diplomatic mission when he mysteriously disappeared. At nearly the same time a hermit calling himself Priest Serapion suddenly appeared in the vicinity. Then one day Count P—— of M—— recognized him as his lost nephew. Arrested after a violent struggle, he was committed to a lunatic asylum in B——.

The medical men there found only one thing wrong with his mind: the fixed idea that he was the same Serapion who fled the Theban desert in the days of the Emperor Decius (in the third century) and suffered martyrdom in Alexandria. Probably with the help of Dr. S——, he escaped from the asylum and was allowed to live in a hut he built in the forest.

Himself an amateur psychologist, the storyteller decides to go back to the forest and cure Serapion by attacking his fixed idea at its source. The story reaches its climax in their debate. Serapion insists that centuries ago he had survived a gruesome martyrdom, "his limbs being torn asunder at the joints, and his body thrown down from a lofty rock." Even now there are reminders, he says, "a severe headache, and occasional violent cramps and twitchings in my limbs."

At that point, the storyteller attempts his cure. First he explains the malady of the fixed idea, citing the case of Abbot Molanus, "who conversed most rationally upon every subject, but would not leave his room because he thought he was a barleycorn, and the hens would swallow him." At last he stands up, takes Serapion by both hands, and cries loudly, "Count P—— awake from the pernicious dream."

Serapion, however, is not moved. Instead he responds by reducing his adversary's position to an absurdity with the observation that only a lunatic would try to reason another lunatic out of his lunacy, if it were lunacy, or if it were not. Because time and space themselves are relative and not fixed, their conquest is a feat his mind can perform.

Overwhelmed by "the very rationality of his irrationality," the storyteller realizes the folly of his own undertaking and begins to understand how the madman can consider his madness "a priceless gift from heaven." Serapion goes on to describe several supernatural visits from geniuses who died long ago, and he further demonstrates the power of his imagination by relating several spellbinding romances before their encounter comes to an end.

Converted from cynicism to fascination, the storyteller returns often to Serapion's hut, though he never again tries to play the role of a psychological doctor. Then one day, after an absence of three years, he returns to the forest one last time, only to find the amazing man dead.

Themes and Meanings

The storyteller's debate with Serapion epitomizes the conflict between Romanticism and rationalism. Based largely on the scientific theories of Isaac Newton, Francis Bacon, and René Descartes, rationalism exalted reason over emotion, and empirical knowledge over faith. Rejecting supernatural explanations, it sought to describe nature as a set of material substances governed by a set of scientific laws revealed by experiments rather than the divine. The new science of psychology was finding its first empirical and experimental bases in E. T. A. Hoffmann's time. With his methodical cynicism, his advanced degree, and his scholarly inquiries, the storyteller embodies the follies of rationalism, as he soon discovers.

In Serapion the storyteller finds his nemesis. No rational man would claim to be a martyr who died centuries ago, but Serapion does. For him, a firm conviction can make something so because mind controls matter and not the other way around, as some scientists suppose.

Serapion espouses a kind of religious idealism. "If it is the mind only which takes cognizance of events around us," he argues, "it follows that that which it has taken cognizance of has actually occurred." Further, he declares that the mental power of men is not their own, but only "lent to them for a time by that Higher Power." Several times he chides the storyteller for underrating the omnipotence of God. He ridicules the rationalistic concept of a watchmaker-God who wound up the universe only to watch it run down without interfering.

His chosen name, Priest Serapion, associates him with the beginnings of a religion called Christianity. Surviving martyrdom like the Savior himself, Serapion remembers awakening from death when "the spirit dawned, and shone bright within me." Even the rationalistic storyteller recognizes in him a "lofty, invulnerable higher spirit."

Serapion emerges from the story as a portrait of the Romantic artist. At first sight the storyteller likens him to a figure in one of painter-poet Salvator Rosa's wild mountain scenes. He tells the storyteller tales "only the most imaginative poet could have constructed." Dr. S—— finds in him "remarkable poetical gifts" and "a most brilliant fancy." The departed spirits who visit him are fit companions, Ludovico Ariosto, Petrarch, and Dante, early heroes of Romantic sensibilities in literature.

For artists such as Serapion, faith, art, and imagination are synonymous. All command a prophetic power that penetrates material reality to expose deeper, unexpected truths. Serapion's notion that time and space are relative, for example, was considered hopelessly visionary and impractical until, almost a century later, Albert Einstein demonstrated its truth.

Serapion's isolation from society typifies the predicament of the Romantic artist. Art in the Age of Reason had been, for the most part, more concerned with public life, common sense, and general truths than with cultivating private fantasies and personal eccentricities. Romantic artists' obsessions with introspection and personal visions, however, cut them off from society. Serapion's hermitage symbolizes the Romantic artist's alienation from society.

Serapion goes back to nature as many Romantics have longed to do since Jean-Jacques Rousseau explained how under such natural, primitive conditions, devoid of the corrupting influence of society, humanity could enjoy his innate goodness in simple happiness. Serapion does live a placid, cheerful life in his hut. However, he is not quite the untutored noble savage Rousseau had in mind. Indeed, his return to nature is an ironic enterprise, undertaken as an alternative to incarceration in a lunatic asylum. His whole attitude toward nature is ambivalent. He considers it a desert. Like many Romantic artists, he loves the immortal spirit more than mortal nature. His death occurs not in the Theban desert but in a German forest.

Style and Technique

Hoffmann helped make the short story a viable literary genre. His influence on Washington Irving and Edgar Allan Poe was profound. Brief prose narratives and tales had been around longer than the written language, but before the nineteenth century they were usually written down in ways as unstructured, rambling, and episodic as the stories themselves happened to be. Hoffmann was among the first generation of writers who deliberately set about to give those amorphous forms more artistic shape.

The conflict between Serapion and the storyteller follows a pattern that became virtually definitive of the short story as a literary form. First comes a complicating incident (the puzzling reply in the forest) that draws the opposing forces into conflict. The action mounts to a climax (their debate) where the forces do decisive battle. Then the action falls to a point of final resolution (Serapion's death).

The tales of Hoffmann have been called the culmination of gothicism. The Romantic revival of emotionalism, supernatural faith, noble savagery, and the like precipitated in Europe a craving for things gothic. Dark forests, melancholy, superstitious peasants, misty ruins, mystery, and other obstacles to rationalism came back into vogue. The gothic style can be felt in the forest setting, supernatural events, numerous medieval allusions, and the eerie, supernal tone that pervades this story.

Hoffmann cleverly uses an unnamed narrator to enlist the reader's sympathy for Serapion. Namelessness suggests a lack of individuality, which is appropriate to an avatar of rationalism, and it helps make his clash with Serapion philosophical rather than personal in nature. He is the Everyman of rationalism who adopts a cynical attitude toward imagination. Ordinarily, most readers would share his initial reaction to Serapion's madness. Thus, when he begins to appreciate the madman, the reader is tempted to do the same.

Because this story is a mental adventure, philosophical dialogue plays a greater role in it than action. Even the lively details of an atrocious martyrdom, the capture and escape from the lunatic asylum, are rendered narratively rather than dramatically. Serapion's astonishing character is revealed by words and scarcely developed through action, while the storyteller's character is developed largely through dialogue.

John L. McLean

THE STORYTELLERS

Author: Fred Chappell (1936-   )
Type of plot: Psychological
Time of plot: The 1940's
Locale: Western North Carolina
First published: 1985

> *Principal characters:*
> JESS, the narrator, a young boy
> JOE ROBERT, his father
> UNCLE ZENO, a master storyteller

The Story

The narrator begins by questioning whether the events he is about to recount actually occurred. Certainly, Jess says, there was an Uncle Zeno in his Appalachian childhood, but he cannot remember much about him as a person. What lingers in his memory is primarily a voice, telling stories. Uncle Zeno then takes over the narrative.

Zeno's first story concerns a great hunter, Lacey Joe Blackman, whose dearest possession is an heirloom watch; a retired farmer, Setback Williams, who now spends his time growing apples; and a bear who is protected by the park service, even though he steals Setback's apples and destroys his trees. The tale has a surprising ending. When the bear finally has to be shot, his body gets caught on a tree limb, and as it swings, Lacey times it with his prized watch and comments that it is slow. Jess's father, Joe Robert, does not understand the story, but when he asks for an explanation, Zeno simply ignores him.

Jess now describes the efforts of his father, Joe Robert, to compete with Uncle Zeno. Feverishly, Joe Robert searches for stories to tell. He looks in the books around the house for old fairy tales and legends, and he collects anecdotes from people in the community. With a fine flourish, he tries out his discoveries on the family. Joe Robert always spoils even the best stories with his own embellishments and his theatrical endings. In contrast, Zeno seems to be a mere vehicle through which stories tell themselves.

The narrative now returns to Uncle Zeno, who is reminded of Buford Rhodes and his favorite coonhound, who is so smart that he can find a coon whose skin will fit any flat surface he sees. Unfortunately, seeing the ironing board, the hound sets off on an impossible quest, and Buford has to go in search of him.

By now, Joe Robert is so frustrated over Uncle Zeno's inconclusive endings and so jealous of his skill that he cannot let his guest continue. Despite his mother-in-law's expostulations, Joe Robert leaves to find the real Buford Rhodes, in order to ask him whether Zeno's account is a true one. During his father's absence, Jess happens on

Uncle Zeno, sitting all alone, and finds that he is continuing with the story in progress, which now involves a cave and a Cherokee woman.

Late that afternoon, Jess's father returns, reporting that he has not been able to find any trace of Rhodes. Joe Robert is sure that by casting doubt on Zeno's truthfulness, he has invalidated his story of Buford and maybe all the others. As usual, he has missed the point. Unlike his father, Jess understands that the value of a story does not depend on its being factual. Jess, however, now has a rather unsettling theory about the relationship between fact and fiction. Because Buford Rhodes has disappeared as surely as the characters in Homer's *Iliad* (750 B.C.E.; English translation, 1611) and *Odyssey* (725 B.C.E.; English translation, 1614), Jess now suspects that any individual who appears in fiction will promptly disappear from the real world.

At the supper table, Zeno's story brings Buford home to his family, who are being supported by Elmer, now a teacher at the high school. Joe Robert has had enough. First he confronts Zeno with the news about Buford Rhodes, and then he launches angrily into the tale of a man who married a mountain girl and enjoyed entertaining her family, except for his wife's storytelling relative, who drove him crazy.

After Joe Robert leaves the table, the mother and the grandmother try to understand his rude behavior toward Uncle Zeno, who they agree is harmless. Then Uncle Zeno begins another story. This time, to Jess's dismay, the main character is his father. Recalling his theory about what fiction does to real people who are incorporated into it, Jess goes out to the porch to check on Joe Robert, who indeed admits that he feels a bit weak. When Jess says that some apple pie might help, Joe Robert gets up to go indoors. Just as Uncle Zeno's voice falls silent, Jess sees his father disappearing into the darkness.

Themes and Meanings

"The Storytellers" is one of Fred Chappell's ten short stories about Jess's childhood in North Carolina that make up the novel *I Am One of You Forever* (1985). Throughout the novel, the adult Jess tries to come to terms with his past, to deal with the question that even the dead come back to ask him: "Are you one of us?" The volume ends with Jess's affirmation, which is the title of the book.

This affirmation is much more than just an assurance that Jess will always remember the place and the people who made him what he is. One could do that while still maintaining a comfortable emotional distance. What Jess means is that he has become incorporated into the life of his people, so that there is now no distinction between the subject and the object: They are one. In "The Storytellers," Chappell suggests that such a mystical surrender of the self is essential if one is to deal effectively with personal memories or, through the creative imagination, to produce a work of art.

Thus the two storytellers of Chappell's own story can be seen as symbols of the right way and the wrong way to approach both art and life. Jess's father is not a bad man; he has a good heart and an abundance of charm. Nevertheless, the same lack of self-discipline that sends him off to fish when he needs to work the farm, and impels him to play practical jokes without contemplating the consequences, also makes it impossible for him to become an artist. He cannot give himself to his story. When he recounts Homer's *Iliad*, Joe Robert adds props, such as the photograph of the film actress Betty Grable, whom he casts as the legendary beauty Helen of Troy; he interpolates his own comments on the action; and he concludes with a wild chase, with a sofa pillow used as the body of Hector. None of this is in the spirit of the original; all of it seems to be just an opportunity for Joe Robert to show off, like a schoolboy.

In contrast, Uncle Zeno acts as a medium through which his stories tell themselves. The fact that his art controls him, instead of the reverse, is evident in the way he starts and stops talking, without regard to the needs of his listeners, and even, as Jess discovers, without any listeners at all. The secret of Uncle Zeno's power, as well as of his serenity, is his capacity for surrender to a higher power. At the end of the story, the young Jess sees that his father will never understand the lesson to be learned from Uncle Zeno; however, in the way he stands aside to let "The Storytellers" be told by his narrators, the adult Jess shows that he is living by Uncle Zeno's rules.

Style and Technique

Like the other stories in *I Am One of You Forever*, "The Storytellers" is firmly rooted in a literary tradition that pervades southern literature, that of the Old Southwest humorists, who set their stories in the frontier settlements of Alabama, Georgia, Mississippi, and Tennessee. Their humor, which often involved accounts of coarse practical jokes, and their tall tales, based on folklore and merging into myth and fantasy, influenced writers from Mark Twain, the author of *Huckleberry Finn* (1884), to William Faulkner.

Uncle Zeno's final story refers to a practical joke, described in detail in "The Good Time," which involved substituting pullet eggs for the fillings in some fine chocolates that Annie Barbara Sorrells would naturally bring out on the next social occasion. Such anecdotes, showing a triumph of crude nature over what pioneers saw as pretentious and artificial gentility, are typical of the Old Southwest humorists. Like them, the author of "The Storytellers" also delights in tall tales, such as Uncle Zeno's accounts of the clocklike bear and the analytical dog.

It is just a step from such comic exaggerations to more serious fantasy, and here Chappell's technique most clearly reflects his theme. In Jess's confusion about Uncle Zeno's actual visits, in his final description of his father's disappearance, and even in Zeno's unstructured stories themselves, there is more mystery than certainty in "The Storytellers." Thus Chappell illustrates his belief that, as the true artist knows, there is no real distinction between the seen and the unseen, the world of fact and the world of fiction.

Rosemary M. Canfield Reisman

THE STRANGE RIDE OF MORROWBIE JUKES

Author: Rudyard Kipling (1865-1936)
Type of plot: Horror
Time of plot: The 1880's
Locale: A city of the living dead in the desert between Pakpattan and Mubarukpur, India
First published: 1885

> *Principal characters:*
> MORROWBIE JUKES, a British civil engineer stationed in India
> GUNGA DASS, a Brahman, formerly a telegraph master
> DUNNOO, Jukes's dog boy

The Story

Morrowbie Jukes's strange ride occurs when he is weakened by a fever. Baying dogs disturb his sleep. He kills one of them and displays its body, hoping to deter the other dogs from their baying. Instead, they devour the body "and, as it seemed to me, sang their hymns of thanksgiving afterwards with renewed energy." Morrowbie tries to shoot the loudest of the dogs, but the lightheadedness that accompanies his fever makes him miss the offending dog even though he unloads both barrels of his shotgun in its direction.

Finally, Morrowbie decides to go after the dog with his boar spear. He has his pony, Pornic, saddled and sets out. The pony runs at breakneck speed in a straight line, galloping past the baying dog and running for several miles beyond it. Suddenly Morrowbie sees the waters of the river Sutlej before him; then his pony stumbles and the two roll down a slope. Morrowbie loses consciousness.

When he awakes, he is inside a horseshoe-shaped crater, three sides of which are enclosed by high slopes slanting at about sixty-five degrees. The river provides the remaining boundary. Morrowbie tries to ride out of the crater, but he cannot conquer its steep slopes. Then he hears a gunshot from across the river, and a bullet lands close to Pornic's head.

Some time passes before Morrowbie becomes aware that other people inhabit this wilderness. Slowly, about sixty-five people emerge from badger holes that Morrowbie thought were untenanted. Among them is Gunga Dass, a Brahman and a former telegraph master, whom Morrowbie once knew. Gunga Dass cries, "Sahib! Sahib!" Morrowbie recognizes him only by a scar on his cheek for which Morrowbie was apparently responsible. Gunga Dass commences to tell Morrowbie about this city of the living dead on which he has stumbled.

The crater and its barrows are inhabited by people who, thought to be dead from cholera, had been taken away for hasty cremation. Some of them were not dead, and when they stirred, those who were to have cremated them plastered their noses and mouths with mud. Those who did not die from suffocation as a result of this ministration were set loose, and many of them, including Gunga Dass, who almost died, ended up in this crater. A gunboat cruises the Sutlej by daylight to make sure that no one escapes from the place.

Gunga Dass takes all of Morrowbie's money and wants to take his boots as well. He tells Morrowbie that he will look after him for a while but suggests that in time Morrowbie should wait on him, a suggestion that Morrowbie rejects. All at once, however, Morrowbie finds himself in the middle of a role reversal. He is no longer master. Gunga Dass controls him. On Morrowbie's first night in the crater, its residents kill his pony to use as food, a meat much better than the crow that they usually catch and roast for their daily meal.

Morrowbie learns that there is only one way out of the crater, an intricate course along the riverbank, most of which is composed of deadly quicksand. He also learns that one other Briton has stumbled into the crater and that Gunga Dass murdered him.

Morrowbie gets possession of the murdered man's mummified body and buries it in the quicksand, but not before he has secured the man's possessions, including his journal. Out of the journal's binding falls a piece of paper on which the dead man has written the secret of how to escape from the crater. Just as Morrowbie discovers this piece of paper with its burned edges, Gunga Dass appears, knows that Morrowbie has found the piece of paper for which he himself has been searching, and takes it from Morrowbie.

When Gunga Dass drops it, calculatedly, Morrowbie rushes to pick it up and Gunga Dass hits him in the head from behind. When he regains consciousness, Morrowbie is aware that someone is calling, "Sahib! Sahib!" He looks up to see the face of his dog boy, Dunnoo, staring down at him from a considerable distance. Dunnoo knots together a few leather punkah ropes with a loop at one end. He lowers them to Morrowbie, who puts the loop under his arms. Dunnoo hauls him up the side of the crater and tells him that he has followed Pornic's hoof prints fourteen miles to this place to save his life.

Themes and Meanings

"The Strange Ride of Morrowbie Jukes" is rich in meaning. One theme that Rudyard Kipling explores here is that of the social stratifications that exist both within Indian society, with its caste system, and between the local Indians and their British masters. One is reminded of the exploration of similar themes in Sir James Barrie's *The Admirable Crichton* (1902) and in William Golding's *Lord of the Flies* (1954). In the Kipling story the master prevails, but not without the help of the faithful servant.

Morrowbie must prove his mastery to the people confined in the crater: "I have been accustomed to a certain amount of civility from my inferiors, and on approaching the crowd naturally expected that there would be some recognition of my presence." These people, however, first laugh at Morrowbie and cackle after him. He thrashes one or two of them, and then they keep a respectful distance. Morrowbie realizes, "I had left the world, it seemed, for centuries. I was as certain then as I am now of my own existence, that in the accursed settlement there was no law save that of the strongest."

When Morrowbie's pony is killed, Gunga Dass explains to him that horse is "better than crow, and 'greatest good of greatest number' is political maxim. We are now Republic, Mister Jukes, and you are entitled to a fair share of the beast." This political statement, written in the 1880's, must have been startling for its time.

This story is in many ways a commentary on all humanity. The microcosm that Kipling creates in the crater is a discouraging one. Gunga Dass torments the representative of the ruling class because in the crater the classes that exist outside have little meaning. Gunga Dass reminds Morrowbie of a schoolboy who enjoys watching the death agonies of a beetle impaled on a pin, but Morrowbie is not much better than Gunga Dass in this respect. One must remember that life does not mean much to him. He kills a dog because it disturbs his sleep. He has no feeling for the Indians, whom he regards as his inferiors.

The human race, Kipling seems to be saying, feeds on itself, just as the baying dogs eat the dog that Morrowbie has slain. Gunga Dass uses live crows, Judas crows, to attract other crows so that he can capture them and eat them. Survival for the British, according to this philosophy, can be assured only if, figuratively, they feed on their own species, the Indians and other colonials.

In the crater, Morrowbie depends on Gunga Dass for his survival, and Gunga Dass moves toward assuming the role of master. However, Morrowbie also depends on his Indian servant, Dunnoo, for his escape from the crater and from the city of the living dead. Once Morrowbie is back in his own world, Dunnoo will be the inferior, Morrowbie the master.

Style and Technique

At the center of "The Strange Ride of Morrowbie Jukes" is a pattern of reversals: Servants become masters, and the dead rise up to live again. Morrowbie Jukes seems almost to be living through a bad dream, except that the horrors he experiences are real. Kipling achieves a plausible basis for this dreamlike atmosphere, however, by presenting his readers with a protagonist who has been suffering from a fever that has weakened him and left him disoriented, as one sees when he tries to shoot the baying dog.

"The Strange Ride of Morrowbie Jukes" can be seen as the strange ride of humankind. The galloping pony takes Morrowbie to the brink of the crater, and they both fall in. Morrowbie is powerless to control the force that takes him to the crater, just as people, perhaps, are powerless to control the forces that direct their destinies.

R. Baird Shuman

THE STREET OF CROCODILES

Author: Bruno Schulz (1892-1942)
Type of plot: Fantasy
Time of plot: The early twentieth century
Locale: A small town anywhere in the Western world
First published: "Ulica krokodyli," 1934 (English translation, 1963)

> *Principal characters:*
> A TOWN
> THE INHABITANTS OF THE TOWN
> A STORE CLERK
> OTHER SALESCLERKS, young women
> CITY CABS
> TROLLEYS
> TRAINS
> PROSTITUTES

The Story

A discussion of "The Street of Crocodiles" must begin with the difficulty of identifying its central figure or hero. The first sentence reads in a deceptively clear and straightforward fashion: "My father kept in the lower drawer of his large desk an old and beautiful map of our city." Later, very little is clear. As in the works of Franz Kafka, a "terrible ambiguity" seems to hang over the story. It is not a story about the father, nor is it really a story about the narrator's town, even though that town is the principal character. It is a story about modern life, its degeneration as a result of the triumph of commercialism and cheap values (see the metaphoric title), a story about the "degradation of reality" as a modern Polish critic (Artur Sandauer) has called it. There may not even be an actual city—at least none is ever named, and its geographic location would be difficult to pinpoint except to say that it is a city in the Western world where Western goods are traded. The reader knows no more of it except that an "old and very beautiful map" exists of this city where the engraver entered with great care every significant detail: "streets and alleyways, the sharp lines of cornices, architraves, archivolts, and pilasters." The city has an old and a new section, and it is the new section with its "pseudo-Americanism" and its "shops with the stigma of some wild Klondike" that the author uses as his metaphor for the decrepitude and illusoriness of life in the twentieth century. Here, starting with the vegetation, everything is cheap and shoddy. There are no individual distinctions, but a pervasive grayness and barrenness reigns everywhere. The goods in the outfitters' shops are gray and colorless and the bales of cloth form "imaginary jackets and trousers." The young salesperson drowns the shopper with his "cheap sales talk."

The outfitters' shops, however, are nothing but a disguise for antiquarian book-stores with "collections of highly questionable books and private editions." They are facades of a world of corruption underneath where the young salesclerk and the sales-women play out erotic poses in front of one another. The narrator, who has observed these activities, uses the moment of their absorption in one another's suggestive poses to escape out into the street in order to view the larger panorama of the new district of the city.

What he saw in miniature in the outfitters' stores, alias pornographic bookstores, now is viewed in the larger dimension of street life. It is a "reality as thin as paper." It is a sham reality without substance where cabdrivers do not drive cabs but cavort through the town with their fares, engaging in meaningless and dangerous antics; the trolleys are not trolleys but conveyances made of papier-mache and lacking a front section, and the trains stop in the middle of a street and temporarily transform the street into a cavernous railroad station. Nothing is certain here, nothing can be de-pended on, not even the normal purchase of railroad tickets. Around it all—the cabs, trolleys, and trains—prostitutes wend their way, women who are not a special group but could be the wives of the barbers, the coffeehouse conductors, or anyone else.

The narrator asks in conclusion, is this corruption, this sham reality, only imagi-nary? Where does it go once it has reached its apogee? It recedes, he says, like an ocean wave. Corruption, like virtue, is too banal to last. Nothing, not even vice, can endure. It, too, comes and goes, impermanent like everything else. "The Street of Crocodiles" is a phantasmagoria created of corruptible material like papier-mache, which disintegrates when confronted with the true reality. What is the true reality? That question is not answered. The world is like papier-mache; it came to life and died in the imagination that produced it.

Themes and Meanings

The central theme in "The Street of Crocodiles" is an examination of the nature of twentieth century life. The mode of presentation is surrealistic and the title an ex-tended metaphor. Life in the new district is a caricature of life in the old; it has degen-erated to the extent that it has lost what was once called reality. It is not real. Life in the city—which the narrator examines by looking at a "beautiful map" that is extended over a "sheaf of parchment pages"—is illusory. It presents a mere "bird's eye pan-orama." The narrator's imagination fills it with life, peoples its stores and streets, per-mits motion and activity to flow through its boulevards and alleys, observes and as-sesses. This observation and assessment reveal the vanity of life, its illusoriness, its deceptiveness (the outfitters' shops as facades of pornographic bookstores), its impo-tence. Its reality is a sham, for it exists, after all, only on a map, despite the beauty of its engraving.

Does this view of "The Street of Crocodiles" not possess any reality at all? It does. The grotesque possesses elements of the real, but its forms are misshapen as in a dis-tortion mirror. Great predecessors of Bruno Schulz in the art of the grotesque were the painter Hieronymus Bosch (1450?-1516), the Russian writer Nikolai Gogol (1809-

1852), and the Austrian writer Franz Kafka (1883-1924). The upheavals of the twentieth century gave further impetus to a presentation of the grotesque in painting (George
Grosz, 1893-1959), in literature (Stanisław Ignacy Witkiewicz, 1885-1939), and even
music (aleatory music and its practitioners, such as Karlheinz Stockhausen, born
1928). The presentation of reality in grotesque forms raises questions about the nature
of reality itself. Where does it exist if not in the human mind, and does one not create it
for oneself every moment of one's life again and again? It may appear to one appealing or unappealing. The artist Schulz saw his reality and transformed it through his
imagination and creative talent. He made it "strange," so that the familiar should once
again become unfamiliar to his readers and should rouse their own imaginative sensibility. Finally, reality is ambiguous.

Style and Technique

The artist proceeds as a painter by addressing first and above all the visual sense.
The design of the map from which he creates his city is shown in precise visual detail.
Such visual detail applies to aspects of the city, its people and transport. Because the
proportions are out of shape, what one sees is grotesque. Schulz makes rich use of adjectives that refer to decay and disintegration. The most widely used color epithet is
"gray": a gray day, gray-glassed display windows, that gray, impersonal crowd, those
dirty gray squares. The author pays special attention to his language (the use of adjectives is only one element), and by means of certain pronouns tries to create the effect
of an oppressive atmosphere, of the hopeless treadmill of life, of delusion and
irreality. His paratactic syntax carries the effect of a certain monotony, appropriate to
the setting of unrelieved grayness, of life beyond redemption. The story is very short
(eight pages in the original Polish), yet its power rests on its concentrated linguistic
texture, the incongruity of its pictures, and the unique and hypnotic imaginative flight
of its creator.

Joachim T. Baer

STRONG HORSE TEA

Author: Alice Walker (1944-   )
Type of plot: Social realism
Time of plot: The mid-twentieth century
Locale: The rural American South
First published: 1968

> *Principal characters:*
> RANNIE MAE TOOMER, the protagonist, a poor southern black
>   woman
> SNOOKS, her dying infant son
> "AUNT" SARAH, a local expert in country medicine and home
>   remedies
> THE MAIL CARRIER, a white man in whom Rannie places her trust

The Story

Snooks, Rannie Mae Toomer's infant son, is dying of double pneumonia and whooping cough. Rannie has no one else in the world, is unmarried, and lives in an unheated, drafty shack somewhere in the South.

Sarah, a neighbor who is expert in country medicine and home remedies, suggests that one of these remedies might help Snooks, but Rannie will have none of it. She has supreme confidence in white medicine and wants a white doctor for her son. She is also certain that the white mail carrier whom she has begged to call for the doctor will send him as soon as possible. Despite the drenching rain and bone-chilling winds that enter the shack, Rannie is sure that the doctor will soon arrive and give Snooks an injection that will make him well again.

Rannie recalls two past meetings with the mail carrier. Once, she had inquired whether the advertising circulars she received meant that someone would come later to deliver the things she needed: sweaters, shoes, rubbing alcohol, a heater for the house, a fur bonnet for Snooks. When he explained to her the meaning of the word "sale," which was always written on the circulars in red capital letters, Rannie was amazed, for she could never afford to buy any of the items advertised. Her conclusion was that this was simply the way things were; no one could do anything about it.

She met the mail carrier again on the morning Snooks was so ill. She had waited in the winter rain, had no umbrella, and had only leaky plastic shoes. At this second meeting she insisted that he send her a real doctor. The mail carrier first suggested Sarah's home remedies, but when Rannie remained adamant that a real doctor give Snooks real medicine, he said that he would do what he could and stuffed a new consignment of advertising circulars in Rannie's hand. Rannie recalls that she had once asked the mail carrier for any extra circulars he had so she could patch the drafty walls of her house with them.

A doctor finally arrives, but it is Sarah, not the white doctor whom Rannie has expected. Sarah is the "doctor" the mail carrier sent. At this point, Rannie realizes that no white doctor will come, and she places all the confidence she can muster in "Aunt" Sarah. Sarah frankly tells Rannie that Snooks is dying but suggests that she has one remedy if Rannie has the stomach to help. Snooks must drink some "strong horse tea," and Rannie must collect it.

Once again Rannie ventures outside in rain, thunder, and lightning. She waits for nearly an hour in the pouring rain before the gray mare begins to spread its legs, only to realize that she has brought nothing in which to catch the "tea." Nevertheless, Rannie is determined to save Snooks, so she quickly slips off one of her plastic shoes and runs after the mare. When she realizes the shoe leaks, she places her mouth over the tiny crack so as not to lose any of the precious "medicine." Even as Rannie slips and slides through the mud to return with the "tea" that Sarah needs, the reader is told that Snooks's frail breathing has already stopped with the thunder.

Themes and Meanings

Rannie Mae Toomer is twice a victim of her own childlike need to trust. Her naïveté is clear from her belief that the items in the advertising circulars she receives will be delivered to her house for free if only she requests them. Significantly, the items she most wants are hardly luxuries (rubbing alcohol, sweaters, shoes, a heater, a baby's bonnet); they are not even for herself but for her child. The mail carrier and the circulars he brings are Rannie's only contacts with the world of white people, a world that seems infinitely superior to her own.

As Rannie waits in the drenching winter rain to beg the mail carrier to send a real doctor for Snooks, she has the same innocent confidence that all will be well once she makes her request, but to the mail carrier she merely appears "more ignorant than usual." Indeed, Rannie is ignorant, but only in the sense that she possesses the childlike simplicity that most people quickly lose. Ironically, as a poor black woman living in a remote country shack, Rannie stands as little chance of getting the doctor her son requires as she does of receiving for free the items she sees advertised in the circulars the mail carrier brings. Clearly, the word "ignorant" more accurately applies to the mail carrier, who never sees beyond Rannie's unkempt appearance to the desperate nature of her plight. He does not understand that Rannie's request for a white doctor is implicitly a rejection of Sarah's home remedies and, by extension, of her own background. Rannie has told Sarah that she does not want "witch's remedies" for her son and is therefore at the mercy of whoever might help.

Still, Rannie is victimized a second time, in this instance by Sarah. Though Sarah probably does believe that "strong horse tea" might help Snooks, she nevertheless exploits Rannie's courage when for a second time Rannie ventures into the rain and waits, this time to collect urine from a mare. The final irony is Rannie's use of her leaky plastic shoe to catch the "tea" and her sealing the crack by holding her mouth to the toe. All at once, ignorance is triumphant, and Snooks is dead.

Style and Technique

Alice Walker often writes works in which a black protagonist, usually a woman, is caught between black and white cultures and inevitably becomes the victim of both. At her best, Walker neither indulges in polemics nor seeks to blame; indeed, here, as third-person narrator, she distances herself from her characters and allows the story to tell itself. The effect of this technique is akin to high tragedy. The reader of "Strong Horse Tea," for example, knows that the white doctor will not come, that either Sarah will refuse to help once Rannie has rejected "witch's remedies" or that Sarah's help will probably come too late. What comes as a surprise is the grotesque indignity to which Rannie submits in order to do what she desperately hopes will help her child. Here, most of all, Rannie's guileless innocence comes into its sharpest focus.

The winter storm, which continues in varying degrees of fury, serves as an important symbol. Rannie cannot escape; it pours through the walls of her shack, and it drenches her on her two errands to help Snooks. All the while, tears pour down Rannie's face, left unwashed for five days because of her concern for her son, and leave "whitish snail tracks." This is a late winter rain, and the death that that season brings is matched in the death of Snooks, whose breathing stops with the thunder.

Those who have read Walker's celebrated novel *The Color Purple* (1982) will recognize similarities between its narrator, Celie, and Rannie, the protagonist of "Strong Horse Tea." The common humanity and simple faith of these country women are easy to recognize, and Walker's skill in portraying these qualities gives her work a lyricism that is far above the racial polemic that might have come from a less gifted author.

Robert J. Forman

STRUCTURAL ANTHROPOLOGY

Author: Adam Mars-Jones (1954-   )
Type of plot: Didactic, parody
Time of plot: The late twentieth century
Locale: The British Isles
First published: 1982

> *Principal character:*
> AN EXPERT in the field of structural anthropology

The Story

"Structural Anthropology" begins in the form of a lecture on its title subject, as an authority in the field explains how the social science discipline might be seen as an application of the methods of psychoanalysis to an entire social community rather than to an individual person. In his introductory remarks, he notes that the separate approaches of the two techniques that "seek to discover the workings of the human mind" might be combined so that the anthropologist's traditional field of exploration—a culture "at a distance conducive to objectivity"—could be expanded to "uncover much that is startling in our own culture." To support his position, he shows how Sigmund Freud, the pioneering practitioner of the psychoanalytic method, was intellectually linked across space to President Woodrow Wilson, across time to scientist Leonardo da Vinci, and across time and space to Greek mythological king Oedipus, setting an example of resistance to "self-imposed limits" that restrict and restrain imaginative extrapolation.

The theoretical conceptions of the speaker, familiar in academic discourse, are temporarily set aside as he recounts an incident that he will use to demonstrate the efficacy of the method he is championing. Maintaining a tone of objectivity, the speaker describes how a woman, returning unexpectedly to her home, discovers her husband in an adulterous liaison. She leaves unnoticed, returns at the usual time, and puts sleeping-pills in his dinner. While he is sleeping, she sticks "his hand to his penis with Super Glue." The doctors and nurses treating the man are compelled to devise a number of original procedures to restore everything to its natural arrangement. The point of the story, according to the speaker, is that it has mythic resonance and that its deeper meanings can be revealed through the techniques of structural anthropology, which he will apply and illustrate in the remainder of the narration.

Following this section, which functions as a kind of prologue, Adam Mars-Jones divides the story into five discrete units, each of which establishes a dichotomy: nature/culture, limp/stiff, food/drug, private/public, and comedy/tragedy. Within each unit, the speaker delves further into the motives of the parties in the story and links their actions to larger cultural trends. The first unit is focused on glue, which the speaker sees as a figure for the degree of adhesion between mutually opposing entities, as well as an inert substance that the wife chooses because it lacks the capacity for resurrection. As the narrative progresses, various examples of disconnection are mentioned ("the collective unconscious" independent from "chronological sequence"), leading toward the next unit, which the speaker labels "the secondary axis of oppositions."

Here, the physical dimensions of the wife's actions are examined. The social and personal requirements regarding arousal and containment are analyzed in terms of their effects on "social order and the next generation" The speaker contends that the purpose of the wife's revenge is to parody virility, as artificial stiffness in this case reveals incapacity. The point here is that any permanent condition, unmediated by change, is a pathological state, laughable and disgusting to an impartial observer.

The third unit considers the contrary forces operating in terms of a choice to sacrifice variety for consistency. Marriage requires the diminution of momentary excitement in the interest of the future generation, so that in an "economy of duties and pleasures," the speaker asserts, a man "renounces sex as drug" and accepts "sex as food"; thus, he explains, hunger will be satisfied rather than stimulated. However, in the case of the adulterous husband, a demand for excitement has been met by the wife "*drugging his food*," using the drug (glue) as a narcotic rather than a stimulant in order to publicly dramatize her feelings about the betrayal of the marriage agreement.

In the fourth unit, the speaker discusses the ways in which a private commitment is ratified by a public ritual, one of the crucial components of a myth. The ritualistic accouterments of a marriage ceremony are reversed in the wife's actions, the church replaced by its "symbolic inverse," a hospital. The speaker shows how this has a direct appeal to the "collective unconscious" and notes that in practice, structural anthropology "increases mystery in the process of explaining it."

The final unit continues the concept of counter-ritual, aligning it with folktales in which a character (the wife) metamorphoses from one character (Captive Maiden) into another (Witch). The speaker explains how the wife has involved the community—surgeons and nurses—in her action, with attending women in the hospital representing a suppressed cultural desire as they "re-enact the transformation of the female from subservient employee to ambiguous manipulator." In concluding, the speaker claims that the "sordid or trivial" details of the original story have been absorbed into "the tangled richness of myth," a strong argument for a method that can reveal hidden, sometimes forbidden, truths about a contemporary social construct.

Themes and Meanings

One of the more influential concepts brought into literary analysis by critical theoreticians during the 1960's was the technique known as structuralism, which attempted to understand literary production as a form of social practice, maintaining that what is most valuable in literature is determined not by character, setting, or theme, but by the structuring of events. The structural anthropologist Claude Levi-Strauss, whom Mars-Jones mentions, developed an idea of the basic human social relation in terms of "raw" and "cooked" with respect to food or meaning, and Mars-

Jones uses this distinction to fashion a structural arrangement in his story that both exhibits and parodies a methodology. Originally designed as a corrective to criticism that ignored historical factors, structuralism evolved through the 1970's into a device that some critics used to disregard many of the most appealing aspects of literature, producing jargon-clotted quasi-scientific analyses repellent to both readers and writers. Mars-Jones attempts to counter this trend by using what appears to be a structuralist technique that is dazzling in its brilliant explanation of the cultural significance of a "sordid story" while at the same time making claims that are unsubstantiated, far-fetched, or overblown. At the crux of his conception is the question of whether the technique offers anything beyond the entertainment of self-regarding wit, abstract learning, and cross-disciplinary blending.

At the core of Mars-Jones's query is the nature of narrative and the essential value of a story. The "story" that is the subject of the expert's deconstruction is an amusing trifle at most, but the "story" of "Structural Anthropology" is dependent on the progressive revelation of the character of the narrator. The emerging outlines of his mind, in conjunction with his enthusiasm for his discipline and the ways in which he presents it, are the elements of "Structural Anthropology" that make it a work of imaginative literature rather than a lucid lecture.

Mars-Jones anticipates the trend toward cultural studies in university departments of literature, in which other disciplines of the humanities (sociology, psychology, ethnography), as well as newer areas of inquiry (feminist studies, homosexual studies) enlarged the field, sometimes to the extent that more traditional and still viable aspects of literature were subsumed or disregarded. The continuing appeal of "Structural Anthropology" is that it manages to function as a "story" in the more conventional sense while offering some intriguing glimpses of how an evolving theoretical perspective might enhance a reader's comprehension.

Style and Technique

Because the expert on the methods of structural anthropology is essentially located outside the action of the story, the voice that he employs in the course of the narration is the fundamental determinant of his character. As he is the only character in the story—what might be called an approximation of a protagonist, to indicate his relationship to the action, which could be said to take place in his mind—his manner of speaking is responsible for the emergence and development of his character. Mars-Jones controls and manipulates this voice as he explains and demonstrates the techniques of a discipline that fuses aesthetic and scientific terminology, maneuvering deftly in an unmarked area in which the fields are in uneasy symbiosis.

The opening paragraph, which introduces the discipline, is a learned exposition of fundamental facts, replete with references, reasonable and measured in tone. The rational, sensible approach of the speaker, designed to instill confidence, is exemplified by the words, "if applied with care and thoroughness." Then, in a radical shift in style, the anecdote of the spurned wife's revenge is told in crisp, descriptive phrases, conversational and vivid in detail, somewhat like a tale told in a pub. The contrast between professorial removal and personal participation sets the style for the flow of the narration, sometimes distant and analytical, sometimes direct and almost delightfully engaged. Scientific examination requires total objectivity; literary criticism that does not distort or completely betray the spirit of literary inspiration may engage the full spectrum of feeling of the critic.

Commentators from previous centuries such as Samuel Johnson, Virginia Woolf, and D. H. Lawrence, among others, remain vital for the play of a distinctive, even quirky sensibility on the work that their formidable intelligence has chosen to discuss. The speaker in "Structural Anthropology" has something of this quality, as his objectivity recedes while he relates, with evident relish, the brilliance of the wife's strategy. The overall effect is the formation and presentation of an individual personality, which, in the course of its narrative and interpretive actions throughout the story, also becomes the agent of the collective unconscious that contains the kind of universal truths that are the ultimate aims of artistic endeavor.

Leon Lewis

THE STUCCO HOUSE

Author: Ellen Gilchrist (1935-　　)
Type of plot: Psychological
Time of plot: The 1990's
Locale: New Orleans and Mandeville, Louisiana
First published: 1994

> *Principal characters:*
> TEDDY, a seven-year-old boy
> RHODA, his mother, a poet
> ERIC, his stepfather, a photographer
> HIS MATERNAL GRANDPARENTS, who live in nearby Mandeville

The Story

"The Stucco House," told mostly from a young boy's perspective, is a glimpse into a failing marriage with one parent abdicating her role as a mother and the other realizing that he prefers his young stepson to his wife.

As the story opens, Teddy, asleep with his stuffed animals, is awakened at daybreak by his stepfather, Eric, who wants Teddy to go with him to find Rhoda, who did not come home the previous night. They locate her on the staircase of a duplex, unconscious, wearing nothing but pantyhose. The father suspects alcohol and an affair but tells Teddy that she fell down the stairs. Young though he is, Teddy recognizes that his mother is drunk.

After his stepfather brings his mother back to their upscale New Orleans home, Teddy watches over her. She awakens and irrationally confides in him that Eric tried to kill her and that he must inform his grandparents. Although he silently dismisses the accusation and expresses concern to himself about her sanity, he, later, does as instructed. Thinking of Teddy's welfare, Eric has the gardener, who obviously cares for the boy, drive Teddy to his grandparents' house in Mandeville. Anticipating the boy's visit, his grandfather readies the horses and searches for the archery equipment, and his grandmother bakes a caramel cake. Even so, Teddy would prefer to remain with Eric.

In one of the few scenes not narrated from Teddy's point of view, Eric goes into Rhoda's room, looks at her watercolors (a new venture of hers), thinks that she is talented, and reads from a journal that she intentionally left out. He is curious about any new affairs. The entry shows him that there have been some, but it also reveals that she is despondent and unhappy with her life as a wife and mother. Although he questions their marriage, he realizes that he loves Teddy and that Teddy depends on him. When Rhoda recovers, she bemoans her fate as a failed poet because some of her poems were rejected by an obscure journal, suggests that she and Eric go out to dinner, and then abruptly denies that she had sex the previous night.

However, Eric is more concerned with his actions than hers. He had used Teddy to protect himself against her possible accusations, thus exposing the child to the sight of his unconscious and nearly naked mother. Leaving Rhoda (and it is not clear if it is for an afternoon or if it signals the end of the marriage), he goes to the farm to get Teddy and thinks about taking a trip with him to Disney World.

Themes and Meanings

In many of Ellen Gilchrist's stories, the central character is a self-centered girl or woman. However, in "The Stucco House," the protagonist is a young boy, but his self-indulgent mother is the same Rhoda who appears in many of Gilchrist's short stories. She is introduced as a young girl in *Land of Dreamy Dreams* (1981). She appears in both *Victory over Japan* (1984), the winner of the National Book Award for Fiction, and *Age of Miracles* (1995), which contains seven stories about Rhoda, including "The Stucco House." The Rhoda stories have been assembled in *Rhoda: A Life in Stories* (1995), and Gilchrist chose "The Stucco House" as one of the thirty-four stories to be included in her *Collected Stories* (2000). Taken together, the Rhoda stories chart the development of Rhoda Manning from childhood through adolescence, marriage and divorce, affairs, and her career as a writer. Even though Rhoda, as an adult, is financially well off and talented, she is dissatisfied. She, as well as some of Gilchrist's other female protagonists, is searching for an identity, a search often curtailed by the demands of a family. Although some characters find satisfaction and a balance between career and family, many do not.

In "The Stucco House," Rhoda, portrayed as a writer with a drinking problem, considers herself to be a failure not only as an artist and poet but also as a wife and mother. She realizes that Teddy prefers Eric, and she sees her two other sons, who are at camp during the time frame of the story, as obstinate teenagers. Because she feels the traditional gender roles are too restricting, she does not want to define herself by them. She abrogates her role as a parent to her current husband, who willingly accepts it, at least as far as Teddy is concerned. She has one failed marriage, and her present marriage seems to be headed for divorce as well. She does not find fulfillment in her poetry or painting, although her photographer husband thinks her watercolors are promising. In many ways, Rhoda is trying to chart a course but is unsure of her destination. The extent of the difficulty that Rhoda faces in her search is suggested in the first paragraph, which contains a brief mention of a poet who committed suicide (a reference to Gilchrist's friend the poet Frank Stanford).

Gilchrist in "The Stucco House" presents a dysfunctional family, but at the same time, she stresses the importance of family and community. Without such support, Teddy would not be coping as well as he is. Even though he lacks maternal guidance, Teddy has Eric who embraces the role of parent, correcting his grammar and providing food, albeit soda and pizza. Eric also welcomes him into his darkroom and encourages Teddy's own interest in photography. He takes him on excursions to the mountains and to the beach. In addition, Teddy has the support of his grandparents who love him and provide needed discipline, which Teddy, a typical child, resents. Even Big George, the gardener, is part of his network of support.

Although Rhoda might not realize it, she, too, has a support system provided by Eric (at least for the time being) and also by her parents and her brother Ingersol, who wonders why she always disrupts things but still travels into New Orleans to attend to her. Thus the story depicts a woman's desire for autonomy, but it also shows the consequences on those around her.

Style and Technique

The first and last parts of the story are narrated from the viewpoint of Teddy, whose name suggests one of the stuffed animals on his bed, thereby not only implying his innocence but also suggesting his mother's lack of concern and her tendency to treat him like a teddy bear or a toy. The reader is presented with a picture of how a seven-year-old's mind works. The boy reads a book about magic and believes that with the right spell he can be transformed into an animal or be rendered invisible. He thinks that God plays a game devising bad things to do to people then arbitrarily changes his mind. He thinks that if there is a divorce, he will be able to choose to live with Eric and that they will be bachelors together. Clearly his interpretations of the events are a child's. Juxtaposed with Teddy's understanding are the views of Eric, Big George, Ingersol, and his grandparents; the reader is given multiple perspectives of the mother and her behavior, none of which is flattering. Even though Teddy is only seven, the reader is provided with enough evidence to trust the child.

The ending is ambiguous. Does Eric leave for a few hours or for good? It also implies a solution that is fanciful and unrealistic. Going to Disney World does not address the problems in the marriage. One cannot remain in a make-believe world but must eventually return to the stucco house, a house that appears solid because of the facade but may be cracked underneath the stucco. In a similar fashion, the family in the story appears solid, having an expensive home in New Orleans, a gardener and housekeeper, and artistic friends, but underneath there are deep divisions.

"The Stucco House" benefits from the southern roots of Gilchrist, who was born in Mississippi and lived in New Orleans and Arkansas. The setting in the story is New Orleans, home of Gilchrist from the mid-1960's to the mid-1970's, and Mandeville, a town on the other side of Lake Pontchartrain. References are made to New Orleans streets, food, and the heat and humidity of its summer. The region also influences Gilchrist's characters. The Rhoda stories challenge southern assumptions about girls and women, questioning the southern tradition as exemplified by New Orleans and the delta plantation where Gilchrist spent her summers as a child. Thus the young Rhoda is energetic and ambitious. In the later stories, including "The Stucco House," Rhoda rejects the confining roles of wife and mother and searches for her own voice, refusing to be satisfied with what society dictates. Gilchrist, who published her first book at forty-four after raising her three sons, would recognize Rhoda's struggle.

Barbara Wiedemann

A SUDDEN TRIP HOME IN THE SPRING

Author: Alice Walker (1944-   )
Type of plot: Psychological
Time of plot: The late twentieth century
Locale: New York and Georgia
First published: 1971

> *Principal character:*
> SARAH DAVIS, one of two African American students attending a
> prestigious women's college in New York

The Story

An external narrator presents a few days in the life of Sarah Davis, a popular college student, one of the only two black students at a prestigious women's college in New York. Sarah faces many conflicts, both external and internal. Her environment is perfect for her in some ways, but also troubling. She is studying art at a college with the best teachers, yet she has difficulty with her art because there are few models for the black faces she wants to draw. She particularly feels unable to draw black males, because she cannot bear to trace defeat on her blank pages. Although she is popular with the other students, they do not understand her or her culture and unknowingly patronize her. One day, Sarah receives a telegram telling of her father's death and has to make a sudden trip home to Georgia to attend her father's funeral. Her father's death precipitates another conflict: Sarah begins to wonder about a child's duty to her parents after they have died. As she packs for her trip home, she talks to a suitemate about the difficulties that the black novelist Richard Wright had with his father.

Sarah's old bedroom at home now houses her father's body. As she looks at her father lying in his casket, Sarah reflects on her feelings about him and her mother. She blames him for her mother's death; her mother died in her sleep, seemingly from exhaustion from the difficult life that she led. Sarah views her father as the weak parent, the one not able to care properly for the family. However, as she looks into her father's face and tries to find there the answer to her question of what a child owes to her dead parents, she begins to realize that perhaps her views are faulty. She begins to doubt if she is taking the correct route in her life by attending a college in the north.

While home, Sarah spends time with her grandmother, grandfather, and older brother. Her genuine interest in art and education becomes clear as she gently deflects her grandmother from looking too soon for a great-grandchild. Her interaction with her grandfather begins the resolution of Sarah's conflicts. Watching the strength in her grandfather's dignified face as he stands at his son's grave, Sarah wonders why it never occurred to her to paint his face. She promises her grandfather to make such a portrait, but he asks instead to be done "up in stone." Talking with her older brother furthers the resolution of Sarah's conflicts. He assures her that her interest in art is a worthy pursuit, and that once she learns to draw his face and sculpt her grandfather's, she can return to the South or go anywhere she wants. With the knowledge that her grandmother is looking to her to continue the generations and that her grandfather and brother have faith in her ability to fulfill her artistic dreams, Sarah returns to college. When a student who does not know the reason for Sarah's trip south asks her how her trip home was, Sarah responds that it was fine.

Themes and Meanings

"A Sudden Trip Home in the Spring" is an initiation story about a young woman coming to terms with adulthood, both by resolving the conflicted feelings she has about her father and by becoming more confident about her own artistic endeavors and life. The story implies that by coming to terms with her own inner struggles, she will be better able to deal with the external difficulty of living in an atmosphere in which her heritage is not valued or even understood. Sarah's internal and external struggles are connected: She doubts her father's strength because of the way he was treated by his white employers; envisioning her father as a weak man, she feels unable to portray strong men in her art; once she recognizes the strength in the males of her family, her artistry is released and her connection with her own culture becomes healthier, making her more able to deal with external obstacles.

Although the story is cyclical, in that it begins and ends with Sarah at the northern college, it is cyclical geographically, not psychologically. The doubts and questions Sarah has at the beginning are resolved by the end. She is back at the college to master her creative abilities, but she is now more confident about the direction of her life. Sarah identifies her life with that of the black novelist Richard Wright, an important novelist to her, yet one that the other women at Cresselton do not know; in Sarah's mind, they are identified more by the world of the writer F. Scott Fitzgerald, whose novel *The Great Gatsby* (1925) presents the lives of the leisured rich.

Style and Technique

Alice Walker clearly focuses on Sarah in "A Sudden Trip Home in the Spring." Although Sarah's family members are important in helping her come to a healthy acceptance of her heritage and a confidence in her own artistic abilities, Walker keeps the grandmother, brother, and grandfather in minor roles, in part by not giving them names.

Twice in the story, Walker refers to a rat that Sarah must stare down. The first reference to the rat is when Sarah is alone in her bedroom with her father's body lying in the casket. She calls to her brother that there is a rat under the casket, but her brother does not hear anything, leaving Sarah alone to deal with it. The rat here is both literal and symbolic. Sarah stares straight at it until it finally runs away, but her thoughts just before she notices the rat are also important. As her father lies dead, Sarah is also forced to face the unpleasant feelings she harbors about him and their somewhat estranged relationship. After her mother's death, Sarah avoided her father as much as she could, spending much of her time in her own room. Thinking now about how

Wright came to terms with a father who betrayed him, Sarah wonders whether unre-solved feelings about her own father may keep her from achieving a healthy connec-tion with her own roots and with herself.

As an adult, understanding the hardships her father endured working as a farmhand for white farmers, Sarah begins to see that what she felt was her father's weakness may have actually been a strength. By this point in her life, Sarah herself has been placed in uncomfortable and humiliating circumstances by her white friends at col-lege. Her father endured humiliations and hardships in order to keep the family to-gether so that her generation could prosper; his and her mother's difficult life brought forth a daughter who received a scholarship to attend a first-rate college. Sarah does not now see her father as a perfect man, but she begins to question her youthful as-sumptions about his weakness and what she saw as a lack of love for her mother. She recognizes now that he understood love much better than she did.

At the story's end, Walker again writes of the rat. A collegemate, who does not know the reason for Sarah's journey home, asks how her trip was. Sarah knows she is back in a world that has no comprehension of her own; she is back in an environment peopled by young women whose hair blows freely in the wind as they travel to the ten-nis courts and back. Sarah now is able to accept that world and yet hold tight to her own: "Stare the rat down, thought Sarah; and whether it disappears or not, I am a woman in the world. I have buried my father, and shall soon know how to make my grandpa up in stone." Just as Sarah stares down the literal rat, she learns to accept both the strengths and the flaws of her father's life and to tolerate the superficial view her college acquaintances have about her own life.

Marion Boyle Petrillo

THE SUICIDE CLUB

Author: Robert Louis Stevenson (1850-1894)
Type of plot: Suspense
Time of plot: The late nineteenth century
Locale: London and Paris
First published: 1878

>   *Principal characters:*
>   PRINCE FLORIZEL, the heir apparent to the Bohemian throne
>   COLONEL GERALDINE, the Master of the Bohemian Horse and
>   aide-de-camp to Prince Florizel
>   THE PRESIDENT OF THE SUICIDE CLUB, a notorious villain
>   DR. NOEL, an English expatriate in Paris, a former associate of
>   the president, now assisting the prince

The Story

Three related stories make up the larger plot of "The Suicide Club," although each of the separately titled stories might be understood if read alone. The larger plot concerns the work of the hero, Prince Florizel of Bohemia, and his assistant, Colonel Geraldine, in pursuing and finally destroying the unnamed president of the Suicide Club, an organization that provides desperate men with ways to escape unhappy or disastrous lives without the scandal of overt self-destruction.

The first part, "The Story of the Young Man with the Cream Tarts," establishes the personalities of the major characters and the nature of the club. The prince and the colonel, both of whom are visiting London and are interested in life's more eccentric opportunities, are seeking adventures in an oyster bar near Leicester Square. Among the pair's many attributes is the capacity to disguise their true characters so as to meet and talk with all classes of people—the prince being less proficient in disguise than his assistant because the nobility of his nature makes it impossible to hide its quality altogether.

As they are enjoying the bar's fare, the young man enters, accompanied by two men carrying trays of cream tarts, a rich pastry. The young man proceeds to offer tarts to each of the patrons in the bar, including the Bohemian pair; by the rules of the sport he has invented, he eats any tart that is rejected by the person to whom he first offers it. The prince and Geraldine accept his offer on the condition that the young man join them for supper after the remainder of the tarts are consumed. The young man agrees, and the three soon find themselves in the private dining room of a Soho restaurant.

After a pleasant meal, the prince and Geraldine persuade the young man to explain his unusual sport with the cream tarts. He tells of an insufficient fortune, of an excessive love that could not be returned, and, finally, of bankruptcy. Playing to the young man's apparently morbid concern, the Bohemian pair succeed in discovering that he is actually preparing himself to die by suicide, although he tells them that he is not going to commit the act himself. Intrigued and alarmed, they convince the young man that they are in the same circumstances themselves, and they persuade him to take them along as he visits the club where the matter will be taken care of.

Once they arrive, the prince and Geraldine are admitted as members only after an elaborate interview with the president, which includes the signing of a solemn pledge not to violate the secrecy of the club or to fail in completing the tasks assigned to them as members. Afterward, they enter the club room to find what appears to be an ordinary party of men talking, drinking, and playing at cards, although with a particularly feverish air. Many of the members are quite young or in the prime of life, but the attention of the prince is arrested by a crippled man of considerable age, Mr. Malthus, who, although apparently suffering from many afflictions, is nevertheless intensely interested in the affairs of all the members. After a period of conversation and gaming, doors at the end of the room are opened and the company retires to another room containing a large table at which the president sits, carefully shuffling a deck of cards.

As soon as the members take their seats around the table, the prince and Geraldine find out how the business of the club is transacted: by dealing, one at a time to each of the members, the whole pack of cards until the ace of clubs and the ace of spades have been turned over. The man receiving the spade will die that night at the hands of the man receiving the club, who will follow the plans laid out by the president. Both Bohemians are suddenly concerned that, should chance turn against them, the prince might be put in a position that would be intolerable, for either his honor or his life would suffer. As it happens, however, the spade falls to Mr. Malthus—who almost collapses when he sees his fate—and the club to the young man with the cream tarts. The prince and Geraldine extricate themselves as quickly as possible and depart, discovering in the papers the next day the news of Mr. Malthus's death by accident in Trafalgar Square. The prince decides to return to the club the next evening in order to destroy it, hoping in that way to help the young man work through his guilt for the death of Malthus.

In the evening's hand, however, the worst happens: The prince is dealt the ace of spades and prepares to meet his doom because of his word of honor to follow the rules of the club. Following the instructions of the president, he sets out, only to be captured and stolen away by a gang of apparent thugs, who turn out to be his own servants under the direction of Geraldine. The colonel tells the prince that all has been taken care of, and the two return to Box Court, the location of the club, where the prince metes out justice. He invites the president to take a trip to the Continent with the younger brother of Geraldine—an implicit sentence of execution because the younger Geraldine is under instructions to dispose of the man by duel. With that, the first and most elaborate of the stories concludes.

The second part, "The Story of the Physician and the Saratoga Trunk," continues the story from a somewhat different perspective. Mr. Silas Q. Scuddamore, a wealthy New Englander visiting Paris, is tricked by a series of strange coincidences into keeping an assignation with a woman who never appears at the rendezvous. When he returns to his lodging, he is horrified to find on his bed the body of a man recently killed. In his horror and fright, he attracts the attention of a neighbor, Dr. Noel, who promises to help him out of the obvious difficulty that the body represents. The next day the doctor departs for a while to make arrangements while Scuddamore keeps grisly watch over the body.

When the doctor returns, he tells Scuddamore that he can transport the body to England and dispose of it there, the transportation being possible because Dr. Noel has arranged to convey his luggage through diplomatic channels, where it will not be opened at customs inspection, and the disposal of the body being possible because of Dr. Noel's connections in England. Scuddamore is too much in a state of shock to notice how quickly and easily this serious problem is solved; in this period of shock, his only real response is a feeling of disgust when the doctor tells him that the body must be transported in the Saratoga trunk that stands in his room and that Scuddamore himself must load the body into the trunk.

Scuddamore discovers the next day that he will be traveling in the suite of Prince Florizel. Despite great anxiety, he arrives in England without trouble and tries to take the Saratoga trunk to the address that Dr. Noel has given him; the prince's servants, who drive him to the address, evidence surprise when he instructs them to go to Box Court. Returning to his hotel and made anxious by a man who appears to be trailing him, he keeps the trunk with him overnight, then tries again to deliver it. He is immensely surprised when the occupant at Box Court turns out to be the prince himself, who has taken over these quarters as he tries to dismantle the damage done by the club. The prince is even more surprised, however, when he opens the trunk to find the dead body of Geraldine's brother.

After hearing Scuddamore's account, the prince explains that Dr. Noel is an erstwhile colleague of the president and that the entire coincidence seems providential in the matter of punishing the wicked. Recognizing his own implicit guilt in the death of the younger Geraldine, the prince announces that he will even more steadfastly undertake to bring the president to vengeance, on which note this second section closes.

The final part, "The Adventure of the Hansom Cab," introduces Lieutenant Brackenbury Rich, a young war hero who has returned to England after his service in India. Feeling out of place on his arrival in London, the lieutenant sets out to explore the streets of the city and to familiarize himself with a scene from which he has long been absent. A sudden downpour of rain drives him into the shelter of an unoccupied cab, and he instructs the driver to drive about as he will, for lack of a better destination. The driver immediately sets off to a large and well-lighted house, where a party of gentlemen is being entertained. Assured that he will be well received, the lieutenant finds there a group of strangers who nevertheless have in common an air of independence and self-sufficiency. When only a half-dozen guests remain, the host declares his purpose: He is looking for courageous and iron-willed men who will assist him in a matter of honor. Four of those remaining decline to participate and retire, leaving the lieutenant and Major O'Rooke, another war hero, to accompany the host.

As the three make their way to the rendezvous for the duel, the host—who is in fact Colonel Geraldine—explains that the masquerade at the house was a device by which he hoped to acquire the services of the most courageous and most honorable men. On arrival at a large but dilapidated house in extensive grounds, they are introduced to their host's principal, whom the major recognizes as Prince Florizel. The prince explains that he is now about to conclude the dangerous business of destroying the president of the Suicide Club, with the assistance of Geraldine and Dr. Noel, who is also present. The two war heroes are to serve as seconds in the duel between the prince and the president, who attempts to ambush the prince but is forestalled by the party. The principals and seconds in the duel retire to the grounds, leaving Geraldine and Dr. Noel to wait anxiously. The prince and the heroes soon return with word that the president has been dispatched, and thus the story ends.

Themes and Meanings

"The Suicide Club" is an interesting representative of the so-called sensational fiction of the nineteenth century, in which peculiar circumstances and exciting action sometimes replaced narrative and psychological realism. As a result, the story lacks some of the more intensely conceived ideas and themes that mark other, perhaps more serious, fiction in the period. In this story, one recurrent idea appears in all three sections as a unifying motif: the idea of personal honor. Florizel's situation, as Geraldine frequently reminds him, requires that the prince consider not only his own interest but also the interest of Bohemia, the throne of which he is to inherit.

In the exciting events of the story, the prince is thus constantly placing himself at risk, and he seems to depend on his wit, strength, and honor to defend him. In the first and third parts, however, the prince is actually in danger of sacrificing his life for the sake of his honor, the result being that his personal virtue will remain intact, although his country will then be without a fitting successor to the crown. Geraldine, as the active partner in this relationship, is always having to place his own interest and safety at the disposal of the prince. As the story develops, one may reasonably ask whether the continual reference to and discussion of honor is not a device by which the author ironically points out the ephemerality of honor in the kind of extreme behavior that the prince both confronts and represents.

Style and Technique

"The Suicide Club" was included in a collection called *The New Arabian Nights* (1882). As the title would appear to suggest, the stories in the collection are highly mannered and artificial in character. Robert Louis Stevenson does not represent either the life of Victorian London or the character of a crown prince with any psychological reality; his intention seems rather to have been the production of a story with peculiar and exciting incidents, however unlikely the circumstances they depict might actually have been.

In structure and technique, the story has the same superficial character. Besides the elaborate and peculiar events of the plot, Stevenson indulges the habit of introducing characters without developing them beyond the few bold strokes in which they are drafted at their first appearance. As a result, recognizable stereotypes—the completely amoral villain, the young man disappointed in love, the miserly New Englander, the war hero—predominate in the action of each story. Even the prince (the name and country of whom Stevenson borrows from William Shakespeare's *The Winter's Tale*, c. 1610-1611) is conspicuously lacking in developed personality, serving for the most part as a mere representative of an extraordinary notion of honor. The only significantly developed character is Colonel Geraldine, who must be more fully represented if his actions are to be at all credible. Nevertheless, the absence of any explicit indications of his grief at the death of his brother suggests that even in his case, Stevenson had in mind not a portrait of human beings as they actually are but an exciting story that would engage and entertain readers with a taste for suspense.

Dale B. Billingsley

SUICIDES

Author: Cesare Pavese (1908-1950)
Type of plot: Psychological
Time of plot: 1938
Locale: Turin, Italy
First published: "Suicidi," 1953 (English translation, 1964)

> *Principal characters:*
> THE NARRATOR, a civil servant
> CARLOTTA, his deceased lover
> JEAN, a boyhood friend

The Story

As the narrator sits at a café watching people pass, he falls into a guilt-stricken sense of loneliness. A solitary, brooding character quick to revert to memories of the past, he has suffered for years from delusions and remorse, but now he merely wishes to maintain his self-control and observe as life goes on all around him. This is one of the simple pleasures of his life, although at times it leaves bitter aftertastes. He wishes he were more astute or clever as, for example, women are in justifying their actions even to themselves.

On this particular morning, the narrator is amused by two café customers who are playing a trick on the young woman at the cash register. He is suddenly reminded of his own stupidity in certain situations and that when he reacts against other people, it is usually in a cruel fashion. These thoughts recall memories of Carlotta.

It has been a year since Carlotta died, but the narrator is constantly reminded of her. Carlotta was a simple person who worked as a cashier and lived in a little two-room apartment. He went to her house one evening, made love to her, told her he wished to be alone afterward, and went away for three days. On his return, he treated her coldly and spoke to her very little. When he first met Carlotta, he had just been humiliated by another woman, a bitter blow that had almost driven him to suicide. He understood that he was taking his revenge for one woman's cruel and unjust treatment on another woman, but continued to see Carlotta and leave her in the evenings after indulging his passion. He liked to walk the deserted streets at night; they reminded him of his youth, and allowed him to feel the resentment he harbored against women at its fullest. He thought that Carlotta was naïve and because she was separated from her husband, merely turned to him for some comfort.

One evening, however, they went to the cinema together, they stopped for a drink at a café, and the narrator ended up spending the entire night with Carlotta. This intimacy made him feel tender toward her, but soon he reproached himself for this. It made him furious to see Carlotta looking blissful and content because the woman he really loved never showed such happiness to him. On such occasions, he would walk in the cool morning air and promise himself to be firmer and harsher. On his return, he would tell her that their relationship was strictly physical and that she would never be a part of his life. Often, he would try to avoid Carlotta, and when they did get together he would be cold and distant. Although this made her think of leaving him, she lacked the courage to do so.

Some evenings the narrator talked and talked to Carlotta to the point that he forgot his bitterness and became like a boy again. On these occasions, Carlotta served as an audience and he would offer his opinions on love ("To enjoy love to the full, it must also be a betrayal") and youth ("We fell nobly in love with an actress or a girlfriend and devoted all our finest thoughts to her"). One evening, he tells Carlotta about a boyhood friend, Jean, who committed suicide.

Jean and the narrator loved the same girl, and they often talked together about love and death. Because they were both unhappy youths, the narrator suggested that they kill themselves. They had a revolver, which they took to the hillside to fire one winter day. In a deserted lane, Jean put the revolver into his mouth. The gun went off and killed him.

As the affair with Carlotta dragged on, the narrator became more sullen and cruel. He told Carlotta to go with anyone she wished as long as she does not catch a venereal disease. When she told him that her husband came to see her, he responded that she should try to get him back. After that, they saw each other sparingly at the café or talked briefly on the phone, until one evening when he visited her at her apartment. When he left her, they both knew that it was final. For weeks the narrator waited for a telephone call from Carlotta, but it never came. One day he went to the café where Carlotta worked and noticed that there was another woman at the cash register. He went to her apartment and learned from the concierge that a month earlier they had found her dead in bed, with the gas turned on.

Themes and Meanings

Cesare Pavese was obsessed with the idea of suicide, a recurring theme in his works. When he was still in school, a close friend of his killed himself with a revolver in the manner described in "Suicides." At his funeral, Pavese, wild with grief, was prevented at the last moment from following his friend's example. The subject was constantly in his thoughts, as many entries in his personal diary attest. The protagonist in "Suicides" is, in effect, a neutral version of Pavese himself.

Pavese's work expresses with painful clarity the crises and despair of modern humanity. A major theme in all of his works is that of solitude or alienation. Pavese wrote in his diary that the "greatest misfortune is loneliness. The whole problem of life, then, is how to break out of one's own loneliness, how to communicate with others." The protagonist in "Suicides" is continuously seeking to be alone with his innermost thoughts. His efforts at integrating into the city fail, and the only comfort he derives from it is to wander its deserted streets or to gaze unseen at its inhabitants. With Carlotta, the protagonist jealously preserves his privacy and attempts at all costs not to strive for any kind of human bond because he knows that this is impossible with the human condition.

Love also becomes a marginal aspect of human solitude. When Pavese was at the university, he fell in love with a woman with whom he had an affair that lasted five years. In 1935, he was arrested for alleged antifascist activities and spent ten months in exile. On his return, the woman he loved abruptly left him and married another man. A hatred for women as deceitful, self-centered, and treacherous subsequently appears in almost all of his works. He portrays women savagely and with a certain degree of violence. In "Suicides," his brooding spirit of revenge against women reaches its extreme limit when the protagonist not only makes Carlotta suffer but suggests to her the idea of suicide by telling her how his young friend had killed himself. Love is not a solution, and the narrator in "Suicides" reproaches himself for even a kind thought or tender moment shared with Carlotta.

Style and Technique

"The style of the twentieth century expresses but does not explain. It is a never-ending revelation of inner life, manifesting it in moments when the subject of the story is the link between reality and imagination." These words from Pavese's diary hold the key to the author's style in "Suicides." It is objective, rather than descriptive or moralistic, in nature. The narrator's views on love and Carlotta as a symbol of all women are seen through his actions, which reflect his inner thoughts. It is his actions, the solitary walks or the cruel words to Carlotta, that reveal his pessimistic ideas on the human condition.

The manner in which the protagonist treats Carlotta also reflects the author's opinion of the impossibility of communication, of any sincere human relationship. Pavese does not treat the problem of the inability to communicate from a philosophical point of view; he describes what he sees around him, in the atmosphere and social surroundings. Thus the introspective nature of the narrator in "Suicides," his lack of participation in the life of others, conveys a basic division between self and the world, between individual and society. This expresses in painful clarity the crises and despair of modern humanity.

Victor A. Santi

THE SUITOR

Author: Larry Woiwode (1941-   )
Type of plot: Domestic realism
Time of plot: 1939
Locale: North Dakota
First published: 1969

> *Principal characters:*
> MARTIN NEUMILLER, a young Catholic man
> ALPHA JONES, his intended bride
> CHARLES NEUMILLER, his father
> ED JONES, Alpha's father

The Story

The Neumiller and Jones families live on neighboring farms in rural North Dakota. Martin Neumiller, in love with Alpha Jones, visits her parents' home on New Year's Eve to propose marriage. A fierce winter storm kicks up, the wind howls, the temperature drops below zero, and snow piles up to the axle hubs on Martin's Model A Ford. Alpha Jones accepts her suitor's proposal, but Martin is still uneasy about what her parents think of him. Because of the bad weather, Alpha's mother reluctantly agrees to let Martin sleep overnight on the sofa. Martin's anxiety over Alpha's parents confuses him, causing him to doubt whether Alpha has actually accepted his marriage offer. As he drops off to sleep, he thinks about what has happened that day.

Martin says prayers before going to sleep: Hail Marys, a decade of the rosary, the Our Father, and an Act of Contrition. The Neumillers are a devout Roman Catholic family—which may explain why Martin's and Alpha's parents have never been in each others' houses although they live only five miles apart. Martin's mother thinks Alpha's father, Ed, is a devil and an insane atheist. Martin's parents have often seen Ed Jones walking along the railroad tracks into town, his gray hair wildly flying in the wind and his eyes full of devious animal energy as he sings obscene songs and disrupts the quiet countryside.

Ed walks into town because he does not have a car and does not want to wear out his horses just so he can go out and get drunk. Ed has told Charles that getting drunk is his only release; Ed says he is killing himself trying to rid his farm of the quack grass that is choking the wheat crop. He has tried cutting, burning, and digging, but nothing seems to help. Ed feels he was duped after buying the old Hollingsworth farm and discovering its poor soil. The farm has been put under the plow for only ten years and needs more work to make it productive. Drinking is Ed's way of running away from his problems on the farm—the impending loss of his daughter, a difficult relationship with his wife, the lack of sons to help him, and his inability to fight quack grass. After hearing this, Charles tells his family nothing is wrong with Ed Jones. Martin's mother disagrees and tells Charles and Martin to stay away from Ed because they will be judged by the company they keep.

Alpha's mother was raised in the Missouri Synod Lutheran Church, known for its strict observance of ritual. She believes that every Catholic is up to no good. Ed Jones seems outwardly nonreligious and more open to Martin's courtship of Alpha. Ed claps Martin on the shoulder during his visits and calls him "boy." Outside the house, Ed discusses politics, government, horses, and his low opinion of mechanized farming. Ed thinks horses can do all farmwork and is proud of his team; he even worries over the condition of the barn where the horses sleep. Inside the Joneses' home, however, Ed is taciturn and silent.

Ed echoed his wife's anti-Catholic feelings once as Martin listened in the next room. Ed may have been getting drunk with one of his friends when he yelled that Catholics were sanctimonious and hypocritical. Ed has warned Alpha against marriage to a Catholic, because the union would create many children. Alpha has told Martin that her father's angry remarks do not mean anything.

When Martin wakes up the morning after the storm, Ed is stomping around the house; Ed has been awake since 4 A.M. fixing a rattling windmill and sheltering the livestock. Ed has awakened Martin so he can help him pull his car out of a snowdrift. Ed irritates Martin because he turns Martin out before he has a chance to say good-bye to Alpha and confirm her acceptance of his proposal. Ed protests that Martin moves too slowly and the day is getting on.

Martin dresses and goes outside with Ed. It is still nearly dark, despite Ed's frenzied call to arms. Martin's fingertip becomes frozen to a metal buckle on his overshoes as he tries to put them on, further angering him. Martin decides now is the time to speak to Ed about his desire to marry Alpha.

Ed stops Martin short, saying he already knows about Martin's plans to marry. Alpha stayed up all night because of her excitement and told her family. The reason Ed has roused Martin so early, which was not obvious to the suitor, was to get Martin to church on time. Ed assures Martin that their marriage will work out, despite the two families' differences. Ironically, it is Ed, not his churchgoing wife, who remembers it is the Sabbath. The story ends with the apparently atheistic, possibly alcoholic father asking the pious Martin, "Do you think I might be Christian?"

Themes and Meanings

The story of the young man who falls in love with a young woman and asks her antagonistic father for her hand in marriage is universal in appeal. One theme is how love transcends family differences in its patience, kindness, and strength. The background of the family discord between the Neumillers and Joneses presents another thematic issue: a confident, educated, successful, faithful Roman Catholic family confronts a suffering, semitransient, regressive Protestant family. "The Suitor" echoes William Shakespeare's star-crossed lovers in *Romeo and Juliet* (c. 1596) and even the legend of Tristan and Isolde; each of these stories concerns young people who must reconcile cultural differences in order to love each other.

However, the enigmatic Ed Jones, not the lovers, stands as the emotional and thematic center of "The Suitor." He represents the guardian of old ways (symbolized by traditional farming) and the keeper of the treasure (Alpha), but suffers from personal difficulties with drinking and trying to support his family. Despite his problems, Ed attempts to celebrate life in his drinking and singing, evading his problems on the wings of a different type of love—narcissism.

"The Suitor" explores the spiritual potential of the half-beaten Ed Jones. Darkness and light are mixed in equal proportions in him, making his a dynamic, complex personality. Ed's love of animals, his pride in his horses, and his painful battle with weeds place him close to nature. Although Ed is partially defeated, he lives life to its fullest and enjoys harassing the youthful Martin Neumiller. Ed's proper role is resistance to the kind of change Martin represents: education, business, machinery, and marriage. Metaphorically, Ed guards his fortress by protecting the things dearest to him, but his complexity allows him to transcend his own limitations.

Ed resents the dogmatic religion of both his wife and Martin's family. "The Suitor" suggests the possibility that this rebellious and unpredictable character is, in fact, the most genuinely spiritual. This is proven by his "offices," such as care for animals, and his observance of Sunday despite the storm and Martin's apathy. Ed accepts Martin as a surrogate son and receiver of his daughter, despite the fact the Neumillers have rejected him. Martin's mother is judgmental of Ed's behavior, while Ed suspends his biases in favor of giving his blessings to the marriage of Martin and Alpha. Ed thus shows the true path of unconditional love.

Style and Technique

To understand "The Suitor" fully, one must study the mythology of the Neumiller family in other stories. Larry Woiwode's stories create a system of family history and a complex web of relationships among people spanning several generations.

"The Suitor" is traditional and realistic in style, based largely on the author's autobiographical memories. The character of Martin Neumiller is modeled after Larry Woiwode's father. Critics have written that in his stories and novels, Woiwode revives a neglected literary form—the family album. Many of Woiwode's stories describe the plight of the Neumillers living in North Dakota, their German ancestors who emigrated to the United States, and the lives of their children as they move on to various professions in Illinois and New York.

Woiwode uses rich description, limited dialogue, and an omniscient narrator in "The Suitor." The word choice is clean and especially beautiful and poetic when Martin reflects on his feelings toward Alpha. The story uses nonchronological organization, freely moving from the present to Martin's memories about what his family knows about the Jones family.

Jonathan L. Thorndike

SUMMER EVENING

Author: Kay Boyle (1902-1992)
Type of plot: Psychological
Time of plot: The late 1940's
Locale: Germany
First published: 1949

> *Principal characters:*
> MAJOR HATCHES, a military officer and host
> LIEUTENANT PEARSON, a guest
> THE YOUNG MAN IN THE BLUE SUIT, an intelligence agent
> THE HAUSMEISTER (POP), a houseboy servant

The Story

Like many of Kay Boyle's stories written while she was a foreign correspondent for *The New Yorker*, the events of "Summer Evening" take place during the post World War II reconstruction of Germany under the American occupation. The story relates the events of a cocktail party given by one Major Hatches and his wife. Their guests include military officers, government personnel, and their spouses. Although little action occurs during the course of the story, as the party progresses, the reader is introduced to a variety of sharply etched characters and is permitted to overhear their various conversations.

As the story opens, Major Hatches comments to Lieutenant Pearson about choosing a Hausmeister: "You have to be as careful about who you take as a Hausmeister as who you marry. . . . You have him underfoot twenty-four hours every day of the week." Hatches is cruel in his remarks concerning the Hausmeister's desperation, exemplified by his having to retrieve cigarette stubs for his own use. Pearson continues the discussion by relating the story of a fellow in Nuremberg who would drop his butts out the window so that his Hausmeister would have to crawl through the shrubbery for them.

Marcia Cruickshank, the flirtatious wife of Captain Cruickshank, is one of the lonely, unhappy Americans among this ensemble of characters. Unlike another member of this party, Wendy Forsythe, who is unhappy in her realization of humankind's cruelty to its fellow creatures, Mrs. Cruickshank is unhappy because of her own empty life. She gets so drunk, as she does at all the social gatherings she attends, that she openly seduces the young man in the blue suit, an "intelligence" operative whose name is never revealed. Disgusted, her husband eventually must carry her to their car.

Captain Pete Forsythe, as he views the castle across the valley, is forced to think of the war: "There's a tank, a big Sherman tank, rusted and gutted and turned on its back, with field flowers growing through the carcass of it," an example of "the meaningless paraphernalia of war." As Forsythe remembers the Americans' defeat of the Germans, he maintains a strong conviction against further humiliating the former enemy. It is his wife Wendy's sensitivity to the extinction of the whooping crane that stimulates his thoughts: "The wheat growers came down across the plains and the marshes and the open prairies, . . . and the whooping crane lost its breeding ground. Like the Indian, the bison, the poets, their time is finished. There is no role left for them to play." Like other creatures similarly exploited by Americans, the Germans are made to feel like foreigners in their own land.

The Americans' exploitation of the Germans is further exemplified by the last conversation between Hatches, Pearson, and the intelligence agent, regarding the museum-quality treasures—the Biedermeier silver coffee set that had been in a German family for generations, the seventy-four-piece Dresden dinner service with gold inlay, the tablecloth that took a professor's wife twenty years to make—all bought "for a song." They are amused that the hungry Germans are willing to trade their "back teeth" for coffee and lard.

The Americans not only have cheated the Germans out of their material possessions but also proceed to strip them of any dignity that they may have left. At the end of the story, Hatches, Pearson, and the intelligence agent play their cruelest prank on the Hausmeister. When he is invited by Major Hatches to partake of a nightcap, the Hausmeister divulges his American background. He was born in "New Joisey" and desires to return to his homeland. The Hausmeister is led to believe that the young intelligence agent is the General Consul and that a golf-score card is a passport. To their embarrassment, the Hausmeister breaks down in tears of joy. Hatches expresses his disgust at what they have become during their stay in Germany: "What are we doing here, any of us? he asked himself, in sudden bewilderment, almost in fright. What has become of the lot of us here?" Boyle's stories typically end in this kind of revelation.

Themes and Meanings

"Summer Evening" portrays humanity's injustice to humanity. The references to the Americans' mistreatment of the Indians and to the German's systematic annihilation of the Jews both echo the Americans' present exploitation of the Germans. The character of the Hausmeister and the Americans' ridicule of him particularize the general helplessness of Germany. The major's statement that the Hausmeister will "make enough out of what's left in the ashtrays after one of these shindigs to keep him in luxury six months" not only belittles the subservience of the Hausmeister but also alludes to the falling social status of the entire German population.

The Hausmeister is a broken old man who must resort to alcohol to escape his pain. He has no purpose in life because of the destruction of the war ("Everything bombed out. Everything lost. Nothing left to Pop"). Although Boyle does not sympathize with the Nazis, she exhibits compassion for a proud and defeated people. While the Hausmeister symbolizes the broken spirit of Germany, the young man in the blue suit (the intelligence agent) represents the strength of America. He is naïve about the frailty of human feelings, just as the Americans were practically taking over a country that did not belong to them. He exhibits no conscience in his taking advantage of Mrs.

Cruickshank's loneliness or his taking part in the practical joke played on the Hausmeister.

The setting is not merely background for the story, but further supports its theme. The party is held on "a dreamy, bluish summer evening" in a terraced villa overlooking an eleventh century Hessian town. The villa and the wealth associated with it symbolize America's exploitation of postwar Germany. Across the valley, the ancient castle, which appears "to watch, as it had watched for century after century, for armored knights on horseback . . . or for armored vehicles and low-flying planes," represents an ennobled German past. Unfortunately, the view of the castle elicits sympathy only from Captain Forsythe. The others are interested in filling themselves with Scotch-and-sodas and chopped-egg-and-anchovy canapes. The absence of German guests and the presence of German musicians and a German servant indicate that the Americans are interested, not in socializing with the Germans, but in using them for their entertainment and service.

Style and Technique

Although the story does not contain a plot in the traditional sense, "Summer Evening" does contain a coherent structure and well-developed characterization. It is framed by two incidents that humiliate the Hausmeister: the discussion of his collecting cigarette stubs and the prank of the make-believe passport. Within this frame, Boyle moves in and out of various conversations, in the manner of tracing shots by a motion-picture camera. These conversations take place between a few individuals whose lives are unfolded by Boyle's delicate touch. The characters are first introduced by third-person description. Mrs. Hatches, for example, is described as one who "flew at her guests with cries of pleasure, her bosom swollen like a pigeon's in her flowered dress." The words "flew" and "cries" make vivid Mrs. Hatches's image as a pigeon. Similarly, Lieutenant Pearson is described as a good-natured, youthful man who has been "larded" since childhood with excessive fat. This quintessential "ugly American" is so fat, in fact, that he has three rolls of flesh overlapping his jacket collar. It is no wonder that Boyle has a strong reputation as a stylist, a manipulator of language in her striking metaphors and her ability to create sharp, vivid pictures.

What the characters say also supports the narrator's description of them. Mrs. Hatches's own statements reveal her personality: "That's twice you-all gave you' wud you'd come on ovah and play bridge with the Majah and me!" "You promised me that lemon-meringue recipe two weeks ago . . . an' you nevah kep' you' wud!" Not only do these lines portray Boyle's ear for dialect, but also the trivial, cocktail-party subject matter exposes Mrs. Hatches as the superficial person she is. It is not surprising that she, unlike her husband, achieves no moral growth during the course of the story.

Boyle once stated in a lecture that, more than technique, it is the writer's profound belief in something that is essential in creating a story. Boyle's belief in the need for pity and understanding is evident in "Summer Evening."

Patricia A. Posluszny

SUMMER LEAGUE

Author: Danny Romero (1961-   )
Type of plot: Realism
Time of plot: The 1960's
Locale: Southern California
First published: 1989

> *Principal characters:*
> MICHAEL, an eight-year-old Chicano boy
> ANTONIO and
> PAUL, his friends
> MR. GARCIA, his softball coach

The Story

Three young Chicano friends meet at a baseball field on the first Saturday after school closes for the summer. Although Antonio and Paul decide to sign up for a summer softball league, Michael hesitates to commit himself. When he gets home, it becomes clear that his reluctance to sign up is caused solely by the fact that his family can ill afford the two dollars that joining the team will cost. Michael's mother cannot buy him a glove, but he is permitted to join the team.

When practice begins two days later, Michael and Antonio show up but discover that Paul has gone to Tijuana. The boys are placed on two different teams, with Michael being coached by Mr. Garcia, a dark, sweating man with a strong accent, bloodshot eyes, and a silver front tooth. On the first day of practice, the boys play no ball at all, but instead do jumping jacks and run laps. As the summer wears on, Michael plays mainly in the outfield, where there is little action, and he gets only one or two hits during the whole season. After Michael plays Antonio's team, he goes to Antonio's house for lunch, and the boys talk about who is the best pitcher in the major leagues. They also talk about who would win if the two of them had a fight and then playfully wrestle.

Just before the season ends, Michael's mother takes him to a sporting goods store and buys him an inexpensive glove, which he wears during the last game of the season. Because the pitcher on Michael's team walks ten batters in a row, Michael has nothing to do in the outfield. His team loses by a score of 23-0, with the game being called after the third inning. Michael decides not to attend the awards ceremony the following week, but thinks that maybe he will play again next season.

The story ends as Michael looks at his new glove and reads the name of some left-handed ballplayer that no one would recognize—"much like himself," he thinks.

Themes and Meanings

Danny Romero's brief story of a boy playing in a summer softball league seems simple and straightforward. It is about a young Chicano who spends an uneventful summer playing softball on a Little League-type team. However, it is precisely this lack of significant events that defines the boy and his summer. In fact, it hardly seems a story at all, more like a realistic slice of life with little or no thematic importance. What gives the story its significance is just the feeling of insignificance that Michael feels.

Romero chooses the summer sport of softball—a variation of baseball—purposely, for baseball, more than any other sport, takes on almost mythic significance as the great American pastime. As such novels as Bernard Malamud's *The Natural* (1952) and W. P. Kinsella's *Shoeless Joe Comes to Iowa* (1983; adapted into the film *Field of Dreams* in 1984) demonstrate, there is a heroic potential, typically American, about the "boys of summer" that does not characterize football or basketball. The fact that a young Chicano wants to play the game so he can feel like "big stuff" is thus ironic, for it signifies the immigrant's efforts to carve out an identity for himself by means of his adopted culture's icons and conventions.

The ultimate failure of the game to provide a sense of importance and identity for Michael is emphasized throughout the story. It begins with his sister's teasing him for being in the "tiny league" and yet acting as if he were so "big." It continues when Michael gets Mr. Garcia as his coach, a stereotype of the unkempt Chicano who wears baggy pants and drinks too much beer. There is no indication in the story that Michael has a father, for it is only his mother who attends to his needs; his coach certainly does not provide a strong male image for him. Indeed, Garcia seems more interested in selling firecrackers to the boys for the Fourth of July celebration—another allusion to ironic images of heroism in a story about Mexican immigrants, for the framers of the Declaration of Independence are not Michael's own forefathers. The fact that Michael may be missing a father image to emulate is also suggested by how pleased he is at the attention that Antonio's father pays to him when he goes to his friend's home for lunch. This lack of a father is an important thematic element in this story that centers on a sport in which a father and son playing "catch" is a conventional stereotype.

The image of Michael stranded in the outfield, having to tear off his borrowed right-hander's glove so he can throw the ball with his left hand during the few moments that it comes his way symbolizes the failure of the game to fulfill Michael's needs. It is a further irony that only one game remains in the season when his mother, who knows little about the game, finally takes him to the Big Five Sporting Goods store (another reference to the "big stuff"/"tiny league" dichotomy introduced early in the story) to buy him a glove.

The failure of the game to meet Michael's needs to have a father/hero figure and to feel important is finally emphasized at the conclusion of the story, when Michael tries to read the name of the left-handed pitcher in the center of his glove and realizes that the name is one that no one would recognize, "much like himself." However, in spite of this realization, the story ends on a note of hope with Michael thinking that he will return for the summer league next season.

Style and Technique

While the theme of "Summer League" focuses on the loneliness and lack of identity of a young Chicano immigrant seeking importance by means of the great American mythic sport of baseball (Romero uses softball because it is a diminutive of hardball, just as Tiny League is even smaller than Little League), the subtle way in which Romero communicates the thematic significance of this seemingly insignificant story places it within the modern short-story tradition of lyrical realism.

In the tradition of Anton Chekhov, the great late nineteenth century Russian short-story writer, Romero knows that it is better to say too little than too much. "Summer League" is written in an economical and straightforward narrative style, with no exposition, explanation, or commentary. What readers know about Michael's situation, they infer from the apparently realistic details of the story. They guess that Michael has no father because no father is ever introduced and because Michael goes to his mother for what he needs. They know that his search for a heroic father figure in the league meets with failure because Mr. Gomez, who should provide an image of the surrogate father as coach, is merely a stereotype of a sloven drunk.

Other details in the story subtly suggest the strife and tentativeness of Michael's life as an immigrant. A brief scene in which a group of black children taunt a Latino snack truck vendor by calling him a "honky-ass" and the vendor responds by calling the children "jungle bunnies" establishes the ethnic isolation and conflict that serves as a backdrop for the story. The simple fact that the friend Paul cannot play ball because he has abruptly left for Tijuana suggests that he and his family may have been deported by immigrant officials.

Perhaps the most poignant scene in the story occurs when Michael goes to eat lunch at his friend Antonio's house in Antonio's father's new car. As Michael goes to the bathroom, he looks at the pictures on the hallway wall of Antonio and his family—who are all smiles at the beach, at Disneyland, at the circus, and in the mountain snow. When Antonio's father pats Michael on the shoulder and tells him that he has real heart, Michael almost burns his tongue on his soup. The fact that Michael is acutely aware of his lack of a father to make his family whole is finally suggested at the conclusion by Mr. Garcia's asking the boys to attend the awards banquet on Tuesday night and to "be sure to bring your family." As Michael turns to head for home, he knows that he will not show up on Tuesday night.

Romero is not only keenly aware of the sense of isolation of the young Chicano in the United States, he is also skillful in using an economical writing technique that communicates what Frank O'Connor once called "the lonely voice" of the short-story form.

Charles E. May

SUMMER NIGHT

Author: Elizabeth Bowen (1899-1973)
Type of plot: Psychological
Time of plot: World War II
Locale: Ireland
First published: 1941

> *Principal characters:*
> EMMA, an errant wife
> THE MAJOR, her husband
> FRAN, the Major's aunt
> DI and VIVIE, Emma's daughters
> ROBINSON, Emma's lover
> JUSTIN CAVEY, a city man visiting the small town
> QUEENIE CAVEY, Justin's sister, who is completely deaf

The Story

An unnamed, bare-legged young woman, who later turns out to be Emma, is driving rapidly south, alone, on an Irish road. She pulls into a "Do Not Park" space in order to make a long-distance call from a hotel. She has a brief conversation with an unnamed man, who is later called Robinson. He cautions her not to drive too fast in the treacherous light because they have the whole night before them, and he inquires about the Major, Emma's husband.

Robinson, having hung up rather abruptly, returns smiling slightly to the two guests in his living room: a pretty, middle-aged, deaf woman named Queenie Cavey, and her brother, Justin Cavey, who, because of the war in Europe, is spending his vacation visiting his sister in their native town. Tonight for the first time they have taken up Robinson's invitation to call at Bellevue any evening. Queenie sits by the window drinking tea and enjoying the view of the distant beeches of the old feudal domain while Justin discourses on the war, life, identity, and love, and Robinson keeps glancing at the clock. Robinson is a factory manager who arrived in town only three years ago and does not socialize with the townspeople. The local ladies, having discovered that he is a married man living apart from his wife and that he frequently disappears for the weekend, whisper that Bellevue is a Bluebeard's castle. Suddenly Justin asks: "What's love like?" Robinson utters a short, temporizing, and unnaturally loud laugh that reaches Queenie.

Justin is angered, and Robinson apologizes; to change the subject, he asks if Queenie is fond of children. "You mean why did she not marry? There was some fellow once . . . " Justin answers. Robinson takes photos of his two sons over to Queenie, who says that it is a wonder that he has no little girl. He returns for a third photo, passes his hand "as though sadly expunging something, backwards and forwards across the glass." He does not know how to tell Queenie that the child is dead.

Without transition, the Major is introduced in his orchard sixty miles away: a tall, unmilitary-looking man with a stoop, whose frown has intensified in the last months. He is called to the phone by Aunt Fran. Emma has rung up ostensibly to say good-night. He asks if the people with whom she is going to stay will be waiting up for her. Aunt Fran protests that Emma said goodnight before she left and comments that she seemed undecided about going all afternoon.

The Major goes up to the bedroom of his daughters, Di and Vivie: The latter is a miniature of his wife. Di reports that Aunt Fran is frightened that something will happen. Vivie says that her mother likes things to happen and was whistling all the time she was packing. She suggests that her mother may not come back.

When Di is asleep, Vivie prowls through the house naked, her body covered with chalk drawings of stars and snakes. Her bouncing on the bed in her mother's room causes the chandelier in the drawing room to tinkle. Aunt Fran insists on investigating. Told to kneel and pray, Vivie objects: "In my skin?" Aunt Fran rolls Vivie up like a great sausage in the pink taffeta eiderdown.

Again with no transition, the reader is back at Bellevue, where Justin and Queenie are taking their leave. At this moment a car pulls up at the gate and its lights go off. Emma has arrived.

Robinson is very much at ease, while Emma is nervous and asks for a drink. This is her first visit to Bellevue. She says that the friends expecting her have no phone and that he will have to think of something that went wrong with her car. She remarks that she hardly knows Robinson and asks if she was wrong to come. During a visit to his garden, Emma is intrigued by the domain in the distance and its destroyed castle. When Robinson observes that they do not want to stay outdoors all night, Emma becomes frightened by his experienced delicacy on the subject of love. He has ruined her fairy tale.

On his return to the hotel, Justin writes a lengthy, accusatory letter to Robinson and adds that he prefers they should not meet again. "Justin, trembling, smote a stamp on this letter," and walks toward Bellevue to post it. "On his way back he still heard the drunken woman sobbing against the telegraph pole."

Queenie happily undresses in the dark. "This was the night she knew she would find again. On just such a summer night, once only, she had walked with a lover in the demesne. . . . That had been twenty years ago, till to-night when it was now. To-night it was Robinson who, guided by Queenie down leaf tunnels, took the place on the stone seat by the lake."

Themes and Meanings

The psychological complexities of life and of social intercourse, especially the interactions between the public and the secret lives of the characters, are vividly evoked in this story. The "European war" is vaguely upsetting even in neutral Ireland. Emma wants excitement, Robinson wants to enjoy fully his time away from work, Aunt Fran feels threatened on all sides, and Justin, the sensitive thinker, sums up: "Now that there's enough death to challenge being alive we're facing it that, anyhow, we don't live."

Emma's bid for excitement disturbs everyone except Queenie. The Major is apprehensive and worried by her departure from home; her daughters think that she may not return; Aunt Fran urges Vivie to pray after rolling the child up in a protective eiderdown as if she were on fire; Justin is outraged; Robinson evidently has some scruples because he twice suggests that Emma should return to her home. Only Queenie does not react, probably because she has not heard the town gossip or the war talk and apparently does not understand the significance of Emma's car at the gate of Bellevue. Queenie has been touched by Robinson's kindness to her and lives in her own dreamworld.

Critics often mention Elizabeth Bowen's sense of social comedy, but there is no comedy in this story except Aunt Fran's efforts to ward off evil. It is the somber record of humans hurting one another. The author has managed to catch her people at the moment when, through action or speech, their inner lives are exposed.

Style and Technique

"Summer Night" is considered to be one of the best of Elizabeth Bowen's scores of short stories. The style is taut: Every word counts; no detail is unimportant. Tension is created in the very first paragraph by small details. One does not know who the excited young woman is or where she is going at sunset in such a mad rush, but one feels her mood of expectancy because she glances at her watch and reads the mileage on the yellow signposts.

The reader can see the characters as they move about and talk to one another despite the economy of description of the rooms. In the main scene, an open window, easy chairs, and a fireplace mantel with a clock and silver-framed photos suffice. The author displays her extraordinary talent for the creation of atmosphere when she pictures Aunt Fran's room with its feeling of transitoriness.

It is the characters who unfold the plot, not the narrator. Elizabeth Bowen wrote that the action of a character should be unpredictable before it has been shown, inevitable when it has been shown. She does not explain what prompts the actions of her characters. Understanding this story requires the same technique demanded by an Impressionist painter: The reader must synthesize for himself. He must conjecture what has happened.

The most striking symbolism in the story is the use of light and darkness to mark the difference between public and secret lives. Emma watches the sun set on her ride to her rendezvous. It is dark when she arrives, and as soon as she enters the house she wants the top light turned off. When she and Robinson are in the garden and she is still living her fairy tale, there is the light from his flashlight, but no moon. Justin writing the angry letter in his small harsh hotel room is bothered by the hot light. It is well past twelve o'clock on this dark night when he sees the woman sobbing by the telegraph pole. Queenie goes happily to bed in the dark. Because light and darkness also have a moral connotation throughout the tale, one wonders if Queenie will be Robinson's next victim. This lack of conclusion is typical of Elizabeth Bowen's short stories.

Dorothy B. Aspinwall

THE SUMMER OF THE BEAUTIFUL WHITE HORSE

Author: William Saroyan (1908-1981)
Type of plot: Wit and humor
Time of plot: The early twentieth century
Locale: The Central Valley of California
First published: 1940

> *Principal characters:*
> ARAM GAROGHLANIAN, a nine-year-old boy
> MOURAD, Aram's cousin
> UNCLE KHOSROVE, Aram and Mourad's uncle
> JOHN BYRO, a neighbor

The Story

"The Summer of the Beautiful White Horse" is narrated by nine-year-old Aram Garoghlanian, a member of an Armenian community living among the lush fruit orchards and vineyards of California. One morning Aram is awakened before dawn by his older cousin Mourad, who everyone thinks is crazy. Aram is astonished to see that Mourad is sitting on a beautiful white horse. Aram has always wanted to ride a horse, but his family is too poor to afford one. However, the Garoghlanian family is noted not only for its poverty but also for its honesty, so it is unthinkable that Mourad could have stolen the horse.

Nevertheless, Aram asks Mourad if he has stolen the horse, and Mourad invites him to jump out the window if he wants to go for a ride. Now Aram is sure that Mourad has stolen the horse, but he jumps up behind Mourad, and the two of them begin to ride out of the little town in which they live.

As they ride, Mourad begins to sing. Everybody in the family thinks that Mourad has inherited his crazy behavior from Uncle Khosrove, a huge man who can stop all discussions and arguments by bellowing at the top of his loud voice, "It is no harm; pay no attention to it." Khosrove once said this when told that his house was on fire. Although Mourad is not Khosrove's son, this fact does not matter to the Armenians. They think that it is Khosrove's spirit that Mourad has inherited, not his flesh.

When they reach the open country, Aram wants to ride the horse by himself, but Mourad reminds him that it is up to the horse. Mourad can ride because, he says, "I have a way with a horse." When Aram tries to ride the horse, he cannot control the animal, and it throws him. The two boys find the runaway horse, hide him in an abandoned barn, and go home.

That afternoon, Uncle Khosrove comes to Aram's house to smoke cigarettes and drink coffee. John Byro, an Assyrian farmer, also comes by for a visit and complains that his white horse was stolen last month. Uncle Khosrove roars, "Pay no attention to it." John Byro says that he walked ten miles to get to Aram's house, causing pains in his legs, and Uncle Khosrove again bellows that he should pay no attention to it. John Byro points out that he paid sixty dollars for the horse, and Uncle Khosrove shouts, "I spit on money." John Byro stalks out of the house.

Aram runs to his cousin Mourad's house and finds him fixing the wing of a hurt bird. His cousin has a way with birds. Aram explains that John Byro visited and that he wants his horse back. He also reminds Mourad that Mourad had promised to keep the horse until Aram could learn how to ride. Mourad says that it might take a year for Aram to learn how to ride, so Aram suggests that they keep the horse for a year. Mourad roars that the horse must go back to its owner and that no Garoghlanian could ever steal. He says they will keep the horse for only another six months.

For two weeks, the boys take the horse out in the mornings for rides, and every morning Aram is thrown, but he never gives up hope that he will learn to ride like his cousin. One morning the boys meet John Byro as they are putting the horse away. Mourad explains that he will handle the situation, as he has a way with farmers. John Byro asks the name of the horse, and Mourad tells him that it is My Heart. The farmer says that he looks exactly like the horse that was stolen from him and, after inspecting the horse's teeth, says that the boy's horse could be his horse's twin. As he leaves them, he points out that, "A suspicious man would believe his eyes instead of his heart."

The next morning, the boys return the horse to John Byro's barn. The farmer's dogs do not bother them because Cousin Mourad has a way with dogs. He presses his nose against the horse's nose, and the boys leave. That afternoon John Byro rides by Aram's house in his surrey to show Aram's mother the horse that has been returned. He says that the horse is stronger and better-tempered than ever. Uncle Khosrove shouts, "Your horse has been returned. Pay no attention to it."

Themes and Meanings

In this gentle story from the collection *My Name Is Aram* (1940), William Saroyan calls into question the nature and the value of conventional morality and even of reality itself. Faced with a situation in which the first impulse of most people would be to punish the thieves, the people of this slow-moving, rural Armenian community (which undoubtedly was modeled on the author's hometown, Fresno, California) do more than recognize that boys will be boys. They also understand that the value and thereby the use of property belong to those with spirit and understanding, not only money. A horse, after all, is a living being, not a thing like the burning house that Uncle Khosrove so easily dismisses. John Byro knows who has taken his horse, and he hints not to the boys but to the boy's relatives that he knows, but he does not force the issue by demanding his horse back. To insult the honor of the Garoghlanian family would cause much more trouble than the loss of a horse, disrupting the peace of the community.

Even when Byro catches the boys red-handed, he does not condemn them. When he mentions that he believes with his heart, not with his eyes, he is telling the boys that he knows that they are basically good boys who do not intend him or the horse injury.

Ironically, all turns out for the best. The daily morning exercise has improved the health of the animal, and he is better than ever, so the boys have done John Byro a favor with their mischief. No harm to it, as Uncle Khosrove would say.

The importance of spirit in Saroyan's writings is shown in the characters of Uncle Khosrove and Mourad. No one is upset because both are crazy, for craziness has its strong points. Mourad really does have a way with animals, perhaps because of his unusual approach to the world, and Uncle Khosrove really is able to calm every conflict, even those involving himself, so who is to say who is crazy or even what is crazy?

Style and Technique

Saroyan adds to the warmth and gentleness of the story of the borrowed horse by making the narrator a child, a technique that also suggests that the story might be viewed by a child as a lesson in human relations to be carried into and acted on in adulthood. Saroyan does not sugarcoat his view of childhood, however, as Aram's continuing inability to ride the horse both reminds the reader that all childhood dreams do not come true and enlists the sympathy of the reader through the technique of the self-deprecating narrator. As such a narrator is not threatening to the reader, it is easier to believe in and participate in his experiences.

Perhaps "listener" is a better term than "reader" when discussing the audience of Saroyan's stories, as the folk tradition from which his works come suggests an oral presentation that is often missing in the modern, media-dominated world. It is much easier to understand the power of a character such as Uncle Khosrove, for example, if the listener can hear the storyteller bellow his remarks, and the emotions behind the apparently off-center conversations of the people in the story can be better grasped if the teller reads the story aloud with an ear and a voice for the underlying meanings.

James Baird

A SUMMER TRAGEDY

Author: Arna Bontemps (1902-1973)
Type of plot: Domestic realism
Time of plot: About 1930
Locale: Mississippi River Delta
First published: 1933

> *Principal characters:*
> JEFF PATTON, an elderly, black sharecropper
> JENNIE, his elderly, blind wife

The Story

Jeff Patton has farmed the same acres on Greenbriar Plantation for forty-five years. He loves the land, but life has been physically demanding and the shares system has kept him locked in poverty. A recent stroke has left him lame, and he fears that another will make him a helpless burden on his wife, Jennie, who has been blind for years and is now frail. Both are sound of mind, but their life has been reduced to a series of losses, including the deaths of five adult children in the last two years. They share a state of constant grief and anxiety.

Jeff struggles to don the moth-eaten formal attire that he wears only on rare occasions, such as weddings. He feels excitement and fear as he and Jennie prepare for a trip. A short time later, driving through the countryside with Jennie in their old Model T Ford, Jeff feels a familiar thrill, as he surveys the vitality of the crops and natural vegetation. He feels again the determination and pride that always have accompanied his sense of his mental and physical strengths, required for survival on the land, but if he takes his hands from the steering wheel, they shake violently.

Jennie has repeatedly prompted Jeff to make this trip, relying on his courage to match her belief in the rightness of their decision. As they near their destination, however, she becomes wracked by grief at the thought of leaving everything behind. Crying like a child, she questions whether they should continue. Jeff is tortured by his knowledge of what they are about to do and would like to turn back, but he assures his wife that they must be strong. He knows that they have fully considered their fate, and that more reflection would merely lead to the same, inevitable conclusion. They both know that life has become intolerable, and would only get worse. After they regain their resolve and composure, Jeff drives the car into the deep water of the Mississippi.

Themes and Meanings

The story's title words, "summer" and "tragedy," suggest its theme: the shock of recognition that the cyclical fullness of life inevitably depletes the lives of individuals, calling into question the significance and nobility of human existence.

Historically, the concept of tragedy has implied that human life is very valuable, and that suffering, especially when it results inevitably from the pursuit of happiness, reveals that human life is richly meaningful. The combination of positive and negative connotations in the title hints at the potential for such irony. The author generalizes the truth of his perception by illustrating it with an instance from the common lives of simple people, even persons whose fated suffering would typically be ignored. The universality of what his characters face makes the story broadly applicable, and the way they face their fate demonstrates the possibility of heroic action, even by ordinary people.

The suffering experienced by the characters is easily recognizable by readers as something that could happen to them or someone dear to them. The author gains the reader's sympathy and even admiration for the tragic protagonist, Jeff Patton, by showing his affectionate goodwill, ability and dedication, mental strength, moral innocence, goodness of purpose throughout his adult life and in his final action, and pain and courageous struggle. Given his world of natural and societal forces that require strengths that those same forces limit and finally take away, Jeff's purposes—to provide happiness for his family and prevent further suffering by his wife—are likely to be interpreted by readers as reasonable, understandable, and courageous. His tragic decisions to kill his wife and himself, and then in fact driving into the river, challenge the reader to understand these characters' thoughts, place a value on their lives, and finally make a moral judgment regarding suicide, particularly a suicide and murder that might be interpreted as euthanasia.

Both Jeff and Jennie are grieving over the loss of their own children, the difficulty that daily life poses for persons who are infirm and are becoming a burden on others, the casting off of what good they yet find in their present life, the realization that they do not have the potential of an enjoyable future, and the prospect of death of their beloved partners and themselves, within the hour. Jeff's suffering is especially significant, because ultimately he must make the decision, exercise the will, and accomplish the action that brings about his own death and his beloved's.

The African American heritage of these characters, in a racist locale, is important within the context of the principle that labor and life are cheap. Slaves, and then sharecroppers, like mules, have provided inexpensive labor, and therefore have been considered expendable. This story, however, suggests that its characters share with readers of any ancestry a common human reality of fatal suffering. It elevates the psychological and moral status of its characters by showing them taking ultimate control of their lives through difficult and decisive action. While the author leaves it for the reader to judge whether his characters' actions are wise, their thoughts and feelings serve as an enlightening model of what readers might observe or experience under a similar crisis of age and health.

Style and Technique

In simple and straightforward language, such as his characters would use in their thought and conversation, Arna Bontemps tells a deceptively unassuming story about the last day in the life of an elderly couple. Only the literary and quasi-philosophical word "tragedy" in the title signals an alert reader that something portentous might be coming. That word places the story's protagonist in the company of characters such as Aeschylus's Agamemnon, William Shakespeare's King Lear, and Arthur Miller's Willy Loman, men who in old age take fatal action with more or less awareness of what they are doing, and more or less wisdom about the inevitability of human suffering.

Within his first few sentences, however, Bontemps cues the reader not only to his characters' age and health, but also to their social status, more like a Loman than like a king or conquering general. With a few early details and images, the author foreshadows their impending deaths: Jeff Patton is turning away from vanities, his coat is moth-eaten, his mouth twists "into a hideous toothless grimace" like a skull, his wife's voice comes like an echo, and she has a "wasted, dead-leaf appearance." Conversation, like life for this couple, is sparse, and therefore dialogue is used sparingly in the telling of their story, but when it comes, with a touch of the African American dialect of the Delta, the reader hears the direct, plain emotions of affection and fear that permeate the characterization and plot. The way the author establishes the decline and impending loss of life, paralleling the understated, ironic nobility of his characters, evokes the reader's sympathy and acquiescence in a violent death.

Simplicity of language and detail also creates an unpretentious, realist style of storytelling that makes the reader feel like a neighbor watching this couple pass by. There is nothing unusual or unnatural in the setting; the world is presented just as the Pattons would see it. When Jeff's or Jennie's emotions are revealed, they seem normal to the situation. Their thoughts then seem appropriate to both the situation and emotions; and the story's line of action follows convincingly from the characters' inner motivation.

There is also a touch of naturalism in the style, as the characters are so driven by the socioeconomic system and the effects of time that the fate of such simple lives might appear to be determined by external forces beyond their control. On the other hand, the author deftly uses mythic motifs of cyclical vitality; the eros of the vegetation of the countryside and of Jeff's love of the land, his wife, and life itself; the journey that the Pattons are taking; and even the donning of formal attire for a heroic task, to provide an epic dimension to his story, raising his characters above naturalistic victimhood into a conscious acceptance of suffering that glorifies them.

Tom Koontz

A SUMMER'S READING

Author: Bernard Malamud (1914-1986)
Type of plot: Social realism
Time of plot: The mid-twentieth century
Locale: New York City
First published: 1956

> *Principal characters:*
> GEORGE STOYONOVICH, a nineteen-year-old high-school dropout
> SOPHIE STOYONOVICH, his twenty-three-year-old sister
> HIS FATHER
> MR. CATTANZARA, a change-maker in a subway booth

The Story

Because George Stoyonovich left school on an impulse when he was sixteen, he has been through a string of unsatisfying jobs. Now he is almost twenty years old and unemployed. He does not go to summer school because he feels that the other students will be too young. He does not go to night school because he does not want the teachers to tell him what to do. Instead, he stays in his room most of the day, sometimes cleaning the apartment, which is located over a butcher store. His father is poor, and his sister Sophie earns little, so George has little money to spend.

Sophie, who works in a cafeteria in the Bronx, brings home magazines and newspapers that have been left on tables. George sometimes reads them along with old copies of the *World Almanac* that he owns. He has begun to dislike fictional stories, which now get on his nerves. At night, he roams the streets, avoiding his old friends and seeking relief in a small park that is blocks beyond his neighborhood, where no one will recognize him. In the park, he thinks of the disappointing jobs that he has held and dreams of the life he would like to lead: He wants a good job, a house of his own, some extra money, and a girlfriend. Around midnight, he wanders back to his own neighborhood.

On one of his night walks, George meets Mr. Cattanzara, a man who lives in the neighborhood and works in a change booth in a subway station. George likes Cattanzara because he sometimes gave George a nickel for lemon ice when George was a child. Cattanzara sometimes comes home drunk, but on this night, he is sober. He asks George what he is doing with himself, and George, ashamed to admit the truth, says he is staying home and reading to further his education. He then claims he has a list of approximately one hundred books that he is going to read during the summer. George feels strange and a little unhappy about what he has said, but he wants Cattanzara's respect. After commenting that a hundred books is a big load for one summer, Cattanzara invites George to talk with him about some of the books when George finishes reading them, and then walks on.

After that night, George notices that people in the neighborhood start showing respect for him and telling him what a good boy he is. His father and Sophie also seem to have found out about the reading. Sophie starts giving him an extra dollar allowance each week. With the extra money, George occasionally buys paperback books, but reads none of them.

George starts cleaning the apartment daily. He spends his nights walking through the neighborhood, enjoying his newfound respect. His mood is better. He talks to Cattanzara only once during the next few weeks; although the man asks George nothing about the books, George feels uneasy. He starts avoiding Cattanzara, once even crossing the street to keep from walking by him as he sits in front of his house, reading *The New York Times* from cover to cover. On that occasion, Cattanzara shows no sign that he is aware of George's presence. George stops reading entirely, even neglecting the newspapers and magazines that Sophie brings home.

One night, Cattanzara, obviously drunk, approaches George. He walks silently past George but then calls George's name. He offers George a nickel to buy some lemon ice. When George tries to explain that he is grown-up now, Cattanzara argues that he is not. He challenges George to name one book he has read that summer. When George cannot, Cattanzara tells George not to do what he did, then walks on.

The next night, Sophie asks George where he keeps the books he is reading because she sees only a few trashy books in his room. When George cannot answer, she says she will no longer give him the extra dollar, calls him a bum, and tells him to get a job.

George stays in his room for almost a week, in spite of the sweltering weather and the pleas of Sophie and his father. One night, he goes out into the neighborhood and discovers that the people there still show him respect; Cattanzara has not told anyone that George is not reading. George feels his confidence slowly coming back to him. He learns that the rumor has gone through the neighborhood that he has finished reading all the books, and wonders whether Cattanzara has started the rumor.

One fall evening, George leaves the apartment and runs to the library. After counting off a hundred books, he sits down at a table to read.

Themes and Meanings

A central theme of "A Summer's Reading" is George's lack of self-confidence and self-respect. Early in the story, Bernard Malamud says that George believes that teachers do not respect him, but the one who really does not respect him is himself. He is so ashamed about quitting high school on an impulse that he hesitates to hunt for jobs, feels dissatisfied with the jobs he gets, avoids his old friends, and does not date the neighborhood girls. He is so uncomfortable in his neighborhood that he seeks escape in a park blocks away from where he lives. His lack of self-confidence and self-respect also keeps him from returning to school, going to night school, or even beginning to read the hundred books.

By telling people that George is reading one hundred books, Mr. Cattanzara helps create a sense of self-confidence and a feeling of self-worth in George. He enjoys being respected by his sister, his father, and the people in his neighborhood. When

Cattanzara discovers that George is doing no reading, he helps George even more by cautioning him not to make the same mistake that he made, and by not telling anyone that George is not reading. George thinks that Cattanzara is the one who has spread the rumor that George has finished the hundred books, a rumor that enables him to save his pride and feeling of self-worth and eventually enables him to begin reading. With the support of Cattanzara and of the neighborhood, George learns that it is all right for him not only to dream of a better future but to try to make that dream come true.

The story also emphasizes the importance of an education and of reading. George is uncomfortable with formal education, but Malamud indicates that the alternative of independent reading is available. At first, George feels unable to take advantage of that possibility, but at the end of the story, he begins to work on advancing his education.

Style and Technique

Irony lies at the heart of "A Summer's Reading," beginning with the story's title. During the summer, George reads none of the books he has planned to. As critic Robert Solotaroff points out, he instead reads his own psyche and the psyches of the people in the neighborhood. He learns that the people in the neighborhood support him, and that with their support, he just might be successful in his planned reading and thus in his life.

The greatest irony lies in Cattanzara's not telling the people of the neighborhood that George has done no reading; instead, George thinks that Cattanzara is the one who spreads the rumor that he has done all the reading he planned. This rumor enables him to retain the respect of the people in the neighborhood and, finally, to do something to make himself worthy of that respect.

Malamud uses a third-person narrative in "A Summer's Reading," but often the narrative seems to reflect what George is thinking. For example, Malamud writes of George's neighborhood, "George had never exactly disliked the people in it, yet he had never liked them very much either. It was the fault of the neighborhood." The rest of the story makes it clear that the sentence about fault reflects George's ideas rather than reality. Before the story is over, George finds himself liking the people of his neighborhood, largely because they begin showing that they like, support, and respect him. As a result, he begins to respect himself and finally is able to begin the process of reading that may lead to his being worthy of that respect and to his bettering his life.

Richard Tuerk

SUN

Author: D. H. Lawrence (1885-1930)
Type of plot: Psychological
Time of plot: The 1920's, or possibly earlier
Locale: Sicily
First published: 1926

> *Principal characters:*
> JULIET, a New York matron
> MAURICE, her husband, a stuffy, conventional businessman with "a grey city face"
> JOHNNY, their son
> MARININA, a Sicilian woman more than sixty years old, probably of Greek descent
> A SICILIAN PEASANT, about thirty-five years old

The Story

Divided into five parts, D. H. Lawrence's story of initiation into rites of the healing, vital process of connection with the universe begins with the doctor's command: "Take her away, into the sun." Juliet, a middle-class young matron, leaves behind her tepid-souled husband Maurice as she travels by ocean passage with her son, a nurse, and her mother to the south, to Sicily. There, in a landscape known to ancient Greek colonists of the Italian isle, she strips off her clothes—symbolic of her former prudish conventions—to be naked in the sun. In part 1, by the roots of a cypress tree, she feels the sun warm her into renewed physical consciousness; revitalized, she invites her young son, Johnny, to play in the sun.

In part 2, mother and son make a ritual of sunbathing by the cypress tree. Marinina, a wise old Sicilian woman in whose veins probably flows the Greek blood of her ancestors, acts as priestess of the sun cult, encouraging Juliet to appreciate the beauty of her nude body. Part 3 treats Johnny's encounter with a golden-brown snake, which slithers to escape into the rocks, unharmed by Juliet. In part 4, Maurice visits his wife and son; his pale, unhealthy appearance contrasts with the sun-brown vitality of his wife and son. Ashamed to cast aside the clothes that represent his civilized constraints, he is an awkward presence, and Juliet senses an estrangement between themselves. In part 5, Juliet fantasizes of an affair with a healthy, "rather fat, very broad fellow of about thirty-five," a married Sicilian peasant, but she rejects her fantasy to have the peasant father her next child. Instead, she will—with regret—return to Maurice, who will give her a pallid child. "The fatal chain of continuity would cause it."

Themes and Meanings

Unlike most of Lawrence's fiction, "Sun" avoids the basic conflicts arising from problems of mating (or of erotic selection and fulfillment). Although Juliet and Maurice are temperamentally estranged throughout the story, the wife decides finally (although unenthusiastically) to resume her marriage and, after a time, to conceive another child by her listless husband. Attracted to the "quick animal" vitality of the Sicilian peasant, she nevertheless rejects this man as a lover, following the dictates of prudence and convention rather than the impulses of her emotions. Head wins over heart, and the narrative line of this story deviates—in a pattern not typical for Lawrence—from one that has an end result in erotic fulfillment. Instead, the pattern resembles that of such late fiction by the author as "The Woman Who Rode Away" and *St. Mawr* (1925), in which the female protagonist similarly discovers spirituality by merging her ego with the universe, thus attaining a substitute gratification for physical passion.

In this story, the substitute "lover" for Juliet is the animating force of the sun. This force provides more than the healthful values of sunbathing or physical culture: It provides a close contact with blood consciousness. Warmed by the sun, Juliet is restored in her blood to a consciousness of her essential nature, so that her body is in harmony with external Nature.

Lawrence contrasts the physical and emotional well-being of Juliet and her child, devotees of the sun, with the pallor of Maurice. With his "grey city face," Maurice represents effete civilization, the brain instead of the instincts, a man who smells "of the world and all its fetters and its mongrel cowardice." Compared to the Sicilian peasant, healthy in his vitality and "quick energy," Maurice is "like a worm that the sun has never seen." Unlike the snake, which Juliet and the boy observe with fascination but do not disturb, Maurice is wormlike in his fear of the sun.

To Lawrence, the golden-brown snake, a fertility (indeed, phallic) symbol, is perfectly at home in both worlds—that of the sun and that of the underworld (the dark or blood consciousness). In his poem "Snake," Lawrence develops in much greater complexity his concept of the snake as a "lord of life," symbol of the deepest instinctual and procreative powers. In this episode of the story, the snake simply represents the unity of all creatures, unself-conscious in their natural roles. The snake is "part of the place, along with her and the child." By accepting the "place," Juliet also becomes part of the whole design of nature, a "worshiper" not only of the sun but also of the harmonizing force that unites humankind with the source of vitality in all life—the anima.

Style and Technique

To express the theme of revitalization, Lawrence uses symbols for a rite of initiation into the "mysteries" of the anima. His major symbols are the golden-brown snake, symbol of the unconscious that can return to the rocks—the "underworld" of blood instinct—after sunning itself in the external (conscious) world; the orange and the lemons, symbols of the vitality of the sun; and, above all, the cypress tree. The cypress was sacred to the ancient Greeks who once colonized Sicily and whose descendants, such as Marinina, still carry their ethnic traits. For example, in the sanctuary of Aesculapius at Kos, Greeks of the classic age were forbidden to cut down cypress trees. Once sacred both to Osiris, the "Dying and Reviving God," and to Dionysus, worshiped for his vitality and ecstatic excesses, the cypress is also significant in this story as a link between the sun and the earth.

Being fully aware of the classical-mythological attributes of the tree, Lawrence symbolizes the cypress as "a low, silvery candle whose huge flame was darkness against light: earth sending up her proud tongue of gloom." Like the snake, at home in both the underworld and the sun-heated rocks, the cypress is treated as though it were a "candle," kin to the sun, but whose flame is "darkness" from the underworld (subconsciousness). Similarly, in the great poem "Bavarian Gentians," Lawrence describes a dark-blue flower with "torch-like" points that serve as a connection between the consciousness and the subconsciousness, and that serve to illuminate the rites of the "marriage of the living dark."

Through means of ritual—suggested, not directly stated, by the writer—Juliet first takes off her clothes as she sits by the cypress tree, as though she were an acolyte to the god. When her child has similarly been initiated into the sacred rites, he also responds to the tree. By that sacred place, mother and son are made whole, and "she herself, her conscious self, was secondary, a secondary person, almost an onlooker." Ruled by the sun, she is reanimated; the true Juliet is "this dark flow from her deep body to the sun."

Leslie B. Mittleman

SUNDAY DINNER IN BROOKLYN

Author: Anatole Broyard (1920-1990)
Type of plot: Social realism
Time of plot: 1954
Locale: Brooklyn
First published: 1968

> *Principal characters:*
> PAUL, the narrator and protagonist
> HIS MOTHER
> HIS FATHER

The Story

A young man named Paul, who is apparently in his twenties, travels from his Greenwich Village apartment to his parents' Brooklyn home for Sunday dinner. As he walks toward a subway station, he glimpses the colorful characters who populate his path and draws vivid correlations among them, the local landmarks, and the associations they inspire in him. Among an almost circuslike array of people, the reader sees "the Italians . . . all outside on stoops and chairs or standing along the curb in their Sunday clothes . . . mothers with their hair pulled back and their hands folded in their laps . . . like Neanderthal madonnas . . . [and] girls [with] long pegged skirts which made their feet move incredibly fast."

The subway itself is an exotic realm. Paul states, "I took a long breath like a deep-sea diver and went reluctantly underground." In the subway train the passengers ignore one another, yet exhibit an uncanny attunement to one another's movements as they silently exchange seats in an undulating, almost somnambulistic underground ballet.

The scene surrounding Paul's arrival in Brooklyn proves that he has transported himself to still another world. The borough's empty streets remind him that in stable, middle-class Brooklyn, everyone conforms by eating dinner at the same hour. Paul walks to his parents' house where they greet him as a prodigal son. His mother and father strive to please him by providing him every comfort and by filling him with the food they hope will sustain him. In their eagerness to provide a perfect Sunday evening, Paul's parents revise and repress their own beliefs and desires, a fact that Paul understands, and a truth that ironically increases, rather than decreases, his anxieties.

Following dinner and conversation, Paul's father accompanies him back to the subway station. As the father starts to descend the subway steps, Paul stops him, telling him to remain where he is so as not to overexert himself or to breathe in the station's polluted fumes. Paul's father protests, but finally acquiesces, and as the disaffected son disappears down the underground stairs, he feels his father's sadness.

Themes and Meanings

"Sunday Dinner in Brooklyn" is a story about the bittersweet nature of love. Concentrating on the awkward, often painful, affection between parents and their adult children, Anatole Broyard's central theme is an exploration of how parent-child relationships evolve, rather than remain static, as children enter adulthood. Just how such relationships evolve is what interests Broyard; rarely can even the most psychologically well-adjusted families suspend their emotionally symbiotic attachment to one another in lieu of some sort of traumatically sanitized affection, and Broyard suggests they should not even if they could. Broyard's theme also extends to encompass the pain inherent in all types of love—physical, divine, and societal—as time necessarily transforms love into longing.

The story reverberates with subtle sexual messages. For example, the narrator describes a group of adolescent girls: "All of their movements seemed to be geared to this same tempo, and their faces were alert with the necessity of defending the one prize they had against mother and brother alike" and "the uninteresting boys they would eventually wind up with, older girls between affairs, older boys on the lookout for younger girls . . . [where] they stood, Fifth Avenue dribbled to its conclusion after penetrating Washington Arch." These sad observations show love—and society—not at its apex, but in its decline, a decline almost akin to dissipation.

Similarly, Broyard writes of religion, if not of spirituality:

> There was a tremendous vacuum left by God. In contrast to the kitchen-like intimacy of the church on Thompson Street—which in its ugliness succeeded in projecting its flock's image on the universe—the spiky shells on these blocks had a cold, punitive look, and seemed empty except for those few hours in the morning when people came with neutralized faces to pay their respects to a dead and departed deity.

As time withers passions into memories and human frailty erodes faith into duty, Paul's love for his parents and theirs for him evolves from a playlike existence wherein actors infuse life into lines written for them, to a more experimental scene in which the actors anxiously improvise in the hope of creating meaning. Paul travels to his parents' house as a gesture of respect, but more important he visits his family because he seeks the unencumbered, primary affections of his youth. As he arrives in Brooklyn, the sun hits him in the eye and he reflects, "It seemed to me that the sun was always shining in Brooklyn, drying clothes, curing rickets, evaporating puddles, inviting children out to play, and encouraging artificial-looking flowers in front yards." In other words, the Brooklyn in which Paul was raised, and where his parents still reside, nurtures Paul and his imagination more in his imagination than in reality. For in reality, just as clouds often shadow Brooklyn's sun—which cannot, after all, cure rickets—Paul and his parents' thwarted attempts to communicate with one another make them ache from their mutual desire so intense that pathos practically smothers them.

When Paul's mother declines the rocker—the home's prize chair—for him, he leans back to appease her, despite his desire to remain erect. When Paul eats his mother's food he recalls how, as a child, his first restaurant meal made him realize that she was not the world's best cook. Now, however, as he finishes his Sunday dinner he becomes "flatulent with affection." He knows, "belly to belly, that was the only true way to talk."

According to Broyard, after love's language loses its distinct expression, as it must, only the instincts that constitute love's metaphors can comfort. The failure satisfactorily to communicate as love struggles to transcend life's transformations is not a matter of fault, but of fate. Paul muses:

> When I was a boy, these streets had quickness and life for me, each detail daring me to do something to match my wits, my strength, my speed, against them. Then I was always running. I saw things on the run and made my running commentary on them without breaking my stride, hurdling, skipping, dodging, but still racing forward . . . until one day I ran full tilt into myself and blocked my own path.

So it is with love in all of its manifestations. Growth involves change, and the most painful aspect of that change, Broyard notes, is that those who are loved realize the intentions and needs of those who love them, but cannot adequately acknowledge or fulfill them. As it is with an individual such as Paul, so it is with society itself. Like a moth hovering too close to a flame, individuals and societies consume themselves by seeking the light that shines brightest in their fantasies.

Style and Technique

Broyard's decision to write "Sunday Dinner in Brooklyn" in the first person and in the past tense provides the intimacy and perspective necessary to convey the story's theme. Paul's surname is not mentioned, nor are the first or last names of his parents. Such names are not only unnecessary for the purpose of communicating the story, they are even inappropriate designations when perceived from the narrator's viewpoint. The lack of such names reinforces the idea that Paul is indeed Everyman. Like most young adults, Paul is incapable of conceiving of his parents as entities whose identities can be separate from his; to him they are "my father" and "my mother," not "Mr. and Mrs."

To achieve a rich, yet declarative style punctuated by subtle humor, slight ennui, and startling imagery, Broyard loads his language with similes, metaphors, and personifications. The story's first sentence reads: "I took a roundabout route to the subway, and because I was going to Brooklyn the Village seemed to have at the moment all the charm of a Utrillo." Comparing Greenwich Village to a Maurice Utrillo painting creates a specific visual image, while also allowing Broyard to suggest something of Paul's eager worldliness, education, and self-conscious, youthful snobbery.

The story's second paragraph begins: "Since it was summer, the Italians were all outside on stoops and chairs or standing along the curb in their Sunday clothes, the old men in navy blue and the young men in powder blue suits, as though their generation was more washed out than the last." Broyard's simile here reinforces his theme that Paul's generation relinquishes stability for seemingly less-substantial individuality. This is especially true of those like Paul who seek their identities away from the steady sameness of their parents' solid lives in favor of finding new, post-World War II identities in such teeming communities as Greenwich Village.

Broyard's dependence on figurative language permits him to avoid overwriting so that what remains unstated is implicit, ensuring that his occasional short, simple sentences deliver a punch.

L. Elisabeth Beattie

SUNDAY IN THE PARK

Author: Bel Kaufman
Type of plot: Domestic realism
Time of plot: The 1980's
Locale: A city, probably New York
First published: 1985

> *Principal characters:*
> A WIFE AND MOTHER, the protagonist
> MORTON, her husband, a university professor
> LARRY, their three-year-old son
> JOE, a boy about Larry's age
> JOE'S FATHER

The Story

The title suggests how ordinary a scene this brief story presents. In a quiet corner of an unnamed park in an unnamed city, an unnamed woman sits in the sun with her family—what could be more typical, more universal? Her husband, Morton, who works at a university, is pale and intelligent, enjoying some time out-of-doors with the Sunday paper. Their three-year-old son Larry is playing in the sandbox, earnestly digging a tunnel. The mother sighs, content with her life.

Suddenly another child about Larry's age throws a shovel of sand at Larry's head, narrowly missing him. Clearly, he does this on purpose, and he stands with feet planted, waiting for Larry's reaction, but Larry barely notices. His mother scolds the child as she would her own, reminding him kindly that throwing sand is unsafe. In response, the child throws more sand, and this time some lands in Larry's hair.

Larry now comes out of his concentrated stupor and notices the boy's behavior, but he waits for his mother to act. She speaks sharply, scolding more forcefully, while the two boys continue to look expectantly at her. Morton is still reading his newspaper, not paying any attention. The other boy's father does react, however. He announces that because they are all in a public park, his son Joe can throw sand if he wants to.

Now, as the mother has run out of resources, Morton finally becomes aware of what is going on. He tries to reason pleasantly with the other father, as he would reason with an erring student. However, the other man is not impressed with his calm manner, his "civilized" intellectual approach. He would rather settle the dispute with blows.

As the two men stand facing each other, the mother wonders how she can stop the inevitable battle. Morton is clearly off balance, not used to settling things this way. He stands unsteadily, and his voice trembles. "This is ridiculous," he says. "I must ask you . . . " "You and who else?" the man asks.

Finally, Morton turns his back and walks away awkwardly, gathering up his family as he heads out of the park. For reasons that she cannot articulate, even to herself, the mother is angry and ashamed. Always before she has been proud of her husband's and her son's sensitivity and delicateness. Now, although she is relieved that the confrontation was resolved without a fight and agrees with her husband that a fight would not have solved anything, she feels defeated.

As they leave the park, Larry struggles and cries. He does not want to go home. The mother cannot calm him, and Morton finally threatens that if she cannot discipline the boy he will do it himself. "Indeed?" she replies. "You and who else?"

Themes and Meanings

The story of the two boys and the two fathers is a story of the conflict between reason and force, between man and beast. Larry is smaller, quieter, and weaker than Joe; the two boys ignore each other and manage to play side-by-side for a time. Morton is smaller and weaker than the other father, and he, too, ignores the scene in front of him at first. So long as neither engages, they are safe.

The family's security and contentedness is built, however, on a false view of the world. Morton is in his element at the university, out of the sun, where all disagreements are rational, where reason has power. On an ordinary Sunday in the park, however, he confronts a man who is not like him, who relies on physical power. The fact is, there are both kinds of people in the world. When push comes to shove (in this case, a literal possibility), force can beat reason every time, at least over the short term. Although Morton walks away from the fight and no one is physically hurt, his views of the world and himself have changed.

The role of women in this conflict is a complex one. The only person whose thoughts and feelings are presented is the mother; the reader can judge the other characters' thoughts only by their actions. However, the mother's part in the external events is a passive one. She is the one who first notices Joe's aggressive actions, and she feels comfortable scolding the three-year-old boy, but as soon as Joe's father joins in the confrontation, she steps aside, leaving her husband to deal with both bullies. Interestingly, the only other female characters in the story are two women and a little girl on roller skates, who leave the park just after the first spadeful of sand is thrown.

Women have traditionally left brute force to men—not necessarily repudiating violence themselves, but relying on their men to deal with it for them. The mother in this story does not consider fighting herself, but she comes to wish her menfolk were more forceful and less exclusively rational.

With whom, then, is the mother angry at the end of the story? Why does she, at least in words, take on the role of the bully? It seems too simple to say that she is angry at Morton for not defending the family honor. She has always been proud of him before; she agrees that reason should be used instead of force. If she is disappointed in Morton for appearing weak, she must also be disappointed in herself—not because she should have punched the other father herself, but because she now doubts whether wisdom and intellect can really hold their own against brute force. If they cannot, what grounds has she for her secure contentment at the beginning of the story? If they cannot, what chance does a woman have in this world?

Style and Technique

"Sunday in the Park" relies heavily on sharp contrasts to make its points, beginning with the conflict between what the reader expects from the peaceful title and the brutality that lurks in that park. The peaceful scene becomes a battle between the forces of civility and barbarity, and Bel Kaufman plays up the differences in the two families to the point that they are almost allegorical figures.

At first glance, the two boys seem much alike. They are about the same age, and they are squatting calmly side-by-side in the sandbox. The boys are not sharing or playing together, but happily ignoring each other, in what child development experts call "parallel play." As soon as sand is thrown, however, the differences are made clear. Larry has a pointed little face and a small frame; Joe is chubby, husky, with "none of Larry's quickness and sensitivity in his face." After the mother scolds Joe, Larry looks to her to see how he ought to react, but Joe (whose name is pointedly not the diminutive "Joey") never looks at his father.

The fathers might also appear similar at first. Both men are sitting on park benches reading, ignoring their young sons playing in the sandbox. However, Morton is small, able comfortably to share a park bench with his wife, while the other father is big, taking up an entire bench himself. Morton reads the Sunday *Times Magazine* while the other man reads the comics. Morton speaks pleasantly and shows his anger by tightening his jaw, while the other speaks rudely and scornfully, flexing his arms and waiting for a punch.

No fight ever develops; the only fists in the story are the boys', and their fists are clutching sand shovels. The boys listen and stare, but the conflict soon stops being about them. In fact, Larry does not want to leave the park; the sand-throwing that starts the disagreement does not affect him.

Kaufman uses these contrasting details to shift the reader's focus, first to the boys, then to the fathers. The mother, the observer, is not paired with anyone, just as she plays no part in the potential fight. As details of her thoughts and actions reveal, she carries within her elements of both fathers. She can speak civilly or brutally, she can move gently or sharply. Ultimately, the conflict between reason and force is not between people, but within them.

Cynthia A. Bily

THE SUPPER AT ELSINORE

Author: Isak Dinesen (Baroness Karen Blixen-Finecke, 1885-1962)
Type of plot: Gothic
Time of plot: 1841
Locale: Elsinore and Copenhagen, Denmark
First published: 1934

> *Principal characters:*
> MADAME BAEK, an old servant of the De Coninck family
> FERNANDE (FANNY) DE CONINCK, the eldest daughter
> ELIZA DE CONINCK, her sister
> MORTEN DE CONINCK, their brother, a privateer

The Story

Madame Baek, who lives as the caretaker in the now empty De Coninck house in Elsinore, reflects on her memories. She has spent most of her life with the De Coninck children and senses the doom that hangs over the breed. For the two sisters, this doom takes the form of restless dispositions, which causes them to be bitterly unhappy despite their great beauty, family wealth, and social success. As young ladies growing up in the family home, they were the bright lights of Elsinore society, surrounded by admiring friends and beaux and much in demand at parties, balls, and outings.

However, even as young women they were obsessed with the dark side of life and gave themselves up to bitter tears in the privacy of their own rooms, dwelling on the sham and hypocrisy about them. At the time of the story, they are "old maids" of fifty-two and fifty-three, for they have found it impossible to accept any of their suitors.

As a young man, their brother, Morten, exceptionally handsome and elegant, was pursued by every girl in Elsinore. He became engaged to Adrienne Rosenstand, a friend of his sisters, but then he went to serve in the Napoleonic Wars. As the commander of a privateer, he engaged in many thrilling encounters with British ships, which earned for him public adulation. When privateering was finally prohibited, everyone thought that he would marry his sweetheart and settle down. On the morning of the wedding, however, he disappeared.

In the ensuing years, however, strange rumors of him drifted back to Denmark. It was rumored that he was a pirate, that he had distinguished himself in wars in America, that he had become a wealthy landowner in the Antilles. Eventually, the townspeople came to think of him as a legendary figure, much like Bluebeard or Sindbad the Sailor.

Fanny and Eliza, initially overcome with grief and shame at the sudden disappearance of Morten, inflated the rumors into portents of great honors that would befall him. As years have passed, however, they have come to accept the worst. Someone has seen Morten in New Orleans, poor and sick, and the last news that the sisters hear is that he has been hanged. As for Adrienne, she waited fifteen years for Morten to return, then finally married another. At her wedding, the two De Coninck sisters appeared for the last time as the belles of Elsinore.

Now, in the present time of the story, Madame Baek begins to decline, with fainting, shrieking, and deep, silent spells. Her friends believe that she is near death, but she rallies and sets off for Copenhagen, where the two sisters now live. She arrives on the day of Fanny's birthday and waits in the kitchen. Upstairs, the two maiden ladies entertain their guests, talking happily of the past, on which they love to dwell. They also enjoy talking about their married friends with pity and contempt, as those whose fates are sealed. Eliza, particularly, is as lovely as ever, and wears an air of expectation, as if extraordinary things might still happen.

When the guests leave, the sisters meet with Madame Baek. She tells them that Morten has returned to Elsinore, that he "walks in the house." She has seen him seven times. The sisters journey to Elsinore and assemble in the room in which they shared so many secret suppers with their brother in the old days. He appears and takes the chair between them, as he had in the past. His noble forehead bears a strange likeness to a skull. He soon reveals that he comes from Hell.

Morten questions his sisters about their lives, then tells them of his five wives. What he loved best, however, was his life as a pirate on the finest schooner that ever flew over the Atlantic, the loveliest thing he ever saw. He was sent to buy the schooner by a wealthy old shipowner, but he fell in love with it and kept the ship himself. That was the beginning of his downfall. He named the ship *La Belle Eliza*. Eliza now admits that she knew of the ship, having heard of it from a merchant captain of her father. She has guarded the secret from all the world, and it has kept her happy throughout the years.

Fanny asks Morten to tell her one or two things he knows that they do not. He tells them that he has learned one thing, "that you cannot eat your cake and have it." Morten was eventually hanged for stealing the ship. Before he died, he asked the priest for one more minute of life, to "think, with the halter around my neck, for one minute of *La Belle Eliza*." Fanny, exhausted from the strain, turns on Morten and bitterly complains that he has at least lived. She is always cold, she says, so cold that her warming pans in bed do not warm her. When the clock strikes midnight, Fanny stretches out her arms to Morten, but at the last strike he is gone. Eliza, in great pain or joy, repeats Morten's last wish on earth, "to think, with the halter around my neck, for one minute of *La Belle Eliza*."

Themes and Meanings

Isak Dinesen set her gothic tales in the past because, as she said, "Here, no temptation for me to fall back into realism, nor for my readers to look for it." She explained that the word "gothic" in the title of the collection in which this tale appears refers to her affinity with the Romantic age of Lord Byron. The erotic heroes and demoniac daredevils of Romantic literature gave Dinesen her earliest notions of emotional freedom, the theme that is embodied in the three main characters.

Morten, although of an aristocratic family and hero to all Elsinore, abandons his fiancé and his place in society for the wandering life of a pirate. When he loses his heart to a ship, the essence of his heart's desire, he seals his doom by stealing it. In this way, he lives out an unconventional, heroic morality that is based on the freedom to incur risk and take the consequences. The individual is free to fulfill his destiny, to become himself. Although this act eventually leads to his hanging, he has lived his dream. About to be hanged, he is not repentant but wishes only for another moment of life to think of *La Belle Eliza*.

Eliza has also lived out her Romantic destiny. Although she has remained an "old maid," her beauty and grace are realized by her namesake, *La Belle Eliza*. When she thinks about the ship, imagining it with its full white sails billowing, "She looked once more like a girl, and the white streamers of her cap were no longer the finery of an old lady, but the attire of a chaste, flaming bride."

Although Fanny seems to be the only one unfulfilled at the end of the story, she has nevertheless kept the faith by refusing to tread the path of mediocrity. When Morten must finally return to Hell, she begs him to take her with him. He cannot, but there is a strong suggestion that she will soon join him in the nether world, which is her own Romantic destiny.

Style and Technique

The Romantic mode has left its mark on the style of Dinesen's story no less than on its theme. The two sisters are described in hyperbolic terms, as befits Romantic heroines. Not only are they the "heart and soul of all the gayety in town," but also "When they entered its ballrooms, the ceilings of sedate old merchants' houses seemed to lift a little, and the walls to spring out in luminous Ionian columns, bound with vine." Morten, a match for his sisters in all things, is "the observed of all observers, the glass of fashion and the mold of form."

Even nature conspires to set the stage for the return of the hero. It is not until the unusually severe winter of 1841, when the "flatness and whiteness of the sea was very strange, like the breath of death over the world," that Madame Baek sees Morten returned from the dead.

The first part of the story, which recounts the early years of the three De Coninck siblings, is told primarily from the point of view of Madame Baek. Her speculations on their strange behavior serve to heighten the air of mystery that surrounds them. After she has unburdened herself of her secret, however, "A weight and a fullness had been taken from her, and her importance had gone with it."

Her importance is gone structurally, as well, for now the point of view changes, and a new omniscient narrator relates the reunion of the three siblings. While the reader has glimpses of the inner thoughts of both Fanny and Eliza, Morten is revealed solely through his dialogue and the reactions of his sisters. All three main characters are embodiments of Romantic ideals rather than the fully realized, rounded characters that are typical of more realistic fiction. Dinesen has resurrected the Romantic short story and given it philosophical overtones.

Sheila Golburgh Johnson

THE SUPREMACY OF THE HUNZA

Author: Joanne Greenberg (1932-   )
Type of plot: Social realism
Time of plot: The 1970's
Locale: A Western American mountain region
First published: 1971

> *Principal characters:*
> TED MARGOLIN, a professor of anthropology
> REGINA MARGOLIN, his wife
> LARRY WESTERCAMP, a civic activist and conservationist

The Story

Ted Margolin, an anthropologist and university professor, commutes to work from his home in the mountains because he enjoys the unspoiled surroundings. His serenity is suddenly broken by the installation of ninety-foot power lines across the countryside. He protests through his lawyer, to no avail. Then he is invited to a citizens' protest meeting, where Larry Westercamp, an avid campaigner for citizens' rights, tries to enlist his active support in helping to fight the installation of the lines. On the way home, Westercamp fumes to Margolin about how he is especially angry at having been made the butt of a humorous television news clip in which he was seeding a stream with trout while the state's governor was fishing downstream.

During the next weeks, Margolin is besieged with telephone calls and mail seeking his support for various causes. He becomes irritated with what he sees as an infringement on his personal life. When he speaks to Westercamp again, he is curt and evasive about his unwillingness to become personally involved in the protest over the power lines. In the course of the conversation, Westercamp explains to Margolin how civilization has ruined the harmony enjoyed by primitive societies such as the Chontal Indians. Margolin, with superior knowledge of ancient settlements, counters Westercamp's Utopian vision with hard facts about the primitive lifestyle that Westercamp idealizes.

The power lines continue to disturb Margolin, but he goes on with life during the fall; he learns later from Westercamp that the protest movement is almost dead. In December, Margolin goes to the state hospital to help therapists there on three cases involving Indians. He leaves home believing that his knowledge of ancient cultures may be of some help; he returns sobered, realizing that the Indians he sees are far removed from their culture and have become victims of "civilization" in its worst form. Almost immediately on returning, he calls Westercamp, who is now trying to solicit support to stop water pollution. On this occasion, Westercamp laments modern society by comparing it to the civilization of the Hunza, a Tibetan group. Though Margolin knows that this vision is flawed, he says nothing to change Westercamp's opinion.

The conversation disturbs him so that, unable to sleep all night, he rises early in the morning and begins hurling a primitive spear, which he keeps to show his classes, to release the tension he has built up inside himself.

Themes and Meanings

Joanne Greenberg's main concern in "The Supremacy of the Hunza" is with the encroachment of civilization and technology on human society. The central question raised by the events of the story is: What role can, or should, an individual take to preserve a way of life about which he or she feels strongly? The simplicity of the question belies the complexity of the answers suggested by this story. The central characters, Margolin and Westercamp, present two contrasting attitudes toward the question.

Westercamp is an idealist, but his idealism appears at first to be founded in a kind of blind naïveté. He has only a superficial knowledge of more primitive civilizations. They exist for him not as real communities but as symbols of a pristine form of human society that has become overwhelmed by the march of progress. He comes alive when he is working for a cause; he wastes away when he cannot generate enthusiasm for his ideals. His vision is Utopian, and he is willing to work to bring about his ideal society in the real world.

Margolin perceives Westercamp's activism as folly. Unlike his neighbor, Margolin takes only those steps that he believes will not interfere with his own routines: He calls his lawyer and he calls the power company. These are clearly civilized responses. On the other hand, Margolin has what he believes is a firmer understanding of societies such as the Chontal and the Hunza. His anthropological studies have provided him some insight, it is true: He knows, for example, that such societies were racked with disease, that hard work caused the population to age prematurely, that living in these communities often amounted to no more than grubbing out a day-to-day existence against the harsh elements of nature.

His experience with the young Indian in the mental hospital shocks Margolin into realizing that the heritage of these primitive societies is in fact disappearing; civilization has indeed destroyed what was good in these peoples as it alleviated their physical deprivations. Further, he realizes that his own knowledge of such societies is also defective. His wife's observation that he does not "know primitive man any more than" Westercamp does hits home. As a result, as he comes to understand the commitment that drives Westercamp to continue his activism in the face of defeat and disappointment, he realizes that such beliefs are necessary if modern humanity is not to be overwhelmed by its own inventions.

Style and Technique

The narrative style of this story belies the complexity of its construction. Greenberg balances major scenes carefully, pivoting them on the central experience of Margolin's visit to the state mental hospital. The story opens with Margolin's measured protest against the construction of the towers. After an encounter with Westercamp, he feels annoyed at what he perceives as an intrusion into his private life by someone trying to get him involved in a movement for social change. His frustration is exhibited in his curt response to Westercamp's description of the Chontal society. When he has chastised his neighbor, he feels smug and satisfied.

Margolin's interview with the Indian at the mental hospital shows him the hubris that lies at the center of his own personality. That scene is followed quickly by another encounter with Westercamp, one in which Margolin refrains from criticizing his neighbor's mistaken views of the Hunza. Feeling upset and irritable, he ends up making a primitive response to release his frustrations: He begins hurling the spear he had hitherto used only for classroom demonstrations, making this symbolic gesture as a protest against the towers.

The balanced structure is supported by carefully crafted descriptions of scenery that focus on the beauty of the countryside and the imposing, ugly towers. Greenberg portrays the towers as animate objects that have invaded the countryside. They symbolize all that is wrong with the encroachment of technology and civilization on nature. Further, since the point of view is limited to Margolin's vision, the reader is led only gradually to realize that there is much merit in Westercamp's view and that the story is really about Margolin's conversion to appreciate the supremacy, in a sense, of communities such as that of the Hunza.

Laurence W. Mazzeno

SUR
(A Summary Report of the Yelcho Expedition to the Antarctic, 1909-1910)

Author: Ursula K. Le Guin (1929-　　)
Type of plot: Adventure
Time of plot: 1909-1910
Locale: Antarctica
First published: 1982

> *Principal characters:*
> THE NARRATOR, the unnamed "Supreme Inca" of the expedition
> JUANA, the narrator's cousin
> ZOE, the one with a gift for naming
> BERTA, a sculptor, "La Araucana" of the expedition
> EVA, with Berta the chief architect and builder of Sudamerica del Sur
> TERESA, the mother of Rosa del Sur
> CARLOTA, "The Third Mate" of the expedition
> LUIS PARDO, the captain of the *Yelcho*

The Story

Despite its apparent objectivity as "A summary report of the *Yelcho* expedition to the Antarctic, 1909-1910," the story "Sur" is a surprising piece of gently subversive fiction, narrated by an unnamed woman some years after the events of the story take place. The surprise and the subversion result from the story's feminist stance and from the attendant replacement of the value of "achievement" by "what is large."

In the early paragraphs of the story, its feminism remains latent, hinted at only by the items with which the report will be kept—children's clothes and toys, wedding shoes and finneskos—and by the atypical purpose stated for the expedition: "[T]o go, to see—no more, no less." Further, the trouble encountered in gathering an expeditionary force hints at the narrator's dissatisfaction with what women are or have been made to be, with the stark limits imposed on the average woman by her socially determined role: "So few of those we asked even knew what we were talking about—so many thought we were mad, or wicked, or both!" The following sentences, with their references to parents, husbands, children, and the responsibilities to family that are traditionally a woman's concern, prepare the reader for the first explicit indication that this is to be an all-female expedition: the list of its participants. The knowledge of this expedition's special character colors the rather ordinary story of travel and exploration that follows.

The report of the expedition itself proceeds naturally enough with accounts of the voyage to Antarctica on the Chilean vessel *Yelcho*, the choice of a site for base camp and the building of "Sudamerica del Sur," the sledge-journey to the South Pole, and the return to base and, finally, to civilization. Each part of this report, however, reveals in various ways its feminist character. During the initial voyage, for example, the *Yelcho* is nicknamed *la vaca valiente* (the valiant cow) in memory of the "far more dangerous cows" of Juana's past, and the members of the expedition find themselves "oppressed at times by the kindly but officious protectiveness of the captain and his officers." Such details are embedded in expected surroundings: discussion of the best route for the voyage, celebration of the first iceberg sighted, descriptions of the Ross Sea and the Great Ice Barrier.

Male superiority is subverted in the report's next stage by contrasting the slovenly housekeeping found at Captain Robert Falcon Scott's base hut with the home built by the women of the *Yelcho* Expedition. Having described the surroundings of Scott's camp as "a kind of graveyard," the narrator details the dirtiness and "mean disorder" of the hut's interior: an open tin of tea, empty meat tins, spilled biscuits, even "a lot of dog turds" on the floor. The narrator's excuse for the men who have left this mess is scathing: "[H]ousekeeping, the art of the infinite, is no game for amateurs." By contrast, the home created by the women provides "as much warmth and privacy as one could reasonably expect," then becomes at the hands of Berta and Eva "a marvel of comfort and convenience," and is the setting, finally, of the "beautiful forms" Berta sculpts from the ice.

After the *Yelcho* steams north, leaving the women "to ice, and silence, and the Pole," the southern journey is a model of good planning, good practice, and amazing perseverance. The narrator meticulously details the establishment of supply depots, the superiority of the food they carry, the organization of the southern party, the pain, weariness, even craziness of the terrible trek to the Pole. Even in this account, so fact-filled, the narrator's condescension toward men is clearly revealed: "I was glad . . . that we had left no sign there, for some man longing to be first might come some day, and find it, and know then what a fool he had been, and break his heart."

The story draws swiftly to its close with the return to base and the laconic report of the return to civilization: "We came back safe." Two feminist moments color these final paragraphs. The matter of Teresa's pregnancy raises the central biological fact of femininity—menstruation and childbearing. The narrator's response of "anger—rage—fury" is directed first at Teresa for apparently having concealed her pregnancy, but the emotions are quickly directed away from Teresa to the society that has kept her ignorant of what it means to be a woman. In the wider context of the story's feminism, the anger is both self-directed and competitive: The narrator's earlier frustration with female ignorance becomes anger at an unavoidable fact of normal female life, and her anger at Teresa is also recognition that the party's womanhood could have caused the expedition to fail. The story ends, though, on a lighter note, ostensibly added as a postscript years later, but still echoing the narrator's condescension toward other explorers; her grandchildren, she says, may enjoy the secret of her expedition, "but they must not let Mr. [Roald] Amundsen know! He would be terribly embarrassed and disappointed."

Themes and Meanings

The subversion of male superiority that colors the story's progress is balanced by its aim of personal fulfillment and freedom and by its positive feminine acts, revealed in the expedition's command structure, in its making of a home, and in its emphasis on forethought over prowess.

The narrator's natural human curiosity—the sort that might begin any story of travel—provides the first impetus to the *Yelcho* Expedition; she is drawn to "that strange continent, last Thule of the South, which lies on our maps and globes like a white cloud, a void, fringed here and there with scraps of coastline, dubious capes, supposititious islands, headlands that may or may not be there: Antarctica." The expedition's real justification, however, seems more specifically personal and feminine, the desire to break out of biologically and socially imposed limitations; this sense is revealed in the narrator's grief for "those we had to leave behind to a life without danger, without uncertainty, without hope." The freedom the women find on the ice of Antarctica is a freedom achieved by shedding familiar securities and points of reference, a freedom that leaves them with only themselves: "It was overcast, white weather, without shadows and without visible horizon or any feature to break the level; there was nothing to see at all. We had come to that white place on the map, that void, and there we flew and sang like sparrows."

The women's establishment of a command structure that is never used, their delight in making a home in the ice, and their patient preparation for the trek to the South Pole are possible because of a fundamental difference between their expedition and those of male explorers. Their goal contrasts with the "scientific accomplishments" of earlier and later explorers, with their desire "to be first." This contrast is explained partly by the narrator's sense that as women the members of the *Yelcho* Expedition are "by birth and upbringing, unequivocally and irrevocably, all crew" rather than officers, and it is provided with a more explicit rationale as the narrator comments on the ugly traces left by earlier expeditions. She muses that "the backside of heroism is often rather sad; women and servants know that. They know also that the heroism may be no less real for that. But achievement is smaller than men think. What is large is the sky, the earth, the sea, the soul." If her final words, written years later, contain any regret, she hides it well: "We left no footprints, even."

Style and Technique

In her introduction to *The Left Hand of Darkness* (1969), Ursula K. Le Guin wrote, "A novelist's business is lying." She noted further that novelists may "use all kinds of facts to support their tissue of lies" and that "this weight of verifiable place-event-phenomenon-behavior makes the reader forget that he is reading a pure invention." Her story "Sur" foregrounds this "peculiar and devious" practice, for in it the factive and the fictive, explorer's log and wanderer's yarn, strive for dominance. The fictive wins.

The level, reportorial tone of "Sur" is established partly by the narrator's distance in time from the events she reports—memory, like reflections in a glass, levels what would in fact be three-dimensionally alive—but more concretely by the selection and organization of details in the story told. The account of the origin of the expedition, for example, carefully outlines the sequence of the narrator's growing interest in Antarctica, naming names, indicating dates, supplying the reader with the sources of her knowledge. However, these are also the sources of her desire, and the reader cannot miss the vocabulary of emotion that laces the list of facts ("my imagination was caught," "I . . . followed with excitement," "filled me with longing"), the telling hyperbole of "reread a thousand times," and the romantic inversion of the world in the phrase "last Thule of the South," appropriating centuries of geographic lore in a single act of the making mind.

Careful indications of position, records of temperatures and other weather conditions, meticulous accounting for distances traveled, even the qualification of the accuracy of such measurements with a note that "our equipment was minimal"—these details enforce the illusion of factuality that the story seeks to create, yet even a quasi-scientific explanation may in this narrator's hands become the occasion for metaphor. Her explanation for "footprints standing some inches above the ice," for example, segues into a logically unnecessary simile, then checks the aesthetic impulse with a neutral remark:

> In some conditions of weather the snow compressed under one's weight remains when the surrounding soft snow melts or is scoured away by the wind; and so these reversed footprints had been left standing all these months, like rows of cobbler's lasts—a queer sight.

The narrator is quite conscious of the fictive role she and her companions play in Antarctica and later at home. Zoe, with her "gift for naming," for example, begins to fill "that white place on the map" with names that the women recognize as having effective factual status only for them. The "invisible cattle, transparent cattle pastured on the spindrift snow" are recognized, too, as products of minds "a little crazy," but this is the insanity of art, more formally realized in later years as the narrator's children hear stories of "a great, white, mad dog named Blizzard . . . and other fairy tales."

Like Berta's ice sculptures the narrator's experience of Antarctica can be preserved only in stories. Because its truth—more human, at last, than strictly feminine—cannot be truly said in words, it cannot be brought north: "That," says the narrator with sadness, perhaps, but also with a sense of freedom, "is the penalty for carving in water."

Jonathan A. Glenn

SUSANNA AT THE BEACH

Author: Herbert Gold (1924-   )
Type of plot: Parable
Time of plot: The 1950's
Locale: Lake Erie, near Cleveland, Ohio
First published: 1954

> *Principal characters:*
> THE DIVING GIRL
> A FAT SWIMMER
> FREDDY, his friend
> AN OLD POLISH WOMAN
> HER PLUMP FRIEND
> A PRETTY GIRL ON THE BEACH
> HER MOTHER

The Story

As an unnamed adolescent girl practices diving into Lake Erie, a crowd of people watch her on the beach. The girl concentrates so fully on perfecting her dive that she does not notice a tear developing in the side of the worn, black bathing suit that she is outgrowing.

One of those watching the girl is a fat man who lolls in the water talking to his friend Freddy about business; both ogle the girl lustfully, making remarks about "biting off a piece" of her. Other watchers include an old Polish woman and her overweight friend, who talk about caring for their parents and who criticize the girl for having no shame. Also on the beach is a pretty young girl with a junior-miss nose who hugs herself the way her favorite starlet does. The men are not interested in the pretty girl on the beach; they sense that she would fear to dive into the tricky, polluted lake water. Her mother declares, with some satisfaction, that the diving girl will get an earache because of the organisms in the water.

The diving girl has fled all the billboard schemes of a pretty girl in order to focus on a grand design: perfecting her dive. Although her exercises are simple, she has an idea of what they should be and she has the will of perfection. The men who watch her from the beach think that her self-sufficiency is a pity and a waste, and it makes them sad. The women on the beach envy her youth and devotion to her art, but consider themselves morally superior to her.

As the girl repeatedly dives into the murky water, the tear in her worn suit lengthens, revealing the side of her budding breast and threatening to show more. The girl feels the rip just once, but she is so intent on the demands of perfection that she closes the split with her fingers, then forgets it and lets it go. If she thinks of her body at all, it is only to think of her skill and her practice for her body's sake, for she is an expert.

Finally, the girl's breast is fully revealed, "its pink sprouting from the girl's body like a delicate thing nurtured in the dark." The old Polish woman screams, "You're nekked, girlie! Nekked!" and the fat man and his friend cheer her on. When the girl finally notices the observers, she is at first incredulous, then, turning from them toward the water, she runs into the lake. Thinking that she wants to drown herself, several men swim after her. However, although the "righteousness" of the mob's laughter urges them on, the girl is strong, skillful, gifted, and "encumbered by nothing but her single thought."

Themes and Meanings

The title of Herbert Gold's story and its basic situation clearly signal his intention to retell the story of Susanna and the elders from the Book of Daniel in the Apocrypha. The biblical story is a simple account of Susanna, a young married woman who walks daily in her garden, where she is seen by two elders who lust after her. One day when she is alone in the garden, the elders rush up to her and tell her that if she does not yield to their desires they will say that a young man has been with her. However, Susanna is a righteous woman who says that she would rather be at their mercy than lie with them and sin against the Lord. Susanna is vindicated when Daniel tricks the elders into giving conflicting testimony. The biblical story embodies the conflict between the sacred and the profane and exemplifies the triumph of the spirit over the things of the world.

In giving this universal situation and theme a modern setting, Gold has no trouble creating a similitude for the lusting elders in the men on the beach who watch the girl and wait for her suit to rip. However, Gold transforms Susanna's trust in God in the Apocrypha story to the diving girl's single-minded demand for perfection, and he also expands the profane world to include not only the lustful men, but also the women who envy the girl's innocence, purity, and quest for perfection.

The girl is obviously elevated from the crowd on the beach, sufficient unto herself, dedicated to her discipline, concerned only with the demands of perfection. Her ambition has no practical purpose and thus seems madness to the watchers. Although the watchers focus on the body of the girl, which is desired by the men and envied by the women, the girl herself is seemingly unaware that she even has a body; the complete perfection of her dive, if such were possible, would mean the use of the body as a means of its own transcendence; she wishes to create an alternate world superior to ordinary reality. As a modern-day treatment of the Susanna and the elders story, the end of the story is a vindication of the girl's innocence and superiority.

Style and Technique

Although "Susanna at the Beach" focuses on a modern-day event and seems to feature realistic characters engaged in everyday activities, both the title and the style of the story suggest its parable nature. The story's point of view is that of an anonymous observer who watches the events but does not place himself in the story. Because the narrator does not know the girl's name, the only reason he gives her the name

"Susanna" in the title is to identify her situation thematically with that of the beautiful and devout Jewish woman in the story of Susanna and the elders.

The style of the story is like a parable in that its single-minded focus throughout is on the meaning of the girl's elevation above those people on the beach because of her devotion to her craft. Whereas the people on the beach are real and fleshly, the girl herself—although her body is an object of desire and envy—has no consciousness of the physical. Gold's style makes it clear that her diving symbolizes her devotion to an idea: "The girl used herself hard, used her lightness hard." Moreover, like Susanna in the story in the Apocrypha, the girl is the embodiment of innocence, not responsible that she is the object of fleshly desire. "Her innocence—an innocence of lessons— was informed by the heart and by the pressure of her blood."

Gold's language also makes it clear that what motivates the people on the beach is not merely physical desire and prudery, but also an intense jealousy that they do not have the same dedication and single-minded focus on an ideal that the girl has. For example, as the old Polish woman looks at the girl, she shivers "at her own memories of paleness, of resiliency, of pink colors." The fat man and his friend Freddy are not interested solely in sexual attractiveness; they ignore the pretty girl on the beach, for they know that despite her prettiness she has put herself apart from "risks of pleasure."

The rip in the bathing suit makes it possible for Gold to emphasize a fundamental difference between the girl and the people on the beach: While the people cannot ignore her body as mere flesh, the girl thinks of her own body, if at all, as only that which must be transcended to perfect her art. In his elevated parable style, Gold says that all the people on the beach lean together to watch the tear widen, "sharing the girl and sharing each other, waiting for their world's confirmation against the challenge she brought it, an assurance of which they were in need before the return to autumn and the years rapid upon them."

"Susanna at the Beach" is an effective example of a writer's ability to transform a simple everyday event into a moral parable by paralleling to a traditional mythic tale and by maintaining a style that emphasizes the transcendent significance of events.

Charles E. May

SWADDLING CLOTHES

Author: Yukio Mishima (Kimitake Hiraoka, 1925-1970)
Type of plot: Horror
Time of plot: The mid-twentieth century
Locale: Tokyo, Japan, near the Imperial Palace
First published: "Shimbungami," 1953 (English translation, 1966)

>   *Principal characters:*
>   TOSHIKO, a twenty-three-year-old mother of a new son
>   HER HUSBAND, an actor
>   A NURSE, who gives birth to a son in Toshiko's home

The Story

After a shocking incident in their home two days earlier, Toshiko and her actor husband meet friends in a Tokyo nightclub. The young wife and mother is dumbfounded to hear her husband recounting the incident—which has disturbed her greatly—as merely an amusing story for their companions' entertainment. Troubled and vulnerable, Toshiko feels acutely aware of her husband's insensitivity, neglect, and lack of consideration for her. Her mind swells with loneliness and her fears of the future provoked by her horror at the scene she has so recently encountered in her son's nursery.

The story that so horrifies Toshiko began with the arrival of a new nurse, a woman with an oddly distended stomach and a prodigious appetite. Not long after she arrived, loud moans came from the nursery. Toshiko and her husband rushed in to discover the nurse giving birth on the floor. Toshiko's husband rescued the family's good rug and placed a blanket under the nurse to prevent damage to the parquet floor.

Although two days have passed, Toshiko, in contrast to her husband, is still preoccupied by this experience. In particular, she obsesses about one scene that she alone witnessed. The doctor who finally arrived to attend the nurse derided her and her bastard child so strongly that he had his attendant wrap the newborn boy in newspaper. Appalled by the doctor's cruelty, Toshiko rewrapped the child in new flannel. The image of the innocent child in his soiled paper wrappings, however, remains.

As Toshiko's husband sets out from the nightclub for other engagements, she goes home alone in a taxi. Riding through the darkened streets of Tokyo, she reflects on the nurse's child and the secret shame of his birth. What if this boy, twenty years hence, should meet her own son? The one, reared in solid comfort, might be savagely attacked by the other who will have been turned into a brute by a life of deprivation and disgrace. The bloody newspapers in which that newborn was briefly wrapped would mark him for life; they would be a blight on his being, the secret emblem of his entire existence, his inescapable doom. She imagines one day going to the boy to tell him of her secret knowledge of his first moments of life.

On impulse, Toshiko leaves her taxi and walks beneath the cherry blossoms in the dark deserted park near the Imperial Palace. She wanders until she encounters the form of a man, asleep on a bench, wrapped in newspapers. Standing beside the dirty anonymous figure, she imagines this young man as the future manifestation of the baby recently born in her house. With a rustle of newspaper, a powerful hand seizes her wrist. Instantly, Toshiko realizes that both her foreboding and her powerful sense of connection to the baby in newspaper swaddling have been realized.

Themes and Meanings

"Swaddling Clothes" explores the barren geography of the alienated human. On one level, the story maps the painful terrain of an empty Japanese marriage, a union characterized by a husband absent emotionally and physically. The wife is ignored and the child tended by a surrogate. The devaluing of human life is boldly marked by the image of a child alone on the floor, wrapped like trash, degraded. The protagonist, suffering in silence, half mad with loneliness, vulnerable to her own thwarted sensitivity and caring, devalued and disregarded, falls prey to morbid preoccupations, obsessive fantasies, and a powerful pull to self-destruction.

The bastard child that will become the brutal killer of the future is perhaps a projection of Toshiko's own husband's domination of her spirit as well as the outward sign of the murderous oppression of her culture's patriarchy. In this tale women and children are ignored and demeaned by adult males. The bastard child imagined as killer of her own son and assassin of herself is the true offspring of her man's inhumanity to man.

Also implicit is an indictment of the social order in which Toshiko resides. The doctor, the supposed epitome of compassion and caring, disdains an innocent life, degrades it, dishonors it. The whole society is characterized by willful disregard for human dignity. The locale that Yukio Mishima chooses for the climax of his story suggests that this evil, this menace, is asleep at the very heart of Japanese culture, beside the Imperial Palace at the hub of the ethos of Japanese life. In the enigmatic ending it is the female who is threatened, the silent but sole source of compassion. The grip of the mysterious male hand is a death grip; Toshiko's fate is to be destroyed by the homeless disfranchised offspring of her own heartless and mercenary society.

Style and Technique

Scholars say that a literal translation of the title of this story is "waste newspapers." Although the English title, "Swaddling Clothes," is not entirely accurate, ironically, it captures a central tension of the tale. With this title the warm white flannel evoked by the English term is conflated with the dirty newspapers that first swathe the newborn child. The child in the dramatic birthing scene is visible throughout the tale in a series of tensions; the cherished child in clean flannel contrasts with the bloodied paper wrappings that declare this child trash, a piece of meat, a throwaway life.

As the pristine flannel and the soiled papers are held in tension, so are other objects and persons united. Two powerful images are conflated in the story: images of cherry blossoms and images of newspapers. To Toshiko the artificial cherry blossoms on the theater marquee are revealed to be shreds of paper; she walks down the park path beneath an umbrella of blossoming trees with heaps of waste paper at her feet, and at first the sheets of paper draping the vagrant on the bench glow in the darkness like a blanket of cherry blossoms. Both the blossoms and the newspapers suggest transience, one the transience of events natural, the other the transience of events humanmade. The blossoms evoke an entire genteel aesthetic and the most ancient traditions of Japan. The other suggests the blaring emptiness of modern Western lifestyles of conspicuous consumption. Most dramatically, the newspapers unite the bastard child born in Toshiko's nursery with the malign force of the shadowy figure of her future destruction. This small tale of horror lifts a corner of the veneer of Japanese contemporary life and reveals the madness and violence beneath.

The conjunction of oppositions is a pattern woven in the very fabric of the story. The boundaries of familiar dualities are broken as the commonplace becomes the bizarre and the domestic transforms into the public. East and West, traditional and modern, birth and death, past and present, nature and humankind unite until inner and outer realities merge at a park bench. Doubles people the landscape of Toshiko's life: two babies, one legitimate and one a bastard; two mothers, united in silence and powerlessness; two males, powerful forces of personal and social control; and finally the bastard and the vagrant, both swaddled in newspapers, both social discards. Two acts of personal violation mirror each other as well. The dishonoring of the newborn is the psychic seed of the impending violation of Toshiko. The horrific union of the wraithlike female protagonist and the menacing phantom embodiment of the newborn suggests Japan's fate, an impending destruction of personal, social, economic, and political orders.

Part of the dramatic power of this tale arises in its use of point of view. The narrative voice is omniscient, yet the narrator's power to reveal people and the world is not employed. In the tale the reader never goes outside Toshiko's mind. One does not hear others' words or views; one sees other people's actions in the indistinct impressions that they register on Toshiko's consciousness. Certainly the mode of presentation conveys the alienation and isolation of Toshiko in her world. More important still, the point of view suggests Toshiko's alienation from herself. Lost, she bumps into her own thoughts and feelings like strangers on a crowded street. The effect of this narrative technique on the reader is profound. One cannot identify with the protagonist. She walks like an automaton into a death grip, seemingly never speaking and never being spoken to, scarcely seen or felt. As she is estranged from herself so she is estranged from the reader. An omniscience that could tell all but reveals nothing is a strategy for creating that paradoxical preternatural quality of events. The narrator can show and tell all but reveals nothing. Is Toshiko a mad housewife intent on suicide? Or is she a symbol of the fragile spirit of a nation inexorably, blindly, walking into the hands of its own murderer? In the context of the social, economic, political, and moral upheavals of post-World War II Japan, after the incineration of Hiroshima and Nagasaki, Mishima sought to ring an alarm for his people, to cry for renewal of human dignity and compassion for others in both personal and social realms.

Virginia M. Crane

SWEAT

Author: Zora Neale Hurston (1891-1960)
Type of plot: Psychological
Time of plot: The 1920's
Locale: A village in Florida
First published: 1926

> *Principal characters:*
> DELIA JONES, a black washwoman
> SYKS JONES, her husband of fifteen years
> BERTHA, his mistress

The Story

The story covers several weeks in the lives of Delia Jones and her husband, Sykes, from a Sunday evening to a Monday morning, with a brief flashback to the course of their relationship during fifteen years of marriage. The action begins at a crucial moment that is to lead to Sykes's death and Delia's liberation. For the first time, Delia stands up to Sykes's abuse. She has just returned from church and has begun her week's work as a laundry woman for white people, sorting out the clothes that she collected the day before. Sykes, who has spent the day with his mistress, Bertha, lays a bullwhip across her shoulders to frighten her. She is deathly afraid of snakes. He also kicks her clothes around, grinding dirt into them, and complains not only about her working for white people but also about her hypocrisy, for she goes to church and receives the Sacrament but still works on Sunday. This irreligious, adulterous man, making such accusations and physically and psychologically abusing her, suddenly causes her to alter the relationship: She drops the meek posture of the subservient wife, takes up a heavy frying pan as a weapon, and threatens Sykes with retaliation. She declares herself willing to defend not only her person but also the house that she has paid for with "sweat" for the past fifteen years. She refuses to let him drive her out to make room for his new woman.

The following Saturday, Delia takes the laundered clothes to town. During this second segment of the story, Zola Neale Hurston chooses to present her heroine's situation from the town's point of view, as an assortment of men gossip on the porch of a general store. The men sympathize with Delia, recognize the abuse she has suffered from Sykes, and condemn Bertha as the dregs of a neighboring town, the only woman during the past fifteen years who would succumb to Sykes's advances. Sykes and Bertha show up at the store to buy groceries. Sykes flaunts his importance before the townspeople and before Delia, who is passing by on her way home. Such public indignity heightens the conflict.

The third and final section of the story takes place several weeks later. No longer able to intimidate Delia with physical abuse, he plays on her fears by bringing home a real snake, a six-foot rattler in a soap box. After living with the snake for two or three days, Delia finds her Christian patience at the breaking point: She declares that she is moving her church membership to another town, because she does not want to take the Sacrament with her husband, and that she hates this man she married. The next day being Sunday, she goes off to church and does not come home until evening. As she passes the soap box and notices that the snake is gone, she imagines that perhaps Sykes has taken seriously her threat to seek justice from the white community. As she prepares to begin the week's washing, however, she discovers, to her shock, the rattlesnake at the bottom of the clothes hamper. Frightened almost senseless, she runs out to the barn to spend the night. When Sykes returns later in the evening, he finds no matches left to light the candles. As he stumbles about drunk in the dark, the rattlesnake bites him. Hearing his cries, Delia ventures out from the barn and watches through a window as Sykes dies from poison. Unable to endure the final moments before death, and unable or unwilling to help him, she goes to sit under a chinaberry tree to imagine the look on Sykes's face.

Themes and Meanings

Hurston's story derives from the black folk tradition that she first came to know in her hometown, the black community of Eatonville, Florida. Christianity was a part of that tradition; her father was a Baptist preacher. Even after her years of study under anthropologist Franz Boas, her fieldwork as an anthropologist collecting folklore among her own people and in the Caribbean, and the consequent influence of Voodoo on her thinking, Christianity remained a living part of Hurston's work. She continued to prefer biblical settings and stories; a character in *Jonah's Gourd Vine* (1934) calls the Bible a "hoodoo" book. "Sweat," one of her earliest stories, records her thinking before the Voodoo period. It assumes a Christian cosmology, as yet unmodified by Voodoo traditions, but adapted to the perceptions of a folk culture—that of poor blacks in the American South.

Hurston's theme of extreme love and extreme hate within the black family acquires, in the story "Sweat," the magnitude of a cosmic struggle between good and evil, God and Satan. The central principle, which almost has the force of a moral, Hurston pronounces through the voice of Delia: "Whatever goes over the Devil's back, is got to come under his belly. Sometime or ruther, Sykes, like everybody else, is gointer reap his sowing." Faith in a Providence that will reward good and punish evil is a refuge of people who on earth know nothing but suffering.

Within the religious scheme of this fictional world, Sykes is the representative of those who defy the Christian God. He rebels against the principles of love and compassion, and, hence, his soul becomes hardened. A proud, vengeful creature, he is already damned. He cannot see goodness in others and elevates himself to the role of god. In an ironic assertion of his own powers, he claims, "Ah aint got tuh do nothin' but die," disclaiming responsibility to anyone on earth. He brags to Bertha that "this was his town and she could have it if she wanted it."

The reader knows where his or her sympathies ought to lie. Sykes is clearly wrong throughout the story, and Delia is right in living out the principles of Christian love, tolerance, and humility. In addition, she has those virtues closely associated with Christian principles in America, hard work and "sweat." She earns her way in life. The ending bears out her prediction of poetic justice. God does not forget the faithful.

Nevertheless, the ending of the story struggles against a strictly Christian reading. The pattern does not go so far as to challenge the Christian order. The man who plays with snakes and defies Christian ethics is not a hero, a conjure man of another cultural order, but a villain. However, Hurston does not allow the Christian scheme to dictate the psychology of her heroine. She has Delia at last defy her husband, call him the same names that he has called her, and in the end disclaim any responsibility for him. When he is dying of poison, she feels compassion but refuses to aid him. In the sense that Sykes is pure evil, one can see this as consistent with Christian eschatology, but in the sense that he is a man, one may read it as human, female vengeance. She not only does nothing to help him but also wills his destruction. She must live with the knowledge, too, that he sees her and knows that she lets him die.

"Sweat" is thus one of many literary accounts of Christianity's impact on the black psyche and its modifications under the stress of psychological pressures. It is also, perhaps, an indirect comment on the economic consequences of a racially split society. What is more noticeable, however, is the absence of white society. The story pits black against black. Whites are far in the background. They appear only once, in Delia's threat to complain to them if Sykes ever beats her again. In this respect, Hurston anticipates by forty years the fiction of Alice Walker and Toni Morrison: She affirms black culture by ignoring or subordinating the white; she allows the culture to speak for itself; she subordinates the male to the female consciousness. This last characteristic in itself dictates a modification of the Christian tradition.

Style and Technique

Though written in a southern folk idiom, "Sweat" has none of the humor of Hurston's predecessor in the genre, Charles Waddell Chesnutt. Her message is somber from beginning to end. What the story offers is a naturalistic slice of life combined with some heavy Christian symbolism. The most potent symbol is the rattlesnake, known for its ubiquitous ("ventriloquist") death rattle. Having already introduced evil into their house, Sykes next brings the snake itself. Delia's known fear of worms and snakes and Sykes's vain belief that he possesses a magic power over them are both symbolic attitudes toward evil. When he releases the snake from the box, giving it free rein in the house in order to drive out Delia (goodness), he only prepares the scene for his own destruction. Worked into this major symbol is that of the matches, Sykes's practice of using up all the matches (light) without ever replacing them. When Delia returns home there is only one left, but it is enough. When he returns there is no light for him to see the rattlesnake. In total darkness "Satan" kills him.

Other symbols complete the Christian scenario. The experience of the Passion— suffering and triumph over it—is central. Delia's whole life is the Passion experience, yet Hurston does not use the symbolism explicitly until Delia goes through the agonizing months of Sykes's affair with Bertha: It is then that "Delia's work-worn knees crawled over the earth in Gethsemane and up the rocks of Calvary." On returning home from church on the fatal Sunday evening, Delia sings of the River Jordan that "Chills de body, not de soul." The sacramental experience has begun her resurrection. (Another "cold river," the poison of the snake, destroys both Sykes's body and his soul.) Delia's actual resurrection, however, comes in another symbolic place, the barn behind the house, clearly a reminder of the stable. There she ends her suffering and momentarily achieves peace.

Even the structure of the story at first seems to insist on a Christian salvation. It begins on a Sunday and the final act begins on another Sunday. Delia's symbolic rebirth in the barn comes before Sykes's death on Sunday evening. In fact, however, consistent with the psychological turn already noted, Hurston adds a twist to the symbolism in the final paragraph, for the real ending to the story comes not on Sunday, but on Monday morning. Life is not over for Delia. She must bear up under the knowledge that Sykes still had hope. The sun has revealed to Sykes signs that Delia had returned home and that she was close by watching. Though it seems clear that Delia is helpless—the doctors are too far away, and her fear of snakes keeps her from entering the house—the torment of imagining Sykes's plaintive and accusing eye in the final moment of life gives the closing statement of the story the psychological horror of the macabre rather than the peace of resurrection. On that symbolic Monday morning, the agony of the Passion continues. The Passion is not simply a biblical story; it is human experience.

Thomas Banks

THE SWEETHEART OF THE SONG TRA BONG

Author: Tim O'Brien (1946-   )
Type of plot: Impressionistic, frame story
Time of plot: The 1960's, during the Vietnam War
Locale: Vietnam and Minnesota
First published: 1990

> *Principal characters:*
> RAT KILEY, an American soldier
> MARK FOSSIE, an American soldier in Vietnam
> MARY ANNE BELL, Mark's fiancé

The Story

In "The Sweetheart of the Song Tra Bong," Rat Kiley, a soldier with a reputation for telling tall tales, claims to have witnessed the transformation of Mary Anne Bell, a typical American girl who visits her fiancé, Mark Fossie, in Vietnam, into a wild jungle beast.

At the start of the story, Rat is in a small medical detachment overlooking a village called Tra Bong and a river called the Song Tra Bong. The area had been a Special Forces outpost, and a squad of Green Berets still bivouacked on the perimeter. The "Greenies" were secretive, antisocial, and sometimes gone for days—or weeks—in the jungle.

One of the men in Rat's unit, Mark Fossie, arranges for his fiancé to visit. Mary Anne Bell is an all-American girl—a "tall, big-boned blonde," with long white legs, blue eyes and a complexion "like strawberry ice cream." She is naïve, friendly, and curious. She wears a pink sweater and white culottes.

At first things go well for the couple. They hold hands, talk, and plan their all-American wedding and marriage—complete with a house in the suburbs and three blond children. Mary Anne participates in camp life. Although she is flirtatious and sexy, the men realize that she is just being friendly, and they like her. She is curious about everything: the weapons, cooking, medical equipment, geography, and the local people and language.

The second week of her visit, Mary Anne persuades Mark to take her to the village of Tra Bong. He argues that going there would be too dangerous, but she prevails. In the village, she behaves like an ordinary tourist unaware of danger. She is outgoing, friendly, and curious. On the way home, she removes her outer clothing and swims in the Song Tra Bong—a symbolic baptism that marks the beginning of her transformation.

At the end of the second week, Mary Anne helps treat some casualties and is not intimidated by blood or ugliness. She cuts her hair and wraps her head in a bandanna, stops wearing makeup, and lets her personal hygiene go. Even her voice changes, becoming lower. She learns how to disassemble, assemble, and shoot an M-16 rifle. Mark becomes uneasy and begins to mention her going home, but she refuses, saying that she has never been happier.

Mary Anne begins coming back to the soldiers' hooch late at night. One night she does not return at all. The men search the camp, finally finding her with the Green Berets. She is asleep, and they realize that she has gone out on a patrol with them in the jungle.

By the third week, tension between Mary Anne and Mark is evident, and he begins to arrange for her departure. Mary Anne becomes morose and silent, sitting alone, staring at the jungle. Rat says that she seems both terrified and enthralled by it. Abruptly, she disappears into the jungle for three weeks with the Green Berets.

When she returns, her transformation is complete. Rat does not recognize her when she walks out of the jungle like a silent shadow. Even her eyes have changed from blue to a "jungle green." She disappears into the hooch of the Green Berets.

Mark waits outside the hooch all day for her to emerge. By nightfall, she is still inside, and strange noises, sights, and odors are coming out of the hooch. Mark and Rat enter. The scene is unsettling. Candles flicker in the darkness. There are two smells, one of incense and the other a "stench that paralyzed your lungs . . . a mix of blood and scorched hair and excrement and the sweet-sour odor of moldering flesh—the stink of the kill." Next to a pile of bones is a sign that says, "ASSEMBLE YOUR OWN GOOK!! FREE SAMPLE KIT!" Mary Anne is singing to Vietnamese music. Her face is flat and expressionless, no longer open and friendly. She wears a necklace of dried human tongues strung on a copper wire. She says that she has become captured by the mystery of the war, and she has never felt so alive as she does out in the jungle. She tells Mark that there is really nothing more to say and she orders him and Rat to leave the hooch because they do not belong there.

Rat does not know firsthand what happened later because he was transferred, but he has heard that Mary Anne finally disappeared into the jungle and was never seen again, although rumors cropped up about half-seen odd shadows or movements, or a feeling that the "Greenies" on patrol had of being watched by the jungle itself.

Themes and Meanings

"The Sweetheart of the Song Tra Bong" is one chapter of a loosely connected collection of stories about Vietnam, *The Things They Carried* (1990). One major theme that runs through this story and the book is the nature of truth and of history. Tim O'Brien has said that fiction is more truthful than fact because the author can shape the facts to extract the essence and meaning in a way that fact alone cannot.

The form of the narration also highlights an important theme. The story of Mary Anne is a story within a story within a story. The fictional narrator "Tim O'Brien," who frames the whole book, is looking back on the Vietnam experience and describing it from a distance of twenty years. Within the story of Mary Anne, "O'Brien" describes Rat Kiley telling a story. The narrative emphasizes Kiley's unreliable grasp of facts and his tendency to exaggerate. Additionally, only part of what Kiley tells is his own experience; part is hearsay and myth. This layered narrative form reveals another theme: that history is composed of fact, hearsay, and myth. Sometimes one cannot know the difference, and maybe the difference does not even matter. O'Brien, during a lecture at Ohio State University in April of 1999, insisted that the story of Mary Anne had a basis in fact, but when students asked him whether it was "true," he replied that this was irrelevant.

Another theme is that war corrupts the innocent. O'Brien, in the lecture at Ohio State, said that one major motivation for writing the story in the first place was his feeling that it was not fair that only men should fight and die in war and that women should remain innocent. Like Mary Anne—as Rat Kiley points out—the men are also innocent when they arrive in Vietnam. They too are changed—not only by the horror of the experience but also by the insidious seduction of danger and violence.

Heart of Darkness (1899, 1902) by Joseph Conrad is a tale about a similar journey, although it leads out of civilization and into evil in the Congo, not Vietnam. In Conrad's story, women remain protected from ugly reality. The fiancé of Kurtz, Conrad's main character, remains in civilization and hears from the returning narrator a sanitized version of how her fiancé died. Mary Anne, on the other hand, experiences what the men in Vietnam experience, and her reaction demonstrates the theme that women are as capable of savagery as men.

Style and Technique

The story within a story within a story is a technique that removes the reader from the action, making the action less immediate and less verifiable. Emphasizing this effect, the story of Mary Anne is broken up at several points as Rat comments on the story. His comments point out some of the themes and also remind the reader that this is a story. The listeners tell Rat not to interrupt the story but to "tell it right." Then, at the end of the story, the truth of the facts recedes even farther when Rat says that he did not see the end of Mary Anne himself but just heard tales about what might or might not be seen, heard, or felt by men going into the jungle. Mary Anne has left the world of fact and gone into the realm of myth.

Mary Anne's transformation is pointed out by details of her appearance and manner. Pretty, friendly, and outgoing at first, the details of her appearance gradually change: She becomes careless of her looks and dress, cuts her hair, and begins wearing dark clothes—the fluffy pink sweater disappears, and she begins to wear army fatigues and a dark bandanna.

Communication is one hallmark of humanity. Mary Anne's communication changes as the story progresses. Talkative and friendly at first, she goes so far as to learn some Vietnamese words and phrases. Then she gets less talkative, and even the pitch of her voice gets lower. The necklace of human tongues that she wears at the end is a final powerful symbol of the cutoff in communication between her and the civilized world. She tells her fiancé that there is no use talking. As a contrast in this final scene, she is once again wearing her pink sweater and white culottes, and at first appears like her old self—heightening the irony of how complete the transformation has really been.

The river, which appears in the title of the story, is a symbol of her change. At the point when she begins to change, she swims in the river, a kind of baptism. She emotionally crosses the river.

The story has elements of Magical Realism, the Latin American literary movement of the 1960's that juxtaposed magical or fantastic elements into an otherwise realistic story. O'Brien has said that he admires the writers in this movement. Mary Anne herself is a figure of Magical Realism. Through Magical Realism, O'Brien emphasizes the essential mystery of life and the human inability to understand it.

Myra H. Jones

THE SWIMMER

Author: John Cheever (1912-1982)
Type of plot: Psychological
Time of plot: The early 1960's
Locale: Bullet Park, a fictional suburb of New York
First published: 1964

> *Principal character:*
> NED MERRILL, a youthful-looking man of middle age

The Story

In "The Swimmer," John Cheever experiments with narrative structure and chronology. Apparently realistic on the surface, the story is eventually revealed as reflecting the disordered mind of the protagonist. When the story opens, Ned Merrill is youthful, strong, and athletic; by the end, he is a weak and broken man, unable to understand the wreckage of his life. Proud of his wife and his four beautiful daughters, Merrill at first seems the picture of health and contentment. This initial image quickly disintegrates as Merrill weakens and is confronted with his loss. However, the action of the story takes only a few hours.

One summer day, Ned decides to swim a series of pools between the home of his friends the Westerhazys and his own home eight miles away. He imagines the string of pools as a river, a "quasi-subterranean stream that curved across the county," and names it Lucinda, after his wife. He begins his peculiar trip with great gusto, imagining himself "a legendary figure" or "a pilgrim, an explorer, a man with a destiny."

As Ned begins his journey, Cheever establishes the social context of a typical Sunday in Bullet Park. People go to church, it seems, but once there they commiserate with one another about their hangovers. Once home from church, most of their activities are athletic: golf, swimming, tennis, and perhaps some bird-watching at the wildlife preserve. Ned's desire to swim across the county is presented as the quintessence of the athletic optimism that characterizes his whole community. However, the ubiquitous hangovers undercut the otherwise rosy picture of life in this beautiful suburb. Similarly, Ned's apparent health and vigor mask the reality of his distress.

At first Ned's trip goes well. He swims unnoticed through people's backyards, or is welcomed by surprised friends who are enjoying a Sunday swim, or entertaining at poolside. At several houses he accepts drinks. By the time he has swum half the Lucinda, he is tired but satisfied. However, the second half of the journey goes less well. He is caught in a sudden storm, which turns the weather cooler and creates an autumnal feeling. He is disappointed when a friend's pool is empty of water, the bathhouse locked, and a "For Sale" sign nailed to a tree. When he has to cross a highway, he is embarrassed to be seen in his swim trunks by passing motorists, some of whom throw beer cans or jeer at him. He considers returning to the Westerhazys, but finds rather to his surprise that he feels unable to return. Somehow it is impossible to go back.

The worst part of the trip is yet to come. First, he must swim with distaste through the crowded, unclean public pool. Then, as he travels from yard to yard, old friends and neighbors make strange remarks to him. One couple, who happen to believe in nude sunbathing, offer sympathy for his recent misfortunes—yet Ned has no sense of what they mean. In two places, rude comments are made about his financial situation. His former mistress, who cried when he broke off their affair, now scorns him. He even perceives rebuff at the hands of a bartender working at one of the parties through which he passes. At the last few pools he can barely swim and must stop repeatedly, holding on to the side. When he reaches his own house, he finds the garage doors rusty, the rain gutters loose, and the door locked. Looking in the windows, he sees that the house is empty.

Themes and Meanings

"The Swimmer" has as its primary theme the power of the mind to deny unpleasant truths, or, to put it more positively, the determination of the ego to preserve itself in the face of events that might erode or obliterate one's self-confidence. In order to grasp this theme, the reader must figure out roughly what has happened to Ned and how he has responded to those events.

The recent events of Ned Merrill's life can be tentatively reconstructed once the story has been read. Evidently a few years past he had been living a comfortable suburban life with his wife, Lucinda, his four daughters, and a house boasting not only a cook and a maid but also a tennis court. When the story opens, the reader accepts Ned's description of such a life as reflecting his present condition. However, clues quickly begin to mount that something has happened to Ned—a financial ruin that led to social ostracization and eventually to a psychological breakdown. Even while his journey is going well, he shows signs of dislocation. He cannot remember whether a neighbor had been in Japan last year or the year before. Another family, the Lindleys, has dismantled their riding ring, but he has only a vague memory of having known this. He asks another friend for a drink only to be told that "there hasn't been anything in this house to drink since Eric's operation. That was three years ago." When he arrives at the house of his former mistress, he cannot remember how long ago their affair ended, and he has apparently lost all memory of having sold his house. In the last paragraph of the story, he still clings to the idea that his wife and daughters are due to return home at any moment.

Ned is determined to hold on to his past despite the many signs that his former life has disappeared. This determination underscores the theme of the mind's willfulness in the face of disaster. Ultimately, however, this strength of mind is impressive without being admirable because Ned's conviction cannot restore to him his former happy life.

Style and Technique

Despite the many realistic details included in the story, from the detailed descriptions of the various pools (specifying, for example, whether they are fed by a well or a brook) to the nuances of suburban social climbing, the story contains an element of fantasy. Although the action of the story covers at most several hours, Ned seems to age appreciably. Midway through the journey, he notices that his swim trunks are loose, and wonders if he could have lost weight in the space of the afternoon. The youthful vigor he exhibits in the early pages of the story gives way to a fatigue that leaves him unable to swim even one length of his last pool.

In addition to his own sense of aging, the summer itself gives way with inappropriate suddenness to autumn. After he is caught in the rainstorm (an event that exhilarates rather than depresses him), he notices a maple bare of leaves and feels sad at this sign of autumn, even while rationalizing that the tree must be blighted to have lost its foliage in midsummer. However, the signs of autumn persist. He smells wood smoke and wonders who would be burning wood at this time of year. Toward the end of his trip, the water of one pool has a "wintry gleam," he smells the autumn flower chrysanthemum, and the constellations of the oncoming night are those of the winter sky.

In "The Swimmer," then, Cheever veers from conventional realism to experiment with a style that emphasizes psychological veracity. Although the structure of the narrative is unconventional, the story manages both to convey a conventional plot line (Ned's loss of money and status) and to reveal the complexity of a man's interior reaction to personal disaster. Cheever's juxtaposition of realistic detail and fantastic plot elements enables him to explore the workings of a mind out of touch with reality in a broad sense, yet acutely aware of the minor details and realities that compose the social fabric of life in Bullet Park.

Diane M. Ross

THE SWIMMERS

Author: Joyce Carol Oates (1938-   )
Type of plot: Social realism
Time of plot: 1959-1971
Locale: The Chautauqua Mountains of New York State
First published: 1989

> *Principal characters:*
> SYLVIE, the narrator, a woman recalling an incident during her
>   youth
> JOAN LUNT, an attractive woman in her mid-thirties
> CLYDE FARRELL, Joan's lover, Sylvie's uncle
> ROBERT WAXMAN, Joan's former husband

The Story

Sylvie looks back at a sequence of events that occurred in 1959 when she was thirteen years old and observed the relationship between her uncle, Clyde Farrell, and Joan Lunt, a mysterious new woman in town.

Clyde and Joan meet when both are swimming one early morning at the YMCA. Clyde admires Joan's style of swimming even before he sees her up close. Although they swim together in the pool, they do not speak to each other. The next time he sees her at the pool, he introduces himself. Strongly attracted to each other, Clyde and Joan soon begin spending most of their time together.

Clyde is a good-looking man, an athlete, with well-defined shoulder and arm muscles, who had been a boxer in the Navy and has worked as a truck driver, factory foreman, and manager of a sporting-goods store. He likes to gamble at cards and horses. Although he is powerfully attracted to women, no one expects him to marry.

Joan Lunt is a good-looking woman with dark eyes, thick dark hair, and a thin scar at the corner of her mouth. She has been in Yewville about a month when she meets Clyde. She lives in a tiny furnished apartment and works at the most prestigious department store in town. The townspeople perceive her as arrogant because she is independent and values her privacy. She attends church but leaves without speaking to anyone, and she drinks alone at the Yewville Bar and Grill. She remains a mystery to the townspeople, who grow suspicious of her.

Sylvie's relationship with Joan also begins at the YMCA pool. One day after their swim, Joan waits in the lobby for Sylvie and invites her to her apartment. Although the apartment is shabby, to Sylvie, who is pleased to be Joan's first guest, it has a makeshift glamour. Sylvie thinks it strange that although Joan has been living in the apartment for weeks, she still has not unpacked the two suitcases that lie opened on the floor. When she asks Joan about the scar beside her mouth, Joan tells her that a man once hit her and warns Sylvie never to let a man hit her.

The relationship between Clyde and Joan becomes more serious as they spend time at Clyde's cabin, the racetrack, and the local bars and restaurants. They are happy in each other's company, but when Joan disappears for a day or two without an explanation, Clyde becomes angry and upset. The real trouble comes when Rob Waxman, Joan's former husband, shows up, and Clyde sees that Joan is terrified of him. When Clyde steps between Joan and Rob, the two men scuffle, and Rob pulls a gun and shoots Clyde in the shoulder. Despite the wound, Clyde attacks Waxman and beats him until someone pulls him off. Joan is upset by the fight. Although she loves Clyde, she has such a fear of violence that seeing him beat Waxman terrifies her. Clyde wants to forget the incident, and the two discuss their situation at length. Clyde thinks that they will continue their relationship, but Joan leaves town and the two never see each other again.

Although Clyde searches for Joan, he never finds her. Sylvie goes away to college and never sees Joan again either. Clyde lives a typical bachelor lifestyle for a time but eventually retreats to a solitary life. The last time Sylvie speaks with Clyde about Joan it is 1971, twelve years after the end of the affair. Clyde's face, with its "look of furious compression" and the dents that resemble animal tracks, shows his unhappiness. Observing him closely, Sylvie wonders if she is "seeing the man Joan Lunt had fled from or the man her flight had made." Sylvia and Clyde never learn what became of Joan.

Themes and Meanings

As in many of Joyce Carol Oates's works, violence is an underlying theme of "The Swimmers." The violence that took place in the past is an ominous presence, and fear of more violence is at the core of the story. Joan Lunt is a wounded person, struggling to build a new life for herself, still held captive by the fears of her past. Just as her relationship with Clyde is strengthening, an act of violence breaks them apart. When Clyde hits Joan's former husband, he is reacting as many men would in the same situation. It may be said that he is actually acting as her protector. Joan, however, sees only the act of violence and runs away.

Another characteristic of Oates's characters is their fear of commitment. Joan is fighting to overcome her past, to survive on her own, unencumbered by possessions or people. Her suitcases remain packed so that she can flee quickly if necessary. The contradiction in her personality is shown in the contrast between her clean, strong, self-confident strokes as a swimmer and the frightened woman who drinks alone at the bar, always watching for trouble. She is suspended between her love for Clyde and her fear of involvement. Her previous experience has left her unable fully to commit to a new relationship. Although Clyde has a number of friends, he has never made a serious commitment to anyone either. A powerful attraction draws them together, and their feelings for each other are intense. The tension in their relationship charges the atmosphere. The failure of the relationship is a result of a lack of understanding and an inability to make a commitment.

Isolation is another theme that pervades "The Swimmers." Joan is an outsider, different, an object of curiosity. The townspeople regard Joan with suspicion, and she does not want to become involved with the community. Joan guards her privacy, and

Clyde leads a solitary life. These people who swim so expertly in the safety of the YMCA pool seem unable to deal with the forces of life on the outside.

Style and Technique

By using the device of an observer-narrator, Oates is able to tell the story from the point of view of a young girl, but with an emphasis on the actions of the adults. Sylvie observes and records the actions of the main characters, but she does not see into their minds. There are gaps in the story because of Joan's flight and the narrator's confusion about what has happened. Although Sylvie continues to observe her uncle, she never really understands him either.

Oates describes the small details of ordinary contemporary scenes. The love story begins in the harsh, cold light of the swimming pool of the YMCA with its antiquated white tiles, wired glass skylight, and sharp medicinal smell of chlorine. Joan's apartment building is shabby and worn with a "weedy back yard of tilting clotheslines and wind-blown trash."

The sentence structure itself reflects the action. In two long, smooth sentences of almost eighty words each, Oates describes Joan's style of swimming as "a single graceful motion that took her a considerable distance." Oates uses a long, graceful sentence to describe this type of stroke. The only scene of violence in the story comes up suddenly. Waxman appears without warning and the situation explodes in violence almost immediately. Oates describes this scene with speed. Clyde reacts with quick actions, animal-like responses. She uses phrases such as "Waxman leapt after her" and "Clyde . . . scrambled forward . . . bent double . . . and managed to throw himself on Waxman." Everything happens so fast that, in retrospect, Clyde cannot even remember his "lightning-swift action."

Oates's choices of images and metaphors show her underlying concern with violence. In the opening paragraph of the story, the narrator says that this story lodges in the memory "like an old wound never entirely healed." The inanimate objects in Joan's apartment are described in terms of violence, "battered-looking furniture" and "injured-looking Venetian blinds." The pool, on the other hand, is a symbol of security and safety. The water provides an environment in which Joan is "sealed off and invulnerable." Later, Oates juxtaposes the shelter of the pool where Joan and Sylvie are "snug and safe" with the icy "pelting" rain that hits the skylight overhead.

In describing Joan, Oates piles up details of physical description to show that she is a cautious person, trying to get her life under control. Joan focuses on the details as a way of establishing some sense of order in her life. Joan's face is "carefully made up" with an "expertly reddened mouth." Her hair is "carefully waved," and her nails are "perfectly manicured, polished an enamel-hard red." Joan's appearance provides a picture of a person who is in control, as if these details of grooming protect her from intrusion. In contrast to these details, the small scar "is like a sliver of glass" that shows her vulnerability.

Judith Barton Williamson

SYLVIE

Author: Gérard de Nerval (Gérard Labrunie, 1808-1855)
Type of plot: Fantasy
Time of plot: Around 1838
Locale: France
First published: 1853 (English translation, 1922)

> *Principal characters:*
> THE UNNAMED NARRATOR
> ADRIENNE, a girl he loved as a youth
> AURÉLIE, an actress in Paris
> SYLVIE, the girl he might have married

The Story

The narrator goes night after night to a theater in Paris to sit at the feet of Aurélie, an actress who approximates his distant feminine ideal. Aurélie remains distant. She is said to love a pale young man who echoes the romantic ideal then in fashion in a society where the narrator seems to be a marginal participant. When the narrator leaves Paris and returns to the Valois in the countryside, he remains equally an outsider, referred to by his old friends as "the Parisian."

Several associations, begun when a newspaper headline reminds him of a country festival from his past, have prompted the narrator to hasten to the Valois in time to see his childhood friend Sylvie at an all-night dance honoring Saint Bartholomew's Day. His destination, however, recalls another festival, at which he once abandoned Sylvie for the fascinating but unattainable Adrienne. A daughter of a noble family of the region, Adrienne had enchanted him with her singing, but her family expected her to follow a religious vocation.

Back in the country, the narrator quickly finds Sylvie. Once again he is torn between two societies, a somewhat mythic past that he associates with Adrienne and the traditions she represented, and the present, where Sylvie lives. Alone on a path at night, he alternately races toward a convent that may house Adrienne and the village where, in the morning, he is reunited with Sylvie.

Sylvie seems to appropriate some of the traditional past. She once tried on her aunt's old wedding dress and costumed the narrator as her bridegroom. This masquerade is now past. He must recognize that Sylvie has redecorated her house in a modern style and no longer keeps up her traditional craft of lacemaking. In one last scene of intimacy, Sylvie sings an old folk song to him. The song, a story of three beautiful girls, parallels the narrator's situation.

There is no indication which of the women in his life would be the most beautiful. Sylvie reveals to him that Adrienne had had bad luck, without giving further details. Sylvie also becomes inaccessible. On hearing of her impending marriage to one of their old friends, the narrator abruptly returns to Paris.

The story then moves ahead in time. The narrator does have a chance at the love of Aurélie, but the actress must have a man who is totally devoted to her. When the narrator avows his continuing fascination with Adrienne, Aurélie abandons him. At the very end Sylvie, now happily married, reveals to him that Adrienne had died in the convent many years before. He has lost both the women he might have loved because of the memory of a woman who no longer existed.

Themes and Meanings

The nature of this story, composed in the first person and consisting largely of the narrator's thoughts, makes it perfect as a vehicle for extensive descriptions. Through his choice of material in the descriptive passages, Gérard de Nerval introduces a series of value judgments on the people and places described.

At first the presence of description seems ironic. In the first scene at the theater, after commenting on the dress and jewels of members of the audience, the narrator asserts his lack of interest in them. The ensuing description of Aurélie, however, already contains elements calculated to enhance the reader's perception of her by specific associations.

Aurélie is as beautiful as "the divine Hours . . . of the frescoes at Herculanum." This analogy with the recently discovered classical paintings heightens the degree of beauty ascribed to Aurélie, but by the distance implied, reinforces the idea of her inaccessibility.

In the case of these romantic allusions, Nerval draws on concepts popular in his day with which his readers would already have specific associations. In his portraits of Adrienne and Sylvie, he creates a more personal system of association where older, traditional things appear good, while their modern replacements seem crass and uninteresting. Adrienne's strong link to the traditions of her aristocratic forebears establishes her as having a superiority to which Sylvie can only briefly aspire.

The chapter that introduces Adrienne presents a brief glimpse of her in the context of a traditional local festival. Before she appears, a lengthy description of a chateau from the time of Henri IV, with young girls dancing and singing, establishes the important role of girls and singing in this landscape. Thus when Adrienne sings, her beauty and mystery captivate the narrator. She has become his only link to the desired, mythic past.

In contrast to this invocation of authentic French culture, the narrator's encounters with Sylvie are marked by two temples of neoclassical style, ornaments of the past century now falling into ruin. He recalls previously escorting Sylvie to a festival on an island where such a temple formed a part of the setting. Recalling the image of Antoine Watteau's painting *Voyage à Cythère* (1717), he characterizes this as the temple of love. When he seeks Sylvie again later, he comes across the temple of philosophy. This temple marks an end to festivity, for the narrator notes that the young girls dressed in white are absent from it. This, together with the distressingly modern objects he observes in Sylvie's house, portrays Sylvie in a context that is cut off from the beauties of the past.

Style and Technique

The events of "Sylvie," composed largely of an erratic journey the narrator makes through the Valois region of France, are of secondary importance to the memories that the places he visits evoke. The central element of the story involves the narrator's mental and emotional travels, of which his actual physical movement gives only a limited approximation.

Contrasting social customs serve to distance the narrator from the women he loves. At first readers see the contrast of Paris with the provinces. Chapters set in Paris at the beginning and end of the story form an enclosure for the narrator's trip, showing him as traveling away from Paris, even though he is returning to the scenes of his youth. In fact, the narrator remains an outsider in both settings.

The descriptive flashbacks in "Sylvie" go beyond mere decoration. Through them Nerval re-creates an entire past society, much as Marcel Proust later did in *À la recherche du temps perdu* (1913-1927; *Remembrance of Things Past*, 1922-1931, 1981), but with the exception that, lacking Proust's linking device of the madeleine, Nerval's associations remain essentially visual.

The society of late medieval France had a special importance for Nerval, who, seeing himself descended from heroes of that time, felt that he had a continuing association with them. This dual perception of himself seems to have figured in his crises of mental illness, but his intimate association with the past was also something that he valued greatly.

The transition from a present to a past life may be irresistible, but it is not easy. The narrator easily slips into remembering scenes from his past, but his true enchantment with Adrienne comes through a series of initiatory steps that recall the entry of a knight into an adventure. While he begins by imagining a château and many girls dancing, his attention narrows until he loves only one. As they are drawn together by the ritual pattern of the dance, it becomes appropriate for him to kiss Adrienne. With his kiss, even before Adrienne begins her enchanting song, he declares that an unknown trouble took hold of him.

This kiss as turning point recalls Nerval's line from "El Desdichado," the sonnet that reflects his descent into the hell of his madness. After that experience, he declared that his forehead was "still red from the queen's kiss." The identity of this queen, linked in the poem to both pagan and Christian tales, remains unclear. Still, the important image of the woman marking him with a kiss parallels Adrienne.

Although elements of episodes with Sylvie also parallel chivalric antecedents, the crossing over water to reach the temple on the island for example, they do not result in the same evocation of the past. The trip to the island produces the relatively modern image of a painting by Watteau.

Engagement with the past, as represented by the narrator's infatuation with Adrienne, corresponds to Nerval's overwhelming wish. Its dangers are apparent in that it costs the narrator the happiness he could have had with either of the two women who might have loved him.

Dorothy M. Betz

THE SYMBOL

Author: Virginia Woolf (1882-1941)
Type of plot: Sketch
Time of plot: The late nineteenth or early twentieth century
Locale: An alpine resort, possibly in Switzerland
First published: 1985

Principal character:
THE NARRATOR, an elderly English woman

The Story

This brief story begins with a description of the mountain, the focal point of the alpine village in which the story is set. The mountaintop is like a crater on the moon, filled with iridescent snow whose color changes from dead white to blood red. The mountainside is a vast descent from pure rock and a clutching pine to the village and graves in the valley.

An elderly English woman sits on her hotel room balcony. She starts to write to her sister in England that the mountain "is a symbol," but she pauses to observe the mountain, as if to think about its symbolic significance. While the woman is musing, the omniscient narrator comments on the theatrical nature of the alpine resort: The hotel balcony is like a box at a theater and human behavior appears as "curtain raisers." From this omniscient perspective, life looks artificial and temporary: "Entertainments to pass the time; seldom leading to any conclusion." When the English woman sees young men on the street below, she recognizes one of them as a relative of the mistress of her daughter's school. She remembers that young men in the past have died climbing the nearby mountain and becomes again mindful of its symbolic presence and power.

Continuing her letter to her sister, the woman recalls the time that she spent with their dying mother on the Isle of Wight. This remembrance stirs her to disclose that she longed to hear the doctor say that her mother would die soon, when in fact she lived another eighteen months. She writes that she regarded the mother's death as a symbol—a symbol of freedom. She goes on to say that "a cloud then would do instead of the mountain" as a sign of having reached the top. Her memory then turns to her Anglo-Indian uncles and cousins who were explorers, and she reveals her own great desire to explore, though marrying was a more sensible choice.

After turning her attention to a woman routinely shaking out a rug on another balcony, the woman resumes her letter to her sister. After mentioning the local villas, food, and hotel, she returns to the subject of the mountain and what a splendid view she has of it, as well as of everyone else in the village. She says that the mountain is always the center of conversation; people discuss whether it is clear and seems close, or it looks like a cloud and seems farther away.

Just the night before, she confesses, she hoped the storm would hide the mountain, and then asks if she is being selfish to want it concealed in the face of so much suffering. Admitting that this suffering afflicts visitors and native residents equally, she quotes the hotel proprietor as saying that only an earthquake could destroy the mountain and that no such threat exists there.

The woman again notices the young men, who are now roped together and climbing the mountain; she stops her letter midsentence: "They are now crossing a crevasse." The pen falls from her hand as the men disappear.

Later that night the men's bodies are uncovered by a search party. The story ends with the woman finding her unfinished letter and writing that the old clichés seem appropriate: The men tried "to climb the mountain"; peasants put flowers on their graves; and the young men have "died in an attempt to discover . . . " Because no conclusion seems fitting, the woman tacks on the conventional line, "Love to the children" and signs her pet name, closing the letter and the story.

Themes and Meanings

Virginia Woolf finished "The Symbol" less than a month before her death in 1941. The story explores the issues associated with her experimental interests in the novel—how to blend objective and subjective reality in ways that capture the sensuous and tangible qualities of experience, while suggesting its ephemeral and elusive nature. In essays such as "Modern Fiction" and "Mr. Bennett and Mrs. Brown," Woolf explores the new aesthetics involved in presenting a fiction reflective of modern behavior. For the twentieth century sensibility, as Woolf and other modernists perceive it, life is in a constant state of flux where nothing is stable and the mind constantly receives "myriad impressions." Life, unlike its treatment by Edwardian novelist Arnold Bennett, is not a tightly plotted Aristotelian drama with a clean beginning, middle, and end. Instead, life—like character—is always in a state of becoming—a state of uncertainty and change in which decisive moments are internal and subjective, moving the individual upward in a spiritual quest of self-knowledge.

Woolf's concerns lay the groundwork for understanding how "The Symbol" reflects themes characteristic of her experimental art. Her unnamed woman writer, an outsider in the alpine village who is removed from its street bustle, muses on what a symbol is and how it relates to the mountain—the recurring focus of her thoughts. The mountain becomes identified here with the human quest, the "longing" to reach the top and whatever the perceived goal suggests. For the protagonist, it is a desire to be free of traditional restraints—first her mother and then her sensible marriage. It is a longing to transgress conventional boundaries like the male explorers in her family—her Anglo-Indian uncles and cousins. This family is a blend of the West and the East, of British pragmatism and Indian spirituality, a mix conducive to successful exploration. The young alpine explorers, distinguished in the past by their valley graves and in the present by being roped in their upward climb of the mountain, are not so different from the woman's own uncles and cousins in their quest for the unknown. The protagonist, through apparently limited by gender expectations, manages to eke out a life of adventure through her role as writer/observer—the onlooker who records the life and death of the young explorers as well as the ups and downs of her own emotional life.

Many of Woolf's characters, particularly in her novels, are imaged as being on literal and symbolic journeys leading to something that continually beckons and eludes the human imagination. The symbol, like the quest, escapes definition and summary. The suggestive and abstract significance of a mountain, cloud, letter, or death depends on the changing context of the perceiver. When the protagonist is responsible to her dying mother, she says that a cloud signifies freedom as well as a mountain and that death itself becomes a symbol of release. For Woolf, the process of questing, of scaling the mountain, of writing the letter seems more important than the goal itself. Indeed, the process of discovery seems to take precedence over physical death as the protagonist closes her comments on the young male mountain climbers with the unfinished line, "They died in an attempt to discover . . . " This inconclusive ending reaffirms death as yet part of the discovery process that may continue beyond material life as humans know it.

Style and Technique

Woolf constantly experimented with style, searching for ways of presenting character that explore the unconscious self. Dissatisfied with the summary treatment of character in terms of external events, she was primarily interested in character as a fluctuating interplay of the mind in response to ordinary experience. Physical sensation, as described in her fiction, provokes thought and memory, and the latter also nudge each other, unfolding in a series of images. In "The Symbol" the protagonist is suggested largely by her thoughts and memories, which are spurred initially by the view of the mountain and the village life and subsequently revealed in the letter. For her, the past, present, and future clearly shape who she is. As she reflects on the mountain and the aspiring climbers, she remembers an earlier balcony on the Isle of Wight. There she entertained her mother by describing the travelers who disembarked on the isle after an ocean journey. Like a dutiful daughter, the young protagonist attended to the requests of her dying mother, perceiving death then as a symbol of freedom, of unlimited possibility to be explored.

The protagonist's past and present experiences, subjective and objective reality, are connected by her musing on the symbol and trying to understand its significance. Woolf's characteristic style is to shift the narrative back and forth between memory and present experience, as mediated through the protagonist's perceptions and the omniscient narrator's description. The shifting narration symbolizes Woolf's notion of how to describe character in terms of a fluctuating play between external sensation and internal reaction. Ultimately, the story itself can be read as a symbol of how character depends on, and is shaped by, imaginative desire and longing.

Chella Courington

THE TABLES OF THE LAW

Author: William Butler Yeats (1865-1939)
Type of plot: Fantasy
Time of plot: The 1890's
Locale: Dublin
First published: 1896

> *Principal characters:*
> OWEN AHERNE, the protagonist, a mystic
> THE NARRATOR, Aherne's friend

The Story

After dinner and an evening of conversation, the narrator feels comfortable enough to ask his old friend Owen Aherne a question that has been troubling him for many years: For years Aherne has cared for nothing but theology and mysticism—why has he not followed through on his original vocation for the church? Aherne considers his answer, meditatively holding a glass of red wine in his hand, "its deep red light dyeing his long delicate fingers," making him look as if he were "holding a flame in his naked hand." As he waits for Aherne's answer, the narrator reflects on the character of his friend. When the narrator and Aherne had been students in Paris, they had belonged to a group devoted to "speculations about alchemy and mysticism." Aherne, it seems to the narrator, has in his beliefs "a fanciful hatred of all life," and this hatred has ripened into a strange mélange of beliefs, in part self-created, in part borrowed, "that the beautiful arts were sent into the world to overthrow nations, and finally life herself, by sowing everywhere unlimited desires, like torches thrown into a burning city." It seems to the narrator that Aherne is the sort of person for whom "there is no order, no finality, no contentment in this world."

As the narrator so reflects, Aherne rises and offers to show the narrator the cause of his seeming loss of interest in the church and of his apparent reserve and indifference of recent years. He leads the narrator down a long corridor to his private chapel, passing engravings and portraits that Aherne has acquired on his travels, pictures depicting "enraptured faces of the angels of Francesca," "sibyls of Michael Angelo," seeming to hold an "incertitude, as of souls trembling between the excitement of the spirit and the excitement of the flesh," and "faces like thin flames," wrought by the Symbolists and Pre-Raphaelites. As he looks, "that long, grey, dim, empty, echoing passage [has] become to my eyes a vestibule of eternity."

In the chapel, the narrator is shown the object that has changed Aherne's life: On the altar is a bronze box that stands before six unlighted candles and an ebony crucifix. The box, decorated with "gods and demons, whose eyes are closed to signify an absorption in the inner light," holds a secret book, the only surviving copy of a book written by Joachim of Flora, who had been an abbot in Cortale in the twelfth century. The book, *Liber inducens in Evangelium aeternum*, has been carefully hidden and guarded by generations of the family of Aretino after Pope Alexander IV had the original cast into the flames for its heretical views. Aherne has acquired the book from Giulio Aretano, an artist and a Cabalist. Aherne puts the book in the narrator's hands, and the narrator turns the "gilded, many-coloured pages." This book, claims Aherne, has "swept the commandments of the Father away," and it "goes to the heart." In it are the names of "great artists who made them graven things . . . and adored them and served them," as well as "the names of the great wits who took the name of the Lord their God in vain." It praises the "breakers of the seventh day and wasters of the six days" and tells of "men and women who railed upon their parents." Those "heavy with love and sleep and many-coloured raiment" and "noble youths who loved the wives of others" fill the pages of this secret book. Murder, the violation of chastity, the bearing of false witness—all such deeds find their place in the book. Persons who had become "stars shaken out of the raiment of God" are its characters.

The narrator then sees that the ivory tables on which the Ten Commandments were written, and which stood in the chapel, are now gone and have been replaced by blank tables, on which Aherne plans to write his "secret law." Aherne sees himself as the messiah for a new and terrible religion.

> Yes, I shall send out of this chapel saints, lovers, rebels, and prophets: souls that will surround themselves with peace, as with a nest made with grass; and others over whom I shall weep. The dust shall fall for many years over this little box; and then I shall open it; and the tumults, which are, perhaps, the flames of the last day, shall come from under the lid.

The narrator tries to dissuade Aherne, pointing out the danger of such beliefs, but Aherne is adamant: "How then can the pathway which will lead us into the heart of God be other than dangerous?" he asks. The first part of the story ends at this point, as the narrator expresses his regret and sorrow for not having tried more forcefully to dissuade Aherne.

The second part finds the narrator walking along a quay in Dublin ten years later. Suddenly he sees Aherne, his face a "lifeless mask with dim eyes." Aherne seems to see the narrator but turns away, hurries down a side street, and disappears. The narrator searches for him for weeks, then again spots him in a narrow street behind the Four Courts and follows him to his house. He seems, to the narrator, like a man "whose inner life had soaked up the outer life." At first, Aherne tries to keep him away ("I am lost, and must be hidden!") but finally allows the narrator to come into his house. Again the narrator follows Aherne down the long corridor, now "choked with dust and cobwebs," the pictures "grey with dust and shrouded with cobwebs." Dust also covers the "ruby and sapphire of the saints on the window," making it very dim. Aherne points to the tablets, which are now "covered with small writing." "You have a right to hear," Aherne tells the narrator, "for since I have told you the ideas, I should tell you the extreme danger they contain, or rather the boundless wickedness they contain." The ideas had made him happy at first, he relates. He had felt "a divine ecstasy, an immortal fire in every passion, in every hope, in every desire, in every dream." He thought that he "was about to touch the Heart of God." Then everything changed, and he realized that "man can only come to that Heart through the sense of separation from it which we call sin, and I understood that I could not sin, because I had discovered the law of my being." Because he has learned to see the world from the perspective of the angels, he can no longer sin, for everything he does is in accordance with a self-given law. Thus, because he sees creation in its entirety, he is no longer "among those for whom Christ died." He has "lost my soul because I have looked out of the eyes of the angels."

Suddenly, the room darkens. As Aherne sits, listless and dejected, the narrator sees faint purple-robed figures, holding faint torches and sighing "with sorrow for his sorrow." The narrator, in terror, flees the house as a voice cries, "Why do you fly from our torches that were made out of the trees under which Christ wept in the Garden of Gethsemane?" The narrator realizes that if he turns back, "all that bound me to spiritual and social order, would be burnt up, and my soul left naked and shivering among the winds that blow from beyond this world and from beyond the stars." He thus leaves the house forever. As for Aherne, the narrator relates that he has been "driven into some distant country by the spirits whose name is legion, and whose throne is in the indefinite abyss, and whom he obeys and cannot see."

Themes and Meanings

The interest in matters mystical, and in their relation to destruction, derangement, or apocalypse is a strong element in William Butler Yeats's poetry, early and late. Owen Aherne, protagonist of "The Tables of the Law," is an important speaker in poems central to the Yeats canon, as well as playing a prominent part in *A Vision* (1925, 1937), the poet's prose summary of his own mystical divinations. The story's emphasis falls on the protagonist's daring, longing, loneliness, and ultimate desolation. The elapse of ten years between the close of the first part of the story and the opening of the second underlines a preoccupation with initiation and aftermath, with longing and its consequences. It also suggests that Aherne's experience will forever remain a mystery. It necessarily remains beyond the realm of collective and typical experience. The remoteness of Aherne's spiritual adventures is accentuated by the obvious psychological distance between him and the narrator during their second encounter. Reappearing in the second half of the story as a haunted, and haunting, travesty of his original ambitions, Aherne is less a neo-Mosaic legislator than an alarming caution against spiritual overreaching.

The quest for and desire to codify a new spiritual dispensation is a lofty goal, appropriately reserved for Aherne, "the supreme type of our race." However, for all of his learning, intensity, and commitment, he cannot escape his human limitations. His shockingly misguided but strangely exultant efforts to do so leave him the prisoner of an unending tragic dream, a hell of his own making.

The sense of ardent pursuit, the conception of an extreme, the possibility of swift, temporary uplift followed rapidly by a condition of endless deterioration and damnation—these and various ancillary preoccupations constitute the fabric of "The Tables of the Law." Such interests lend the story a distinct *fin de siècle* tinge. Aherne—in effect, a mind at the end of its tether—is reminiscent of such protagonists as the Duc des Esseintes of Joris-Karl Huysmans's *A rebours* (1884; *Against the Grain*, 1922) and Oscar Wilde's Dorian Gray.

Aherne conveys much perturbation of spirit. Despite excellent cultural credentials, he is rootless and disaffected. He is at pains to distinguish himself from "those . . . who have only the world." However, his radical revision of contemporary orthodoxy in the name of one fabricated by himself and Joachim of Flora leads only to his coming face-to-face with himself. Aherne's inability to renounce or transcend his own nature, his incapacity to break the bonds of worldliness, his failure to inhabit a realm of pure spirit reveal a mind unable to consolidate its own impulses. "The Tables of the Law," then, may be seen as a precursor of the vision of cultural and spiritual dissolution central to the Modernist movement, a vision to which the more mature Yeats bore witness even as he abhorred it.

The story also strikes a contemporary note by appearing to create an association between decay of energy and decadence. Aherne is a would-be mythmaker, a seeker of paradise, a trustee of a sacred text, a sage who can declare, but not finally uphold, the belief that "the world only exists to be a tale in the ears of coming generations." Clearly, he possesses all the qualifications to bring out the revolution in consciousness that he envisages. However, the greater his abilities, the more catastrophic their deployment. The more of himself he puts into his visionary enterprise, the more significant his losses. He ends up in exile, which in this case is a condition of spiritual entropy.

In addition, and perhaps as a corollary, the story offers a covert but elaborate reproof to the imagination. Here Yeats seems to be worrying tacitly about a dictum of one of his own imaginative ancestors, William Blake: "The road of excess leads to the palace of wisdom." Aherne's imaginative excess may lead him to a more profound assessment of his human destiny, but his habitation does not have the sense of ease and scope that "palace" and "wisdom" usually connote. However, Aherne has appointed himself seer, visionary, and seeker after strange gods, offices frequently arrogated to themselves by poets, particularly those of the Romantic tradition, as Yeats was. Ultimately, however, the imagination may not overrule the world. To coexist with it is a sufficient challenge.

Style and Technique

"The Tables of the Law" is much more obviously sustained by the sonorities of its style than it is by the accessibility of its ideas or the cogency of its plot. The story's rather elaborate prose is as inimitably part of Yeats's schooling by the leading stylists of the day, Walter Pater and Oscar Wilde, as anything else in this typical period piece. Yeats's protracted sentences, the rhetorical flair of Aherne's monologues, the pervasive sense of distracted brooding—all are the fruits of the fundamentally overripe, dandified prose of the author's stylistic mentors.

However, style in the story is not merely a matter of language: The language's florid effects also influence other aspects of the material's presentation. Gesture, large and small, and invariably mannered, is a case in point. Aherne is a character of large gestures (all of them expressing repudiation and the usurpation of tradition), intended for dramatic effect and, ultimately, to influence public events. His presence, and particularly his conversation, has a theatrical aura—understandably, perhaps, given Yeats's growing interest in the theater and in its techniques of narration, which date roughly from the story's year of publication. Additional theatrical features are especially prominent in the first part of "The Tables of the Law"—the ritualized meal, the ceremonious initiation of the narrator into the secret history of Joachim, Aherne's declaration of heretical faith.

The story cunningly and critically contrasts this careful (perhaps too careful) orchestration of gestural effects in the opening section with the at once fugitive and overblown effects of part 2. Here, none of the evidently stabilizing factors of a familiar civilization (located by Yeats, typically, in the Aherne family home) is at work. On the contrary, the reader witnesses the ruins of thought's edifice, an apocalypse rendered primarily in fastidious and exalted prose. The witnessing, however, consists of monitoring the story's emotional atmosphere and registering the seismic shocks of Aherne's spiritual experiences. These attain imaginative plausibility as a result of the story's style and technique, its language and use of image and symbol.

George O'Brien

TAKE PITY

Author: Bernard Malamud (1914-1986)
Type of plot: Fable
Time of plot: The early 1950's
Locale: New York City
First published: 1956

Principal characters:
ROSEN, a former coffee sales representative
DAVIDOV, a census-taker
EVA KALISH, a widow

The Story

Rosen, an elderly former coffee sales representative, lives in a drab and spartan room, into which Davidov, a census-taker, has limped without knocking. Davidov is surprised that the worn, black shade over the single narrow window is closed, but Rosen grumbles that he does not need light. After cryptic—and, for Rosen, uncomfortable—preliminary exchanges, Davidov opens a notebook and prepares to write. Finding his pen empty, the census-taker pulls out a pencil stub and sharpens it with a razor blade, letting the flakes fall to the floor.

Davidov finally prods Rosen into revealing the nature of his acquaintance with Eva Kalish and the charities that Rosen extended to her. Eva, thirty-eight years old and the mother of two young girls, is the recent widow of a nearly bankrupt immigrant Jewish grocer who died at Rosen's feet. Rosen's subsequent efforts to aid the new widow clearly play a critical role in the census-taker's inquiry.

Rosen is made to relate his persistent attempts to help Eva and her children as she struggles, and fails, to keep her dead husband's business afloat. Drawing on his own experience, he repeats to Eva the advice that he once gave her husband: The store is in a bad neighborhood; it was a mistake to begin with; it will be a grave for him and his family; they should get out. After Mr. Kalish's capital was exhausted, he had agreed with Rosen, just as he fell dead. Rosen tells the widow to take the insurance money bequeathed to her, leave the business to creditors, and go to relatives.

Rosen is secretly in love with Eva, and his pleading becomes more insistent, but Eva is deaf to him. She cannot go to relatives; Adolf Hitler has killed them. She refuses his offer of credit. She even becomes upset when he brings her a piece of sirloin. She will not consider rent-free living in part of a house Rosen owns. She will not even allow him to pay for someone to watch her children while she looks for a job. Rosen fails, too, when proposing a platonic marriage, from which he seeks nothing but to care for her. Eva steadfastly rejects each of Rosen's overt and covert offers of charity.

Each rejection, none of which he comprehends, plunges Rosen more deeply into despair. Nevertheless, he is determined. Drafting his will, Rosen leaves all of his worldly goods to Eva and her girls, turns on the gas, sticks his head in the stove, and commits suicide.

Rosen is a suicide looking out the window of his coffin; Davidov is an angel sent to record Rosen's charities. When Eva appears at the coffin window to apologize, Rosen screams at her: "Whore, bastard, bitch. Go 'way from here."

Themes and Meanings

Best known as a Jewish American writer, Bernard Malamud frequently created characters that are poor, sad, benighted, and living on the margin. However, they somehow manage to preserve, maintain, or regain a semblance of self-worth in the teeth of implacable circumstance. Rosen's suicide represents an assertion of a sadly comic human dignity in a chaotic, often merciless and incomprehensible world. Rosen has literally killed himself trying to succeed in what he believes is a worthy effort. Feeling that he has been pained and abased by endlessly entreating Eva to accept his unselfish help, Rosen salvages something of himself by angrily rejecting the apologetic and beseeching Eva when she appears outside his coffin window. As he lies in limbo awaiting judgment, he may even meet the angel Davidov's standards.

"Take Pity" is one of several stories appearing in *The Magic Barrel, and Other Stories* (1958), Malamud's first collection, most of which are tragicomic tales of long-suffering Jews. Although they are that, it would be superficial to see them as that alone. Although his characters often are Jewish, they are created less to realistically chronicle aspects of traditional Jewish life than to serve as moral metaphors. In "Take Pity," for example, Malamud emphasizes the horror and comedy of Rosen's frustrated need to share, to enjoy a communion prized by many people throughout most cultures. The story, then, is a moral fable with near-universal spiritual relevance.

Within this context, however, Malamud fills his tale with ironies. The angel, Davidov, like the people he scrutinizes, is shabby, poorly equipped, somewhat frazzled, and bored. Kalish, the grocer, saddles Rosen with his burdens as he dies at the feet of the old, sick, lonely coffee sales representative. It is ironic that Rosen, a skeptical and experienced person, is willing to visit all of his money and goods on a widow whom he scarcely knows. Woven throughout the story is the crowning irony that those who are eager to savor the joy of giving unselfishly must suffer from the would-be recipient's hatred and endure personal anguish and humiliation. Even worse, with the Holocaust still excruciatingly etched in Jewish memories, Rosen dies by gas. When Rosen is stripped of everything with nothing remaining to give, proud Eva appears, repentant and importuning.

Ironies aside, however, "Take Pity" stands as a testament to the enduring Jewish—and human—spirit.

Style and Technique

This is the first of Malamud's stories to be written from an omniscient point of view. This device more readily evokes a gothic mood, one characterized, that is, by desolate settings and macabre, mysterious, and violent events. The dialogue superbly demonstrates the Yiddish idiom. One example is when Davidov asks Rosen how the grocer died. "On this I am not an expert," Rosen replies. "You know better than me." "Say in one word how he died," Davidov impatiently demands. Rosen answers, "From what he died?—he died, that's all." Davidov presses, "Answer, please, this question." Laconically Rosen responds, "Broke in him something. That's how." Davidov asks, "Broke what?" and Rosen retorts, "Broke what breaks."

Malamud masterfully blends the banal and commonplace with the mystical and the spiritual. Through the first part of "Take Pity," for example, Rosen speaks with an angel whose appearance, speech, and demeanor are anything but angelic. Davidov behaves like a drab, ordinary, Yiddish-speaking mortal. Rosen also speaks and acts as if, despite his death, he were alive. The reader accepts these characterizations until Malamud reveals, smoothly and without explicit explanations, Davidov's real identity and Rosen's true condition.

In "Take Pity," Malamud facilitates this merger of the real and the unreal by using a spare setting and employing almost cryptic prose. This allows his characters to move easily between worlds—a device that Malamud often employed—without things seeming in the least out of the ordinary. Neither Rosen's nor Davidov's actions or speech betray their incongruities to the reader, and Malamud introduces no digressions or distractions. His writing rivets on the essential. Rosen and Davidov are not engaged in chit-chat. Rosen is not interested in the latest news, gossip, trends, fads, fashions, or politics. He is grappling with frightening glimpses of his own inner nature. Through his intense concentration on the essentials of Rosen's inner struggle, Malamud permits Rosen to discover an inner resilience and depth, although partly discovered in death, that Rosen never knew he possessed.

Critics generally do not rank "Take Pity" among the finest of Malamud's short stories. Some find that it suffers from the author's omniscient narration, that is, from the absence of Malamud's own voice. Others find it too gothic and pessimistic. Still others question the discrepancy between its supporting structure and its abrupt ending—Rosen's cursing of Eva. There is general agreement, however, that "Take Pity," like much of Malamud's writing, is powerful, distinctive, and rare in its ability to join the commonplace with the mystical and spiritual and, by doing so, encourages readers to explore their own inner realms.

Clifton K. Yearley

TAKING CARE

Author: Joy Williams (1944-   )
Type of plot: Psychological
Time of plot: The 1960's-1970's
Locale: A small town in the northeastern United States
First published: 1972

> *Principal characters:*
> JONES, a Protestant minister
> HIS WIFE, who is seriously ill
> THEIR MARRIED DAUGHTER, who has run away to Mexico
> HER INFANT DAUGHTER, who has been left with Jones

The Story

Jones, a preacher, has been in love all his life, yet his love has apparently not helped anyone. When the story opens, he is sitting beside his wife's bed in a hospital fifteen miles from their home, waiting for the results of blood tests that the doctors hope will make possible a diagnosis of her illness. In addition to his sick wife, Jones is responsible for their daughter's six-month-old baby girl and her German shepherd, for the daughter has left her husband and run away to Mexico (where she will soon have a nervous breakdown). Little happens in the story proper—Jones will probably visit other parishioners in the hospital, he writes a cheery card to his daughter in response to a letter from her, and each day he brings a yellow rose to his sick wife—but much happens in flashbacks, which reveal how the wife first fell ill and the early signs of their daughter's problems. In the present, the overwhelmed Jones plays his multiple roles of husband, father, and mother as best he can.

In the seventh section of this eleven-part story, Jones delivers a sermon from the pulpit of his church, baptizes the baby, and serves communion, but all his actions seem to happen in slow motion, as if in a dream. In the next section, his wife is operated on to remove a large tumor as Jones takes care of the baby and cleans the house. His wife will be coming home for Christmas, and Jones puts up a tree but waits for her to help him decorate it. In the last section of the story, Jones picks up his wife at the hospital. They drive home with the baby, and together "they enter the shining rooms."

Themes and Meanings

"Taking Care" seems on first reading to have two opposite or contrary meanings. On one hand, the story is about the power of human (and perhaps divine) love. As Jones says in his sermon, "We are saved not because we are worthy. We are saved because we are loved." His sermon is a blur to him, however, and as Joy Williams says in the opening sentences of the story, his love for others has never seemed to help anyone. For, in spite of what he does, as loving husband and father, his wife is sick and probably dying, and his daughter has abandoned her family only to face a mental breakdown. Also, in spite of Jones's profession, there is little evidence of God's immediate presence in "Taking Care." The ambiguous meaning of the story is captured best, perhaps, in a series of vivid images: on a drive into the country, during which Jones sees "a holiness in snow, a promise," and he and his baby granddaughter delight in the sight of a snowshoe rabbit running across a field. The rabbit is suddenly shot by a hunter and skids across the road in front of their car, however, just as his wife has been struck down by disease. The beauty in this world, in short, is constantly being undercut by its pain. Jones plays a record of Austrian composer Anton Bruckner's *Te Deum* ("Thou, Lord") left by his daughter and is overwhelmed by the music but cannot remember enough of his college German to understand the meaning of the words. It is not easy to grasp the meaning of what goes on in life, Williams implies—even if you are a minister.

Jones says at one point that in his profession, he is concerned with both justification and remorse, that is, with explaining life and then grieving for it. The story demonstrates that there are really no explanations for many things in life, however, and that all people can do is to grieve and to take care of one another, and those are the tasks Jones has taken on in the story. He takes care of his sick wife, his infant granddaughter—even his daughter's dog. His parishioners, for their part, try to take care of Jones and his family, and his refrigerator is stuffed; when he opens it, "A brilliant light exposes all this food."

At the end of the story, Jones, his wife, and their infant granddaughter "enter the shining rooms" of their house. Their home is filled with some almost supernatural glow (even inside the refrigerator), because it holds the love that Jones and others have poured into it. In spite of the multiple problems he faces, Jones has taken care of others, and the story reflects that love.

The story's title may convey this complex meaning as easily as any other element. "Take care" is an expression people use all the time without thinking about its meaning, as Jones himself does in the story. However, "taking care" is really the most important action humans can perform, Williams implies, for taking care of someone fulfills what it means to be human. What distinguishes humans from other life-forms is that they can "take care" of one another, take responsibility of and care for one another. The epiphanic ending cannot erase all the abandonment and sickness taking place in the story, but it certainly balances them with something more spiritual, if not grace then surely redemption for Jones.

Style and Technique

Jones is certainly "taking care" of more than his required load in this life, and there is a heaviness, a sadness, to the story that is expressed appropriately in Williams's flat, terse prose style. The most noticeable element of "Taking Care," however, is its structure, eleven separate sections divided by Roman numerals. This numbering divides the sections more completely than simple line breaks or even Arabic numerals might, giving the story a staccato, fragmentary quality. The story's structure demonstrates that the events of life are unconnected, as people themselves are. (His daughter wandering the beaches of Mexico seems the strongest example of this last idea.) The order of the sections is also choppy, moving abruptly back and forth in time, with no smooth or clear progression or logic. Uniting the disparate sections of the story, bringing them together, is human love in the form of Jones "taking care" of others and his parishioners "taking care" of Jones with their bowls and bottles of food in his refrigerator.

The tone of the story is objective and neutral, as if readers are looking down at its characters and events from a great distance. The point of view in the story reinforces this feeling because Williams tells readers details (such as the daughter's future breakdown) that Jones himself cannot know. In certain sections (for example, Jones's sermon), there is a surreal, nightmare quality to the prose, as if characters are walking in a dream.

The intense quality of this prose is heightened in a series of images and metaphors that are charged with meaning. In the opening section, for example, Jones compares himself to an animal in a traveling show who "wears a vital organ outside the skin, awkward and unfortunate, something that shouldn't be seen, certainly something that shouldn't be watched working." It is his heart, readers suspect. He chews his communion bread, "but it lies unconsumed, like a muscle in his mouth." Earlier he imagines his wife as "a swimmer waiting to get on with the drowning," and her blood moving as "mysteriously as constellations" of stars. Like Joyce Carol Oates and Flannery O'Connor before her, Williams creates a prose of vivid, even frightening texture and intensity, but like them, she also conveys central truths of the human heart.

David Peck

THE TALE

Author: Joseph Conrad (Jósef Teodor Konrad Nałęcz Korzeniowski, 1857-1924)
Type of plot: Psychological
Time of plot: World War I
Locale: At sea
First published: 1917

> *Principal characters:*
> THE COMMANDING OFFICER, the protagonist and narrator of the
>   tale
> THE NORTHMAN, the master of a cargo ship
> THE WOMAN, who listens to the officer's tale

The Story

Twilight is falling through the window of a long, gloomy room. In the gathering darkness, a woman asks her companion, a man of the sea, for a tale. He begins, awkwardly, deliberately, reminding her that what he is about to relate is a story of duty, war, and horror.

During the early days of the "bad" war, a commanding officer—the narrator himself—is taking his ship past a dangerous rocky coast. The weather is foul, a thick, impenetrable fog obscuring the coast so that the commanding officer can see nothing and can only sense the danger before him. What he can see is small flotsam, perhaps cargo from a ship sunk by an enemy submarine reported to be near. The officer suspects that the cargo may be intended for the enemy, left there for the submarine by another ship. He knows that certain supposedly neutral ships have violated their neutrality for profit and that one of these may be close by.

As the fog thickens, the commanding officer orders the ship to be brought closer to land and to lower anchor in the shadow of the coast and wait for the weather to clear. Here he sees another ship, sitting quietly at anchor, as if in hiding. He begins to wonder if this ship is an innocent neutral or if, indeed, it is guilty of providing the submarine with supplies. Does it intend to sneak out when the fog lifts?

Alarmed yet puzzled by his suspicions, the commanding officer boards the mysterious cargo ship. The master, a Northman, is congenial, even loquacious. He insists he really is lost. The Northman tells his own tale, a brief account of his getting lost in the fog and of having engine failure. This voyage was his first in these waters. The ship is his own, providing a meager living for his family. The Northman's tale is credible enough, but the commanding officer is unconvinced. Cleverly he implies that the Northman is making a profit from the war, but the Northman denies trading with the enemy, insisting that his cargo is bound for an English port.

Although the Northman has given a good account of himself—even his manifest is clear—the commanding officer is increasingly suspicious. Looking firmly into the

Northman's face, the commanding officer suddenly becomes convinced that this honest-seeming, slightly drunk captain has forged an enormous lie. Seeing no way out, convinced of some monstrous villainy, the commanding officer declares that he is letting the Northman go and orders him to steer south by southeast, which would take him past the rocks and into the safety of the open sea. Tired but trusting, the Northman steams off.

The commanding officer ends his tale here, but in a final summation to the woman in the darkening room he declares that the course he gave the Northman led not to safety but to destruction on the rocks. The Northman had been telling the truth; he had been lost. The commanding officer has been left bitter and despairing of never knowing the real truth.

Themes and Meanings

As in so many of Joseph Conrad's works, meaning is at once contained in and amplified by the setting. In "The Tale," the setting of the sea in fog takes on metaphorical and symbolic significance. The crux of the story is the commanding officer's attempt and ultimate failure to find certitude. Has the Northman violated his neutrality by supplying the enemy? The commanding officer is unable to verify his suspicions. The Northman seems to be telling the truth—he is, indeed, at sea, unable to find his way out of the fog. The commanding officer is also fog-bound, unable to see, to distinguish truth from falsity. A philosophical dilemma faces the commanding officer, a dilemma pertinent to all humankind: How can one know the truth in a world in which the truth is obscured by the fog of human fallibility?

The commanding officer is at war not only with the enemy submarine or the mysterious cargo ship but also with himself, with his frailty as a creature fog-bound by intellectual limitations. Although in command of his ship, he is full of doubts and prejudices, capable even of mean-spiritedness. When he sends the Northman to destruction on the rocks, he is guilty of a cleverness verging on the diabolic. The truth as he learns it is that the Northman really was lost, but the commanding officer realizes that he will never know whether he committed murder or exacted justice.

The commanding officer discovers that his actions and motives are shrouded in fog, that the controlling agency of his endeavors is ignorance. Such fog, such ignorance, pervades not just the sea but the room in which he tells the tale. The twilight setting makes his companion only a disembodied voice. He cannot see her clearly but can only respond to her questions. The relationship thus implicit between them is as uncertain as the darkening room. When the commanding officer turns away from her at the conclusion of his tale, he signifies his despair. The enormous lie that he perceived as part of the faithlessness of war has now become for him part of the faithlessness of human conduct, even in acts of compassion and love.

Style and Technique

Conrad's technique of the frame narrative is integral to the story's meaning. The central story of the commanding officer is told as part of a larger narrative, the frame, involving the narrator of the tale and the woman who asks him to tell it. Such a device, awkward as it may be in lesser works, is at least as old as Giovanni Boccaccio's *Decameron: O, Prencipe Galetto* (1349-1351; *The Decameron*, 1620) or Geoffrey Chaucer's *The Canterbury Tales* (1386-1400), works in which short tales appeared as independent narratives supporting an overall plan. In "The Tale," the device is used not only to create suspense, but also to reinforce the theme of uncertainty and confusion. By connecting the wartime experience of the narrator with the personal relationship implied between him and the woman listener, the device emphasizes the narrator's inability to trust or to love.

The narrator's revelation of guilt and uncertainty at the end of his story connects with the end of the frame narrative when the woman compassionately seeks to comfort him. The narrator cannot accept her comfort. He merely turns away, suggesting that he has carried his doubt into his personal life, shutting him off from her tenderness and, perhaps, her love.

Within the narrator's tale, the Northman relates his own story. Brief as it is, the account provides still a deeper obscurity to the narrator's attempt to see the light. Credible as the Northman's tale appears, its presence within the narrator's tale to the woman merely emphasizes confusion. "The Tale" is thus constructed like a nest of Chinese boxes: a tale within a tale within a tale, obscurity within an enigma within a puzzle.

Finally, the sentence structure reinforces the theme of uncertainty and forms a kind of rhetorical subtext to the settings of fog and twilight. The commanding officer speaks deliberately, haltingly; his opening narrative to the woman is awkward, filled with pauses, punctuated with unfinished declarations and cryptic remarks. In turn, the woman's own dialogue comprises a series of questions, probings into the narrator's halting observations. Even when the tale has advanced, the narrator is still speculative, his remarks circling around the puzzle, seeking certainty. Both style and technique, then, are not merely reflections of Conrad's Victorian manner of storytelling, but are directly integrated with the theme and meaning of the tale itself.

Edward Fiorelli

TALL TALES FROM THE MEKONG DELTA

Author: Kate Braverman (1950-)
Type of plot: Psychological
Time of plot: The late 1980's
Locale: West Hollywood, California
First published: 1990

> *Principal characters:*
> THE UNNAMED NARRATOR, a recovering alcoholic divorced
> woman who teaches creative writing
> LENNY, a Vietnam veteran, former drug addict, and former
> convict

The Story

The unnamed protagonist is a thirty-eight-year-old California woman who is divorced and raising a young daughter, has been a recovering alcoholic for five months, and is currently seeing an analyst. As she walks across a parking lot in West Hollywood one day on her way to an Alcoholics Anonymous meeting, she is accosted by a short, fat, pale man with bad teeth who introduces himself as Lenny. He invites her for coffee, inquires about her life, and tells her that he will show her the other side and give her the ride of her life. She turns him down.

The next day, Lenny is at the narrator's noon Alcoholics Anonymous meeting and has brought the narrator a bouquet of roses. Again he invites her out, and again she refuses, but Lenny persists. After watching her for two weeks, he knows every move that she makes. Lenny calls it "recon," the kind of reconnaissance he used to do in Vietnam, and promises to tell her some tall tales from the Mekong Delta. She again cuts him off, but later, sitting in her car, she notices the sky in a different way. It is China blue, and Lenny's talk of Asia has given her exotic fantasies of emperors and concubines.

At her meeting the following day, she finds herself looking for Lenny. Sure enough, he is there, holding two cups of coffee as though awaiting her arrival, and he seems younger and tanner than she remembers. Walking out later, she looks at her watch, but Lenny admonishes her, and makes her take it off and give it to him. Time is not important, he says; besides, he will give her something better, a Rolex. He claims to have a drawerful of them, along with a bundle of cash in a safe-deposit box. He offers to take her for a ride around the block on his motorcycle and extends his hand. She takes it and fantasizes once again about blue Asian skies and China seas.

Over the next week, the narrator tries to avoid Lenny. She changes the times and locations of her meetings, but she trembles when she thinks of him and is irresistibly drawn back to the earlier meeting place. She finds him sitting on the front steps of the community center as though he were expecting her. She begins to cry. Lenny consoles her, offers to buy her dinner, and tells her not to worry about the way he looks. He is in disguise, on the run from Colombian drug dealers, and he shows her a knife he has hidden in his sock. He has another under his shirt and is carrying guns. The narrator feels dizzy, lost, but Lenny reassures her: He is in her dreams; he is her ticket to the other side, and she can never get away from him. She lives in a dreamlike state, another time almost, because she no longer has a watch.

Days later, when Lenny says he wants to have sex with her, she finds herself helpless, although rationally she knows better. He needs to get an AIDS test, he is a drug addict, he is pathological, and he has spent time in prison. Lenny reassures her by telling her that if she contracts a disease, he will see that she never suffers. He will take her to Bangkok, keep her loaded up with dope, and will kill her with his own hands before she suffers too much. With Lenny, she is like a child, frozen in time as though under a spell, and she allows him to take her to a place in Bel Air vacated by one of his acquaintances. On the way there, Lenny tells her about his experiences as a drug runner, flying planes from Arizona to Colombia. In fact, that is how he got into trouble with the Colombians.

The narrator now fantasizes about living with Lenny in Colombia, dancing barefoot in bars and fanning herself with handfuls of hundred-dollar bills. At the Bel Air mansion, she and Lenny swim naked in the pool and make love in the bedroom, her body draped with expensive diamonds.

The narrator does not see Lenny for a while, but on Christmas Eve he shows up on her doorstep in blue jeans and a black leather jacket, riding a motorcycle. The Colombians are after him, and he is on his way out of town. He needs a drink; despite the fact that the narrator is in Alcoholics Anonymous, she agrees to have one with him. He wants her to come with him, but she refuses. She has a daughter to think about. Nervous and anxious to leave, Lenny heads for the door, tells her it was some ride and that he gave her a glimpse of the other side, and roars off into the darkness. She takes another sip of vodka and knows that when the bottle is empty, she will buy another and another. The air seems a pool of blue shadows, an enormity that will enter her, finding out where she lives and never letting her forget.

Themes and Meanings

"Tall Tales from the Mekong Delta" concerns a woman whose inner emptiness makes her vulnerable to a crude and dangerous man who taps into her deepest fantasies. She is a bored, upper-middle-class Beverly Hills woman who, at the age of thirty-eight, has fallen prey to the conventional twentieth century modes of self-destruction—divorce, alcoholism, and drugs—and is trying to patch things back together through Alcoholics Anonymous and psychotherapy. She is, however, a woman of intelligence and rich imagination; she teaches creative writing and is a writer herself. It is precisely this inner life that makes her vulnerable.

Lenny, for all of his vulgarity and physical unattractiveness, comes from another side of life about which the woman has only fantasized. He is the rebel, the outlaw, who offers her a glimpse of the forbidden, the dangerous, and the deadly. He knows exotic places such as Vietnam, Colombia, and Thailand; has experienced war and adventure; has been in prison and smuggled drugs; and has access to luxurious homes, cars, and diamonds. He even wears black leather jackets and rides a motorcycle, conjuring up images of an aging James Dean, Marlon Brando, or Elvis Presley. When Lenny is with her, the narrator envisions blue skies with sunsets of absinthe yellow and burnt orange, warlords and concubines, and villages on the China Sea. He is an exotic passport into a world about which she has only dreamed—a Mekong Delta of possibilities that fill the emptiness of her life.

Lenny proves to be no better than the alcohol that once removed her from the painful reality of her life, however, and after she has a farewell drink with him, there is every indication that she will return once again to the bottle for her fantasies. The color blue, used throughout the story, has become an infected blue at the end, a kind of contagion that fills up the protagonist. Her dreams of a richer, fuller life depart with Lenny, and the emptiness within her is still there. He has become just a tall tale to tell her friends, like his own tall tales of the Mekong Delta, and although she may have gotten a glimpse of the other side, she knows she will never reach it. The China blue sky of possibility will always be inside her, never letting her forget.

Style and Technique

Kate Braverman wrote "Tall Tales from the Mekong Delta" as a series of dramatized encounters between the protagonist and Lenny, each involving them more deeply in their relationship with each other. After the initial meeting in the parking lot, there are encounters in the meeting room of the community center, in the basement of a church, in a public park, and in a Bel Air mansion. The more open settings—the park, the mansion's swimming pool—are appropriate for the fantasies of the protagonist, who envisions skies, rivers, sunsets, and flowers. The dramatic encounters also point up the differences between the woman and Lenny. Lenny's speech is crude, profane, bullying, and selfish; the protagonist's is direct, defensive, apologetic, and spare. The most poetic passages are the protagonist's fantasies, gracefully written passages that are full of color and beauty, a stark contrast to her simple speech.

Braverman places the final scene on Christmas Eve. Although there are other religious references in the story, such as an AA meeting that takes place in the basement of a church, the final encounter between the protagonist and Lenny suggests the Christian virtues that are lacking between them: love, charity, and selflessness. Lenny's departure takes place on an evening of tall tales about Santa Claus and flying reindeer, an appropriate setting for his final appearance in the woman's life and for the tall tales he leaves behind.

Kenneth Seib

TALPA

Author: Juan Rulfo (1918-1986)
Type of plot: Philosophical realism
Time of plot: 1926-1929, during the Cristero uprisings
Locale: Western Mexico
First published: 1953 (English translation, 1967)

> *Principal characters:*
> TANILO SANTOS, a Mexican man who goes on a pilgrimage to
>   seek a cure for his life-threatening disease
> NATALIA SANTOS, his wife, who accompanies her husband
> HIS BROTHER, the narrator, who accompanies his brother
> HIS MOTHER-IN-LAW

The Story

"Talpa" is one of Juan Rulfo's best-known short stories. The story is related by the unnamed narrator, Tanilo's brother, who accompanies Tanilo Santos and his wife, Natalia, on their pilgrimage to Talpa, where they hope Tanilo's illness can be cured at the shrine of the Virgin Mary. The story begins after Tanilo has died and the travelers have returned to Zenzontla, with Natalia seeking solace from her mother. The reader believes that the narrator will be an objective observer of the events until he reveals in the second paragraph that he helped Natalia bury Tanilo and in the fifth paragraph that he and Natalia are responsible for Tanilo's death. The rest of the short story is a series of flashbacks in which the narrator describes the events leading to Tanilo's death.

According to the narrator, the idea of going to Talpa comes from Tanilo, but he and Natalia agree to accompany the sick man there out of a sense of duty. The narrator knows that Natalia has not been sleeping with her husband since he became ill. The inevitable happens, and during the journey to Talpa, Natalia and the narrator leave Tanilo on the side of the road and go off into the fields to consummate their passion. However, when they get to Talpa, the story takes a sinister turn.

The three of them left their hometown, Zenzontla, in mid-February, and twenty days later, in early March, they reach the outskirts of Talpa, where they join up with a number of other pilgrims who are also making their way along the main street of Talpa toward the Virgin Mary shrine. At this point, Tanilo suddenly gets very ill and asks to turn back, but because they want to get rid of him, the narrator and Natalia ruthlessly force him to keep walking. The pilgrims are singing the Gloria while walking along the main street, and just before they enter the shrine, they begin a dance, in which Tanilo, though very sick, participates. All the pilgrims then enter the church and take part in the ceremony, but immediately afterward, Tanilo is found dead.

Natalia and the narrator subsequently take Tanilo's body to a nearby field, and they bury him deeply enough so the animals will not get him. On the way back to Zenzontla, Natalia is suddenly overcome with a terrible sense of guilt at what she has done, and she will not let the narrator come near her. The story ends where it began. The narrator is trying to come to terms with the crime he has committed, and he is bitter that Natalia will no longer have anything to do with him.

Themes and Meanings

This story expresses in realistic images the philosophical notion of being cut off from God. Juan Rulfo lived through a period of great social unrest in Mexico. When Plutarco Elías Calles came to power as president of Mexico in 1925, he continued the social reforms of his predecessor, General Alvaro Obregón, distributing land to the landless and restoring communal holdings to villages, but he also, more controversially, initiated some vigorously anticlerical measures. He challenged the Roman Catholic Church's control over the national educational system and reclaimed vast tracts of land from the church for his land reform program. In retaliation, the church closed all the churches in Mexico and whipped up support for the Cristeros Rebellion. The common people began an armed struggle against the government's anticlerical policies that lasted from 1926 until 1929, and Rulfo, as an impressionable young boy, witnessed the horrors of the war, especially as it lay waste to the rural areas of Jalisco in western Mexico. Some of the despair of this period filtered into his literary work. The collection of short stories from which "Talpa" is taken, *The Burning Plain, and Other Stories* (1967), indeed, depicts violence in the countryside of Jalisco as well as the moral stagnation of the people who live there. Though not overtly evoked in these stories, the Cristero Rebellion acts as a backdrop, underpinning a world that has been cut off from God.

The world portrayed in "Talpa" is weighed down by the heaviness of sin without any hope of forgiveness. It is no coincidence that the journey that Tanilo, Natalia, and the narrator make takes place between mid-February and mid-March, at about the time of Lent in the Christian calendar. The physical and mental pain that Tanilo experiences when trying to walk to the shrine in Talpa, as well as the wounds on his skin, suggests that Rulfo is deliberately drawing a parallel between Tanilo and Christ's Passion. In Rulfo's novelistic world, however, there are the tribulations of Lent but not the resurrection. At the climactic point of the story, Tanilo simply dies and is unceremoniously laid to earth.

Style and Technique

Rulfo underlines the philosophical significance of this story by using proper names to indicate symbolic significance. It is ironic that Tanilo's last name is Santos, for he and his wife are anything but saints. Talpa is a fictional place-name and was chosen to emphasize the spiritual blindness of the characters in the story as *talpa* is the Latin word for the genus of the mole. The narrator and Natalia are therefore to be understood as comparable to moles because they hide from the sun. This symbolism is further underlined by the description of the pilgrims who accompany them into Talpa, who are described unflatteringly as a mass of writhing worms. Worms, like moles, travel underground, and both images are intended to underline the spiritual blindness of the pilgrims. These metaphors undercut the notion of transcendence normally associated with the idea of a spiritual pilgrimage.

Zenzontla is also a fictional place-name, but this name is sufficiently similar to *tezontle*, the name of a light and porous volcanic rock common in Mexico, to be understood as a subtle, glancing allusion. This fits in with the symbolism of the story because the earth on which Natalia and the narrator lie when they are committing adultery (which is even more heinous because it is incestuous as well) is hot, Natalia's body is described as "heating up" when she comes near the narrator, and their bodies are described as like a fire. The story is about the ways in which an uncontrollable, volcanic passion erupts and destroys three people's lives—Tanilo's literally, and the narrator's and Natalia's metaphorically, because they are both lonely and guilt-ridden by the conclusion of the story.

The style used in Rulfo's story is one of deliberate understatement characterized by flat descriptions. The scene in which Natalia and the narrator bury Tanilo's body is a prime example. Natalia and the narrator are portrayed as simply digging a hole with their bare hands to a sufficient depth to prevent animals from getting to the body. It is difficult to imagine a more sparse description. Nothing is embellished, and there are no descriptive adjectives. Another hallmark of Rulfo's style is that, in spite of the horror of the events depicted, the reader does not get a sense of what is going on inside the characters' heads. The reader does not hear their anguished thoughts; rather their anguish is simply expressed in physical terms as air "smelling of death" or the heart feeling "squeezed." The reader also learns that Natalia and the narrator are carrying an "enormous weight" on their shoulders. Psychological pain is typically expressed in physical terms. These two techniques—flat, unadorned descriptions and the translation of psychological emotions into physical metaphors—are the hallmarks of Rulfo's literary style.

Stephen M. Hart

TATUANA'S TALE

Author: Miguel Ángel Asturias (1899-1974)
Type of plot: Surrealist
Time of plot: Probably the Spanish colonial period
Locale: Probably Guatemala
First published: "Leyenda de la Tatuana," 1930 (English translation, 1945)

> *Principal characters:*
> MASTER ALMONDTREE, a priest who can assume both human and
>   tree form
> BLACK ROAD, who is granted part of the priest's soul
> THE MERCHANT OF PRICELESS JEWELS, who gains the priest's
>   soul from Black Road
> TATUANA, a beautiful slave whom the merchant purchases with
>   the priest's soul

The Story

This delightful legend, retold by Miguel Ángel Asturias, introduces the reader to the imagination of the Guatemalan Indian, an imagination that still reflects the worldview of the old Maya. It is a worldview that seems at first totally strange, but its dissolving categories of time, place, and being are familiar to the modern Western mind in dreams, fairy tales, and surrealism.

Master Almondtree, the protagonist, can take either human or tree form. As a priest, he is so brilliantly arrayed that "the white men" think that he is "made of gold." Well-versed in curative herbs, he can also understand the messages of obsidian and the stars. He is old, with "a frosty beard," and as a tree, "the tree that walks," he mysteriously appeared in the forest already mature.

During the full Owl-Fisherman moon, Master Almondtree decides (no reason is given) to apportion his soul out to the four roads. Each road has a color and name: "the black one, sorcerer night; the green, spring torment; the red, Guaycamayo or tropical ecstasy; white, promise of new lands." The last three roads go off and meet something with a corresponding color—a white dove, a red heart, and a green vine—which tries to get their portions of the Master's soul from them, but the three roads refuse to listen and keep going. Not so careful is the Black Road, "speediest of all," which goes into town to the marketplace. There the Black Road meets the Merchant of Priceless Jewels and swaps him the Master's soul "for a little rest."

When the Master hears, he assumes human shape and heads for the city. In the marketplace he finds the Merchant of Priceless Jewels, who has the portion of his soul locked away in a box. The Master tries to buy it back, making numerous offers—"a hundred arrobas of pearls . . . a lake of emeralds . . . amulets, deers' eyes to bring water, feathers against storms, marihuana for his tobacco"—but the Merchant will not sell. Instead, the Merchant intends to use the Master's soul to purchase a beautiful slave girl. The Master departs, leaving behind his curse.

A year later, the Merchant and thirty of his servants are traveling on horseback along the mountain highways, returning home with the purchased slave girl. She is naked except for long black hair sweeping to her feet, while the gold-clad Merchant sports "a mantle of goat's hair" on his shoulders. After telling her that she is worth her great price, the Merchant describes the life of ease they will enjoy together and the old woman who will tell their fortunes: "My destiny, she says, is the fingers of a gigantic hand." Not replying, the slave girl stares at the horizon. Then, out of the peaceful sky, a fierce storm breaks on them. The horses spook, and the Merchant's horse falls, dumping him at the base of a tree hit just then by lightning: "It seized him by its roots as a hand picks up a stone and flung him into the abyss."

Back in the city, the Master has been roaming the streets during this time like a crazed man, speaking to animals, knocking on doors, and frightening people, who are "amazed at his green tunic and frosty beard as if confronted by an apparition." As the full Owl-Fisherman moon comes around again, he knocks on the Merchant's door. The beautiful slave, the only survivor of the terrible storm, answers. He twice asks her the question he has been asking everyone else: "For how many moons did the roads go traveling?" She does not reply; instead, they stand gazing deep into each other's eyes.

They are interrupted by rude sounds, followed by the authorities, who arrest them "in the name of God and the King." He is charged with "sorcery," she with "being possessed by a demon." After seven months in prison, they are sentenced to death by burning. The night before their scheduled execution, the Master comes to the beautiful slave girl, Tatuana, and uses his fingernails to tattoo the figure of a boat on her arm. He tells her to trace the same figure on the ground or in the air, step into it, and escape any danger. She will become as "free" and "invisible" as his thoughts. Following his instructions, Tatuana escapes. The next morning when the guards enter the prison, all they find is "a dry tree . . . on whose branches were two or three still frosty almond flowers."

Themes and Meanings

Characters who take different forms or become invisible appear in legends throughout the world. Legends summon up the prescientific mind, such as the European mind before Aristotelian logic decreed that one thing cannot be something else or in two places at the same time. In "Tatuana's Tale," the reader is back in a world similar to the ancient Greek poet Homer's.

There is, however, an important difference. In European and Semitic legend, the legends themselves are a means of asserting humankind's control over nature, of bringing order out of chaos. Humankind imposes its personality on nature, viewing it anthropomorphically and slaying its monsters. In "Tatuana's Tale," the process works the other way. Humankind is not separate from nature but continuous with it, part of it. Instead of fighting nature, humankind joins it, reading its messages and learning its secrets. This view of nature, which undergirded Mayan worship of the corn god and possibly the later practice of human sacrifice, is embodied here in the old priest. He changes into human or tree form at will, and even in human form, wearing his "green tunic," he seems like "an apparition." Perhaps he distributes his soul to the four roads because, growing old, he desires to merge back into nature entirely, which seems to be all that death amounts to (at the end, the "dry tree" has apparently died).

In European and Semitic thinking, merging back into nature has never meant a consummation but rather a loss of personality and control, a return to night and chaos, home of John Milton's Satan. The Christian view is indicated by the ending of "Tatuana's Tale," where the Master and Tatuana are arrested "in the name of God and the King" for "sorcery" and "being possessed by a demon." This ending is like a coda to the legend, as though added at a later stage to deal with the colonial experience. It articulates a theory of liberation: People who can merge back into nature cannot be controlled. Trying to own or control them is like trying to own or control nature. The Merchant's fate should be adequate warning.

Style and Technique

The style of "Tatuana's Tale" shows the influence not only of a native surrealism, the tradition of *arte fantastico* stretching back to pre-Columbian times, but also of a superimposed European surrealism that Asturias picked up in Paris. The European surrealism is most apparent in several poetic descriptions, such as the following: "It was the hour of the white cats. They were walking back and forth. The rosebushes were amazed." Sheep return home "conversing with their shepherds," and "a thread of tobacco smoke separated reality from the dream, black cats from white cats." These descriptive touches hold up the action, but they also contribute to the story's strangeness and to its sense of continuity within nature.

Also strange are the legend's many references to numbers: the four roads, "the twenty months in the four-hundred-day year," the seven months in prison, and so forth. These references give the legend a ritualistic aspect, but their specific meanings are part of the mystery of the Maya, who were geniuses with numbers. The Maya's calendars and astronomical calculations indicate that they were obsessed with time, whose circular quality in nature might be suggested by the Master's reunion with his fragment of soul (Tatuana) precisely on the Owl-Fisherman full moon.

Harold Branam

TEARS, IDLE TEARS

Author: Elizabeth Bowen (1899-1973)
Type of plot: Coming of age
Time of plot: The 1930's
Locale: London
First published: 1937

Principal characters:
> MRS. DICKINSON, a widowed mother who tries always to do the right thing
> FREDERICK, her seven-year-old son, who cries constantly
> A YOUNG WOMAN, who befriends Frederick

The Story

Seven-year-old Frederick bursts into tears in the middle of Regent's Park on a beautiful, sunny May afternoon as he and his mother are on their way to the zoo. His elegantly dressed mother is mortified at his crying, yet it is her reproach that draws the attention of the passing people to the scene. She has been so troubled by her son's frequent crying that she is unable to speak about it with any of her friends or relatives. Once she had started to write to a mother's advice column for assistance but never sent the letter because she could not think of the correct way to sign it.

Frederick cries often and long. He never knows why or what happens to make him cry. He just cries. Nothing matters to him when the tears take over; this day in the park his mother refuses to take him to the zoo, but he does not care. His lack of self-respect makes others look at him and respond in unkind ways; he gets no sympathy. His mother tells him at least once a week that she does not know how he will fit in at school because of his crying. Mrs. Dickinson hates the fact that when she takes a privilege away from him for crying, he seems not to care. She seldom openly punishes him, but she rebukes and belittles him almost constantly. When he seems to feel no emotion about not going to the zoo, she tells him she wonders what his father would think of him. She goes on to say that his father, a pilot who had died after an airplane crash, used to be so proud of him that she is almost glad that he is no longer with them. After this strong reprimand, Mrs. Dickinson walks on ahead so as not to be embarrassed. She tells Frederick to pull himself together before he catches up to her.

Frederick stays behind, knowing that his mother is really ashamed of him. He makes little noise as he sits composing himself and watching a duck. Mrs. Dickinson keeps walking, and as the distance extends, so do her emotions. She had been a pillar of strength when her husband died five years ago. While she sat by his bed for two days waiting for him to die, she never shed a tear. After his death, she remained unnaturally composed, only crying once when she went to see her baby, Frederick. At the age of two, Frederick lay awake while his mother's tears had put her to sleep. The look in Frederick's eyes caused the servant to comment that it seemed as if he knew what had happened. Since then, however, Mrs. Dickinson has stood straight and tall, accepted no pity, and needed no support. Her response to men who wanted to marry her was always that Frederick was now the man in her life, and she had to put him first.

Once Frederick stopped crying, he knew he could go after his mother, but he did not want to. Instead, he climbed over the rail to go down and pat the duck. As he reaches out and the duck swims away, he hears a voice warning him about being over the rail and on the grass. He looks and sees a young woman sitting on the park bench, and he thinks that she does not really look or act like a woman. He is intrigued. She gives him an apple and asks about his crying. She has been sitting on the bench during the whole crying fit and wants to know what makes him cry. Something in her tone and her remarks comfort Frederick and make him talk with her: She is not demeaning to him; she really wants to understand. She tells him a story about a boy named George who used to live in a place where she worked. He was a boy, older than Frederick, who also cried out of control. She says he cried as if he knew about something that he should not know. She tells Frederick that he should stop crying so that he does not become like George. Frederick's mother comes into view, and the young woman tells him to go to her before there is more trouble. They shake hands and part.

Mrs. Dickinson is coming down the walk, being careful not to look or seem anxious because Frederick has been gone so long. Appearance is everything to Mrs. Dickinson; she remains calm and unflustered at any cost. As she waits for Frederick to come, the young woman stays on the bench and thinks about George and Frederick; their eyes "seemed to her to be wounds, in the world's surface, through which its inner, terrible unassuageable, necessary sorrow constantly bled away and as constantly welled up." As the young woman is thinking about her meeting with Frederick, he is running toward his mother shouting that he has nearly caught a duck.

Although years later Frederick still recalls with pleasure the afternoon that he spent trying to catch the duck, he has never again thought about the young woman or George.

Themes and Meanings

"Tears, Idle Tears" is about innocence versus experience; it is a coming-of-age story about a young boy's feelings being ignored by one member of the adult world and being restored by a stranger. Frederick is made to feel so bad about disgracing his mother when he cries that he withdraws within himself and becomes apathetic, but he overcomes the disgrace of crying when a young woman on a park bench is friendly to him. The years of being badgered have started to affect Frederick. He never knows why he cries, it just happens. He is a sad little boy.

Mrs. Dickinson must have everything in her life appear to be proper. She dresses and behaves in an elegant manner; she also dresses Frederick elegantly and expects him to behave accordingly. The expectations she places on Frederick are too cumbersome for him to carry. He has become the man in her life; therefore, she expects him to act like a man. She cannot understand where the tears come from when he cries, nor does she want to understand. Frederick behaves like a child because he is seven years old. Mrs. Dickinson shut down her emotions five years ago and now performs rather than lives life. She is incapable of feeling; she acts rather than reacts.

Tears are viewed as a bad thing. When Mrs. Dickinson's husband lay dying, the chaplain and the doctor gave thanks that Mrs. Dickinson was so brave. In the five years since her husband's death, Mrs. Dickinson has alienated women but attracted men. Elizabeth Bowen is showing a social difference between men and women by their reactions to the crying.

The title comes from Alfred, Lord Tennyson's poem "Tears, Idle Tears":

> Tears, idle tears, I know not what they mean,
> Tears from the depth of some divine despair
> Rise in the heart, and gather to the eyes,
> In looking on the happy autumn-fields,
> And thinking of the days that are no more.

Frederick's idle tears are not understood by most of the adult world.

Style and Technique

Bowen is known as an exceptionally descriptive and detailed writer. Landscapes and colors are very important to her stories. Frederick cries in the middle of Regent's Park where "Poplars stood up like delicate green brooms; diaphanous willows whose weeping was not shocking quivered over the lake. May sun spattered gold through the breezy trees; the tulips though falling open were still gay; three girls in a long boat shot under the bridge." At once, the reader is in the park with Frederick and his mother. Bowen's description of her characters manages to present their attitude as well as their appearance. Mrs. Dickinson is "a gallant-looking, correct woman, wearing today in London a coat and skirt, a silver fox, white gloves and a dark-blue toque put on exactly right." Frederick's "crying made him so abject, so outcast from other people that he went on crying out of despair. His crying was not just reflex, like a baby's; it dragged up all unseemliness into view. No wonder everyone was repelled." The young woman in the park has a smile and a cock of the head that was "pungent and energetic, not like a girl's at all."

This detail and description help make it possible for Bowen to weave the difficulty of love throughout her story. The boy's hysteria and the mother's coldness can be explained by the fact that the boy's father died five years earlier. Because Bowen has realistically presented the past and present experiences of her characters, the reader can see how previous wounds have scarred them and made them who they are today.

Rosanne Fraine Donahue

TEENAGE WASTELAND

Author: Anne Tyler (1941-   )
Type of plot: Psychological
Time of plot: The early 1970's
Locale: An unnamed city
First published: 1984

> *Principal characters:*
> DONNY COBLE, a troubled fifteen-year-old boy
> DAISY and
> MATT COBLE, his parents
> CALVIN BEADLE, his tutor

The Story

When Daisy Coble receives a telephone call from the principal of her son Donny's private school, the boy's problems do not seem serious. He is described as "noisy, lazy, disruptive, always fooling around with his friends." At a conference with the school's principal, Daisy is ashamed to be regarded as a delinquent, unseeing, or uncaring parent. She describes the restrictions that she and her husband have placed on Donny: no television on school nights, limited telephone calls, and so on. Following the conference, Daisy conscientiously follows the principal's suggestion that she personally supervise Donny's homework and is discouraged by the weaknesses she finds in Donny's work.

In December, the school reports that Donny shows slight progress, as well as new problems: cutting class, smoking in the furnace room, leaving the school grounds, and returning with beer on his breath. Psychological testing is undertaken and a tutor recommended. "Cal" Beadle, the tutor—whom Donny resists at first—quickly establishes himself as being on the boy's side: against the school, which he calls punitive, and the parents, whom Donny calls controlling and competitive—words that he has obviously picked up from Cal.

Donny apparently enjoys his sessions with Cal, who encourages his students to hang around by listening to records and shooting baskets at the backboard on his garage. Donny's grades do not improve, but the school notes that his attitude is more cooperative. This proves to be an illusion, however, as in April Donny is expelled after beer and cigarettes are found in his locker.

Instead of coming home after his expulsion, Donny goes to his tutor's house, where Daisy finds him looking upset and angry. When Donny refuses to accept any blame for the incident, Daisy recalls the bold-faced, wide-eyed look on his face when, as a small boy, he denied little mischiefs, despite all the evidence pointing to his guilt.

Donny proposes that he apply to another school, an idea about which Cal is enthusiastic, saying that he works with many students at the other school. Cal adds that this other school knows "where a kid is coming from." Daisy does not like the sound of the school and is troubled by Cal's smile, which strikes her as "feverish and avid—a smile of hunger."

Shortly after this conference, Donny's parents enroll him in a public school and terminate his tutoring sessions. Although both decisions are against Donny's wishes, he plods off to his new school each morning, without friends, looking worn out and beaten.

In June, Donny disappears. The police try to find him, but their remarks about the hundreds of young people who run away every year are not reassuring. Three months pass without word from Donny. Both his parents have aged, and his younger sister tries to stay away from home as much as she can. Daisy lies awake at night going over Donny's life, trying to understand their mistakes and wondering whom to blame.

The story ends as Daisy, falling asleep, glimpses a basketball sinking through the hoop, onto a yard littered with leaves and striped "with bands of sunlight as white as bones, bleached and parched and cleanly picked."

Themes and Meanings

Anne Tyler's focus in this story is the gradual disintegration of the relationship between a teenage boy and his parents. The title of the story, taken from the lyrics of "Baba O'Riley," a song popularized by The Who in the early 1970's, clearly suggests Tyler's theme, although in an oblique way. "Teenage Wasteland" is a metaphor for the place where Donny's parents see him when they pick him up at Cal's: Students there are idly shooting baskets; loud music pours out through the windows; and Donny, "spiky and excited," looks like someone they do not know. To Daisy and Matt, all the students look like hoodlums. When Daisy murmurs, "Teenage Wasteland," recognizing the song, Matt, misunderstanding, replies, "It certainly is." Thus in only a few lines, Tyler encapsulates the enormous distance between them and the youngsters playing in Cal's backyard. The distance increases as Donny moves further from them, until communication between them nearly ceases. When Donny is expelled, the fact that he heads for Cal's house instead of home signifies both his preference for his tutor and his inability to make his mother accept his lame explanation of the incident that precipitated the expulsion.

The image with which Tyler closes the story is subtle and moving. Lying awake at night, Daisy tries to understand what has happened and has a vision of Cal's yard, where a neighbor's fence casts narrow shadow bars across the spring grass. As she drifts off to sleep, she recalls that scene, the stripes of sunlight "as white as bones, bleached and parched and cleanly picked." It is a fearful image, one that Tyler does not explain, leaving it to the reader to interpret as an expression of Daisy's defeat and despair.

Style and Technique

The narrative viewpoint of "Teenage Wasteland" is that of Donny Coble's mother, Daisy. The entire story is told in the third person as an omniscient author might tell it, but one who knows only the thoughts and feelings of Daisy. All events are presented as Daisy experiences or observes them, and the dialogue always includes her.

Daisy is not given to introspection and emotionalism, as one may expect, considering the disappearance of her son, with whom she cannot communicate. The boy wants to be trusted and treated as an adult, even as he behaves in childish and self-indulgent ways. These are judgments that the author's style leads the reader to make; Tyler herself does not judge. Her style is unemotional, detached, and objective. Her characteristic use of brief, telling descriptions and natural, credible dialogue keeps the pace of the story swift; there is not an unnecessary word. For example, when Daisy catches up with Donny at his tutor's home after his expulsion, she merely says, "Hello, Donny." It is a simple greeting that conveys her inability to express her deep feeling of relief, her uncertainty about how to approach her son, who replies by simply flicking his eyes at her.

In addition to concise, sketchy narration, and dialogue that seems exactly suited to the speakers' personalities, Tyler uses images to convey tone and mood. The brief scene in Cal's backyard, for example, is made visible and meaningful through the image of a fence casting shadows across the grass in narrow bars. The suggestion of a prison is not made, but the connection is undeniable. The scene is echoed in the closing sentence of the story as Daisy sighs and tosses sleeplessly, unable to come to a clear understanding of what has happened.

It is possible to read this story in terms of superficial facts. However, the reader who searches for what those facts suggest beneath the surface of brief conversations and simple, straightforward narration in which every word is essential, will be rewarded. As usual, Tyler transforms ordinary people in familiar situations into a moving tale that can appeal to readers who recognize themselves or someone they know.

Natalie Harper

TELL ME A RIDDLE

Author: Tillie Olsen (1913-   )
Type of plot: Realism
Time of plot: The 1950's
Locale: America
First published: 1961

> *Principal characters:*
> EVA, the protagonist, an elderly woman dying of cancer
> DAVID, her husband
> NANCY,
> HANNAH,
> VIVI,
> CLARA,
> LENNIE,
> PAUL, and
> SAMMY, their children
> JEANNIE, the one grandchild who understands

The Story

"Tell Me a Riddle" is the story of an elderly immigrant couple who, after forty-seven years of marriage, disagree bitterly over how to live out their retirement. The wife looks forward to having her house to herself now that the children are all gone, "of being able at last to live within, and not move to the rhythms of others." The husband wants to sell the house and join his lodge's cooperative for the aged, where he hopes to find a "happy, communal life." As the bickering continues and threatens to "split the earth between them" now that they are no longer "shackled" together by the needs of the family, the children enter the dispute, siding with their father, whose jokes and sociability seem to be more reasonable than their mother's moodiness and introspection.

One night the wife, Eva, feeling strangely sick, asks her husband, David, to stay home with her. He has been planning to stay home anyway, watching television, but when she makes this request, he leaves, just to spite her. When he returns, she is asleep on the sun porch; this is the beginning of a week sleeping in separate beds, apparently for the first time in their married life. In the middle of Eva's last night on the porch, David awakes to her singing a Russian love song from their youth. "I can breathe now," Eva announces and finally returns to their bedroom. This passage marks an important turning point in the story. Though David proceeds to find a buyer for the house, the family soon discovers that Eva's body is riddled with cancer and that she has at best a year to live.

During the rest of the story, David rushes Eva around the country to visit each child in succession while she begs to return home. Though he worries about the money going quickly and fears his own weakness in coping with her disease, he does his best to hide her impending death from her, to cater to what he perceives to be her final needs.

At each stage of this journey, the reader learns more about Eva's past and the sources of the gap that separates her from her children. With Hannah, it is religion; Eva associates her daughter's Judaism with the superstition and backwardness of prerevolutionary Russia, a world she fought to destroy. David is more accepting of Hannah's perspective as she defends the need for tradition and the pleasure of ritual.

With Vivi, it is nurturance. Eva refuses to hold Vivi's new baby; she helps with ironing, with cleaning, "but to none tended or gave food." She had given everything to her own children, "had borne them to their own lives" and now fears a distraction that will draw her out of her self once again. Vivi responds to this unnatural behavior by "remembering out loud deliberately, so her mother would know the past was cherished" and that she appreciates the sacrifices Eva made despite her present strangeness. Instead of responding to these memories, Eva hides in a closet, where she returns to a more distant past, her own girlhood in Russia and the martyrdom of her beloved friend Lisa, "who killed one who betrayed many."

The final stage of their journey brings Eva and David to Los Angeles, where they move into an apartment set up for them by their granddaughter, Jeannie. Here they spend days at the ocean side where Eva marvels at the sand and stones, evenings visiting relatives and an old friend, Mrs. Mays, who lives in a one-room tenement, her husband dead, her children scattered. Though Tillie Olsen describes Los Angeles as the "dwelling place of the castoff old" like Mrs. Mays, Eva finds peace in the rhythms of the sea and especially in the relationship she develops with her granddaughter Jeannie, who alone understands her needs and can speak openly to her of death. Most important, because of her refusal to report a Mexican family that is preparing a dead child for burial at home according to its own customs but in violation of United States health laws, Jeannie reminds Eva of Lisa.

Eva's last few days of life are filled with memories of the past; bits and pieces of songs and poems associated with the Russian Revolution pour out of her, "a girl's voice of eloquence that spoke their holiest dreams" but said nothing of her adult life in the United States. At first David feels betrayed by these memories that so totally exclude him, but then he realizes that he too once shared the same dreams, the same youthful idealism. He tries desperately to question her, to measure his loss of faith against her continued belief, but it is too late; she is too far gone to respond to him. Overcome by his own despair, David sees a sketch Jeannie has drawn of the two of them, "their hands . . . clasped, feeding each other" as "the tall pillar" feeds her veins:

> And as if he had been instructed he went to his bed, lay down, holding the sketch (as if it could shield against the monstrous shapes of loss, of betrayal, of death) and with his free hand took hers back into his. So Jeannie found them in the morning.

That day, which is her last, Eva's body is wracked by convulsions of agony, and members of her family must hold her down. David, who feels he cannot go on, leaves the room. Jeannie follows him, reassuring him that his wife is "not there," but is now "a little girl on the road of the village where she was born," reveling in the joy and music of a wedding. "Leave her there, Granddaddy. . . . Come back, come back and help her poor body to die."

Themes and Meanings

"Tell Me a Riddle," though it is simple in plot, is complex and rich thematically. It is at once a story about failed dreams, love and marriage, old age in America, the healing power of art, mothers and daughters, and the meaning of freedom. Above all, it is a powerful tale of a caged bird who longs to soar free and who recovers her youthful ability to sing only in dying. The key line is the repeated refrain "Of being able at last to live within," a poignant restatement of Virginia Woolf's famous call for a room of one's own. The story suggests that in loving and nurturing her seven children, Eva necessarily sacrificed her own personal needs. The few moments she found for herself and a book after the children were in bed were often snatched from her as David returned home and would coax her, "Don't read, put your book away." She does not resent those years but now wants time and space for herself, freedom from living for other people.

Ironically, as Eva begins to break out of her cage and sing, the songs she recalls all date from the time when she may have been "free" of family responsibilities but was "imprisoned" by political repression. The story thus plays on the meaning of freedom. For the children it means the rights and liberties of American citizenship, freedom from poverty and anti-Semitism. For David, it also means to be "carefree," to have freedom in particular from constant worries about money. With Eva's death David remembers another freedom, "that joyous certainty, that sense of mattering, of moving and being moved, of being one and indivisible with the great of the past, with all that freed, ennobled," and that his struggle to be "carefree," to live the American Dream, may have had as its price the loss of this more precious freedom.

Style and Technique

"Tell Me a Riddle" received the O. Henry Award as the best American short story of 1961 and continues to receive critical acclaim. By far the most ambitious and powerful of the four stories collected in the book *Tell Me a Riddle* (1961), it might be more appropriately labeled a novella. Its complex themes are supported by an equally rich narrative voice capable of modulating from bitter to funny, from sad to joyful, from serious to ironic. The lyricism of the language itself combined with her ability to involve and move her reader has earned Olsen high marks as a prose stylist.

Olsen deserves equal praise as a dramatist for her creation of character and dialogue. Eva and David, in all their pain and anguish, are brought to life with humor and affection. The authenticity apparently derives from Olsen's own familiarity with the world she describes and her careful rendition of the dialect her characters speak. David and Eva's English is filled with the colorful Yiddish metaphors they have brought to the New World from their native Russia. Whether used as a curse ("like the hide of a drum shall you be beaten in life, beaten in death") or in self-mocking honesty ("Vinegar he poured on me all his life; I am well marinated; how can I be honey now?"), such poetic language marks the distance between the generations. The generic English of the American-born children suffers in comparison and seems to underline the aesthetic poverty with which they have paid for their material affluence.

Olsen sees herself as the spokeswoman for the uneducated, for the working classes, for all those whose creativity has been suppressed by the day-to-day pressures of earning a living and tending to the needs of a family. In her collection of essays *Silences* (1979), she speaks of "the gifted" who have remained mute "because of circumstances, inner or outer, which oppose the needs of creation." Olsen's own work demonstrates how beautifully such voices can sing, once freed.

Jane M. Barstow

TELL ME HOW LONG THE TRAIN'S BEEN GONE

Author: James Baldwin (1924-1987)
Type of plot: Domestic realism, coming of age
Time of plot: The 1930's
Locale: Harlem, New York City
First published: 1968

> *Principal characters:*
> LEO, the narrator, a ten-year-old boy
> CALEB, his seventeen-year-old brother
> MR. PROUDHAMMER, their father
> MRS. PROUDHAMMER, their mother

The Story

   "Tell Me How Long the Train's Been Gone" tells the story of a ten-year-old African American who struggles to make his way in a racist world and encounters various obstacles interfering with his growth and development. His family, the Proudhammers, provide a strong barrier against those obstacles. Leo describes how he and his brother Caleb are the best of friends and how they protect each other. His father, an immigrant from Barbados who has been crushed by life, still retains a strong sense of racial pride and an absolute commitment to his family. He believes that he comes from royalty, a race that was greater and nobler than the citizens of Rome or Judea and mightier than those of Egypt. He tries to instill this sense of background in his children and is frustrated by the fact that no one else recognizes his lineage. Leo recognizes the futility of his father's vision. Already, as a ten-year-old, he recognizes that the most important part of life depends on learning how to fit into a world that shows him no mercy.

   Mrs. Proudhammer is a model of the strong black woman who does what is necessary to provide for her family. Leo tells of a shopping trip during which his mother commands the storeowner to give them the food she requires although she lacks the money to pay for it. She tells the storekeeper to put the charge on her bill. It is evident that Leo takes pride in his mother for her willingness to do what it takes to take care of her family.

   Caleb and Leo get into an argument about washing out the tub in the morning. When Leo claims that Caleb never cleans the tub, Caleb demands that Leo apologize. Their father comes to Leo's defense and states that it is not necessary for Leo to apologize because the allegation is true. A major part of the relationship between the boys is that Caleb is responsible for Leo when they go out together. Caleb takes Leo along with him to the motion picture theater so that Leo can provide "cover" for Caleb when he in fact takes off to go out with his friends. Leo, small, frail, and sensitive, does not like Caleb's friends, whom he views as aggressive and coarse. Leo describes himself as living in fear around those boys.

If Caleb fails to take Leo to the motion pictures, Leo has to hang around the box office and wait for some obliging adult to take him in. However, the worst part is the walk from their apartment to the theater several miles away. Each new neighborhood through which he must walk poses new dangers. He fears the other children, who are bigger and stronger, and white people, particularly police, whom he hates.

Leo describes his subway adventures. Usually, he can ride for free by sneaking under the turnstile. He loves to people-watch. However, on one Saturday evening, he forgets to get off the subway and gets lost. The train takes him far beyond his usual stop, and soon he finds himself surrounded by white people. As his panic rises, he loses any sense of how to find his way back to Harlem. Eventually, he speaks to a black man on the train, who is decent enough to respond to his situation. The man stays with him until he is sure the boy is on the right train to go home. Leo gets home without further incident but is grateful to the stranger for helping him.

Another evening when Caleb takes Leo to the motion picture theater, he leaves him there and goes out with his friends. When Leo leaves the theater, he decides to look for Caleb. Because it is a rainy night, Leo gets drenched. Worse, he is frightened of the night and hides out in the cellar of an abandoned house. Soon he hears the sound of scurrying rats and then the sound of two people making love, which he thinks is some form of violent activity. He panics, then runs out into the rain and straight home to Caleb, who calms the hysterical boy.

One evening, Leo and Caleb are confronted by a white police officer. The officer humiliates both of them by making threats and innuendoes that suggest they are up to some kind of criminal activity. When the boys come home and share the information with their father, he becomes enraged, partly at the indignity to his boys and partly at his helplessness to protect them. The discussion turns to the question of whether any white person is good. The story ends with the issue of justice for the black person unresolved.

Themes and Meanings

The major theme of this story is racism and its affect on the lives of people. The story is first and foremost about the impact of that racism on Leo, a sensitive ten-year-old boy. Leo's description of himself as small, frail, and a sissy in the eyes of Caleb's friends suggests that Leo is a stand-in for the author and that the story may well describe his own situation. If so, then James Baldwin's lifelong struggle for social justice and equality for African Americans can be seen as developing from his emerging consciousness as a boy just like Leo, who already, as a ten-year-old, is fearful of whites and hates white police officers.

As the story develops, ample justification for this hatred is evident in the harassment and humiliation Leo and his brother experience during their encounter with the white police officer. This kind of humiliation is part of what it means to be African American in Harlem and by extension in the entire United States. The humiliation extends to the father, the man descended from royalty, who is unable to protect his children. Instead, Mr. Proudhammer has to swallow the indignity and accept his own impotence.

The story raises the issue of the humanity and goodness of white people. In the minds of the major characters, because of their behavior toward blacks, white people are seen as devoid of goodness and humanity.

Style and Technique

This first-person narrative is told through the eyes of a ten-year-old African American boy, who describes himself as timid, fearful, sensitive, and creative. This technique requires the reader to be alert and to evaluate the responses of this boy in the light of a mature awareness. One quality of the story as the boy tells it stands out in sharp relief: the sense that the story is about people living in the dark. There is no mention of sunshine or brightness, only night scenes. Perhaps this exclusive focus on the lives of the Proudhammer family living in darkness is a way of conveying to the reader that the consciousness of the storyteller is in a state of darkness, a state of ignorance. Despite his awareness of what is going on around him, he does not see a way to deal with it. At this point in his life, no light is available—he has no understanding—to guide him to comprehend how to free himself from this darkness.

The episode in the subway serves as a metaphor for this situation. Leo states that he loves subways, and they taught him the geopolitical construct of the city. Black people got on and off the train in certain stops, white people at others. His recognition of this neighborhood segregation terrorizes him and eventually leads him to get hopelessly lost. This getting lost can be understood symbolically: Not only is he lost physically, but he has lost his ability to cope with a racist world beyond his comprehension.

From the standpoint of style, the story is told simply, as if from the consciousness of a ten-year-old. Leo has no awareness of politics or economics, of history, or intellectual movements of great figures. Nonetheless, politics, economics, history, and intellectual movements impinge on his consciousness through the reality of his life. He knows he is black and the world he lives in is dominated by whites and also repressive toward his people.

Richard Damashek

THE TELL-TALE HEART

Author: Edgar Allan Poe (1809-1849)
Type of plot: Horror
Time of plot: The 1840's
Locale: An American town or village
First published: 1843

> *Principal characters:*
> THE NARRATOR, a man whose madness drives him to murder
> THE OLD MAN, the victim who is apparently cared for by the
>   madman

The Story

This is a chilling tale of madness and murder. "True!—nervous—very, very dreadfully nervous I had been and am," admits the narrator, "but why will you say that I am mad?" In a vain effort to prove his sanity by detailing how carefully he planned the gruesome deed, the narrator makes it abundantly clear from the first that he is dangerously deranged. Little is revealed about him, or about the old man that he kills. He did not hate the old man; indeed, he says he loved him. However, he had to kill him because he was tormented beyond distraction by the old man's eye—"a pale blue eye, with a film over it." In the first two paragraphs, the narrator draws the reader into the terrifying yet fascinating world of madness that has led him to murder.

Having decided to kill the old man, the narrator recalls with obvious pleasure how calculatingly he set about to do it. For seven successive nights, he slipped into the old man's room just after midnight. He moved ever so slowly, first lifting the latch and then gradually insinuating himself into the room. Once inside, he would open his darkened lantern so that a single ray of light fell on his tormentor, that "vulture eye." On each of those nights, however, the eye remained closed when the light fell on the old man's face, and the narrator found it "impossible to do the work; for it was not the old man who vexed me, but his Evil Eye." Although the old man possessed some wealth and was wary enough of robbers to have the shutters of his bed chamber nailed shut, the narrator insists that his victim suspected nothing. During the day, the narrator explains, he was kinder to the old man than ever before.

On the eighth night, the narrator was especially cautious, though almost ecstatic with feelings of power and triumph, certain that the old man knew nothing of what he was doing or planning to do. Reveling in the moment, he may well have laughed. At any rate, the old man startled in his bed. Moving steadily into the darkened bedroom, the narrator began to open the lantern, but his thumb slipped, and the old man cried out, asking who was there and sitting up in his bed. The narrator says that he did not move for more than an hour, for the room was pitch black; nor did the old man move. Finally, the old man groaned slightly, and the narrator knew that it was the sound of one overcome by deathly fear, for he too had experienced that terror deep in the night. "I knew what the old man felt," he claims, "and pitied him, although I chuckled at heart."

Slowly opening the lantern, the narrator found that its single ray fell directly on the vulture eye—"all a dull blue, with a hideous veil over it that chilled the very marrow of my bones." No other part of the old man's face was visible, but presently he heard "a low, dull, quick sound, much such a sound as a watch makes when enveloped in cotton." He was sure it was the old man's heart, and as the beat grew louder, he feared the sound might be heard by the neighbors. Enraged by the thought, he threw open the lantern, sprang into the room with a yell, dragged the old man to the floor, and pulled the heavy bed over on him. He was shortly dead, and the heart beat no more. To conceal his crime, the narrator dismembered his victim and hid the corpse under the floor of the old man's chamber. A tub caught all the blood. The murderer asks if a madman would have been so sagacious.

It was about 4:00 A.M. when he finished doing away with the body. Shortly thereafter, there was a knock on the door, and, sure that no one could discover what he had done, the narrator was not at all worried when three police officers explained that a neighbor had heard a scream and suspected foul play. The narrator answered that he had cried out because of a bad dream. The old man was away visiting friends, he said, but the police should search the house, see that nothing was taken, and be assured that all was well. As they finished their work, the narrator bade them to sit down a few minutes, placing his own chair over the planks that covered the old man's remains. The pleasant conversation of the police convinced him that they suspected nothing. The officers seemed to be reluctant to leave, however, and the narrator began to feel uneasy. He then heard what sounded very much like the old man's heart beating again, and he became very anxious, talking loudly and moving about the room, hoping that the police would not hear the heartbeat. "I foamed—I raved—I swore! I swung the chair on which I had been sitting, and grated it on the boards, but the noise arose over all and constantly increased." He suddenly felt that the police knew, though they pretended to ignore him. In desperation, he admitted his crime and urged them to tear up the boards and uncover that "hideous heart."

Themes and Meanings

This is largely a study in human terror experienced on two levels, both horrifying to behold. First, there is the narrator, the maniac, driven by his compulsive hatred of the "evil eye" to kill a man he says he loved. He is a case study in madness, tormented by that satanic eye that he simply must destroy. His madness is quite convincing and profoundly disturbing because it seems so capricious and meaningless. Indeed, seldom has the mystery and the horror of mental illness been so vividly portrayed. The "eye" also has a double meaning. The narrator is driven to self-destruction, though his suicidal urges are objectified in the old man's diseased eye.

The other level of terror is that experienced by the old man. His terror is made all the more realistic because it is related from the perspective of his tormentor, the mad narrator, who takes sadistic delight in knowing that the old man is quaking in his bed. Given the appearance of three police officers not long after the murder, one is tempted to speculate that the old man knew more than the narrator thought he knew. Perhaps he had conveyed his suspicions to a neighbor, or perhaps the young man has been demented for years, and the old man has been caring for him. If he did suspect the narrator, the terror that the old man felt during the hour before his death must have been excruciating.

The story is replete with double meaning and irony. The narrator destroys the "evil eye," thus ensuring his own destruction, or incarceration at least. Fearful that the neighbors would hear the heartbeat growing increasingly louder, the anxious maniac yells as he bludgeons the old man, and the neighbors certainly heard that. The arrival of three police officers suggests that they knew something was amiss and that the old man had tipped off someone, though the narrator is sure that his victim suspected nothing. There is also the beating of that tell-tale heart. Was it really the old man's heart, or was it the narrator's own heart betraying him? The mystery—and the story is to a considerable extent a mystery—is thus maintained to the very end. The irony is exquisite, a tribute to the literary genius of Edgar Allan Poe.

Style and Technique

Poe had definite ideas about the style and composition of the short story. To begin with, despite his wonderfully realistic descriptions in this and other tales, he advocated art over reality and believed that the artificial contrivances of the writer's imagination could reveal more truth about the human condition than faithful adherence to observed reality. As Poe saw it, the short story was the ideal medium for conveying artistic insight because the reader was likely to give it his or her concentrated attention for the brief time it took to read it. Above all else, he insisted that the writer should make every part of the short story contribute to its total effect. "If his very initial sentence tend not to the outbringing of this effect," wrote Poe, "then he has failed in his first step." His devotion to that injunction is clearly demonstrated in "The Tell-Tale Heart." Indeed, he excels in creating and developing that fascinating mood of mystery and madness that makes the story so irresistible.

Poe had the ability to portray his protagonists, mad though they might be, in sympathetic terms. The reader comes to understand the demented narrator, or at least to pity him, because his obsession is so overpowering.

Poe was a master of the first-person narrator, and that technique, so treacherous in the hands of a lesser artist, makes for unusual intimacy between the reader and the storyteller. Indeed, one is drawn into the tormented mind of the madman. The mind is especially Poe's domain, with its interplay of emotions, its mixture of reality and fantasy, and its ultimate mystery. To convey the impressions and feeling that he wanted, Poe relied on a variety of rhetorical tools, and he carefully crafted every sentence. However, "The Tell-Tale Heart" is convincingly spontaneous and filled with those little details that heighten the realism. Devoted to art for art's sake, Poe probed the limits of human reality in stories shaped by both intuitive genius and literary craftsmanship.

Ronald W. Howard

TELL THEM NOT TO KILL ME!

Author: Juan Rulfo (1918-1986)
Type of plot: Social realism
Time of plot: The early twentieth century
Locale: Jalisco, Mexico
First published: "¡Díles que no me maten!" 1953 (English translation, 1959)

> *Principal characters:*
> JUVENCIO NAVA, the owner of a small farm and herd, an escaped
>   criminal
> JUSTINO, his son
> COLONEL TERREROS, the son of a man whom he murdered

The Story

Juvencio Nava cries out, "Tell them not to kill me!," pleading with his son, Justino, to help him. Juvencio, who is in his sixties, has just been arrested for a crime he had committed thirty-five or forty years earlier. At first, Justino is reluctant to interfere, fearing that the police or the soldiers may arrest him too or even shoot him. Then there will be no one left to care for his wife and children. He finally relents and offers to see what he can do to assist his father.

As he waits, tied to a post, Juvencio recalls the past events that led up to his present predicament and circumstances. Years earlier he killed Don Lupe, his neighbor and the landowner in the areas of Alima and Puerta de Piedras. The two men had been feuding over grazing and water rights during a particularly dry spell. Don Lupe refused to let Juvencio's animals graze on his property. After several warnings, Don Lupe finally killed one of Juvencio's animals for wandering onto his land. In retaliation, Juvencio killed Don Lupe.

Juvencio then bribed the judge to release him and bribed the posse not to follow him, but they came after him anyway. He finally escaped and went into hiding with his son in Palo de Venado. He later learned that Don Lupe's widow had soon died; their two small children had been sent far away to live with relatives. Therefore, Juvencio thought that he might be relatively safe and that the incident would gradually be forgotten. He still lived in fear of detection, however, hiding out or going on the run whenever he heard that outsiders or strangers were in the area.

Meanwhile, Juvencio's son grew up, married a woman named Ignacia, and fathered eight children. Juvencio's own wife abruptly left him one day, but he dared not go searching for her because he still feared capture. He did not want to leave his hiding place to go into town. All he had left to save was his own life. He thought and hoped that after so much time, he would finally be left in peace, an old man in his last years, a threat to no one.

Now they have arrested him after all. They have even tied him up, even though he is too old and weak to try to escape. They say that they will execute him. After so many years of dodging capture and death, he cannot imagine being caught and dying so suddenly now. He simply cannot accept the dreadful idea. He continues to think and to hope, pondering a possible way out, but he can find none. He wonders if he can convince his captors to release him, but he is afraid to speak to them. He remembers when he first saw the men coming, back on his own land, as they came trampling his field. Instead of hiding or fleeing, he went down to tell them not to damage his bit of property. That was a very serious mistake, a very foolish and costly error. He was caught, and none of the four men would respond to his pleas for mercy.

The group's sergeant finally stands up in front of the door to the headquarters, speaking with his colonel, who remains inside. Only the colonel's voice can be heard as the sergeant relays his questions to Juvencio about the town of Alima and the Terreros family. Eventually the colonel reveals that he is the son of Don Lupe, that he grew up as an orphan, deprived of his father's protection. He learned several facts about the brutal nature of his father's murder. He tried to forget this information but could not. He had vowed to capture his father's murderer because he could not forgive such a man; he could not permit him to continue living.

The colonel then orders that Juvencio be shot by the firing squad. Juvencio pleads for his life, repeating that he is no threat because he is so old and worthless; he says that he has been punished enough through all the years of living in fear and hiding, plagued by constant dread. The colonel finally tells his men to get Juvencio drunk first, before the time of execution, so that he will not feel the bullets.

In the final scene, Justino returns to collect Juvencio's body. The son places his father's body on a burro and covers his father's head with a sack, because the corpse is shocking to see. As he departs, heading home to arrange his father's funeral, Justino thinks that the family will hardly recognize the old man, he was so full of holes.

Themes and Meanings

This work is from Juan Rulfo's 1950's collection of short stories *El llano en llamas*, which presents scenes from life in rural Jalisco, Rulfo's native region of Mexico. The collection has been translated by George D. Schade as *The Burning Plain* (1967). Many of its stories, like this one, involve family relationships in difficult situations. Rulfo himself was an orphan; his father was killed in the long years of the *cristero* revolts during the time of the Mexican Revolution and his mother died several years later. The theme of the search for the father, for family roots, and for personal or even national identity permeates Rulfo's writings.

Both sons in this story, the colonel and Justino, feel a sense of family loyalty and duty. The colonel is seeking justice as well as revenge for his father's murder. He does not attempt to face the guilty man directly, lest he feel some sense of compassion for him. Justino is hesitant, yet he tries to help his father. He seems to accept Juvencio's admitted guilt, and he finally claims the body for burial. Although Justino had his father with him during his youth, he felt the fear of a life constantly in dread of his father's potential capture and death. The colonel spent most of his life without a father; he came to be overwhelmed by the desire to see his father's murderer punished, perhaps as much to avenge his own lost childhood as to avenge his father.

Juvencio tries to avoid death almost up to the very end, as he has all of his life. However, there is a certain inevitability and fatalism in his ultimate demise. He knows that his family suffered along with him all those years, but his primary thought is for self-preservation. The reader is left to ponder the limits of rights and responsibilities, of justice and revenge, of mercy and forgiveness. The story offers a strongly evoked regional setting, vividly described, which is elevated to a broader level by the sobering consideration of deep, universal themes.

Style and Technique

Rulfo is noted for his powerful evocation of scene, for the sense of place created in his work. He employs dialogue and popular speech to add to the realism of the social situations depicted. All five senses are invoked as the sights, sounds, smells, textures, and tastes of the landscape are described. The reader can feel the impact of the hard, rugged life of the region. Rulfo's literary devices include some repetition, as in this story, to underscore a character's desperate psychological state. The reader can feel Juvencio's fear and dread as he thinks about the events leading up to his capture. The heat, the dust, the harshness of the scene are all conjured up for the reader's imaginative consideration.

Rulfo also varies verb tenses in order to illustrate alternations between past and present, between memory and current reality; events are not revealed in a directly linear, chronological order. A character's memory is used to portray the past, and dialogue among characters is interspersed with the protagonist's own thoughts. Rulfo utilizes language in a disciplined, economical style. His setting often is one of intense and grinding poverty, desperation, and desolation; towns are seen to be depopulating as people seek a better life elsewhere. Sometimes only the dead are left behind, as in his novel *Pedro Páramo* (1955), with its use of Magical Realism (joining the possible with the imaginary). His stories, in contrast, are predominantly and truly realistic.

Margaret V. Ekstrom

THE TENDER SHOOT

Author: Colette (Sidonie-Gabrielle Collette, 1873-1954)
Type of plot: Psychological
Time of plot: May, 1940, and 1923
Locale: Paris and a region of Doubs in Franche-Comte
First published: "Le Tendron," 1943 (English translation, 1959)

> *Principal characters:*
> THE NARRATOR, a woman
> ALBIN CHAVERIAT, the storyteller
> LOUISETTE, the young girl
> THE MOTHER, the mother of the young girl

The Story

The opening dialogue of "The Tender Shoot" introduces the reader to an unidentified woman and an old friend of hers to whom she gives the name Albin Chaveriat. Evidently this name is chosen to hide the real identity of the storyteller. The setting is Paris, in May of 1940. Over dinner, the woman persuades her seventy-year-old bachelor friend to tell her a story of his love life, a secret life that limited, for the woman at least, a deeper sense of their friendship.

The woman has just encouraged Chaveriat to spend his time in the country, while the war lasts, at the Hersent home, a home filled with young daughters and nieces. Chaveriat refuses to go there for that very reason. He has renounced the two great passions of his life, young girls and shooting. Chaveriat begins his story by telling the woman that it was because of the dissolution of a masculine friendship that he acquired his taste for young girls. Chaveriat considered his friend Eyrand's marriage a betrayal of their mutual affection, refused to forgive him, and the friendship ended. It was with this estrangement that he became unsociable with everyone but very young girls.

Chaveriat proceeds with his story by telling of a late summer in 1923 spent at the estate of a wealthy chemist friend in the region of Doubs. Though he no longer hunted, he still accepted his friends' hunting invitations. He is especially bored with the others present, their constant eating and drinking, and so he keeps to himself. Being an ardent walker, one day Chaveriat wanders outside the domain and finds himself at the top of a hill where a stream flows by. From the other side of a crumbling wall, the horned forehead of a she-goat nudges his hand. As he is about to touch the she-goat, a girl's voice warns him not to or the she-goat will chase him. He does so, and the she-goat bounds after him. The girl wrestles the she-goat to the ground, and it runs off.

Chaveriat's passion for young girls is sparked by the presence of this lovely, nearly sixteen-year-old country girl named Louisette. A flirtation begins with very evident romantic intentions on the part of Chaveriat. Several times he offers Louisette trinkets to flatter and charm her. Each time she adamantly refuses, saying that her mother would disapprove, would not understand. After a week of these late-morning lovers' meetings, Chaveriat, because of a social conflict, invites Louisette to meet him in the evening.

More than two weeks of meetings follow when Louisette changes their meeting time to much later in the evening. By that time her mother will be in bed, and Louisette's work will be finished. One late evening, Chaveriat takes leave of his host to rendezvous with Louisette. The threatening weather prompts him to carry his mackintosh and his pocket torch. Their lovemaking is interrupted by a rainstorm, and Louisette leads him to the shelter of her nearby home, a run-down château. Quietly they sneak into the darkened château and settle on a sofa. The rain subsides and he is about to leave when the downpour redoubles.

Chaveriat's uneasiness grows in this strange place, and he is eager to escape from these unfamiliar, eerie surroundings. Suddenly a candlelight appears on the staircase. Louisette's mother appears, a small, white-haired woman with a magnificent gaze, resembling her young daughter. To no avail Chaveriat attempts to explain his behavior with her daughter. She asks him how old he is and then rebukes him, a man of fifty with white hair and wrinkles under his eyes, for having forced himself on her daughter. She could have understood such behavior with young boys but not with an old man.

With Louisette and her mother becoming increasingly enraged and threatening, Chaveriat streaks out of the house with them in pursuit. As he escapes down the dilapidated, stone-walled path, the two women push stones from the top of the wall that strike him on the shoulder, ear, and foot. Finally Chaveriat arrives at his host's home. After a long and violent bout with fever, he recovers to renounce his passion for all the Louisettes of the world.

Themes and Meanings

Estrangement and ensuing loneliness are the motivating forces that drive Chaveriat to find some sort of fulfillment in the arms of young girls—his tender shoots. It is with his boyhood friend Eyrand's betrayal of their friendship that Chaveriat enters into his world of solitude, never again to establish a truly meaningful bond with another person. Even the secrecy of Chaveriat's love life has limited an otherwise deeper relationship between him and his woman friend, the narrator. He confesses that he has been just like any other man in his involvement with women, his attraction toward a sensible marriage. However, he rejects any close or permanent relationship in a kind of self-willed effort to remain separate and alone.

The lonely world in which Chaveriat has chosen to live has prevented him from entering into an adult relationship on an intimate basis. He was unwilling to give up the deep abiding friendship he had with Eyrand. Not wanting to be hurt again, he substituted those to whom he would not and could not become deeply attached except on a superficial and physical basis. As Chaveriat stated, his friendship for Eyrand surpassed the faithful devotion of a lover for his mistress. Old boughs for tender shoots, he says to his woman friend, is the lie he tells to excuse himself for the lust he feels for young girls.

Though there appears at times to be some yearning for a deeper meaning in his relationship with young girls than simple sexual gratification, he has not been able to go beyond treating them as a species, as a sexual symbol that must be studied and then consumed. Louisette reinforces the theme of loneliness, for he sees her showing no fundamental gaiety and living in dangerous solitude. They increase in each other this sense of separateness in their game of mutual exploitation. He saw her exploiting him as a lecherous man who has found a willing girl, and he saw himself as one relieving Louisette of her youthful boredom. However, to give some kind of meaning to their relationship he wished she could show some affection, could treat her unselfish lover as a friend, perhaps the friend that Eyrand once had been. Chaveriat noted at their parting that no words of tenderness, desire, or friendliness had been exchanged. She would not let him into her secret life and refused any show of affection, his gifts, and any attempts to know her better. In this way Louisette intensified his sense of rejection and loneliness. Their only intimacy was physical, and her only way to communicate with him was with kisses.

Chaveriat's hope for meaningful, adult intimacy ended at the time of his estrangement from Eyrand. He was left alone, rejected and abandoned. From that point in time Chaveriat did not mature psychologically in his relationship with women. In fact he confesses that Louisette's sensuality in a grown woman would have revolted him.

This conflict between his self-imposed loneliness and his escape from reality created a life for him of empty romantic intrigues, the shallowness of which is climaxed and revealed in his final amorous episode with Louisette. Chaveriat's reaction to his own story is one of sadness, this sadness he also felt emanating from Louisette. The result of his adventure with her was a feeling of disgust and a desire to reject all the Louisettes of his past. His compensation was freedom from this bondage of empty and meaningless sexual gratification with young girls. Finally healed, at least in part, of the loneliness that estrangement had thrust on him, he could now turn to those other than the Louisettes of the world to comfort him.

Style and Technique

The writer of "The Tender Shoot," Colette, introduces Albin Chaveriat, the teller of the story, which is, in essence, a psychosexual study. If Colette, the writer, and Chaveriat, the teller, are the same person, then the interpretations of sexual inferences and connotations leave room for speculation. The relationships between Chaveriat and his Louisettes reflect a female rather than a male psychology. The implied meaning of the relationship is very much central to the mystical qualities of the story itself. Colette places the reader in two worlds, the real world of Chaveriat's woman friend and the chemist, and the illusory world of Louisette. These are the same two worlds in conflict in which Chaveriat finds himself. His Louisette world is that of sexual adolescence. His other world is finally that of adult reality.

The author's description of nature is lyric and evokes a sense of eerie loneliness that adds color and movement to the mystical tone of the story and intensifies Chaveriat's innermost feelings. Suspense and mystery are very much interwoven throughout the story. The web of intrigue concerning the secrets of Chaveriat's love life immediately engages the reader's attention. His friend's betrayal, the ensuing realization of loss, and his sudden hunger for young girls cement the reader's attention very early in the story. The suspense intensifies as the reader is drawn into the young girl's world. Who is Louisette? Does she symbolize and reinforce the empty, lonely, and nearly desperate nature of Chaveriat's essence? It is in this unreal world of the Louisettes that he is driven to choose and to accept the real world of Chaveriat.

David J. Quinn

TENNESSEE'S PARTNER

Author: Bret Harte (1836-1902)
Type of plot: Social realism
Time of plot: 1853-1854
Locale: Sandy Bar, a fictional Western mining town
First published: 1869

> *Principal characters:*
> THE NARRATOR, an unnamed resident of Sandy Bar
> TENNESSEE'S PARTNER, a devoted friend of Tennessee
> TENNESSEE, a notorious gambler and thief who is hanged
> JUDGE LYNCH, who captures Tennessee and presides at his trial

The Story

The unnamed narrator explains that the real name of Tennessee's Partner has—in accordance with Sandy Bar's quixotic practice of rechristening new arrivals—never been known in the mining town. The locals have dubbed the man "Tennessee's Partner" because he teamed up with Tennessee, a wholly disreputable character whose own real name has been similarly obliterated from communal memory.

The narrator goes on to relate the story of Tennessee's Partner's search for a bride. A year earlier, in 1853, the man set out for San Francisco from Poker Flat but got no farther than Stockton, where he was attracted by a waitress in a hotel. During a courtship, the waitress broke a plate of toast over Tennessee's Partner's head, then agreed to marry him before a justice of the peace. With his new bride in tow, the man returned to Poker Flat, and then went to Sandy Bar, where the couple took up residence with Tennessee.

Some time after his partner's return, Tennessee began making indecent advances to the new bride until she ran off to Marysville. He then followed her there and set up housekeeping without the aid of a justice of the peace. A few months later their relationship ended; the woman took up with yet another man and Tennessee returned to Sandy Bar. To the disappointment of the townspeople, who gathered to witness a shooting, Tennessee's Partner was the first man to shake Tennessee's hand, and he greeted him with affection. With no trace of bitterness, and without apology, Tennessee and his partner resumed their former relationship as if the woman had never existed.

The narrator goes on to explain that the residents of Sandy Bar suspect that Tennessee—already known to be a gambler—is also a thief. These rumors are confirmed when Tennessee is caught red-handed after robbing at gunpoint a stranger traveling between Sandy Bar and Red Dog.

After frantically escaping from Sandy Bar, Tennessee is cornered in a canyon, where Judge Lynch finds him. Armed with a better "hand" than Tennessee—two revolvers and a bowie knife—the judge calls Tennessee's bluff and takes him prisoner. During the ensuing trial, conducted by Lynch, Tennessee's Partner tries to buy his friend's freedom, offering a watch and seventeen hundred dollars in raw gold, his only belongings of any real worth. This offer is construed as a bribe, so rather than help the accused, it merely hastens his date with the "ominous tree" atop Marley's Hill. Tennessee is convicted and sentenced to hang.

Tennessee's Partner does not attend the hanging. Afterward, he arrives with a crudely decorated donkey cart and rough coffin to claim Tennessee's body. Followed by a curious crowd, he drives the makeshift hearse through Grizzly Canyon to an open grave near his cabin. There he gives a brief, rustic funeral oration, thanks those in attendance, and buries Tennessee.

After this primitive funeral, the health of Tennessee's Partner declines. He visibly wastes away until he takes to a sickbed and dies. In his final delirious moments, he envisions his reunion with Tennessee in death: "Thar! I told you so!—that he is—coming this way, too—all by himself, sober, and his face a-shining. Tennessee! Pardner!"

Themes and Meanings

"Tennessee's Partner" chronicles an inexplicable bond between two men, Tennessee and his partner, both crude, unlettered mining camp men. The basis for their bond is never explained, but its durable strength is revealed in the fact that their friendship survives a breach of its faith: After Tennessee runs off with his partner's wife, he returns to Sandy Bar and is welcomed back by his friend without rancor or resentment. Theirs is a friendship that transcends marriage ties—at least for the protagonist, Tennessee's Partner.

Although Bret Harte's story is in the tradition of local-color realism, its essential idea is romantic in origin. It argues that no matter how primitive a man appears to be, he may still possess some indelible virtue, such as loyalty. The devotion of Tennessee's Partner to his friend is not contingent on refined sensibilities honed through schooling or sophisticated social codes. In fact, Tennessee's Partner cannot even articulate the code by which he lives or the feelings that bind him to his friend. When he is asked to speak on Tennessee's behalf at his friend's trial, he can only ask, "What should a man know of his pardner?" To him, loyalty is simply a fact of his life—one as unfathomable to him as it is to the reader.

The fact that rough-and-tumble frontier mining camp existence scarcely seems a promising incubator for the kind of sensibilities that underlie the protagonist's behavior makes his loyalty all the more remarkable. It is also unique in the story, for the citizens of Sandy Bar do not share Tennessee's Partner's simple virtue. In contrast, they tend to be cruel spectators. When Tennessee returns to Sandy Bar after having been jilted by his partner's wife, the townspeople gather in Grizzly Canyon, not because they hope there will be an amiable reunion between Tennessee and his partner, but because they assume there will be a shooting. When Tennessee's Partner takes his friend home for burial, the townspeople follow, not from respect for the dead, but from idle curiosity. Some even jest, mocking the ceremony.

From the community's point of view, Tennessee's Partner's selfless devotion is an aberration, to be ridiculed, not admired. He has no other relationship, no friends; outside his relation with Tennessee he is basically a pariah figure, a familiar sort in the fiction of Harte. Presumably, the bond between the two men is forged in part because, in reality, frontier life could be desperately lonely. No matter how wretched a man Tennessee is, he fills the fundamental need for human companionship that his partner and any sensitive person might feel in such an environment.

Style and Technique

Although some modern commentators have complained that "Tennessee's Partner" strains credibility and borders on the maudlin, it remains one of the best pieces of short fiction to come out of the western, local-color tradition in which Harte played such an important part. Its sentimentality is balanced by the sort of rawboned, understated humor, borrowed from the tall-tale oral tradition, that marks the stories of Harte's contemporary and one-time acolyte, Mark Twain. Harte uses a variety of comic elements, such as malapropisms, verbal irony, and inappropriate tone, to good effect, offsetting the sentimentality that otherwise might overburden the reader.

By employing an unidentified narrator who plays no other role in the story, Harte also distances the reader from the inward feelings and thoughts of his main character, making a psychological probing of his consciousness impossible. The narrator offers no explanation for the friendship of Tennessee and his partner; it is just there, inexplicable and mysterious. A simple, uncultured man, Tennessee's Partner cannot articulate his feelings, except, by implication, in his artless but quaint funeral oration and his rhapsodic meandering in his death throes. Only the narrator, who is the thinly veiled author, and Judge Lynch are articulate. In fact, the story's main flaw is perhaps the tendency of the author to editorialize, to orchestrate the reader's feelings in an attempt to evoke pathos. Harte also strains in some of the descriptive passages, using the pathetic fallacy familiar from romantic literature to achieve a desired mood. For example, the forlorn plight of Tennessee, on the eve of his trial, is heightened by the vastness of the surroundings. Harte describes the nearby Sierra Nevada as being "etched on the dark firmament . . . remote and passionless, crowned with remoter passionless stars." To the contemporary reader, such writing may seem turgid, but it would hardly have seemed excessive to the readers of Harte's own period.

By carefully blending humor and pathos, Harte manages to skirt emotional clichés, keeping readers intrigued with his story. One may complain that he never really investigates the motives behind Tennessee's Partner's devotion to his friend, but that objection arises in the wake of modern psychological theories that did not impact fiction until some decades after Harte wrote the story. In his fictional world, characters are often what they are by virtue of an innate proclivity that circumstances can only reveal but not necessarily explain.

John W. Fiero

TERRIFIC MOTHER

Author: Lorrie Moore (1957-   )
Type of plot: Psychological
Time of plot: The 1990's
Locale: American Midwest and northern Italy
First published: 1998

> *Principal characters:*
> ADRIENNE, a woman in her late thirties who is a visual artist
> MARTIN PORTER, her academic husband
> ILKE, a masseuse

The Story

Although "Terrific Mother" follows Adrienne's life for almost a year, the dominant event in the story takes place at a Labor Day barbecue, at which she is involved in an accident that results in a baby's death. When the picnic table on which Adrienne is sitting collapses, she lets go of the child she is holding, inadvertently causing its death. Adrienne becomes devastated by guilt. This guilt is exacerbated by the fact that, shortly before this event, friends advised Adrienne that she should have her own baby because she would make a fine mother. Suffering a numbing depression, Adrienne retreats into her attic apartment for seven months, taking pains to avoid contact with people.

Martin Porter, a professor in economics, attempts to wrest her from Adrienne solitude and eventually convinces her to marry him, although she feels that her role in the baby's death has made her a pariah unfit for normal life. Martin wins a scholarship that allows him and his spouse to spend a month in a luxurious mountain villa in northern Italy. There, amid other academics and their partners, he revises a book, and Adrienne is given a studio to pursue her artwork. Much of the story takes place over mealtimes at the resort, occasions during which Adrienne meets numerous scholars, most of whom are self-absorbed specialists. She is not taken seriously by the academics because of her status as a spouse. Obsessed by the earlier accident with the baby, Adrienne cannot do much in her studio except kill spiders, and dissatisfied with the pretension she encounters at the villa, she grows restless and begins visiting Ilke, a masseuse who has been recommended by a fellow spouse at the villa.

Becoming aware of her body once again, Adrienne discovers that her time with the masseuse also takes her deeply within her psyche, and she repeatedly returns for more of the therapeutic sessions. Under the trancelike state of mind created by the masseuse's hands, Adrienne recalls her parents' deaths, ponders loss, and ruminates on her childlessness and her ambivalent feelings about her marriage. Strengthened by self-awareness and less self-conscious than when she first arrived at the villa, Adrienne eventually adopts a position of playfully aggressive irony when conversing with the other guests. As the month progresses, however, Adrienne begins to feel estranged from her husband, who seems completely at ease with his academic colleagues and the esoteric intellectual atmosphere at the retreat.

After one particularly intense massage and then an annoying encounter with a tarot card reader, Adrienne wanders off to a meadow, where she removes her clothes. Resting, she imagines that she has crossed into the underworld, and when a tourist guide interrupts her reverie, Adrienne momentarily confuses the elderly woman for a somewhat ludicrous looking spiritual guide. At the end of the story, Adrienne surprises Martin with her knowledge that he has been secretly visiting Ilke, an act that, to her, constitutes a kind of betrayal. From Adrienne's perspective, Martin has trespassed on the intense privacy and spiritual sojourn she experienced with the masseuse. During this marital confrontation, Adrienne experiences an epiphany when she suddenly perceives all of her dead reflected in the eyes of her largely misunderstood husband, and she recognizes that she must ask both them and him for forgiveness.

Themes and Meanings

The final story in *Birds of America: Stories* (1998), "Terrific Mother" offers a coda for the entire collection in which many of the collection's themes and images are elaborated on and given a final reprise. This story follows Lorrie Moore's famous "People Like That Are the Only People Here: Canonical Babbling in Peed Onk," a story detailing the dilemmas faced by a mother whose infant son is diagnosed with cancer. In many ways, Adrienne embodies the concerns explored in the book's other stories. Her life is disrupted by the persistent contingency that undermines human experience. Her lengthy trauma after the shock of the baby's accidental death exiles her from community, and during this period of mourning, she is nakedly exposed to existential doubt and metaphysical lawlessness. Learning that the only authentic act available to people is forgiveness—both for themselves and also for others—Adrienne has an insight that could offer a kind of provisional redemptive knowledge to the characters who occupy the other stories in the collection.

Very different from the project-oriented academics at the villa, Adrienne is adrift. If people generally understand their lives as containing choice and a certain degree of predictability owing to the apparent laws of cause and effect, Adrienne finds herself cut loose from daily life and its organizational structures because of the baby's accidental death, an event that signals cosmic chaos. Her mental state has more in common with the unconscious than the rationality through which the scholars govern themselves. Adrienne is often disconnected from the present; existing in a prolonged state of trauma, her mind gives her glances of the dead infant as a ghostly toddler walking alongside her dead parents. As the masseuse rubs her feet with oil and covers her in a blanket, Adrienne feels that she is the baby Jesus but also simultaneously the grown man and the corpse after the crucifixion. However, Adrienne does not believe that she is a messianic figure. Rather, she perceives her life not so much as a gradually unfolding linear narrative but as a kind of anarchic dream in which certain associative images and philosophical problems—the nature of pain, the boundaries of the self, and the relation between appearance and reality—recur in endlessly fluctuating forms, defying a method of understanding that depends on chronological progression and causal connections.

Style and Technique

Moore engages irony as a philosophical and aesthetic mode perhaps more than any other contemporary short-story writer in English. Beginning with Adrienne, one perceives that her remarks to other people make sense within the context of the conversation; however, most of what she says also refers to the dead baby, something that other people cannot by necessity understand. Adrienne uses irony because she is at a loss to find the right person to whom she can communicate her pain. Perhaps no one could ever be the listener she needs. Accentuating her protagonist's use of irony, Moore hints at the story's overall ironic strategies. For example, Adrienne finds herself seated next to an anthropologist during one meal at the villa; the anthropologist, having just returned from China, informs Adrienne of the mass infanticide that has occurred in that country owing to the government's strict population control policies. A detail such as this creates a degree of pathos in that the anthropologist is not aware of Adrienne's past.

More important, however, the dramatic irony allows Moore to evoke the multitude of children who die annually across the world without seeming heavy-handed. Offhand references to the Russian Revolution, fascism in World War II, and an overheard tidbit of conversation in which one scholar castigates another for not knowing about the Peasant's Revolt—each of these details summons a world of grief that is extraneous to the plot of the story. That the Peasant's Revolt is not everyday knowledge, even among academics, points to the fact that most of human history is irrelevant to the present. Past terror and actual human suffering disappears into the past; only arcane scholarship remains.

Moore is so adept at creating vivacious and convincing dialogue, so skilled at casually sketching in the intricacies of her characters, that this radical skepticism appears very far in the story's background. Adrienne—whose name contains nothingness inside it through the pun on the French *rien*, or nothing—is consumed by rage for most of the story, which implicitly repudiates not only a world in which children die in domestic accidents, but also a world in which Nazis murder children as the result of ideology. None of these ideas is stated blatantly; rather, they are manifested through Moore's ironic indirection.

"Terrific Mother" does not overtly engage political questions; instead, it subtly poses anguished ethical and metaphysical problems. Beneath its quirky humor and satire, the story borders on philosophical nihilism. Furthermore, literature as a mode of discourse is treated ambivalently. Moore takes the epic convention of a journey to the underworld and uses it irreverently insofar as Adrienne's descent is meant to be understood as a realistic component of her psychological situation, not as a clever allusion to a time-honored literary device. Put differently, the story relies on literary conventions to demonstrate their limitations in depicting human life.

Michael Trussler

TERRITORY

Author: David Leavitt (1961-   )
Type of plot: Domestic realism
Time of plot: The 1980's
Locale: California
First published: 1982

> *Principal characters:*
> NEIL CAMPBELL, a twenty-three-year-old homosexual, who is home visiting his mother
> MRS. BARBARA CAMPBELL, his mother
> WAYNE, his twenty-eight-year-old lover

The Story

After a two-year absence from home, Neil Campbell, a twenty-three-year-old homosexual, visits his mother with his current lover, Wayne. Mrs. Campbell, a beautiful, sophisticated, and politically committed woman, generously welcomes Neil and his lover, but the visit soon proves painful for both mother and son. Mrs. Campbell tries to maintain her normal schedule: playing music with her friends, caring for her three Airedales, and running errands, but her nonchalance soon dissolves into doubt and recrimination as lines are drawn between her and Neil. Neil's return sparks for him uncomfortable memories of his early sexual awakening and unresolved anger at his mother concerning how understanding she has always been about his sexual inclinations. He is embarrassed at how "she located and got in touch with an organization called the Coalition of Parents of Lesbians and Gays. Within a year she was president of it. . . . He winced at the thought that she knew all his sexual secrets and vowed to move to the East Coast to escape her."

Wayne, Neil's twenty-eight-year-old lover, is charming and natural; he gets along well with Mrs. Campbell. It is Wayne who reaches across the dinner table to take Neil's hand in plain sight of his mother, and later that evening, when Mrs. Campbell finds them in the garden where they have gone to make love, it is Wayne who "starts laughing" after being discovered. Wayne's ease with the situation, however, soon ends. The next day, when the three are returning from the dog groomer, one of the Airedales urinates on Wayne, and Mrs. Campbell responds by saying, "I'm sorry, Wayne. . . . It goes with the territory" using the word that effectively draws the boundaries between her lifestyle and that of her son.

Neil's "territory" is his sexual inclination, and in a flashback he reveals how his mother impinges on it. At Neil's first Gay Pride Parade, Mrs. Campbell manned a booth for the Coalition of Parents of Lesbians and Gays; "they had posted a huge banner on the wall behind them proclaiming: OUR SONS AND DAUGHTERS, WE ARE PROUD OF YOU. She spotted him; she waved, and jumped up and down." Mrs.

Campbell's territory is her house, an orderly environment that she shares with her three female dogs, Abigail, Lucille, and Fern. Her discovery of Neil and Wayne in the garden the night before has made her "very frightened—and worried," and she defends her territory by saying, "I lead a quiet life. . . . I don't want to be a disciplinarian. I just don't have the energy for these—shenanigans." Neil accuses her of being uncomfortable with his "having a lover," and she responds by saying, "No, I'm not used to having other people around, that's all. Wayne is charming." However, Mrs. Campbell is clearly disturbed by her son's arrangement. When the three of them go to an Esther Williams film and Neil attempts to put his arm on her shoulder, "it twitches spasmodically, and he jumps, as if he had received an electric shock." Neil, reaching out to her through a touch, unnerves Mrs. Campbell, and when they come home from the film, she rebukes Neil for "what you were doing at the movie" and admits that "I can only take so much. Just so much. . . . I remember, and I have to stop remembering. I wanted you to grow up happy. And I'm very tolerant, very understanding. But I can only take so much." With all her good intentions gone and her hopes for her son put aside for all time, Mrs. Campbell returns to her house, to her territory, after Neil cautions her not to feel responsible for his life, but also not to make him responsible for hers.

On the plane trip home, Wayne, the outsider in this story, remarks to Neil that he has a "great mother and all you do is complain," but Neil responds by saying that no outsider would understand how "Guilt goes with the territory." As the plane nears New York City and the image of his mother fades, Neil settles back into the life that is right for him, into his self-defined territory of two men holding hands, eyes closed, and "breathing in unison."

Themes and Meanings

Mrs. Campbell's and Neil's relationship raises basic issues about parenting and sex, the boundaries of family love and obligation. In a family as liberal and understanding as the Campbells, there are still shame and thwarted expectations. Neil is ashamed of his own sexuality, while his mother treats it as a worthy political cause that she eventually loses. By coming to terms with each other's limitations, Neil and his mother reenact the painful but inevitable process of separation that takes place between parent and child. Because this is a mother-son separation, it has a sexual dimension. Because it involves a homosexual son, the usual separation rituals are inoperative; as much as Wayne is a part of Neil's life, a long-term partner perhaps, he can never be a potential daughter-in-law, and this fact must naturally bewilder Neil's mother and influence her responses.

Mrs. Campbell is not the kind of mother who shows anger toward her son for being homosexual, but one can speculate on the sublimated anger implied in her having three female dogs. Are Abigail, Lucy, and Fern daughters who will never betray her as her much-absent husband and her sexually deviant son have? David Leavitt teases the reader to infer as much when he has Neil recount how his first dog, Rasputin (obviously male), licked his torso, thereby igniting his first sexual feelings. The respective sexual territories that Neil and his mother come to occupy were marked off at that moment.

Style and Technique

"Territory" is a third-person narration that alternates between the present action of Neil's visit and the past action of his sexual history, which is disclosed in a series of flashbacks. These flashbacks bring Neil into focus in a way that the present action of the story cannot. Certain information is divulged in these flashbacks to which only Neil and the reader are privy, Neil's sexual history, for example. By learning Neil's sexual history, the reader becomes more sympathetic to his situation. In fact, Neil's sexual behavior is no different from most heterosexual behavior; he has settled down with Wayne after a more promiscuous stage that he admits "had been brief and lamentable."

On another level, the flashback technique affords a more telling description of Mrs. Campbell. Though she is seen as gracious and liberal in the present action, a more fragile side of her character emerges in the flashbacks. During the gay pride march, her political savvy and her motherly good intentions crumble when confronted with "a sticklike man wrapped in green satin [whose] eyes were heavily dosed with green eyeshadow, and his lips were painted pink."

Finally, the alternating narrative structure is itself a territory of sorts. One moment the reader sees a group picture, something at a medium distance, the next moment a closeup, a memory, something more revealing and microscopic. Neil's consciousness acts as a lens, a focusing mechanism, a surveyor's tool that delineates for the reader where one boundary ends and another begins.

Sylvia G. O'Sullivan

TESTIMONY OF PILOT

Author: Barry Hannah (1942-   )
Type of plot: Social realism
Time of plot: The 1950's to 1970's
Locale: Clinton, Mississippi
First published: 1974

> *Principal characters:*
> WILLIAM HOWLY, the narrator
> ARDEN QUADBERRY, a saxophone player and pilot
> LILIAN FIELD, Arden's girlfriend
> EDITH FIELD, her sister

The Story

In a rambling but effective manner, William Howly recalls the story of his odd friend, Arden Quadberry. They first meet by accident. Seeking to punish a nearby black family for what he believes was the savage treatment of a pig, William and another boy, Radcleve, shell the black family's home with Radcleve's homemade mortar. The shells, actually batteries, fall short, landing on the house occupied by the Quadberrys. Mr. Quadberry is a history professor and his wife is a musician; their son, Ard, with his Arab nose, saxophone, and mud-caked shoes, is not accepted by the other boys. Sent by his parents to tell the boys to stop the shelling, Ard is nearly blinded on the return trip when Radcleve nonchalantly tosses an M-80 firecracker packed in mud in his direction.

Made uneasy by his own silent complicity in the act as well as by Ard's strangeness, Howly keeps his distance until their senior year, when Ard joins the school band. As their lives begin to intersect, Howly, the band's drummer, has the opportunity to observe Ard more closely. Once he enters the band room and comes on Ard and a small, red-faced ninth-grade euphonium player who calls him "Queerberry," and is beaten for his temerity. At the state championship, held in nearby Jackson, Howly sees a different side of his unusual friend. When Prender, the much-loved band director, is killed en route to Jackson in a head-on crash with an ambulance, Quadberry takes charge. Not only does he direct the others, he plays so brilliantly that the judges applaud, an attractive woman in her thirties walks up to Ard and introduces herself, and the beautiful Lilian, the majorette and third-chair clarinetist who missed the start of the performance because she was drowning her sorrow in two beers, offers Ard both her apologies and herself.

Howly's band, the Bop Fiends, which includes Ard, becomes well known, able to command twelve hundred dollars a night. Howly's success is also his undoing, as his loud drum playing soon makes him deaf. Ard goes off to the United States Naval Academy, the only school that wants him, charging Howly with looking after Lilian, who, like Howly, will attend the local college. Six years later, Ard, having given up his saxophone for a much bigger gleaming metal tube, a navy fighter plane, arranges to meet Lilian at the Jackson airbase. He touches down and, without even bothering to deplane, delivers to Lilian, and through her to Howly, this one-size-fits-all message: "I am a dragon. America the beautiful, like you will never know."

In Vietnam, much the same good technique that had made him so fine a saxophonist makes him a successful fighter pilot, flying escort for B-52's on bombing missions. Immediately after downing his first enemy plane, killing its pilot, Ard's luck changes. Hit by a ground missile, he flies back to sea, ejects, and lands right on the carrier's flight deck. He spends a month recovering from a back injury. Returning to action, his plane fails on takeoff and drops off the end of the carrier's deck into the ocean. Again he ejects, this time under water, after waiting for the ship to pass over him. Again he hurts his back, this time so severely as to preclude his ever flying or playing again.

Sometime later, Lilian, now an airline stewardess, dies when a hijacker's inept bomb explodes a few miles off the Cuban coast. Two weeks after the memorial service, the handicapped and previously abstemious Quadberry returns home to Clinton, drunk and smoking a cigar. Howly is there to greet him and to tell him of Lilian's death. His mother shows up and his father, who had opposed Ard's participation in the war, is waiting in the car. Seven months later, Ard calls Howly, who now lives with Lilian's younger sister, Edith, to ask whether he should undergo a new surgical procedure that has a 75 percent chance of curing him, but a 25 percent chance of killing him. Howly tells him to trust his luck and have the operation. Quadberry does and dies, his luck having run out.

Themes and Meanings

"In Mississippi, it is difficult to achieve a vista." This line, delivered early in the story, proves doubly important. First, it underscores the strong southernness of Barry Hannah's fiction, its links to a particular region and culture and to certain of the South's most important writers: Edgar Allan Poe, Mark Twain, William Faulkner, and Flannery O'Connor. Second, the line underscores the story's concern with how well one sees and how one is seen. How well one sees is highlighted in the opening pages in the number of times the narrator as a boy of ten or so manages to misjudge the small world that makes up his rather limited vista. How one is perceived proves especially significant in the case of the story's titular subject, with his Arab nose, white halo, and odd name. Although Quadberry's inspired saxophone playing represents the school's best hope for winning the state championship, it also represents, at least to Howly, a "desperate oralness" that neither he, nor Lilian, nor the small, red-faced, ninth-grade boy can satisfy. That Ard is, or may be, homosexual only compounds his difficulty in trying to find a place either in his small Mississippi town or in the aggressively male world of Annapolis and navy pilots during the Vietnam War.

When he goes to Annapolis, he begins the process that will take him from playing the saxophone to flying fighter aircraft, from soloist and musical genius to the no less intense but certainly more deadly isolation of a plane's cockpit. In the sky, he achieves the widest vista possible and the greatest distance from all that is merely human. Howly moves in a parallel but opposite direction. Just as Ard must give up his saxophone because of his bad back, Howly must give up his drums because of his deafness. Howly's deafness, however, brings him closer to people, including Edith Field, Lilian's younger sister, "a second-rate version of her and a wayward overcompensating nymphomaniac." With Howly, she finds what Ard, with his chronic sneer and Arab nose up in the air, and the haughty Lilian never do, a measure of happiness, some relief for her desperate loneliness. In Hannah's world of odd characters, freakish accidents, and thwarted lives, the moral seems to be that less is often more.

Style and Technique

The one exception to the less-is-more rule is the narrator's style. The aptly named William Howly is a latter-day Huck Finn, although older, wiser, and better educated, who, instead of lighting out for the Territory, has settled into the relative comfort of a job as lead writer at a Jackson advertising agency. The story is told in the vernacular and follows a more or less straightforward chronological line. The delivery may be deadpan but the phrasings are often startling: hyperbolic, comically grotesque, the matter-of-fact rendered with a manic touch of southern gothicism. Ard's "ugly ocher Chrysler," for example, "was a failed, gay experimental shade from the Chrysler people." Syntax is at times decidedly and comically colloquial ("I didn't know but what he was having a seizure"). The narrative often swerves from one scene to another; one section, for example, ends, "Now Quadberry's back was really hurt. He was out of this war and all wars for good," and the next begins, "Lilian, the stewardess, was killed in a crash."

Hannah's art is one of stark juxtapositions rather than intricate designs, an art of extravagant verbal effects and broad, cartoonlike strokes rather than the careful building up of realistic detail. It is an art in which comic antics are deployed to keep despair at least momentarily at bay, and in which finely tuned psychological motivation plays a less important role than raw emotional force. "Testimony of Pilot" thus resembles Quadberry's playing, which combines technical brilliance with sudden transcendence: "desperate oralness" and a private ecstasy, dignified because of what came out of his horn. The story follows essentially the same dramatic idea that the Bop Fiends do—to "release Quadberry on a very soft sweet ballad right in the middle of a long ear-piercing run of rock-and-roll tunes"—and achieves precisely the same result, astonishing its audience with its tenderness.

Robert A. Morace

TEXTS FOR NOTHING 3

Author: Samuel Beckett (1906-1989)
Type of plot: Absurdist
Time of plot: The mid-twentieth century
Locale: Dublin, Ireland
First published: "Textes pour rien 3," 1955 (English translation, 1967)

>   *Principal characters:*
>   THE NARRATOR
>   VINCENT, his friend

The Story

This is one of Samuel Beckett's intellectually and perversely teasing monologues about existence, which are quite common in his later work. As the unnamed narrator considers what he should do, he seems to be trying to prove his own reality by constructing a story that he keeps chopping and changing. It may be a story of a journey, out and back, that takes place in the spring. There is to be no serious action, so the voice assures itself that there is nothing to fear. Nevertheless, there is a constant sense of anxiety and reluctance involved. The voice decides to be the character in the story, and there is a sense that it is to be a male character, an old man, cared for by a nanny called Bibby.

The narrator faces the problem of how to describe himself, perhaps with the help of memory, although he admits that he cannot remember much, so he abandons that idea. He will instead write of the future. As an example of that method, he thinks about how sometimes at night he says to himself that on the morrow he will put on his dark blue tie with the yellow stars. This thought seems to upset him, but he hurries on with his proposed action and decides to be accompanied by an old naval veteran, who may have fought under Admiral Jellicoe in the British navy in World War I. There is considerable gritty detail about this proposed companion, and about the narrator's physical state. The veteran's lungs are bad, and the narrator himself suffers from a prostate condition, which he alleviates in unpleasant detail. There is a sense that what he is saying is not simply being made up, but, in fact, actually occurred in the past, as numerous minor acts in his characters' lives are recorded with tangible details. The narrator imagines spending time with his companion trying to keep warm, and their pleasure in betting on horses and, occasionally, on dog races.

The narrator thinks for a moment of going alone, but reconsiders and decides to take his old friend, whom he calls Vincent, with him. He spends some time imagining what it would be like to start off with Vincent stumbling along behind him. However, this consideration of how to make something of himself outside his loneliness fails, and he abandons the idea of making his trip with Vincent.

He tries again, thinking about how to describe himself physically, and concludes that he might find it easier just to be a head, rolling along, but with some sort of leg to deal with the hills, starting out from Duggan's (which may be a name for a Dublin betting shop) on a rainy spring morning. The voice admits that it is all for naught—that none of this exists, that his attempt to make flesh of his plight of being nothing but a voice fails him. He is reduced to his state of seeming nothingness, in which nothing will happen. There will be no departure or stories about tomorrow, and the voices he seems to hear have "no life in them."

Themes and Meanings

Beckett was always interested in problems of existence, particularly the simple fact that human beings have no certainty that anything or anyone exists outside their own consciousness. Beckett's characters, therefore, are battling against the nightmare of solipsism. He often expresses the battle to discover existence in stories about characters who try to give themselves life by contemplating existence in invented stories. There is something appropriate, if maddeningly circular, in the idea of Beckett writing about characters who are trying to confirm their existence by writing about making up stories about themselves.

In this story, the narrative voice goes quickly to the problem as if one were writing a story, choosing a character, a plot, a setting, and a time frame. There is some specificity in the naming of two characters, and the suggestion that the story is taking place in Dublin. For example, the reference to "the Green" may mean St. Stephen's Green, a park in the center of Dublin. There is also specificity in various graphic descriptions of the physical states of the narrator and his friend Vincent.

The story may be seen as a metaphor for the human condition, which Beckett always views with considerable pessimism as physically difficult at best, psychologically not worth the bother, and, ultimately, impossible to make any sense of, however hard one tries. For Beckett's characters, life is also difficult to prove. The philosopher René Descartes was assured by the proposition "I think, therefore I am." Beckett, by contrast, seems to think that the idea would be more accurately expressed as, "I think, but I am not so sure that I exist, and thinking does not necessarily clear up the problem or make things any better."

The story may be taken also as a metaphor for the difficulty of artistic creation—a frequent theme with Beckett narrators, who often weave it into their attempts to discover who and where they are. Beckett is called an "absurdist" because his stories are absurd in the sense of seeming to be meaningless, and they are absurd in the sense of reflecting his belief that life has no meaning.

Style and Technique

Beckett's fiction looks much more difficult than it actually is, but it does require careful attention, almost word to word, and certainly sentence to sentence because his narrators are constantly changing their minds. Beckett's strength lies not in telling the usual narrative with a beginning, middle, and end, although there is a rudimentary structure of such in this tale, but in the texture of his monologues. His characters (if they can be called such) may be down and out, both physically and socially, but that is sometimes taken to suggest that they are stupid—which they are not. His is a plain, oral style, but the content and manner of his expression are often highly intelligent.

From early in Beckett's career, he was interested in the nature of human existence. By the time he got to this kind of work, he was almost exclusively concerned with the question of how one knows things, and particularly, with how one exists within one's own mind. This story is best read in the context of the other tales in *Stories and Texts for Nothing* (*Nouvelles et textes pour rien*, 1955; English translation, 1967) because, as a group, they form a kind of tone poem of musings, sometimes poignant, sometimes angry, sometimes self-pitying, about the nature of living at the lowest level of self-perception, cut off from most normal social connection, and living a bare-bones existence.

The story can also be read by itself, with the understanding that there is no action, no plot, and no resolution as one expects in the usual short story. What there is must be read carefully and slowly to keep track of the constant changes. Simply, it seems to be the musings of an old man, though his bodily aspects are clearly played down, who seems to be trying to make sense of his life by inventing it in the form of a story, but cannot make up his mind what or who or where or when to do it.

The aesthetic pleasure in this story lies not in its conclusion, nor in its incidents, but in listening to its cranky, eccentric, but intelligently wayward voice. As a result, the standards for judging the quality of the tale lie not in plot, or in characterization in the ordinary sense, but in the act of entering the mind of this odd creature. It requires, in a sense, an abandonment of the usual touchstones of short-story judgment, although it can be argued that Beckett is using a rather narrow form of the "dramatic monologue" in which the speaker reveals problems, and sometimes solutions thereof, while often inadvertently revealing character. It is an old literary form, which can be seen in Geoffrey Chaucer's Pardoner, in William Shakespeare's soliloquies, and in some of the poems of Robert Browning, T. S. Eliot, and W. H. Auden. The real standard for its credibility as a work of art lies in the experience of keeping track of what is happening in the mind of an interesting character. It is quite possible to do so, but it demands the reader's close attention, patience, and willing suspension of disbelief in much of what is ordinarily presumed to be the normal elements of the short-story form and content. Form illustrates meaning.

Charles H. Pullen

THANK YOU, M'AM

Author: Langston Hughes (1902-1967)
Type of plot: Sketch
Time of plot: The 1950's
Locale: An American city
First published: 1958

Principal characters:
MRS. LUELLA BATES WASHINGTON JONES, a large woman
ROGER, a fourteen- or fifteen-year-old purse snatcher

The Story

It is eleven o'clock at night as a large woman carrying a large purse slung over her shoulder walks down a deserted city street. Suddenly a boy dashes behind her and with one tug jerks the purse from her. Its weight throws him off balance and he falls, legs flying up. The woman calmly kicks him.

Pulling the boy up by his shirt and shaking him, the large woman demands that he return her pocketbook. When she asks if he is ashamed, the boy finally speaks. He answers yes and also denies that he meant to snatch the purse. Not deceived, the woman tells him that he lies, discovers that he has no one at home, and drags him off. Frightened, the boy begs to be released, but the woman simply announces her name: Mrs. Luella Bates Washington Jones. The now sweating boy struggles desperately but finds the woman's half nelson difficult to resist.

As they enter her furnished room, Mrs. Luella Bates Washington Jones leaves the door open. She asks the boy's name; he replies that it is Roger. Calling him by name, she tells him to wash his face, then turns him loose—at last. Roger looks at the open door and looks at the large woman; he chooses to wash.

When the woman asks if he took her money because of hunger, the boy replies that he wanted blue suede shoes. The woman only says that she has done things that she would tell no one. Then, leaving him alone by her purse and the open door, she steps behind a screen to warm lima beans and ham on her gas plate. The boy does not run; he does not want to be mistrusted.

While they eat, the woman asks no questions but talks of her work on the late shift at a hotel beauty shop. After they share her small cake, she gives the boy ten dollars for some blue suede shoes and asks him to leave because she needs her rest.

Mrs. Luella Bates Washington Jones leads Roger to the barren stoop and says that she hopes he behaves himself. He barely manages to say thank you before the large woman shuts the door. He never sees her again.

Themes and Meanings

Merely alluding to the economic problems that cause widows to work late shifts and parents to leave unemployed teenagers unsupervised, Langston Hughes focuses on the universal power of love and trust in "Thank You, M'am." Hughes portrays the nobility of common people and the vitality of his African American culture in his works. Mrs. Luella Bates Washington Jones, whose name ironically recognizes both the slavery codes of the founders of the United States and the dignity of the common person, gives spiritual and physical gifts to the young boy.

This large woman first recognizes the dignity of the boy's name, Roger. Then she offers him cleanliness and self-esteem. Equality and trust are other spiritual gifts. As a woman who must heat ham and beans on a hot plate, Mrs. Luella Bates Washington Jones knows that food and money are necessary to maintain dignity. Finally, she gives Roger the greatest gift of all: the right to direct his own life. She closes the door; he is left to choose what he will do. As in most of Hughes's poems, satires, and sketches, circumstances and society may be unfair, but the individual has a choice. Roger, like Mrs. Luella Bates Washington Jones, must create his own dignity and freedom.

Style and Technique

Hughes chose to write in the idiom of black America and for more than forty years experimented with its cadences and accents. Most of "Thank You, M'am" is written in an urban dialect. This reliance on colloquial dialogue to reveal personality is one characteristic of the traditional African American oral style that Hughes often employs. Other characteristics are a deceptively simple sentence structure and a presentational style of narration. Hughes has the woman and the boy speak directly; they seldom demand or declare but simply ask or say. Hughes also has the narrator speak in a colloquial voice. The narrator tells the reader, "The large woman simply turned around and kicked him right square in his blue jeaned sitter."

In addition to capturing speech cadences in his works, Hughes experimented with the sound of the blues in his poetry and prose; the blues, which sing of the common person and of survival, are heard in "Thank You, M'am."

Charlene Roesner

THANKSGIVING DAY

Author: Susan Minot (1956-   )
Type of plot: Social realism
Time of plot: The mid-1960's
Locale: Motley, Massachusetts
First published: 1984

> *Principal characters:*
> MA and PA VINCENT, the grandparents
> GUS, their son
> ROSIE, Gus's wife
> UNCLE CHARLES, another son
> AUNT GINNY, Uncle Charles's wife

The Story

Gus and Rosie Vincent arrive at Ma and Pa Vincent's home, followed by the other aunts and uncles and cousins. Coats are taken off, there are greetings, and then the adults line all the young cousins up outside for the annual photograph. After the picture has been taken, Rosie Vincent instructs her children to go to the kitchen and greet Livia, the large, sweating woman cooking the family's holiday dinner. Livia drills the Vincent children in the catechism, and when they do not respond, she answers her own questions.

Sophie, Bit, and Churly snitch candy from the dinner table while the adults, except for Rosie, have cocktails in the living room. Some of the children drift into this adult sphere, keeping silent while their parents and grandparents talk. Readers see the details of the room through the wandering eyes of the quiet children: books, a photograph of Ma when she was young, the portrait of Dr. Vincent over the mantelpiece, the fancy shoes with flat bows that Ma is wearing and that her granddaughters like best. Interwoven through these details is the superficial, anecdotal conversation of the adults, who talk without looking at one another.

Delilah, sticking close to her mother in this uncertain adult world, says she wants to go look at the lion. Rosie tells her daughter to ask Pa, but Delilah and Sophie cross the room to examine a shadow box rather than address their grandfather. Finally Rosie speaks for her daughter, telling Pa that the children would like to go see the lion. His affirmative response is snapped out as a threat: "Watch out it doesn't bite you."

A troop of cousins ascends the stairs to the third floor, where the lion lies on the floor of the farthest attic room. In the thin light, amid the scent of cedar, the cousins approach the dead animal. Bit is the only one who will dare touch the tongue, made of fired clay, and Sophie lies down next to it to touch her cheek to the lion's soft ears.

Leaving Caitlin and Churly at the red-leather bar, Sophie, Bit, and Delilah proceed to the owl room, some of the boy cousins following. In this room are all kinds of ornamental owls. Along the hallway, stretching away from the owl room, are photographs and silhouettes of Vincent family members: Pa's pictures of himself from his sporting, Harvard, and political speechwriting days; a picture of Pa's famous brother. When the wandering children return to the living room, the grown-ups are arguing over whether the lawn at the grandparents' house had ever frozen over and the kids skated on it. Uncle Charles remembers this and is corroborated by Gus and Ma, but Pa, in the stubbornness of his old age and contrariness, says no.

Dinner is served. Most of the cousins sit at the wobbly children's table. Plates arrive at their places with everything already on them. Sophie leaves the table to go to the bathroom, and she stands in the hallway for a moment, listening to the sounds of the meal in the other room—the sounds of silverware on plates, voices, echoes. She returns to the table in the middle of a conversation that the adults are attempting to squelch, but that Churly wants to know more about. Ma has called someone a crook and Churly wants to know who it is and what he stole.

At this point Ma makes a strategic turn, changing the subject to the vacation house in Maine. This also turns out to be an unsafe topic of discussion: There is an argument about a porch that the house used to have. Was it torn down or did it burn down? Pa insists that it was torn down, but Aunt Fran says she thought it burned. Ma agrees and gives the signal to end the conversation. True to form, Churly disregards Ma's cue and presses the subject, asking how it burned down. There is tension at the table; Sophie feels flushed. Pa repeats that it was torn down. Ma explains that the remainder was torn down. Pa glares at Ma.

Ma starts to stack dishes on the turkey platter, getting ready to remove the dinner things from the table. Pa and Ma argue over whether he is finished eating. Aunt Fran tries to move forward by tempting Pa with dessert. Pa obstinately curses Livia's pies and then follows with a non-sequitur that silences the table: "Only occasionally you will disguise a voyage and cancel all that crap." The children are uncertain amid this tension. As the family eats dessert, Pa mumbles a series of phrases that seem unconnected to anything presently going on. When his wife whispers something in his ear, he loudly responds, "Why don't you go shoot yourself?"

The family dinner ends, and the family members disperse. Ma and Aunt Fran take Pa upstairs and then join the other grown-ups for coffee in the living room. To Uncle Charles's query, Ma answers with finality that everything is fine. This time it is Delilah, not Churly, who challenges the signal to be silent. Unlike Churly, who pushes argumentatively, Delilah challenges out of bravery. Delilah asks whether Pa was mad at them. The question forces the issue of Pa and the family's treatment of him. Gus says Pa didn't know what he was saying. Rosie keeps silent, pouring the coffee. Ma says Pa wasn't mad at Delilah. Aunt Ginny says that the turkey was delicious. Uncle Charles tells her to shut up. The family exchanges compliments over the meal. Ma gives all credit to Livia. Rosie says that Ma arranged it beautifully, to which Ma replies, "Actually, I don't think I've ever arranged anything beautifully in my whole life." Silence reasserts itself, and the vignette of the Vincent family Thanksgiving Day ends on a note of strained quiet and stillness.

Themes and Meanings

Susan Minot's story, which does not have a conventional plot, derives its meaning from the rich collection of details depicting the Vincent family. Carefully selected and skillfully expressed, these details work together to describe various family members and, most important, the habits and rules of the family's interaction. The occasion for the family gathering is an annual holiday, and this, coupled with Minot's use of language and verb tense, suggests that readers are witnessing a ritual that has occurred before and will come again.

The economical, minimalist style used to narrate the story of the Vincent family's holiday communicates more about the characters than an initial read might suggest. The story reveals the peculiar habits and roles of several family members: Churly is argumentative, Rosie is patient and a peacemaker, Sophie is pensive and sensitive, and Pa's senility is filled with anger. The details about the family members and snippets of their conversation also provide a blueprint for the family's dynamics—who talks and who does not, who has the power to stop a conversation, how the three generations interact. Minot reveals that much of the power in the family now resides in Ma, which contains implications for Pa's deep anger. Also, the aunts and uncles function fairly rigidly within the confines of the family blueprint; but Churly challenges it aggressively, Delilah questions quietly, and Sophie studies it. Ma's retort at the end of the story is another breach of the family contract; the unexpected comment throws the family so effectively off-center that they are unable to respond.

Style and Technique

Minot's economical use of language and detail does not withhold information; readers should not conclude that there is no meaning beyond these details, that is, that the surface is all there is. The narrative economy forces one deeper into these details in any attempt to extract meaning.

Minot's style encourages readers to mine the surface and reveal the profundity of the ordinary. For example, Sophie's trip to the bathroom during dinner is not an irrelevant detail. Minot tempts the reader with such facts, in effect asking what one can make of them. Treated this way, the ordinary detail becomes metaphoric, and the reader must explore the possibilities of meaning that these metaphors might contain. When Sophie walks down the hall to the bathroom, she leaves the family. This separation can be seen as merely physical, but it may also signify deeper distances between this pensive girl and her family. When she listens to the noise of the family, she is studying these people with her ear. Perhaps Minot is suggesting a role for this little girl—a role of family observer, the one who pays attention, although from a safe distance.

Julie Thompson

THAT EVENING SUN

Author: William Faulkner (1897-1962)
Type of plot: Psychological
Time of plot: About 1915
Locale: Jefferson, a small town in Mississippi
First published: 1931

> *Principal characters:*
> NANCY, a part-time domestic servant, the protagonist
> JESUS, her husband
> JASON COMPSON, SR., for a time Nancy's employer
> QUENTIN COMPSON, Jason's son, the narrator
> CANDACE CADDY COMPSON, Quentin's younger sister
> JASON COMPSON, JR., Quentin's younger brother

The Story

Nancy is a black woman who has been filling in as cook in the Compson household during the illness of their live-in servant Dilsey. She has an unreliable husband, and she has taken to prostitution to supplement her income. She has been knocked down and kicked in the face by a white client from whom she demanded payment, after which she, not he, has been jailed. While in jail she has made an attempt on her own life.

At the time of the story she is visibly pregnant, and Jesus, her husband, has gone off, first vowing vengeance against the father. Afraid that he will return and menace her, Nancy begs Mrs. Compson to let her sleep at the Compsons' house, but Mrs. Compson will not permit it; therefore, except for one evening when she sleeps in the Compson kitchen, Mr. Compson and the three children escort her home in the evening. Between the Compson house and her cabin is a ditch, which she views as the likely place for an ambush.

After Nancy's final day with the Compsons, when Mr. Compson will no longer accompany her, she cajoles the children, all under the age of ten, to accompany her. On their arrival at the cabin, she is so terrified that she uses every ploy she knows to delay the children's return, offering to tell them stories and make them popcorn, but her hospitality falls short of pleasing the children.

Finally Mr. Compson comes for the children and offers to take her to a relative's house, but she will not leave. When the Compsons depart Nancy is sitting, petrified, in her house and moaning. The author does not reveal whether her fears are groundless.

Themes and Meanings

Although the story touches on such aspects of early twentieth century southern life as the imposition of technology on a culture of traditional handicrafts, the awkward and frequently cruel adjustments of the races to social change, and the inequality of the races under the law, "That Evening Sun" is mainly a story about fear—fear rendered all the more terrible by Nancy's total isolation among others who cannot understand, share, or relieve it.

The title of the story derives from a well-known blues song. Nancy's moaning, which Quentin, one of the Compson children, describes as "not singing and not unsinging," occurs when the evening sun goes down and her imagination is most active. Her state exceeds ordinary blues melancholy, with the result that her "unsinging" lies beyond the control of music to give pleasure or consolation. Quentin, the narrator, knows what has happened to Nancy, but neither he nor anyone else in the story understands her despair or the all-consuming nature of her terror.

Although her husband has vowed vengeance against the presumably white father of Nancy's child, she realizes that any such act against a white man would be suicidal and that if Jesus does take action, she can expect to be the target. The Compson family are uncomprehending in their various ways. Mrs. Compson simply resents her husband's leaving her to take a part-time servant home, the children are too young to understand what besides skin color and external subservience distinguishes blacks from themselves, and Mr. Compson's suggestion to Nancy that she "let white men alone" indicates how little he fathoms her vulnerable situation.

On the night that the family allows Nancy to sleep in the kitchen, she awakens them with her moaning but is too frightened even to respond to the question of whether she has actually seen her husband lurking outside. Given a cup of coffee, she cannot hold it and does not notice that the coffee has spilled out. The children's naïve questions concerning what she has done to make Jesus so angry only add to her despair.

Nancy has neither the sense of belonging to a settled familial and social order, such as that to which her slave ancestors could cling, nor any enforceable legal rights such as those a person in her position might begin to enjoy a half century later. Her nominal rights have been ignored, her unfortunate relationship with a contemptible white man has disfigured her face, and her husband's subsequent abandonment of her has destroyed such stability as her life had offered. Unlike the earlier slave generations, she must contend with the threat of unemployment and the caprices of her white employers. Although Dilsey has steady work and an obviously secure place within a household, Nancy represents the nominally free black woman at the mercy of a husband who himself suffers, without any possibility of legal redress, bitter insults to his own manhood and may avenge himself by cruelty to her. She is, as she several times observes, "just a nigger," and although she is religious, she feels that God will no more stand by a "hellborn" creature such as herself than will the Compsons.

Ultimately, she is left to the mercy of the Compson children. If they leave her, she must face the uncertainty of the night alone. Her story to the children about a queen winds up with that royal lady pursued by a "bad man" in a ditch. Knowing that queens do not have to cross ditches, the children reject the story. In this and in a remarkable variety of other ways William Faulkner conveys her fear. She burns her hand on the hot globe of a lamp and does not notice the damage until Caddy calls her attention to it. She cannot concentrate on as simple a task as popping corn for the children and burns it all. She breaks into a cold sweat and inadvertently recommences her eerie moan. The arrival of Mr. Compson temporarily relieves her tension, but he has come to take the children home, and she is left to her private hell.

It is important to realize that Faulkner not only has given a graphic picture of southern intolerance, injustice, and violence, which generates lonely terror in a person such as Nancy, but also has enacted fictionally a sensitivity and sympathy for such a victim that is ordinarily beyond the scope of those who have not lived in a town such as Jefferson. Even when, as in this story, there are no characters who share this sympathy—Dilsey is too much a mainstay of the Compson family to share the burdens of her temporary replacement—Faulkner's story implies a moral responsibility unknown to the millions of Americans who have not been compelled to live with, or even notice the existence of, the Nancys and Jesuses of Faulkner's region. "That Evening Sun" communicates not only the sins but also the conscience of the South, and the "I" who hates to see the evening sun go down is not only Nancy but also any reader whose conscience Faulkner's story has constructed or reconstructed.

Style and Technique

Faulkner deploys more narrative resources in developing his themes than any other American writer. The effect of his stories is a function of his way of telling them; therefore, no summary of action or theme can do them justice.

In "That Evening Sun," Faulkner uses a retrospective point of view. Quentin, the oldest of the three children, relates events of fifteen years earlier. Between 1915 and 1930, as he observes at the beginning, much has changed in Jefferson, the seat of Faulkner's mythical Mississippi county. Shade trees have yielded to electric poles and wires, unpaved streets to asphalt, and black women lightly bearing laundry bundles on their heads to black women at the same task in automobiles. Immediately the author establishes the distance between the time of the action and that of the telling. By the absence of any comment on changes in attitudes and by Quentin's matter-of-fact tone, Faulkner implies the lack of any humane compensations for the loss of the old rhythms of small-town life.

The retrospective method also allows Quentin latitude for necessary exposition of facts that as a child he could not have understood, while at the same time the narrator can attempt to achieve immediacy and vividness by reporting recollections of an experience from his tenth year. When he focuses on the scenes that he witnessed with his brother and sister, Quentin's narrative becomes childlike in its language and sentence rhythms, as if he is striving to replicate the perceptions of fifteen years ago. Thus Faulkner achieves an unusual blend of the perspectives of the adult and the child, with the transitions managed so skillfully that they blend smoothly.

Another effective technique is the juxtaposition of the adult conflicts and the children's more circumscribed world. Faulkner creates a counterpoint consisting of Nancy's troubles with men and her remonstrations with the elder Compsons, on one hand, and, on the other, the naïve questions, petty quarrels, and self-seeking artifices of Quentin's younger siblings, Caddy and Jason, most of which are ignored or shushed by the adults. To a certain extent the children's talk mirrors the preoccupations of the older generation. Young Jason, for example, is particularly interested in determining the status of blacks, while he and Caddy both spend much of the time on the path between their house and Nancy's debating whether Jason is indeed a "scairy cat."

The overall effect of the counterpoint of children and adults, however, is one of stark contrast. The youngest child's attempts to establish who is and who is not a "nigger" represent only an embryonic version of the adult code that condemns Nancy to insecure servitude and Jesus to base humiliation, and the children's utter incomprehension of the nature of adult fear heightens the reader's sense of Nancy's isolation. The world of the children is not precisely innocent, for they have already absorbed many of their parents' attitudes, but they have no intimation of Nancy's inner turmoil. As yet they are cruel and pitiless only in the manner of inexperienced children against whose naïveté Nancy's hopelessness stands out in sharp relief.

One more aspect of the narration deserves comment. Faulkner expected his readers to "see through" his narrators in two different senses. It is only through Quentin that the story is available at all, yet the reader must also see through Quentin in the sense of seeing beyond his field of perception. In his objective account there is no sympathy. In Nancy's hour of need, the Compsons, though in no way legally responsible for her, nevertheless abrogate their moral responsibility not to abandon her. Quentin shows no sign of recognizing this responsibility fifteen years later. He can be trusted to get the facts correct, but the author leaves it to his audience to appreciate their significance.

Robert P. Ellis

THAT IN ALEPPO ONCE

Author: Vladimir Nabokov (1899-1977)
Type of plot: Sketch
Time of plot: Around 1941
Locale: Nice, France
First published: 1943

> *Principal characters:*
> THE NARRATOR, a former poet, fleeing from the Germans
> HIS WIFE, a younger woman

The Story

The narrative of the struggle of a nameless man to preserve his sanity, this story is told through a letter that he addresses to a literary colleague whom he seems to have known since an early age. His letter tells the bizarre story of his marriage to a seemingly nonexistent wife, their eventful flight from Paris to Nice to escape the Germans, and the strange events that arise from their unfortunate separation in Faugères, so close to their destination.

When the narrator gets off the train to get food in Faugères, the train leaves without him—several minutes ahead of schedule. He leaves messages at the train station for his wife, has the station call other stations, and leaves messages with several station agents, all to no avail. He cannot find his wife in Faugères, Montpelier, or Nice, where he finally stays to look for her.

A week later, after the police try to convince the narrator that they have found his wife, he sees her, by coincidence, standing in line outside a store in Nice. She tells him of her misfortunes with the train, how she joined a group of refugees who lent her money to get to Nice, and how she boarded the wrong train but finally made it to Nice.

Reunited, they start the task of applying for exit visas to the United States. Soon afterward, however, the narrator's wife tells him that she lied about her disappearance. She admits that she had really been staying with "a brute of a man" whom she met on the train. This throws their relationship into disarray, as the narrator tries to find out every detail of her infidelity, believing that the truth will make it easier for him to bear.

Meanwhile, their quest for visas goes on. One day, the narrator's wife confesses "with a vehemence that, for a second, almost made a real person of her," that she had not done it.

Their wait for visas continues until, finally, the narrator comes home carrying two exit visas and two tickets for a boat to New York. When he gets home, however, he finds his wife has gone, along with her suitcase and clothing. The only memento she has left is a rose in a glass.

After several inquiries, the narrator finally finds an old Russian woman who tells him what his wife has told everyone else—that she has met a wealthy aristocrat and that she wants a divorce, but that her husband would not give his consent. On the narrator's way out, the old lady tells him she will never forgive him for killing his wife's dog before they left Paris. She is referring to the same dog the narrator's wife told him she would have missed had they had a dog.

After deciding to go on alone, the narrator goes to Marseilles to catch a ship for New York. Four days later, he goes on deck and runs into an acquaintance from Paris, who says he saw the narrator's wife a few days before in Marseilles, with her bag, saying that her husband would be along shortly. Taking this in, the narrator decides to write to his former colleague, who is also in New York now. He realizes that somewhere he has made a fatal mistake. This reminds him of Othello's similar situation, and he realizes that he may end up a victim of his own delusions—or worse—if he is not careful.

At the end, the story loops back to the beginning and explains the title. From the title it did apparently end in Aleppo for the narrator.

Themes and Meanings

Only Vladimir Nabokov could have written "That in Aleppo Once," an unusually complex short story with several levels of meaning. Chief among these are geometric patterns, word games, human relationships, and allusions to other authors. From its title through its end, "That in Aleppo Once" mimics the pattern of William Shakespeare's *Othello* (1604), and Nabokov's story follows a similar theme of love, perceived betrayal, and the progressive decline of the hero until he is consumed, like Othello, by despair and delusion.

When he is late for a train, he loses his wife for a week. When his wife shows up, she tells him that she has slept with three refugee women. Later, she changes her story to having slept with a hair-lotion salesperson. Shortly afterward, she tells other people that an aristocrat was courting her, and that the narrator had threatened to shoot her and himself if she left him. On another level, the narrator marries (gains) her, loses her on the train, gets her back, loses her again when she leaves, almost gets her back through the friend on the boat who saw her in Marseilles, and loses her definitively when he sails without her.

In his quest for a visa, the narrator talks about the hopeless spiral: "We were trying to get . . . certain papers which in their turn would make it lawful to apply for a third kind which would serve as a steppingstone towards a permit enabling the holder to apply for yet other papers."

The narrator refers to an embankment on which he pictures his wife standing. It first appears as an "endless wind-swept embankment." Later, at the end of the story, it becomes "the hot stone slabs" with "tiny pale bits of broken fish scales" on which he pictures his wife walking.

Even the narrator's choice of words shows a devolving pattern: He starts the letter with sublime prose: "the sonorous souls of Russian verbs would lend a meaning to the wild gesticulation of trees," but, by the end, he is reduced to inane, slanted rhymes: "How is Ines? How are the twins. . . . How are the lichens?"

To make matters worse, the narrator's wife lives in her own world, and the narrator's attempts to understand her lead him to further confusion. For example, on the train from Paris, she starts crying about the dog they have left behind. When the narrator tells her they had never had a dog, she replies, "I know, but I tried to imagine we had actually bought that setter." The narrator does not recall ever talking about buying a setter. However, the dog takes on a life of its own, so that, near the end of his stay in Nice, the narrator is rebuked by an old Russian matron for hanging "that poor beast . . . with your own hands before leaving Paris."

The downward spiral ends in the narrator's recognition that he has made "a fatal mistake," just as Othello had in killing Desdemona, and the subsequent realization that he must pay for this mistake. The unfortunate implication of the title is that, as the author himself fears, he will ultimately lose control and end up killing himself— hence the line, "It may all end in *Aleppo* if I am not careful."

Style and Technique

Nabokov uses a variety of literary devices in this story. Most obvious to the reader is the first-person "confessional" narrative, seen in several other Nabokov works, notably *Lolita* (1958), and *Pale Fire* (1962). In "That in Aleppo Once," this device allows the author to express his own opinions without signing his name. Thus, when the narrator recalls "With all her many black sins, Germany was still bound to remain forever and ever the laughing stock of the world," it is really Nabokov expressing his contempt.

The title is an innovative example of foreshadowing: Readers familiar with *Othello* will recognize the line as a symbol of the impending death of a man whose illusions have overtaken him.

The narrator, being a poet, has a natural tendency to write in a descriptive manner, and, although he claims he is not a poet just now, he manages to slip in several rhymes and poetic allusions. The repetition and variation on certain themes, such as the loss of love and the embankment, seem like stanzas of a long, complex poem. In the middle of the story, when the narrator finds that his wife has gone with all of her belongings but has left a rose on the table, the narrator (and the astute reader) see this as what French rhymesters call *une cheville*—a word used to maintain the meter in a line of poetry.

In using so many literary devices and allusions, Nabokov is asking his readers to be as well educated as he. Without a knowledge of *Othello*, for example, the reader will miss the references throughout to that play, which reinforce the title's meaning. Furthermore, without a knowledge of some French, Russian, and historical background, the reader is equally blocked. Perhaps Nabokov's message, therefore, is that all of life depends on interwoven pieces and chance occurrences, and the more one knows, the better one can understand—and prevent—tragedy.

Gregory Harris

THEATER

Author: Jean Toomer (1894-1967)
Type of plot: Social realism
Time of plot: The 1920's
Locale: Harlem, New York City
First published: 1923

> *Principal characters:*
> JOHN, the brother of a theater manager
> DORRIS, a chorus girl

The Story

The "theater" of the title is Howard Theater, an urban cabaret in the 1920's, set amid the "life of nigger alleys, of pool rooms and restaurants and near-beer saloons." As its afternoon rehearsal begins, the manager's brother John sits in the center of the theater and watches. He is a light-skinned African American, educated, urbane, and conscious of his social status.

The chorus girls themselves hold no interest for John. He coldly contemplates them and rejects them. They are beautiful, but beneath him socially; all of their movements are studied and routine. Although the women are unworthy of John and of his attention, the music and the glitter and the artificial passion soon begin to excite him. He wills his mind to put the excitement down, but when he sees Dorris appear on stage, he senses that there is something different about her. Unlike the other dancers, she is really engaged, really "throwing herself into it." He cannot help noticing and desiring her. Dorris has bushy black hair, a lemon-colored face, and full red lips. John tries to suppress his desire for her; she is beneath him socially, despite her beauty. It would never work.

Dorris notices John noticing her. She desires him as well and asks her partner about him. He identifies John as the manager's brother, and "dictie" (slang for blacks who are overconscious of their social class). This makes Dorris angry. She knows she is just as good as John is, even if she is not educated or working in a respectable profession. She doubles her efforts in the dance, trying her best to impress John. If he is to refuse her, he may as well know what he is passing up. Soon her involvement takes her beyond trying to impress. The dance takes over her mind and body. All the men in the theater, and even in the alleyway, stop what they are doing to watch. Her spontaneity and energy are contagious; the other dancers start to move more freely as well.

John cannot take his eyes off Dorris as she swings her body and bobs her head. Beautiful and exciting, she is clearly dancing and singing for him now. No longer can he use his intellect to control his feelings for her. For her part, Dorris is imagining what she might have with John: passion, love, marriage, a family, and a stable home. He seems to be the sort of man who can give her all that. Her dance expresses the joy of possibility. John gazes at her and daydreams about meeting her, touching her, and watching her dance in private.

When the music finally ends, John is still dreaming about Dorris and does not realize that the dance is over. Dorris looks at him for approval, but he is not looking at her because he is staring off into space, seeing her in his dreams. Hurt to think that John has become indifferent to her so quickly, and saddened at the death of her own dreams, Dorris flees the stage in tears. The story ends. The two never even speak.

Themes and Meanings

In the sketches and stories that make up his collection *Cane* (1923), Jean Toomer often returns to the idea that African Americans who live in cities have lost an important part of themselves. A connection with the soil is, in an essential way, a connection with the soul. John, the "dictie" black man, is an example of this. Urbane and educated, he is also emotionless and controlled. When he begins to feel excited by the music and the dancers, he wills himself to ignore or suppress his excitement. He has developed the ability to control his feelings through his intellect, and Toomer shows that this trait, although it may be useful for urban life, is ultimately sterile and self-defeating. What excites John about Dorris is her spontaneity, her willingness to surrender control (or her inability to control herself). Her singing makes him think of "canebrake loves and mangrove feastings"—of earthy, rural pleasures that John's inner self craves. Every time that he rejects spontaneous pleasure because it "wouldn't work," he denies himself an opportunity to be a whole person.

Although Dorris is beautiful and can help John reconnect with his own soul, he talks himself out of wanting her. Because of the difference in their social classes, he will not approach her. Instead, he will touch her only in his mind, passing up what the reader realizes may be an important chance for his own happiness.

Dorris understands social class in the same way that John does, although she resents it. Because of the difference in their social standing—because he is "respectable" and she is not—she also will not approach him, and she can think of only one reason for his not approaching her. Dorris and John might be able to find a lasting and fulfilling relationship with each other, but the urban concept of social class—a bankrupt concept, Toomer believes—stands between them.

The theater is one place in a city where the two worlds meet, where "black-skinned life" will not be pushed aside. It is the only place where John can, for a time, connect with the world of feeling and spontaneity, and in fact there seems to be no other reason for him to be there. (He is not working at the theater and he never speaks to his brother, the manager.) However, it is only a place, and he can leave it any time. For Dorris, there is no escape if John rejects her. The dazzling theater is a symbol of the city, glittering but essentially artificial and unsatisfying for everyone.

Style and Technique

Stylistically, "Theater" can be confusing at first, because its points of view are fluid, changing every few paragraphs. A narrator of sorts opens the story, but this voice changes from objective reporting to speaking for the characters. John and Dorris also speak for themselves, and many of their speeches begin with their names followed by a colon, as with lines in a play. Many lines are fragmented sentences, with spaces and repetitions: "Arms of the girls, and their limbs, which . . . jazz, jazz . . . by lifting up their tight street skirts they set free . . . (Lift your skirts, Baby, and talk t papa!)" The dream passage comes in short phrases and sharp images. Clearly, Toomer is manipulating point of view and language to capture the feeling of the music, and to force the reader to surrender intellect to feeling, just as John is asked to do.

A device that ties everything together is the image of walls. The opening paragraph describes the walls of the city buildings that seem to have a life and a music of their own. The singing and shouting of jazz mixes with the "tick and trill" of the walls. During the day the walls sleep, but at night they become soaked with songs. When John walks into the theater, "they start throbbing with a subtle syncopation."

As the pianist begins rehearsal, the walls awaken; as the men and women dance, the walls begin to sing and press inward. It is this pressing inward, toward him, that John first notices as his excitement builds, and his blood starts to press in also. As Dorris dances for John, the walls press in toward them both, until they feel as though they are in the same small space. John feels walls pressing within him also, pressing his mind within his heart—containing his intellect but not his emotions.

The image of the walls echoes Toomer's themes of boundaries, between social classes, between heart and mind, and between city life and country life. Here, the walls are boundaries, but living ones, with their own songs. If John would listen to the right songs, if he would wall up the right things, he and Dorris could build a room of their own together.

Similarly, images of light and darkness echo John's involvement with Dorris and with his emotional center. As he first sits in his seat, a shaft of light from above illuminates half his face. Dorris is backstage, in the shadows. When Dorris begins to dance, she glows herself, and as her intensity increases she moves to the front of the stage where she is in the brightest light. (The rest of the dancers are in shadow.) In his ecstasy, John feels himself rising on the shaft of light, and his dream is full of soft warm lights. However, John's dream is just a dream—a shadow—and he is turning toward it instead of toward the real Dorris. When she looks to him, his face is entirely in shadow, and there he stays.

Cynthia A. Bily

THEFT

Author: Katherine Anne Porter (1890-1980)
Type of plot: Psychological
Time of plot: The late 1920's
Locale: New York City
First published: 1929

> *Principal characters:*
> THE UNNAMED NARRATOR, a woman who has lost her purse
> CAMILO, her rejected Spanish escort
> ROGER, her longtime friend
> BILL, her drama collaborator, who cheats her
> THE JANITOR, the woman who steals her purse

The Story

A woman living alone in New York City's bohemian area during the late 1920's discovers that her treasured gold cloth purse is missing. Aware that she had the purse in her hand when she came in the night before and dried it with her handkerchief, the woman recollects the events leading up to its loss.

The previous evening, the woman attended a cocktail party. When she left, she had the purse, and it contained forty cents in a coin envelope. It was raining and she was accompanied by Camilo, who was escorting her to the train. Observing that Camilo's new hat was being destroyed by the downpour, she compared him with her sweetheart, Eddie, whose hat never looked out of place, no matter the weather or the hat's general shabbiness.

At the stairwell to the train, Camilo left, to her relief. She immediately met up with Roger, a longtime friend, who suggested a taxi for the trip home. Soon they were in a cab making small talk. Roger casually mentioned that his wife, Stella, had written and would be coming back to him. The woman told him about a letter she had received. He asked her for ten cents to pay for the cab and commented on her purse's beautiful appearance. She gave him the dime and remarked that her purse was a birthday present. Their last comments were on Roger's new play and his determination not to compromise his integrity.

On entering her apartment building, the woman was met by Bill, a struggling playwright, who offered her a drink while he unloaded his personal problems. He told her that his latest work was in trouble. The play's director had rejected the script after casting and rehearsing it for three days. Bill then began to criticize his estranged wife because she demanded ten dollars a week for their baby.

The woman attempted to change the subject by commenting on Bill's pretty rug. Bill told her it cost fifteen hundred dollars when it belonged to a celebrated actress, but he had paid only ninety-five dollars. She then asked him about the fifty dollars he had promised her for revising part of his third act. Angered, Bill chastised her. She reminded him that he was paid seven hundred dollars, but he did not relent. Despite herself, she told him to forget the money, had another drink, and left for her upstairs apartment.

The woman remembered taking the letter out of the purse before drying it. She again read the letter, which was from a lover (possibly Eddie). The letter writer blamed her for the collapse of the relationship. She tore the letter into narrow strips and burned them in the coal grate. The following morning, while she was in the bathroom, the female janitor came into her unlocked apartment, called out that she was examining the radiators, and left abruptly, closing the door sharply.

The woman remembers all these events while she dresses, smokes a cigarette, and drinks her coffee. She determines it was the janitor who stole the purse. Angry, she goes down to the basement, confronts the culprit, and demands the purse's return, stating that it was a present she did not want to lose. The janitor swears that she did not take the purse, so the disbelieving woman tells her to keep it. Climbing the stairs, the woman reflects on rejection, the ownership of possessions, and the loss of love.

The janitor follows her upstairs and hands her purse back to her. She claims that she took it for her teenage niece and thought it would not be missed. The owner retorts it was missed because it was a present from someone. The thief replies that the owner could easily get another one, but the niece might not; besides, the older woman has had her chance at love. The owner holds out the purse and tells the thief to take it. The janitor now refuses, saying her niece is pretty and young, but the woman needs it more. After another exchange of recriminations, the janitor leaves and the woman puts the purse down and reflects that it is she who will end up with nothing.

Themes and Meanings

"Theft," despite its brevity, contains several interlocking themes that lie at the core of Katherine Anne Porter's work. Foremost is the theme of alienation that permeates the story. Porter creates a modern alienated wasteland, populated by characters suffering from empty human relationships. None of the individuals portrayed connects emotionally to another. Of the five marriages or love affairs to which the story alludes, for example, none is successful.

Paralleling the theme of alienation is that of rejection. The woman, nameless because she has lost her identity, experiences rejection of one sort or another from all the characters. She rejects Camilo as unworthy of her and, in turn, is rejected by Roger, possibly a current lover, who chooses reconciliation with his wife. When she arrives at her apartment building, Bill rejects her contributions to his script by refusing to pay her the promised money. Rereading the letter from a lover who blames her for the deterioration of their relationship, she symbolically rejects him by destroying the letter. Her final rejection involves the loss of the purse and the janitor's unwillingness to take it once it is freely given.

Porter underlines the themes of alienation and rejection with another one involving loss—the loss of the stolen purse and the woman's feelings regarding it. On one level, the purse signifies a material possession that she is willing to give up; on another, deeper level, it is not just her possession, but an extension of her personality. It probably was given to her by Eddie and symbolizes not only their love and life together, but also her youth. Now older, she is forced to face this painful reality when the janitor throws the purse back and taunts her about no longer being young, thereby precipitating her spiritual isolation. Her latent feelings of isolation, loss, and rejection merge by story's end. She is left with an empty purse and cold coffee, devoid of love.

Style and Technique

"Theft" is a unique short story in the Porter canon for several reasons. It is the first effort at incorporating autobiographical elements into her work. Porter developed an intense relationship with Matthew Josephson, her literary mentor and lover. His wife, after discovering the affair, told him to choose between them. Josephson chose his wife and wrote Porter a letter detailing the decision and the fervent hope they could continue working together and remain friends. Porter was crushed and humiliated by the rejection, which is echoed in the experience of this story's protagonist.

Porter creates an atmosphere entirely different from those of her earlier efforts by placing "Theft" in a contemporaneous urban setting. She also uses flashbacks more extensively than in her previous work, and as integral parts of the story. Most of it takes place in the woman's mind. Her heroine is defined slowly and with a myriad of small details not present in her earlier characters.

Porter employs a number of effective stylistic devices. She uses the weather to set the story's tone through her use of the rain, establishing the bleak mood that distorts vision. Her use of material objects, such as the purse, hats, letters, and a cup of coffee, are skillfully and symbolically woven into the story. Camilo's hat being destroyed by the driving rain is contrasted to Eddie's stylish wearing of a hat under any circumstances and Roger's protection of his. Porter uses the letter device for both reconciliation and termination. For Roger, the letter means the renewal of the severed relationship with his wife; for the nameless protagonist, a letter triggers a rejection of part of her past and precipitates her feelings toward the thief and the stolen purse. The use of the cup of coffee is masterful. The woman had a hot cup of coffee before descending into the infernolike basement to confront the janitor. By story's end, after her heated altercation with the janitor and the realization that she is fully alone, the now-cold cup of coffee, combined with the rejected purse, symbolically drives home the sense of isolation and loss of love. It is easy to understand why most literary critics hail the subtle and complicated "Theft" as one of Porter's minor masterpieces of short-story writing.

Terry Theodore

THEME OF THE TRAITOR AND THE HERO

Author: Jorge Luis Borges (1899-1986)
Type of plot: Mystery and detective
Time of plot: 1944, 1924, and the early nineteenth century
Locale: Ireland
First published: "Tema del traidor y del héroe," 1944 (English translation, 1962)

> *Principal characters:*
> AN UNNAMED NARRATOR, the writer of the story
> RYAN, a historian and the great-grandson of Fergus Kilpatrick
> FERGUS KILPATRICK, a patriot in the Irish rebellion of 1824
> JAMES ALEXANDER NOLAN, Kilpatrick's oldest companion

The Story

On the eve of the rebellion in Ireland in the year 1824, Fergus Kilpatrick, a patriot, is assassinated. One hundred years later, his great-grandson, Ryan, who is compiling a biography of the hero's life, tries to discover the identity of the assassin. His search entails the examination of historical records that prove to be enigmatic rather than illuminating. The contents of these documents recall episodes and characters from literature. For example, an unopened letter found on the cadaver forewarned of the assassination attempt in the same way that Calpurnia's warning did not reach Caesar in time to save him.

Ryan wonders about the possibility of a secret form of time, a drawing of lines that are repeated, like the systems proposed by the Marquis de Condorcet, George William Friedrich Hegel, Oswald Spengler, and Giambattista Vico, and like Hesiod's degeneration of humankind. However, Ryan notices that history has copied not only history but also literature because certain words recorded from a conversation between Kilpatrick and a beggar are originally from William Shakespeare's *Macbeth* (1606). Another discordant element in the investigation is a death sentence, signed by the usually merciful Kilpatrick, from which the name has been erased.

Finally, Ryan is able to piece together the clues. At Kilpatrick's request, Nolan, Kilpatrick's oldest companion, had learned the identity of the traitor to the cause: Kilpatrick himself. Because of the latter's popularity among the Irish people, Nolan conceived a strange project in order not to compromise the rebellion. It was arranged for Kilpatrick to be assassinated under deliberately dramatic circumstances that would endure throughout history. To this end, Nolan, who at one time had translated the principal works of Shakespeare and written about the *Festspiele* (vast theatrical representations with thousands of actors, which reiterate historical episodes in the cities and mountains where they occurred), wrote a script for the assassination. The play was performed, although not without a certain amount of improvisation by Kilpatrick, who, getting carried away with his part, would often speak lines more dramatic than those of Nolan, who had, in turn, plagiarized material from Shakespeare. Ryan suspects that Nolan intended those scenes to be clues for a future investigator.

Themes and Meanings

"Theme of the Traitor and the Hero" narrates the deeds of Fergus Kilpatrick and the events surrounding his assassination, but it is about the nightmarish fatalism that is existence. The story takes the form of an investigation into a century-old unsolved crime, conducted by a biographer who deciphers the enigma through the interpretation of some historical documents. However, although this evidence furnishes the information that leads to the final solution of the riddle, in the process it has raised disturbing questions about such notions as a secret form of time and reality copying the imaginary.

Various passages contained in the documents remind the biographer of certain texts, authors, and protagonists (historical as well as literary), dating from classical and biblical times to the present. Patterns emerge that not only enable the reconstruction of an incident in the past but also partially reveal the essence of being. The explanation of what actually happened—that Kilpatrick was a traitor who agreed to act out a staged assassination in order to save the rebellion—may satisfy Ryan's curiosity, but at the same time, it advances a malevolent hypothesis about how reality occurs. The solving of one mystery leads to another, greater and virtually unresolvable one.

In "Theme of the Traitor and the Hero," there are three story lines: an assassination, an investigation, and an invention. The story is told by a first-person narrator who "perhaps" devises a plot about a contemporary narrator, the latter, in turn, a biographer of his great-grandfather's life as set down by Nolan and others. These characters belong to three distinct time periods: 1944, the present of the anonymous writer; 1924, the year in which Ryan carries out his investigation (retold using the historical present tense); and the early 1800's, the era of Fergus Kilpatrick. Certain texts correspond to the different narrative threads, each having a source in other writings.

All the texts are linked: the first-person narrator acknowledges the influence of Gilbert Keith Chesterton and Gottfried Wilhelm Leibniz in the construction of his plot about Ryan's biography, which is based on historical records, including Nolan's drama, which derives from both the works of Shakespeare and the Swiss tradition of *Festspiele*. Furthermore, the three texts are products of discoveries: The first narrator has had certain partial revelations about history, Ryan figures out Nolan's strange project, and Nolan discovers the identity of the traitor. Common to all three stories, then, is the author-discoverer who rewrites texts from the past that are to be rewritten in the future. The same pattern is repeated again and again, like infinite mirrors creating a labyrinth with no exit.

Such interminable reflections are evocative of the type of existence envisioned by Leibniz: the perceiving and being perceived among all elements in the universe. In "Theme of the Traitor and the Hero," writing is the particular mode of perception: It confers existence on its subjects and its authors or creators by its practice (they are perceived through the text); conversely, it derives its being from (perceiving) what already is. Inasmuch as writing represents existence, it becomes an act of creation, literally as well as figuratively, demonstrated when, for example, history copies literature, written documents anticipate future readers, and plots justify their inventors.

From Kilpatrick's double identity (not as traitor and hero but as patriot-hero and protagonist-hero), other heroes and traitors may be inferred. For example, Ryan is the protagonist-hero of the invented plot, and, at the same time, he is a traitor in that he sustains the myth of Kilpatrick, that is, through his role as author. Nolan also commits treason through literature in the form of an elaborate, deceptive drama. However, these specific acts only serve to point to the larger betrayal that is writing itself, the perpetuation of existence as it is known.

Style and Technique

"Theme of the Traitor and the Hero" belongs to the genre of mystery stories, Jorge Luis Borges adapting its conventions in order to express his message. The writer after whom he models his story is Chesterton, whose detective fiction is characterized by reasonable explanations of the apparently inexplicable. This is clearly the case in "Theme of the Traitor and the Hero," as Kilpatrick's culpability (leading to Nolan's plan) accounts for various incongruencies and gaps in the original testimony. This, however, is only one aspect of the interest Chesterton holds for Borges.

In an essay in the collection, *Otras inquisiciones* (1952; *Other Inquisitions: 1937-1952*, 1964), the Argentine author concludes that Chesterton's work consistently has traces of the demoniac, the nightmarish, with such images as jails of mirrors or labyrinths with no center. It is this dimension of the mystery writer that seems to lend meaning and impact to the other borrowing, the structural device, in "Theme of the Traitor and the Hero." Evidence in the story itself may be found, for example, in Ryan's noteworthy absence of reaction to the discovery of Kilpatrick's guilt, in contrast to his utter astonishment before the possibility of a secret form of time. Although the former is at the literal center of the text, it is a much less significant moment within the narrative. Furthermore, mention of Leibniz's preestablished harmony introduces a metaphysical concept more akin to an atrocious observation than a reasonable explanation.

Besides supplying background information about the inception of the story, the first-person narrator in the initial paragraph creates an immediate subjectivity, shrouding the remainder of the story with a veil of uncertainty. His use of the Spanish future of probability, "*escribiré tal vez*" ("perhaps I am writing"), coupled with an obscure view of history, places the subsequent fabrication within the realm of the conjectural, precise dates notwithstanding. The epigraph taken from William Butler Yeats's *The Tower* (1928) suggests that what he will be guessing about is that which makes men move.

Krista Ratkowski Carmona

THERE WILL COME SOFT RAINS

Author: Ray Bradbury (1920-   )
Type of plot: Science fiction
Time of plot: August 4, 2026
Locale: Allendale, California
First published: 1950

The Story

This futuristic story has no characters but centers instead on the single house left standing after a nuclear blast has destroyed the remainder of Allendale, California, in the year 2026. It is the story of one day in the life of the house: the day the house finally dies after having lived on for days after its inhabitants were killed in the blast. All that remains of the couple and two children who once lived there are four silhouettes in paint on the otherwise charred west exterior wall of the house. Such is the technology of Ray Bradbury's twenty-first century world, however, that the house continues to go about its daily business, oblivious to the total destruction around it and to the total absence of human life: "The house was an altar with ten thousand attendants, big, small, servicing, attending, in choirs. But the gods had gone away, and the ritual of the religion continued senselessly, uselessly."

Mechanical voice boxes hidden in the house's walls announce the date, weather, and noteworthy events of the day. A voice clock sings out the passing hours. The mechanical stove makes breakfast for family members who will never return to eat it, and robot cleaning-mice scurry out of their burrows to carry away any chance bit of debris. The family dog, the only remaining living creature, starves to death outside the kitchen door while inside the kitchen the uneaten breakfast is swept down the garbage disposal. The mice, sensing decay, scurry out again to carry off the corpse and toss it into the incinerator.

Time ticks away as the house prepares for a bridge party that never takes place, draws baths for its missing inhabitants, prepares dinner, warms the beds, and even lights a pipe for its absent master. At ten o'clock, the house starts to die. A falling branch breaks a window and sends a bottle of cleaning solvent shattering across the kitchen stove. Fire races through the rooms as the house fights desperately to save itself. All of humankind's twenty-first century technology is brought to bear as the battle rages. Voice boxes scream out warnings to the inhabitants for whom the warning comes too late, chemical foam gushes from the attic, and mechanical rain showers down from the walls. Finally, however, the reserve water supply that has kept the house functioning for days is used up, and the fire rages out of control.

As the house's wiring, its nervous system, starts to shrivel and burn, pandemonium breaks loose. The stove turns out huge quantities of breakfast as the flames eat up what has already been prepared, the mice rush out to try to carry away the growing mounds of ash, and the walls resound with a crazy chorus of voices, one quietly reading poetry as the study around it burns. When the house finally comes crashing down, dawn is showing in the east, and from the one wall still standing a single, last voice repeats over and over, "Today is August 5, 2026, today is August 5, 2026, today is . . ."

Themes and Meanings

By 1950, Bradbury was well aware of the looming threat of nuclear holocaust and of the irony that the technology that could be used to make life more comfortable for humanity could also be misused to bring about humankind's ultimate destruction. In creating the house that is the focal point of the story, human beings have made their scientific knowledge work for them to render daily life orderly and carefree. Before the nuclear explosion, the inhabitants of the house clearly lived a pampered existence, and it was the house itself, humankind's creation, that pampered them and that indeed even did much of their thinking for them. The house cooked, cleaned, and protected itself without the expending of any human energy. Martinis and sandwiches appeared readymade for the bridge party, and the cards were even mechanically dealt. The children were entertained with fantasy worlds on film projected on the walls of the nursery, and their parents with poetry read at their request by a voice box. The house also reminded the owners to pay their bills, to acknowledge birthdays and anniversaries, and to take along galoshes and umbrellas. Ironically, once the house made possible by humankind's technological advances started to function, it no longer needed humankind. So smoothly did the house run itself that it might have lived on much longer had not nature interfered.

In Bradbury's prophetic look at the future of modern society, human beings by the year 2026 have advanced to the point where they can control their material realm, but they cannot control their own destructive tendencies. The implication is that the nuclear blast is the result of an act of aggression against the West Coast of the United States. Whether war or nuclear accident is responsible for the devastation, however, human beings' power to use science for their own benefit is juxtaposed to their powerlessness to control their scientific developments in their more destructive forms.

The end of the story also illustrates humankind's powerlessness in the face of natural forces. The manner in which the house dies emphasizes the ability of nature to endure in spite of human beings' ultimately fatal attempts to control their environment. The wind blowing down a tree branch starts the series of events that end in the total destruction of the house. Dawn breaks in the east as the destruction is complete. The natural cycle goes on regardless of whether there is a single human being left alive to witness it. A human's puny recorded voice calls forth that a new day has begun, but the sun rises to shine only on a heap of rubble.

Style and Technique

At the heart of the story's irony is a poem by Sara Teasdale that the mechanical house chooses to read when the former lady of the house, Mrs. McClellan, is no longer there to express a preference. The title of the story comes from the first line of the poem: "There will come soft rains and the smell of the ground." Teasdale goes on to create a poetic world in which swallows, robins, and frogs continue their singing, oblivious to humankind and its wars:

> And not one will know of the war, not one
> Will care at last when it is done.
>
> Not one would mind, neither bird nor tree,
> If mankind perished utterly;
>
> And Spring herself, when she woke at dawn
> Would scarcely know that we were gone.

The irony exists in the way in which Bradbury's fictional world in "There Will Come Soft Rains" parallels the imaginative world of Teasdale's poem. By placing this poem in the middle of the story, just before the house starts to die, Bradbury draws attention to the role that nature plays in its death, but also to nature's lack of concern for humanity. There is also the additional irony that this poem about nature's lack of concern for human life is picked at random by a house designed to operate at the beck and call of people who are no longer even there. The house, with its mechanical voices, carries on, unconcerned, just as do the birds and frogs of the poem, with their natural voices.

The personification of the house throughout the story serves to make even more obvious, by contrast, the absence of human life. The house is full of voices, but not one of them belongs to a living human being. When danger arises, the voices scream and wail as if the machines behind them were capable of feeling fear. The house fights valiantly to save itself, and the fight becomes a battle as between two human entities. The fire lies in beds, feeds on paintings, stands in windows, feels the clothes in the closets. The fire is clever. It sends flames, as with conscious intent, to destroy the attic brain that controls the water pumps. The house's defeat is described in anatomical terms: "The house shuddered, oak bone on bone, its bared skeleton cringing from the heat, its wire, its nerves revealed as if a surgeon had torn the skin off to let the red veins and capillaries quiver in the scalded air." Its collapse becomes a burial: "The crash. The attic smashing into kitchen and parlor. The parlor into cellar, cellar into sub-cellar. Deep freeze, armchair, film tapes, circuits, beds, and all like skeletons thrown in a cluttered mound deep under."

Humans, in their attempt to be godlike, have succeeded in creating a dwelling that practically takes on a life of its own. In the absence of its human creators, however, the religion for which the house itself serves as an altar is reduced to an empty ritual. The ritual continues for a time, but the "gods" that it is designed to serve have gone away. All that remains is nature, which scarcely knows that they are gone.

Donna B. Haisty

THESE HANDS

Author: Kevin Brockmeier (1973-   )
Type of plot: Impressionistic
Time of plot: The 1990's
Locale: An American town or suburb
First published: 1999

> *Principal characters:*
> LEWIS WINTERS, a thirty-four-year-old man who writes fairy tales
> and works as a nanny
> CAROLINE MITCHELL, an eighteen-month-old child for whom he
> cares
> LISA MITCHELL, her mother
> THOMAS MITCHELL, her father

The Story

Although Lewis Winters, the protagonist/narrator, writes fairy tales, he insists that this story is not one of them. He also says that although the one he loves is eighteen-month-old Caroline Mitchell, the only thing padded in his room is the furniture and the only thing barred is the wallpaper. For those who suspect this is a Lolita story, he says he has never read Vladimir Nabokov's novel.

Hired by Lisa Mitchell to baby-sit her daughter Caroline, Lewis falls in love with the child and wishes they could spend their lives together. He tells her stories, watches her play, and takes her for walks. When people think Caroline is his daughter, he begins to think of her in that way. Much of the story is taken up with descriptions of Lewis's caring for Caroline. Although one such description is a lovingly detailed account of giving her a bath, Lewis makes no sexual approaches to the child. However, he is so obsessed with her that he makes a list about how many times he has dreamed about her, how many stories he has told her, how many diapers he has changed, and how many songs he has heard on the radio with her name in them.

Lewis's idyllic relationship with the child ends one day when her mother comes home early, distressed because she has lost her job. Lewis tries to comfort her, allowing her to rest her head on his shoulder and to cry. When he runs his fingers through her hair, she pulls away and tells him he had better go. The next morning when he arrives at the house, the husband, Thomas Mitchell, tells Lewis they will not be needing his services any more. When Lewis asks to say good-bye to "her," meaning Caroline, his true love, Mr. Mitchell thinks he is talking about his wife.

The story ends with Lewis standing outside Caroline's window, thinking of her sleeping in her bed and wondering if he should find a way to tell her good-bye. However, he does not and simply leaves. He often dreams of Caroline resting in his lap, running away with him in his car, pulling to the side of a quiet street, lying on the hood and watching white stars and soaring red airplanes, asking which is the more beautiful and the more real.

Themes and Meanings

When a thirty-four-year-old man becomes obsessed with an eighteen-month-old girl whom he is baby-sitting, the reader, accustomed to kidnap and child abuse shock stories, may initially feel uneasy. If the man were the girl's father and the word "love" were used instead of "obsessed," the reader would smile approvingly. So why cannot a man, even though he is not the parent, idealistically love a little girl for her grace and beauty and innocence? This is the thematic question that Kevin Brockmeier—a dreamer, a writer of fairy tales, and a fabulist—poses in "These Hands."

Although it is certainly risky for Brockmeier to write a story in which a grown man's love for an eighteen-month-old baby is described in terms usually associated with a man's erotic love for an adult woman, in the first paragraph, Lewis says that what he longs for is something that is not ugly, false, or confused. He believes in the possibility of grace and kindness, and beauty. Later in the story, he talks more about this notion of ideal beauty when he says as a matter of simple aesthetics, the ideal human form is that of the small child because people lose all sense of grace as they mature.

Lewis says that what he loves about Caroline is the concept of the heart known as the "salient point"—that point at which people merge with the universe. What Brockmeier risks exploring in this story is the mysterious nature of love itself, which, in its primal, polymorphous perverse form, knows no limitations of gender or age or species, but simply is the uncontrollable desire to be completely at one with the loved one. This is the basic desire of love in all fairy tales and romance literature, from Cathy's cry in Emily Brontë's *Wuthering Heights* (1847), "I am Heathcliff," to Aschenbach's agonizing fall from restraint and order into the beauty of the young boy Tadzio in Thomas Mann's *Der Tod in Venedig* (1912; *Death in Venice*, 1925). The lover does not want something so coarse as sexuality; Lewis thinks of Caroline not as a physical being but rather as a form of pure beauty, innocence, grace, and perfection. The misunderstanding at the end of the story that he wants something so mundane as a sexual encounter with Caroline's mother is sadly ironic in that it makes any further relationship with Caroline impossible. Like Wing Biddlebaum in Sherwood Anderson's story "Hands" (1919), it is the physicality of the hands that desire to touch in a purely nonphysical way that creates misunderstanding. What Lewis wants, what the romantic dreamer always wants, cannot be "handled" physically.

Style and Technique

"These Hands" opens with a self-reflexive reference to the teller of the story itself: "The protagonist of this story is named Lewis Winters. He is also its narrator, and he is also me." The technique that changes the story from simply one in which a man feels paternal love toward an eighteenth-month-old baby is Lewis's use of such words as "lover" and "my love" to refer to the baby Caroline. Because such terms are usually reserved for adults, the story could be taken initially for one in which Lewis has a Lolita-like sexual love for the infant. Although Lewis says at the beginning of the story that this is not one of his fairy tales, his use of several fairy-tale motifs challenges a possible sexual misinterpretation of the story.

Lewis uses several fairy-tale references to help him understand his love for Caroline. For example, he tells the story of a man who grows so fond of the sky that he makes a kite out of his heart and sails it into the sky. Never looking down for fear that he might be pulled to earth, he sails the world. Talking about love, Lewis says, is like the story he is telling, for it is always difficult to articulate what love really means. Lewis creates fairy tales that feature Caroline as an innocent who is able to see the imaginary constructs of fairy tales as if they were of the physical world. In one such story, Caroline floats around in a giant bubble and sees a man's heart sail by like a kite.

Another technique Brockmeier uses in the story is the list that Lewis makes about his relationship with Caroline, in which he itemizes the number of days he has known her, the number of puzzles he has constructed with her, the number of diapers he has changed, the number of lies he has told the reader, the number of times he has dreamed about Caroline, and more. The list suggests that Lewis sees all the events of his life solely in terms of his relationship with Caroline, for nothing else seems important to him.

The story ends with Lewis dreaming that Caroline is beside him and that they pull to the side of a quiet street and lie across the hood of the car, watching the stars and soaring red airplanes above, asking which is the more beautiful and which is the more true. This reference to English poet John Keats's notion of "Truth is Beauty, Beauty is Truth," suggests the ultimate idealism of Lewis's love for the child.

Although Brockmeier is compared with writers such as T. C. Boyle, Steven Millhauser, and George Saunders for his fantasy constructions, his work is sweeter than theirs; there is no smirking satire here, and there are no intellectual puzzles or metafictional mysteries. Instead, his stories explore an adult nostalgia for the fantasies of childhood, whether they came from the Bible or the Brothers Grimm. Without lapsing into the simplistic or the sentimental, "These Hands" evokes a basic human desire to recall that childhood realm of fairy tale, which, even as it seemed fantastic, embodies truths more profound than those evoked in the news that lands daily on people's doorsteps.

Charles E. May

THEY

Author: Rudyard Kipling (1865-1936)
Type of plot: Psychological
Time of plot: The early twentieth century
Locale: An Elizabethan house in the Sussex Downs, England
First published: 1904

Principal characters:
AN UNNAMED NARRATOR
AN UNNAMED BLIND WOMAN, the owner of the house

The Story

When driving through the Sussex countryside in early summer, the narrator, who appears to be an English gentleman of adequate means and impeccable manners, loses his way. In order to regain his bearings, he stops at an impressive mansion, where he sees two children at an upstairs window and hears a child's laughter coming from somewhere in the garden, two events that are of far greater significance than he can possibly realize. A woman approaches him from the garden, and he realizes that she is blind. In the ensuing discussion, it becomes clear that the narrator is fond of children, and the woman (whose relationship to the children in the house is unstated, although it is clear that she is not their mother) asks him to drive around the grounds so that the children may see the motor car—the presence of a car in that area being something of a novelty. The children, however, are extremely elusive, always hiding and leaving only reminders, such as a toy boat in the fountain, of their presence. There is something very mysterious about them. "Lucky you to be able to see them," the blind woman says, but her words contain an irony of which neither narrator nor reader is yet aware.

One month later, the narrator returns to the house. Curious about the children, he tries to attract their attention by making an elaborate show of repairing his car. He hears the faint tread of a child's feet on the leaves, but the children flee when he makes a sudden sound. Then, as he sees the blind woman approaching, he appears to discern a child clinging to her skirt, but the child disappears into the foliage as the woman draws closer. The children are so shy, she explains. They come and stay with her because she loves them. She does not know how many there are. They are not her own because she never married.

The narrator is puzzled by his conversations with this woman. She has beauty, sweetness of voice, and depth of soul, and yet she is marked by sadness and regret. He discovers that she possesses telepathic powers; other people's thoughts appear in her mind as colors. Some colors hurt her; others make her happy.

Their conversation is suddenly interrupted by the appearance of a distraught woman who is running frantically toward them. It transpires that her grandchild has fallen seriously ill, and the local doctor is unavailable. In the hectic events that follow—the search for a doctor and a nurse, the rush to collect medicine—the story snaps into dramatic action and becomes charged with the sense of the fragility and uncertainty of human life, and the reality of human suffering.

It is not until autumn that the narrator returns to the area. He learns that in spite of all the efforts made, the child had died within two days of becoming ill. On arriving at the house, he hears the blind woman singing:

> In the pleasant orchard-closes,
>   God bless all our gains, say we—
> But may God bless all our losses,
>   Better suits with our degree.

She shows him around the house for the first time. The evidence of children is everywhere: toy guns, rocking horses, dolls. However, the children themselves are nowhere to be seen; only the rustle of a dress or the occasional patter of feet betrays their presence. An odd kind of chase ensues, from room to room, passage to passage. The children have plenty of places to hide. Finally, as the narrator reaches the hall, he sees them, deep in the shadows, hiding behind a leather screen. He resolves to make them reveal themselves by pretending not to notice them. It was, he thought, a game between them. When the blind woman is distracted by the arrival of one of her tenants, he slides his chair back and taps on the screen. Moments later he feels his hand being clasped and kissed by the soft hands of a child. Instantly he knows the truth and senses that he has known it since the day he first saw the children at the window of the house: They are the happy ghosts of the youthful dead. The woman, realizing that he knows her secret, confesses that she feels undeserving, as if she had no right to hear the children because she has "neither borne nor lost." They came "because I needed them. I—I must have made them come." The toys were unnecessary, but she disliked having empty rooms.

The narrator listens and ponders the meaning of his realization with increasing emotion. He seems to be grappling with an equal measure of joy and sorrow. He knows that he can never return to the house. He reassures the blind woman that it is right for her to possess spiritual insight, but it would be wrong for him to cultivate it, even though it seems to come naturally to him. He gives no reason for this belief. The story ends as he sits silently by the screen, lost in the intensity of his contemplation.

Themes and Meanings

The origins of "They" can be traced to a tragic event in Rudyard Kipling's own life. He and his family had traveled to New York in 1899, and during the trip both Kipling and his seven-year-old daughter became seriously ill. Kipling recovered, but his daughter did not. Kipling's grief was deep and enduring. Back at his home in England, according to his father, he would see his daughter—like the children in "They"—"when a door opened, when a space was vacant at table, coming out of every green dark corner of the garden, radiant—and heart breaking." There is no doubt that "They," underneath the luxuriousness and beauty of the setting and the apparent gaiety of the children's presence, carries a heavy weight of sorrow, which only gradually unfolds itself.

The theme of the story is of the continuity of life and the continuity of grief, in the face of the raw facts of "losin' and bearin'," the human experience of birth and death. The theme has two crosscurrents. In one sense the story is uplifting; the ghost-children, after all, seem happy enough, and they can be perceived by those who possess love and spiritual insight. Love reaches beyond the grave, and the dead are a comfort to the living. However, they are a torture also. There is no mistaking the sadness and sense of regret in the unnamed blind woman; her voice "would have drawn lost souls from the Pit, for the yearning that underlay its sweetness." It is as if her psychic gifts must somehow be paid for, and in this respect she resembles the character Mrs. Ashcroft in "The Wish House," another of Kipling's short stories set in the Sussex countryside.

In the final pages of the story the full force of the sorrowful aspect of the theme is brought out, as the inner life of the narrator comes to the fore. His soul is "torn open," and his realization that he can never return to the house where the presence of the dead is so vivid is "like the very parting of spirit and flesh." Perhaps here the autobiographical strain of the story surfaces once more; Kipling, as the narrator, must put his grievous loss behind him and channel his psychic energies into further creative work.

Style and Technique

Structurally, "They" falls into three sections, corresponding to the three visits the narrator makes to the Sussex Downs. The very first paragraph effectively but unobtrusively leads the reader into the unusual world in which the story takes place. The references to Roman roads, Norman churches, and an old smithy that had once been a hall of the Knights Templars evoke the vast reach of time in English history. The narrator enters a world that is full of the passage of time and the imprint it leaves. Paradoxically, however, it is also a fairy-tale world that is beyond time; retracing his route on a map the narrator can find no name or information about the old house on which he has unwittingly stumbled. He realizes that he is "clean out of [his] known marks," a thought that has more significance than he realizes: He is entering a place that is unknown to him not only geographically, but spiritually as well.

The anonymity of the two central characters—they are never named—contributes to this effect. Not only does it surround them with a slight aura of mystery, but it also suggests that they possess some kind of universal significance, beyond the localized boundaries of time and place and larger than their individual personalities. As a significant contrast, all the characters in the poignant little episode that makes up the second section of the story are named: Arthur the sick child, Jenny the mother, Mrs. Madehurst the grandmother. The subtle and the mysterious gives way to the concrete and the real, and this prepares the reader for the revelation contained in the final section.

The force of the third section comes largely from the unexpected shift in focus from the house, the children, and the blind woman, to the sudden intensity of the narrator's feelings. Up to this point in the story, he has been a model of politeness and courteous detachment, as much the observer of sights and events as their direct participant. The fact that the sudden surfacing of his inner life is so dramatically effective is a tribute to Kipling's skill as a storyteller. Throughout the story he has inveigled the reader into seeing and experiencing with the eyes and the mind of the narrator, in his puzzled innocence. When the carefully cultivated sense of suspense, strangeness, and mystery is resolved in the final, overwhelming flash of realization, in which all the events of the story fall into place, readers find that they have been inexorably drawn into the experience, and as the story closes they find themselves, like the narrator, silently contemplating thoughts beyond the reaches of their souls.

Bryan Aubrey

THEY WON'T CRACK IT OPEN

Author: Yong-Ik Kim (1920-   )
Type of plot: Social realism
Time of plot: The 1950's
Locale: Sarasota, Florida
First published: 1969

> *Principal characters:*
> CHO, the narrator, a Korean schoolteacher visiting the United
>   States as a student
> DICK, an American who served in the Korean War
> MA, Dick's mother, a first-generation Romanian immigrant to the
>   United States

The Story

A schoolteacher from a village close to Pusan, South Korea, Cho comes to the United States to further his education. Before reporting to campus, he decides to visit his American friend, Dick—a soldier who was stationed in South Korea during the Korean War. Dick often visited the blind children's school where Cho was teaching and entertained students with stories about the United States. He told students that he came from a town where they had "the greatest show on earth" and once took a circus issue of *Life* magazine to show children its colorful pages. Cho described to the blind children what they themselves could not see: an elephant dancing, lions obeying their trainer, odd-looking animals with stripes, and the circus parade.

The blind students had trouble distinguishing the words "clown" and "crown." Cho tried to explain the difference to them but to no avail. After one student with limited vision touched Dick's big nose, the word "crown" stuck. Dick thereafter was known to the students as "Crown Dick."

Cho is surprised that Dick is not at the bus station to meet him. He takes a taxi and discovers that Dick does not live in one of those homes "whose large glass windows seemed to hold an underwater richness," homes with "shiny cars in the driveways and televisions inside." Instead, he lives in a worn clapboard shed with a battered old car parked outside.

During the visit, Cho learns that Dick's parents are first-generation Romanian immigrants. His family moved from Iowa to Florida after Dick's father passed away. Cho witnesses squabbles between Dick and his mother over jobs and money. Dick's mother, for example, does not want Dick to pay Cho's cab fare because they need the money for Christmas. However, Dick worries about what Cho will think of them and insists on paying it. Dick's mother tells Cho that Dick is a good boy, but he always wants to show off. Dick's friends have offered him jobs, but he has been trying to find a "big job" by himself.

As they drive back to the bus station, Dick starts drinking. They take a detour to the beach where Dick tells Cho that one reason he decided to visit Cho's school was that his mother complained to the army about her eyes and asked them to send him home. He wanted to learn what people with weak eyes look like and fell in love with the students. Dick confesses that he told Cho's students "fairy stories" about what he would do when he returned home, and he asks Cho to promise not to tell them anything to disillusion them. He loves them now more than ever.

After Dick passes out, Cho decides to leave by himself. Walking back to the foot of a long, white bridge, he sees a pile of coconuts for sale and buys one. Carrying the strange fruit under his arm, he makes his way back to the city and finds the street where Dick said the greatest show on earth marched.

There Cho mails the coconut to his students in Korea and imagines them putting their heads together, touching and hugging the strange fruit and even its shadow. He can hear them say: "No, no! We will not crack it open to see what is inside. We want to keep it whole."

Themes and Meanings

The thematic concern of this story revolves around the conflict between illusion and reality. Dick is a complicated character who is amusing, kind, and generous. His affection for the blind Korean students is sincere. He makes them laugh with his stories about the circus and gives them hope by describing what they cannot physically see. He promises the children that once he gets home, he will buy them candies, clothes, and shoes. By misleading the students into believing that everything in the United States is rosy and by painting a glorified picture of his own life, Dick instills false hopes into their hearts. The conflict between lies and truth is emphatically pronounced by Cho's discovery that not all Americans live in "beautiful homes with shiny cars in the driveways." It is also expediently demonstrated and accentuated by the physical conditions of the students. Their physical blindness mirrors and underlines their mental blindness. Their naïveté reveals their vulnerability.

Dick is not weaving "fairy stories" merely for the Korean children's benefit. He also wants to create an unreality for himself to block out unpleasant memories and to hide from reality. Dick is not happy at home. His parents are poor first-generation Romanian immigrants, who have been struggling to establish themselves in the United States. The squabbles between Dick and his mother are also often occasioned by cultural conflicts. Dick is more in tune with the mainstream American culture than with the culture that his parents brought with them to the United States. He is independent and lives in his dreams. He does not worry about finances and often takes his guests out to buy them dinner and drinks. Dick's mother, on the other hand, is pragmatic and frugal. She once asks Dick to pick up cow dung from the street. It can be used as fuel in winter. She believes Dick is ashamed of her, ashamed of her secondhand clothes, and ashamed of her broken English.

Telling "fairy stories" is one way for Dick to avoid facing reality. Alcohol is the other. Dick's mother has complained to Cho that Dick has been drinking heavily lately. On the way to the beach, Dick never stops drinking. He finally passes out in front of Cho, leaving the latter to figure out how to get back to the bus station.

The complexity of the story, however, lies in the fact that Dick is doing the wrong deed for the right reason. The blind Korean students remind him of his mother. He knows that they have been through a lot in life. He does not want to disappoint them by sharing the miseries of his own life with them. He wants to hear them laugh. He wants to inculcate and rekindle hopes in their tormented young hearts. As Cho recalls, their school "was in a bleak building that had once been a warehouse. Everything at the home for the blind children of refugees was bleak." However, when Dick walked into that school, he "had heard for the first time" the blind students' "laughing shouts."

It is apparently for the same reason that Cho decides to send a coconut home. He can see in his imagination the children touching and hugging the strange fruit and its shadow while laughing and shouting: "We will not crack it open to see what is inside. We want to keep it whole."

Style and Technique

A first-generation Korean immigrant, Yong-Ik Kim came to the United States in 1948. He has published many stories and three novels, *The Happy Days* (1960), *The Diving Gourd* (1962), and *Blue in the Seed* (1964). The novels have been published in several languages. Several of Kim's works describe a first-generation immigrant's observations and experiences in the United States. They enable readers to look at the United States through the perspective of a new immigrant.

Typical of Kim's writing style, "They Won't Crack It Open" intermingles memory with reality. The narrative jumps back and forth from the present to the past and from the United States to Korea. The approach is effective. By juxtaposing the "fairy stories" about the circus Dick tells the blind Korean students and what Cho discovers in the United States, Kim is able to highlight the conflict between illusion and truth and between memory and reality. It also reveals the narrator's concerns for his students and his strong tie with his home country.

The narrative pace of the story is slow, deliberate, and almost leisurely. It follows the narrator's innocent view as he struggles to determine which America is the real and which one is the fake: the America he has heard in Dick's stories and the America he sees with his own eyes. Cho's misconception about the United States is subtly suggested in the beginning of the story. When he is waiting for Dick, he thinks that his Asian face should get someone's attention at the bus station. He is forced to face his own false conceptions of the United States, however, when "no one at the station" gives him "even a curious stare that might invite a foreigner to ask a question."

Qun Wang

THIEF

Author: Robley Wilson (1930-   )
Type of plot: Fable
Time of plot: The 1980's
Locale: An airport
First published: 1980

> *Principal characters:*
> AN UNNAMED MAN, waiting for a plane
> A WOMAN WITH BLACK HAIR
> A WOMAN WITH BLOND HAIR

The Story

A man waiting at an airline ticket counter sees a beautiful, black-haired young woman and stares at her in an openly admiring way. She sees him and looks away. Later, while having a drink in the airport bar, he sees her again, this time talking to a blond woman. He wants to attract her attention and buy her a drink, but he cannot catch her eye. The third time he sees her, he is buying a magazine, and she jostles him. When he remarks, "busy place," she blushes, frowns, and vanishes in the crowd.

This seems like the end of the encounter, until the man reaches in his back pocket for his wallet and realizes that it is missing. He thinks about the credit cards, the money, and the identification in it, and all at once knows that the black-haired woman has picked his pocket. As he considers the difficult process of canceling the cards and getting new identification, he feels suffocated and wonders what he should do. He curses the woman for pretending to be attentive to him, for letting herself stand so close, and for blushing—not out of shyness—but out of anxiety over being caught. Just as he decides to report the incident to a guard, he sees the woman sitting in the terminal reading a book.

When the man sits down and says he has been looking for her, she claims that she does not know him and accuses him of trying to pick her up. He accuses her of stealing his wallet and demands its return. Although the woman first denies it, she then takes a wallet out of her purse, gives it to the man, and runs away. Realizing that it is not his wallet, the man chases her through the crowd, until he hears a woman's voice behind him crying, "Stop, thief! Stop that man." A young marine trips him and he falls. The woman who has been chasing him is the blond whom he saw the brunette talking to earlier, and she has a police officer with her. The blond accuses the man of stealing her wallet, and indeed the wallet the black-haired woman has given him belongs to the blond.

Two weeks later, after the embarrassment and rage are gone and his lawyer has been paid, the man gets his wallet back in the mail, with no money or credit cards missing. Although he is relieved, he knows that he will feel guilty around police officers and ashamed in the presence of women for the rest of his life.

Themes and Meanings

Although "Thief" at first seems like a realistic story about real people in a real situation, it is actually an ironic fable about how men treat women as if they were anonymous things and steal their identity when they stare at them and have sexual fantasies about them in public places. The fable nature of the story is initially suggested by the implausible nature of the events that take place. Rather than being realistic, they have been calculated purposely by the author to illustrate his ironic theme. It is unlikely, for example, that the two women haunt the airport just to trap men who stare at them; it is also unlikely that they have just met at the airport and plan their revenge on the man spontaneously. Thus, if the actions of the story cannot be accounted for realistically, they must be accounted for in terms of the author's purposeful plan for the story's illustrative point.

The thematic significance of what the women do depends on the reader's realization of the fact that the man has first stolen something from the black-haired woman; thus her stealing his wallet so he can then be accused of stealing from the other woman becomes an ironic example of poetic justice. What the man steals from the woman by staring at her is her identity as an individual because he is interested in her only as a conquest or as a sexual object. As the black-haired woman says when the man sits down and accuses her of stealing his wallet: "Is this all you characters think about—picking up girls like we were stray animals? What do you think I am?"

Although the man, like many men, may feel that his admiration of the woman and his desire to have a drink with her is innocent and harmless, the story seeks to illustrate that women may feel differently; indeed, they may deeply resent someone openly staring at them or trying to pick them up. Such an action is an invasion of a woman's freedom to be in public without being the victim of some man's sexual fantasies, for such fantasies drain a woman of her personal identity and transform her into a mere object. Robley Wilson's story is about how two women turn the tables on such a man and steal his identity instead.

Style and Technique

Because the generic type of this story is ironic fable, its basic technique is ironic reversal and poetic justice. Indeed, its plot is a carefully controlled narrative about the two women who give the man a taste of his own medicine. The story's parable nature is also suggested by its being told completely in present tense, a point of view that conveys the sense of an illustrative picture. The point of view suggests the working out of a sequence of events to support a premise. For example, the story begins, "He is waiting at the airline counter when he first notices the young woman." The illustrative nature of the story is further emphasized in the chase scene, which the narrator says is like a scene in a motion picture, for as he chases her, the bystanders go scattering and she zigzags to avoid a collision. The scene also resembles a film in that present tense is the basic time frame of all film. The man is not telling about a remembered event from which he has learned something, nor is some disinterested party who witnessed the scene recounting it in a narrative. Rather, the point of view suggests something taking place before the reader's eyes as a purely illustrative incident. That the story is like a film or lurid little drama for the tabloids is also suggested by the man's thinking how the newspapers will refer to the woman as an "Ebony-Tressed Thief" and by his feeling pleased with himself by his use of the word "lifted" instead of "stole," "took," or even "ripped off" to describe what the woman did, for it sounds more like a word used in a film.

Everything that happens in the story is ironically appropriate to illustrate the poetic justice of the man having his own identity taken from him (his credit cards, driver's license, and identification cards) in revenge for his trying to steal the identity of the black-haired woman by staring at her as an object of his own sexual desire. It is ironically appropriate that the blond woman says to the police officer, "He lifted my billfold," thus echoing the word the man was so pleased with using earlier. It is also ironically appropriate that the man cannot even prove his identity to the police officern, because that which proves his identity has been stolen from him.

At the end of the story, the man is embarrassed but cannot really tell anyone why, for he knows that he has brought the incident on himself. He only knows that because he deserved what happened to him, he will feel guilty around police officers and ashamed in the presence of women for the rest of his life. This final awareness emphasizes the story's parable nature.

Wilson has called his fiction "premise fiction," a genre that occupies something of a middle ground between realistic fiction and dream fiction. Even as the event he describes seems real, there is something wildly improbable and fabulistic about it. Like much of Wilson's fiction, "Thief" is based on following an idea out to its logical conclusion, not on following real people as they interact with one another in actual life. The events of the story proceed along highly improbable lines, even as Wilson uses simple realism to recount them. In such a way, Wilson can take advantage of the techniques of both fantasy and realism simultaneously and thus illustrate the themes of his premise fiction in an economical and uncluttered way.

Charles E. May

THE THINGS THEY CARRIED

Author: Tim O'Brien (1946-   )
Type of plot: Psychological
Time of plot: The late 1960's
Locale: Vietnam
First published: 1986

> *Principal characters:*
> FIRST LIEUTENANT JIMMY CROSS, a boyish army platoon leader
> MARTHA, a college student who writes to him
> KIOWA, a Native American soldier
> TED LAVENDER, a terrified soldier

The Story

A platoon of seventeen American foot soldiers is on the march in the booby-trapped swamps and hills of Vietnam. They have been ordered to set ambushes, execute night patrols, and search out and destroy the massive tunnel complexes south of Chu Lai constructed by Viet Cong guerrillas. Young and frightened, most of the Americans are ill prepared emotionally for the stresses of war. The story does not follow a traditional linear plot but instead offers fragments of their experience, including seemingly unending lists of gear and personal effects that they carry with them. What they carry links them, yet distinguishes them.

Chief among the men and one of the oldest is First Lieutenant Jimmy Cross, twenty-four years old and not long out of college, who is smitten with love for a girl back home. He carries with him two photographs of Martha, an English major from Mount Sebastian College in New Jersey, whom he briefly dated. He yearns for her sweatless perfection, her white skin and clear gray eyes, fantasizing a relationship with her that never existed. Although she writes to him and he carries her letters, re-reading them each night, it is clear that his passion for her is not reciprocated. When Martha sends him a talisman, a white pebble from the Jersey shore, Lieutenant Cross carries it in his mouth, savoring its salty taste as something almost holy. Dreams of Martha help him escape Vietnam.

On April 16, the men draw lots to see who will wire a Viet Cong tunnel with explosives. The soldier selected to search the tunnel is the one about whom they are concerned, for his risks are great. When he finally emerges, covered with filth, all are relieved, but just as the tension eases they hear a shot. Ted Lavender, who stepped away from the group to relieve himself, is killed without warning by an enemy sniper. The incident stuns the platoon. Death in a firefight is one thing, but this swift and meaningless death is quite another.

Ted Lavender has always carried tranquilizers and top-grade marijuana to numb himself against his own terror, but his obsessive fear and caution do not help him; the twenty pounds of ammunition that he has carried makes no difference. He dies, as his friend Kiowa marvels, without time to react. His horrified comrades place him in a body bag and summon a helicopter. While they wait, they smoke Lavender's marijuana and crack jokes to mask their emotions. Then they burn a nearby Vietnamese village in retaliation, shooting the dogs and chickens.

That night Kiowa, who carries moccasins and his grandfather's hunting hatchet, tries to make sense of Lavender's death and to grieve, but he feels nothing. He pillows his head on the New Testament that he carries with him, a birthday gift from his father, and is glad simply to be alive. This fact comforts him, and he sleeps soundly.

Lieutenant Cross, on the other hand, weeps; he accepts full blame for Lavender's death, although in truth there is no blame. He suffers with guilt because he was thinking of Martha at the moment that Lavender was killed—he has loved her more than his men. He realizes now that his distant Anglo-Saxon virgin is nothing more than a dream. In his foxhole he burns her letters and photos, surrendering his illusions, and determines to conduct himself as an officer, a leader. He will be strong, tough, and silent—a man's man. He will protect his men, maintaining discipline and order so that they will live.

Themes and Meanings

A major theme that this story explores is the initiation of young men in wartime, when youths must become men. Pranksters must become killers, dreamers must become realists—or someone dies. The world of the intellect (Lieutenant Cross is a college graduate, Martha's letters express her admiration for Geoffrey Chaucer and Virginia Woolf) is of little relevance here; neither is romance or idealism. Courage becomes a concept without meaning. Getting through the experience alive is the important thing, as Kiowa knows too well. Fear paralyzes them all, yet somehow they manage to continue their march, to put themselves at risk, to carry out their orders. The trick is to survive.

The weight of their burdens is real. What these men have to nourish and protect them is only what they bear on their backs. Scarcely past boyhood, a medic packs his comic books and M&M candies for the relief of particularly bad wounds. A gentle soldier carries a rubbery brown thumb cut from a Viet Cong corpse. A third, a big, stolid man, packs with him the delicacy of canned peaches and his girlfriend's pantyhose. The men also carry infection, disease, and the land itself in the particles of dust and mud. They carry fear. They carry the weight of memory; they carry ghosts. They carry the burden of being alive; they carry "all they could bear, and then some."

Each man likewise carries within himself a longing for escape from the senseless and terrible reality of war. Some make their escape through sleep, as Kiowa does. Others manage to survive through daydreams, like Lieutenant Cross, or through drugs, like Ted Lavender. Every man waits for the blessed moment when a plane, or "freedom bird," will lift him above the ruined earth, the sordidness and death, his own shameful acts, into the lightness of air and the promise of home. The phrase "Sin loi! . . . I'm gone!" echoes in their real and imagined nightmares.

Style and Technique

This story is not told in chronological sequence. Rather, the random observation of one character after another alternates with a deliberate litany of weights and masses, the things they carry. Tim O'Brien's style here is fragmentary, close at times to pure stream of consciousness. His language is largely flat and understated, except where it is salted with slang, military jargon, and obscene black humor. The men's conversations are brief, punctuated by dashes rather than quotation marks, so that their spoken words are not easily distinguished from narrative.

Lavender's death is announced matter-of-factly in the second paragraph. Again and again the story returns to this event, each time revealing a little more detail, a new perspective, almost as if in a dream. The story spirals away from, circles around, focuses momentarily on this death.

The style is the story—a plodding, monotonous narrative punctuated by brief flashes of action. The catalog of objects carried, the accumulating weight of things, extends in steady, numbing procession. Gradually the repetition of weights and measures acquires meaning. This is what their lives have become, step after step, ounce after ounce.

Even the names seem symbolic. Jimmy, a boy's name, is paired with a man's title, lieutenant; these two qualities meet or cross in the protagonist. The boy inside the man's body is forced to become an adult and shoulder the burdens of an adult. Kiowa is also one in whom past and present views of race, war, and religion collide. His Indian grandmother remained an enemy of white people during her lifetime, yet his father now teaches Baptist Sunday school in Oklahoma City. Although Kiowa still carries his moccasins and an ancestral hatchet, he also carries boots and modern weapons. Finally, the delicacy of lavender, both scent and hue, suggests Lavender, the fragile youth who cannot bear to meet war face to face, and who quite literally loses his mind when he is shot in the head.

O'Brien's story is heavy with irony. Lavender, weighted down by extra ammunition and sheer panic, is the only American to die. Jimmy Cross leaves behind his love for Martha, choosing instead to bear responsibility and guilt for a death that could not have been foreseen. The story's emphasis on their innocence and vulnerability, coupled with the repeated date of Lavender's death, suggests poet T. S. Eliot's opening lines from *The Waste Land* (1922):

> April is the cruellest month, breeding
> Lilacs out of the dead land, mixing
> Memory and desire, stirring
> Dull roots with spring rain.

In this cruel month, in this cruel war, all these young men carry in their hands and on their backs their damaged, terrified, desperate lives.

Joanne McCarthy

THE THIRD AND FINAL CONTINENT

Author: Jhumpa Lahiri (1967-   )
Type of plot: Domestic realism
Time of plot: The 1960's to 1990's
Locale: London, England, and Cambridge, Massachusetts
First published: 1999

> *Principal characters:*
> THE NARRATOR, an immigrant from India
> MALA, his wife
> MRS. CROFT, his 103-year-old American landlady
> HELEN CROFT, her daughter and caregiver

The Story

"The Third and Final Continent" is the story of how a young immigrant adjusts to his new home and new bride. The heroine of the work is an eccentric, elderly widow, who manages to help the young man feel less lonely. She shows him qualities in his wife that he had not noticed and provides him with a model for his future life.

The narrator's account starts with his departure from his native India and continues with a summary of his five-year stay in London. After obtaining a job at a library at the Massachusetts Institute of Technology, he returns to Calcutta, marries, then flies to the United States, leaving his bride behind, with the understanding that she will join him six weeks later. In the meantime, he intends to stay in a room at the Young Men's Christian Association (YMCA) in Cambridge, Massachusetts. However, when he happens across an advertisement for a room in a much quieter area, he decides to look it over and ends up renting it.

At first, he is puzzled by the eccentric behavior of Mrs. Croft, his elderly, widowed landlady. Every evening, she announces that there is an American flag on the moon, pronounces the fact "splendid," and insists that her roomer repeat the word loudly enough so that she can hear it. This becomes a ritual. So does his presenting his rent envelope personally, rather than leaving it on a ledge. To his amazement, this considerate act elicits an expression of gratitude from the crotchety old woman. When her daughter Helen Croft makes her weekly visit, she tells the narrator that he is the first tenant her mother has ever referred to as a gentleman. He also learns from Helen that Mrs. Croft is 103 years old and so fiercely independent that she insists on eating only soup and heating it herself. From that time on, the narrator takes a little more time conversing with Mrs. Croft, and he often checks to make sure that she has not fallen.

During his six weeks with Mrs. Croft, the narrator often thinks back to his wedding and to the five unsatisfying nights he and his wife, Mala, spent together before he left India. He feels no affection for his wife and does not look forward to her arrival. He thinks back on the years he spent caring for his mother, who went insane after becoming a widow. However, he will be a dutiful husband just as he had been a dutiful son. He rents an apartment, meets Mala at the airport, and installs her in her new home. However, they remain strangers.

On one of their walks, they stop at the home of Mrs. Croft, who is now bedridden in the parlor. When the narrator responds to a comment by Mrs. Croft with his usual "splendid," for the first time, he sees Mala laugh. He wonders what the old lady will make of his wife, dressed as she is in a sari, with a red dot on her forehead. However, after looking her over, Mrs. Croft pronounces Mala a lady. Not long after their visit, the narrator is saddened by the news of Mrs. Croft's death.

Thirty years later, the narrator and Mala have a happy marriage, a comfortable home, and a son at Harvard. They have become American citizens and plan to spend their remaining years in the United States.

Themes and Meanings

Many of Jhumpa Lahiri's stories deal with the difficulties immigrants have in adjusting to alien cultures. Lahiri admits that "The Third and Final Continent" was based in part on what her father told her about his coming from Calcutta to the United States, where he, too, became a university librarian. The author stresses the fact that any immigrant from a country like India, where everyone lives surrounded by a large extended family, will feel alienated in a society in which people so value their privacy that they are content to live as strangers. Thus the narrator of "The Third and Final Continent" can adjust to a diet of corn flakes and bananas but finds it more difficult to get used to being isolated. Therefore it means a great deal to the narrator when Helen tells him that he has gained the approval of her mother, who judges everyone by the high standards of an earlier time. By accepting him, she becomes his friend.

It would seem that the arrival of his wife would end the narrator's isolation. However, Lahiri typically presents marriage as a source of problems, not a solution to them. Arranged marriages may work out when there is an extended family to provide support for the couple, but when the new husband and wife are alone together in a new country, their prospects are not good. In "The Third and Final Continent," the narrator has even more reason to dread his wife's arrival. Because of his experience with his mother, he cannot imagine how a woman's presence could bring him happiness.

Again, it is Mrs. Croft who solves the narrator's problem. What she does is to change his perspective. When she pronounces his wife a "lady," she validates his marriage, for he knows that she seldom applies the term to anyone. Moreover, during that encounter with Mrs. Croft, he sees qualities in Mala that she had not previously revealed, notably, a kind heart and a sense of humor. Following the lead of Mrs. Croft, he observes Mala closely, and for the first time, he finds himself feeling some tenderness for her. He later realizes that it was then he began to fall in love.

"The Third and Final Continent" is also a story about courage. Mrs. Croft keeps calling the narrator's attention to the landing on the moon, which is the third continent of the title. As he learns more about her, the narrator begins to see why she identifies with the astronauts. Like them, she finds herself in an alien world, and like them, she forges ahead anyhow. Unlike the narrator's mother, Mrs. Croft has not allowed her widowhood to destroy her life. When he hears of Mrs. Croft's death, the narrator grieves because she has become his role model. Thirty years later, he can say that his own life proves one can do anything; all it takes is courage and determination.

Style and Technique

Lahiri is a writer who knows the value of restraint. Although there are a great many realistic details in her fiction, none of them is gratuitous. When she describes the narrator's room at the YMCA in "The Third and Final Continent," for example, she mentions the cot, the desk, the cross on the wall, and the sign on the door to the effect that cooking is not permitted. Outside the window, which has no curtains, there is a steady stream of noisy traffic. The room that the narrator rents in Mrs. Croft's house is described much more fully. For instance, instead of a cot, it has a twin bed. The walls are papered, there is a rug on the floor, and it has both a closet and a bathroom. Again, the author leads the narrator to the window, which, unlike that in the YMCA, has curtains. Outside, he sees a backyard and two fruit trees. The reason for using so many details in the description of this room is to point out how inferior the other one was and to suggest that the narrator expects to be much happier in his new lodgings.

Lahiri is just as restrained and just as effective when she describes the inner lives of her characters. For example, all that the narrator of "The Third and Final Continent" remembers about the bride he left in India is the cold cream on her face, her braided hair, and her constant weeping. From that recollection, Lahiri has her narrator move immediately to the memory of his mother's final days. The author leaves it to the reader to understand why the two women have become linked in her character's mind. Similarly, she does not have him consciously contrast his mother with that other widow, Mrs. Croft; again, it is enough that he is inspired by the American woman's courage.

"The Third and Final Continent" demonstrates that Lahiri has the technical skill of a far more experienced writer. That skill, along with her originality and her insight into human nature, earned her a Pulitzer Prize for her first book, *Interpreter of Maladies: Stories* (1999). "The Third and Final Continent" was one of the stories included in that collection.

Rosemary M. Canfield Reisman

THE THIRD BANK OF THE RIVER

Author: João Guimarães Rosa (1908-1967)
Type of plot: Mystery and detective
Time of plot: Perhaps the twentieth century
Locale: Probably central Brazil
First published: "A terceira margem do rio," 1962 (English translation, 1968)

Principal characters:
THE UNNAMED NARRATOR
HIS FATHER
HIS MOTHER
HIS SISTER
HIS SISTER'S HUSBAND
HIS BROTHER

The Story

One day, quite unexpectedly, the narrator's father orders a canoe made. His wife thinks it absurd for a man his age to think about hunting and fishing, but the man offers no explanation. When the canoe, sturdy and built to last, finally arrives, the man solemnly paddles it into the middle of the river. During the first few days after this strange withdrawal, the narrator worries about his father and regularly leaves some food along the riverbank for his father's sustenance. The days become weeks, months, years, and it finally becomes clear that his father will never return to his family. His father manages somehow to ride out the floodwaters every year, though he barely touches the food left for him by his son and by other members of his family. The daughter marries and has a son, and the family gathers by the river in the hope that the man will come to see his new grandson, but he does not appear.

The daughter moves away, and finally the mother goes away to live with her sister. Finally, only the narrator, out of some profound sense of duty, stays. When he realizes how aged he has become, he knows that his father must be very old, and he goes down to the bank at last and calls out that his father's duty is finished, that he, the narrator, will take his place in the canoe. The father approaches in the canoe, but the son panics and flees. His father is never seen again. Finally, the son longs for a place to die, a canoe.

Themes and Meanings

A story of such open-endedness, in which characters have no names and nothing is explained, is naturally one that invites a great variety of interpretations. The story's lack of specificity is complicated by its title, which calls for the reader to identify a third bank, a process that would require an evaluation of the extant two to determine which is the first and which the second.

The easiest procedure for approaching the third bank phenomenon is to consider the story in the context of the volume in which it was published, which in the original Portuguese was entitled *Primeiras estorias* (first stories), although it was João Guimarães Rosa's fourth book. Although nothing more than authorial perversity may be the reason, it is true that ordering, numbering, and ranking are rational procedures that depend on a grasp of the external configuration of things, a perception of the real. However, the author is demanding a perception of essence, not subject to ordering, numbering, or ranking, because it cannot be seen with the eyes alone. The stories in this volume are all about human beings who are disconnected or alienated from the mainstream of social machinery; thus, their perceptions are not received community perceptions, which tend to be linear and symmetrical, but rather eccentric and individualistic, ranging from childhood wonder to second sight and across to the third bank.

When the father leaves in his canoe, he is doing so in response to some imperative that remains a mystery to the community. The only one who approaches an understanding of that imperative is the narrator, who never explains, at least not in any ranked or ordered fashion, his understanding of it. The narrator's perception is that the father had waited all that time for the son to take over the task of staying in the canoe in the middle of the river, and that when he turned and fled he somehow failed. However, it is also apparent that when the offer is made, the ordeal, with whatever outcome, is over, for the father is never seen again.

It is probably possible to interpret this story in a psychological fashion, or as a problem of family communication, or even as a religious tale, but that would reduce it to allegory or treatise, in which the force of the tale is at least partly derived from the evanescent nature of the imperative. The characters in other stories in the volume are eccentrics, madmen, murderers, and children, who share with the father of "The Third Bank of the River" a distance from received community perceptions that allows them to see things that normal people cannot see, and their gift of perception leads them into a state that transcends the literal and the ordinary.

Style and Technique

Guimarães Rosa is Brazil's monster of style, in the sense that James Joyce was such a monster in English. Anyone who knows his work can identify a single line read aloud as his or not his, because the diction of all of his works is "strange"—he is fond of neologisms, back formations, foreign words, Latinisms, pleonasms, expletives, unfamiliar word order, internal rhyme, onomatopoeia—the list is long. Such diction is difficult to render into English, with the result that those few works that have been translated are all much more "flat" in English than they were in Portuguese: The story is still there, but the surprises and delights produced by language alone are largely absent.

The stories in the volume in which this story appears are probably less dizzying from the perspective of language than are many of his others, which may be one reason that this volume is one of the few translated. However, even in English the story is too elliptical, not sufficiently informational, to satisfy readers who desire full understanding on a first reading. There is great range in the length of Guimarães Rosa's stories, from some early ones of more than one hundred pages to later ones that barely cover two printed pages. In all these stories, two elements of composition, language and perception, are at once stumbling blocks to the reader and keys to understanding the fictions. Guimarães Rosa did not write about the fantastic, but the world about which he writes is one in which the rules are not those of the rather more banal world that most people inhabit, and because the world is perceived as larger and more open to such things as three-banked rivers, the language used to narrate the tales is more elastic and less ordered than the banal language that most people speak.

Though the mystical sense of language is necessarily flattened by a rendition into English, a less elastic tongue than Portuguese, the mystical sense of the world remains intact, and sensitive readers may even discover that some of the rivers in their world have three banks as well.

Jon S. Vincent

THE THIRD PRIZE

Author: A. E. Coppard (1878-1957)
Type of plot: Realism
Time of plot: The late 1890's
Locale: A medium-sized English town
First published: 1928

> *Principal characters:*
> GEORGE ROBINS, an attractive young clerk
> NABOTH BIRD, his friend, a bicycle mechanic
> JERRY CHAMBERS, a "cockney ruffian"

The Story

George Robins and Naboth Bird are young men for whom footracing is "their pastime, their passion, their principal absorption and topic of conversation"; although neither is a champion runner, each occasionally wins "some sort of trophy."

On an August bank holiday, they go to a garrison town on the coast of England, where the holiday is being celebrated with a carnival of games. The crowd attending includes a medley of soldiers, sailors, most of the population of the town, and a number of blind beggars. The young men meet two girls who have come from London for the holiday; the "short snub" Naboth devotes his attentions to Minnie, the more demure of the girls, while the "cute good-looking" George offers "his gifts of gallantry" to Margery, who displays "some qualities not commonly associated with demureness."

After George and Margery engage in some trivial flirtation, the young men enter the mile race. George wins third prize. When the men are dressing after the race, they are pursued by Jerry Chambers, a "cockney ruffian living by his wits," who suggests that he could get the first and second place winners disqualified so that George could claim the first prize of five pounds. They reject his offer with appropriate scorn.

When the prizes are awarded by a portly countess, the only titled person the young men have ever seen, the name of W. Ballantyne is called out for the third place winner in the mile race. When no one comes forward, George quickly exchanges his tweed cap for Nab's bowler and claims the prize as W. Ballantyne. The prize is a sovereign, a gold coin worth one pound. After the awarding of the prizes is completed, George, again wearing his tweed cap, disappears, leaving his friends wondering what he is "up to." When he returns, he says that he has been to claim the third prize as George Robins. He reports that after some "palavering and running about" the persons awarding the prizes apologize for their mistake and give George a second sovereign.

Margery and Minnie rather fatuously admire George's cleverness, but Nab is perturbed by this dishonesty: All may be fair, as Margery says, in love and war, but sport is something else. To Nab, George's trick is "a bit like what Jerry Chambers might have done himself." Margery maintains that George was "jolly smart" and that Nab was actually his confederate because he lent George his hat. George offers Nab half of the questionable sovereign, but Nab resolutely refuses it. In spite of their disagreement over the ethics of George's claiming the same prize under two different names, the foursome remains amicable and continues to wander through the festive crowd.

In the midst of the stream of people a blind beggar is trying, without much success, to get contributions from the crowd by playing a hymn tune on a tin pipe. In spite of his ragged appearance, the beggar stands erect and maintains a sort of dignity; his feeble wife holds his arm with one hand and reaches out with the other for the few pennies that are given to them. George, Nab, and the girls are astonished to see Jerry Chambers standing in front of the pathetic couple, brazenly drawing attention to them with "excruciating gestures and noises." Maintaining that looking at the old couple "just breaks my heart," Jerry says that he is going to sing a comical song, dance a jig, and perform some other antics "to collect bullion for this suffering fambly." Jerry abandons his plan of dancing a jig when he discovers that the only tune the beggar knows is the hymn "Marching to Zion," but he aggressively passes his hat to collect money for the couple, whom he openly refers to as "those two old bits of mutton."

While Margery is searching for a coin, George takes the "glittering questionable sovereign" and, before Margery can prevent him, drops the coin into Jerry's hat. Then, "curiously shamefaced," he hurries away. The girls are dazzled by the generosity of George's contribution, and even Nab is "mute before its sublimity."

After they leave, Jerry counts the money and loudly thanks the crowd for the "very handsome collection" of eight shillings and fourpence. Then he hurries away, murmuring "Beau-tiful beautiful Zi-on." He keeps the golden sovereign for himself.

Themes and Meanings

The theme of this story turns on the comparison that the author invites among the varying degrees of honor exhibited by the principal male characters. Naboth, the mechanic, is clearly the most honorable: He objects to his friend's trickery in getting the second sovereign and resolutely refuses George's offer of half of the questionable prize. He cannot imagine what George is up to when he goes to get the second sovereign and is astonished when George describes his trick. The other extreme is represented by the totally unprincipled Jerry Chambers. He has lost money by betting on George, and he wants to make good his losses by inventing reasons to have the first and second place winners disqualified. His antics in calling attention to the pathetic old beggar and his wife are pure exploitation, as he is simply using them as an occasion to collect money, and, as he keeps the largest contribution, George's sovereign, for himself, giving the beggar a sum amounting to less than half the value of the sovereign.

George, the clerk, wavers between these two extremes. He is as quick-witted as Jerry in conceiving his plan to get an extra sovereign, but Nab's disapproval—significantly Nab condemns the trick as "a bit like what Jerry Chambers might have done himself"—arouses qualms of conscience that prompt him to give the sovereign to the old couple. There is a vast difference between George's extorting an extra sovereign from the sports committee and Jerry's brazen and vulgar exploitation of the impoverished old couple for the same coin.

Although Nab's steadfast integrity and George's conscientious sacrifice of the sovereign that he got by deception win the praise of the girls—and, presumably, the approval of the reader—it is significant that Jerry escapes unscathed with the sovereign to which he had no legitimate claim. Honor deserves—and wins—respect in the kind of world the story depicts, but a grossly vulgar charlatan escapes with the cash.

Style and Technique

Among the most notable aspects of A. E. Coppard's technique in this story are his skillful drawing of character and his deft presentation of significant details of description. The holiday crowd gathered for the games is festive, but also a little vulgar; it is made up of "soldiers, sailors, and quite ordinary people." George and Nab are from the lower ranges of the stratified English society of the 1890's; Margery and Minnie seem typical of the "jolly girls" who "hunt in couples." Margery opens her conversation with George by complaining that the train on which they came from London was filled with "boozy men" with "half of 'em trying to cuddle you." This conversational gambit naturally invites similar flirtation from George, and the triteness of their flirtation helps define the characters. Similarly, the blatant vulgarity of the conversation of Jerry Chambers identifies him as a "cockney ruffian."

Although one hesitates to insist dogmatically on the precise significance of small details, they can often provide important clues to the author's values and attitudes. What is the importance, for example, of the fact that the blind beggar, who has a "strange dignity inseparable from blindness in his erect figure," wears a clerical hat? The town where the games take place has a garrison and a dockyard and would have been considered a city except for the fact that the "only available cathedral" was "just inside an annoying little snob of a borough" that keeps itself outside the "real and proper" town. The cathedral further isolates itself from the public by charging sixpence admission. The only titled person the young men have ever seen is the countess who helps award the prizes, but Coppard says that she has "a stomach like a publican's wife." Traditionally, the institutions of the church and the aristocracy were supposed to give England its moral fiber, but such representatives of these institutions as appear in this story seem conspicuously deficient. In a world where the church is either impoverished or snobbishly withdrawn and where a countess is indistinguishable from a publican's wife, it is hardly surprising that the vulgarity of Jerry Chambers prevails.

Erwin Hester

THIS INDOLENCE OF MINE

Author: Italo Svevo (Ettore Schmitz, 1861-1928)
Type of plot: Psychological
Time of plot: The 1920's
Locale: Trieste, an Austrian town occupied by Italy
First published: "Il mio ozio," 1957 (English translation, 1969)

> *Principal characters:*
> ZENO, the narrator, an aging bourgeois man
> FELICITA, his enterprising mistress
> CARLO, his nephew, a medical man
> MISCELI, a rival for Felicita's "affections"

The Story

The narration begins with a pronouncement that the present established by calendars and clocks is merely arbitrary; that the self and the people around the self constitute the true present. The reader is thus introduced to the ensuing interior monologue and its obsession with time.

The narrator's present is dominated by his retirement from business and an impending inertia. It is also largely dedicated to medicine. In arming himself against disease, the narrator, Zeno, is aided by his nephew Carlo, just out of the university and conversant with the most up-to-date remedies. Guided by Carlo, Zeno is committed to preventive treatments. Having determined that Mother Nature will maintain life in an organism only so long as there is hope that it will reproduce, he prescribes a mistress for himself.

Zeno and the tobacconist, Felicita, to whom he becomes attracted, agree at the outset on a monthly allowance. Felicita rarely neglects to mention the stipend falling due by the twentieth of the month. For his part, Zeno never lets on that his interest in her is primarily medical. Zeno learns, however, that another person is a "complex medicine," impossible to take in doses. On one of the two days of the week he is scheduled to visit his mistress, he decides that he would be better off listening to Ludwig von Beethoven's *Ninth Symphony* (1823). The next day, however, he determines to take advantage of what is due him. He reminds himself that he must pursue a treatment "with the utmost scientific exactitude" to gage its effectiveness.

After arriving at Felicita's flat, Zeno is surprised to find there fat old Misceli, a man about his age. Regaining his composure, Zeno orders some cigarettes. Felicita's scolding of him for visiting her on an unappointed day offends him. He declares an end to their arrangement.

As he starts down the stairs, Misceli appears and announces that he, too, is leaving, having placed his own order with the tobacconist. Zeno takes considerable satisfaction in comparing his fitness favorably to Misceli's. After a discussion on maintaining health and stability, the two part.

Motivated by a sense of economy, Zeno calls on Felicita once again before the paid-up month is through. She is on her way out, and can only say that she will consider the matter. Zeno's response is an ineffectual "Ouf!"

Thus Felicita has educated him in his "present role of old man." Now he attempts to "deceive" Mother Nature simply by following women with his eyes, "trying to discover in their legs something more than a mere motor apparatus." The story closes with an episode in which Zeno's gaze at a lovely young girl on a train is met with an accusation of "Old lecher" from an aged maidservant, which he parries with, "Old fool!"

Themes and Meanings

As one of five fragments that constitute an unfinished continuation of the novel *La coscienza di Zeno* (1923; *Confessions of Zeno*, 1930), "This Indolence of Mine" treats many of the same themes: signs of health and disease, the aging process, preoccupation with death, and human motivation. Much of the narrative deliberates over medical theories and health regimes. Such deliberations dominate not only Zeno's musings but also his conversation. He even interrupts his narrative to check his blood pressure.

The marking of time is a related concern, as its loss is a reminder that one is approaching death. Zeno unsuccessfully tries to "claim" his due from Felicita before the end of his paid-up month. Following her evasions, his futile attempt to find solace in music reinforces his betrayal by time, the art of music depending on temporal relationships. Instead of the joy and harmony that he expects from listening to the last movement of Beethoven's Ninth Symphony, he senses only violence.

Presumably influenced by Freudian psychology, Italo Svevo delineates his characters by their drives: Zeno's thoughts and actions are taken up with "hoodwinking" Mother Nature into allowing him to remain alive; Felicita's every move is calculated to ensure her material well-being. Svevo also humanizes his characters, however, as he reveals the vulnerability showing through the cracks of their singlemindedness. Zeno, convinced that only surrender to love will prove an adequate health regime, is powerless to explain to Felicita how he wants her to be. Felicita, meanwhile, spoils the treatment that she is to provide by her habit of remarking that, strangely, Zeno does not repulse her.

In the story, as in other works of Svevo's later period, the author seems reconciled to human helplessness and to the inevitable dualities of character and situation, and ambition and real life. The years following World War I arguably parallel the decline of the Roman Empire, when civilization seemed threatened as much from within as from without, and people feared that the end of the world was near. At that time, both Augustinian Christianity or Stoicism offered compelling visions of the future. Zeno the Stoic characterized the world, every few thousand years, as degenerating into chaos only to rise anew, as a phoenix from its own ashes. Given his portrayal of time as an inveterate prankster, Svevo may very well have been thinking of the Stoic when he named his protagonist.

After the failure of his early novels, Svevo gave up writing for twenty years and became a successful businessman. In the 1920's, he took up his pen again, encouraged in part by his friendship with James Joyce, who had tutored him in English. In May, 1928, Svevo wrote regarding the "score of pages" he had written of his follow-up to *The Confessions of Zeno*, "I'm having a whale of a time. It won't matter if I don't get to finish it. I'll at least have one more good laugh in my life."

Style and Technique

Svevo is generally considered to have pioneered the use of interior monologue as a narrative technique. Critics write admiringly of the insightful and innovative probing of character in his work. Svevo is also identified as one of the first fiction writers to experiment with psychoanalytic concepts, with which he became acquainted because of cultural ties to Trieste, his hometown, and Vienna, the center of Freudian analysis. From *The Confessions of Zeno* on, his narratives present two levels of action. The first is a loosely connected series of events linked thematically; the second takes place in the mind of the narrator.

The irony that suffuses Svevo's work derives in part from this dual structure. Motives and intentions are contrasted with the stated perceptions of others and also with their end results. Zeno is shocked when told by Felicita that she does not find him repulsive, as he has never imagined himself that way. Instead of protecting him from death and decay, Felicita ends up teaching Zeno that he is an old man. Even Zeno's ordering of cigarettes as a way of avoiding humiliation backfires: The brand, which is duly delivered to him, is one he despises. Such skillful use of irony enables Svevo to balance humor and pathos in this and other works successfully.

Svevo's style was denounced by contemporary Italian critics for its lack of polish and luster. They thereby remained loyal to the current cult of literature promoted by the poet, novelist, and dramatist Gabriele D'Annunzio and defined in his phrase, "beauty is all." Svevo's bemused and bumbling narratives could scarcely be more antithetical to D'Annunzio's virtuoso style. Thus began the "Svevo case," an extended debate among critics on the literary quality of Svevo's works. Supporters have claimed an appropriateness for his homely prose, given the transparency with which it reflects his characters' less-than-lofty preoccupations. Nobel Prize-winning poet Eugenio Montale has noted that, in translation, the "sclerosis" of Svevo's characters tends to be lost.

Svevo's "pidgin Italian," as many critics characterize his language, is reflected in his pseudonym, which means "Italus the Swabian." Here he salutes his mixed linguistic heritage: his father's in the German Rhineland and his mother's in Italy. In defense of his idiosyncratic prose style, Svevo wrote in 1925, "For me, growing up in a country where, until seven years ago, our dialect was our true language, my prose could not have been other, unfortunately, than what it is." With characteristic self-mockery, he added, "and now there is no time to straighten out my crooked legs."

Amy Adelstein

THIS IS WHAT IT MEANS TO SAY PHOENIX, ARIZONA

Author: Sherman Alexie (1966-   )
Type of plot: Psychological
Time of plot: The 1980's
Locale: Spokane Indian Reservation, Nevada, and Phoenix, Arizona
First published: 1993

> *Principal characters:*
> VICTOR, the protagonist; a young, alienated Native American who
>   lives on the reservation
> THOMAS BUILDS-THE-FIRE, his childhood friend, a storyteller
> CATHY, a gymnast and a passenger on the plane to Phoenix
> NORMA MANY HORSES, a respected Native American woman who
>   saves Thomas

The Story

"This Is What It Means to Say Phoenix, Arizona," a story about reclamation, focuses on the relationship between Victor and Thomas Builds-the-Fire, two young Native American men who have grown up together on the Spokane Indian Reservation. Estranged from each other since they were teenagers, Victor is presented as the modern Indian, a man who has lost faith in himself and in everything Indian and traditional. Thomas Builds-the-Fire is Victor's antithesis, a dreamer and a traditional storyteller.

The central action of this story is a journey these two men take together to Phoenix, Arizona, where Victor's father, who left Victor and his mother when Victor was seven, has died of a heart attack in his trailer. They take this journey to claim Victor's father's "savings" and ashes. Having just lost his job at the Bureau of Indian Affairs (BIA) and financially unable to make the trip with the one hundred dollars given to him by the Tribal Council, Victor runs into Thomas Builds-the-Fire, who offers to lend him the money he needs on one condition. Thomas says Victor must allow him to go along, since Thomas had promised Victor's father that he would "watch out" for Victor. Aside from their childhoods, Victor's father is the link that ties these two men together.

The two men take a plane to Phoenix, and on the plane, they meet and talk to a passenger named Cathy, a gymnast who says she was first alternate on the 1980 U.S. Olympic team. Thomas Builds-the-Fire initiates contact with her, and this impresses Victor. As they ride in a taxi to Victor's father's trailer, Victor apologizes to Thomas for beating him up when they were children. They both go inside the trailer where Victor retrieves a photo album and a stereo. With three hundred dollars from his father's savings account and his father's pickup truck, Victor and Thomas drive back to the reservation through the Nevada desert.

Back at the reservation, Victor gives Thomas half of Victor's father's ashes. Both Thomas and Victor plan to travel to Spokane Falls to throw the ashes into the water. Significantly Thomas tells Victor that his father will then "rise like a salmon, leap over the bridge, over me, and find his way home." The story ends with Victor promising Thomas that one time, "just once," he will stop and listen to one of his stories. Victor acknowledges this as a "fair trade," and they part with Thomas going into his house to hear a "new story."

Imbedded within the story are six flashbacks, four of which tell the story of a more innocent time, when Victor and Thomas were children and close friends. In one flashback, Thomas predicts that Victor's father will leave, and tells Victor why. In the second, Victor asks Thomas for a story, and he tells him a story about two modern-day Indian boys who could still be warriors but in a different way. In the third, Thomas saves Victor from being stung to death by wasps. In the fourth, Thomas "flies" by jumping from the roof of the tribal school to the cheers of all the Indian children. Though Thomas crashed and broke his arm, he was a hero to Victor that day.

As Victor gets older, he loses his belief in Thomas's visions and, while drunk, beats up Thomas for no apparent reason. In this flashback, all the Indian boys sit back and watch, and Thomas is saved only when another character, Norma Many Horses, comes along to stop the fight.

In the last flashback, presented right before Victor and Thomas arrive back at the reservation, Thomas is all alone, an orphan and a storyteller to whom no one on the reservation listens anymore.

Themes and Meanings

The meaning of Sherman Alexie's "This Is What It Means to Say Phoenix, Arizona" is amplified by the story's symbolism. The story's title, among other elements in this story, is significant. Phoenix is not only a city in Arizona but also the name of a bird in Egyptian mythology that rises from its own ashes and is reborn, making it a symbol of immortality and regeneration. Victor and Thomas Builds-the-Fire travel to Phoenix and, in the hot Arizona summer, step inside Victor's father's trailer to reclaim, literally and figuratively, that which has been lost. It is not only Victor's father's ashes, but also the ashes of Victor's own life, which Victor seems ready to grasp by this story's end. Thomas Builds-the-Fire is the character and agent, as his name literally indicates, who has built the fire under Victor.

Fire is a symbol of the passions and of the heart. Though Thomas is an outsider, even on the reservation, his "fire" is the transforming agent for Victor, for Thomas is a man filled with magic, dreams, and visions. When he tells Victor the story of his journey to Spokane Falls to find Victor's father, Victor recognizes the tie between his father and Thomas and that Thomas is a part of Victor's own story. When Victor abandoned Thomas, he abandoned a part of himself; this is part of what Victor reclaims.

This story embodies a journey motif that literally takes place via the plane ride to Phoenix, the stop at Victor's father's trailer, and the road trip back to the reservation.

On the plane they meet Cathy, the gymnast, whose physical flexibility stands in contrast to Victor's mental inflexibility. With Cathy, an athlete involved with the 1980 Olympic games—which the U.S. government boycotted—and the only "white" character in the story, Alexie implies that the U.S. government is self-serving, whether it is dealing with athletes or Indians.

Once in Phoenix, Victor goes into his father's trailer because "there might be something valuable in there." He is not talking about something that will be valuable in the material sense but sentimental things—letters or photographs. After entering his father's "house," Victor is then able see his father in a more human light.

On the way home, Victor drives his father's pickup for sixteen hours. When Thomas takes over at the wheel, halfway through the Nevada desert, he accidentally runs over a jackrabbit. Victor and Thomas both agree that the jackrabbit committed "suicide," which alludes to both Victor and his father, men who both had the ability to escape the symbolic "desert" of their own lives but refused. With this realization, Victor takes back the wheel and drives home, for now, he, unlike the jackrabbit and his father, is more consciously in charge of his own path.

The real journey takes place inside Victor, the protagonist and initiate, who emerges by story's end not as an obviously changed man but as one who now has the capacity for change. During the course of this journey, Victor recalls his childhood innocence and his pain, remembers what is bad and good about his father, acknowledges that his actions have hurt Thomas, and gives Thomas half of his father's ashes. Significantly, Thomas and Victor return to the reservation "as the sun [son] was rising."

Style and Technique

The seventh story within Alexie's short-story collection *The Lone Ranger and Tonto Fistfight in Heaven* (1993), "This is What it Means to Say Phoenix, Arizona" continues the story of Victor, an alienated young Indian man. Dialogue is used extensively. Alexie wrote the screenplay for the film *Smoke Signals* (1999) based on this short story.

Told in the third person, mainly through the consciousness of Victor, the tone is bleak, even cynical at times, with small details carrying great weight. Though this story is more psychological than political or social, references to the BIA, Thomas Builds-the-Fire's HUD (U.S. Department of Housing and Urban Development) house, poverty, alcohol, and the reservation underscore the tragic history of the Native Americans' interactions with the U.S. government and their psychological consequences.

In the first two sentences of the story the reader learns that Victor has just lost his job, that his father has died of a heart attack, and that soon Victor will be in great pain. However, this tone is offset by the character of Thomas Builds-the-Fire, who brings into the story both hope and comic relief. Although the reservation is presented as a place where history has produced poverty, alcoholism, and disillusionment, Thomas, himself a product of the reservation, seems to have transcended this. Though he is ignored, his Indian name links him with everything Indian and traditional. Like Norma Many Horses, who is described as a "warrior," Thomas is, in his own way, "powerful." Therefore, his connection with Victor produces the seeds for Victor's transformation. In the same way that Thomas Builds-the-Fire's name is meaningful, Victor's name indicates that he will be victorious.

By using a central story told within a number of smaller stories, Alexie weaves a tapestry from the threads of the past, which allows Victor, through his own memories and his connection with Thomas, to rise above his circumstances. Thomas envisions Victor's father rising like a salmon when he throws his ashes over the water of Spokane Falls. However, Alexie implies that it is Victor who will rise from the ashes, a young man who will be reborn, like the phoenix, from the flames of his own suffering and pain—flames kindled by his journey with Thomas Builds-the-Fire.

Candace E. Andrews

THIS MORNING, THIS EVENING, SO SOON

Author: James Baldwin (1924-1987)
Type of plot: Social realism
Time of plot: The 1950's
Locale: Paris
First published: 1960

> *Principal characters:*
> THE NARRATOR, an African American singer and actor living in
> Paris
> HARRIET, his Swedish wife
> PAUL, his seven-year-old son
> JEAN LUC VIDAL, the French director of his films

The Story

On the eve of the narrator and his family's departure for the United States after twelve years of residence in Paris, the narrator is being chided by his wife and visiting sister about his nightmares. He is worried about his return to the racist United States after such a long absence and what effect it will have on his multiracial family and his career.

The story is structured around a series of social interactions. The first concerns the narrator's family and his Paris existence. He puts his son to bed in the concierge's apartment, and his wife and sister go out on the town. The narrator slips into the first of his reveries on his apartment balcony overlooking the Eiffel Tower as he revisits his first years in Paris as an expatriate and struggling artist. He speculates on the whereabouts of his old North African friends and the conditions of the current Algerian conflict. He is in love with Paris and the French because they do not judge him on skin color, but he deplores their colonial war.

The narrator has an extended flashback about his visit to the United States eight years before for his mother's funeral. He describes the boat trip on which he sings spirituals and blues for a white audience, and his arrival in New York, where he is called "boy" by a white officer as he descends the gangplank and is engulfed by the "cunning and murderous beast" of New York City.

The flashback ends and the narrator welcomes his French friend and director, Jean Luc Vidal, into his Paris apartment. Over drinks, they reminisce about the narrator's defining role as Chico in *Les Fauves nous attendent*, a movie about a young mulatto man from Martinique who dies tragically in the underworld of Paris. Vidal drew a great performance out of the narrator by forcing him to confront his own interior demons, including the hateful summer after his mother's death that he spent in the American South working as an elevator boy.

The final section of the story takes place on Paris's Left Bank. In a discotheque, the narrator is recognized and approached by four African American students on tour in Europe. On their way to a Spanish bar, they hook up with Boona, an old Arab friend of the narrator. In a Spanish bar, one of the American girls has ten dollars stolen. Boona is accused and the narrator intercedes. Boona denies he stole the money. The matter is finally dropped, but not without an argument that forces the narrator to think about his position in relation to Africans. In the early hours they separate, and the narrator goes home to stand over his sleeping son's bed pondering father-son relationships. He awakens his son and they set out on their journey to the new world.

Themes and Meanings

The story is about an African American male expatriate who finds personal and career success in a foreign country. It shows his fears about returning to the United States after many years. He is concerned about the reception facing his interracial family, and wonders about his ability to continue his career in the United States. Examples of prejudice that he and his father experienced lace the story, giving credence to the narrator's apprehensions for his son.

The narrator is at the crux of many conflicts. He is an African American male living in Paris with an adopted language and culture. He has a white wife and mulatto son whom he loves, yet he fears for their safety. He wonders whether his successful career as a singer and actor can continue, and he debates the merits of being famous. Finally, he questions his place in French society because of France's colonial war in Algeria and his personal relationships with many poor North Africans.

At the center of the narrator's concerns is the question of color. Much of the story relates in telling detail, subtle and blatant forms of racism experienced or witnessed by the narrator. The narrator has not been able to express all of his anger. When he was asked to play a disturbed mulatto from Martinique in Vidal's film, he faltered. It was only after Vidal confronted him about his own repressed hatred of racism that he was able to perform the role with the passion it deserved.

The narrator is caught between his freedom and success in Paris and his past, marred by racism, which he is again about to confront. Using the flashback episode as an example of what he expects on his return, the narrator details the horrible feelings of helplessness and hatred generated by racist behavior. His family in the United States experienced prejudice firsthand and it damaged them forever. His father's and sister's lives were destroyed by racism, and the narrator escaped to France to avoid the same fate. Now famous, he must come to terms with his expatriate status, and find a way for his son to live without the same scars of racism.

The narrator also doubts that his identity as a black actor and singer has any validity in the United States. Having become famous in France for singing the blues, he fears ridicule in his own country, which often denigrates black creations. Coupled with this fear of failure is his suspicion of success. Fame has brought recognition, but not peace. The final section of the story deals with this conflict when the narrator is confronted by the African American tourists and finds himself absorbed into their circle.

When Boona is accused of stealing, the narrator is caught between commitment to his fellow countryman and loyalty to his old, but less than honest, friend. A similar conflict is expressed in his loyalty to the French, which is strained by their colonial war. The story ends without resolution.

Style and Technique

When James Baldwin wrote "This Morning, This Evening, So Soon," he was already famous, as is the nameless narrator of his story. The story reflects some autobiographical details much in the same way as his first novel, *Go Tell It on the Mountain* (1953), suggested the author's early life in Harlem. As an expatriate writer, Baldwin was indebted to the French for accepting his blackness and cradling his creativity. Although Baldwin himself never married and had no son, his tormented relationship with his stepfather bothered him all of his life. Finally, success never satisfied Baldwin, and his fight against racism continued until his death.

Baldwin writes in the first person in a confessional style that manages in a few short pages to cover much historical and geographical territory. With his ability to weave flashbacks into the present narrative, he provides a picture of two cultures and demonstrates the conflicts inherent in the narrator's ambivalent position. As an African American living in France with a white wife and a small son, he must make important choices. Baldwin expertly increases the tension by having the story occur on the eve of the narrator's departure. Caught between two worlds, Baldwin uses a close confessional style to create tension. The narrator's psychological dilemma is reinforced by his night on the town. Once again he is caught between loyalties and must mediate some kind of compromise. The story is a good example of Baldwin's mature writing style, in which he is able to depict white and black characters with considerable compassion while still showing the horrible effects of racism in American life.

Stephen Soitos

THIS WAY FOR THE GAS, LADIES AND GENTLEMAN

Author: Tadeusz Borowski (1922-1951)
Type of plot: Social realism
Time of plot: World War II
Locale: Auschwitz
First published: "Proszę państwa do gazu," 1948 (English translation, 1967)

> *Principal characters:*
> THE NARRATOR, the protagonist, a Polish inmate at Auschwitz
> HENRI, a French inmate at the camp and the narrator's friend

The Story

Through the first-person narrator, the author describes in harsh detail the daily routines and horrors of the concentration camp. The opening scene is a surreal picture of thousands of men and women, naked, waiting through the heat and boredom until another transport, carrying thousands of Jews to the gas chambers, arrives. Like the narrator's friend Henri, many of the inmates are members of the Canada Kommando, the labor gangs who work at unloading the transports. Henri and the narrator are introduced as they discuss the transports while lying in their barracks, eating a simple snack of bread, onions, and tomatoes. The transports mean survival. As the guards look the other way, the laborers can "organize" food and clothing from the piles of personal possessions collected from the Jews on the way to their death. As Henri states, "all of us live on what they bring."

The monotony is finally broken by the approach of a transport. For the first time, the narrator joins Henri as part of the labor gang heading to the station. The station is "like any other provincial railway stop" except that the regular freight here are those sentenced to the gas chambers. While the laborers wait, Henri barters with a guard for a bottle of water, on credit, to be paid for "by the people who have not yet arrived." As the freight cars pull into the station, the desperate cries for water and air from the prisoners crammed into the cars are quickly silenced by the gunfire ordered by an officer annoyed by the disturbance.

Once the doors are opened, the prisoners surge toward the light like a "multicolored wave." The Canada Kommando members work feverishly, taking bundles from the crowd, separating those destined for the labor gangs from those for the chambers, loading trucks marked as Red Cross with the dazed prisoners. In sharp contrast to the mayhem on the ramps, an SS officer, with calm precision, marks off the new serial numbers, "thousands, of course."

A more odious task yet remains for the laborers as they are ordered to clean out the dead and dying from the cars. The narrator describes the trampled bodies of infants he carries out "like chickens." He begins to be affected by the terrors. At first intensely tired, he slips into a confused and dreamlike state as he sees the scenes repeated over and over. His own feelings of helplessness and terror turn to disgust and hatred for the Jews themselves—for, as he tells Henri, he is there, acting so brutally, only because they are.

Just as the last cars leave, the tired laborers hear a whistle and "terribly slowly" a new transport pulls in. The cycle of atrocities begins anew. Now the Kommandos are impatient and brutally rip the bundles from the prisoners and hurl them into trucks. The scenes of horror intensify as a mother tries to abandon her children in the hope of making the labor gangs (for all mothers and their children are gassed together). A couple locked in each other's arms, "nails in flesh," are pulled apart "like cattle." In the cars are seething heaps of bloated corpses and the unconscious. The narrator can no longer overcome his mounting terror and runs blindly away from the horror. When Henri finds him, he tries to reassure him that one becomes seasoned to the work, as has Henri himself. There is another whistle and the "same all over again" begins but slowed by night. There are the same motionless mountains of bodies in the cars, the same cries of despair. The narrator can no longer bear the repulsion he feels, and he vomits. However, with the vomiting, the narrator rids himself of all the horrors he has witnessed. He suddenly sees the camp as a "haven of peace" for its inmates and realizes that he and his fellow prisoners survive, that "one is somehow still alive, one has enough food." He is seasoned. As the labor gangs finish their ungodly work and prepare to return to the camp, the narrator remarks how the camp will be fed by this transport for at least a week, how this was "a good, rich transport."

Themes and Meanings

Tadeusz Borowski drew on his own experiences as a prisoner at Auschwitz and Dachau for his stories on camp life. This, the first, published shortly after his release, graphically gives testimony that people are capable of doing anything to other people. More troubling is the realization that ordinary people, good people, will do anything to survive. The inmates of the camp learn to survive by assisting in the atrocities. For the Canada Kommando, the piles of plunder—jewelry, money, gold—taken from the nameless thousands are not as precious as the pair of shoes or can of cocoa that they can "organize."

By using a first-person narrator (one never given a name), the author clearly identifies himself with the responsibility and guilt to be shared by all. The narrator senses his responsibility when he lets his disgust turn to anger at the thousands who go passively to their deaths. He is forced to act inhumanly to survive as a human. As often noted, the narrator is both executioner and victim. He suffers the knowledge of his collaboration. Borowski called his stories on the concentration camps "a voyage to the limit of a particular experience." That experience is the realization of what a person can and will do to survive.

Style and Technique

The true horror of Borowski's experience is the routine of the collaboration in the atrocities. He has his narrator speak with the detached, objective voice of a reporter in most of the story. The phrases are simple and direct; the incredible brutality of the events needs no commentary. "I go back inside the train; I carry out dead infants; I unload luggage; I touch corpses." The normalcy of events is heightened by the descriptions and actions of the SS officers and guards. Against the backdrop of feverish action left to the camp inmates, the SS officers "move about, dignified, businesslike." They discuss the routines of their lives—children, family—as thousands are routinely executed. There is nothing out of the ordinary taking place there at Auschwitz.

There are several key images in the story. Food—the bare essence of survival—is a recurring motif. The narrator is first seen eating "crisp, crunchy bread," bacon, onions, and tomatoes. The Greek prisoners find rotting sardines and mildewed bread; as Borowski simply states, "They eat." The gangs rest with vodka, cocoa, and sugar "organized" from the transport. Even the bodies of the dead, trampled infants, are described as chickens. As the gangs return to camp, they are weighed down by the "load of bread, marmalade, and sugar" that they collected. Food as the image for survival occurs throughout the Auschwitz stories.

Another recurring image in Borowski's stories is that of insects. The mindless drive to eat and live surfaces in humanity as well as in insects. The Greek prisoners sit, "their jaws working greedily, like huge human insects." What Borowski calls the "animal hunger" of the camps drives them to eat whatever is available.

The relentless machinery of the transports and the corresponding helplessness of the prisoners are seen in the author's use of the wave simile. Borowski describes the prisoners of the first transport as a wave of "a blind, mad river." Nothing can stand in its way. However, it is not an isolated phenomenon. The last transport also discharges its freight that is like a wave that "flows on and on, endlessly."

Joan A. Robertson

THE THREE-DAY BLOW

Author: Ernest Hemingway (1899-1961)
Type of plot: Psychological
Time of plot: About 1920
Locale: Northern Michigan
First published: 1925

> *Principal characters:*
> NICK ADAMS, the protagonist
> BILL, Nick's close friend

The Story

"The Three-Day Blow" has little external action. The story focuses on the conversation of Nick and his friend Bill as they take refuge from an autumn storm in the cottage of Bill's father. The two close friends get drunk on whiskey belonging to Bill's father and speak of common interests: baseball, fishing, favorite books and writers, their fathers, and, as the whiskey takes effect, the recent breakup of Nick's relationship with a girl named Marge. The most important action, however, occurs inside the mind of Nick Adams.

The story begins as Nick walks through an orchard to join Bill at Bill's cottage while taking note of the way the field and woods are windblown by the autumn storm. Inside the cottage, the boys warm themselves by a roaring fire and reveal that they are eager sportsmen and avid readers. They refer to the talents and limitations of particular ballplayers and speak of unscrupulous trades, corrupt managerial strategies, and baseball monopolies that have ruined many good athletes and kept certain teams on top and others at the bottom of the baseball ladder. Suggesting a conspiracy among owners, Nick says, "There's always more to it than we know about." They agree that the "Cards" will never win a pennant—that even when the Cardinals did get going once, a train wreck ruined a promising season.

On their second glass of whiskey, the boys convey their admiration for certain writers over others—favoring writers they perceive as personally honest and whose works issue from firsthand knowledge. Books are as real to the boys as is fishing or whiskey, and they wish that they could share their personal passions with writers to whom they feel close. Gilbert Keith Chesterton is a "better guy" than Horace Walpole, but Walpole is "a better writer." They would like to take both of them fishing.

With the pouring of a third glass of whiskey, the boys propose to get really drunk and question whether they are not drunk already. Warmed by the whiskey, the fire, and their camaraderie, each praises the other's father, but it is clear that Nick is bothered by the fact that in contrast to Bill's father, a painter who is a bit wild, his own teetotaler father, a doctor, has missed out on too much in life. However, Nick notes philosophically, "It all evens up." As if to prove his father wrong about drinking, Nick vows to show that he can hold his liquor and still be practical. Knocking a pan off the kitchen table, Nick shows that he is far less in control than he pretends, and his unnatural rigidity is comical.

Moving to a fourth glass of whiskey, forgetting their promise to themselves to drink only from the bottle already open, the boys are more than tipsy now. On his way back from fetching water for the whiskey, Bill winks at the "strange" face that peers back at him from the mirror. The intensity of camaraderie, fueled by the biggest drinks yet, climaxes in toasts to writers and to fishing, which the boys declare is better by far than baseball. Filling their glasses a fifth time, they congratulate themselves on their wisdom.

At this point, referring to Nick's breakup with his girl, Bill speaks of "that Marge business"—which, it seems, has been on the minds of both boys all along. Bill argues that "busting it off" was Nick's only choice because marriage, especially to a girl who is evidently Nick's social inferior, would destroy his personal freedom. Bill tells Nick, "Once a man's married, he's absolutely bitched. He hasn't got anything more. Nothing. Not a damn thing. He's done for. You've seen the guys that get married." For a while, Nick says nothing or merely nods in quiet acquiescence to Bill's insistence that Nick "came out of it damn well." However, one can see that Nick is far more affected by the breakup than he is willing to admit; despite a sixth glass of whiskey, the knowledge that the relationship is over forever is dramatically sobering and saddening. When Bill reminds Nick that the marriage would have infringed on their male camaraderie, that they might not even "be going fishing tomorrow," Nick seems reconciled. "I couldn't help it," he says. . . . All of a sudden everything was over. . . . I don't know why it was. . . . Just like when the three-day blows come now and rip all the leaves off the trees." They agree that the breakup was no one's fault—that, as Bill puts it, "That's the way it works out."

Rationalizing that he and Marge were not even engaged, Nick determines to get truly drunk and go swimming and simply to avoid thinking about Marge anymore, or he might get back into it again. Ironically, he is consoled by the realization that he can get back into it if he wants to—that nothing was "irrevocable." Now quite drunk, the boys load shotguns and go out into the blowing gale to hunt. Feeling that he has escaped a trap, Nick concludes, "None of it was important now. The wind blew it out of his head."

Themes and Meanings

In a story such as "The Three-Day Blow," the reader must be warned against too easily accepting what happens literally in the tale, which hardly seems to constitute a story at all. What holds this story together is not its developing action but its haunting vision of a world in which human ideals and aspirations are too often thwarted by cupidity or incompetence or by the destructive forces of nature. Love ends just as suddenly and without warning as "when the three-day blows come now and rip all the leaves off the trees." When Bill says, "That's the way it works out," he refers specifically to the end of young love. However, he also voices the growing awareness of the young men that the world is unceasingly hostile and unsympathetic, that nothing of value lasts very long, and that only the tough-skinned survive.

As with life itself, love is subject to the cruel flux and dissolution of nature. It, too, has its seasons, like baseball or hunting, youth or old age. The fire that blazes up and dies down, the "second growth timber," even the autumn storm itself, reminds one that cyclical change is the great law of life. "All of a sudden," Nick says, "everything was over. I don't know why it was. I couldn't help it." At first Nick condemns himself, but then he consoles himself with the thought that everything in life dissolves into nothingness and that no one is to blame.

Marrying and settling down represent the stifling of soul, the death of male independence that every Ernest Hemingway hero abhors. This is evidently what Bill has in mind when he tells Nick, "If you'd have married her you would have had to marry the whole family. Remember her mother and that guy she married." Domesticity is seen also as a condition in which one is more vulnerable to life's storms, more subject to self-betrayal or the kind of double-cross that has ruined many good baseball players and writers. Fishing is preferred to baseball and living alone is preferred to marriage. The solitary game allows one to guard against losing control of oneself and to guide one's own destiny.

Nick's disenchantment with love may say more about his own disturbed emotional condition than about the institution of marriage. However, if sensitivity to life's traps and storms makes both boys a bit paranoid about marriage, that same sensitivity heightens their love of that perishable physical world whose loss they know is one day inevitable—that lovely fire, for example, that warms Nick but that may "bake" him if he is not careful. Nick is especially attuned to the sensual delights of the world about him—he is intoxicated with life. The shiny apple he puts in his coat pocket, the "swell smoky taste of the whiskey," the "dried apricots, soaking in water," the feel of the heavy wool socks, even the storm itself—all are simple, concrete experiences safely removed from the troublesome world of women.

Not only do such pleasures seem most available in the out-of-doors world of male camaraderie—the world of hunting, fishing, and baseball—but also the rules for survival in that world are clear and manageable. The boys are competent with guns just as they expect writers and baseball players to be competent and to behave with integrity. It is understandably to this world that they look for consolation against the threat of the "Marge business" at the end of the story. Nick, however, may still be more pained than consoled about this world of sudden, unpredictable storms. He has not really resolved the paradox of life as both preserver and destroyer. He knows that even the lasting power of the best of logs, one to be saved against bad weather that "will burn all night," is short-lived, yet his youthful illusions lead him to insist that nothing is "absolute," nothing is "irrevocable."

Style and Technique

"I always try to write on the principle of the iceberg," Hemingway said about his craft. "There is seven-eighths of it under water for every part that shows." In drawing attention to the often unsuspected depths in his work, Hemingway provides the ground for instruction in one of the major aesthetic principles of modern fiction: the art of indirection. What most modern writers have realized, and what is achieved so well in "The Three-Day Blow," is that it is possible to convey a great many things on paper without stating them at all. The art of implication, of making one sentence say two or more different things with a minimum of description, and the possibilities of conveying depths of emotion and the most intimate and subtle of moods through the interplay of image and symbol were grasped by Hemingway as well as by any modern writer.

The surface effects of this story are so astonishingly clear and simple at first encounter, and its language so unambiguous and lucid, that the casual reader may be deceived as to the actual movement of the iceberg beneath the water. The unadorned dialogue and lack of emotional commentary, for example, reflect the boys' fear of emotional complexity as well as their emerging stoic attitudes about life and love. The concentrated use of concrete, specific physical details and the avoidance of philosophical generalities reflect in turn the boys' reliance on physical experience as an antidote to moral complexity. Finally, the essential worldview of Nick and Bill is portrayed through a series of subtle, interlocking contrasts: dry and warm, wet and cold; country and city; weak and dishonest men, strong men of integrity; male camaraderie, marriage and domesticity. On the one hand are the initiated, such as Bill's father and those writers and sportsmen who function honestly and courageously in the world. These men know about life's treacherous storms but also know how to cope. On the other hand are the uninitiated or the defeated, such as Nick's father or the husband of Marge's mother—those who have been unalterably "bitched" or ruined by life.

On encountering the stylistic subtleties of "The Three-Day Blow," the casual reader might worry that little of importance is happening. However, Hemingway obtains a maximum emotional response from his reader more by what is not said than by what is. Understanding this should enable the reader to see that indirection in storytelling may be an integral part of the meaning of the story and a way of distinguishing fiction of genuine value.

Lawrence Broer

THREE DEATHS

Author: Leo Tolstoy (1828-1910)
Type of plot: Symbolist
Time of plot: The nineteenth century
Locale: Russia
First published: "Tri smerti," 1859 (English translation, 1902)

> *Principal characters:*
> MARYA DMITRIYEVNA, an upper-class woman in her mid-
> twenties who is dying from consumption
> VASILY DMITRICH, Marya's solicitous and sentimental husband
> EDWARD IVANOVICH, Marya's doctor
> MATRYOSHA, Marya's maid
> UNCLE FYODOR, a poor old carriage driver, who is dying from
> consumption
> SERYOGA, a young peasant carriage driver
> NASTASYA, a peasant cook at a post station on the route to
> Moscow

The Story

In the story's four numbered sections are described the actions of two sets of characters, one from the upper class and one from the lower. Each set revolves around a character dying from consumption: Marya Dmitriyevna, attempting to flee the harsh Russian winter to reach the warm Italian climate in the hope of curing her illness, and Uncle Fyodor, lying in the last stages of his illness in the carriage drivers' quarters at a post station. The two sets of characters intersect in sections 1 and 2 of the story, when the two carriages of the small upper-class entourage make a brief rest stop at the post station, where most of the lower-class characters work.

At the station, all the passengers except Marya disembark to eat; Vasily and Edward also have wine and further discuss what should be done about Marya, who in the doctor's opinion will certainly not live to reach Italy. At the opening of section 2, the young driver of Marya's carriage, Seryoga, enters the drivers' quarters to ask for the dying Uncle Fyodor's new boots as replacements for his own worn-out ones, which are woefully inadequate in the inclement weather. Fyodor assents, subject to Seryoga's promise to provide a headstone for his grave.

After the carriages' departure, the remainder of section 2 shifts to focus on the comfort Nastasya attempts to provide for Fyodor, who dies that night and appears in Nastasya's dream. Section 3 focuses on the family of Marya gathered, along with a local priest, at a Moscow house, where she is bedridden, too ill to continue her futile flight. At the section's conclusion, she dies, and at her wake an inattentive deacon reads psalms in a lonely vigil. Section 4 shifts back to the peasant group, recounting Nastasya's chastisement of Seryoga for not fulfilling his promise to Fyodor and subsequently Seryoga's dawn venture into the forest to begin to make good his word. The "death" of the tree (described in very human terms by the narrator) that Seryoga chops down to provide a cross on Fyodor's as-yet-unmarked grave is the third death referred to in the story's title.

Themes and Meanings

As suggested by its title, the story's main subject is death, an interest in much of Leo Tolstoy's fiction, most notably in "The Death of Ivan Ilyich," perhaps his most famous short work. In "Three Deaths" the questions of how the different social classes respond to death, how the dying respond to it, how the living respond to those who are dying, and finally what role God has in the cycle of life and death are explored.

The story, structured as an elaborate network of implicit comparisons and contrasts, shows underlying similarities despite surface differences between the upper and lower classes in how they are affected by this certain fact of experience. Marya is surrounded by family, is relatively young, is impatient with slight physical discomforts caused by her maid, attempts to flee from death, holds off serious thought of it to the end, and dies in the spring. In contrast, Uncle Fyodor is without any family, is old, puts up with cramped discomforts over a stove, seems resigned to what will shortly happen, and dies in the autumn. However, what is important, Tolstoy shows, is that both characters come to the same terminus.

Those around Marya attempt to show almost every consideration and hesitate to speak to her explicitly about death (Marya finds even the word "die" frightening); in contrast, Seryoga bluntly asks for Fyodor's boots (tantamount to saying that a dead man will not need them), and the cook, Nastasya, explicitly comments on corpses not needing new boots and complains (demurring "God forgive me the sin") that Fyodor has too long been an inconvenience and should have died some time ago. However, Tolstoy shows through the exact inversion of these qualities in each class that whether rich or poor, humanity reacts with fundamental similarity to the dying. Marya's tearful husband exclaims to God and covers his eyes while unfeelingly giving directions to a servant about where to put the wine he and the doctor are to enjoy; and, as Marya notes, he comes out of the station to inquire after her while insensitively still munching on his meal.

Similarly, though Nastasya is frank and unsentimental, she is sympathetic to Fyodor, apologizes for her earlier wish for his death, tries to make him comfortable, and dreams about him (the latter suggesting her spiritual sensitivity or only her concern about the old man, or both). To the two young peasant girls from the station, who are trying to peep at Marya in the carriage, the dying person is simply a curiosity; to Marya's two very young children, she is a matter of indifference, as they continue to play their games just before and after her death. Thus, no matter what their social class, those around the dying are shown to have both their altruistic and their selfish, unconcerned moments.

God is referred to several times in the story, often in the exclamation "My God!" The emphatic allusion at the end of section 3 to Psalm 104 implies, considering all thirty-five verses of the psalm, that God has created a symmetrical, cyclical universe with an orderly round of spring and fall, day and night, delights and miseries, life and death, and goodness and wickedness. Nature, including several references to trees and birds, is described at length in the psalm, applying to the death of the tree in section 4, which, though sad for the tree, will happily supply a marker for Fyodor and space for the flourishing of other surrounding trees.

Style and Technique

The story has much realistic, specific detail. Details of setting, including not only sights and sounds but also smells, are described with great vividness and emotional effect, such as the closeness of Marya's carriage, which "smelt of eau de Cologne and dust." Also, like his fellow realists Gustave Flaubert and Anton Chekhov, Tolstoy does not shun the scatological component of reality, considering it not only the basest but also the most basic level of experience, noting that with the advent of spring in Moscow comes not only beauty: "Streams of water hurried gurgling between the frozen dung-heaps in the wet streets of the town."

However, like Fyodor Dostoevski, Tolstoy in this story—as in much of his work— endows realistic details with symbolic import. The smell of Marya's carriage, for example, is part of the network of symbolic contrasts in the story, the eau de cologne of the upper-class setting representing a foil to the smell of the confined carriers' quarters: "a smell of human beings, baking bread, and cabbage, and sheepskins." Similarly, the careful physical description of Matryosha in the story's opening paragraphs creates a symbolic antithesis between her robust vitality and Marya's moribund decay.

Besides the symbolic applicability of Psalm 104 to the story (its own cyclical symmetry corresponding to the story's) and the symbolism of Nastasya's dream (which suggests that death has been a joyful release for Fyodor), perhaps the most clearly demarcated symbolic portion of the work is the long, descriptive passage in section 4, personifying the tree. The tree "trembles in dismay" in its roots as it is about to come down, while surrounding trees display "their motionless branches more gladly than ever in the newly opened space." The tree's death thus is shown to be a parallel to the human deaths. The concluding sentence of the story recalls both the hymn of praise to God the creator in Psalm 104 and the mixed joy and mourning of the human deceased's loved ones, who are happy to be alive but not unmindful of their loss: "The sappy leaves whispered joyously and calmly on the treetops, and the branches of the living trees, slowly, majestically, swayed above the fallen dead tree."

Norman Prinsky

THE THREE HERMITS

Author: Leo Tolstoy (1828-1910)
Type of plot: Didactic
Time of plot: The nineteenth century
Locale: The White Sea, in the Russian Arctic
First published: "Tri startsa," 1886 (English translation, 1887)

> *Principal characters:*
> AN ARCHBISHOP, a prominent figure in the Church
> THE THREE OLD MEN, rumored to be holy men living on a remote
> island
> THE SHIP'S PASSENGERS AND CREW, including a little "muzhik",
> or simple peasant fisherman, the captain, and the helmsman

The Story

On a ship sailing from Archangel into the White Sea is an Archbishop and several of his followers. While on deck, the Archbishop overhears a little fisherman telling the other passengers about three old men, "servants of God," who live on an island barely visible on the distant horizon.

At the Archbishop's request, the fisherman tells about his encounter with the three old men, who had once helped him when his boat struck on the remote island. The old men, he tells the Archbishop, were most peculiar in appearance. One was very old and hunchbacked, with green hairs mingled in his gray beard. Another, who had a yellowish gray beard and wore a ragged caftan, was also very old, but taller than the first and strong enough to turn the fisherman's boat over "as if it were a pail." The third was the tallest of the three, and he had a snowy beard that reached to his knees.

The Archbishop, having heard the fisherman's story, asks the helmsman about the presence of three "holy men" on the distant island. The helmsman's response indicates that the fisherman may have been merely "spinning yarns." Nevertheless, the Archbishop goes to the captain and requests that the ship be brought close enough to the island that he can be rowed to it. This request does not please the captain, who tells the Archbishop that it would not be worth his while to see the old men. They are, he has heard, "imbeciles who understand nothing and are as dumb as the fishes of the sea."

Neither the helmsman nor the captain, however, is able to dissuade the Archbishop, who offers to pay the captain well for changing the ship's course so that he can visit the island. Thus, the captain changes the ship's course and in a short while brings it to anchor near the island. A rowboat is lowered, and several rowers are commissioned to take the Archbishop to the beach, where, by telescope, three old men can already be seen standing near a large rock.

When the Archbishop lands on the shore, he finds the three old men just as the fisherman described them, all ancient in age, with long beards of varying shades of gray, and very poorly dressed. The old men say very little but are impressed by the presence of the Archbishop, who asks them how they make their devotions and how they pray to God. The oldest of the three answers for the others that they do not know how to make any devotions but know only how to serve and support themselves. As for prayer, says the old man, they only know to say, "Three are Ye, three are we. Have Ye mercy upon us." As soon as the one old man says this simple prayer, the others look to Heaven and repeat in unison, "Three are Ye, three are we. Have Ye mercy upon us."

The Archbishop is amused by the old men's simple prayer. Citing Holy Scripture, he endeavors to teach them a prayer that he considers more pleasing to God, the Lord's Prayer. Over and over he has them repeat the words after him: "Our Father, who art in Heaven." The old men are very slow to learn this prayer, but at last they do manage to say it without the Archbishop's prompting.

At dusk, the Archbishop takes his leave of the old men and returns by rowboat to the ship. He is very satisfied with himself, giving thanks to God that he has been able to provide such simple old hermits with instruction in the proper way to pray. As the island fades into the distance and the gathering darkness, however, he suddenly spots a flicker of light coming from its direction. The light seems to be overtaking them. He asks the helmsman what it might be—"a boat, or not a boat; a bird, or not a bird; a fish, or not a fish?" The helmsman, seeing the light take the shape of the three old men "moving rapidly over the sea," drops the tiller and cries out: "Oh God of Heaven! There are three old men running upon the sea as upon dry land!"

As the ship's company gathers at the stern to witness this miraculous event, the three old men, holding hands and moving rapidly over the sea "without moving their feet at all," come up to the edge of the ship and address the Archbishop. "O servant of God," they say, "we have forgotten . . . all that you taught us. So long as we repeated it, we remembered it. But for an hour we ceased repeating it, and every word escaped us. . . . Teach it to us again."

The Archbishop is struck by this experience. He crosses himself and tells the old men, "Your prayer has also been suitable enough for God. It isn't for me to teach you. Rather you should pray for us sinners!" He then bows down to their feet, whereupon they move back over the sea toward their island, from which a faint glimmer is visible until morning.

Themes and Meanings

In Russian, there is a small rhyme, "*Bog i ya, my druzya . . . zachem nuzhna religiya?*" that means "God and I, we are friends . . . what do I need religion for?" This rhyme epitomizes Leo Tolstoy's attitude toward organized religion as he saw it in czarist Russia. After his own development of strong pacifist beliefs in the early 1880's, Tolstoy was critical of the dominant Russian Orthodox Church for its sanctioning of the czarist government's warring and social oppression. In his stories of this period, he tried to awaken people to the superiority of individual belief over religious dogma. In "The Three Hermits," the Archbishop's self-satisfied piety is shown to be inferior to the old men's simple and direct relationship with God. Through the story,

Tolstoy attempted to teach people not to allow others, no matter what institutional support possessed or authority cited, to mitigate their moral beliefs. In support of this lesson, he cited as an epigraph to the story a verse from the New Testament: "And when ye pray, make not vain repetitions as the heathen do; for they think they shall be heard for their much asking. Be not like unto them, for your Heavenly Father knows what ye have need of before ye ask Him."

Style and Technique

Tolstoy's stories, especially his later ones, are very didactic in nature. He saw himself as a teacher, one whose task was to distill the truth as he found it so that it could be understood by people whose understanding was not as profound as his own. That is why he wrote "The Three Hermits" in a simple style, recalling the apocryphal religious legends of Russia's earlier centuries. These legends are primarily an oral genre, rife with repetitions of detail and with a straightforward moral message that is clearly stated at the end.

The style relies heavily on the device of triplication: three old men, three reported descriptions of them from three different sources, one of whom is referred to in three different ways (little muzhik, peasant, and fisherman), and so on. Even the syntax reflects this device, with many sentences having a tertiary structure: "What could it be—a boat, or not a boat; a bird, or not a bird; a fish, or not a fish?" The true function of this stylistic device is mnemonic. A triple repetition of story elements on all levels ensures that the lesson transmitted by the story will be well learned. The story's main stylistic device, then, fits well with Tolstoy's perception of himself as a teacher of spiritual truth. This triplication, common in the telling of folktales and other oral narratives, reflects as well the trinity of Father, Son, and Holy Spirit that is central to Orthodox theology.

Lee B. Croft

THE THREE OF THEM

Author: Edna Ferber (1885-1968)
Type of plot: Character study, domestic realism
Time of plot: World War I
Locale: Chicago
First published: 1918

> *Principal characters:*
> MARTHA FOOTE, the head housekeeper at the Senate Hotel
> GEISHA McCOY, a gifted entertainer
> ANNA CZARNIK, a Polish refugee who has become a scrubwoman
> BLANCHE, the mulatto maid who waits on Geisha McCoy
> IRISH NELLLIE, a maid at the Senate Hotel

The Story

The story opens with an overview of the furnishings and atmosphere in the homely, even unfashionable, suite of Martha Foote, the head housekeeper at the Senate Hotel. Her black walnut bed, chest, and desk are substantial pieces of furniture and sparkling clean. Martha's taste differs from that of the hotel decorator, who responds to the latest fashions and has supplied the guest rooms with modern, fragile furnishings. Martha is a model of midwestern values and virtue, and her substantial furniture suggests the strength of her character.

A crisis occurs when one of the guests at the Senate Hotel develops insomnia and becomes hysterical. The resident in room 618, Geisha McCoy, has been terrorizing the hotel for two days. Geisha is so successful an actor that she is paid a thousand dollars a week, but everything at the Senate Hotel seems to be getting on her nerves. She first charges that the blankets are vile and filthy. In fact, the blankets are dirty because Blanche, Geisha McCoy's maid, gave her a massage with them in hopes that she could relax enough to fall asleep. Geisha claims that she has been unable to sleep because of the clanking of chains and strange howls. Blanche is convinced that ghosts are responsible for the noises, and she, too, is becoming hysterical.

Martha solves the mystery of the disturbance by producing the cause of the noise: Mrs. Anna Czarnik, clad in her awkward boots. The clanking noise was her pail, the swishing, her rag, and the wail, her singing. Anna has been singing a *dumka*, a song of mourning. She is expressing grief and bitterness against the armies who have invaded her Polish homeland.

Geisha threatens to have Anna dismissed, but Martha dissuades her by telling her that Anna is a natural comedian. By describing Anna very sympathetically as a gallant entertainer who makes the other scrubwomen laugh, Martha ingeniously suggests a parallel between Anna and Geisha. Realizing that more lies behind Geisha's nervous hysteria than simple insomnia, Martha encourages Geisha to confide in her. It is clear that Geisha feels that she has lost her talent for relating to her audiences. The actor says that she is driven crazy by the people who sit where she can see them and knit, wondering how she can be funny when she is hypnotized by three stone-faced women knitting olive-drab wool. She then breaks down and confesses that she is also worried about her son who is now in France, but she lashes out when Martha tries to comfort her.

Martha then sums up the moral of the story by pointing out that when people brood about their troubles, they lose the human touch that enables them to sympathize and communicate with others. This is a particularly apt concern for Geisha because her art, and her success as a performer, is based on empathy and communication. She is amazed at Martha's insight and expresses incredulity that Martha is actually the hotel housekeeper, believing that she must be an aristocrat who has seen better days. Martha quite complacently assures her that she is the housekeeper and that she is not a gentlewoman fallen on hard times but that her father drove a hack and that her mother ran a boarding house. Geisha, relieved and refreshed after confiding her fears, assures Martha that she can now sleep, even in room 618. Just as Martha is about to leave the room, Geisha asks her if she thinks that Anna might be willing to sell her shoes. The question indicates that Geisha will now be impersonating Anna in her performance and that she has regained her common touch.

As the story concludes, Irish Nellie, another maid, asks Martha how her son is, and the reader learns that he, too, is in France and that he has been wounded. In contrast to Geisha McCoy, who has become so apprehensive about her son that she cannot function as an entertainer, Martha continues to do her job even though her son has been wounded. Nellie has brought Martha her evening meal, a dinner that Nellie regards as much too plain. Pointing out that Martha could have any number of delicacies, from strawberries to ice cream, she marvels that Martha would select corned beef and cabbage and assures her that if she had the status of housekeeper, she would definitely select something more exotic than corned beef and cabbage. Martha insists that if Nellie were in her place, she, too, would dine on homely fare.

Themes and Meanings

Edna Ferber was a novelist and playwright as well as the author of short stories. Most of her short stories were sketches that were published first in magazines and then reprinted in collections. "The Three of Them" appears in the collection *Cheerful, by Request* (1918). She is noted for her creation of powerful and memorable female characters. "The Three of Them" focuses on Martha Foote, a strong woman who exhibits courage as well as homely virtue. Martha is like the central figure in Ferber's popular and successful stories about a traveling salesperson named Emma McChesney. Emma is a middle-aged divorcée who supports her son by selling Featherloom petticoats on the road. *So Big* (1924), the novel for which Ferber received the Pulitzer Prize in 1925, focuses on Selina DeJong, another woman with a strong character, who is widowed early and later survives even the disappointment of her only son's failure. Martha, the protagonist of "The Three of Them," belongs among Ferber's gallery of strong heroines.

Style and Technique

Ferber attributed her descriptive economy to her training as a journalist in which she learned to describe human beings with only a few words. In "The Three of Them," as in many of her short stories, Ferber begins with a description of the locale that has a direct bearing on her characters' reactions to events. When Ferber is entirely in control of her material, as she is in writing "The Three of Them," physical details introduced in the description function symbolically to represent the psychological realizations of her characters. The reader may recognize the three stern knitting women in Geisha's audience as modern representations of the classical Fates, but the effect is not dependent on the reader's recognition of the allusion.

Critics have charged that Ferber's style is overly didactic and that she uses her narratives to moralize on contemporary issues. Because Ferber writes in the third person, using the point of view of an omniscient author, it is easy for her to explain to the reader exactly what point she is making. This makes her work seem dated to those who are accustomed to a more suggestive, less direct approach to narrative. Ferber does sometimes use her omniscient narrators to reveal the perceptions and values of a particular character, but she also manages to suggest these values in brief dialogues. In "The Three of Them," the concluding dialogue between Nellie and Martha over Martha's preference for plain and homely fare, suggests the wholesome values that Martha represents.

Jean R. Brink

THREE PLAYERS OF A SUMMER GAME

Author: Tennessee Williams (Thomas Lanier Williams, 1911-1983)
Type of plot: Psychological
Time of plot: The 1940's
Locale: New Orleans, Louisiana
First published: 1952

> *Principal characters:*
> BRICK POLLITT, an alcoholic Delta planter
> MARGARET POLLITT, his wife
> ISABEL GREY, a young widow
> MARY LOUISE, her twelve-year-old daughter
> THE UNNAMED NARRATOR, Mary Louise's ten-year-old friend

The Story

Brick Pollitt, a former college athlete, has married a New Orleans debutante and settled down to the life of a Delta planter. For some reason of self-disgust, the reason for which is not made explicit, he has become an alcoholic. His own excuse is that his wife, Margaret, a powerful, domineering figure, has psychologically and sexually castrated him and taken away his self-respect.

When a young doctor who has treated Brick's alcoholism dies of brain cancer, Brick befriends the doctor's genteel widow, Isabel, and her plump daughter, Mary Louise, and provides them with financial support. Although the widow becomes Brick's mistress, the reason that he turns to her has less to do with sexual desire than with the mysterious nature of Brick's need for something that remains unexplained. Much of the story centers around the croquet game that the three of them play during the summer the story takes place. It is told by a man who witnessed it all several years previously when he was a ten-year-old friend of Mary Louise.

Although Brick insists that he is curing his drinking problem and that Isabel has helped him regain his self-respect, he is not strong enough to resist the powerful personality of his wife or the strong allure of alcohol that helps him escape into a fantasy world. Before the end of the summer, Brick's self-destructive behavior increases and threatens to destroy the widow and her daughter as well. As his behavior deteriorates, Brick returns to the control of his wife and neglects the widow and her daughter, who then leave town. In the last scene of the story, the narrator reports seeing Brick, grinning with senseless amiability, being driven through town by his wife, the way some ancient conqueror such as Alexander the Great might have led the prince of a newly conquered state through the streets of a capital city.

Themes and Meanings

The central thematic mystery in the story is the motivation behind Brick's self-disgust, something that Tennessee Williams has called a basic sense of unknowable dread. The narrator in the story simply says that it came on him with the "abruptness and violence of a crash on a highway. But what had Brick crashed into? Nothing that anybody was able to surmise, for he seemed to have everything that young men like Brick might hope or desire to have." Brick says the reason for his malaise is the fact that his wife has castrated him by taking away his respect and that he must prove that he is a man again. He tells a group of painters working on the widow's house that the meanest thing that one human being can do to another is take away his self-respect. "I could feel it being cut off me," he says.

The fact that Brick tries to regain his self-respect through the passive young widow and what he himself calls the sissy game of croquet is the central irony of the story. Brick's problem is not simply sexual, or even psychological, but rather aesthetic and metaphysical. His impotence is not a reaction against the castrating Margaret but rather a revolt against the flesh itself. His flight into the chaste arms of Isabel—which have been purified by the death of her husband—is the search for truth in the basic romantic sense of its equation with beauty. It is an attempt to escape from flesh into art, to escape intolerable contingent reality into the bearable—because detached and fleshless—ideal of aesthetic form.

This attempt to escape the contingency of existence by means of aesthetic patterning and idealization is doomed from the start. His desire for a romantic relationship with Isabel, as well as his effort to play the superior game of art and form with human beings as the pawns, comes crashing up against the real physical and psychological needs of the other two players—the widow and her daughter.

Style and Technique

At the beginning of the story, the narrator establishes the metaphor that identifies the summer game of croquet with the nature of the artwork. The game, he says, seems to be composed of images the way a painter's abstraction of the game would be built of them. The wire wickets set in the emerald lawn and the colorful wooden poles stand out in a "season that was a struggle for something of unspeakable importance to someone passing through it." The formal design of the game is like a painter's abstraction; likewise, the characters become images and abstractions. They are not so much real people as stylized gestures pictorially woven within the lyrical narrative that is the legend of Brick Pollitt. The narrator says that the bits and pieces of his story are like the paraphernalia for a game of croquet, which he takes out and arranges once more in the formal design of the lawn. "It would be absurd to pretend that this is altogether the way it was," he says, "and yet it may be closer than a literal history could be to the hidden truth of it."

The narrator's engagement in the formally controlled patterning of the artwork that one uses to control the contingency of life is the same game that Brick plays with croquet. He is drawn to Isabel because her actual encounter with the contingency and horror of flesh during the time her husband was dying reflects his own fear of flesh. To engage in the summer game is thus to run out of something "unbearably hot and bright into something obscure and cool"—to run out of the unbearable world of existential reality into the cool, ordered, deathless world of the artwork.

When Brick realizes that form must inevitably become involved and entangled with the reality of flesh, he becomes caught in an unresolvable metaphysical dilemma. Because there are other players involved in his game, human beings who have real emotional and fleshly needs, the game becomes contaminated because it must be played at the expense of Isabel and Mary Louise. When Brick realizes the hopelessness of his efforts to escape life into the romantic pattern of art, he is transformed from tragic actor to clown and the croquet lawn becomes a circus ring. His desire to live within the formalized world of art and idealization is doomed to failure, and thus the mysterious metaphysical problem that plagues Brick is left unresolved.

Near the end of the story, after Brick realizes the impossibility of his summer game and no longer comes to the widow's house, the narrator says, "The summer had spelled out a word that had no meaning, and the word was now spelled out and, with or without any meaning, there it was, inscribed with as heavy a touch as the signature of a miser on a check or a boy with chalk on a fence." Any attempt to spell out Brick's problem, even the attempt the story itself makes, is inadequate to get at the truth of Brick's ultimately romantic desire for beauty.

Brick's tragicomic efforts reach a climax one night when he turns on the water sprinkler, takes off his clothes, and rolls about under the cascading arches. No longer a Greek statue, he is a grotesque fountain figure and a clown. This degeneration into what the narrator calls unintentional farce is suggested by a trivial conversation carried on between Mary Louise and her mother about using ice to cool her mosquito bites. An aesthetic game that begins as an effort to transform something hot into something obscure and cool takes place among frozen stylized figures on a cool lawn of a house that itself looks like a block of ice; it finally becomes a banal banter in which the ice is reduced from its symbolic function to the practical utility of cooling Brick's drinks and easing Mary Louise's bites.

The narrator learns that when one uses human beings in an effort to play the game of art and reach the beauty and detachment of form, the result is the loss of the human. The beauty of the artwork alone can remain pure, but only because of its inhumanness.

Charles E. May

THE THREE STRANGERS

Author: Thomas Hardy (1840-1928)
Type of plot: Realism
Time of plot: The 1820's
Locale: Southwestern England
First published: 1883

> *Principal characters:*
> THOMAS SUMMERS, the first stranger, an escaped prisoner
> THE HANGMAN, the second stranger
> THE PRISONER'S BROTHER, the third stranger
> SHEPHERD FENNEL, the host to a christening party
> MRS. FENNEL, the shepherd's wife

The Story

Higher Crowstairs is an isolated cottage some three miles from Casterbridge, the county town where the county jail is situated. It is late winter, in the evening of a very rainy day. Shepherd Fennel and his wife are holding a christening party, to which about twenty relatives and neighbors have come, all well known to one another. Inside it is warm and snug, with a blazing fire in the hearth. Mrs Fennel, a somewhat frugal lady, is hoping to strike a balance between dancing and talking, so that no one gets too thirsty or too hungry. The musicians are a twelve-year-old fiddler and the parish clerk, who plays the serpent, an old-fashioned brass instrument.

Into this festive scene, three strangers intrude, one by one. The first has come from the direction of town and asks shelter from the rain. He dries off by the hearth but is evasive when asked about himself. Although he enjoys smoking, he has neither pipe, tobacco, nor pouch.

Shortly after, a second stranger knocks, this one is headed toward Casterbridge. Again, he wishes to dry off and sits down at the table, right next to the first stranger, penning him in. He is much more jovial than the first stranger and asks for drink. He drinks the mead (a fermented honey drink) in large quantities, much to Mrs. Fennel's consternation. When asked about his occupation, he sings a song for the locals to guess. Only the first stranger joins in the chorus. It is obvious from the song that he is a public hangman, coming to hang a prisoner slated for execution the next day at the county jail.

A third stranger enters during the song, looks terrified, and rushes out. Just then a gun is heard firing from the town, indicating a prisoner has escaped. One of the guests, "the engaged man of fifty," declares himself a constable and, after some knockabout humor, eventually sets off in pursuit of the third stranger with a posse.

While the women exit upstairs to comfort a wailing baby, the first two strangers creep back into the cottage, having made little effort to search for the man supposed to be the prisoner. After eating and drinking a little more, they part.

The posse captures the third stranger. By the time they return, the local magistrate and two jailers are at the cottage. They realize the third stranger is not the escaped prisoner, but his brother, come to pay his last respects. The real prisoner was the first stranger, but now it is too late and too dark to look for him. In the morning, a desultory search is made for him, but as his crime was only that of stealing a sheep to feed a starving family, there is much local sympathy for him, and the search is soon abandoned. His calmness has saved him.

Themes and Meanings

This short story is typical of Thomas Hardy's writing in that it occurs among country people within the bounds of Wessex, the fictional name he gave to Dorset and its surrounding counties in the southwest of England. It is told humorously but with deep insight into the local people's sense of community, manners, and speech. Many of Hardy's short stories, especially in his collection *Wessex Tales* (1888), deal with the "rustic chorus," as they appear in his major novels. Many of these tales are set in the past, having been supposedly handed down for two or three generations, remembered for some quirky event or character.

"The Three Strangers" is a good example of this. Set two generations before the time of its writing, it deals with a particular quirky episode concerning a hangman. By the time the story was written, hangings had ceased to be public, and the offences for which the death penalty was given had been greatly reduced. Sheep stealing no longer carried the death penalty, for example.

Hardy, like Charles Dickens before him, was fascinated by public hangings and the folklore that grew up around them. Such folklore is reflected in another of the *Wessex Tales*, "The Withered Arm," where the superstition that touching a hanged man's neck cured certain diseases is made a central motif. Even his major novel, *Tess of the D'Urbervilles* (1891), climaxes with Tess's hanging, an incident based on a boyhood memory. However, unlike Dickens, Hardy did not protest the method of execution nor examine the causes of the crimes that led to hanging.

In "The Three Strangers," the furthest that Hardy will go politically is to suggest the considerable sympathy felt for the escaped prisoner, based on the sense that sheep stealing does not merit such a severe punishment. The usual alternative, penal deportation to the colonies, is not, however, mentioned. Hardy makes no attempt to comment on the economic conditions that led to men starving. The emphasis is on the humor of the situation: the audacity of the prisoner, the coincidence of the hangman joining him, and his brother finding him in the situation.

Such avoidance of political statement is interesting in the light of the controversial reception of Hardy's novels written after 1883, particularly *Tess of the D'Urbervilles* and *Jude the Obscure* (1895), both of which deal with poverty and repression in a principled and systematic way, placing the causes in the rigid English social system. Here in the short story, social class is not an issue, except that the depiction of peasants and shepherds, it could be argued, is for the amusement of a middle-class readership wanting to see a pastoral but archaic lower class. Whether Hardy himself is a mediator of a rather superior patron in doing this could be argued.

Style and Technique

The main plot technique employed is that of the use of a stranger intruding on a close-knit society and in some way disrupting the normal rhythm of its lives. Although Hardy uses three intrusions rather than just the normal one, they are only vaguely threatening or suggestive of the supernatural, climaxing at the moment when the hangman sings his song of self-disclosure and his audience backs off in shock. Otherwise the tone is kept at a humorous level, through such well-used devices as the depiction of rustic talk, fondness for drink, and the miserliness of Mrs. Fennel, particularly as it is opposed by her naïve but generous husband.

Mrs. Fennel's efforts to keep the dances short are particularly comic, perhaps made more realistic by Hardy's memories of his boyhood, when he was a musician at such occasions and would play for hours. The pursuit of the fugitive is particularly reminiscent of William Shakespeare's comic petty officials, such as Elbow and Abhorson in his *Measure for Measure* (1604). Their clumsy efforts are, the reader knows, doomed from the start.

Hardy's characterization of country folk and country customs is as well done here as in any of his novels. His depiction of community has been especially praised. So also has his description of the local landscape. The sharp division of town and country seen in *The Mayor of Casterbridge* (1886) is seen here as well, but this time from the rural point of view. The cottage stands remote and isolated, even though only three miles from town. Its isolation is further emphasized by its weather, the nighttime, and the rugged contours of the downland. Hardy's tale takes on its solidity from the sense of *real* place, closely detailed. The rainy night may be described as a gesture to some supernatural tale, but the concrete emphasis is on what life was really like for the shepherds, where a baptism was one of the few causes for celebration and a stranger's visit the highlight for the year.

David Barratt

THROWN AWAY

Author: Rudyard Kipling (1865-1936)
Type of plot: Social realism
Time of plot: The 1880's
Locale: India
First published: 1888

Principal characters:
THE BOY, a Sandhurst graduate serving as a subaltern in India
THE MAJOR, who has kindly feelings toward The Boy
THE NARRATOR, a British military man

The Story

The protagonist in "Thrown Away" is never identified other than as The Boy. A young subaltern in India, The Boy led a sheltered life with his family in Great Britain and never had to deal with unpleasantness. After his years at Sandhurst preparing for military life in the colonies, The Boy is sent first to a third-rate depot battalion and then to India.

At first, he finds India attractive. The ponies, the dancing, the flirtatious women, and the gambling all appeal to him. However, The Boy has been quite protected until now. He has developed no sense of humor. He takes life and its petty tribulations very seriously. Rudyard Kipling likens The Boy to a puppy, saying that if a puppy bites the ears of an old dog, the old dog will properly chastise it, making it wiser. However, if the puppy grows to be a dog with its full set of teeth and bites the ear of an old dog, never before having learned that there are limits to what it does, it is likely to be hurt. The Boy apparently has never been placed in the situation of having to learn his limits and is now like the grown dog with a full set of teeth who is about to bite the ear of an old dog.

The Boy falls into gambling, and his losses mount alarmingly. He takes these losses seriously and broods over them. For six months, The Boy makes one personal mistake after another, and the people closest to him know that he is making them but presume that he will learn from his mistakes and will fall into line as do most other people who come out from Great Britain.

When the cold weather ends, The Boy's colonel talks to him with some severity, but not much differently from the way colonels typically talk to subalterns: "It was only an ordinary 'Colonel's wigging'!" the reader is told. The Boy, however, takes the "wigging" very much to heart. Shortly after it, one more event contributes substantially to what is ultimately to happen: "The thing that kicked the beam in The Boy's mind was a remark that a woman made when he was talking to her. There is no use in repeating it, for it was only a cruel little sentence, rapped out before thinking, that made him flush to the roots of his hair." Again, he has something to brood about.

For three days after this unfortunate occurrence, The Boy keeps to himself. Then he takes a two-day leave, presumably to go shooting for big game at the Canal Engineer's Rest House, about thirty miles out from his base. People laugh at his going after big game there because the only thing worth shooting in that area is partridge, hardly the big game that The Boy seems to seek.

One of the majors has grown fond of The Boy and becomes alarmed when he hears that he has gone out shooting. He alone suspects what the big game might be that The Boy seeks. He enters The Boy's quarters and discovers that he has taken with him a revolver and a writing case, hardly the equipment for game hunting. The Major enlists the aid of the omniscient narrator, asking him if he can lie, and the two set out for the Canal Engineer's Rest House in a wagon drawn by a pony, which is pushed so hard to get there in a hurry that it is almost dead when they arrive three hours later at their destination thirty miles away.

When they get to the Rest House, the Major calls for The Boy's servant and calls out The Boy's name. There is no answer. The two men notice that a hurricane lamp is burning in the window, although it is four in the afternoon and quite light. They hear only the buzzing of hordes of flies. They enter the building and find that The Boy, having written farewell letters to his loved ones, has all but shot his head off with his revolver.

The narrator reads the letters, which are filled with self-recrimination, and he and the Major decide that they must cover up the suicide in order to spare The Boy's family grief. They decide to say that he has died of cholera, attended by them until the end. They burn his letters, then burn the bed and bedding and dispose of the ashes. They gather up The Boy's watch, locket, and rings to send to his family. The Major thinks that The Boy's mother will want a lock of his hair, but because of the mode of his death, they cannot find one fit to send her. The Major's hair is about the same color as The Boy's, so the narrator cuts a lock from the Major's head, which sets them both to laughing, supporting the argument that in India it does not pay to take anything too seriously.

The two buy hoes and dig a grave for The Boy. They wait a day before going back to their base with the news of the death. They send letters off to The Boy's loved ones telling them of his death. In due course, they receive a letter from The Boy's mother saying that she is grateful and will be under an obligation to them for as long as she lives. The story ends with the line, "All things considered, she was under an obligation; but not exactly as she meant."

Themes and Meanings

Much of Kipling's writing focuses on problems peculiar to and generated by British colonialism, and this story certainly fits that mold. Early in the narrative, Kipling tells his readers, "Now India is a place beyond all others where one must not take things too seriously—the mid-day sun always excepted. Too much work and too much energy kill a man just as effectively as too much assorted vice or too much drink." The Boy cannot survive in India because he takes things too seriously. He cannot accept the indolence and the inefficiency that characterize service in India.

On the other hand, the Major and the narrator will survive because even in the face of The Boy's gruesome death, they can laugh. They are not heartless, otherwise they would not think to spare The Boy's family the grief of knowing that their son committed suicide. In Kipling's presentation, the Major turns a deaf ear to those who criticize him for not bringing back The Boy's body for a regimental burial on base. Kipling shows here a man who is at peace with himself, one who knows he has done what is best and who does not care what public opinion is regarding his action. He will certainly never repeat The Boy's mistake even though he understands it and once goes so far as to say that he had gone through the same "Valley of the Shadow" as did The Boy.

The Boy is never given a name because Kipling emphasizes early in the story that in colonial India, if one man dies, he will be replaced in the eight hours between death and burial. He also points out at the end of the story that The Boy and his act will be forgotten before a fortnight has elapsed. Life here is impersonal, attachments ephemeral. Early in the story, Kipling writes that flirtations do not matter because one will not be in any one place for long.

Style and Technique

"Thrown Away" is essentially a story about anonymity. Told through an unnamed omniscient narrator, the story centers on a protagonist who remains anonymous and on a Major who is fond of The Boy but who has long since lost the sensitivity that might lead him to the same end as that of The Boy.

Kipling allows the Major emotions. When the narrator reads him the letters that The Boy has written to his loved ones, the Major "simply cried like a woman without caring to hide it." Kipling leaves little doubt, however, that the Major will recover quickly from the shock of The Boy's suicide. Before he returns to base, he is laughing and joking with the narrator. Then he has a long sleep that apparently erases what is left of this horror from his mind.

What Kipling shows here is that people are quite replaceable in India—perhaps everywhere. Kipling holds his characters in this story at arm's length; readers see them but do not know them. This is not a failing on Kipling's part but is rather a reflection of the harsh realities of colonial India.

R. Baird Shuman

TICKETS, PLEASE

Author: D. H. Lawrence (1885-1930)
Type of plot: Psychological
Time of plot: World War I
Locale: The English Midlands
First published: 1919

> *Principal characters:*
> ANNIE STONE, a young conductor on a railway line
> JOHN THOMAS "CODDY" RAYNOR, a handsome inspector
> NORA PURDY, one of several other women conductors

The Story

"Tickets, Please" is a story of unrequited love and the vengeance that it spawns. In its psychological depth and detail, however, it also reveals the sexual war that D. H. Lawrence believed always raged between men and women. The setting is of crucial importance to this story, for it reflects in several significant ways Lawrence's themes. The background is World War I; because most of the healthy young men are away fighting in France, the trains are being driven by "cripples" and "hunchbacks," and the conductors on this "most dangerous tram-service in England" are all women.

The chief inspector on Annie Stone's line is John Thomas Raynor (nicknamed "Coddy" by the women), who is young and good-looking and who takes full advantage of his situation. He flirts with the conductors by day and "walks out" with them by night, and not a few have been forced to leave the service in "considerable scandal."

Annie has kept her distance from John Thomas (she has a boyfriend of her own), but one night they meet unexpectedly at a local fair and spend an exciting, romantic evening together. With their continued intimacy, Annie becomes possessive. "Annie wanted to consider him a person, a man: she wanted to take an intelligent interest in him, and to have an intelligent response." However, here, Lawrence says, "she made a mistake." John Thomas has no intention of becoming an intelligent, serious person to her. He "walks out" with another young woman conductor on the line.

Annie is devastated by the rejection and vows revenge. She plots with Nora Purdy, another of John Thomas's former girlfriends, and together they round up half a dozen former conquests of John Thomas. One dark Sunday night, when Annie has again agreed to walk home with John Thomas, they all meet in the "rough, but cosy" waiting room in the depot at the end of the line.

When John Thomas comes into the depot, he apparently senses the situation and says that he is going home by himself. However, the girls insist that he choose one of them to walk with: "Take one!" They force him to face the wall and guess which one touches him, and then, "like a swift cat, Annie went forward and fetched him a box on the side of the head that sent his cap flying and himself staggering." All the other girls attack him now, and a game turns into a battle between the hunters and the hunted: "Their blood was now thoroughly up. He was their sport now." They beat and subdue him until he is on the floor "as an animal lies when it is defeated and at the mercy of the captor."

Even in defeat, however, John Thomas is clever, and when the women still demand that he choose one of them, he names their ringleader: "I choose Annie." Annie, however, no longer wants him—"something was broken in her." The women release him, John Thomas leaves in tatters, but there is no sense of triumph in the waiting room; the girls leave "with mute, stupefied faces." They have wreaked their revenge and defeated their enemy, but in doing so they have also somehow destroyed the object of their desire, and there is no satisfaction in this victory.

Themes and Meanings

Like so many other Lawrence stories and novels, "Tickets, Please" concerns the sexual and spiritual war that is being waged just beneath the surface of civilized life. When that veneer is scratched, the psychological jungle is revealed.

It is appropriate that it is wartime. Aside from furthering the plot, the wartime setting is also a metaphor for the constant struggle between men and women. It is a "dangerous" but "exciting" time and, as in the stories of Ernest Hemingway at about the same time, wartime tends to show life in an exaggerated but intense reality.

This is particularly clear in the crucial battle between John Thomas and his vindictive captors. "Outside was the darkness and lawlessness of war-time," Lawrence tells his readers at the beginning of this section. Inside, there is also "war" or "lawlessness" waiting in the depot, as in the hearts of these women.

When the women corner John Thomas, something happens to them, and they are transformed into powerful sexual animals. "Strange wild creatures, they hung on him and rushed at him to bear him down." They have become the aggressors, and their new, animal, sexual power makes them feel "filled with supernatural strength." However, this conquest of the male brings them no satisfaction; it is, Lawrence writes, a "terrifying, cold triumph." Ironically, when they bring John Thomas down they destroy not only his male sexual advantage but also his sexual attractiveness; in his tattered tunic, John Thomas is nothing to them now. They have succeeded only in making him like themselves; they have gained nothing new.

Lawrence is thus predicting failure in the sexual revolution. When women band together (as they can here, under the special conditions of wartime), they can win. Their victory, however, is hollow, for they have destroyed the object of their "lust" at the same time that they have destroyed his superiority. They leave the depot "mute" and "stupefied" because they did not know their own, irrational, animal strength—and because they have really lost, not won. There has been a sexual revolt, but once the old order has been overthrown, the slaves have no new order to install and have lost the privileges of the old. It is a sad and pessimistic message. John Thomas and the women need each other as they are, Lawrence is saying, and there is apparently no way to undo the cruel and patriarchal sexual domination.

Lawrence's story treats themes and motifs that would not be treated in such depth and detail again for half a century, until the women's sexual revolution in the second half of the twentieth century became a literary revolution as well. In his sexual psychology and symbolism, Lawrence is a father of much of that literature.

Style and Technique

As in so much of Lawrence's fiction, the style in "Tickets, Please" helps to control the raw power of his content and thus becomes an integral part of the meaning. "Tickets, Please" opens almost like a children's story, and the description of the Midlands tramway system reads like something out of "The Little Engine That Could" or—in a parallel from the story itself—the carnival rides that Annie takes with John Thomas. However, even in these opening paragraphs, there is a crucial contrast between the playful personification of the train and the "sordid streets" and "grimy cold little market-places" of this depressed and depressing industrial England. From the beginning, there is a contradiction in tone as there is in content (between, for example, the two conditions of women in the story, before and after their overthrow of John Thomas).

The narrator of "Tickets, Please" helps to mask this gap. There is a casual, familiar "we" in the opening narration: "Since we are in wartime." This editorial "we" tends to moralize: "The girls are fearless young hussies," the voice intones. After Annie starts seeing John Thomas and some of the other conductors are "huffy" to her, this voice is consoling: "But there, you must take things as you find them, in this life." The narrator is preparing for the defeat at the conclusion; it is a voice of order and stability.

The language of the story also carries these themes. In the beginning of the story, the imagery is military: The tram-car is Annie's "Thermopylae" (a famous battle site in Greece); she watches John Thomas "vanquish one girl, then another." In the battle with John Thomas, however, this language becomes animal, and the girls become wild hunting creatures and bring John Thomas "at bay." Throughout the story, the language is sexual. John Thomas's name (especially his nickname, "Coddy") refers to the male organ (as in "codpiece"), and there are several other phallic references; the sight of his "white bare arm," for example, maddens the girls. Although at an intellectual level the story is about an attempted overthrow of the old patriarchal order, at the level of language and imagery the story is an example of Lawrentian "blood-lust," in which the animal in woman tries to pull down the sexual power in man.

Although a novice reader of the story may be struck by the sexual symbolism and the psychological realism of the story, the humor and irony of "Tickets, Please" may not be as obvious. The playfulness of the opening sections is not only in its tone; serious as this struggle is, it is also inherently comic (and here the narrator's voice helps). Similarly, the use of language can be highly ironic. When John Thomas quips to the girls in the waiting-room, "There's no place like home," the word "home" has several levels of meaning. It is ironic because it is "home" (security) with John Thomas that the girls want, and it is "home" that John Thomas assiduously avoids. Lawrence's language, in short, can be as rich and bottomless as his meaning.

David Peck

THE TIME OF HER TIME

Author: Norman Mailer (1923-   )
Type of plot: Social realism
Time of plot: The 1950's
Locale: New York City
First published: 1959

> *Principal characters:*
> SERGIUS O'SHAUGNESSY, the narrator
> DENISE GONDELMAN, his lover

The Story

Sergius O'Shaugnessy has tried to live entirely by his own lights, to establish the time of his time. Sergius is a sexual adventurer, a man of action asserting his manhood. He has even established a bullfighting school in Greenwich Village. He is a loner, living on the fringes of society, refusing to conform, and behaving like an artist, which means abiding by his own code and creativity.

Sergius has come by his identity the hard way. He is an orphan who grew up in a Catholic orphanage. To make himself, he has had to jettison not only the teachings of traditional religion but also allegiance to institutions of any kind. He lives in the moment, free of guilt (he claims) and any emotional baggage. His life is only as stable as his own stamina; his truths are the product of experience. He recognizes no authorities or limitations, except the ones he imposes on himself.

Sergius's conception of himself is challenged by Denise Gondelman. She is bright, Jewish, and full of the psychiatric jargon that puts off the hipster, who sees her as the typical intellectual Jew. She uses words to type people and to assert her superiority. She is obviously dissatisfied with her conventional boyfriend, and she is attracted to the nonconformist, belligerent Sergius. They become enmeshed in a love-hate affair.

Denise confesses that she has never had an orgasm. She doubts that Sergius would find her a good lover, but he takes her admission of inadequacy as a spur to his male ego and sets out to rectify her sex life by conducting a war against her frigidity. His masculine power-grabbing alienates her, yet like him, she craves intense experience, and she believes that through him she will finally achieve a sexual climax.

At first Sergius disappoints her. His own climax comes too soon for her, and she angrily accuses him of selfishness. Then they struggle in another round of sexual intercourse, each trying to pound into the other his or her own sexual rhythm. Finally, Sergius seems to triumph. Denise has an orgasm—on his terms, he believes.

Denise does reach a sexual epiphany with Sergius, but she rejects him because of his predatory code. He acts in bed like a bullfighter; his violence excites and repels her. When Sergius claims credit for satisfying Denise sexually, she retorts that he has not changed her in any fundamental way. She implies that she has gotten just as much as she wanted from him, but she has not actually put herself in his power. Sergius admits the truth of her retort when he compares the look in her eyes to that of the bullfighter ready for the kill. She has used him at least as much as he has used her. Denise's parting shot is to quote her psychiatrist, who has told her that Sergius's whole life is a lie, that he has done nothing but run away from his own homosexuality.

Sergius does not defend himself against her allegation. He simply calls it her truth. Her words define her psychological state, not necessarily what he thinks of himself or what their relationship has meant to him. He ends the story admitting that she has been a worthy opponent.

Themes and Meanings

How seriously can Sergius O'Shaugnessy be taken? Bearing a name reminiscent of a mythic Irish hero, he has come out of nowhere, so to speak, to make an impression on his times. Still, is establishing a bullfighting school in Greenwich Village really such a heroic thing to do, or is it ridiculous? Denise Gondelman's words imply there is something absurd in Sergius parading himself as a man of action defying death. He has killed bulls in Spain, but what bulls are there to kill in New York City? His real adversary is a woman and, Denise implies, himself. His tough talk and violent streak mask an uncertain identity. He is not the master of reality but its fool. He is not in control of his time but the servant of her time.

The feminine pronoun in the story's title is a profound rewriting of the romantic, heroic quest story. Denise, in some ways, displaces Sergius as the story's hero. She refuses to submit to his code of male superiority, even though he brags that she cannot experience sexual satisfaction without him. Her strength comes from knowing that her orgasm has been possible because she has fought Sergius in bed, not because she has given in to him. In effect, she expresses contempt for him as a sexual object even as he supposed she was his instrument.

Denise's truth does not displace Sergius's so much as it shows his limitations. Her comment that he has denied his homosexuality is simplistic, and is made more so because she is quoting her psychiatrist who has not even met Sergius. Nothing revealed about Sergius makes the charge of homosexuality seem relevant to his attitudes. Denise lives in the world of second-hand diagnoses. She has made real contact with Sergius, yet she resorts to jargon rather than confronting him in all of his individuality. She denies the mutuality they have shared, however briefly.

In this sense, the title is ironic and belittling of Denise. She has had the time of her time and emerged triumphant in her own mind, but where else? She has walked out on Sergius, denying him the role of conquering hero, but she also has turned him into a cliché: the macho man hiding his vulnerable side. She is, in a way, a parody of Sergius, declaring a hollow victory, slaying a bull where there are no bulls to be slain. She does not admit or wrestle with her contradictory desires to be totally in control and to abandon herself to a moment of complete ecstasy, a moment that would take her beyond her categorical view of reality. Both Denise and Sergius have been the bull and the bullfighter; their relationship is about how they constantly shift between their passive and active selves, their roles as heroes and victims.

Both characters are romantics in that they blow up experience, making of it a life-and-death battle, in which the self suffers either defeat or victory. Neither is satisfied with mediocrity or with half-success. Each sees their relationship as a duel of identities.

Style and Technique

As in "The Man Who Studied Yoga," the companion piece to Norman Mailer's "The Time of Her Time," the key to the story's meaning is the narrator. Although Sergius is Denise's antagonist, he shows remarkable sympathy and respect for her, almost as if she is his other half. He can portray her as frigid and reductionist in her judgments, yet he acknowledges her as a genuine quester to whom he feels compelled to accord a tribute, however ambivalent.

Sergius's mixed feelings about Denise do mask his own internal divisions. He wants to be strong, but he also wants to have the courage to admit his fear and inadequacy—which, in a way, Denise has done in her own case by coming to him. By allowing her to speak so clearly and boldly, he is implying not only that she is a match for him but also that he has learned something from her, grown in his ability to scrutinize himself.

The true heroism of "The Time of Her Time" is the narrator's willingness to recognize his own absurdity and powerlessness. Paradoxically, he asserts power by dramatizing how he has been stripped of it. It is not his physical prowess but his mental agility and sensitivity that triumph in the story.

If Mailer makes fun of his hero, he also gives him a full and honest voice that honors the objective of his quest: to be the best at what he does, in both the bullring and the bed. Denise has been attracted to that authentic quality, even though she seeks to deny it at the end of their affair. For Sergius, Denise is another encounter with reality, in which he simultaneously loses and gains control of himself, succumbs to and dominates his times. He makes his story, and Denise's, into a fable of all romantic quests—doomed to failure and yet assertive of self-growth.

Carl Rollyson

TIME THE TIGER

Author: Wyndham Lewis (1882-1957)
Type of plot: Satire
Time of plot: 1949
Locale: London
First published: 1951

> *Principal characters:*
> MARK ROBINS, a bureaucrat in the Socialist Ministry of
> Education
> CHARLES DYAT, Mark's old friend, a petty bourgeois black
> marketeer
> IDA DYAT, a widowed landowner and the sister of Charles

The Story

Mark Robins (the "red," or Marxist) and Charles Dyat (the diehard reactionary) became friends when they attended Oxford University together in the early 1920's. They
were both from professional, upper-middle-class families. As students, Mark was the
conservative and Charles was the radical, sporting a red tie. Twenty-five years later, in
the aftermath of World War II, Great Britain has a Socialist government, and Mark has
swung to the Left, while Charles has swung to the Right. However, they have remained friends: As the story opens, Charles is visiting Mark and has just spent the
night in Mark's "Rotting Hill" apartment in the suburbs of London.

Wyndham Lewis's portrait of postwar Britain is comically grim: It is a satire of the
same sense of cultural and material debasement, shoddiness, and deterioration conveyed more somberly by George Orwell in *Nineteen Eighty-Four* (1949). In Mark
Robins's apartment, the water heater has broken down, the bread is gray and hard as
brick, the buttonholes on his shirts are too skimpy to push buttons through, his shoe-
laces are too short to tie in bows, and his nail clipper falls apart when applied to his
nails. The telephone lines are fouled up, and food shortages continue, leaving nothing
but bad tea, bad butter, and bad jam. All this adds up to a bad mood for Mark, who nevertheless represses his mood, dismisses the problems, and believes that soon enough
the progress of socialism will cure these ills.

Unlike Mark, Charles places no faith in the current regime. As they begin to talk
over breakfast, their political differences quickly become apparent, over the topic of
tipping, or "oiling palms." Charles confesses that in order to get preferential treatment
he always gives tips, but Mark is scandalized by this vestige of upper-class patroni-
zation. Their conversation takes up the question of the food shortages: Mark thinks
that they are actual, Charles declares that they are part of a Socialist plot to beat the
population into political submission. Mark declares that Charles is an "egotist" with

an "individualist itch to pick holes," and Charles retorts that Mark is a "yes-man" who has opportunistically but foolishly joined the Socialist cause.

Still, they leave the apartment in good spirits, "jabbing each other mirthfully with their forefingers," and begin a round of errands in downtown London. Mark must get a blood test, and Charles needs an eye examination, which sets up a running debate concerning the National Health Service and the question of socialized medicine. Then Mark exchanges a shirt shrunken to an unwearable size after one wash. Charles attempts to make conversation with his eye specialist by criticizing the welfare state: The doctor ignores him and then sends him to a public glasses shop. This episode puts Charles's pretensions to gentility and his prejudices against the lower classes in general and women in particular into action: He ends up in a private shop where his ego can be appropriately massaged.

Late that evening, the two are back at Mark's apartment discussing a film they have just seen, a French existentialist film called "Time the Tiger." Mark finally lets all the day's irritations get to him, and Charles sees his chance to score some ideological points. They debate life, time, and progress, with Charles nostalgically evoking the year 1900 and Mark maintaining that popular culture is not all bad. They talk about the powers unleashed by technology, "the fantastic power conferred upon the politicos in this new era of radio, automatic weapons, atomic bombs." Charles denounces the legacies of Karl Marx and Charles Darwin, and Mark denounces the British Tories: They reach no agreement.

A reunion with Charles's widowed sister Ida, whom Mark dated many years before, has been scheduled for the next day; that night Mark dreams about her. When the three of them actually meet the following afternoon, Ida appears to "step out of a dream," seeming to Mark not to have aged a bit. Their conversation dwells on visions of their more youthful days, and all the while Mark fantasizes about marrying Ida and bringing her into his new way of life. Then "Time the Tiger" leaps: "Ida—an Ida at least twenty years older—was denouncing the Socialist Government. . . . His love transformed herself with nightmare suddenness into a Tory soap-boxer." The reunion falls apart: Mark will never see Ida again; rather, he resolves to make a date with a Socialist woman of his acquaintance. Several months later, Mark replies to a letter from Charles, "I suggest you find some other correspondent."

Themes and Meanings

"Time the Tiger" is a study of friendships tested and demolished by political pressures, the interplay among political beliefs, social class, personality, and nostalgia. As the petty bureaucratic supporter of the Socialist regime, Mark is presented as a repressive type, a self-denier and a stoic, a man who is moral (that is, conformist) out of sheer lack of imagination: "Where Mark would be apt to respect the most pernicious by-law, Charles would be quite certain to break it." Mark dutifully submits to regulation and has rationalized the social need for such submission, whereas Charles defies and defames the new order. In opposition to Mark's self-denial, Charles would be self-indulgent, if he were not so broke. Mark is law-abiding, Charles, the black marketeer and free marketeer, is an outlaw. These opposing characteristics represent the standard dramatization of the antagonism between public and private, collectivist and individualist sensibilities, Mark and Charles representing the progressive Socialist mass and the beleaguered elite, respectively.

Mark is comically naïve, but Charles is comically selfish. Mark can envision a future, and his Socialist idealism buffers him a bit from the sordid bumps and bruises of actual life, but Charles despairs of his chances in this new society and longs for the halcyon era of class privileges. Mark's naïveté sets him up for the reversal delivered at the climax of the tale by Ida's metamorphosis from timeless sweetheart to time-bound ideological foe: The transition to the new social order will not be as seamless as he dreams. At this point, Charles and Ida Dyat merge in a composite portrait of petty conservatism: They are reactionaries motivated by self-interest, by the losses of power and prestige that they must suffer under the ongoing Socialist upheavals. The future appears to be Mark's, but with a distinct sense that Mark has acquiesced, and forgotten his own acquiescence, to a life of "second best." Moreover, his new world must be purchased at the price of the collapse of his old connections.

Style and Technique

For an author whose anticommunism is proverbial, Lewis delivers "Time the Tiger" with considerable restraint. The narration is deft, hard-edged, understated, sardonic, and deployed with a confident, ironic hand. This is Lewis's mature or late prose style: There is none of the syntactic experimentalism, the "blasting and bombardiering" of his earlier stories. The world of Mark and Charles is viewed not through the lenses of Lewis's earlier Vorticism but through the trained and focused eyes of the aging visual artist finding his effects in ludicrous juxtaposition of concrete objects and persons actually presented by postwar British life.

Lewis makes Mark the central character, and although Mark is not the brightest man, he is not unsympathetic: Mark has cast his lot with the new order and patiently awaits a glorious future. One suspects that Charles is primarily the spokesman for Lewis's own attitudes, but Charles is in no way idealized: He is witty but bitter, and his anarchism is not heroic but suffering. When the true antithesis to what Mark represents materializes, it does so as Ida Dyat, a walking mirage of nostalgia who then turns into a bloodthirsty female fascist. Both as literal description and as allegory for class conflict, the politics in "Time the Tiger" are never heavy-handed. Lewis has transposed his vision of ideological conflict into a fine and enduring ironic fiction.

Bruce Clarke

TLÖN, UQBAR, ORBIS TERTIUS

Author: Jorge Luis Borges (1899-1986)
Type of plot: Fantasy
Time of plot: 1935-1947
Locale: Buenos Aires, Argentina
First published: 1940 (English translation, 1962)

> *Principal characters:*
> THE NARRATOR, presumably Jorge Luis Borges
> ADOLFO BIOY CASARES, a friend of the narrator (and of the real Borges)
> HERBERT ASHE, an English engineer involved in the encyclopedia plot
> EZRA BUCKLEY, the Tennessee millionaire who financed *A First Encyclopedia of Tlön*

The Story

"Tlön, Uqbar, Orbis Tertius" depicts a fantastic world, which gradually, during the course of the story, acquires a tenacious and undermining hold on reality. The story is told in the form of a memoir that mixes the narrator's personal reminiscences with essayistic account, plausible events in Buenos Aires with the fantastic inventions of an imaginary land (Tlön), and fictional characters (Herbert Ashe, Ezra Buckley) with the names of Borges's real friends (Adolfo Bioy Casares, Carlos Mastronardi, Nestor Ibarra, Ezequiel Martinez Estrada, Drieu La Rochelle, Alfonso Reyes, Princess Faucigny Lucinge, Enrique Amorim). Reality and imagination are constantly intermingled: Real books such as the *Encyclopaedia Britannica* are mirrored by invented ones such as *The Anglo-American Cyclopaedia* and *A First Encyclopedia of Tlön*; nonexistent books are ascribed to real authors; and preposterous theories share paragraphs with Benedict de Spinoza, Arthur Schopenhauer, and David Hume. Assumptions about how to separate what is true from what is untrue are challenged, parodied, and subverted. Amid the chaos of the world, a human desire for order and organization at any cost is seen as understandable but very dangerous.

The story is divided into three parts. In the first section, the narrator and his friend and collaborator, Adolfo Bioy Casares, discuss a hypothetical "novel in the first person, whose narrator would omit or disfigure the facts and indulge in various contradictions that would permit a few readers—very few readers—to perceive an atrocious or banal reality," a novel that is this very story. The mirror in the hallway, which reflects and monstrously distorts reality, reminds Bioy of an article in *The Anglo-American Cyclopaedia* (which mirrors the 1902 *Encyclopaedia Britannica*) about a country named Uqbar. An extensive search reveals that it is only Bioy's copy of the encyclopedia that contains the extra pages about Uqbar and its imaginary regions of Mlejnas and Tlön. The apparent hoax article is disquieting but more puzzling than ominous.

The second section describes the narrator's discovery and perusal two years later (in 1937) of the eleventh volume of *A First Encyclopedia of Tlön*, left behind in a bar by a shadowy Englishman, Herbert Ashe. The encyclopedia has on its first page a stamped blue oval inscribed "Orbis Tertius," and it describes a "vast methodical fragment of an unknown planet's entire history," its languages, philosophy, science, mathematics, and literature. Because, says the narrator, "the popular magazines, with pardonable excess, have spread news of the zoology and topography of Tlön," he will attempt to expound its concept of the universe.

The people of this imaginary planet are "congenitally idealist" and do not believe in the material, objective existence of their surroundings. They believe only what they themselves perceive, and hence the "world for them is not a concourse of objects in space; it is a heterogeneous series of independent acts. It is successive and temporal, not spatial." In language, this means that there are no nouns for concrete objects, only aggregates of adjectives that describe the immediate moment. Cause and effect are not thought to be related. Objects are held to disappear physically when no one is thinking about them. Innumerable sciences and philosophies abound on Tlön, as many as one can imagine. Materialism is merely the most unacceptable one of a vast number of possible ways of considering reality. The happiest hypothesis is that everything in the universe exists within one supreme mind. Thus, plagiarism in literature cannot exist if all works are the creation of one supreme author, who is timeless and anonymous and whose stories are all variations on a single plot.

The narrator describes how many centuries of idealism have changed reality. Lost objects can be duplicated through memory; anyone who remembers an object can find it. These duplications are called *hrönir*, and their quality varies as they are reproduced again and again through successive memories. Objects may also be produced through hope; anything people wish to find and can imagine appears as an *ur*. Thus archaeologists reshape and document the past according to their own imaginations.

The third section of the story, the postscript, supposedly appended to the text several years later and thus confirming the historical nature of the account, appeared (labeled 1947) in 1940, as an original part of the story. It creates at once a sense of future time having passed already and a somewhat bewildered uneasiness. When the narrator makes the observation that "ten years ago any symmetry with a semblance of order—dialectical materialism, anti-Semitism, Nazism—was sufficient to entrance the minds of men," he is describing the world of the immediate moment, not the world of ten years before. He is describing that ominous time just before World War I, when anti-Semitism and Nazism had invaded the reality of Germany (and Argentina) just as the reality of Earth is invaded in this story by the ideology of Tlön.

The postscript purports to clear up the mystery of Tlön. It tells how a secret society of the seventeenth century set about to invent a country and describe it. In 1824, the project was financed by Ezra Buckley, an eccentric millionaire from Tennessee. It was Buckley who suggested that a *Britannica*-like encyclopedia of the invented planet be written and in 1914 (just at the onset of World War I), the last volume of the secret *A First Encyclopedia of Tlön* was distributed. By 1942, strange objects from Tlön have begun to appear on Earth: a compass inscribed in one of the alphabets of Tlön, and a mysteriously heavy cone, identified as an image of the divinity in certain regions of Tlön.

In 1944, a complete set of the forty volumes of *A First Encyclopedia of Tlön* are found in a Memphis library, and the importance of this event is (according to the narrator) recognized by everyone. The encyclopedia is phenomenally popular; a mad proliferation of summaries, editions, commentaries, and pirate editions of this "Greatest Work of Man" flood the earth. The order, symmetries, and rigor of Tlön seem infinitely superior to the confusion and doubts of ordinary human existence. Tlön appeals irresistibly to those who yearn to live in an ordered and comprehensible universe, a labyrinth of complexities perhaps, but a labyrinth that has been designed to be deciphered by men. The inventors of Tlön have triumphed; they have "changed the face of the world" and will continue, unimpeded, to change it until the human world becomes Tlön.

In the meantime, the narrator disassociates himself from this eagerly changing world around him. In its enthusiasm for an orderly universe, humanity forgets that the tidy logic of Tlön is "a rigor of chess masters, not of angels." The narrator is acutely aware of the attraction of idealism, but his nostalgia is more important to him, nostalgia for a culture that believes in the mysteries of angels and for a past that includes his own childhood and its familiar (though often illogical) languages. He retreats to the hotel where he spent happy days as a child (although it is also the hotel where Herbert Ashe left *A First Encyclopedia of Tlön*) not to act decisively but to continue a revision, to continue to take pleasure in words from the past, that past that the Tlön revisionists are now obliterating and replacing. Sir Thomas Browne's *Urn Burial* of 1658 traces the inevitable mortality of humankind through all of Western history. The narrator's translation of the *Urn Burial* is both a refuge from a terrible present and an indication of the futility of all intellectual effort. Within a labyrinthine, incomprehensible universe, man creates further mental labyrinths, such as totalitarian ideologies. The most absurd and unrealistic of these ideologies is, in this story, the invention of a planet, whimsically presented through the provisional encyclopedia that describes it. However, absurd as it is (far more unrealistic than Nazi expansion), the invented world begins to impinge on and gradually to dominate reality. The world as one knows it disintegrates. There is nothing the narrator can do but watch in horror. He retreats to another futile intellectual game: the translation of a difficult seventeenth century English Baroque writer into the no-less-difficult seventeenth century Baroque Spanish of Francisco Gomez Quevedo y Villegas.

Themes and Meanings

Borges's interest in philosophical idealism and its implications is evident in "Tlön, Uqbar, Orbis Tertius." Men imagine the world as they wish it to be and then try to impose this vision on others; Borges describes how seductive yet how dangerous this penchant can be. The chaos of the real world cannot be understood by human beings, and yet men are endlessly tempted to define and control reality by establishing rules. Tlön offers this illusion of order and purposefulness, but it is shown in this story to be a human plot to take over the earth. Borges suggests some parallels with the expansion of the Nazi movement and with Marxism; "Tlön, Uqbar, Orbis Tertius" is one of his more political stories.

Style and Technique

"Tlön, Uqbar, Orbis Tertius" plays off an indisputably real account against a preposterous fantasy, managing to make reality seem unreal and fiction seem plausible. Readers trained to believe what they see in the *Encyclopaedia Britannica* and the newspapers find themselves manipulated in this story by a worldwide mysterious plot. The story is extensively documented (like a credible encyclopedia article) with real and fictional sources so intertangled that the truth is lost. However, amid the shambles of Western civilization, the narrator in the end holds out some hope for humanity: Aggregates of words (manifestos, revisionist histories, political propaganda) may destroy, but words may also provide comfort, refuge, and communion with the past.

Mary G. Berg

TO BUILD A FIRE

Author: Jack London (1876-1916)
Type of plot: Naturalistic
Time of plot: 1900
Locale: The Yukon territory, some seventy miles south of Dawson
First published: 1902

> *Principal character:*
> A TENDERFOOT, who is attempting to travel across the Yukon
> wilderness in winter

The Story

"To Build a Fire" is an adventure story of a man's futile attempt to travel across ten miles of Yukon wilderness in temperatures dropping to seventy-five degrees below zero. At ten o'clock in the morning, the unnamed protagonist plans to arrive by lunchtime at a camp where others are waiting. Unfortunately, unanticipated complications make this relatively short journey impossible. By nine o'clock that morning, there is no sun in the sky, and three feet of snow has fallen in this desolate Yukon area. Despite the gloomy, bitter, numbing cold, the man is not worried, even though he has reason to worry. At first he underestimates the cold. He knows that his face and fingers are numb, but he fails to realize the seriousness of his circumstances until later in the story. As the story unfolds, the man gets progressively more worried about the situation. At first, he is simply aware of the cold; then be becomes slightly worried; finally, he becomes frantic.

His only companion is his wolf-dog. The animal, depressed by the cold, seems to sense that something awful might occur because of the tremendously low temperatures. The dog is frightened, and its behavior should show the man that he has underestimated the danger.

At ten o'clock, the man believes that he is making good time in his journey by traveling four miles an hour. He decides to stop and rest. His face is numb, and his cheeks are frostbitten. He begins to wish that he had foreseen the danger of frostbite and had gotten a facial strap for protection. He tells himself that frostbitten cheeks are never serious, merely painful, as a way to soothe himself psychologically and force himself not to worry about the cold. He knows the area and realizes the danger of springs hidden beneath the snow, covered only by a thin sheet of ice. At this point, the character is very concerned about these springs but underestimates the danger. Getting wet would only delay him, for he would then have to build a fire to dry off his feet and clothes. Every time he comes on a suspected trap, he forces the dog to go ahead to see if it is safe. He begins to feel increasingly nervous about the cold.

By twelve o'clock, he is still far away from his camp and anticipates getting there by six o'clock, in time for dinner. He is pleased with his progress, but, in reality, he is simply reassuring himself that there is no need to worry. He decides to stop and eat lunch, a lunch he had planned to eat with his friends at the camp. His fingers are so numb that he cannot hold his biscuit. He reflects back to the time when he had laughed at an old man who had told him how dangerous cold weather could be. He now realizes that perhaps he had reason to worry and that he had forgotten to build a fire for warmth. He carefully builds a fire, thaws his face, and takes "his comfortable time over a smoke." Then he decides that he should begin walking again. The fire has restored his confidence, but the dog wants to stay by the warmth and safety of the fire.

The man's face soon becomes frozen again as he resumes his journey. Lulled into a false sense of security by the fire, he has become less and less aware of his surroundings and steps into a hidden spring, which wets him to his waist. His immediate reaction is anger because he will be delayed by building another fire. He carefully builds a fire, well aware of the importance of drying himself. He remembers the old man's advice at Sulphur Creek that circulation cannot be restored by running in this temperature because the feet would simply freeze faster. His fire is a success and he is safe. He now feels superior, because although he has had an accident and he is alone, he has saved himself from possible death. He decides that any man can travel alone as long as he keeps his head.

Although confident because of his swift action of building a fire to dry off, he is surprised at how fast his nose and cheeks are freezing. He can barely control his hands; his fingers are lifeless and frostbitten. Suddenly, his fire exists no more; he has built it under a large tree that is weighed down with snow, and when he pulls down some twigs to feed the flame, the snow in the tree is dislodged and falls on the man and his fire. He thinks again about the old man at Sulphur Creek and realizes that a partner at this time would be helpful. He begins to rebuild the fire, aware that he will lose toes, and possibly his feet, to frostbite. Because his fingers are nearly useless, he has difficulty collecting twigs. He is so sure that this fire will succeed that he collects large branches for when the fire is strong. His belief that the fire will succeed is the only thing that keeps him alive. He finishes the foundation of his fire and needs the birch bark in his pocket to start it, but cannot clutch the wood. He panics, drops his matches, and is unable to pick them up. He succeeds in picking them up, finally, and by using his teeth, he rips one match out of the pack. By holding it in his teeth and striking it against his legs twenty times, he lights it but drops it again when the smoke gets into his nostrils. He then strikes the entire pack of matches against his leg and tries to light the wood but only burns his flesh. He drops the matches, and the small pieces of rotten wood burn. He knows that this is his last chance for life and that he cannot allow the matches to go out.

Because he cannot operate his hands, in his attempt to keep the fire burning, he spreads it out too much and it goes out. Now he can only think of killing the dog to put his hands in the carcass to relieve their numbness. The dog senses danger, however, and quickly moves away. The man goes wild and catches the dog but soon realizes that he cannot kill it because he cannot use his hands. He knows that death is near and begins running, just as the old man had warned him not to do. The man hopes that he has a chance to run to camp but knows that he really has no chance, for he lacks the strength. He curses the dog, for it is warm and alive. The dog runs on but the man crumples after running a few yards. He decides to accept death peacefully and admits to himself that the old man at Sulpher Creek had been right. The dog stays with him, but when it smells the scent of death, it runs off in the direction of the camp, where reliable food and fire providers can be found.

Themes and Meanings

The main conflict in this story of survival is between human beings and nature. Another central conflict, however, is that between youth and confidence as opposed to wisdom and experience. The main character is a young man who believes that he knows the frozen wilderness, but he is still a tenderfoot who has not yet learned to respect the power of nature. Jack London shows early in the story that the tenderfoot lacks imagination, an asset he sorely needs when tested to the extreme by the harsh wilderness.

The man's egotism is in conflict with his common sense. He does not understand humankind's frailty and is too proud to admit his own. He does not comprehend the danger posed by an alien, hostile environment in which he can only survive by the full exercise of his native wit, instincts, skill, and cunning. Before the coming of winter, the old-timer from Sulpher Creek had warned him that one should always travel in winter with a partner and that one should never attempt to travel alone in temperatures colder than fifty degrees below zero. In his ignorance, the tenderfoot had laughed at the old-timer's advice. Caught in the bitter cold, he is made to realize the value of the old man's warning.

The tenderfoot scorns other precautions. Once caught in the wilderness, for example, he realizes the value of having a partner. He realizes, moreover, that a facial strap would have protected him against frostbite. Still, he manages to build a fire after he has broken through the ice, and, his confidence momentarily revived, he laughs again at the old-timer. Ironically, the man is doomed by his egotism and his stupidity. When the fire goes out, he has second thoughts about his superiority.

The plot development is incremental as the tenderfoot's dilemma gets more desperate and as he unwillingly learns his lesson. His absurd belief in himself and his ability to cope with the situation is retained until the very end. Although he refuses to give up hope, it becomes increasingly clear that he has lost touch with reality. "When he got back to the States," he fantasizes, as he is freezing to death, "he could tell the folks what real cold was." Ultimately the man will die and be survived by his dog. The animal, a creature of instinct untainted by pride, is better adapted to the environment than the man.

Style and Technique

The fiction of London, in tandem with the work of Frank Norris, Stephen Crane, and Hamlin Garland, helped to shape an American naturalism, a particular strain of scientific realism that was influenced by European writers of the later nineteenth century, particularly the French writer Emile Zola, who described the role of the novelist as that of "a scientist, an analyst, an anatomist" who interprets reality through the application of scientific determinism. In "To Build a Fire," London places his protagonist in a harsh natural setting that tests to the limits his ability to survive in the wilderness.

The style of this particular brand of realistic fiction depends on the cold, objective presentation of detail that respects the force and power of nature and reduces the individual to a position of relative insignificance. The central character of London's story is a vain creature, supremely and ironically confident of his ability to survive.

The story is carefully structured around the building of several fires. The first two fires the tenderfoot builds are merely matters of convenience, when he stops on his journey to rest and eat. In both instances, the dog is reluctant to leave the safety of the fire. The third fire is built to stave off an emergency because the man has gotten his lower body wet. This fire is foolishly built, however, because the tenderfoot has no foresight or common sense.

The fourth and final fire the tenderfoot attempts to build is crucial to his survival, but he is too far gone to accomplish this task. His hands are by then too frozen to manipulate his matches, and his mind is so far gone that he cannot fully understand the seriousness of his peril. All he can do is believe in the possibility of his survival. The story provides an interesting study in the psychology of an unhinged mind.

London's story depends for its effect on situational irony. An ironic strain that runs throughout the story is the tenderfoot's sense of superiority and contempt for the old trapper on Sulphur Creek. The irony is dramatic in that the reader soon realizes that the old man was right, a realization that escapes the tenderfoot until the very end of the story.

James M. Welsh

TO HELL WITH DYING

Author: Alice Walker (1944-   )
Type of plot: Domestic realism
Time of plot: The 1960's
Locale: An unspecified southern state
First published: 1967

> *Principal characters:*
> MR. SWEET LITTLE, an old African American man
> THE NARRATOR, a young African American woman

The Story

Mr. Sweet Little was a diabetic, alcoholic, guitar-playing, tobacco-chewing, tall, thin, dark-brown man whose hair and straggly mustache were the color of Spanish moss. He lived alone on a neglected cotton farm down the road from the narrator and her family. Over a period of many years, Sweet Little and the children participated in a ritual that was an important element in the lives of all. When Mr. Sweet was feeling the worst, the bluest, the sickest-at-heart a man could be, he would take to his bed and the doctor would declare that old Mr. Sweet was dying. The narrator's father would declare, "To hell with dying, man, these children want Mr. Sweet!" and the children would swarm around the bed and throw themselves on top of the dying man. Always the youngest child would kiss the wrinkled brown face and tickle the motionless body until it began to shake with laughter. These things were done to keep Mr. Sweet from dying. The children performed the ritual naturally for many years. No one told them what to do—they played it by ear. So it was that Sweet Little was repeatedly rescued from the brink of death by love, laughter, and the innocent belief of children. As the youngest child in the neighborhood, the narrator led these revivals for the last part of Mr. Sweet's life.

Sweet Little was kind and gentle, even shy with the children—an ideal playmate. Often so drunk that he was as weak as they, he was able to act sober when drunk, a talent that enabled him to carry on fairly coherent conversations. The narrator's mother never held his drunkenness against him and always let Mr. Sweet and the children play together.

Once an ambitious person, Mr. Sweet had wanted to be a doctor or a lawyer or a sailor, but he found out that black men got along better if they were not. He had loved another woman before he had had to marry Miss Mary. He was not even sure that their son, Joe Lee, was his. The narrator had learned these things about Mr. Sweet's past from the many sad and wonderful songs he made up while he played the guitar and entertained her family. She remembers how beautiful Mr. Sweet made her feel, how she listened to his songs, watched him cry, and held his woolly head in her arms, and how she wished that she could have been the woman he had loved so long ago. He was her first love. When Mr. Sweet began to cry, it indicated that he was about to die again, so the children would get prepared, for surely they would be called on to revive Sweet Little yet again.

Mr. Sweet was in his eighties when the narrator went away to a university. On his ninetieth birthday, she receives a telegram requesting her to come home immediately because old Mr. Sweet is dying again. She is finishing her doctorate but, sure that her professors will understand, she does not hesitate. When the dying man sees her, his eyes look spry and twinkly for a moment, but this time death cannot be stayed. The twenty-four-year-old doctoral student cannot believe that she has failed to revive the old man: He "was like a piece of rare and delicate china which was always being saved from breaking and which finally fell." The narrator sits strumming Mr. Sweet's old guitar that he has left to her; she hums "Sweet Georgia Brown," the song he used to sing especially to her; and she relives her memories of him—her first love.

Themes and Meanings

Alice Walker's first published short story, "To Hell with Dying" is an initiation story, an account of first love and first death. It depicts how, through innocent faith, laughter, love, ritual, and memory, people triumph over death. The theme of the story is that of the blues, overtly suggested by Mr. Sweet's guitar playing and indirectly suggested by the tone of the story, which is both sweet and sad, like the blues. The story also serves as the narrator's song, or celebration, of Mr. Sweet.

In an initiation story, someone—usually the main character but, in this case, the narrator—moves from a certain plane of innocence into a new realm of knowledge and, having attained knowledge, can never claim innocence again. The novice is often accompanied on the journey to enlightenment by a guide, usually an elder. Sweet Little is the narrator's guide through at least two inevitable occasions of life: love and death. The narrator identifies Mr. Sweet as her first love; he made her feel beautiful and desirable. Ultimately she learns about more than the complexion of love, for she learns the sad truth about death as well.

This story is also about ritual, laughter and celebration, and memory—the various ways people attempt to defeat death. The narrator never states that Mr. Sweet is not really dying all those countless times the neighborhood children revive him. In fact, in the final episode, she seems genuinely surprised that Mr. Sweet actually dies. The reader understands that Mr. Sweet was not really dying all those other times; he was simply drunk and depressed and was resuscitated by the devotion of the children who made him feel needed and loved. That it was the youngest child who always performed the most important part of the ritual strongly suggests that death can only be conquered through a childlike innocence and unqualified faith. Walker's account suggests that the power to stay death not only lies in the hands of children but also exists only for those who, like Mr. Sweet, have the innocence and childlike quality to believe.

In religious terms, a revival is a renewal of faith, and some churches hold revivals often. The repeated ritual of Mr. Sweet's rescue from the brink of death is referred to by the narrator as a "rite of revival." A rite is a ceremony, a certain series of actions performed exactly the same way every time, in order to effect a particular consequence. Much religious symbolism reflects humanity's desire to thwart death. People's general need to be loved and their faith in the healing power of love are both illustrated in this story by the fact that it is the unabashed love and caresses of the children that repeatedly revive Mr. Sweet. It is through memory that humanity best defies death: No one is ever dead if he or she is remembered, that is, lives in someone's memory. When people sing the blues, they are singing of love lost yet remembered, and when the narrator tells the story of Mr. Sweet, she is reviving him. Every time someone reads this story, Mr. Sweet Little is remembered and loved. He is brought to life, again and again.

Style and Technique

In an early interview, Walker offers an autobiographical source for this story and observes, "I was the children, and the old man." The story is better served by focusing on the way Walker transforms an ordinary, recognizable event—an old man thinking that he is dying—into a magical and meaningful experience about the nature of death. The title is a homey variation on the basic human rebellion against death and reverberates like the first sentence of a preacher's sermon. The story stands as a testimonial of faith. The archetypal text gives the congregation of readers an opportunity to draw from common experience. The style is repetitive in the manner of a revival meeting, yet original like a sweet, sad, wonderful song that springs spontaneously from the strings of an old blues guitar. This technique yields both ritual and impromptu experience.

Throughout the story, the narrative tone is loving and warm, compelling by its generosity of spirit. The attention is focused on the plight of the often-dying, beloved old man, while the independence and special achievements of the educated young female narrator are understated. Walker parodies the traditional formula of popular romance by making this hero poor, old, alcoholic, and diabetic—a vulnerable old man, always crying and dying.

The story derives its deep emotional power from universal values, archetypal imagery, and recurrent rhythms. The narrative style springs from an ancient oral tradition of storytelling, a spontaneous and lyric form. The text is musical in its repetition of words and sounds.

Cynthia Whitney Hallett

TO ROOM NINETEEN

Author: Doris Lessing (1919-   )
Type of plot: Psychological
Time of plot: The 1950's and early 1960's
Locale: London, England
First published: 1963

> *Principal characters:*
> SUSAN RAWLINGS, a wife and mother
> MATTHEW RAWLINGS, her husband, a newspaper subeditor
> SOPHIE TRAUB, their au pair

The Story

Susan and Matthew Rawlings are an intelligent, practical, and conventional married couple living in Richmond, a suburb of London. Their twelve-year marriage has produced four children and innumerable sensible decisions. The Rawlingses have a slightly superior attitude toward other couples who allow clichéd problems to disrupt their harmony. When Matthew, a subeditor at a large London newspaper, finally commits adultery, Susan understands and forgives.

Susan, an advertising artist before her marriage, looks forward to the moment when her youngest children, twins, begin school so that she will have some time to herself during the day. Her seemingly perfect family life, however, becomes increasingly insufficient for her, but she is resolved to avoid the typical responses to such inadequacy. She may find some meaning in work but will wait until the children, who need an attentive mother, are older.

Susan battles an increasing depression with her intelligence, trying to find comfort in the always sensible approach she and Matthew take to everything, telling herself she regrets nothing about her life. After the twins finally begin school, Susan finds herself afraid of her new freedom and hides from her depression in cooking, sewing, and other busywork. She is afraid to be alone in her garden, where her loneliness is most likely to manifest itself. Increasingly, she considers her obligations as wife and mother to be pressures that are driving her crazy. Confused by the new Susan whom she seems to have become, she is unable to communicate her fears to Matthew.

Craving privacy so that she can be her true self, Susan retreats to a spare room at the top of her house, but soon her children and Mrs. Parkes, her housekeeper, convert it into yet another family room. After her fears take seemingly human form as a devilish young man grinning wickedly at her from her garden, she takes a solitary walking tour in Wales, but her demon follows her.

After she convinces Matthew to hire an au pair to look after the children when they return home from school each day, Susan begins spending her days in London under the name Mrs. Jones, sitting peacefully in a shabby room in Fred's Hotel, doing nothing but luxuriating in perfect solitude. Room nineteen gives her the identity that her home life denies. Suspicious of her actions, Matthew hires a detective to follow her. Because he wants it to be so, she confesses to having an affair. Matthew admits his own relationship with a friend of theirs and wants the two couples to get together. Confused over how to substantiate her imaginary lover, empty at seeing how easily Sophie Traub, the au pair, fulfills the role of mother, depressed at losing the privacy of Fred's Hotel, Susan goes to room nineteen and turns on the gas.

Themes and Meanings

"To Room Nineteen" appears in a long line of works of fiction dealing with passive resistance to conformity and the resulting mental breakdown. Its antecedents include Herman Melville's "Bartleby, the Scrivener" (1853), in which the title character's preferring not to do anything eventually leads to his death, and "The Yellow Wall-Paper" (1892) by Charlotte Perkins Gilman, whose protagonist, increasingly unsatisfied by her roles as wife and mother, gradually goes insane. This story also has some parallels to one of Doris Lessing's later novels, *The Summer Before the Dark* (1973), whose similarly alienated protagonist leaves her family to escape her depression but eventually returns.

The story of Susan Rawlings can be misinterpreted too easily, especially because of its similarities to "The Yellow Wall-Paper," as simply a feminist parable of an unfulfilled woman driven to her death by an insensitive, male-dominated society, but Doris Lessing hardly presents the world of suburban London, in an obviously unenlightened period, so starkly. Neither does Lessing intend Susan to be simply a case history of disintegration. She is presented too specifically to be merely a type, and despite her hallucinations, she is more depressed than clinically insane.

"To Room Nineteen" is a vivid portrait of the extremes to which the sensitive individual, especially a woman, may go when the resources of everyday life prove inadequate. Susan's problem is not that being a wife and mother is not enough, although she clearly misjudges Matthew's flimsy character. Neither is her predicament so clear-cut that it can be solved by a job or career. Susan is driven to suicide because she cannot find an identity that makes sense to her. If her world makes little sense, she can exert her selfhood only by retreating from it. If this world insists on intruding into her privacy, she loses her battle for identity.

Lessing wants readers to be moved by Susan's suicide and not try to explain it away, but recognize the limits of reason. Susan cannot accept what cannot be rationally understood and wants to consider her unease to be her fault, but blame is not an issue here: "Nobody's fault, nothing to be at fault, no one to blame."

Susan is a prisoner of her rational intelligence, refusing to acknowledge that reason cannot explain or solve everything. Unlike the protagonist of *The Summer Before the Dark*, she has no illusions about freedom because, if achieved, it would place a greater burden of responsibility for her state on her. What she ultimately wants is not freedom from responsibility, obligations, or family, but from the inescapable—herself: "not for one second, ever, was she free from the pressure of time, from having to remember this or that. She could never forget herself; never really let herself go into forgetfulness." A portrait of such extreme alienation takes "To Room Nineteen" well beyond the limitations of any political or sociological interpretations.

Lessing underscores the universality of Susan's story when the narrator comments on the banality of thinking the individual can place all the elements of life in order, can be in complete control. Such reasonable, highly educated people are essentially dry and flat. The Rawlingses are described as "Two people, endowed with education, with discrimination, with judgement, linked together voluntarily from their will to be happy together and to be of use to others—one sees them everywhere, one knows them, one even is that thing oneself: sadness because so much is after all so little." When a thinking person such as Susan realizes the impossibility of truly imposing order on chaos, even greater chaos results.

Style and Technique

"To Room Nineteen" opens: "This is a story, I suppose, about a failure in intelligence." This initial omniscient first-person narration provides considerable ironic distance from the characters. The Rawlingses are first seen almost as mechanical creatures of creation with their pathetic little faith in intelligence and sensibility. As the story progresses, however, this narrating sensibility withdraws, and the reader is plunged slowly into the morbid world of Susan's psyche.

The gradual progression into a desperate mind makes the presentation of Susan's dilemma less potentially didactic and more emotionally engrossing. This approach also makes the reader, who has been cleverly tricked into sharing Susan's concerns, less likely to accept easy answers to a difficult situation. The story's ending reinforces the impossibility of simplistic solutions. Because Lessing's attention to the details of Susan's suburban existence have made her an individual, the suicide is likewise too specific an act to be considered nihilistic.

Lessing employs several devices typical of psychological realism. The demon that Susan first imagines in the garden is a visual manifestation of her mental state, her "irritation, restlessness, emptiness." She fears him because he is an embodiment of all that threatens her. Lessing makes the relationship between Susan and her demon clear when the woman stares into her mirror and sees the reflection first of a madwoman and then of a demon. Susan, the madwoman, and the demon are one.

Color is used to depict the extremes of Susan's world. Her perfect house is white, suggesting sterility and oppression. She escapes from the house into the garden, whose greenness implies the freedom offered by the contrasting natural world, as does the brown river running by it. When the garden no longer provides any escape, Susan goes to Fred's Hotel, where her room has thin green curtains, a three-quarter bed covered with a cheap green satin bedspread, and a green wicker armchair. She dies lying on the green satin bedspread and drifts "off into the dark river," the ultimate escape.

Michael Adams

TOAD'S MOUTH

Author: Isabel Allende (1942-   )
Type of plot: Social realism
Time of plot: The early twentieth century
Locale: Southern Chile
First published: "Boca de sapo," 1989 (English translation, 1991)

> *Principal characters:*
> HERMELINDA, a gregarious young prostitute
> PABLO, a Spaniard who seduces her
> AN ENGLISH COUPLE, the owners of Sheepbreeders, Ltd.

The Story

The rocky, desolate terrain of southern Chile provides the setting for this story, which opens on a sheep ranch. The land is silent and ice cold, and has been decimated by the sheep brought by English settlers. The sheep have eaten the vegetation and trampled the remaining artifacts of the indigenous cultures.

In contrast, the impassive English couple who own Sheepbreeders, Ltd., surround their headquarters with lawns and thorny fences of wild roses. They have not adapted to their surroundings. They stay indoors, observe the formal traditions of the British Empire, and pamper themselves with whatever luxuries their ranch affords.

The South American men who work for Sheepbreeders, Ltd., are underpaid, cold, and lonely, as neglected as the sheep they herd. Their only solace is in knowing Hermelinda, a young woman who lives in a nearby shack, earning her living as a prostitute. She loves them genuinely, and they count on her for a good time. She is known for her playfulness, her enthusiastic sense of humor, and her strong, beautiful body. The only other young woman in the area is from England. The opposite of Hermelinda, the English woman is nervous, fussy, and rarely seen.

On Friday nights, men ride their horses from great distances to spend an evening drinking Hermelinda's bootleg alcohol and playing a variety of games, which guarantee her a profit without cheating anyone. The games are sexual, and the prize is Hermelinda. Sometimes the party is so wild that the English couple hear laughter as they sip tea before bed. They pretend, however, that they hear only the wind.

Hermelinda's most successful game is called Toad's Mouth. She draws a chalk circle on the floor, then lies down on her back inside of it, with her knees spread wide. Thus, she reveals the "dark center of her body" that appears "as open as a fruit, as a merry toad's mouth." The men then toss their coins toward the target. Money that falls within the chalk circle is Hermelinda's to keep. If one of the players happens "to enter the gate of heaven" with his coin, he earns two hours alone with the hostess, an event so prized it is said to transform the winner into a wise man.

One day, an Asturian man named Pablo arrives. He is lean, with the bones of a bird and a child's hands. He looks like a "peevish banty rooster" but is tenacious, and those that threaten his dignity witness his bad temper and readiness to fight. He is a loner from Spain, traveling without obligation or love, and racked by bitterness and pain. He hates the English.

When Pablo sets eyes on Hermelinda, he sees a woman with his own strength and decides life is not worth living without her. He knows that he has a single chance to win Toad's Mouth, and then only two hours to convince Hermelinda to live with him. Under his sharp gaze, Hermelinda becomes motionless on the floor and he tosses the coin perfectly. The onlooking men cheer with envy, but Pablo is nonchalant in his victory. Immediately, he pulls Hermelinda into the bedroom and closes the door behind them.

To the astonishment of the sheepherders, the lovers do not emerge until noon the following day. They leave the shack, carrying their packed belongings. Pablo saddles the horses without glancing at anyone. Hermelinda wears riding clothes; strapped to her belt is a canvas bag with her savings. She has a new expression in her eyes and walks with a satisfied swish. She waves a distracted good-bye, then follows Pablo without looking back.

The sheepherders never see Hermelinda again. They are so distraught that the ranch managers install an enormous open-mouthed ceramic toad from London. This is supposed to cheer the men up, but they are unimpressed. Eventually, the toad ends up on the English couple's terrace. In the evenings, the bored foreigners amuse themselves by tossing coins into its artificial mouth.

Themes and Meanings

In her essay "Writing As an Act of Hope," Isabel Allende explains that she writes in order to illuminate "some hidden aspect of reality, to help decipher and understand it and thus to initiate, if possible, a change in the conscience of some readers." The reality that she describes in "Toad's Mouth" is rooted in Latin American history. In the 1500's, Spanish explorers and soldiers took over the South American continent; the impact they had on indigenous societies was prodigious.

In "Toad's Mouth," the English couple control wealth and labor in a country that is not their own. They represent any imperialist force that takes control of land and people for personal gain. Indifferent to local customs, the owners of Sheepbreeders, Ltd., maintain their prim exteriors by observing tea time and wearing fancy clothes inappropriate to the landscape. They do not interact with the peasants. They treat the native population with so little respect that they blindly allow their sheep to graze atop sacred ruins.

Much of Allende's fiction is set in Latin America, and her characters often face the duality of the poverty and wealth that can exist there. Wealth, Allende explains in her essay, is in the hands of few, yet carries with it the "pretension to dignity and civilization." In "Toad's Mouth," the English couple consider themselves dignified, but Allende depicts them as absurd and misplaced, concerned only with themselves. In contrast, the peasants live with dignity, treating one another with love and respect. It is the peasants, not the wealthy ranch owners, who form a community, work the land they love, and celebrate their passion for Hermelinda.

As a lover, Hermelinda represents the wild and generous strength of the land itself. She also mothers the men, feeding them soup when they are ill, or mending their clothes. Finally, she is their goddess, a symbol of ancient fertility rituals and the perfect recipient of their worship. She loves them as much as they love her, and the relationship is fruitful, benefiting all. Just as the land for centuries gave native people the means to survive, Hermelinda helps the men overcome their hardships.

Pablo, representing Spain, successfully seduces Hermelinda, then draws her away from her friends. He understands the game of Toad's Mouth perfectly and wins at his first try. His passion is angry, defiant, and selfish, but strong as well, and she willingly follows him, as many indigenous people followed the customs of Spain, abandoning their native languages for Spanish and their ancient religions for Roman Catholicism.

The reserved English couple, however, misunderstand the game of Toad's Mouth entirely. They neither know nor love Hermelinda; they fear the joy she initiates and pretend not to notice the laughter that rises from her shack. Trapped in their pretensions, the ranch owners cannot feel the earthy passion of the land they attempt to control. Because they refuse to interact with the culture, they miss its beauty. They shelter themselves from what they think is barbaric and cannot see how they destroy it. In the end, they unwittingly mock their own ignorance by playing with the fake toad themselves.

Style and Technique

Allende has said that she tries "to write about the necessary changes in Latin America that will enable us to rise from our knees after five centuries of humiliations." Specifically, she writes all of her stories for a young woman in Chile whom she hardly knows. Whenever the author is "tempted by the beauty of a sentence" and "about to betray the truth," she thinks of the candid face of the woman in Chile, and then tells the story in honest, unpretentious prose.

"Toad's Mouth" typifies this style. Its descriptions are concise, playful, and rich with metaphor. Tierra del Fuego breaks up "into a rosary of islands," while the headquarters for Sheepbreeders, Ltd., rises "up from the sterile plain like a forgotten cake." The plot itself holds both humor and political commentary; Pablo's seduction of Hermelinda is both sexually outrageous and symbolically tragic.

The characters in "Toad's Mouth" represent forces larger than themselves. This encourages the reader to interpret the story on a broad scale. The peasants at Sheepbreeders, Ltd., are conquered financially by the English couple, then spiritually by the lone horseman from Spain. They are left with nothing to look forward to, because Hermelinda is gone forever. This is not just the tale of one tiny community in Chile. "Toad's Mouth" is the story of Latin America, and of what is lost when a society is dominated by outside forces.

Mary Pierce Frost

TODAY WILL BE A QUIET DAY

Author: Amy Hempel (1951-   )
Type of plot: Domestic realism
Time of plot: The 1970's or 1980's
Locale: San Francisco, California
First published: 1985

> *Principal characters:*
> A FATHER
> HIS THIRTEEN-YEAR-OLD SON
> HIS SIXTEEN-YEAR-OLD DAUGHTER

The Story

The three characters in this story remain nameless throughout. Instead, they are identified only by their relationships to the others: father, daughter, sister, son, or brother. Also omitted is an overt explanation of the reason these three are together in this special way on this particular day. The mother is never mentioned, yet there is little doubt that there has been a divorce and that the children are visiting their father; in fact, they are spending this night with him. The father has canceled the children's music lessons so that the three of them can spend the day together. He wants to find out how his children are doing, but will not ask them outright. He chooses simply to observe them during their day together.

The father takes his children on a long drive out of the city. Rather than attend a men's arm-wrestling competition, the children choose to go to a modified drive-in restaurant: Pete's—a gas station converted into a place to eat. In the car the children fall into the type of competitive banter and pseudo-arguments that siblings often share. Throughout the day the father says all the appropriate "Dad things" that fathers enjoy saying to their children, such as, "Neither of you should be eating candy before lunch."

There are two seemingly trivial but actually important incidents in the story: The girl tells a joke about three men about to be beheaded: The first two are spared because the guillotine does not work correctly, but the third dies after pointing out the device's mechanical problem. The girl learns that a family dog was not sent to a farm to live after it had bitten a Campfire Girl selling candy at their front door, but rather it was dead because the bitten girl's family had insisted that it be destroyed according to California law.

After they eat, the father lets the daughter drive home. When they reach his house, they prepare to sleep on the floor of the master bedroom in sleeping bags positioned in a cozy triangle, as if around a campfire. Nothing significant happens; yet at the end of the day, the father decides that his children are coping well, that "they are all right."

Themes and Meanings

Because readers have no guidance from Amy Hempel's narrator as to what to think about anything or anyone in this narrative, they must become more involved with the story than is typical in order to come to a conclusion. Although there are no explicit or overt explanations or evaluations, many clues are embedded in the text. The story appears to be about relationships, specifically those of a divorced father with his children, in whose lives he has been only marginally involved. It is no small matter that the title of the story coincides with the epitaph for the father's tombstone or with the general connotation of what it means to have a "quiet day" with or without others. Normally quiet time is set aside for some kind of healing, for getting in touch, for listening to inner voices, or for trying to hear better what others are saying. In this story the day is far from being a quiet one; there is much talking going on. The quietness appears to apply to a lack of direct communication and to the soundless situations of a dismembered family and dislocated relationships.

The story also appears to be about the many ways people communicate various feelings without ever speaking the exact words, as well as how people rarely say what they really mean or really feel, but tend to fall into ready phrases, expected responses, innuendo, or euphemism—say it any other way but do not say it outright. The most obvious example of this latter theme lies in the joke that the young girl tells. Even the joke has to be "translated," and therefore is not given in direct speech. In the scenario of the joke, two people are spared execution either because they do not see the problem or because they say nothing. Only the person who recognizes the problem and, more to the point, acknowledges it aloud, suffers negative consequences—he dies. He dies for the knowing and for the telling, for the seeing and saying, for his pointing it out to others.

Many other verbal clues exist in the text of the story, clues that give meaning both to the events and to the characters' behavior, but also that reflect the methods by which this story is told. "But you could read things wrong" might refer both to the father's reading of his children as "all right" or "not all right" and to the reader's interpretation of the story. "Thinking you're invisible because you closed your eyes" might reflect the condition of thinking that pretending makes something so, or that ignoring something makes it cease to exist. There is a pun embedded in the description of the new type of arm wrestling that the family considers seeing: "The best anyone could hope to see would be dislocation." Within the new rules of the sporting event, the worst that can happen now is that someone's shoulder might be "dislocated"; in the arena of life, if "dislocation" is the best that one can hope for, then everyone in the story must indeed be "all right."

Style and Technique

A term frequently applied to Hempel's short fiction is minimalism—a technique that creates fiction that is deceptively simple and realistic. At its best, minimalism creates a concentrated and uncluttered narrative. In addition, it is a style that also reflects the characteristics of the short story, the genre that best houses minimalism. Both minimalism and the short story rely heavily on figures of speech and the baggage of connotation attached to each. Metonymy is the basic trope for realism, and metaphor is the basic trope for poetry. Minimalist stories are realistic in that they use metonymy such as the joke or the arm wrestling references in this story. The joke that the young girl tells is a tiny anecdote within the short story, yet it not only reflects the whole idea of this story, it also gestures toward the larger text of a universal condition in which humanity is no longer located in strong family units and no longer able to address emotions directly. Instead, the human condition represented here disallows words and dislocates language as a means of emotional survival. The references to the arm wrestling contest and the reasons given for the trio not going to the event refer to the same sort of human condition, "The best one could hope for was dislocation"—not just of someone's arm (rather than being broken under the old rules), but also dislocation of emotions, language, and meaning.

Everything left out of a minimalist short story is as important as the things that remain. In this story, for example, there is never any mention of the children's mother (the father's former wife), but she is present as part of the dislocation caused by divorce. Likewise, the names of the characters are left out of the story; this omission gives the story a universal dimension because the characters' anonymity suggests that they could be any father and children who are characters in the drama and effects of divorce. Further, many things are not said by the narrator to the reader; many more things are not said by the characters among themselves. To omit a word, to say something indirectly, to rely on meaningless phrases for communication—all are the most emphatic means of stressing the importance of what has not been said, which in this case seems to be that a divorce has disrupted this family unit, that the father does not feel himself to be a part of his children's lives, and that he is afraid to let them know that he cares about them.

The details of the day's events are relayed by an omniscient third-person narrator, who does not intrude on the story by commenting or making any evaluations, leaving readers to watch and listen to an apparently objective report on the events of this day and the dialogue exchanged among the three characters. The readers are thus left to draw their own conclusions. In employing this type of narrative technique, Hempel presents the reader with a narrator who, in fact, practices what the story appears to preach: Do not point out the problem if you see it; just accept what is what and go on about your business. If you must say anything, say it indirectly, as with the father's assessment of his children's condition: "There is no bad news."

Cynthia Whitney Hallett

TOGETHER AND APART

Author: Virginia Woolf (1882-1941)
Type of plot: Psychological
Time of plot: About 1924
Locale: London
First published: 1943

> *Principal characters:*
> MISS RUTH ANNING, the protagonist, a spinster
> MR. RODERICK SERLE, a man who fancies himself a writer but
> never writes and with whom Miss Anning converses at Mrs.
> Dalloway's party

The Story

Introduced to each other for the first time by Mrs. Dalloway at her party, Miss Ruth Anning and Mr. Roderick Serle are left by their hostess to talk together. Miss Anning had been standing at the window, looking at the evening sky; yet, while "the sky went on pouring its meaning" into her, on Mr. Serle's sudden presence beside her she feels that the sky has changed and is not "itself, any more, but . . . shored up by [Serle's] tall body, dark eyes, grey hair, clasped hands, the stern melancholy face." Just as the sky is "shored up," so too are Miss Anning's perceptions of whatever "meaning" she may have felt able to glean from the sky, for she feels suddenly "impelled" to initiate and carry on a conversation with Mr. Serle, regardless of how "foolish" or superficial the conversation, and regardless of her own feeling that "their lives, seen by moonlight, [seemed] as long as an insect's and no more important."

"Foolish! Idiotically foolish" conversation reveals to Miss Anning, in fact, what she both lacks and possesses as an individual: She lacks the energy needed for "talking with men, who frightened her rather, and so often her talks petered out into dull commonplaces, and she had very few men friends—very few intimate friends at all, she thought, but after all, did she want them? No." Indeed, what she lacks in energy and friends seems insignificant to her when compared to what she possesses: "She had Sarah, Arthur, the cottage, the chow and, of course that . . . the sense she had coming home of something collected there, a cluster of miracles." However, for the sake of the party, for the sake of conversation, and for the sake of Mr. Serle, Miss Anning must put out of her mind those "miracles" that make her life richly and uniquely meaningful, and she must force herself to carry on a meaningless talk with Mr. Serle, a man "she could afford to leave." Miss Anning asks him a question designed to elicit a response from him on a topic, she presumes, about which he cares—Canterbury and the ancestors of his who are buried there.

After presenting Miss Anning's view of this awkward situation, the omniscient narrator then shifts to Mr. Serle's perspective, and here the reader is shown the great need this man has.for such superficial conversation as that which he is having with Miss Anning: "With a stranger he felt a renewal of hope because they could not say he had not done what he had promised, and yielding to his charm would give him a fresh start—at fifty!" Despite the satisfaction he takes from the illusion of a "fresh start" with this stranger, he nevertheless feels that his "extraordinary facility and responsiveness to talk" have proven to be "his undoing" over the years, for he has been unable to refuse invitations to parties, and unable to resist "society and the company of women." Consequently, he has been unable to find the time he needs to be the writer he believes he is—even though he never writes. Rather than blaming himself for putting off his writing and the test of his talent, Mr. Serle finds it easier and less damaging to his exaggeratedly positive self-image to "blame . . . the richness of his nature, which he compared favorably with Wordsworth's." Rather than seeing such parties as given by Mrs. Dalloway, as well as such conversations as his with Miss Anning, as a waste of time and energy, Mr. Serle views such activities as essential to his "deep" life.

The narrator's ironic view of Mr. Serle's existence differs greatly from the man's own view, for underpinning his need for polite society, the attention of women, and idle conversation is the fact that, at home, he has an invalid wife with whom he is "grumpy, unpleasant," and "caustic"—his remarks to her "too clever for her to meet, except by gentle expostulations and a tear or two." Although Miss Anning's displeasure over the superficiality germane to conversations at parties is intensified by her reflection on the "miracles" she possesses at home, Mr. Serle's displeasure with his home intensifies his hunger for precisely such parties as this one of the Dalloways.

Significantly, it is Miss Anning's desire for a meaningful and rich existence that prompts her to tell Mr. Serle "the truth" about her own relationship to Canterbury, and thereby prevent him from going away from her with any "false assumption"; she tells him, therefore, "I loved Canterbury." As a result of her truthfulness, their eyes "collided" and each of them experiences a brief exposure of the other's inner, heretofore "secluded being," and the experience is—while momentary—"alarming" and "terrific." It is, in short, "the old ecstasy of life" made apparent, and its momentary exposure punctuates Mr. Serle's otherwise "yawning, empty, capricious" existence.

Unfortunately, just as quickly as the moment of their communion occurs (that of one "secluded being" with another), it dissipates and becomes a kind of "withdrawal," a "violation of trust," and they are left as before: "She did her part; he his." Caught in awkward silence, they both feel "freed" when Mira Cartwright approaches them and accosts Mr. Serle: To the relief of both Miss Anning and Mr. Serle, Cartwright's intrusion frees them to "separate."

Themes and Meanings

In *Jacob's Room* (1922), Virginia Woolf's third novel, the narrator asserts that "life is but a procession of shadows"; then she asks, "why are we yet surprised in the window corner by a sudden vision that the young man in the chair is of all things in the world the most real, the most solid, the best known to us . . . ? For the moment after we know nothing about him." Although Woolf (through her narrator) is discussing here the difficulty a biographer has in capturing, with words on paper, the essence of an individual, she is also pointing to what she sees as an inescapable fact of human existence: One individual can never completely know another; similarly, one can never completely know oneself because that essentially fluid self is shaded and even, at times, changed by associations with others. This last point (regarding the effect other people have on a personality, as well as on that personality's view of itself and others) is important to understanding Woolf's fiction; indeed, she gave expression to this point in all of her novels, in several autobiographical essays, and in a number of her short stories—one of which is "Together and Apart."

Although both Miss Anning and Mr. Serle naturally have different perspectives and responses to their conversation, and to the party itself (she mildly resents having to abandon her solitary contemplation of the sky for the sake of "empty" conversation with a man whom, she gradually realizes, she does not like; he needs such a conversation because it helps him to forget the person he is at home), the artificial situation in which they find themselves permits them a brief, transcendent moment of communion with each other.

The situation itself demands that the "shallow [and] agile" side of each of these people's personalities "keeps the show going" by "tumbling and beckoning" in talk; yet below the "agile" side of each exists a "secluded being, who sits in darkness." Only when Miss Anning decides that "this man shall not glide away from me, like everybody else, on false assumption," and then decides to express her feelings by saying, "I loved Canterbury," is the reader told that Mr. Serle "kindled instantly." In other words, by articulating her emotions Miss Anning has dived below the superficial and elicited a similar—albeit nonverbalized—response from her companion. Thus they both experience what Woolf elsewhere calls "a moment of being," when, as it is described in this story, the "secluded being" in each of them "stood erect; flung off his cloak; confronted the other."

After such a moment of wordless communication, Miss Anning realizes, as her creator had before her, how inadequate language is for truthful communication—especially in the face of "how obscure the mind [is], with its very few words for all these astonishing perceptions, these alterations of pain and pleasure."

Style and Technique

Reading any of Woolf's stories for the first time, the reader may be struck by how little physical action takes place in them, yet this author's stories always contain much action—thought-as-action—because her characters' conflicts are, with few exceptions, psychological ones. In "Together and Apart," for example, Miss Anning and Mr. Serle sit down on a sofa and—except for when he occasionally crosses or uncrosses his legs—that is all the physical movement the story provides. However, even though the story consists of approximately three thousand words, only a hundred and fifty of which are actually spoken by the two characters, the reader learns about both characters' lives—their feelings of inadequacy and incompleteness, their aspirations and frustrations, and their essentially inescapable feelings of aloneness. It is a testament to Woolf's mastery of prose and storytelling that, while it takes place in a superficial and boring context, the story itself is neither. However, why would Woolf choose such a context?

In *Moments of Being* (1976), Woolf suggests that most individuals are not static personalities but are, instead, fluid and subject to constant changes in being and perception. Although a seemingly constant, continuous identity is imposed on people as they inhabit the finite world of physical and social existence, during "moments of being" this identity is transcended, and the individual consciousness becomes an undifferentiated part of a greater whole; at such a moment all limits associated with the finite world cease to exist. With this in mind, then, the reader is better able to understand why "Together and Apart" takes place in the limited confines of an artificial setting, for the setting itself heightens and intensifies the "moment of being" that Miss Anning and Mr. Serle experience. In fact, the limits imposed on Miss Anning, by the finite setting and the identity that it forces her to project, goad her into demanding more of herself, Mr. Serle, and their situation. Although in the story's first paragraph Miss Anning's perception of the infinite (the sky) is "shored up" by Mr. Serle's presence (himself representing the restrictions of the finite world), she becomes the catalyst for her companion's transcendent moment of communion with the infinite behind the "cloak."

David A. Carpenter

TOMMY

Author: John Edgar Wideman (1941-   )
Type of plot: Psychological
Time of plot: The mid-1970's, not long after the Vietnam War
Locale: Homewood, a decaying black neighborhood in the urban Northeast
First published: 1981

Principal characters:
TOMMY LAWSON, the streetwise protagonist, a directionless black
    youth longing to leave his crumbling home
RUCHELL, his hip, jive partner in crime
INDOVINA, a fraudulent, parasitic white salesperson
CHUBBY, the businessperson's Uncle Tomish sidekick
JOHN LAWSON, Tommy's elder brother who has escaped the
    ghetto

The Story

Tommy Lawson is strolling through the deserted streets of Homewood, a once populous black community now demarcated by boarded-up buildings and cracked sidewalks. Both he and the city streets share a legacy of tough, charismatic individuals: from Tommy's grandfather John French, who jived and jitterbugged until he "got too old and got saved," to the ice-ball vendor Mr. Strayhorn, who in his youth garnered such a reputation that no one yet will shake him down for money. However, now neither the young man nor the blocks where he bebopped have bright futures. Homewood has become a no-man's-land since the 1960's riots, so Tommy shoots pool with the junkies and assorted drifters in the Velvet Slipper.

Today, however, Tommy stalks the Avenue, lost in reminiscence, for he has found a way to escape. He and his running buddy, Ruchell, whose full-time occupation is getting as high as possible, plan to finance their flight by swindling a crooked carsalesperson. They have alerted this hustler, Indovina, to a truckload of stolen television sets that they will deposit at his business for a fee. (Actually, nothing is in their borrowed van except carpeting left there by its owner.) While Tommy closes the deal inside the white man's office, Ruchell will stand guard by the goods. Then, as Indovina's bodyguard Chubby approaches to inspect the cache, Ruchell will corner him with a gun. Tommy simultaneously will hold up Indovina. Certain that the Italian will not report the incident for fear of being charged himself, the two young men will "score and blow" to the West Coast.

However, this scam soon sours. Ruchell shoots Chubby when he sees the hefty man reaching for a concealed weapon. Panicking at the sound of shots, Tommy pistolwhips Indovina and flees toward the van, too hysterical to grab any money first. Hunted now, the unlucky pair hides away from Homewood with Tommy's older brother John Lawson and his family.

Ironically, at last Tommy and Ruchell have severed the old neighborhood's hold. Charged with first-degree murder, they literally cannot return to it. However, their prospects are burdensome rather than uplifting and inspiring.

Tommy especially feels the dead weight of his misbegotten dream. After assuring his brother, "I'm happy you got out. One of us got out anyway," the pursued man lies on a bed thinking about Christmases past. He dwells on not the toys and food, but the sleepless, futile nights spent listening for Santa, watching for the flying reindeer. Again he finds himself with a dream he longs to confirm: being free. Even if it does not make sense given his circumstances, he still yearns for it to come true.

Themes and Meanings

John Edgar Wideman admits that "Tommy," like all the linked tales of *Damballah* (1981), arose from his desire to tell a story whose "theme was to be the urge for freedom, the resolve of the runaway to live free or die." Though Tommy and his peers are not literal slaves, like his great-great-great-grandmother who escaped North, in many ways their struggles are no easier than hers and yield few long-term successes.

As Tommy walks through Homewood at the beginning of the story, he complains to himself that he has "no ride of his own so he's still walking." However, this statement belies the fact that he has tried to thwart the area's encroaching listlessness. He once was lead singer of the Commodores, a group so popular that it drew throngs of listeners to its Sunday jam sessions. A recording deal fell through, however, thanks to a seedy agent, and the group was dissolved.

Tommy's near success has been repeated in many ways by other men from Homewood's row houses and projects. Some have traded apparent impossibilities for the tangible, quick fruition of a junkie's nod. Others have relented unwillingly, their bodies blown asunder in the rice paddies of Vietnam. All have been suppressed by forces outside the community: In lieu of slavers seizing unsuspecting tribes, twentieth century whites use drugs, wars, and legal loopholes to entrap black men.

Tommy admires his brother, once an outstanding basketball player, for skirting a dead-end lifestyle and establishing a career, yet he can never account for precisely why John beat the odds in the first place. With hands "bigger than his brother's," Tommy could "palm a ball when he was eleven," but he did not even try the sport as a means of liberation. On the other hand, Deacon Barclay, a longtime friend of the family, owns a home as a result of a bittersweet victory. He has earned the money by "running around yes sirring and no mamming the white folks and cleaning their toilets," by performing in effect little more than his plantation forebears did.

A slave's paths to freedom (those other than death) were all uncertain long shots: to escape, to purchase himself, to be manumitted in a kind master's will, or to enjoy a superficial independence as the mistress's cook or the master's butler and valet. For many of Homewood's men, the American dream still carries the same measure of unattainability. Thus, as the story closes, Tommy repeats a resolve that echoes the "live free or die" motto of the fugitive slave. He vows, "I ain't going back to prison. They have to kill me before I go back in prison." However, an ugly fact unsettles his declaration: a black man, not a white, died during his heist. In their desperate attempts to use any means necessary for obtaining money and respect, black men all too often hurt their own people: It is as if the final method of containing them is turning them against themselves. The themes of this autobiographical story—John Lawson is Wideman's alter ego—are treated at length in Wideman's acclaimed *Brothers and Keepers* (1984), a work of nonfiction.

Style and Technique

The streets and people of Homewood are moldy grays and jaundiced yellows. The Avenue is "a darker gray stripe between the gray sidewalks," and Mr. Strayhorn peers at passersby out of "yellow eyes." Interestingly, despite his animosity toward this neighborhood, Tommy also is associated with these colors. In one example, he complains about "crawling all sweaty out of the gray sheets. Mom could wash them every day, they still be gray. Like his underclothes. Like every . . . thing they had and would ever have." Similarly, when he and Ruchell plot their ill-fated robbery, the lights about them cast a "yellow pall." Thus, the color imagery stresses Tommy's unfortunate ties to the community. He is already part of its human refuse, and his hopes of climbing out of the pile are as good as dead. However, the images link him to Homewood for another purpose, too. Regardless of his scorn for the winos, methadone users, and ruthless young gangs that have burgeoned over the years, Homewood is his ancestral seat. He walks where his gambling grandfather once strutted, and he passes "rain-soaked, sun-faded" posters paying silent tribute to other relatives' lives. So, though a fresh start and unlimited advancement may never be his, he possesses a history that he cannot lose.

In one well-crafted series of bird images, Wideman vividly underscores Tommy's ineffectual hopes. The young Lawson remembers how, missing the trolley back in high school days, he "wished he was a bird soaring through the black night, a bird with shiny chrome fenders and fishtails and a Continental kit." He describes a car in such terms because a bird, more so than any other creature, suggests freedom. On snapping out of his daydream, however, he discovers a real, dead, barely recognizable bird. This gory corpse, "already looking like the raggedy sole somebody had walked off their shoe," adds a sense of foreboding to the story, as if his teenage aspirations for independence will go the same shredded way as that of the pitiful skeleton fusing with the ground beneath him. Then a similar ghastly memory revives in Tommy's mind. He recalls stoning the winos' camp when he was a child, then fearing the wrath of a foul-breathed boogyman. He would picture his nemesis "behind every bush, gray and bloody-mouthed. The raggedy, gray clothes flapping like a bird and a bird's feathery, smothering funk covering you as he drags you into the bushes." Because the wino of Tommy's reverie metamorphoses into a dead bird, an indicator already of dashed dreams, Wideman again conveys a sense of doom. Tommy is not impatient that opportunities will come too soon; he worries that they will disintegrate before he reaches them.

Barbara A. McCaskill

TOMORROW AND TOMORROW AND SO FORTH

Author: John Updike (1932-   )
Type of plot: Social realism
Time of plot: The 1950's
Locale: An American high school
First published: 1955

> *Principal characters:*
> MARK PROSSER, the protagonist and the story's central
>   consciousness, an eleventh-grade English teacher
> GLORIA ANGSTROM, an attractive student
> PETER FORRESTER, an antagonistic student
> GEOFFREY LANGER, a bright student
> STRUNK, a physical education teacher

The Story

The lesson for the day in Mark Prosser's English classroom is Macbeth's soliloquy on hearing of Lady Macbeth's death:

> Tomorrow and tomorrow and tomorrow
> Creeps in this petty pace from day to day,
> To the last syllable of recorded time,
> And all our yesterdays have lighted fools
> The way to dusty death. Out, out, brief candle!
> Life's but a walking shadow, a poor player
> That struts and frets his hour on the stage
> And then is heard no more. It is a tale
> Told by an idiot, full of sound and fury,
> Signifying nothing.

Macbeth's criticism of life, based on his experience, reflects on the lack of experience or learning taking place in the classroom.

As his students enter the eleventh-grade English classroom, Prosser flatters himself on his ability to interpret their responses to their environment, attributing their restlessness to a change in the weather. The adolescents act out their relationships with one another as they roughhouse their way to their respective seats. Prosser is particularly aware of Gloria Angstrom, whose practically sleeveless pink sweater sets off the whiteness of her arms. His libidinous feelings toward Gloria make him a rival for her attentions with red-headed Peter Forrester, who has not prepared his homework assignment, but has succeeded in making her gasp as they enter the classroom. Prosser expresses his envy in contemplating the shortcomings of redheads in general and Peter in particular by calling on Peter first to be accountable for the homework assignment. Peter is unprepared. Prosser is unable to refrain from mocking his student's superficial, inappropriate answers.

As a teacher, Prosser is very self-conscious; indeed, his self-consciousness matches that of his adolescent students. Rather than concentrating on the subject matter, he reacts to their behavior, or what he assumes to be their reactions to him. His interpretation of William Shakespeare's lines is little better than that of the students, because it depends more on the interaction between teacher and students than on the play. When Peter eventually asks for a better explication, Prosser claims that he does not really know the meaning himself. When the students express their discomfort with this response, he tells them that he does not want to force his interpretation on them; in effect, he abandons the role of teacher to become a "human-among-humans." He is more concerned with what they think of him than with teaching them to understand Shakespeare. When he does start to provide some information about Shakespeare, he allows their disinterest to determine his actions. He is continually evaluating his relationship with them, congratulating himself on what he supposes to be his acuteness of perception.

When the students each attempt to recite the passage from memory at the front of the room, Prosser remains preoccupied with the interaction among them, especially as they relate to Gloria. As he admonishes Geoffrey, the smart boy with whom Prosser identifies himself, Prosser intercepts a note from Gloria to Peter in which she asserts that Prosser is a great teacher and that she loves him. As the period ends, he tells her to stay.

When the others leave, he patronizingly admonishes her for note-passing and suggests that she does not know the meaning of love. He thinks, however, that her emotional sincerity is about to express itself in tears.

After she has left, Strunk, the physical education teacher, comes in to tell how Gloria had played a joke that morning on another of her teachers by letting him intercept a note that said she loved that teacher. Moreover, the same thing had been done to yet another teacher the day before. Prosser feels angry. He does not tell Strunk that he, too, has been a victim of this joke. He leaves the school assuring himself that Gloria had been emotional, about to cry because she really did care about him, regardless of the notes intercepted by the other teachers.

Themes and Meanings

Like Macbeth's soliloquy, this story is concerned with the failure of the passage of time to produce significant meaning. Mark Prosser, as a teacher, is supposed to help his students by guiding them in their search for meaning. Unfortunately, he lacks the self-knowledge, which ought to have come with maturity, that is necessary to do this. His actions are determined by his concern with how others, students or fellow teachers, perceive him. He identifies with Geoffrey Langer, the smart boy, but he behaves like Peter Forrester, the cutup, as he vies with Peter for the attention of Gloria. He picks on Peter through envy of the relationship between the two adolescents.

He wants to retain his authority as a teacher on the one hand; on the other, he wants to be seen as a friend, as a member of the group who happens to have read a little more than the others. Instead of attempting to bring them up to his level, he consistently lowers himself to theirs. When he does attempt to say something significant about the play, he allows himself to become distracted by Gloria, becomes self-conscious about what he is saying, and consciously attempts to sound diffident, as if what he is saying is not important to him either. Naturally he loses the attention of the class. To retrieve their attention, he resorts to reprimanding them and once again attacks Peter, who has taken the opportunity to talk to Gloria. He cannot convincingly answer any of their questions because, regardless of his intellectual maturity, his emotional maturity is no greater than theirs.

Prosser conjectures that all the students want is "the quality of glide. To skip along, always in rhythm, always cool, the little wheels humming under you, going nowhere special." So he accounts for the "petty pace" of their lives. In defining this term, however, he has ranked the work of teachers along with that of accountants and bank clerks. He is inconsistent, unsure of himself, the fool of the soliloquy. His immature need for their fellowship leads him to fall for their joke. The joke itself is somewhat cruel, but it works only because the teachers are so dependent on their students for emotional security. Clearly, the students have the intelligence or insight to realize that. Prosser is a "poor player" because his emotional maturity has not kept up with his age. Time has not endowed him with either maturity or the security that comes with self-knowledge.

Style and Technique

This story is something of a classic in the subgenre of stories about school because of John Updike's ability to capture the sense of being in the classroom. He meticulously re-creates the classroom setting by adding detail to detail in a successful evocation of the interplay between students and teacher and among students themselves. The details of description and dialogue reflect the acuteness of Updike's eye and ear: Students act this way; teachers say these things.

This rich depiction of the setting is matched by Updike's precise manipulation of point of view. Like Henry James, Updike tells his story through a center of consciousness whose intellectual and moral quality delineates theme. The narration is third-person but confined to the consciousness of Prosser. The reader experiences the classroom through the sensibility of the teacher. Thus, the reader not only knows what Prosser knows but also is in a position to evaluate the quality of Prosser's processing of experience into wisdom.

The facile overgeneralizing about students as they enter the room marks Prosser as less than profound. The derogatory generalizations about redheads and about the desire of all adolescents to "glide" through life more precisely define the moral and intellectual limitations of this character. By generalizing, Prosser relieves the anxiety brought about by his need to be liked by his students, the sign of his emotional immaturity. Against the evidence of the notes to the other teachers, he insists that Gloria was sincere in his note. Macbeth's generalizations are rooted deep in his experience; Prosser's, only in the topsoil of his emotions.

William J. McDonald

TONIO KRÖGER

Author: Thomas Mann (1875-1955)
Type of plot: Psychological
Time of plot: The last quarter of the nineteenth century
Locale: A northern German town resembling Lubeck; Munich, the Bavarian capital; and Aalsgaard, Denmark
First published: 1903 (English translation, 1914)

> *Principal characters:*
> TONIO KRÖGER, the protagonist and the author's fictive persona
> HANS HANSEN, Tonio's boyhood friend
> INGEBORG HOLM, a beautiful, blond local girl whom young Tonio admires
> MAGDALENA VERMEHREN, a serious, dark-eyed girl who adores Tonio
> LISABETTA IVANOVNA, an artist friend of the mature Tonio

The Story

Schoolboy Tonio Kröger discovers that he deeply admires, indeed loves, his classmate Hans Hansen. The boys are physical and intellectual opposites. Hans is handsome in a Nordic way with steel-blue eyes, straw-colored hair, broad shoulders, and narrow hips, while Tonio has the dark-brown hair, dark eyes, and chiseled features of the south. Hans's walk is strong and athletic, Tonio's idle and uneven. It hurts Tonio that Hans responds to his obvious admiration with easygoing indifference. When Hans is late for their after-school walk and finally appears with other friends, Tonio almost cries, but when Hans recalls their agreed-on walk and says that it was good of Tonio to wait for him, everything in Tonio leaps for joy.

Though he is aware of the differences between himself and Hans, Tonio never tries to imitate his friend. He knows that Hans will never read the copy of Friedrich Schiller's *Don Carlos, Infant von Spanien* (1787; *Don Carlos, Infante of Spain*, 1798) that he gives him, that even if he did, he would probably never recognize its dual themes of indestructible friendship and forbidden love. Tonio also realizes that he cannot develop Hans's interest in riding. Tonio would prefer to read a book on horses and admire their strength and beauty rather than to be on horseback. Though Tonio recognizes that he is different, he is hurt when Hans calls him by his surname because "Tonio" sounds too "foreign." Tonio likes the unusual combination, "Tonio Kröger."

Tonio's extraordinary sensitivity causes him to feel things more deeply than most boys. Indeed, his ability to recognize sham and ill-breeding, even in his teachers, results in school absenteeism and poor grades, which trouble and anger Consul Kröger, Tonio's fastidious, tall, blue-eyed father. Tonio's beautiful, black-haired mother, Consuelo, seems to him blithely indifferent to his grades, and Tonio is glad about this, though he considers his father's attitude somehow more respectable and dignified.

Tonio, now age sixteen, has suddenly become infatuated by blond Ingeborg Holm. Though he has known her all of his life, she suddenly seems to have acquired a special beauty. Tonio is aware that he feels the same ecstatic love for Inge that he felt for Hans several years earlier, and that this transformation has occurred during Herr Knaak's private dancing class. The perceptive Tonio has considered Knaak's effeminate and affected demonstrations and gestures those of "an unmentionable monkey" and is embarrassed when the dancing master calls him "Fraulein Kröger" after Tonio has taken a wrong turn in the dance.

Mortified by his friends' laughter, Tonio takes refuge in the corridor, wonders why he always seems to feel so much pain and longing, and wishes that he were at home reading *Immensee* (1849; *Immensee: Or, The Old Man's Reverie*, 1858), a romantically joyful story by Theodor Storm. Tonio wishes Inge would come out and console him, but he realizes that she has probably laughed at him like all the rest. Dark-eyed Magdalena Vermehren, "who was falling down in the dances," would be impressed that a magazine has recently accepted one of his poems, but this would mean nothing to Inge. Tonio resolves to be faithful to Inge, even though his love remains unrequited.

By the story's next juncture, Tonio's mother and father have died, the family firm has been dissolved, and the Kröger house has been sold. Tonio goes his own way, lives in various cities in the south, and continues to acquire respect for his intellect and the power of the Word. He comes to think of life as a labyrinth, but even in the throes of depression his artistry sharpens. His exotic name becomes associated with excellence, and his writings gain a large audience. At the same time, Tonio's appearance comes to resemble his work: fastidious, precious, refined.

It is in the southern German city of Munich that the now-established Tonio meets his attractive artist friend Lisabetta Ivanovna. Lisabetta chides Tonio for his formality and fastidious appearance. She claims that he does not look like an author, but Tonio argues that wearing a velveteen jacket or adopting Bohemian ways does not make one an artist. This interview gives Tonio a chance to expound his views on art, specifically the art of writing.

The art of writing is not a blessing but a curse that one begins to feel very early. It begins with a sense of isolation and estrangement from others, and this sense grows deeper with the years until there is no hope of reconciliation. As a result, the true artist is recognizable. The writer, Tonio continues, always speaks most directly to "the same old gathering of early Christians . . . people who are falling down in the dance."

In the last section of the story, Tonio journeys north to the town he had left thirteen years earlier. He finds his boyhood home, even expects to see his father come from its entrance, but discovers that it has now become the town's public library. For a time he is detained by the police, who confuse him with a wanted man, but he proves his identity with the proof-sheets of his latest book. He quietly enjoys this little encounter as he continues his journey north to Denmark.

Tonio enjoys Aalsgaard, the Danish seaside resort where his northward journey ends. One morning after a leisurely breakfast, Hans Hansen and Ingeborg Holm walk through the room. Inge is dressed as she used to be at Herr Knaak's dancing class; Hans wears his sailor's overcoat with its gilt buttons. They are not the Hans and Inge of Tonio's youth but are similar in type. Tonio continues to observe the couple closely in his writer's way and even notices that the nasal pronunciation of the orchestra leader resembles that of Herr Knaak.

In a conversation with Lisabetta, Tonio confides the results of his trip. He has determined that it is his ability to love the ordinary that has made him an artist. Nevertheless, he stands between two worlds, a part neither of the bourgeois world about which he writes, nor of the abstract world occupied by those who coldly adore the beautiful.

Themes and Meanings

This early work of Thomas Mann encapsulates the theory of art he would develop in his novella *Der Tod in Venedig* (1912; *Death in Venice*, 1925) and in many of his subsequent works. It reflects his readings in the works of the philosophers Friedrich Nietzsche (1844-1900) and Arthur Schopenhauer (1788-1860) and uses the device of leitmotif, the short recurring phrase that distinguishes given characters, emotions, or situations in the musical dramas of Richard Wagner (1813-1883).

Nietzsche's theory of balanced opposites as the source of art appears in the story's numerous juxtapositions. Externally, these exist in the story's northern and southern locales and represent northern intellect and southern passion. Tonio's hometown and the Danish town he visits as an adult are balanced by Bavarian Munich (Tonio's place of residence as a successful writer) and the Italian pilgrimage Tonio makes when he leaves his boyhood home. Within the story, Tonio's fastidious father is complemented by his fiery, non-German mother, Consuelo, and opposition continues in Tonio's attraction to Hans and Inge. Significantly, Magdalena and Lisabetta, who more closely resemble Tonio, become the audience for his art. The ultimate fusion of opposites, and by Nietzsche's definition art's origins, is appropriately in the name of the story's protagonist.

Schopenhauer's theory of the will and representation finds expression in Tonio's careful observations of all he sees. He records these from boyhood, and as he grows older and wishes to see pattern and continuity in his life, these impressions return in altered settings. This explains the haunted journey northward that Tonio undertakes as well as his fear that his long-dead father will suddenly emerge from his boyhood home. (A connection between Danish locale, Tonio's father obsession, and the ghost of Hamlet's father seems implied.) His artist's power of will to mold representation also accounts for Tonio's ability to see Hans, Inge, and Knaak in the people at the Danish resort.

Mann loved Wagner's *Der Ring des Nibelungen* (1876) and determined to incorporate Wagnerian-style leitmotifs in his work. The wildflower that Consul Kröger wears, as well as his fastidious appearance, reappear in the dress of the successful Tonio. Similarly, Tonio writes for those "always falling down in the dance," the epithet given originally to Magdalena.

Style and Technique

Mann's works almost plunder his family and circle of acquaintances for their plots, settings, and characterizations. Tonio is the fastidious Mann, and Mann's merchant grandfather, father, and mother appear in the descriptions of Tonio's parents. Mann left Lubeck to live in Munich after his father's death just as Tonio leaves his northern town for the Bavarian capital. Mann felt a deep attachment for a school friend named Armin Martens, Tonio's Hans Hansen.

This intensely personal autobiographical style did not endear Mann to many Lubeck residents, who recognized themselves in his works (or believed they did), and often resented how they appeared. Indeed, it was with the same anxiety that Tonio experienced that Mann revisited the town of his youth when a successful author.

Robert J. Forman

THE TOUGHEST INDIAN IN THE WORLD

Author: Sherman Alexie (1966-   )
Type of plot: Realism
Time of plot: 1998
Locale: Wenatchee, Washington
First published: 1999

Principal characters:
AN AMERICAN INDIAN WRITER, the narrator and protagonist
THE HITCHHIKER, an unnamed Native American prizefighter

The Story

This story about a Native American (Sherman Alexie prefers the term "Indian") who has left the reservation but yearns for his tribe's mythic past begins with a prologue in which the protagonist relates his father's advice to pick up only Native American hitchhikers, warning him that white people will kill you because they smell the dead salmon on you.

When the narrator was a boy, his father would point out hitchhikers on the road: If a hitchhiker were a fellow Native American, he would stop, but if he were a white man his father would drive by without comment. This, the narrator says, is how he learned to be silent in the presence of white people, for Native Americans believe that white people will vanish if ignored enough times. The narrator, a feature writer for a newspaper, says that he now picks up three or four Native American hitchhikers a week. His coworkers at the newspaper office think he is crazy to take such chances.

The central event of the story begins when the narrator picks up a Native American hitchhiker and recognizes from the man's twisted and scarred hands that he is a prizefighter. The man tells the narrator that he goes from reservation to reservation, offering to fight the best fighter there, winner take all. The last Native American he fought was a young man billed as the "toughest Indian in the world," who refused to go down no matter how much the man hit him. Knowing that the young fighter would die before he went down, the hitchhiker sat down on the mat and let himself be counted out.

When the narrator stops at the town of Wenatchee, he invites the hitchhiker to spend the night with him. Later in bed, the hitchhiker begins to fondle the narrator and then says he wants to be inside him. Although the narrator says that he has never done this before and insists that he is not gay, he agrees. After they have sex, the narrator tells the hitchhiker he thinks he had better leave.

After taking a shower, doing some shadow boxing, and searching his body for changes, the narrator goes to bed, wondering if he is a warrior in this life and if he had been a warrior in a previous life. The next morning, he wakes up and starts walking barefoot away from the motel. The story ends with his saying if someone were to break open his heart they would find "the thin white skeletons of one thousand salmon."

Themes and Meanings

Often an outspoken advocate for Native Americans, Alexie explores in "The Toughest Indian in the World" a typical theme of Native American writers—the yearning of the assimilated professional to make some sort of contact with his primal native heritage. The protagonist's continuation of his father's "ceremony" of picking up only Native American hitchhikers reflects his sense of connection with those twentieth century "aboriginal nomads" who refuse to believe that the salmon are gone. Much as the buffalo was a destroyed mainstay of Plains Indians, the salmon is a symbol of the lost hope of the Spokane Indians. Everyone in the Northwest—Indian and white—is haunted by the salmon, the narrator says. The mythic power of the salmon is also suggested by the narrator's recalling how, as a boy, he leaned over the edge of a dam and watched the ghosts of the salmon rise from the water up to the sky to become constellations.

When the narrator picks up the Native American fighter, he wants him to know that he grew up on the reservation, "with every Indian in the world," so he uses Native American slang and shares the hitchhiker's jerky with him. Having moved off the reservation twelve years before to work in the city as a feature writer on a newspaper, the narrator takes pleasure in driving down the road chewing on jerky, talking to an indigenous fighter, feeling "as Indian as Indian gets."

This narrator's admiration for the hitchhiker is further emphasized when the fighter tells the narrator about his fight with a young Native American billed as "the toughest Indian in the world," who refused to go down no matter how many times he hit him. When the narrator tells the hitchhiker he could have been a warrior in the old days both for his power as a fighter and for his honoring his opponent by sitting down and letting him win the fight, he is excited, wanting to let the fighter know how highly he thinks of him.

The narrator's yearning to identify with the world of the warrior establishes a basis for his willingness to have sex with the hitchhiker, even though he is not homosexual. He sees the fighter as beautiful and scarred, a true warrior. In the world of the warrior of the old times, he senses there were no false gender boundaries. The mythic nature of the sex act between the two men is reflected by the narrator's saying that afterward he smelled like salmon. He searches his body for any changes, wondering if he is a warrior now and if he was a warrior in a previous incarnation.

Style and Technique

The stylistic challenge Alexie faces in this story is to convince the reader that it is not merely a story of a homosexual encounter or even a story about a man who is a latent homosexual, but rather a story about the authenticity of the old world of the Indian warrior and its refusal to recognize false gender distinctions. To achieve this, Alexie establishes a first-person point of view to allow the narrator to identify his father's allegiance to Native American hitchhikers with the primitive world of the Native American.

The style of the story is simple and straightforward, for although the narrator yearns nostalgically for a connection to the old mythic world of his forefathers, he is not a particularly philosophical or ruminative man. He often expresses this desire for connection in flippant terms, joking that because Indians believe that if you ignore white people enough they will vanish, perhaps a thousand white families are still waiting for their sons and daughters to return home because they cannot recognize them when they float back as mist and fog.

The narrator does not present himself (as Alexie often does) as a white-bashing polemical voice of his people. In fact, he does not take himself entirely seriously, admitting that he drives a 1998 Toyota Camry because it is the best-selling car in the United States. He also relates, with some humor, his short-term affair with a white woman he worked with, who talked like she was writing the lead of her latest story. The fact that he is not currently involved in a sexual relationship and lives alone in a studio apartment make him vulnerable to the sexual approaches of the fighter he picks up.

The narrator's inability to understand and articulate why he has sex with the hitchhiker does not suggest that he is a homosexual who is unwilling to admit it. Rather, when he says he did it for reasons he could not explain then and cannot explain now, he suggests that he submits to the fighter for mythic rather than personal reasons.

To make the reader accept these mythic reasons for the sexual encounter, Alexie ends the story with a scene presented as reality but suggestive of dream. The narrator says he awoke the next morning and "went out into the world," walking barefoot upriver toward the place where he was born and will someday die. Echoing a statement he made earlier about his father—that the old man wanted to break open the hearts of the hitchhikers he picked up and see the future in their blood—the narrator says that if you were to break open his heart at that moment, you would look inside and see the thin white skeletons of one thousand salmon. This ambiguous conclusion of the story marks a final transition between the everyday, real world to the world of wish, myth, dream; in short, the fantasy world of sacred reality.

Charles E. May

TOWN AND COUNTRY LOVERS

Author: Nadine Gordimer (1923-   )
Type of plot: Social realism
Time of plot: The recent past
Locale: Johannesburg and Middleburg, South Africa, and its environs
First published: 1980

> *Principal characters:*
> DR. FRANZ-JOSEF VON LEINSDORF, a middle-aged Austrian-born
>   geologist who has worked in Africa for seven years
> A SOUTH AFRICAN MULATTO GIRL, a supermarket cashier and
>   Leinsdorf's mistress
> PAULUS EYSENDYCH, a white veterinary college student, age
>   nineteen
> THEBEDI, a black girl living on the Eysendych farm, age eighteen
> NJABULO, a laborer on the Eysendych farm

The Story

When published first in *The New Yorker* (on October 13, 1975), this story was entitled "City Lovers"; the second part was added for publication in *A Soldier's Embrace*
(1980). The two parts are quite discrete stories, connected only by the central theme.

Part 1 gives a detailed account of the professional and cultural background of Dr.
Franz-Josef von Leinsdorf, who has worked in Peru, New Zealand, and the United
States in a senior, though not executive capacity, for companies interested in mineral
research; his special interest is underground watercourses; his cultural interests are
skiing, music appreciation, and reading the poetry of Rainer Maria Rilke. Though he
is thought "not unattractive" by the female employees of the mining company, none
has been invited to go out with him; he lives alone in a two-room apartment.

When Leinsdorf cannot find his preferred brand of razor blades, a mulatto cashier
offers to see that the stock is replenished before his next visit to the supermarket. On
returning home one evening after a trip away, he is told by the cashier that the blades
have arrived; because he is burdened with bags and cases, she offers to get them and
take them to his apartment. Quite uncomfortably, Leinsdorf offers her a tip, which she
declines. He then asks her to come in for a cup of coffee.

Soon, she brings his groceries two or three times a week; he gives her chocolates.
She sews a button on his trousers, and he touches her, commenting, "You're a good
girl." Leinsdorf is impressed by her small and finely made body, her smooth skin, "the
subdued satiny colour of certain yellow wood," and her crepey hair. The two become
lovers—first during the afternoons, then overnight; she tells the caretaker that she is
Leinsdorf's servant, and her mother believes the same.

Near Christmas, three police officers arrive and announce that they have been observing Leinsdorf's apartment over a three-month period and know that he has been living with the mulatto girl. They search the apartment and find her in a bedroom closet. The couple is taken to the police station for a medical examination "for signs of his seed." Leinsdorf's lawyer bails them out, and the girl returns to her mother's house in the colored township nearby. Though she confesses that they have had intercourse, the magistrate acquits both because the authorities failed to prove that carnal intercourse had occurred in violation of the Immorality Act.

Part 2 opens with an account of the childhood association of white, black, and colored children on the farm. This association ends when the white children reach school age, and strict racial segregation is imposed. "The trouble was Paulus Eysendych did not seem to realize that Thebedi was now simply one of the crowd of farm children down at the kraal (village)." The two make love at the riverbed during the summer holidays—sometimes at twilight, sometimes at dawn. When Paulus's parents are away, he and Thebedi "stayed together whole nights—almost; she had to get away before the house servants, who knew her, came in at dawn."

When Thebedi is eighteen and Paulus nineteen and preparing to enter veterinary college, a young black man, Njabulo, a bricklayer and laborer, asks Thebedi's father for permission to marry her. Two months after her marriage, Thebedi gives birth to a daughter. "There was no disgrace in that; among her people it is customary for a young man to make sure, before marriage, that the chosen girl is not barren." The child, however, is very light skinned and has "straight, fine floss," whereas both Thebedi and Njabulo were matt black. Two weeks later, Paulus returned from college and, hearing about Thebedi's baby, visited the kraal to see it, with its "spidery pink hands."

Paulus, ascertaining that Thebedi has not taken the baby to the main farmhouse, suggests that she give it away; then, saying, "I feel like killing myself," he walks out. Two days later, the child is ill with diarrhea, and during the night it dies.

Njabulo buries the baby, but because someone had reported that the baby was almost white and healthy, the police arrive and disinter the corpse. Paulus is charged with murder; Thebedi, at the preliminary investigation, says that she saw him pour liquid into the child's mouth (though she had remained outside the hut when Paulus entered to see the baby). At the court trial, Thebedi recants and the court—finding absence of proof that the child was in fact Paulus's and noting the perjury of Thebedi at one of the trials—declares Paulus not guilty.

Themes and Meanings

Through the juxtaposition of two stories of love, the author has managed to suggest that the laws against interracial association (apartheid) are a cruel interference in what are at times genuine cases of affection, if not love. Leinsdorf comments that he does accept social distinctions between people but does not believe that they should be legally imposed; Thebedi (also in an interview in a Sunday paper) says that her affair with Paulus had been "a thing of our childhood"—a natural outcome of human relationships unaffected by legalisms. Both relationships are terminated through the interference of neighbors rather than through the direct efforts of the authorities: In Part 1, it is suggested that a neighbor or the caretaker at the apartment house was the informer; in Part 2, the other laborers or their women are suspected of informing. However, the situations are alike: There is always someone prepared to adopt a holier-than-thou attitude and to cooperate with officialdom to the discredit of a member of the group.

In both stories one sees parallel elements and can conclude that a general pattern applies in South Africa, regardless of whether love is found in city or country, in youth or middle age, with black or mulatto, by immigrant European or native Afrikaner, with farm girl or city cashier. In both parts one sees that the treatment of whites by courts is more favorable than that of nonwhites. Nadine Gordimer is not an advocate of miscegenation or of interracial romance. Rather, she suggests that interpersonal relationships should remain exactly that and should not become the concern of government policy. Romance or sex between members of different racial groups should be guided by concern for the involved parties rather than by legislative edict.

Style and Technique

Most of Gordimer's stories and novels evoke a sense of compassion for the characters, who are enmeshed in circumstances of their own creation. She manages to develop in her readers a genuine sympathy—even an empathy—for them; understanding, forgiveness, identification are her goals rather than condemnation, advocacy, and partisanship. Further, she manages to show the ineffable bond between individuals of different races, social status, and value systems that can be developed and sustained by respect for individuals as such: Almost all of her characters come from divergent backgrounds, yet they somehow manage to find fulfillment in each other. "Town and Country Lovers" shows the gradual growth and maturation of love between couples and suggests that when that love is fulfilled in sexual relations, it is honest and honorable—though it can be destroyed through the interposition of an artificial, arbitrary, and extrinsic morality. Ultimately, this becomes a question of whether persons should be allowed to decide their own course in life or be obliged to accept a dictated one.

At times, the author distances herself somewhat too much from her characters and their situations: This distance is achieved largely through what seems at times reportage, though because both parts of the story involve police and courtroom investigations, the journalistic quality of the written style may be defended as especially appropriate. In part 1, one can imagine that the Sunday newspaper reporter was responsible for the description of the girl when the police discover her in the closet:

> She had been naked, it was true, when they knocked. But now she was wearing a long-sleeved T-shirt with an appliqued butterfly motif on one breast, and a pair of jeans. Her feet were still bare; she had managed, by feel, in the dark, to get into some of the clothing she had snatched from the bed, but she had no shoes.

However, this factually detailed account is at times found in close juxtaposition with rather coy, Victorian language, as in the description of Leinsdorf making love to his sleeping mate: "He made his way into her body without speaking; she made him welcome without a word." All too often, as here, there is what seems an emotional understatement in which greater feeling and perhaps even passion could be justified. Apparently silent, acquiescent sex is what the lover perceives will make her "like a wife." However, she is notably less passionate than Thebedi, as well as older and more sophisticated. One of the author's achievements is her ability to convey through her style the carefully developed and companionable relationship of part 1 and then the more natural, unrestrained sensuality of part 2.

A. L. McLeod

THE TOWN POOR

Author: Sarah Orne Jewett (1849-1909)
Type of plot: Social realism
Time of plot: The mid- to late nineteenth century
Locale: New England
First published: 1890

> *Principal characters:*
> MRS. WILLIAM TRIMBLE, a widowed businessperson
> MISS REBECCA WRIGHT, her friend
> ANN BRAY and
> MANDANA BRAY, sisters who are the town's poor
> MRS. JANES, a part owner of the Brays' home

The Story

Mrs. William Trimble, an independent and comfortably fixed widow, and Miss Rebecca Wright, a spinster who is dependent and of marginal means, discuss the impact of the severe weather on farmers in nearby Parsley as the two women journey home in Mrs. Trimble's horse-drawn carriage. Although the two women are friends, the author emphasizes the differences between them by having the narrator shift the focus from their conversation to their demeanor—how they respond to the ride and to the cold. Mrs. Trimble, an "active business woman" who has been obliged to handle her affairs in all types of weather, is accustomed to riding in the open air. Miss Wright readily shows that she is uncomfortable.

Mrs. Trimble is more than industrious and self-sufficient. She is a generous woman who takes some interest in the affairs of Hampden's needy; she is a Lady Bountiful of a sort. Miss Wright's dependence on Mrs. Trimble for transportation, her obvious discomfort, and her timidity establish an immediate contrast with Mrs. Trimble. Although the speech of each woman is markedly regional, the differences between Mrs. Trimble and Miss Wright's speech suggests the difference between their social class and reinforces the differences between their personalities.

As the two drive along a rural road, they discover that they are approaching the farmhouse in which two of their friends—elderly sisters on welfare—have been placed by the town. These friends are the Bray sisters, Ann and Mandana, the town poor. They are old, ailing, frail, dependent, and forgotten. After deciding to visit Ann and Mandana Bray, Mrs. Trimble and Miss Wright have some time to reminisce about better times for the Brays, about past sermons, and about the improvident father of the Bray women. His devotion of time and money to the church are the causes of the Bray sisters' impoverished condition.

When the two visitors arrive at the farmhouse, they are greatly concerned: The yard is barren, the chickens are "ragged," the house is drab and isolated. Mrs. Abel Janes, the landlady, is as cheerless as her kitchen. She complains bitterly about her condition and lack of money, and she begrudges her boarders, the Bray women. The cold and drafty attic in which the Bray women live is far more drab than the remainder of the house. It is also poorly furnished. These conditions and the lack of a good view make the sisters virtual prisoners. They have little food to sustain them, and they have no clothing to brave the inclement weather. They speak of getting "stout shoes and rubbers . . . to fetch home plenty o' little dry boughs o' pine." Despite their poverty, the sisters, especially Ann, are hospitable. With her hand in a sling, Ann cheerfully prepares all the food in the room for their guests: tea, crackers, marmalade. In addition to making their guests feel comfortable and welcome, Ann consoles her sister, Mandana, who weeps about their situation. Mrs. Trimble is so touched by the Brays' plight that she vows to approach the selectmen the very next day. The town is going to have to do something to help these women.

Themes and Meanings

Through the descriptions of the topography, the hardships of the farmers, and the plight of the Brays, Sarah Orne Jewett comments on the decline of rural New England. Having her characters reflect on the past and the present enables Jewett to criticize and idealize former days. Because Mrs. Trimble is the only independent character in the story, the only one able to influence positively the town leaders, Jewett is extolling the virtues of self-sufficient women.

At the same time, Jewett recognizes the importance of sisterhood and cooperation. Mrs. Trimble provides transportation for Miss Wright and has made arrangements for Miss Wright to stay in the Trimble home for the night. Both women have great sympathy for Mrs. Janes's complaints. Both demonstrate great sympathy for the Brays. In fact, the visit to the Brays forces Mrs. Trimble and Mrs. Wright to give greater material and emotional support to their disabled friends than they have previously given. The discussions about the Brays explore right and wrong behavior. Ann Bray reinforces the themes of sisterhood and cooperation when she comforts her sobbing sister, Mandana.

Style and Technique

Images of mud, frost, and snow, of stony and sodden fields, foreshadow and symbolize the condition of the Brays; the indifference of the town to its aged and disabled; and the callousness and greed of Mrs. Janes, with whom the Brays live. These images, along with those images of isolation and decay, parallel the aging, the isolation, and the dependence of the Brays. In turn, each symbolizes the decay of the New England region.

A pattern of contrasts between characters—Mrs. Trimble and Miss Wright, Ann and Mandana—between the two sets of women, is an important part of the story's style and structure. Moreover, the speech patterns are correlated with the class and condition of each character; the Brays, who are the poorest, use speech that is the most regional and most obviously different from the speech of the other characters.

Ora Williams

TOWN SMOKES

Author: Pinckney Benedict (1964-   )
Type of plot: Regional, coming of age
Time of plot: The 1980's
Locale: Mountains of West Virginia
First published: 1987

> *Principal characters:*
> A FIFTEEN-YEAR-OLD BOY, the narrator
> DADDY, his father, who has just died in a logging accident
> UNCLE HUNTER, his paternal uncle

The Story

Set during a stormy day in the West Virginia mountains, "Town Smokes" is narrated by a fifteen-year-old boy who has just become an orphan after losing his father in a logging accident that same morning. With nothing but Uncle Hunter, a needy alcoholic, to keep him in his mountaintop home, the boy decides to leave and try to make his way in the world below. Although he tells his uncle that he is going to town to get cigarettes, both he and his uncle know that he will not return from his trip.

During his journey, the boy is robbed by two older boys, poor "ridgerunners" like himself. Though not really interested in stealing his belongings, for sport, the older boys strip the fifteen-year-old of the money, guns, and the knife his father had left him as well as the boy's few earthly goods, including his shoes. Speaking from apparent experience, the robbers leave the boy with a warning, telling him that the people in town do not like ridgerunners and that he would be better off to turn back up the mountain and go home.

Broke and barefoot, the boy wanders into town. He walks into the local drugstore and is met with stories of loss and devastation caused by the storm. The drugstore owner pauses as the boy enters, dirty and shoeless, but continues with his work. The boy proclaims that he has lost his father and has no money but would like a pack of smokes. Given the extraordinary events of the day, the storeowner tells his colleague to get some cigarettes for the boy. Though the narrator is now absolutely destitute, he has found a momentary reprieve from the isolation of the mountains and life without a family.

Themes and Meanings

"Town Smokes" is the title story of a collection of short stories by Pinckney Benedict that examine borders and are populated by independent people with strong personalities. In his first interview about the book in *The New York Times Book Review*, Benedict noted that West Virginia, where the stories take place, is often called a border state because northerners think of it as a southern state and the southerners hold the opposite opinion; Benedict calls the state a doorway. The emotional content of this title story involves borders, the border between boyhood and adulthood and between a dual sense of place and displacement.

"Town Smokes" takes place at a camp on top of Tree Mountain. As the story unfolds, the boy's interpretation of life's events is padded by expressions and understandings that have been passed on to him by his father and his uncle and by a knowledge gained from living intimately with nature. He knows from his father, for example, that a hard rain and a blue sky can happen at the same time, but when such an event occurs at the story's beginning, this is the first he has seen it for himself. He has been prepared and now is witnessing life firsthand. This is his first awakening in a long line of such events. He knows that with his father dead, it is his time to become a man. He knows, too, that he is not yet a man. He is on the border, in between.

The tension at the beginning of the story is between the boy and the alcoholic Uncle Hunter, his father's older brother. As his uncle offers advice on how the boy should conduct himself, it is quickly evident that his advice will hold no sway. The boy has learned from his family all that he will. He is now set to make it on his own. Although the story suggests that he has been launched prematurely, it intimates that what he has learned will be adequate for his survival. He has learned the importance of appreciating the value of one's belongings and, by extension, of valuing his self as a resource. As a point of comparison, the boy later runs across two older boys as he is heading down the mountain. They rob him; they hold power over him. However, ultimately the narrator holds the upper hand. They are missing their teeth, one is mentally slow, and perhaps most pointedly, their gun stock is wrapped with black electric tape and the receiver is rusty. By contrast, the young narrator has learned that the worst thing for any good piece of metal is the touch of a person's hand. Indeed, the knife he has to give over looks shiny even under the cloudy sky. These boys have clearly lived much more of their lives without the guidance and care of their elders.

In "Town Smokes," nature is a personified force, one to be reckoned with, to fight, and to give in to. In fact, the unpredictable power of nature is what has killed the boy's father. The predominant natural element in "Town Smokes" is the rainstorm that causes a geographical transformation and mirrors the boy's personal journey between finding his "place" and being "displaced." As the story begins, the boy is standing out in the rain, large tasteless raindrops falling in his mouth and washing the sweat, dirt, and the past off him. However, the rain is coming down so hard that the boy knows it will run off and not penetrate deep into the earth. Real change, like becoming a man, is slow and steady work. By the story's end, however, he has set out on a path that will lead him away from the shallow creeks on the mountaintop and to the real river that comes through just as it wants, with nothing to hold it back.

Style and Technique

Benedict's style in this early work is often compared to that of his fellow West Virginian writer Breece D'J Pancake, in particular because of his laconic prose, careful attention to local dialect, and portrayal of the colorful, often frightening underclass of the rural South. "Town Smokes" is short fiction at its best: simple and spare but also philosophically complicated.

Written in the present tense, the story unfurls as life does, hinging on the interplay of each decision and its circumstances. As in his story "Miracle Boy" (1998), Benedict strategically places flashbacks, in this case, to reveal more about the father's death. Mixed with the story of the shorthorn sheep called out onto the ice for cruel sport, the flashback of the death of the boy's father illustrates that the present is linked with the past and that people cannot find meaning in one without the context of the other.

Benedict builds tension simply by paying attention to the taste of the rain, the smell of pine from Hunter's wood carving, the sound of the hard rain on the new tin roof, and the unpredictable force of nature. When the young narrator runs into the two older boys along the railroad tracks on his trip to town, the boy gives in when faced with their superior size, experience, and weapons. The boy hates to think of these two possessing what few things remain from his father's life but is powerless to do anything about it. No stunning feats of physical strength and no cunning verbal repartee will get him out of the situation. He gives into stronger forces, then goes on his way. He is in the process of becoming, a story in the process of being told.

In regional fiction, place is voice. In "Town Smokes," the voice of the setting is not only heard but also felt. For example, the rain "throbs" Uncle Hunter these days, and the radio announcer says to watch for flash floods in the narrow creeks coming down off the mountain in a manner that suggests the mountain is to blame. Benedict's writing suggests that life is navigated best when people pay close attention to it. Benedict has said that he works to keep his ego out of his story, to focus his efforts in service to the story. In "Town Smokes," he succeeds. His words do not prevent the reader from paying attention to what matters: to the boy making it through his first solo adventure, to his finding a respite in the momentary kindness of a stranger, and his willingness to build up the strength to go through life just the way he wants with nothing to hold him back.

Karin A. Silet

THE TRACTOR

Author: Peter Cowan (1914-   )
Type of plot: Social realism
Time of plot: Probably the mid-twentieth century
Locale: An Australian suburb
First published: 1965

> *Principal characters:*
> ANN, a painter, elementary-school teacher, and naturalist
> KEN, her fiancé, a suburban land developer
> THE HERMIT, a homeless man

The Story

Ann, a city dweller, and her fiancé, Ken, are visiting the home of Ken's parents in the outer reaches of a new suburban development. Ken reports that one of the two large tractors owned by McKay, the contractor who is clearing away trees and bushes for the expansion of the development, has been sabotaged. Ann, incredulous, cannot believe that anyone would deliberately tamper with clearing or construction equipment, but describes the preparation of marginal farming and grazing land for houses as ruthless. Ken takes pride in his business acumen and entrepreneurship: He is helping to provide people with suburban-style houses and enabling hardscrabble farm owners to realize some income from their land. As Ann acknowledges, he is more perceptive than he chooses to reveal. Ann, however, cannot imagine herself living in a development that has been carved from the bush (the Australian term for the undisturbed countryside).

Ken indicates that he and his friends know who has interfered with the tractors, and also allowed faucets on farm drinking-troughs to run continuously; they are prepared to set fire to the bush in order to flush out the hermit, who has several favorite living-spots in the region. At this, Ann realizes that she can never become one of Ken's group; she has quite different values with regard to both the environment and the homeless, the eccentrics of society, those who commune with nature rather than destroy it in the name of progress.

The summer heat becomes oppressive, and the police cannot find the hermit, who knows every feature of the bush. Ken describes the hermit as a madman, because of his total identification with nature and rejection of conventional domesticity. Although one of his camps is found, the hermit eludes police and a posse for a week. Assuming that the hermit is armed, the posse searches with rifles.

Ken and Ann acknowledge their differing values, which jeopardize their apparent love. She resorts to painting flowers, bushes, and seeds; he states his belief in making domestic use of the land and chastises Ann for being a dreamer, an impractical conservationist. While Ken is out in search of the hermit, Ann helps Ken's mother with household chores. She discerns in her an attractive quietness and insightfulness, but suspects that she has never questioned men's decisions and actions: She epitomizes the wife who accepts male hegemony without demonstration or demur.

At a local birthday party, the conversation inevitably turns to the hermit and the incompetence of the local police in apprehending him. Most people believe that the hermit should be flushed out and killed, if necessary, the way that a nuisance fox or wild dog would be caught. Because Ann's values are so different from those of the others, they question her qualifications to teach their children in the local elementary school.

On her return to her boardinghouse room after the party, Ann is introspective; her sense of anger gives way to dejection and then to fear as she realizes that the men's plan to hunt the hermit and shoot him is likely to be carried out.

A week after the sabotage of the tractor, Ann takes advantage of Ken's absence—he is at a meeting of the posse—and she goes walking, ostensibly to paint wildlife, but in reality to locate the hermit and warn him of the posse's plans in the hope that he will escape. The summer heat exhausts her; although a lover of the bush, she is not experienced in traversing it and becomes lost. Suddenly she is confronted by the hermit. He is thin, his arms are sticklike, knotted and black, and he has a rifle. Ann tries to prevail on the hermit to leave this part of the bush, but his impassivity unnerves her and she cries out helplessly. She sees that he moves in a fashion that is "liquid, unhuman . . . like an animal or the vibration of the thin sparse trees before the wind."

Later in the afternoon, Ann hears shots. Ken explains that the hermit tried to get past the line of the posse, then shot at one of them, so they had to shoot him. Ann is unable to respond. She and Ken drive back to the town.

Themes and Meanings

Almost all of Peter Cowan's short fiction treats a restricted range of thematic material, and most of these themes were introduced in his first volume, *Drift: Stories* (1944): the close connection of individuals to the land, farmers' loneliness without the company of sympathetic women, the incompatibility of city and country life, and the uniformity of values of small-town societies. "The Tractor" introduces all of these, although not all are explored at length. Here the despoiling of the natural environment under the pressure to extend housing and the two central characters' responses to this situation are the principal foci of the story. These, in turn, introduce a number of subsidiary considerations that challenge the thinking of the reader rather than present a set of conclusions. Is there a simple choice between conservation and development? Should the natural environment be preserved at the expense of people who wish to leave the inner cities and have modern housing far from urban blight? Is it wrong for farmers to profit from selling their land to housing developers? Should independent-minded, homeless, or eccentric characters outside the normal social sphere be allowed to wreak their individual vengeance on the representatives of social change, development, or improvement without consequences?

Because it raises so many fundamental social issues, "The Tractor," according to one critic, is a moral fable for modern times. All of its characters and events draw attention to the dominant issue, which is whether the natural environment is something to be destroyed in the interests of wealth and development—the viewpoint of the farmers and the developers—or to be maintained in the interests of nature, beauty, and tranquillity—the viewpoint of Ann and the hermit. Should enforcement of the laws of community be entrusted to society itself, in the form of the police, or to the contesting parties themselves? Because Ann and Ken intend to marry shortly and declare their love despite their fundamental differences, the reader realizes that some compromises or change of belief are essential and inevitable. The solution, however, is left to the reader. Ann's belief that Ken's mother has capitulated to her husband's position makes her reconsider her own stance vis-à-vis male hegemony: In the interest of marriage, should she abandon her own strongly held beliefs or be strong and independent in a matter of concern to her?

Complicating an interpretation of the basic theme of the story is the fact that Ann, although at heart a naturalist, is not sufficiently versed in its ways to avoid getting lost while seeking the hermit; and the hermit, at home in the bush for a decade, has several camps (homes) and a radio (although nonfunctional) that indicate his desire to be connected to the world of commerce and materialism that he presumably disdains. It is he who sabotages the tractor, the sheep-run fences, and the cattle-drinking faucets, and, so far as one knows from the story, he fires the initial shot at the posse. The story, therefore, invites—even demands—considerable thought on the part of the reader on matters of importance.

Style and Technique

In "The Tractor," Cowan uses the device known as metonymy: the presentation of a single case to represent a larger group; in other words, he is making use of symbolic cases. The cost of so doing is the loss of individualized emotional responses. The supposed romance between Ann and Ken is never clearly apparent, so one wonders what they really have in common. Ken's mother is neither affectionate nor markedly maternal. The birthday party is a particularly dull occasion at which jollity, friendliness, and bonhomie seem wholly alien. The posse never seems to have any true cohesiveness or social unity; even the hermit and Ann lack any real common feeling or understanding; it is as if they are as much apart philosophically as they are socially. Cowan seems to suggest that men and women cannot communicate adequately.

Cowan's talent is in showing the sincerity of his characters, although their motivations are not always explored adequately. He reveals—perhaps better than any other Australian short-story writer—the loneliness, monotony, and conformity found in the bush. Earlier writers suggested the importance of mateship—a close brotherhood between men—to the exclusion of women, and tolerance—even exaltation—of the eccentric or loner, but Cowan, a more realistic writer, questions these beliefs.

Some critics have detected a certain poetic quality in Cowan's prose, but this is rare. He does have an excellent ear for incorporating everyday speech and a fine understanding of introspection or philosophical rumination.

A. L. McLeod

TRAIN

Author: Joy Williams (1944-   )
Type of plot: Domestic realism
Time of plot: The 1970's
Locale: A train running between Washington, D.C., and Florida
First published: 1972

>   *Principal characters:*
>   JANE MUIRHEAD and
>   DANICA ANDERSON, ten-year-old friends
>   MR. AND MRS. MUIRHEAD, Jane's parents

The Story

A train moving from one point to another is an appropriate setting for this story about two ten-year-old girls in transition in both space and time. Jane Muirhead's parents fight continuously as "bitterly as vipers," and Danica Anderson's mother has just remarried and has sent her off with the Muirheads for the summer to give her some time to settle in with her new husband. The story begins with the two girls exploring the train on the way home to Florida. Mr. and Mrs. Muirhead spend most of their time in the lounge drinking cocktails, although they do not sit together. Mr. Muirhead talks to young men, because, he says, his wife will not let him talk to young women.

Danica, lonely during the trip, often feels like crying, for she is surrounded by strangers saying and doing crazy things. At one point, Mrs. Muirhead gives her a note to take to Mr. Muirhead, but Jane tells her later that her father ate the note. At another point, the two girls meet a woman, and Jane tells her that her name is Crystal and that Danica is her twin sister Clara. When Jane tells the woman she probably does not believe in men, the woman says it is true, that men are a collective hallucination of women. The woman tells the girls she does research on human pheromones, the chemical substances that people excrete that can lead other people to do or feel a certain thing.

Mr. Muirhead meets a young man who is writing a book on cemeteries of the world, and they talk about famous cemeteries in Paris and Mexico, both of which the Muirheads have visited. What Mr. Muirhead remembers most about those visits, however, is how his wife screamed at him for such things as spilling buttered popcorn on the blazer she bought him or leaving the hammock she bought him out to rot in the rain.

While watching *Superman*, Jane falls asleep and dreams of men in white bathing caps pushing all her grandmother's things out into the street. After Jane tells Danica the dream, Danica feels sorry for herself, because she feels she has no friends and no parents and is aimlessly sitting on a train between one place and another, scaring herself with someone else's dream. When she asks Mr. Muirhead if he thinks she and

Jane will be friends forever, he says that Jane will not have friends—only a husband, enemies, and lawyers. He tells her he hopes she is enjoying her childhood, for when she grows up a big shadow falls over everyone. Danica looks at her postcards, and Mr. Muirhead likes one that has choices—such as "fine," "lonesome," "happy," or "sad"—that you simply check to express how you feel. Danica gives the card to him, and he tells her she is a nice little girl. Then he asks her what she thinks was on the note his wife sent him. "Do you think," he asks, "there's something I've missed?"

Themes and Meanings

The key thematic statements in "Train" belong to Mr. Muirhead, who tells his daughter Jane and her friend Danica that the desires of the human heart have no boundaries and that the "mess of secrets" in the human heart are without number. At the end, he tells Danica that he hopes that she enjoys her childhood, for when people grow up, a shadow falls over them. He also tells her that when he grows up he wants to become an Indian so he can use his Indian name, "He Rides a Slow Enduring Heavy Horse." The sense of life as like being on a train in transition between one point and another is the pervasive theme throughout the story. There is no real stability for the characters, either the parents, whose relationship seems tenuous at best, or for the children, who feel lonely and adrift because of that shaky relationship. There does not seem to be any explanation for this sense of loneliness and isolation beyond Mr. Muirhead's suggestion about some huge black wing that casts a shadow over adults.

As is typical of so-called minimalist realism in the American short story of the 1970's, the thematic strands of "Train" derive not from significant plot events but from the repetition of various thematic motifs throughout the story. One of the most prominent of these motifs is the discussion that Mr. Muirhead has with a young man about cemeteries. In describing his visit to a cemetery in Mexico that had a museum of mummies, bodies preserved by the dry heat of the area, Mr. Muirhead says it is one thing to think of the idea of a Christian heaven or Buddhist incarnation or even the scientific concept of no energy ever being lost, but it is another thing altogether to look at those miserable mummies in the little museum. The horror and indignation on their faces made Mr. Muirhead so aware of the fleetingness of this life, he says, that he almost cried out loud.

The theme of the fleetingness of life is echoed in the motif of Mr. Muirhead always losing things that his wife gives him. She recalls every gift she ever gave him, either monetary or of the heart, and how he has mishandled or betrayed every one of them. This sense of lost opportunities, of the inability to recapture what is lost, is echoed in such seemingly trivial details as the fact that Danica watches *Superman* on television, particularly his spinning the earth backward to return to a previous time so he can keep Lois Lane from being smothered in a rock slide. The inability to recapture lost opportunities receives its final echo at the end of the story when Mr. Muirhead asks Danica about what might have been on the note that he ate rather than read. Mr. Muir asks plaintively, "Do you think there's something I've missed?"

Style and Technique

Joy Williams once said in an essay that the writer cherishes mystery and does not want to advocate or instruct or disclose but rather to escape the obligations of his or her time by transcending them. She also noted that once a writer knows how to achieve a certain stylistic effect, he or she must abandon that method, for repeated effects become false and mannered. However, Williams's writing has been criticized by some reviewers as being merely mannerism, that she writes predictably "laconic little slices of life," each one of which is deceptively inconsequential and indistinguishable from the last one.

"Train" is a classic example of the minimalist style that became popular after the success of Raymond Carver in the 1970's. Nothing of major significance seems to take place; a lot of seemingly trivial details are mentioned; and characters seem isolated from one another by misunderstanding and preoccupation. However, the story differs from the bare realistic laconic nature of Carver's stories by harkening back to the clever precocity of the Glass family of J. D. Salinger more than twenty years earlier. For example, when Jane chides Danica for writing a letter to her dog, she says, "Your writing to Jim Anderson is dumb in about twelve different ways. He's a *golden retriever*, for Godssakes."

As is typical of this kind of story, seemingly inconsequential events and details have thematic rather than plot significance. For example, when Danica and Jane meet a man and woman on the train, Jane asks the man what his line of work is. He says he does not have to do anything for he was injured in Vietnam. When they brought him to the base hospital, they worked for forty-five minutes trying to revive him and then gave up; four hours later he woke up in the mortuary; now he has a good pension from the army. This seeming irrelevant reference is echoed later when Mr. Muirhead talks about the mummies in the museum in Mexico. When the woman tells the two little girls that she does research in human pheromones—chemical substances that lead people to do certain things—this mystery of what makes people do what they do is echoed by Mr. Muirhead's statement that the secrets of the human heart are without number. Finally, the woman's definition of a placebo—as something that makes you think you are getting something that will change you but you are not—is echoed throughout the story in the failed relationships of adults.

The final line of the story—"Do you think there's something I've missed?"—is the epiphany remark that pulls all the seemingly inconsequential references together into a final thematic realization for the reader.

Charles E. May

THE TRAIN FROM RHODESIA

Author: Nadine Gordimer (1923-   )
Type of plot: Social realism
Time of plot: The mid-twentieth century
Locale: Southern Africa
First published: 1947

> *Principal characters:*
> THE WIFE, a passenger on a train
> HER HUSBAND, another passenger
> A LOCAL ARTIST, selling his crafts at the train station

The Story

When a train from Rhodesia stops briefly at a station, its wheels are checked, bread is delivered to the stationmaster's wife, malnourished animals and poor children approach the train for handouts, and artisans walk alongside the train's windows, hoping to sell their crafts to the passengers.

The focus soon is on a young woman (the wife) leaning out a corridor window asking to see a lion, beautifully carved by a vendor. The lion is described minutely, its detail revealing the care and love of the artisan. The young husband joins his wife as she admires the lion. The wife considers the price, three shillings and sixpence, to be too high and decides not to buy it. When the husband asks if she is sure she does not want the lion, she tells him to leave it.

She returns to her train compartment still thinking about the lovely lion with the real fur mane and the black tongue. (It seems the lion is too expensive only when considering the many other carved figures she has already purchased.) However, she also has more serious thoughts. It becomes apparent that the wife is newly married, and the train ride seems to be the end of her honeymoon journey. Her trip to all the foreign places seems unreal to her. She wonders what she will do with all the craft items she has bought on her journey; she wonders how the memories and memorabilia will fit in with her new life. Most significant, she realizes that her young husband is not merely part of her temporary journey, but will be a very real part of her new life.

As the train leaves the station, the young husband enters the compartment proudly displaying the lion. He enthusiastically tells his wife how he bargained with the vendor for fun; at the last moment, with the train moving, the vendor offered him the lion for one and six, instead of three and six. The husband threw down the coins as the train moved, and the vendor flung up the lion.

The wife is upset rather than appreciative. She tosses the lion aside and asks how he could have bargained instead of paying full price if he wanted the lion. The story ends with the train pulling out of the station, the husband looking without understanding at his wife, and the wife feeling empty and sick looking out the train window.

Themes and Meanings

"The Train from Rhodesia" deals with the contrast in the lives between the people
on the train and those in the station and also between the young wife and husband. The
passengers on the train represent those who have both leisure and money: The young
wife on the train is on holiday; other passengers throw unwanted chocolate to dogs at
the station, or sit in the dining car drinking beer. The people in the station represent the
working poor: The vendors at the station squat "in the dust"; the stationmaster's children are "barefoot." The children and animals beg for handouts while the vendors
nearly do so: "All up and down the length of the train in the dust the artists sprang,
walking bent, like performing animals, the better to exhibit the fantasy held toward
the faces on the train."

The physical setting places the white passengers above the local inhabitants: They
sit inside the comfortable train and reach down to throw scraps to the animals or to exchange money for the crafts being held up by the "gray-black" hands. The interior of
the train suggests luxury, but also a lack of life; artificial flowers adorn tables in the
dining car, and the wife, the only passenger whose internal feelings are revealed, feels
a void in her life. The train station suggests poverty but also life and creativity; the
land is poor and the animals are malnourished, but the crafts of the artisans are beautiful. The meeting between the passengers and the local inhabitants is brief and unsatis-
factory. The train itself is presented negatively. Each reference to the train emphasizes
harsh sounds, negative power, or a lack of connection between the train and the landscape. The train brings together the two groups only briefly while actually keeping
them isolated: The "few men who had got down to stretch their legs sprang on to the
train . . . safe from the one dusty platform, the one tin house, the empty sand." The
brief meeting highlights the disparity between the lives of both groups and suggests
that such disparity is harmful to both. The young wife who lives in luxury bears internal scars, while the creative vendors live in poverty.

The young husband and wife are also contrasted. They share the same lifestyle, but
apparently not the same values. The husband appears happy until the contretemps
with his wife over the lion, but the reader who has access to the wife's thoughts and
feelings knows that she is not content. She feels an emptiness and questions the place
of her new husband in her life. When the husband proudly relates his success at buying the lion at a much-reduced price, his wife thinks not of the lovely lion but of the artisan. In anger she tries to explain her view, but her husband does not understand, and
she gives up trying to explain, as if she believes the disparity in their values too large a
gap to be bridged by words.

Style and Technique

Most of the story is told dramatically; its events are presented as if picked up by
a camera and a microphone, with relatively little narrative intervention. Only occasionally the connotations of words—such as the negative ones describing the train—
suggest interpretation. Two passages are important exceptions to the dramatic point of
view: Twice the reader is allowed glimpses into the wife's thoughts and feelings. In

the first passage, the reader discovers that the wife does not buy the lion only because she already has many such memorabilia from her trip. Her thoughts also suggest that she is unsure about her feelings for her new husband. In the second passage, the reader discovers a discrepancy between how the husband and wife think and what they value. The implication of the husband and wife's failure to understand what the other feels about the carved lion suggests that these two people have different values and may therefore be incompatible. The wife finds the lion a wonderful piece of art but does not buy it because, after buying so many other pieces already, she feels that this purchase—not necessarily its price—would be extravagant. The husband believes that she would like the lion at a lower price and does not mind haggling with the vendor for a bargain. The wife is disturbed at her husband's actions. For her, the beauty of the lion is lost at the price of what she views as the humiliation of the vendor. As she is filled with shame at her husband's actions, she feels again a void inside that she expected to be filled by marriage.

Because the train is presented negatively and the inside of the train reflects a kind of sterile luxury, the implication is that the void inside the wife may be caused not by the lack of a husband but by the lack of a life with any real meaning. Her joy at the vendor's lion suggests that perhaps she has the potential for a finer existence and that she would better rid herself of the void by participating in all of life, not just the sterile leisure life the train symbolizes. The separation of the wealthy and the poor is not a satisfactory arrangement for either group.

Nadine Gordimer builds her story on a series of contrasts: white and black, leisured and working, rich and poor, comfort and pain, above and below, sterility and creativity. Because of its dramatic point of view, most of the story is revealed through the contrasts, but on the two occasions when the reader is allowed glimpses into the wife's mind and heart, the themes suggested by the contrasts are confirmed.

Marion Boyle Petrillo

TRAVELER

Author: Ellen Gilchrist (1935-   )
Type of plot: Domestic realism
Time of plot: After World War II
Locale: Mississippi
First published: 1980

> *Principal characters:*
> LeLe Arnold, the teenage narrator and protagonist
> Baby Gwen Barksdale, her cousin
> Fielding Reid, her love interest

The Story

When LeLe Arnold, an Indiana high school student, is invited to spend the summer with her cousin Baby Gwen in Mississippi, she is thrilled. She was recently passed over in a cheerleader election because, she believes, she was regarded as somewhat overweight. She sees Mississippi as a place where she can start over and become a different and more popular person. Immediately on arrival she begins to work on her reputation by telling her cousin that she did make the cheerleading squad and the football team saw her off at the train station.

LeLe and Baby Gwen spend their days sunbathing, playing bridge, and entertaining the boys who call on them. LeLe is attracted to one in particular, Fielding Reid, and about the time that she is beginning to believe her own publicity, that she is special, Fielding finally invites her to go out with him alone. LeLe can hardly contain her excitement but is sorely disappointed when Fielding tells her he has asked her out to talk to her about her weight, which he says is keeping her from being as beautiful as she might be. To save face, LeLe again resorts to lying, telling him that she has a thyroid condition.

When Fielding announces that it is time for his annual swim across the lake, LeLe offers to swim with him against Baby Gwen's protest that it is not a feat suitable for girls. The water empowers LeLe: She feels thin, beautiful, even perfect, and she accomplishes the swim with no trouble, her reputation as "the wildest girl in Mississippi" solidified.

When she returns home with Baby Gwen, LeLe learns that her parents are coming for her. Soon she is back in Indiana, telling a friend there that she was practically engaged to a rich plantation owner's son, while "trying to remember how the water turned into diamonds in her hands."

Themes and Meanings

A young woman's concern with her weight and popularity can be found in much of the fiction of southern writer Ellen Gilchrist. Although LeLe's lies about herself, and her hypocrisy in befriending a girl with a wooden arm only for the sake of her own reputation, give a somewhat negative impression of LeLe, the reader is moved to sympathize with her when she is confronted about her weight by Fielding and to enjoy the clever lie about a thyroid condition that makes Fielding feel bad for bringing up the subject.

Ironically, LeLe comments earlier on how much she likes the fact that her new southern friends are so much less competitive and more polite than her friends in Indiana. With Fielding's rude remarks, the reader realizes that this story can be viewed as part of the body of postbellum plantation fiction that tries to deconstruct images of the South as paradisiacal and all southerners as easygoing and mannerly ladies and gentlemen. Sadly, in spite of Fielding's hurtful remarks about her weight, LeLe still wishes to impress him; that, rather than the accomplishment itself, is the main reason she wants to swim across the lake with him.

Water and swimming also are found repeatedly in Gilchrist's work, symbolizing the source of life and baptism into a new life, and usually associated with her female characters who are empowered in this medium as they are not on land. Until her swim, LeLe's reputation is based on deceit. On immersing herself in the water, however, a change begins to come over her. She senses her inner strength, and this time it comes from an element in which she can compete honestly. She feels weightless in the water and swims easily across the lake, thereby earning her reputation while proving that women's strength is not necessarily found only in their outward appearance.

Back on land, however, LeLe is once more engulfed by the attention paid her, in particular by Fielding, whose unqualified admiration she finally wins. When she returns to Indiana, she is again telling self-aggrandizing lies about her adventures in Mississippi; however, her wistful unspoken thoughts of Mississippi are not of Fielding or her reputation, but of how the water made her feel. That sense of true empowerment is what she is trying to recall as the story closes, reinforcing the reader's awareness of the two LeLes: the seemingly self-confident LeLe who confronts the world, and the insecure LeLe who worries about her appearance and reputation.

Style and Technique

Two complications often arise with first-person narrators: The narrator might be unreliable, and the reader is limited by the narrator's knowledge. In spite of her lying, LeLe is not an unreliable narrator. She reveals the truth to the reader at some point before lying to Baby Gwen, the maid, or Fielding. She even admits that she starts believing in her own lies and has befriended a girl with a wooden arm only for the sake of her own reputation. Such honesty to herself, although ironic given her seemingly uncontrollable compulsion to lie to others, is endearing, allowing the reader to forgive her outward dishonesty and hypocrisy.

LeLe reports at the beginning of the story that she is going to Mississippi to keep Baby Gwen company because Baby Gwen's mother has recently died. She also comments that her father tells her about the invitation just after her own mother has left him for some ambiguous reason having to do with jealousy, which LeLe does not explain. The reader wonders, therefore, if LeLe's father is actually sending her away because he does not want to be burdened with taking care of her by himself, or so that he can continue an affair. Her parents are not mentioned again until the end of the story, reflecting either LeLe's lack of concern about their problems or her desire to forget the family troubles back home. Perhaps she senses that she has been discarded and does not want to think about the implications of this. Either of the latter two possibilities shed light on her drive to be popular beyond the disappointment over her school's cheerleader tryouts. Because she is the one telling the story, if LeLe does not want to think about her parents, then the reader has no further hints to ponder.

The reader can discern the implications of other subtle details in LeLe's narrative that she does not perceive; she may not be an unreliable narrator, but she is a naïve narrator. For example, part of LeLe's joy in going to Mississippi is because her relatives are members of the southern aristocracy, and she looks forward to taking advantage of this. From the moment of her arrival, LeLe basks in the luxuries at the Barksdale home. Gilchrist provides a brief episode that reminds the reader of the nightmarish side of this dreamlike social system: On her first morning in Mississippi, LeLe sees Baby Gwen being bathed by her black maid, Sirena. LeLe is amazed at the oddness of a teenager being given a bath and notices the contrast between Sirena's black hand and Baby Gwen's white skin, but does not comment on the social implications of the scene. The more sophisticated reader recognizes these implications: A system with an aristocracy must also have a subservient class. Again, LeLe's immature idealized vision of the South is undermined by the reader's more insightful perception of the reality.

The story's title provides another example of its multiple levels of meaning. On the surface, the title refers to LeLe's travels from Indiana to Mississippi. At a deeper level, it alludes to LeLe's swim, a trip toward some self-awareness, the realization of her strengths. LeLe's land travels may come full circle, returning her to Indiana where she is still not a cheerleader and where she continues to tell exaggerated versions of the truth, if not outright lies. Her swim across the lake, however, was a one-way journey, giving the reader hope that LeLe will not soon forget the euphoria in earning the respect of others, and herself.

The weight and water motifs employed in this story connect it to the rest of the story cycle of which it is a part (Gilchrist's *In the Land of Dreamy Dreams*, 1981) as well as the rest of Gilchrist's canon. The other stories in *In the Land of Dreamy Dreams* also focus on the issue of reputation and class, and several of them are either narrated by, or have as their protagonists, young girls similar to LeLe, which results in the sense of a composite personality as the single protagonist of the collection. LeLe is reminiscent, in particular, of Gilchrist's most well-known character, Rhoda Manning, who is the prototype for her other female characters and the protagonist of several of the other stories in this collection.

Margaret D. Bauer

A TREE. A ROCK. A CLOUD.

Author: Carson McCullers (1917-1967)
Type of plot: Psychological
Time of plot: The early to mid-twentieth century
Locale: A streetcar café
First published: 1942

> *Principal characters:*
> THE BOY, a newspaper carrier
> THE MAN, a transient
> LEO, the owner of the café

The Story

It is not yet dawn on a rainy morning when the twelve-year-old paperboy decides to have a cup of coffee at Leo's café before finishing his paper route. There are few customers this morning: some soldiers, some laborers from the nearby mill, and an unusual looking man drinking beer alone. Leo, the surly owner of the streetcar café, pays little attention to the boy, and he is about to leave when the man with the beer calls to him. The boy cautiously approaches the man and is taken aback when the stranger declares that he loves him. Though the other customers laugh at this declaration, the man is deadly serious. Embarrassed and unsure of what to do next, the boy sits down when the man offers to explain what he means.

With the boy seated next to him, the man pulls out two photographs and tells the boy to examine them. Old and faded, both are of the same woman, whom the man identifies as his wife. As he begins his story, the boy, anxious to leave the café and finish his paper route, looks to Leo for help; when none is forthcoming, the boy starts to leave, but something in the man's manner compels him to stay. Nervous but resigned, the boy listens, half convinced that the man is drunk.

However, the man seems sober and almost eerily serene as he explains that, to him, love is a "science"; by way of illustration, he tells the story of his marriage. Twelve years ago, when he was working as a railroad engineer, he had married the woman in the picture. He married for love and did everything he could to make her happy, never suspecting that she might be otherwise. Not even two years into the marriage, however, the man had come home one night to find that she had run away with another man. He was devastated: His love for her had made him feel complete, integrated, for the first time in his life. He spent two years traveling about the country looking for her, unable to find even a trace.

Despite Leo's rude and vulgar interruptions, the story holds the boy's attention, and the man goes on with it. In the two years that followed his search for his wife, he continued to be tormented by her memory. Though he could not remember her face at will, he would be reminded of her unexpectedly by the smallest details of daily life.

Miserable, he started drinking. Only in the fifth year after his wife left him did he start to develop his "science" of love. After meditating about love and its failures, he decided that most men go about love incorrectly, falling in love for the first time with a woman. Instead, says the man, people should work up to such a love, falling in love first with less significant things: a tree, a rock, a cloud. He has now mastered this "science," and now he can love anything—at will.

After the man has finished his story, the boy asks him if he has ever fallen in love with a woman again. The man admits that such a love is the last stage of his process, and that he has not yet worked up to it. After reminding the boy that he loves him, the man leaves the café, leaving the boy perplexed but strangely moved by the story.

Themes and Meanings

The desolate setting, the inability of the boy to understand the man's story, Leo's unfailing cynicism—all point to the theme of this story, and that of much of Carson McCullers's fiction: the spiritual isolation inherent in the human condition. The only attempt at communication in the story—the old man's desperate attempt to explain the "science" of love to the adolescent paperboy—is necessarily a thwarted one: Like the Wedding Guest in Samuel Taylor Coleridge's long poem *The Rime of the Ancient Mariner* (1798), the boy is a captive audience, unwilling to listen, but compelled to by the strangeness of the speaker; like the Mariner in that same poem, the man is worn out from having told his story too often. Leo has only contempt for the man, and no words at all for the boy. A sad tale told by a defeated old man to a puzzled boy is the only vestige of human sympathy and communication in the dark world of this story.

Nor is love an answer to the dilemma posed by the story. Clearly, the old man is a victim of love, at least of romantic love: The unexpected loss of his wife was a blow from which he has never quite recovered, even though nearly eleven years have elapsed between her leaving and the time of the story. Having experienced the common reactions to betrayal—the period of obsession to get the loved one back, followed by a period of recklessness and dissipation—the old man has developed a "science" by which he can love everything he observes. Though he is composed, almost unnaturally so, during the telling of his story, it is important to remember that a man who, only somewhat more than a decade before, was happily married and gainfully employed is now little more than a bum. His decline is a testament to the illusory and transient nature of romantic love and to the bitter ways in which it can affect the human spirit.

Though it brings him a certain measure of peace and contentment, the man's "science" is clearly a mechanism that enables him to cope with his lingering misery. By willing himself to love anything or anyone, he thereby avoids the kind of spontaneous, but uncontrollable, love that has nearly destroyed him. The final stage of his "science," the one toward which he presumably is working, is romantic love, the love for a woman. However, by the end of the story, the reader, and perhaps even the boy, knows that he will never again reach that stage, having been hurt by it too badly before.

Style and Technique

"A Tree. A Rock. A Cloud." is a story-within-a-story, that is, the old man's tale is framed by the dramatic situation involving the boy, Leo, and the bleak café. Here, however, the frame does not merely serve as a technical device to justify the old man's narrative; rather, the two stories complement and reinforce each other. Although the tale of betrayal and lost love serves as the centerpiece of the story, an equal amount of space is given over to the action within the café: The boy shifts in his seat, the man lowers his head, Leo prepares food with characteristic stinginess. Both stories are about the failure of human sympathy, and the fact that the old man is unable to find a wholly sympathetic listener makes the story doubly tragic.

Unlike most of McCullers's work, "A Tree. A Rock. A Cloud." is not set specifically in the South; indeed, no specific locale is mentioned. The two principal characters are unnamed, nor is any indication given of the date or of the season. This deliberate indeterminacy lends a chilling universality to the story, transforming it from a story about a tired old man's ramblings to a sort of allegory about the limitations of love.

J. D. Daubs

THE TREE OF KNOWLEDGE

Author: Henry James (1843-1916)
Type of plot: Psychological
Time of plot: The late 1890's
Locale: London, England
First published: 1900

> *Principal characters:*
> PETER BRENCH, the protagonist, a fifty-year-old bachelor of
> independent means
> MORGAN MALLOW, a middle-aged sculptor of independent means
> MRS. MALLOW, his middle-aged wife of independent means
> LANCELOT MALLOW, their son

The Story

At the heart of much of Henry James's fiction is the idea of an education—a gaining of knowledge by a protagonist that changes his or her view of the world. In the longer form of the novel, such as *The Portrait of a Lady* (1881), a number of experiences gradually educate the protagonist, but with the shorter form, such as in this story, James relies on one incident to change a character's view of the world—and himself. The concept of "knowledge"—the key term in the title "The Tree of Knowledge"—is the central concern around which the psychological action revolves. Peter Brench, the protagonist, is a man who loses his innocence, his illusions, through an experience with his godson, Lancelot Mallow.

The action begins with the announcement by Lancelot's mother, Mrs. Mallow, that her son shall not return to college at Cambridge, but instead will go to Paris and learn to become a painter. Peter, a family friend who has been secretly in love with Mrs. Mallow for twenty years, arranges a meeting with Lance in an attempt to persuade him not to go to Paris, but to return to college.

Peter does not wish Lance to go to Paris to study painting because he fears that Lance will learn that his father, who has proclaimed himself a great artist as a sculptor, and who has devoted his life to his sculpting, is without talent. Peter primarily wishes to protect Mrs. Mallow from this knowledge, for he fears that it would bring her great pain and destroy her love for her husband. When Lance questions Peter on why Peter does not wish him to go to Paris, Peter declares, "I've the misfortune to be omniscient." Lance misinterprets the statement to mean that Peter does not believe that Lance has the talent to become an artist. Lance wishes to reassure Peter that he is mature enough to find out the truth about himself, and he replies that his "innocence" no longer needs protecting.

While Lance is in Paris, Peter continues to have Sunday dinner with the Mallows, and he observes the "fond illusion" of the Mallows when it appears that some of the sculpting finally will be sold, and Morgan will gain a reputation as an artist. Peter knows that Morgan will never really amount to anything as a sculptor, for he is without a proper sense of proportion, a necessary aspect of the art. However, because the Mallows are independently wealthy, there is no need for Morgan to become successful, and Peter believes that for the well-being of all concerned, including himself, the present arrangement is best left as it is.

When Lance does return the following year from Paris, he has discovered that he does not have the talent to become a painter, and he also has discovered the lack of value of his father's work—the very knowledge Peter wished to conceal from him. Peter extracts a promise from Lance not to tell his parents the truth about his father. It is Peter's greatest wish that the couple retain their illusion. Peter's goal of protecting Mrs. Mallow from the truth is called into question by Lance's next visit home from Paris. In the final scene of the story, Lance tells Peter of a heated argument with his father, who castigated Lance for not developing his painting. Lance tells Peter that his mother, in order to relieve Lance's feelings, came to him after the argument, and Lance discovered that she had known the true value of her husband's work all along.

On hearing this, Peter is dumbfounded. Lance realizes how very much Peter must have cared all these years for his mother, and at the same time, Peter realizes that Mrs. Mallow is not the woman he thought she was; she was quite capable of living all these years with such knowledge while maintaining a convincing appearance that she believed in her husband's talent: a convincing appearance even to Peter.

When Lance closes the story by declaring how futile Peter's effort was to have tried to keep Lance from Paris, to have tried to keep him "from knowledge," Peter replies that he now realizes his effort was, "without my quite at the time having known it," to keep himself from the very knowledge that he has just discovered. All these years, he has been the one living under a "fond illusion." He was not all-knowing, "omniscient," as he told Lance, but was, indeed, the innocent one in assuming exactly what Mrs. Mallow was as a person.

Themes and Meanings

The nature of a man's illusions about himself is the central theme that James explores in this story. On one level, Morgan Mallow lives a life of self-deception, believing that he is a great artist when, in fact, he has no talent. However, because of this lack of knowledge, he goes on living as a happy, self-satisfied man. His situation is in direct contrast to that of Peter. On a more significant level, Peter discovers that although he always has assumed that he was a man without illusions, it is he who has been living with the illusion, not Mrs. Mallow.

This theme achieves its meaning through the refined sensibility of Peter. He is a man of taste, one who avoids "vulgarity"; he judges himself as one who feels "an extreme and general humility to be his proper portion." For such a man to discover that, for all of his humility, he lived a life based on an illusion calls that very humility into question—in fact, calls his whole life into question.

The age of the protagonist is a central factor in this theme: Peter is not a young man, with his life before him, but rather a man in his fifties, an age when one examines one's achievements in life, when one tries to determine what one's life has meant. He has devoted his life to a woman who is not the person he thought she was, and his illusion has cost him a larger life, one in which he might well have lived more fully.

Style and Technique

James viewed this story as a "novel intensely compressed" without "any air of mutilation" into a short story. The rich psychological dimensions of the protagonist are achieved through the use of language, the famous James style—the sentences are long and complex, with one phrase, one thought, qualified by another, and often yet another. The style is entirely appropriate for the protagonist, for Peter Brench is a man of complex thought, a man concerned with nuance and distinctions.

That the action should be viewed through Peter's mind in third-person-limited point of view is also entirely appropriate, for the real "action" of the story is the psychological processes of Peter's thoughts and feelings. It is this point of view, a character of central intelligence, on whom the action registers, that enabled James to explore the complexities of thought, the nuances of sensibility, for which he is famous.

The complexity of the overall structure in this story parallels the use of language. In attempting to conceal knowledge from Mrs. Mallow, Peter discovers the very knowledge that will lead to his own self-awareness. The structure also gives ironic dimension to the concepts of omniscience, innocence, illusion, and humility. Typical of James, the irony is not stark and biting, but rather complex and satiric. The various elements of the story—its language, structure, irony—are all in proper proportion to create a harmonious whole.

There are those readers who become impatient with the fiction of James on a first reading, who find his prose too dense and his characters and their situations unexciting. To appreciate his work, one often requires multiple readings with a patient sensitivity. Critics and other writers refer to him as "the Master"—one of the greatest artists in the history of prose fiction—for his ability to dramatize complex subjects. In reference to this particular story, James said his "fun" was in dramatizing the material, in making it live on the page, in compressing what was essentially a novel into the short story form. Brevity and physical action are not his forte; instead, his strengths are in portraying the rich life of the educated mind and the complex relationships between persons of sensitivity and taste.

Ronald L. Johnson

A TREE OF NIGHT

Author: Truman Capote (Truman Streckfus Persons, 1924-1984)
Type of plot: Psychological
Time of plot: The 1940's
Locale: Alabama
First published: 1943

> *Principal characters:*
> KAY, the protagonist, a college sophomore
> A WOMAN, her antagonist
> A MUTE MAN, her nemesis

The Story

On an icy winter's night, nineteen-year-old Kay waits for a train. Her tall, thin figure, conservative attire, and stylish hair suggest breeding and wealth. She carries a gray suede purse, on which elaborate brass letters emblazon her name (K-A-Y), as well as several magazines and, incongruously, a green western guitar. Boarding a crowded, littered train, she finds a seat facing a grotesque couple, who share childlike characteristics. The woman's feet dangle, barely brushing the floor; on her enormous head, her dyed red hair is in "corkscrew curls." Tipsy, she behaves erratically, by turns syrupy and then mocking, rude, and rough toward Kay. Her deaf and mute companion has thickly lashed, oddly beautiful, milk-blue eyes, and he reeks of cheap perfume, looks childlike, and wears a Mickey Mouse watch.

As Kay settles in her seat, the woman begins a conversation in which she learns that Kay has been to her uncle's funeral, that she was willed only his green guitar, and that she is a college student. The woman disdains college education. Kay opens a magazine, but the woman prevails on her good manners to talk. As tension builds between them, inexplicably, the woman becomes increasingly able to manipulate Kay. A more emotionally fraught tension bonds the girl and the mute man.

Eventually, under the guise of a polite lie, Kay anxiously tries to flee, but the woman grabs her wrist, demanding, "Didn't your mama ever tell you it was sinful to lie?" Kay denies the obvious, but hastily obeys a terse "Sit down, dear." A tangible sense of history pervading their relationship increases when the woman asks Kay about her hometown. Many cities crowd the girl's mind, but she cannot think which of them it is, then says, "New Orleans." The woman beams, telling Kay that she once ran a lucrative fortune-telling business there. The woman then explains that she and her companion have a traveling act involving the man's being buried alive in a star-studded casket.

As the woman talks, Kay gazes at the mute man, thinking that his face has the same unseeing look as that of her dead uncle. This gaze is not the first between them, for when she first sits down, he swings "his head sideways," studying her; another gaze occurs when the woman briefly leaves them. During the woman's absence, as Kay strums the guitar, the man reaches boldly and delicately to trace her cheek. Kay's mind darts in all directions as he leans closer, and they gaze, searchingly, eye-to-eye, as "keen" pity wells up in the girl, coupling with an overpowering disgust and loathing. Here, Kay feels the first stirring of primal memory.

The story climaxes when the man extracts a peach seed from his pocket. Balancing it in his hand, he catches Kay's eyes in another gaze, obscenely caressing the seed. The woman explains that it is a love charm that he wants Kay to buy for a dollar. Panicky, she refuses. When the woman will not make the man put it away, Kay flees with her purse to the lantern-lit observation platform. There, she clutches at the scant facts of her life, hopelessly seeking perspective. Kneeling down, she warms herself at the lantern's glass funnel until she senses the man hovering nearby. Looking up, Kay makes a last, lucid effort to sublimate her fear in a childhood memory that always "hovered above her, like haunted limbs on a tree of night": the memory evokes aunts, cooks, strangers spinning supernatural stories with threats of a "wizard man" who stole naughty children.

Kay follows the man back inside the compartment, where everyone is asleep—except the woman, who ignores Kay. The man merely sits with his arms folded. Kay's anxiety rebuilds. Near panic, she says that she will buy the charm. The woman does not respond, so Kay turns to the man. His face seems to "change form and recede before her" sliding under water. Immediately, the girl relaxes, succumbing to a "warm laziness," surrendering her purse to the woman, who gently pulls the "raincoat like a shroud above her head."

Themes and Meanings

Truman Capote packs "A Tree of Night" with clues for many themes, all of which relate to the fact that the story is a rite of passage piece that captures the moment when a nineteen-year-old woman passes from childhood innocence to adult sexual awareness. The peach seed, for example, is both masculine and feminine in context: The seed that a male implants in a female produces new life. This shellacked seed in the story, however, is impotent, and thus serves as a symbol of sexual union without reproduction. The mute man's handling of the seed arouses erotic and nameless responses in the innocent college sophomore, who flees to the platform of the car, only to yield compulsively to a desire to fondle the phallic lantern funnel. In doing so, she is fascinated by the tone and texture of her hands as they become luminous and warm while the funnel's heat thaws her and tingles through her.

At this same moment the mute appears. Looking up at him, his arms dangling, Kay recalls the tree of night that she feared in childhood. She remembers that adults in her youth filled her with superstitious fears by saying that a "wizard man" would steal her if she did things that she should not. Back then, a tree tapping against her window played on those fears. Identifying the mute man with her childhood, Kay, at the very edge of passage into full adulthood, follows him back into the coach, where she begs the dwarf woman (a symbol of adult authority) to let her buy the seed for a dollar. The adult influence turns its head, however, leaving Kay alone with the man to strike her own bargain. The man is the one for whom she has felt strong compassion, pity, loathing, nameless fear, and bonding. The story ends with the two characters bonded by a gaze that leads the girl to give in symbolically to her sexual desire, which is now terrifyingly aroused in her.

To understand this story more fully, it is useful to have some knowledge of the early 1940's in the United States, when trains were a common mode of transportation. Young women such as Kay who could afford college were typically sheltered and carefully protected from sexual knowledge of any sort. They were often kept in line by superstitious threats. A woman's vagina was called a "purse," and mothers warned their daughters to keep their purses shut. In "A Tree of Night," Kay gives up the entire contents of her purse. As was also true of sheltered young women in that period, she swoons as she lets it go. As the story ends, she is aswim in waters of sexual surrender.

Style and Technique

Capote believed that what a writer used as subject matter was not as important as how it was used. He told an interviewer that "a very fine artist" can take something "most ordinary" and, "through sheer artistry and willpower, turn it into a work of art." "A Tree of Night" proves his point. Capote makes this work universal by using a "most ordinary" 1940's situation in which there is neither realistic danger, nor tragedy, nor loss. Using psychological realism, he moves his protagonist through the sexualization process. A catalog of nouns defines the stages of her passage, as he has her exaggerate ordinary remarks and events. Her list of nouns, compatible with actual human experience, defines and parodies the universal nature of youth caught at the moment of fully adult sexual awareness.

In the rising action that provides setting, dialogue, character, and plot, Kay moves through amusement, squeamishness, timorous assertiveness, bewilderment, embarrassment, puzzlement, amazement, absentmindedness, and anger. In the story's climax, shame and fear come as she flees the peach seed scene. In falling action come compulsion, preoccupation, and realization, and in resolution come capitulation and copulation. Capote depicts capitulation as a complete "letting-go" of self (the purse identifying the brassy KAY). He depicts copulation as an innocent girl's swoon at the moment of surrender.

Capote, who said that his early stories were attempts to escape the realities of his own troubled life in a quest for serenity, seems to reveal in "A Tree of Night" his self-struggle with primal memories from a dysfunctional childhood filled with aunts, cooks, and strangers and rife with memories of sexual tensions and identity crises.

Jo Culbertson Davis

TRICK OR TREAT

Author: Padgett Powell (1952-   )
Type of plot: Domestic realism
Time of plot: The late twentieth century
Locale: The American South
First published: 1993

> *Principal characters:*
> JANICE HALSEY HOLLINGSWORTH, a middle-aged wife and
>   mother
> JIMMY TEETH, a sexually precocious twelve-year-old boy

The Story

"Trick or Treat" is a story of mutual seduction, told in the third-person through the minds of two characters. The action is what one would expect in an ordinary love story. It begins with the recognition of desire, proceeds through the uncertainties of courtship, and ends with the relationship about to be consummated. What makes the story unusual is that the two people involved are a respectable housewife and a twelve-year-old boy.

The story is set in a small town in the American South. It is fall, a few weeks before Halloween. Mrs. Hollingsworth is walking to the grocery store, thinking about the South and talking to herself. Her monologue is interrupted by a boy in one of the yards she is passing. A brief conversation follows, ending with his suggesting that she is crazy. She replies by suggesting to the boy that he grow up.

After Mrs. Hollingsworth moves on, the boy is furious with himself. For weeks he has been watching her and lusting after her, and now he fears he has insulted her. However, he does not give up hope. A few days later, he appears at Mrs. Hollingsworth's home with a lawnmower, asking for a job cutting her grass. Even though the grass does not need mowing, she agrees. After he finishes, she serves him lemonade in the backyard. However, when a police officer turns up, she finds that the boy has disappeared. It seems that the lawnmower had been reported stolen.

An hour later, the boy telephones Mrs. Hollingsworth to tell her that he will have his lemonade some other time. He addresses her as Bonnie and refers to himself as Clyde, thus identifying the two of them with the notorious bank robbers. Then he hangs up, laughing.

When Mrs. Hollingsworth's husband comes home, she gives him the usual kiss on the cheek. This prompts her to dwell on her own sexual frustration and to imagine how differently she would embrace the boy. She is now convinced that a sexual relationship with him is not an option for her, but a necessity. However, when she remembers that it is almost Halloween, a time that has come to symbolize all her discontent, Mrs. Hollingsworth forgets about the boy.

The next time the boy comes to visit, he is wearing a suit and a hat. After Mrs. Hollingsworth invites him into the house, he immediately removes both the suit and the hat and deposits them in the trash compactor. Mrs. Hollingsworth and the boy sit down at the kitchen table, and she begins to ask questions. Finally she asks him his name. When he responds with "Jimmy Teeth," she introduces herself by her maiden name, "Janice Halsey." During the long silence that follows, she reflects on the strangeness of the situation. Then they start talking again, but Jimmy is only too aware that he is just making conversation because, though he knows what he wants, he does not know how to proceed. It is Mrs. Hollingsworth who takes the next step; she places her hand over his. While they are sitting there, she muses as to how she must behave if this relationship is to be successful. What she has to do, she concludes, is to act as if Jimmy were older than he really is.

Mrs. Hollingsworth now extracts a pledge from Jimmy that if she pays him eight dollars instead of five for mowing the lawn, he will not tell her husband. Then she asks him if he goes trick-or-treating. His answer, that he no longer does, is the one for which she has been waiting. She makes herself another drink and prepares to become Janice Halsey. The story ends with her reflecting that from now on, Jimmy can make his own moves, and so can she.

Themes and Meanings

On the surface, "Trick or Treat" is a story about a relationship that society views as both immoral and illegal. It is generally agreed that no adult should commit a sexual act with a child. The only reason that "Trick or Treat" is not shocking is that as the story progresses, each character gradually develops into someone else. Mrs. Hollingsworth becomes Janice Halsey, a somewhat more sophisticated version of the girl she once was, and Jimmy becomes the adult he one day will be. These transformations suggest that the story is not about lust but about identity. What these characters intend to do is to defeat time.

From the beginning of the story, it is evident that Mrs. Hollingsworth is uneasy in her present role. Her flamboyant cowboy boots are at odds with her prosaic mission, a trip to the grocery store. Her comments to herself also reflect her unhappiness. She seems to be asking whether the South, that is, her whole environment, loves her, but in fact she is deciding whether she will continue to let her society define her. This vague discontent impels her later to speak insultingly to the police officer, whose very uniform represents the rules she resents. It is also what motivates her to hold her husband at a distance. Whatever was once between them has vanished with time. Her husband no longer sees her as an individual. To him and to her children, she is no more than a vague presence. She has a function, not an identity. Mrs. Hollingsworth tries not to be bitter about this fact, for she has to admit that the members of her family are as invisible to her as she is to them.

When someone turns up who regards her as an individual, it is hardly surprising that Mrs. Hollingsworth is drawn to him. However, at first the words in her mind suggest that to her, he has no separate identity. She thinks of him as the child, the boy, or the lawn boy. Not until the final scene does she ask him his name. However, whatever she may think, Jimmy knows exactly who he is. Although he manages to keep his words conventional, his thoughts are as those of an adult, as X-rated as the shirt he is wearing at their first encounter.

Gradually it becomes clear to Mrs. Hollingsworth that, though Jimmy may look like a child, he is more mature than she thought. Certainly his single-minded sexuality seems like something more than adolescent lust. Moreover, Jimmy is very much his own person. Unlike Mrs. Hollingsworth, he gleefully ignores convention. No one but Jimmy would have been self-assured enough to arrive at the home of the woman he hoped to seduce playing the part of a gangster. However, like a mature adult, Jimmy also knows when to keep quiet; Mrs. Hollingsworth believes him when he promises not to tell her husband about their private arrangements and when he assures her that he is too old for trickery. "Trick or Treat" ends happily, for it is evident that though Jimmy will get what he wants, a sexual initiation, Janice will discover her true identity.

Style and Technique

Padgett Powell is admired and, on occasion, criticized for his irreverent style. In "Trick or Treat," there is none of the overblown lyricism that sometimes spoils his effects. Here Powell's prose is precise and controlled. As always, his visual images are effective; the pumpkin head above the pickets is a good example. Typically, too, his dialogue catches the clipped, slangy cadences of everyday speech. Moreover, his characters' mental gymnastics, with all their hesitations and reversals, strike the reader as very real.

Perhaps even more interesting is the author's use of symbolism. Early in "Trick or Treat," Mrs. Hollingsworth concocts a capricious list that she believes sums up the South and accounts for her unhappiness. Halfway through the story, she decides that Halloween belongs on that list, if only because it makes parents, and especially mothers, the slaves of custom and the servants of their children. With Halloween approaching, it is not surprising that Mrs. Hollingsworth should at first see a resemblance between Jimmy's head and a pumpkin. At that point, to her he is just another child. It is significant, however, that once she begins to see him as an interesting individual, the comparison disappears.

Because they reflect the fluctuations in Mrs. Hollingsworth's mind, the references to Halloween in "Trick or Treat" are more suggestive than explicit. However, it is clear exactly what the author means by the allusion to the mythological Orpheus in the final sentence of the story. The god was bringing his wife back from the dead, but he had been warned not to look back. Sadly, he did, and he lost her. Mrs. Hollingsworth does not intend to make the same mistake. When she becomes Janice Halsey for the second time, she knows that she will not be recapturing the past but moving forward into a second youth. As long as she does not look back, either to her distant youth or to her recent past, she will be able to hold her lover, and for a while she will be all right.

Rosemary M. Canfield Reisman

A TRIFLING OCCURRENCE

Author: Anton Chekhov (1860-1904)
Type of plot: Psychological
Time of plot: The late nineteenth century
Locale: St. Petersburg
First published: "Pustoy sluchay," 1886 (English translation, 1915)

Principal characters:
NIKOLAY ILYICH BELYAEV, the landlord
OLGA IVANOVNA IRNINA, his mistress
ALYOSHA, her son
IRNIN, her estranged husband

The Story

The setting for the entire story is the drawing room of Olga Ivanovna Irnina, a woman who is estranged from her husband and is currently involved with Nikolay Ilyich Belyaev. The story opens with a brief description of Belyaev: He is a "well-fed," "pink young man of about thirty-two" years of age. He has three principal activities in life: He is a "St. Petersburg landlord," he is "very fond of the race-course," and he has a "liaison" with Olga.

This opening establishes that, as a landlord, Belyaev lives from the labor of others; that, as a racing addict, he has not closed the gap between his mental and his chronological age; and that, as a paramour, he prefers a liaison with Olga to marriage.

The epithets "well-fed" and "pink" applied to Belyaev are especially unflattering inasmuch as in Anton Chekhov's works the color pink, when referring to a man, suggests the image of a soft, pampered, and effeminate individual, although the expression "well-fed" is an unmistakable sign of pettiness and vulgarity or, more precisely, what the Russians call *poshlost.*

The narrator observes that Belyaev looks on his liaison with Olga as "a long and tedious romance" that he has "spun out," adding parenthetically that this is Belyaev's "own phrase." Here a more serious flaw in Belyaev's character is exposed: He has been insincere about the nature of his relationship with Olga. Moreover, as the words "to use his own phrase" indicate, he has obviously made their "tedious romance" the subject of discussion with others, though not with her.

The inauthenticity of their relationship—its prosaic nature—is further underscored when Belyaev refers to it metaphorically as a romance, the first pages of which—"pages of interest and inspiration"—had been read long ago, leaving only pages containing neither novelty nor interest. Significantly, the word "love" does not appear in the description of even the initial phase of this romance; only interest and novelty are of primary importance to Belyaev. The irony is fully intended when the narrator, after presenting such an unflattering picture of Belyaev, refers to him as "my hero."

As the story opens, Belyaev has come to visit Olga and, not having found her at home, lies down on the drawing-room couch to wait for her. He is greeted by Olga's son, Alyosha, who is lying on a divan in the same room but whom Belyaev does not even notice. This incident betrays Belyaev's treatment of the boy in the past and foreshadows the treatment that he will accord him later.

In describing Alyosha, the narrator notes that the boy is "about eight years old, well built, well looked after, dressed up like a picture in a velvet jacket and long black stockings." Every detail bespeaks Alyosha's excellent material well-being. However, here too, there seems to be a lack of something—an emphasis on the boy's material well-being perhaps at the expense of his spiritual welfare. The single most disturbing detail is his being "dressed up like a picture." He may appear to be "well cared for" but, as is eventually revealed, he is treated as an object—a pawn in a game whose principal players include his separated parents and Belyaev.

A close inspection of the description of Belyaev and Alyosha reveals considerable similarity between the grown-up man and the child: Each is a pampered, spoiled individual; the epithets "well fed" and "pink," used to describe the former, echo the epithets "well looked after" and "well built," used to describe the latter. Similarly, Belyaev's playing the races with his income from tenants finds its parallel in Alyosha's fascination with the circus and acrobats, which his mother's money enables him to see. Even the minor detail that both of them are reclining in the drawing room at the opening of the story underscores their basic similarity. Alyosha strives to behave and talk like an adult but remains a child whose impressions of adults and their standards of morality and conduct are naïve and incomplete. For his part, Belyaev, who is four times Alyosha's senior, demonstrates through his selfishness, irresponsibility, and inconsiderateness of others that in many respects he, too, is still a child.

As he reclines on the divan, Alyosha imitates an acrobat, but his behavior equally conjures up the antics of an insect: "He lay on a satin pillow . . . lifting up first one leg, then the other. When his legs began to be tired, he moved his hands, or he jumped." Next, he "took hold of the toe of his left foot in his right hand and got into a most awkward position. He turned head over heels and jumped up." Shortly thereafter, Belyaev says to him: "Come here, kid" (he uses the word klop, which in Russian basically means "bug" or "bedbug" and colloquially "kid"). He adds: "Let me look at you, quite close." The image of a barely perceptible bug is appropriate for Alyosha. In fact, to Alyosha's greeting, Belyaev responds: "I didn't notice you." The irony and full implication of this statement become apparent when somewhat later Belyaev reflects: "All the time he had been acquainted with Olga Ivanovna he had never once turned his attention to the boy and had completely ignored his existence." Now, as he examines Alyosha (the bug), he asks: "How are you?" In Russian, however, he simply asks "Zhivyosh?" which literally means "Are you alive?"—an ironic question as it reflects Belyaev's attitude toward Alyosha up to now. The "awkward position" that Alyosha has got himself into while imitating the acrobat serves as a foreshadowing of the awkward position in which he will soon find himself vis-à-vis his mother and father after undergoing Belyaev's close "examination."

Alyosha is distracted by Belyaev's watch chain and locket, both of which remind him of his father's—a fact he inadvertently blurts out. Surprised by this information, Belyaev presses Alyosha for a complete confession: He and his sister Sonya, escorted by their nurse, have been seeing their father on a regular basis despite their mother's forbidding them to do so.

To extract this information from Alyosha, Belyaev addresses him as a "friend to a friend," requesting him to speak "openly," "honestly," and on his "word of honor." Alyosha then obtains from Belyaev a promise that the latter will not say anything of it to his mother. When Alyosha requests Belyaev to swear an oath, the latter responds: "What do you take me for?" Belyaev's later custody of the secret gives this question exactly the answer Alyosha—and the reader—feared.

Alyosha informs Belyaev that he and Sonya meet their father at Apfel's sweet-shop, where he treats them to coffee, cakes, and pies, after which, at home, they try to conceal the affair from their mother by eating as much as they can. The father takes advantage of these meetings to extract information about the mother's activities and to set the children against Belyaev. Such statements as "You are unhappy, I'm unhappy, and mother's unhappy" strike even Alyosha as being "strange." Alyosha tells Belyaev (of all people): "I can't understand why mother doesn't invite father to live with her or why she says we musn't meet him." Here Chekhov demonstrates not only Alyosha's naïveté but also his own profound psychological insight into one of childhood's predicaments: the confusion and uncertainty when caught between separate parents.

When asked by Belyaev what their father says about him, Alyosha, after obtaining Belyaev's promise not to become offended, informs him that their father blames Belyaev for their unhappiness and their mother's ruin. Accused of ruining the family's happiness (Olga's in particular), Belyaev explodes with anger. When Alyosha reminds him of his promise not to become offended, Belyaev, in another psychologically authentic response, notes: "I'm not offended," and, after a brief pause, lashes out with: "and it's none of your business!"—a reaction that reinstates the dynamics of the story's opening, in which Belyaev considered Alyosha too insignificant to notice. Belyaev's earlier feelings of being trapped in a dull, drawn-out romance have now become concretized in his image of himself as an animal who has fallen into a trap.

As Olga and Sonya return home, Belyaev continues to rant and rave, completely absorbed in his hurt pride. Behind his hysterics is his desire to end the unhappy romance with Olga. He has been looking for a pretext but has been either unable or too weak to find one. At last the opportunity has presented itself and he seizes it. The animal extricates himself from the trap.

As Belyaev begins to reveal Alyosha's secret, Alyosha experiences a horror that reflects itself in "his face twisted in fright"—quite a contrast to his deliberately, acrobatically "twisted body" described in the story's opening. Alyosha repeatedly reminds Belyaev of his pledged word of honor. Belyaev's brutal response is perhaps the story's best example of irony: "Ah let me alone! . . . This is something more important than any words of honor. The hypocrisy revolts me, the lie." The man who demanded the word of honor from others and easily gave his own has proven dishonorable. Like a child, he has permitted his hurt feelings to take precedence over his word of honor. Now the biggest "hypocrite" and "liar" of all, he accuses others of revolting hypocrisy and lies.

The story comes full circle as Belyaev, absorbed in his insult, "now, as before, did not notice the presence of the boy. He, a big serious man, had nothing to do with boys." The story concludes, however, with Alyosha's final impressions. It is he who appears truly revolted by this entire experience—one that may have scarred him for life. How could a pledged word be so easily broken? How could it have so little value? The narrator concludes that this was Alyosha's first encounter with the world of lies— his first awareness that in this world "there exist many things which have no name in children's language."

Themes and Meanings

In "A Trifling Occurrence," Chekhov demonstrates his profound understanding of a child's psychology. The story shows how impressionable children are. It also demonstrates that what may seem trivial to an adult can be of great significance to a child and may leave a lasting imprint. To depict this "common triviality" at work, Chekhov has chosen a collision of children's emotions with a world of insincere and false relations—a world peopled by petty and dishonorable adults.

At first glance, the story may seem to be about Belyaev's failure to keep his word with Alyosha, thereby insulting the child and putting him through an emotional trauma. Such a reading would lead one to conclude that Belyaev is the villain and Alyosha the injured innocent. On rereading the story, however, one discovers that the situation is far more complex. In fact, no one in this story is innocent, not even Alyosha. To a lesser or greater extent, everyone is guilty of contributing to the tragedy. If Belyaev appears to be all bad (which he is not), Alyosha and the others are certainly not all good. Early in the story, Belyaev looks at Alyosha and reflects: "A boy is stuck in front of your eyes, but what is he doing here, what is his role?—you don't want to give a single thought to the question." The key word here is "role." A closer examination of the story reveals that all characters portrayed are guilty of role-playing rather than leading authentic lives. All of them are caught in a vast web of deceit and betrayal, a web that they themselves have erected.

The "unnatural positions" that Alyosha acrobatically assumes in the opening paragraphs of the story are symbolic of the deceptive lives they all lead. Belyaev deceives Olga about the true nature of his feelings for her and continues playing the role of her lover. Alyosha and Sonya deceive their mother when they meet secretly with their father. Their father deceives their mother by setting up these clandestine meetings; he also deceives his children by telling them "funny stories" and treating them to sweets while pumping them for information about their mother and Belyaev and by faulting Belyaev for all of their unhappiness, without a hint that he himself may have colluded in it. Nor is Olga guiltless in the situation. If she had been completely unselfish, perhaps the liaison with Belyaev would never have been established. She is less than fair by forbidding the children to see their father. The grandeur of her material comforts suggests that she is milking both her husband and Belyaev to support her lifestyle. Even the nurse escorts the children to their meetings with the father, thereby taking part in the deception of her employer.

All the characters, therefore, are connected in a vicious circle of deception. That circle is finally broken when Belyaev, as a result of his egocentrism, betrays Alyosha. In doing so, Belyaev helps to expose all the other deceptions. Thus, the concluding lines of the story, "This was the first time in his life that Alyosha had been set, roughly, face to face with a lie," assume a deeper meaning. Before now, Alyosha himself has been guilty of lying and deceiving; now, he experiences the unpleasantness of being lied to. Given the number of similarities between the adult-child Belyaev and Alyosha pretending to be an adult in the opening two paragraphs of the story, the reader may seriously doubt whether Alyosha will behave any differently once he reaches adulthood. Chekhov's message appears to be that there is no substitute for truly authentic and honorable relationships.

Style and Technique

From its opening to its closing line, "A Trifling Occurrence" is exemplary of Chekhov's mastery of the short story. Its construction is analogous to the best of Chekhov's one-act plays. In fact, it could easily be staged: More than two thirds of its lines consist of dialogue. Another fact common to both story and play is that all major "events" leading up to the conflict take place offstage. As in the indirect plays, so, too, in this story, there are important offstage characters, most notably the father.

The story shows symmetry in its construction: from its bipartite opening, consisting of two paragraphs of ten lines each devoted to the introduction and description of the two protagonists, to its conclusion, consisting also of ten lines. Narrative passages frame what remains, which is essentially dialogue. Chekhov masterfully moves the tempo of this dramatic piece from the leisurely pace of the introductory paragraphs, where one finds both Belyaev and Alyosha reclining on sofas, to the midpoint, where Belyaev and Alyosha become more animated as the former learns the first details of the latter's secret, to Belyaev's real state of excitement once he learns that the father accuses him of the family's ruin, to its crescendo as Belyaev pours out his anger for the insult he has suffered. At this point Olga enters, totally confused, while Alyosha is overwhelmed by terror. Even the lines of dialogue become shorter, thus accelerating the tempo and contributing to the charged atmosphere. In the closing narrative passage the tempo subsides as the narrator sums up the "moral" of the story.

Leonard Polakiewicz

TRILOBITES

Author: Breece D'J Pancake (1952-1979)
Type of plot: Character study, psychological
Time of plot: The 1970's
Locale: Rural West Virginia
First published: 1977

Principal characters:
COLLY, an unsuccessful farmer and amateur fossil hunter
GINNY, his former girlfriend
MOM, his widowed mother
JIM, his elderly friend and a fossil expert
MR. TRENT, a developer who wants to buy his mother's farm

The Story

"Trilobites" is a first-person narrative in which a farmer named Colly describes a single day in his life but also recalls many key events from his past. This day is a turning point for Colly because he defies his mother and reunites briefly, but then breaks dramatically, with his former girlfriend.

As Colly drinks coffee in the Rock Camp café, he considers his unsuccessful attempts to find trilobite fossils in the nearby hills, the recent death of his father, and the loss of his girlfriend Ginny, who now lives in Florida but is back in town for a brief visit. Colly's friend Jim joins him, and they discuss elusive fossils, World War II experiences Jim shared with Colly's father, and the intention of Colly's mother to sell the family farm.

Later Colly drives his farm tractor through blighted, drought-stricken fields and contemplates his failings as a farmer. He catches a snapping turtle in the nearby Teays River and begins to butcher and clean the carcass. When Mr. Trent appears to discuss purchasing the farm, Colly refuses to negotiate and carelessly splatters turtle blood on the developer's trousers. Colly remembers pleasant times from the past (building a barn with his father and his first sexual experience with Ginny in the farm woods), but he also dwells on his father's death (caused by a sliver of metal from a war wound that eventually worked its way into his brain). For no apparent reason, Colly blames himself for his father's death.

As Colly cooks his turtle meat, he overhears his mother's acceptance of Mr. Trent's offer to purchase the farm and her plan to move to Akron, Ohio, where she thinks Colly can get a job at the Goodrich factory. After the developer leaves, Colly argues with his mother about Ginny (whose own mother deserted her and was later murdered in Chicago) and declares that he will not move to Akron.

When Colly goes driving with Ginny, she strikes him as overdressed and quite different from the way he remembered her. They discuss her mother, her overly protective father, her current boyfriend in Florida, and techniques for hitching rides on freight trains. Colly and Ginny break a window to get inside a deserted railroad station, and in doing so, Ginny cuts her arm. Colly binds the wound with his shirt, and it becomes soaked with blood. After a hasty sexual episode on the dirty depot floor, Colly begs Ginny to take him with her. Instead she drives away, leaving him alone at the abandoned depot. The story ends with Colly uncertain and fearful. He is about to lose his home, he cannot go with Ginny to Florida, and he refuses to follow his mother to Akron. What he will do and where he will go remain unclear, but he hints at travels like those of his father and Jim to Michigan, Germany, or maybe even China. With Colly's very thin record of accomplishments, however, such goals may be as elusive as the trilobites he has so often sought but never found.

Themes and Meanings

Breece D'J Pancake's title provides an important clue to the story's meaning. Trilobites are Paleozoic marine arthropods, long extinct, with segmented bodies separated by furrows into three distinct lobes. In several parts of North America, fossilized remains of these arthropods are buried under many layers of rock and soil. Colly's unsuccessful searches for these ancient stone animals parallel his futile attempts to uncover and make sense of his own past. Just as the trilobites suffered extinction, Colly is experiencing many painful losses—the death of his father, estrangement from his mother and girlfriend, and impending eviction from the land he loves but has found unproductive. Throughout the story, Colly probes layers of memory just as he has dug through layers of sediment. In both searches, however, he uncovers little of lasting value that can link his unstable past with his uncertain future. Ironically, Colly can neither uncover a trilobite nor sensibly end his search. Thus, his quest is both enticing and inevitably disappointing. It becomes an emblem of gnawing aspiration that cannot be realized.

Many of Pancake's stories focus on the impoverished lives of West Virginia miners, truck drivers, or minimum-wage gas pumpers. With a bottom-land farm and relatively comfortable house (rather than a rusty mobile home on a jagged ridge), Colly is apparently in a better financial position than that of many Pancake characters. Even so, Colly suffers from the spiritual poverty that pervades Pancake's fiction. In many of Pancake's stories, topography is destiny. The steep mountains and deep valleys of West Virginia allow one to look either down or up, but they permit little horizontal vision. In such an enclosed environment, characters seldom see clearly beyond looming impediments. Instead, they all too often simply stare downward in a mood of resignation. Colly's love of his home valley leads him to scorn the industrial wasteland of Akron, and he has dreams of travel to more fulfilling locations. Thus, Colly does manage to look beyond the enclosing mountains, but his itinerary and plans for the future remain extremely vague, and he has limited inner resources for use in fulfilling those dreams.

Style and Technique

Recurring images of death and decay create powerful effects in "Trilobites." After references in the title and several early paragraphs to dead marine creatures, Pancake presents a graphic picture of Colly's killing a turtle. Just as Colly's valley farm provides no protection from the chilling forces of change and destruction, the calm river is no safe refuge for the turtle. When Colly pulls it out on a long gaff, the turtle bites helplessly at the instrument on which it is caught. Later, in a more obvious image of ineffectual protection, Colly mercilessly breaks the turtle shell with his foot so he can begin to cut up the meat. In killing the turtle, Colly spreads blood on the dusty ground and even on the clothing of Mr. Trent. In like manner, the pain of death in this story stains survivors such as Colly, Colly's mother, and Ginny. Blood once again flows and stains after Ginny cuts her arm at the railroad station.

Although the slaughter of the turtle is deliberate and straightforward, the death of Colly's father is hauntingly insidious. He survived the war wound and lived for many years with a shell fragment inside his body. Only when this tiny dagger migrated to his brain did he suddenly fall dead. Such a scenario may not be entirely plausible, but it serves well to emphasize that death is both intractable and totally unpredictable.

Along with such images of death, the story offers several details of physical decay. In the long span of geologic time, craggy mountains around the town of Rock Camp have eroded to smooth hills. With a deserted, boarded-up railroad station, the town itself is apparently in decline. Pancake's stories contain many images of carcasses or hollow shells, and this empty building is a highly suggestive detail. (One Pancake story is simply entitled "Hollow," and in this case the term is both a noun referring to a place and an adjective describing a personal condition.) The station's shards of glass and other debris parallel the wreckage strewn about Colly's life. In fact, as Colly stands next to the building, he sees himself scattered all over the country with each cell many miles from another one. Inside the desolate station, Colly and Ginny come together for sex, but their activity is not creative lovemaking. It is a detached, almost brutal act.

While negative imagery certainly dominates this story, Pancake includes faint hints of continuity and growth. While Colly sits in the depot, he listens intently to the mud daubers building their nests. As these lowly insects construct homes amid wreckage, they achieve what Colly must try again to do.

Albert E. Wilhelm

TRISTAN

Author: Thomas Mann (1875-1955)
Type of plot: Parody
Time of plot: The turn of the twentieth century
Locale: Einfried, an Alpine sanatorium
First published: 1903 (English translation, 1925)

> *Principal characters:*
> ANTON KLOTERJAHN, a successful, domineering businessperson
> from North Germany
> GABRIELE KLOTERJAHN, his wife, a patient in an Alpine
> sanatorium
> DETLEV SPINELL, a writer of slight reputation who is also taking
> the cure

The Story

At the beginning of January, Anton Kloterjahn and his wife arrive at Einfried, a clinic in the mountain climate once favored by tuberculosis patients. Kloterjahn, who has brought his wife here for treatment of a slight tracheal disorder, is in robust good health and richly enjoys the fruits of his material success. Gabriele Kloterjahn is younger than he; her face betrays fatigue and a delicate constitution; shadows appear at the corners of her eyes, and a pale blue vein stands out under the fair skin of her forehead. Her present complaint—weakness, slight fever, and traces of blood when she coughs—appeared directly after the difficult birth of her first child, a lusty baby who immediately asserted his place in life "with prodigious energy and ruthlessness."

Detlev Spinell, a writer of no particular renown, has been resident at Einfried for a short time already. He has about him an air of illegitimacy, seemingly more dilettante than artist and more vacationer than patient. For some, he is merely amusing, an odd sort who affects the role of the unappreciated, solitary aesthete. Several inmates refer to him privately as "the dissipated baby." Once Kloterjahn returns to his flourishing business in the north, Spinell displays growing interest in his wife, and she finds a certain diversion in his conversation, eccentric as it is. He makes no secret of his dislike for her husband, insists that the name Kloterjahn is an affront to her, and queries her about her own family and her youth in Bremen. On learning that Gabriele and her father are amateur musicians, Spinell laments that the young woman sacrificed her artistic sensitivities to the domination of an acquisitive, boorish husband. Gabriele is vaguely charmed by this devotion; at the same time, her physical condition grows less encouraging.

One day at the end of February, a sleighing party is arranged for the patients, but she prefers not to take part. To no one's surprise, Spinell also remains behind.

Gabriele and her frequent companion, Frau Spatz, retire to the salon. Spinell joins them there and proposes that Gabriele play something on the piano. He knows that her doctors have forbidden it, and she reminds him of this fact, but he invokes the image of her as a girl in the family garden in Bremen, as if to suggest that by satisfying his request she could undo her marriage, her submission to the odious Kloterjahn, and the illness that has resulted from bearing Kloterjahn's child. Finally, she consents and plays a few of Frederic Chopin's nocturnes that have been left lying out in the room.

Then Spinell finds another volume. Gabriele takes it and begins to play as he sits reverently listening. It is the prelude to German composer Richard Wagner's opera *Tristan und Isolde* (1865). The performance is inspired and moving, and when it ends, both sit without speaking. Frau Spatz, by now bored and uncomfortable, retires to her room. As the late afternoon shadows deepen, Spinell urges her to play the second act, the one in which Tristan and Isolde consummate their burning, illicit love. The music completely absorbs the pair at the piano. Gabriele passes to the opera's finale and plays Isolde's love-death. When it is finished, neither can speak until recalled to reality by the bells of the returning sleighs. Spinell rises, crosses the room, then sinks to his knees as if in veneration, while Gabriele sits pensively in front of the silent piano.

Two days later, her condition shows signs of worsening. Kloterjahn is notified and arrives with his infant son, irritated by the interruption of his business affairs. Spinell, meanwhile, writes Kloterjahn a long, laboriously worded letter in which he indulges all of his ecstatic devotion to Gabriele and his hatred of her husband. He calls her the personification of vulnerable, decadent loveliness, consecrated, in his words, to "death and beauty." He denounces Kloterjahn as her mortal enemy for having violated the deathly beauty of Gabriele's life and debased her by his own vulgar existence. When Kloterjahn receives the letter, he reviles Spinell as presumptuous, cowardly, and ridiculous. However, his tirade is interrupted by a message that his wife has taken a turn for the worse and that he is needed at her bedside.

Spinell takes refuge in the garden. He gazes wistfully at Frau Kloterjahn's window and walks on, humming to himself the melody of the yearning motif from *Tristan und Isolde*. His reverie is cut short by the approach of a nursemaid with Kloterjahn's infant son in a perambulator. The sight of the chubby, happily screaming child is more than he can bear; he turns in consternation and walks the other way.

Themes and Meanings

The story's title prepares one for its allusions to the medieval tale of Tristan and Isolde's adulterous, ill-fated love. However, Thomas Mann has transposed a number of its traditional motifs into a new key. Most striking is his casting of the writer-aesthete Spinell as a new Tristan, for Spinell is anything but lyrical, virile, attractive, or heroic, and therein lies the story's parodistic irony. However, it is made thoroughly convincing by the appropriation, not of the medieval courtly epic, but of Wagner's music-drama *Tristan und Isolde*. In "Tristan," the fateful potion that the two "lovers" share is not a magic drink, but Wagner's intoxicating music. The erotic thrall of music and text in *Tristan und Isolde* is potent, and in their susceptibility to the power of musical art both Gabriele Kloterjahn and Detlev Spinell are thoroughly Mannian characters.

One thematic strand reveals this story's kinship with another of Mann's early works, the family chronicle *Buddenbrooks: Verfall einer Familie,* (1900; English translation, 1924). Gabriele Kloterjahn's family had entered a decline reminiscent of that in the Buddenbrook family: a waning of practical, bourgeois vitality and the corresponding emergence and refinement of artistic sensibilities. In Spinell's view, it would have been fitting, even desirable, for the decline to run its course. He harbors such a sublime vision of Gabriele's former life that he feels justified in reproaching Kloterjahn for intervening and presuming to reverse a natural process.

Spinell himself—solitary, unproductive, and even of dubious virility—bears the marks of a twilight generation. Among Mann's portraits of the artist, this is one of the most negative. If disease and artistic creativity go hand in hand, Spinell must be seen as a charlatan. It is questionable whether he is truly ill, and his writing seems to be an agonizing labor. He is clumsy, infantile, and ludicrous in his would-be elitism. Although he lays claim to the intellect and the word as his avenging weapons against a philistine enemy, he is portrayed as unworthy to wield them.

Style and Technique

Richard Wagner's music is not only a subject and a medium of expression in Mann's "Tristan," but also a source of the typically Mannian device of the leitmotif. Like the musical "signatures" that mark characters, objects, and ideas in Wagner's operas, the literary leitmotif may emphasize physical traits, characterize speakers, signal deeper psychological patterns, or suggest characters' affinities and antipathies. Mann most successfully employs it in its full, "musical" value with clusters of associations. Perhaps the most striking example here is Gabriele's reminiscence of her youth, which Spinell embellishes to the point of factual distortion, insisting that a golden crown gleamed in her hair as she sat in the family garden in Bremen. He recalls it in this fantastic version as he "seduces" her to play the piano; he invokes the same images in his overwrought letter to Kloterjahn; and finally he torments himself with it by persisting in the use of Frau Kloterjahn's maiden name at the loathsome sight of the Kloterjahn baby, "Gabriele Eckhof's fat son."

Mann assumes that his reader will recognize Wagner's opera when he introduces it, though neither the composer nor the title is ever named. The clues come through his verbal re-creation of the music itself—its figures, motifs, orchestral voices, and dynamics—and then through quotation of Wagner's text. This distilled evocation of the Tristan and Isolde legend, certainly one of Mann's virtuoso performances, takes Wagner's achievement one step further, as it were: For in the opera the consummation of forbidden love is unambiguously represented in word and music; in "Tristan" it is both sublimated and evaded (if it can be called love at all) in words alone. Spinell and Frau Kloterjahn do not even touch, yet what they partake of is as binding as if they had become lovers. In Mann's terms, Gabriele's ominously rapid physical decline in the days following confirms the fact. Her imminent end was already implicit in the love-death of the legendary Isolde, the musical motif that dominated and ended the rapturous scene at the piano.

As for Tristan-Spinell, his "seduction" does succeed in estranging Gabriele Kloterjahn from husband and child, but only at the price of her physical collapse and his own exposure to Kloterjahn's rage. In the story's last section, the mystical ecstasy has reverted to ironic parody. Life has the final word in the grotesque garden scene, where the shrieking, jubilantly robust baby appears with his nurse before the dazzling aureole of the sinking sun—almost a travesty of madonna and child to mock the defeated Spinell.

Michael Ritterson

THE TROUT

Author: Seán O'Faoláin (John Francis Whelan, 1900-1991)
Type of plot: Sketch
Time of plot: Unspecified
Locale: Rural Ireland
First published: 1948

> *Principal characters:*
> JULIA, a twelve-year-old Irish girl
> STEPHEN, her younger brother

The Story

Julia, a twelve-year-old Irish girl, and her family have come to a place in the country that they have visited often before, perhaps the family's home place. Still innocent enough to enjoy childish pleasure, Julia first races to a familiar dark, dank path nearly overgrown with old laurels, which she calls "The Dark Walk." This is the first year that her brother, Stephen, is old enough to go to the Dark Walk with her, and she delights in his fearful shrieks as she races ahead of him. When Julia and Stephen return to the house and begin squabbling, one of the grown-ups distracts them by asking if they found the well. Although Julia haughtily disbelieves that there can be a feature of the Dark Walk with which she is unfamiliar, she later slips away and returns to the Dark Walk to find out for herself. After much searching, she uncovers a fern-shrouded hole in a rock, which contains about a quart of water and a desperately panting trout.

After sharing her discovery first with Stephen and then with a gardener, she returns to the house to tell the grown-ups, who begin formulating theories to explain how the trout could have gotten there. It is apparent to everyone that the fish cannot survive much longer in the cranny—the summer heat is drying up the water, and the trout already has too little room even to turn over. Julia thinks about the fish all day, returning to visit it often, bringing it bits of bread dough and a worm to eat. The trout, however, will not eat—it simply lies still, panting furiously. Although concerned about the trout, Julia does not think of freeing it; it is too fascinating, and she feels that because she has found it, it is hers to enjoy.

Stephen, apparently much younger than Julia, wants their mother to invent a fanciful story to explain how the trout got in the rock, and he delights in having her tell it to him over and over. Julia scoffs when Stephen repeats the story to her, but while in bed that night she only pretends to be reading her book while she is really listening to her mother recount the story yet again. When her mother tries to turn her story into a lesson about what happens to a naughty little fish who does not stay at home with daddy trout and mammy trout, Julia begs her not to make it a moral story. Her mother obliges by inventing a fairy godmother who sends enough rain for the trout to float safely out to the nearby river. Julia, unlike Stephen, understands that in real life no fairy godmother will save her fish. Sinking into melancholy, she is upset when she hears someone unwind a fishing reel.

Horrified that someone plans to catch—and presumably eat—her fish, Julia grabs a pitcher of water and runs barefoot down the rocky path in the moonlight, frantically searching for the imprisoned trout in the late night dark. When she finally locates the slimy crevice, she grasps the terrified fish, shoves him into the pitcher, and tears down to the end of the path, releasing her trout into the river. Returning unseen to her bed, she again hears the sounds of the fishing reel and giggles with joy at her daring rescue. The next day when Stephen wonderingly announces that the trout has disappeared, Julia suggests with an air of superiority that it must have been saved by a fairy godmother.

Themes and Meanings

A mere four pages in length, "The Trout" has deeper meanings beyond the slight anecdote that appears on the surface. On one level, it may be read as a metaphor for the Irish of the nineteenth and twentieth centuries, trapped in a small country too poor in resources to hold their burgeoning population. Seán O'Faoláin is a chronicler of Irish life and ways, and Ireland has historically been a resource-poor country with a high birth rate. The history of Ireland since the potato famine in the mid-nineteenth century has been marked by periods of massive emigration. During O'Faoláin's lifetime, much of Ireland's young, well-educated population left the rural areas for the cities and suburbs, or left the country for England, the Continent, or the United States—wherever they could find greater economic opportunities.

On a more spiritual level, "The Trout" can be read as a story of a young girl's desire for mystery and her hope to continue seeing the world with wonderment, in conflict with her maturing realization that in the real world, doing nothing has its consequences. After Julia and Stephen return to the house to inform the grown-ups of their discovery of the trout, the adults begin searching for logical explanations of how it could have gotten there—such as being caught as a fingerling by a bird that then dropped it. Julia has no interest in such realistic explanations, but when her mother tries to spin a fairy tale incorporating a moral at the end, she protests and will not accept that either. She wants her trout to remain an enchanted creature that she can visit and ponder at will. Realism wins out, however, when she hears someone getting a fishing reel ready for a sure catch the next day.

By releasing the trout from the death it certainly faces, either from depleting the meager resources of its tiny well or from being caught and cooked, Julia in effect becomes the trout's fairy godmother. In doing so, she has taken a step in the direction of a self-actualizing adult, able to seize control of and change the course of a situation. She has taken a step, perhaps her first, away from being a child who believes that others—such as fairy godmothers—will save the day, and toward becoming a self-actualizing adult responsible for herself and those around her.

Style and Technique

The minimal plot of this brief story offers little opportunity for the development of conflict that might build suspense. Its point of view is that of an omniscient narrator, able to interpret the thoughts and feelings of all the characters, although, in this case, the narrator provides entrée only into Julia's mind. The story is not notable for use of irony, fantasy, emotional impact, or humor.

Although there are an indeterminate number of adults in the story, only Martin—apparently a caretaker or groundskeeper—is mentioned by name. The only character drawn in any depth is Julia, whom the reader sees as she begins her journey from childhood to adulthood, both physically and emotionally. Even she is characterized more through hints than through explicit detail—other than references to her having a long, lovely neck and long legs. Descriptions of her screaming with pleasure at the cold, dank challenge of the Dark Walk, and, at the end of the story, flying like a bird home to bed, suggest a lithe, young girl. On the other hand, she is clearly beginning her journey through adolescence to adulthood, having consciously "decided to be incredulous," because "at that age little girls are beginning to suspect most stories." She is also beginning in the smallest ways to break away from her parents: "She, in her bed, had resolutely presented her back to them and read her book. But she had kept one ear cocked."

The house and the adults are described not at all. On the other hand, the trout and the natural characteristics of the outdoors are rendered, although briefly, in some detail. Opening with his depiction of the Dark Walk as Julia experiences it, and ending with her frantic late-night journey through the walk, to the river, and back home to bed, O'Faoláin's descriptive powers give the reader a small but vivid glimpse of the Irish countryside.

Irene Struthers Rush

TRUANT

Author: Claude McKay (1889-1948)
Type of plot: Psychological
Time of plot: The 1920's
Locale: New York City
First published: 1932

Principal characters:

BARCLAY ORAM, a West Indian émigré working as a railroad car
waiter
RHODA ORAM, his wife, a former school teacher with social
aspirations
BETSY, their four-year-old daughter

The Story

Barclay Oram is viewed by others, and views himself, as just a servant boy who is subject to moodiness. Much like an adolescent truant, Barclay is seeking to define himself in relationship to the dominant social values and to come to terms with his conflicting allegiances. When he immigrated to the United States from the West Indies in search of an education and a better life, it never occurred to him that he could have attained wisdom informally, without sacrificing the "green intimate life that clustered round his village." He was seduced by an image of the cultured life, paying little attention to how his pursuit might transform his world or what compromises he would have to make in order to achieve the trappings of success that he coveted. Thus he finds himself, at the age of thirty-six, imprisoned in a steel-tempered city, cut off from his agrarian roots, playing the role of "dutiful black boy among proud and sure white men."

Throughout his life he gladly has accepted menial jobs as a way to finance his dream. When confronted with his lack of educational preparedness, he spent a year in self-study to make sure that he could pass an entrance exam. Once at the university, however, his studies gave way to his social life. He married the pregnant Rhoda not only because he was enamored of her charm, but also because he did not want her forced to accept menial employment in order to care for their child.

Barclay has been serving as a railroad car waiter on the Eastern loop for three years. He has exhibited all the traits of the loyal employee, foregoing vacations in order to collect the tips necessary to provide for his family and never missing a day of work. Despite his devotion, he has been transferred from a run on which all the employees worked as a cohesive unit to a run on which animosity and mistrust are the watchwords.

In consequence, Barclay has grown weary and bitter. Resenting the fact that he seems "fated to the lifelong tasks of the unimaginative," he decides to abandon his regular ways and play the truant. Rather than rejoining the crew after a stopover in Washington, he malingers, thus missing the train and earning himself a ten-day layoff for his negligence.

Like a suspended truant who revels in his newfound freedom, Barclay is elated and envisions spending his time in carefree pursuits such as parties and movies. Although the thought of lost income troubles him, his concern is only momentary. His wife, Rhoda, however, is less than pleased. Rather than sympathizing with the emotions that have led him to this state, she frets about the impact of his actions on herself, their child, and their social position.

Her concern with social standing leads Barclay into an extended reverie that results in his decision to desert his wife and child. He becomes the consummate truant. He renounces his connectedness to the Western world and swears his allegiance to "other gods of strange barbaric glory"—gods who value the substance rather than the symbols of the life that is lived. At the end of the story, he leaves the apartment bound for a destiny that has yet to define itself.

Themes and Meanings

The primary theme of "Truant" is the dehumanizing impact that modern civilization has on the human soul. From the initial depiction of the subway's cattlelike masses speaking in staccato voices to Barclay's reflections on his own life, Claude McKay makes it clear that in humankind's attempt to achieve progress, much that once imbued human drudgery with an inner dignity has been lost. Rather than being independent, as his ancestors were, Barclay and those around him seem to have become sycophants, enslaved to the whims of others. Because they have settled for passive roles and have become separated from one another, they expect the worst from one another and suppress their own emotional longings. For these reasons, Barclay has come to view service to others as a cruel joke and takes no pride in his own activities. Even as a father, he performs perfunctory rituals that seem to have little connection to who he is. He has so distanced himself from his fatherhood role that, more often than not, he forgets the child, unable to integrate her presence into his own definition of self.

Until he strays from his regular routine, all Barclay's actions are described in terms befitting an automaton. He kisses his wife mechanically; he mechanically accepts the tips that will allow him to support his family; he relates to his daughter in the most distracted of ways. He is a man without purpose and a man without a soul, condemned—as was the Flying Dutchman—to endlessly circle the major cities without ever making a connection or achieving a sense of personal satisfaction or achievement.

When he reflects on his current situation against the backdrop of the life he has left behind, he finds his present sterile by comparison. He misses the verdant countryside and the will-of-the-wisp ethos that made his childhood so endurable. He resents the fact that he allowed an ill-defined dream to uproot him from his homeland and thrust him into an environment that embraces values that are antithetical to those in which he believes.

Even as he rues what he has sacrificed, he is not oblivious to the fact that modern ideals also have polluted the agrarian culture of the West Indies. He remembers watching his own countrymen return from native colleges with a new air, and with a swagger that suggested that somehow they had tapped into a superior universe. He recalls a local teacher who, afraid to admit that she had become pregnant out of wedlock, dies during a botched abortion. These memories stand in sharp contrast to his memories of those he knew during his formative years: aspiring artisans, self-sufficient tillers of the soil, and free peasant girls who, unaffected by social pretense, had gone about their labors as a matter of course.

Barclay's decision to desert his present reality is not a decision to return to the life he has left behind, but a decision to carve out a new niche, to define himself in ways alien to both his homeland and his adopted land. He now has allegiances to no society. His allegiances are strictly to himself and to his tentative set of values. His life, as he defines it, is and always has been "a continual fluxion from one state to another."

Style and Technique

From the opening of the story, McKay relies on wry juxtapositions to underline what might best be termed societally induced alienation. As the tale opens, Barclay and his wife are safely ensconced in "Nigger Heaven," a Broadway theater that caters to those who love clean vaudeville. The show features the Merry Mulligans, a garishly proper vaudeville family who personify the popular cultural ideal of the happy family mindlessly skipping through life.

The show, in all of its mawkishness, appeals to Rhoda's sense of decorum, despite its unreality. This allows McKay ironically to contrast her reaction to that of Barclay. Although she is put off by the "cheap old colored shows," Barclay longs for the dynamism of the Harlem cabaret. It is therefore no surprise that when she chooses to upbraid Barclay for his irresponsible truancy, she is walking out the door to enjoy an evening of whist and dancing. Nor is it any wonder she fails to recognize the internal strife that is gradually destroying their marriage.

"Truant" revolves around conflicting personalities and mind sets. Rhoda, although a caricature of the bright woman who has used marriage as her ticket out of the workaday world, is a foil against which to present Barclay's dilemmas. Within this context, Barclay, although by no means a heroic figure, is a sympathetic character resisting the mindless and mind-numbing forces of his current environment. His decision to surrender to his own wanderlust is, finally, a decision to reclaim both his soul and his identity.

C. Lynn Munro

A TRUE RELATION OF THE APPARITION
OF ONE MRS. VEAL

Author: Daniel Defoe (1660-1731)
Type of plot: Ghost story, frame story
Time of plot: September, 1705
Locale: Canterbury, England
First published: 1706

> *Principal characters:*
> THE NARRATOR of the preface
> MRS. VEAL, a woman who dies and appears as a ghost
> MR. VEAL, her brother
> MRS. BARGRAVE, her old friend whom she visits as a ghost
> MRS. BARGRAVE'S NEIGHBOR, who relates her neighbor's story

The Story

"A True Relation of the Apparition of One Mrs. Veal" is a story in two parts: a preface and a separate account. Daniel Defoe tells a ghost story, but he strives to make the story appear to be factual.

The narrator's preface describes the passage of the story in question from Mrs. Bargrave to her neighbor, to a family member of the neighbor, to a justice of the peace, to a friend of the justice of the peace, and to the narrator of the preface. The narrator of the preface insists that everyone involved in passing along the account of the apparition is trustworthy, sober, and serious. He urges readers to learn from the described events and prepare their souls for the final reckoning.

In the account that follows the preface, Mrs. Bargrave's neighbor affirms the woman's trustworthiness. The neighbor, who heard the story from Mrs. Bargrave, explains that Mrs. Bargrave, who had not seen Mrs. Veal for two and one-half years, answered a knocking at the door and met Mrs. Veal, unaware that her old friend had died on the previous day, September 7, 1705. The women had been friends for a long time and had shared their pains and sorrows, which stemmed mainly from family troubles and hardships. Mrs. Veal expressed her regret at the lapse in the friendship and sought to reaffirm the tie between the two women, pleading for forgiveness for not having maintained contact. She assured Mrs. Bargrave of the perfection of God's plan, even if misery or suffering makes the plan seem harsh. She told her old friend that future happiness would reward her for all her sufferings. Mrs. Bargrave graciously forgave Mrs. Veal for the lapse in the friendship, and a conversation between the women proceeded for an hour and forty-five minutes, with the women recalling their preferred writings, religious books including Charles Drelincourt's *Book of Death* (1675; a translation of *Les Consolations de l'ame fidèle contre les frayeurs de la mort*, 1660) and Dr. Anthony Horneck's *The Happy Ascetick: Or, The Best Exercise* (1681). Mrs. Veal asked Mrs. Bargrave to write to her brother Mr. Veal so that he might properly distribute some of her property.

During the encounter, the ghost of Mrs. Veal made efforts not to reveal her ghostliness to Mrs. Bargrave; she refused a kiss of greeting on the grounds that she was not well, made an excuse for not accepting a cup of tea, and avoided a farewell embrace by making her departure amid the hurried business of the nearby marketplace. Nevertheless, Mrs. Bargrave did touch the dress of her old friend, a dress of "scoured silk," and this detail, according to Mrs. Veal's cousin's wife, was known only to the dead woman and her cousin's wife. In the concluding portion of the neighbor's report on Mrs. Bargrave's statement, the neighbor presents the knowledge of the "scoured silk" as proof of the veracity of her account, and the neighbor adds that the instructions for the distribution of property corroborate Mrs. Bargrave's account, despite Mr. Veal's insistence that the rings and gold were not found in the exact places referred to in the instructions.

The neighbor cannot understand Mr. Veal's rejection of Mrs. Bargrave's statements; after all, Mrs. Bargrave has nothing to gain by making false representations and now seeks privacy rather than publicity. The charges of misrepresentation, the neighbor insists, are unfair because they create unwarranted accusations and discomfort for Mrs. Bargrave, who states that she will not "give one farthing to make anyone believe" that Mrs. Veal appeared after she was dead.

Themes and Meanings

The most obvious question in "A True Relation of the Apparition of One Mrs. Veal" is whether or not ghosts exist. Although Defoe presents various affirmations about the appearance of the ghost of Mrs. Veal, he also includes contradictory information. Furthermore, the information is passed along from person to person, and such a process usually results in distortion and inaccuracy, if not falsehood. The reader is left to see the existence of ghosts as something either proven or unproven. If ghosts do exist, can they be recognized as ghosts? In Mrs. Bargrave's account of her experience, the ghost of Mrs. Veal does not seem to be a ghost. Mrs. Bargrave believes her friend to be alive. Finally, are ghosts always evil, or can they be good spirits? Ghosts are usually presumed to be frightening and evil, but Mrs. Veal's ghost is friendly, pleasant, and morally wise. Is the mortal world the realm of danger while the spirit world is the realm of friendship?

Another important issue in the story is women. The world around Mrs. Bargrave is predisposed to doubt the veracity of women. If an account of an apparition comes from a woman, then corroboration is required. Both the narrator in the preface and the neighbor who recapitulates Mrs. Bargrave's description of events are aware of the doubts raised by her gender, and both strive to clarify that Mrs. Bargrave is a speaker of proven honesty and integrity. In addition to the questions about the truthfulness of women, Defoe gives attention to the circumstances that control the lives of women in England in the eighteenth century. Women were victims of mistreatment and abuse.

Mrs. Veal's father did not provide well for his daughter. Mrs. Bargrave had to deal with "the ill-usage of a very wicked husband" who in one instance of his madness found it necessary to smash teacups. Mr. Veal and his family do not like Mrs. Bargrave's report about Mrs. Veal, and Veal himself charges that a "bad husband" drove Mrs. Bargrave crazy and made her subject to delusions.

Beyond these discussions of ghosts and women, the moral implications of "A True Relation of the Apparition of One Mrs. Veal" are strong. Friendship is a blessing in life. Friends can be supportive of one another, offer courtesies and hospitality to each other, and exchange opinions and ideas. Unfortunately, friendship may falter, perhaps because of changes in residences or family connections. This withering of friendship is regrettable, and if the withering cannot be prevented, then true friends should strive to restore the friendship. Between women, a friendship may be particularly significant. Women who face hardships and abuse gather strength from mutual support. Perhaps the ghost of Mrs. Veal offers the greatest support to Mrs. Bargrave when the ghost assures Mrs. Bargrave of the justice in God's plan. Devotion to God will be rewarded. Even if God's plan includes hardship and suffering in the temporal world, the eternal world offers happiness.

Style and Technique

Defoe is the father of realistic fiction in English. In *Robinson Crusoe* (1719), *A Journal of the Plague Year* (1722), and *Moll Flanders* (1722), Defoe writes fictional pieces that are grounded in history and contemporary reality. Defoe's meticulous attention to detail includes dates, dialogue, place-names, and a journalistic format. In "A True Relation of the Apparition of One Mrs. Veal," Defoe's narrator offers Mrs. Bargrave's neighbor's report as an authentic document. The tone of each of the narrators is insistent, as if the truth about an occurrence could be established by the force behind the spoken word. Setting also is intended to reinforce belief. A ghost story might be doubted, but one cannot be as doubtful if the ghost appears in a woman's private home, in her private seating area, with her familiar elbow chair serving as the seat for the ghost. The home is in Canterbury, a place all readers can identify. The home is part of a neighborhood whose closeness to the marketplace makes the home part of everyday, ordinary life.

In comparison with other short stories, "A True Relation of the Apparition of One Mrs. Veal" does not emerge as a typical story. The events of the story do not constitute a plot. The narrator of the preface is not clearly identified, and then suddenly events are related by Mrs. Bargrave's neighbor. No return to the original point of view occurs. The work is fiction but has the appearance of a journalistic report.

William T. Lawlor

A TRUE STORY
Repeated Word for Word as I Heard It

Author: Mark Twain (Samuel Langhorne Clemens, 1835-1910)
Type of plot: Realism
Time of plot: About 1852-1865
Locale: Virginia and North Carolina
First published: 1874

> *Principal characters:*
> AUNT RACHEL, a sixty-year-old former slave
> MISTO C——, the frame-story narrator
> HENRY, Aunt Rachel's youngest son

The Story

At the close of a summer day the narrator sits on a farmhouse porch atop a hill. A sixty-year-old black servant, Aunt Rachel, sits respectfully on a lower step cheerfully enduring merciless chafing. As the powerful woman roars with laughter, the narrator asks her how it is that she has never had any trouble. Taken aback, she replies, "Misto C——, is you in 'arnest?" Sobered by her manner, he explains that he has never seen her other than cheerful. Aunt Rachel becomes grave and begins her story.

Rachel tells the narrator that even though she was once a slave, she had a husband as loving to her as he is to his own wife, and that they had seven children whom they dearly loved. She was raised in Virginia ("ole Fo-ginny"), but her quick-tempered mother was raised in Maryland and was fiercely proud of her heritage. One day when Rachel's little son Henry cut his wrist and forehead badly, everyone flew around, anxious to help him. In their excitement, they spoke back to Rachel's mother, who snapped, "I wan't bawn in de mash to be fool' by trash! I's one o' de ole Blue Hen's Chickens, I is!" She then cleared everyone out and bandaged the boy herself. Rachel adds that she uses her mother's expression herself when she gets riled.

As Rachel recalls the time when her mistress went broke and auctioned off all her slaves in Richmond, she warms to her subject and gradually rises, until she towers over the narrator. Her recollection of the slave auction is vivid. One by one, her husband and children were sold and she was beaten as she cried in protest. When only her youngest child, Henry, remained, she held him tightly, threatening to kill anyone who touched him. Henry whispered to her that he would run away and work so that he could buy her freedom. Despite Rachel's fierce resistance, Henry was eventually taken away. Since that day, twenty-two years ago, Rachel has not set eyes on her husband or six of her children.

The man who bought Rachel took her to "Newbern" (New Bern, North Carolina?), where she became the family cook. During the war her master became a Confederate colonel, but when the Union took the town, he fled, leaving his slaves behind. Union Army officers then occupied the house and Rachel cooked for them. These officers treated her respectfully and gave her unquestioned command over her kitchen.

Remembering Henry's vow to escape to the North, Rachel one day asked the officers if they might have seen him. She described Henry as very little, with scars on his wrist and forehead, but a general reminded her that after thirteen years Henry would now be a man—something that she had forgotten. She did not then know that Henry had indeed run off to the North, worked as a barber for years, and hired himself out to Union officers so that he could ransack the South looking for his mother.

Now the Union headquarters, Rachel's house was often the site of soldier balls, during which she jealously guarded her kitchen. One night, there was a ball for black soldiers, who particularly irritated her. When a spruce young man danced into her kitchen with a woman, she said, "Gid along wid you!—rubbage!" The remark made the man's expression momentarily change. Other men then came in, playing music and putting on airs. Rachel tried to drive them out, but they merely laughed until she straightened up and said, "I want you niggers to understan' dat I wa'nt bawn in de mash to be fool' by trash! I's one o' de ole Blue Hen's Chickens, I is!" Again the young man seemed to react to her words.

As Rachel finally drove the men from her kitchen, she overheard the young man tell a companion that he would not return with the others that night. Early the next morning, as Rachel removed biscuits from the oven, the same young man unexpectedly reappeared and looked her closely in the eye. Suddenly she knew. She dropped her pan and examined his scarred wrist and forehead. It was her Henry.

"Oh, no, Misto C——," Rachel says, "I hain't had no trouble. An' no joy!"

Themes and Meanings

The essence of this tale is in fact a true story. During one of the many summers that Mark Twain spent near Elmira, New York, he heard the story from Mary Ann ("Auntie") Cord, a former slave who worked at his sister-in-law's farm. Aunt Rachel's "Misto C——" is thus "Mr. Clemens"—Twain himself. In November, 1874, Twain published the story in the *Atlantic Monthly*. It was his first contribution to that prestigious magazine, as well as one of the earliest stories in which he developed a fully rounded African American character and one of the few stories that he ever wrote featuring a strong woman character.

At its simplest level, "A True Story" concerns human endurance in the face of terrible personal loss. Although raised a slave and violently separated from her loving husband and children, Aunt Rachel has remained strong and exceptionally cheerful. So cheerful is she, in fact, that the narrator, who presumably has known her for years, has no inkling of the troubles that she has endured.

At a deeper level, "A True Story" is a tale of revelation—the revelation to a white person that African Americans—even slaves—can share similar feelings of love and devotion. Early in her narrative, Aunt Rachel tells the narrator that her husband

> was lovin' an' kind to me, jist as kind as you is to yo' own wife. An' we had chil'en—
> seven chil'en—an' we loved dem chil'en jist de same as you loves yo' chil'en. Dey was

black, but de Lord can't make no chil'en so black but what dey mother loves 'm and
wouldn't give 'm up, no, not for anything dat's in dis whole world.

The fact that black people have the same emotions as other people was not taken for
granted by whites during Twain's time. He develops the idea more fully in *Adventures
of Huckleberry Finn* (1884), in which Huck gradually understands that Jim, his black
companion who is fleeing from slavery, is as fully human as himself. During their raft
journey, Huck happens to see Jim with his head down, moaning to himself. Sensing
that Jim is thinking about his wife and children, Huck confesses, "I do believe he
cared just as much for his people as white folks does for their'n. It don't seem natural,
but I reckon it's so." The frame-narrator of "A True Story" makes a similar discovery
when he hears Aunt Rachel's story. The common humanity of all peoples is thus a
central theme in both stories.

Style and Technique

As a story within a story, "A True Story" exemplifies the frame-story technique in
which the first narrator (Misto C——) provides the "frame" within which the second
narrator (Aunt Rachel) tells the main story. By alternating the voices of his two narrators here, Twain tells two different stories simultaneously. While Aunt Rachel relates
the dramatic story of her family, the frame-narrator's occasional remarks quietly reveal the shifting relationship between Aunt Rachel and himself.

When the frame-narrator begins his narrative, he is sitting on a high porch, while
Aunt Rachel sits "respectfully below our level, on the steps." As Aunt Rachel unfolds
her story, her position gradually becomes dominant. By the time she recalls the slave
auction, "she towered above me, black against the stars." Although no more is said on
this subject, it is clear that the relative moral positions of the characters are reversed,
with Aunt Rachel clearly in the superior position at the story's end.

The most obvious stylistic technique employed in this story is the use of realistic
African American dialect. Most of the story is narrated in Aunt Rachel's own, unaffected voice. One of Twain's great strengths as a writer was his ear for language and
ability to render it accurately. Here again, "A True Story" anticipates *Adventures of
Huckleberry Finn*, which also makes heavy use of southern black dialects—especially for the character Jim.

In 1992, publicity surrounding the recent rediscovery of a comparatively obscure
article ("Sociable Jimmy") that Twain published in *The New York Times* in 1874 focused national attention on the extent to which the language of *Adventures of Huckleberry Finn* is "black." Recalling the delightfully natural and artless conversation of a
young black boy whom he had met during a stop on a lecture tour, Twain's article resembles "A True Story" in attempting to re-create a conversation word for word.
Twain wrote the *Times* article around the same time that he wrote "A True Story" and
addressed similar questions about African American dialects in both.

R. Kent Rasmussen

THE TRUMPET

Author: Walter de la Mare (1873-1956)
Type of plot: Realism
Time of plot: The late Victorian period
Locale: A village in England
First published: 1936

>   *Principal characters:*
>   PHILIP, a small boy, the son of the rector
>   DICK, another small boy, the illegitimate son of the rector's
>   former parlor maid
>   MRS. SULLIVAN, the rector's cook

The Story

It is nearly midnight on October 31, the night before All Saints' Day. A tiny church is deserted. The beams of the full moon have not yet pierced its darkness directly, but here and there a marble head, a wing tip, a pointing finger gleams coldly.

A stealthy footfall crunches on the rain-soaked gravel, a key is heard turning in a lock, a toy lantern emerges from behind the vestry curtain carried by a small boy. He is shivering from the cold and from qualms and forebodings. He calls low and hoarsely, "Dick, are you there?" When there is no answer, he timidly enters a pew, rapidly repeats a prayer and half-covertly crosses himself. While he is admiring the gilded figure of an angel, he hears a faint shuffle in the vestry. He drops out of sight and wails. No response. He is certain that this must be the friend he is expecting but worries that it is not. He leaps up and flashes the lantern into the glittering eyes of a dwarfish and motionless shape that is wearing a battered black mask. He shudders with rage and terror while Dick roars with laughter.

Philip angrily tells his friend to be quiet and to remember that he is in a church. Dick is at once solemn and contrite. He explains that he is late because he was first waiting for his father to finish reading. Asked if his father would have whacked him much if he had caught him leaving, Dick replies that his mother will not let him punish the boy. Dick then says that his mother came home yesterday with an enormous bundle of old clothes, including a green silk dressing gown, which he is now wearing under his jacket. Philip immediately recognizes it as his own but says loftily that he does not want it now. He suddenly remarks that if Dick's real father had found him skulking in the church he would whack him hot and strong. Dick stiffens and denies this, adding that his real father leaves him alone although he went rabbiting with him one night last summer until the moon came up. Besides, his father is dead.

Philip immediately contradicts this. He heard his people reading aloud from a newspaper only a few days ago and he knows what has become of the man. He says cruelly that if Dick's other father had not been Chapel, he would never have had any father to show and his mother could not have continued to live in the village. Now there is a discussion about ghosts with Philip claiming, unconvincingly, that he does not believe in them and that he came only because Dick dared him to come. He promises to dare Dick in a minute.

Dick goes outside to reconnoiter for ghosts while Philip stares again at a huge figure of the angel clasping a gilded trumpet. This angel has been for some years the habitual center of his Sunday evening reveries whenever he is escorted to church by the family cook. He has asked the cook why the angel was made so that she cannot blow the trumpet, but the real question in his mind is what would happen if she did. Mrs. Sullivan, the cook, has suggested that the angel is depicted as waiting for the Last Day. Philip still wants to know what will happen after the Last Day; he is fascinated by any reference to an angel or a trumpet.

Twelve o'clock strikes; nothing happens. Philip has lost faith in the angel's power. As he sits there, cold and sick, he hears a fiendish screech and sees a lean, faceless shape coming toward his pew. Recognizing Dick, he is despite his terror passionately angry. He dares Dick to stay on in the church alone; if Dick is afraid, he will never again be allowed to enter Philip's house or yard. Philip now proposes several impractical dares and finally orders Dick to climb almost to the roof and blow the trumpet. He says that if anyone blows the trumpet it will be the Last Day. Dick asks what the Bible says about angels, and Philip recounts many instances of their mention and then describes their awesome power, insisting that the Devil has crowds of angels under his command.

Philip starts to leave. Dick detects scorn on his face and says that he has always done anything that Philip asked. He begins to climb. Philip suddenly realizes how enormously high the angel rises. He calls to Dick to come down, but Dick cannot hear him. Philip leaves the church but flies back to tempt Dick with the news that someone, not a man and not a woman, is coming. He is sobbing with rage, apprehension, and despair.

Dick shouts down to ask if they can still be friends if he blows with all his might and the trumpet does not sound. Philip begs him to come down, but Dick declares calmly, "I believe it is hollow, and I think she knows I'm here. You won't say I was afraid now! Philip, I'd do anything in the world for you."

The tapering wooden trumpet splinters off from the angel's grasp and Dick, clutching it, falls to the flagstones below. He is dead. In anguish, Philip creeps home.

Themes and Meanings

"The Trumpet" is considered by some critics to be Walter de la Mare's finest tale, but all find it difficult to classify. Unlike many others, it is not a ghost story, yet it is permeated by a ghostly atmosphere. Strictly speaking, it is not a moral fable, and although it is about children, it is not children's literature. Perhaps it is best termed a symbolic tragedy: the failure of the individual to pierce the veil between the known and the unknown, the natural and the supernatural.

In the ghostly silence of the moonlit church, the marble angel is as real as are the little boys. The recitation of stories of angels in the Bible authenticates their existence while the trumpet due to announce the Last Day poses questions about life, death, and an afterlife for the believer and the unbeliever alike. Mysticism is graphic here. Only Mrs. Sullivan's conversation offers a criterion of normality.

The clue to one meaning of this haunting tragedy lies in its two epigraphs: "For Brutus, as you know, was Caesar's angel." and "And he said . . . am I my brother's keeper?" The two boys are half brothers but do not know it. This suggests that all men are brothers but fail to realize it and to behave as brothers should. Although Philip is the pathetic embodiment of arrogance and cruelty, he is understood and worshiped by the great-hearted, happy, mischievous imp, Dick. Despite social distinctions and differing levels of education, brotherly love is possible, but the price is high. Dick dies in an effort to gratify his brother's obsessive urge for knowledge of life's mysteries.

Style and Technique

The descriptions in the story are pure poetry, but they contain no words for their own sake. Each detail helps to build the atmosphere, to delineate character, or to further the action. The eerie quality is established at once by the date, the midnight hour, the cemetery, the dark church with moonbeams playing on marble tombs, the discussion about ghosts, and the stealthy manner of Philip. His obsession introduces the ultimate mystery.

Character is built by the boys' conversations: Philip's snobbish attitude toward the used clothing that his mother has given to Dick's mother; Philip's very unkind remarks about Dick's mother and presumed father; Dick's praise of the kindness of Philip's mother and his own determination to be a comfort to his mother.

Small details serve to foreshadow the tragedy: The law of gravitation is mentioned, as are the brittle walls of Dick's neat skull; Philip announces that he would like to see Dick's ghost; Dick's beautiful singing voice "would need no angelic tuition—even in a better world." Disaster is implicit from the start.

Although some of the conversation between the boys is completely realistic, that of Philip is less believable when he recounts at length stories from the Bible. It is true that he has been forced to sit through his father's sermons since he was a baby and has searched the Bible for information about angels and trumpets. However, the reader finds the glib recital unnatural in the mouth of a small boy, even one with a haunting obsession. Again there is the mingling of the real and the unreal.

De la Mare's true triumph in this weird story is his use of two little boys and a church monument to create an atmosphere of refined spiritual terror that symbolizes the human urge to find answers to life's mystery.

Dorothy B. Aspinwall

TRUTH AND LIES

Author: Reynolds Price (1933-   )
Type of plot: Social realism
Time of plot: The 1960's
Locale: Kinley, a small town near the North Carolina-Virginia border
First published: 1970

> *Principal characters:*
> SARAH WILSON, a forty-two-year-old schoolteacher, the wife of
>   Nathan Wilson
> NATHAN WILSON, her husband
> ELLA SCOTT, an eighteen-year-old former student of Mrs. Wilson
>   and the mistress of Nathan
> MR. WHITLOW, a stationmaster

The Story

Sarah Wilson has spent her life in Kinley, a rural community in that area north of Raleigh, North Carolina, and south of Richmond, Virginia. She has left the area only for the four years she spent in college preparing to become a teacher. When she finished her training, she had no real reason to return to Kinley. Both her parents were dead, and she was their only child. She decided to take the best offer when she entered the job market, but instead took the first offer. It came from Nathan Wilson, who had been principal for three years of the school in Ogburn, the next small town from Kinley. She married him that June before she began her first and only teaching job.

As the story opens, Sarah is in an open field at night beside the railroad tracks. She sits in her car, and at eight o'clock, she flashes the lights. Someone comes running down the embankment, through the high grasses, to her car. It is Ella Scott, her former student, now an eighteen-year-old woman, who thinks that Nathan is in the car. Sarah has come because when Nathan came home drunk, she found an unsigned note in his pocket, arranging the meeting.

When she shows Ella the note, she comments that Ella's handwriting has improved. The meeting between them is remarkably calm. Ella is properly respectful of Sarah, and she is totally candid in telling her about the relationship between herself and Nathan. Sarah, accustomed to hurt and disappointment, is not going to allow her emotions to control this tense situation.

It is hot, and she suggests to Ella that they will be more comfortable if they drive around and talk. Ella gets into the car, and as they drive the story of her meetings with Nathan, which now have been going on for eight months, unfolds, as does the story of Sarah's childhood and eventual marriage to Nathan.

Sarah drives toward the railroad station, which at this time of night should be closed, because the last train of the day has left. Mr. Whitlow, the stationmaster, is just coming out of the station when they arrive, and he talks with them, revealing elements of Sarah's background. He has known her most of her life.

When they leave the station, Sarah drives down the Ogburn road, past Holt Ferguson's land, which runs on for a quarter mile. She reveals to Ella that this land had once belonged to her grandfather. It passed on to her father, whose marriage house, the house in which Sarah was brought up, was built on it. She tells of how, being an only child, she kept begging her parents for brothers, for company. Her mother always responded, "Sarah, I thought we were happy. Why aren't you satisfied?" When Sarah was twelve, her mother had another child. It was born dead, and four months later, never having recovered from childbirth, her mother died at her twelve-year-old daughter's feet.

Sarah and her father went on living quite happily in the house until her father had a stroke when the girl was fifteen. At that point, Holt Ferguson's wife, Aunt Alice, who was the father's half sister, got Holt to move their whole family into the house with Sarah and her father. Their children were boys, and although Sarah had always wanted a brother, she regarded these children as intruders. Aunt Alice had always had designs on this property that her stepfather had owned.

When Sarah's father died two years later, the girl assumed that the property would be hers. She had always dreamed that one day she would own it. Eventually, however, it was revealed to her that Holt had bought the whole property from Sarah's father for enough money to send Sarah to college.

Sarah goes on to say that she and Nathan, who had spent his life until he came to Ogburn running away from himself, had been unable to have children. She tells Ella that the reason they are childless is that Nathan is sterile. She then begs Ella to give up Nathan.

Ella then reveals that she has been planning to give up Nathan, but she needs to see him one more time. Sarah discourages this final meeting, telling Ella that she will tell Nathan anything she wants conveyed to him. Finally, Ella reveals that she had sent Nathan the note and had tried to see him that night to tell him that she had taken the bus to Raleigh that week and "ditched a baby in a nigger kitchen for two hundred dollars," just as she had promised Nathan she would. She said she would pay her half of the two hundred dollars as soon as she could.

Themes and Meanings

"Truth and Lies" is really the story of a life that has been sustained through compromise. Sarah Wilson never got what she wanted from life, and as the action of this story develops, the reader sees a woman desperately trying to cling to whatever she can. In this case, she is clinging to a marriage that was initially based on need rather than on love. The stationmaster tells Ella that Sarah got out of Kinley, but that her mistake was in coming back. He asks her what brought her back: "Love, won't it, Sarah?" and she replies, "I don't remember that far. Maybe it was," and changes the subject.

Sarah has no illusions about Nathan. The first time she ever saw him, he was drunk, and he has more or less stayed drunk ever since. He told her on the first night she met him at a Christmas party that he was running away from himself, that he had hurt women in the past. By the time Sarah married him, she had grown accustomed to not having what she wanted: She had no siblings, her mother died trying to give her one, her father died, and she learned that the property that she had always thought would be hers would not be. The reader is also told that even in her youth, Sarah's face had "never won praise."

Sarah has lied to Ella, quite unnecessarily, in the hope of making her lose interest in Nathan. When she finally realizes that Ella knows that she has lied to her, Sarah can only say to herself as she drives her car homeward alone, killing a rabbit that runs into its path, "How could I, why should I tell the truth when I thought I could save what was left of our life."

One is left with the feeling that nothing will change. Nathan will go on drinking. He will find other women. However, he needs Sarah, just as Sarah needs him, and they will play out the charade that they began twenty years earlier because they can do little else and because they have grown accustomed to living in this fashion.

Style and Technique

Reynolds Price is a consummate storyteller whose writing has done for Warren County, North Carolina, what Faulkner's did for the area around Oxford, Mississippi. Price, born and reared in rural Macon, North Carolina, is close to his roots, and he tells his tales in the long monologues that are characteristic of much southern conversation. He captures the conflicts and frustrations of people living in relative isolation, people who go to school, sometimes finish, sometimes do not, and then go on to work in textile mills. The women, as he notes in this story, work in the mills until they marry, then they begin producing children in substantial numbers.

Sarah is a cut above the people in her small town. Her father owned land. He earned eighty-five dollars a month as a station agent. The family, although not rich, had been relatively refined, and its members valued one another. The reader also learns that the family never stopped talking except from fatigue, and Sarah's lengthy speeches to Ella are excellent examples of the incessant talk that characterizes southerners of the kind Price writes about in this story.

The rhythm of southern speech obviously resonates in Price's memory, and he records it with a fidelity found in such southern writers as Faulkner, Guy Owen, Thad Stem, and Eudora Welty. His stories are subtle, and in them he drops only the faintest hints at times of the convolutions that are the underpinnings of their action. In the present story, for example, the reader learns that there was no smile when Ella and Sarah recognized each other, and shortly thereafter, the absence of a smile is noted again. The implication is that Sarah's life has been lived without smiles. She has always done what she must, not what she would have preferred.

R. Baird Shuman

TRUTH OR CONSEQUENCES

Author: Alice Adams (1926-1999)
Type of plot: Domestic realism
Time of plot: The 1930's
Locale: Hilton, a fictitious southern city
First published: 1982

> *Principal characters:*
> EMILY AMES, the narrator
> CARSTAIRS JONES, her obsession

The Story

The story opens with the narrator, Emily Ames, reading a gossip column about Carstairs Jones marrying a famous former movie star, and she decides that this man must be the same Car Jones whom she knew many years earlier. She then recounts the history of that extraordinary spring when she first met Car Jones in the seventh grade. She relives the day when she played "truth or consequences" with friends and said that she would rather kiss Car Jones than be eaten alive by ants.

Emily and her mother moved to the university town of Hilton the fall before the principal action of the story takes place. Emily felt like an outsider in this town. As a recent transplant from the North to the South, she felt removed from her classmates; at eleven years of age, she was younger than her seventh-grade classmates; and the fact that her mother was rich embarrassed Emily, who felt "more freakish than advantageous." She felt socially insecure and approached the playground always with excited dread. On one particular April day, she was asked to play truth or consequences with the popular girls. After some innocuous questions, they sprang the big question on her: Would she rather be covered with honey and eaten alive by ants in the desert, or kiss Car Jones? When Emily said that she would prefer the kiss, the other children began to tease her. She did not feel overly embarrassed by the attention, however, because she felt that she had suddenly been discovered after months of invisibility.

If Emily felt socially insecure, Car felt socially removed. The quintessential outsider, he was fourteen, the tallest, the most easily bored, and the most rebellious boy in the class. He was also a "truck child"—the offspring of people living on the farms surrounding the town who sent their children to school in yellow trucks. To Emily, Car was an abnormal person. The narrator recalls him as representing dark and strange forces, although she herself had just come into the light. Although the young Emily could not afford to have anything to do with Car, her literal mind acknowledged a certain obligation. After a number of notes were sent from Car to Emily, a rendezvous was planned: They were to meet in a vacant lot beside the school on a Saturday morning.

The meeting was not what Emily expected. Car was rude and surly; his teeth were stained and his hands dirty. He pulled Emily by her hair, planted a kiss on her, and walked off with a look of pure rage.

When Emily returned home, her mother told her that a boy called. Emily worried that it was Car, but it was Harry McGinnis, a glowing, golden boy. The narrator says that she felt saved because she was normal after all and belonged in the world of light and lightheartedness. Car Jones had not altered her in any way. Emily was embarrassed about seeing Car at school the next week, but to her relief he was not there. After he demanded to be placed in another class, he took a test and was reassigned to the high school sophomore class. Emily never saw him again but continued to hear rumors about him: He attended the university, he went "all the way" with a high school girl, he wrote a play as an English graduate student, and he turned down admission into a fraternity.

The story closes with Emily's conjectures about Car's life. She tries to imagine what his background was really like, what his innermost thoughts were. She concludes that he does not think about the past, that he never thinks about having been a truck child or one of the deprived. However, the story ends with the narrator thinking that perhaps Car may be as haunted by the past as she has been.

Themes and Meanings

"Truth or Consequences" is a story about recognitions, about the discovery of truths and the consequences of actions. It appears to be a story mainly about Car Jones, but it is in fact more about the narrator and her recognition of the truths about her life. The narrator acknowledges at the end that she has no clue about the inner workings of Car's mind, or even about his background. To her he had merely been one of the truck children, greeted by his classmates "with a total lack of interest; he might as well have been invisible, or been black." Of course, Emily does take some interest in him, but she acknowledges, at least in retrospect, that she "was having a wonderful time, at his expense." She won her golden boy, Harry McGinnis, because Car's attention made her visible to her peers. She says she giggles in a "silly new way" when McGinnis asks her out because she has entered the world of normality and left behind Car's "dark and strange" world. She recognizes that her entry into the world of the "popular girls" was effected by her use of the nearly invisible Car.

After Emily is kissed by Car, she dashes from the lot; years later, she reflects that she "was learning conformity fast, practicing up for the rest of my life." She has lived what she considers a normal life for a woman of her age: three children, three abortions, and three marriages to increasingly "rich and prominent" men. Her obsessive interest in Car Jones suggests her disillusionment with the "normal world," with the consequences of her actions that were predicated on conformity, on becoming one with the crowd. She is fixated on Car and on her reinvention of him because he represents the world of rebelliousness, of saying no to the "proper course," whether it be a fraternity that he was invited to join or a career path that would have let him be one of the "rich and prominent" men.

Style and Technique

Because the characters in Alice Adams's story inhabit a larger world, the opening section of the story is devoted to a description not so much of character as of setting. The playground is discussed in terms of levels where the different ages and sexes are assigned. The reader is also introduced to the southern university town and the intricacies of its class system even before the reader meets Car for the first time because the class hierarchies determine to a large extent the type of relationship Car and Emily can have. Given her character, her eagerness to conform and lead a "normal life," it is clear early that rigid social conventions will not allow an intimacy to develop between Car and the narrator. They are separated by too great a gulf.

If the southern social world plays a significant role in the story, so does the southern climate. Emily, who had recently moved from the North, witnesses her first southern spring at the same time that she enters into society. She is "astounded by the bursting opulence" of spring, "enchanted with the yards of the stately houses of professors." This opulence and enchantment seem to conspire against any hope of attachment or communion between Car and Emily; if she is attracted to opulence and stateliness, Car can be no object of desire. He is necessary only because he allows her to have an "altered awareness" of herself. Like the southern spring that seemed so "extraordinary in itself," Emily began to see that she could "command attention," that she was pretty and was no longer invisible.

What is interesting about the "present time" of the story, the moment when she reads the paper in which the bit of gossip about a "man named Carstairs Jones" appears, is that it is without setting, without season, without time. The present of the story encroaches on the past not at all; in fact, it is the past that is richly alive, vibrant, full of color and tension. All we know of the narrator's current life is that she is married to a "successful surgeon" and she is "haunted by everything that ever happened in" her life. She is haunted by Car's memory because of his ability to live at a distance from respectability, from conventionality, from her world.

Kevin Boyle

THE TUMBLERS

Author: Nathan Englander (1970-   )
Type of plot: Holocaust, war
Time of plot: World War II
Locale: The ghetto in Chelm, Poland, and a circus train
First published: 1998

> *Principal characters:*
> MENDEL, an active member of the Mahmir Hasidim
> GRONAM THE OX, his grandfather
> THE REBBE, the religious leader of the Mahmir Hasidim
> A FRENCH HORN PLAYER, a Gentile woman who helps Mendel
> RAIZEL, a widow who helps sew costumes

The Story

"The Tumblers" is told in the third person through an omniscient narrator. The main action in the story occurs during the Holocaust both in Chelm, a ghetto town that in the classic Yiddish tales is traditionally peopled by fools, and on a second-class train filled with a circus troupe.

The protagonist, Mendel, is the grandson of Gronam the Ox, a town leader whose comic actions follow the tradition of the absurd tales involving the fools of Chelm. Gronam won notoriety for his quick thinking when he renamed all the bad things in the ghetto as good things and renamed those items in short supply as those items that were in abundance. When the town's dairy restaurant ran short of sour cream, a necessary ingredient for many traditional dishes during the Feast of Weeks, Gronam told the townspeople to think of water as sour cream and sour cream as water. These examples demonstrated his ludicrous wisdom. Mendel trades gold for potatoes from the surrounding town. He moves from the ghetto to the surrounding town through the sewer passages, thus learning about life outside the confines of the ghetto. He brings news of the German trains that are coming to Chelm.

In Chelm, as in other towns, there are two distinct religious Hasidic Jewish groups: the students of the Mekyl Hasidim, or lenient interpreters of Jewish law, and the students of the Mahmir Hasidim, or strict interpreters of Jewish law. When it comes time to board the German trains and the Jews are told to bring only "essential items," the Mekyls' leader interprets this as meaning that his followers should bring everything one would need to stock a summer home. However, the Mahmir rabbi (or Rebbe) interprets the word "essentials" more strictly—and also in response to what he sees as the shameful indulgence of the Mekyls—so he tells his followers that they should bring only their long underwear.

At the train station, the Mahmir Rebbe orders his followers to stay away from the Mekyls with all of their possessions and heads for a passenger train far down the track, a distance away from the Mekyls. The trains that the Mekyls were waiting for were packed with people; the train that the Mahmirim boarded was filled with circus people, entertainers waiting for clear passage to an important engagement.

On the train with the circus troupe, the Mahmirim are mistaken for acrobats because of their shaved heads, skinny bodies, and colorless attire. Mendel uses his skills with outsiders to infiltrate the non-Jewish circus community. Because he was once a Mekyl and still enjoys drinking excessively, he goes penniless to the club car to try to get someone to buy him a drink. There he meets a woman French horn player who buys him a drink and tells him that the others on the train think they are acrobats. She also tells him that the other trains went away full of people and returned empty. When Mendel returns to the car with the Mahmirim, the Rebbe acts quickly. He realizes that the people in the other trains were being eradicated. He tells his followers that they must learn to tumble in order not to disappear like those in the other trains.

Mendel learns about costumes and acrobatic moves while the Mahmirim practice tumbling moves. The Rebbe keeps the group focused on tumbling practice and religious prayers while Mendel works on gathering discarded articles for Raizel to sew onto the Mahmirim's long underwear for costumes.

On arrival at a large ornate building filled with elegantly dressed patrons, the other circus performers exhibit efficiency, a quality Mendel realizes is lacking in the Mahmirs. The Rebbe acts as a booster for their routine and encourages his followers. During their performance, the audience laughs at them and hurtles anti-Jewish remarks, thinking that the acrobats are not Jews, but individuals who are mocking stereotypical Jewish behavior.

Themes and Meanings

An important theme in Nathan Englander's "The Tumblers" is the struggle of the individual against society. The story takes place during the Holocaust, when being identified as a Jew in areas controlled by the Nazis was a death sentence. It offers a quasi-humorous escape route for the Mahmirim, who are strict observers of Jewish and civil laws. The group is repulsed by the more liberal-thinking Mekyls, who bend the Jewish and civil law to suit their own purposes. The implication is that because the Mekyls behave in a stereotypically greedy manner, they are not as able to shed their acquisitions and thus become trapped by the Nazi regime.

Another point associated with the theme of the struggle of the individual against society is related to how Jews are perceived by the greater populace. If Gentiles view Jews as clumsy and farcical, that perception would be difficult, if not impossible, to erase. The audience laughs at the acrobats, who they believe are mimicking Jewish behavior. When the final scene includes heckling from audience members who demand a longer performance, Mendel impetuously puts his hands out as if he were testing the waters to see if he was safe. There was no other place in the realm of his experience that he would have been able to act as spontaneously.

The entire story is filled with self-deception and self-discovery. From the start, when the townspeople of Chelm hold Gronam in high regard because he renamed all that was scarce as all that was plentiful, it is evident that these people prefer to be deceived rather than to accept the reality that they are trapped in a ghetto. They continue to deceive themselves while they are in the town, but when they are faced with boarding the death train, they must choose between deception and discovery. The Mahmirim discovered that by shedding their possessions they gained an advantage over those who deceived themselves by thinking that everything would return to normal.

Friendship and brotherhood is also an important theme. Mendel is a friend to the Mahmirim and saves their lives by sharing information learned from befriending a Gentile musician from the circus on the train. The Rebbe serves as the leader of a brotherhood of Jewish followers who survive by listening to his advice.

Another theme is illusion and reality. The illusion of the Mahmirim, dressed in their long underwear, being acrobats helps disguise their identity as Jews and protects them from extermination. The revelation of the magical trains that made huge numbers of Jews and others disappear is presented as illusionary but actually is reality. The horror of the Holocaust is masked by absurd scenes of pious individuals in gray long underwear that has been decorated with trinkets and discards from the diner car. Envisioning men and women tumbling in such strange outfits creates a jovial image in an otherwise abhorrent scene.

Style and Technique

Englander uses absurd circumstances in a horrific time to illustrate the interaction of Jews within their community as well as the reactions of others to Jewish people during the Holocaust. Even though he does not mention the Nazis by name, he does state that his story takes place during the Holocaust.

By placing his story in Chelm, Englander connects his work with all the classic Yiddish stories of the foolish inhabitants of that fictional city. He makes Mendel a direct descendant of a well-known character in the Chelm stories, Gronam the Ox. This creates continuity for readers who are familiar with Isaac Bashevis Singer's Shalom Alechem stories. He also offers enough examples of Gronam's faulty logic for any reader to understand the premise on which Mendel's education has been built.

Even though Mendel is somewhat simple, he is a more worldly character than most of the others in the story. He gained his worldliness from his exposure to the world outside the ghetto while trading for food and from his experiences as a Mekyl, when he did not strictly adhere to Jewish law. Mendel's drinking, an activity uncommon for strictly religious Jewish people, enabled him to fit into the drinking crowd in the dining car, so the Rebbe chose him to be the group's undercover agent. Thus, Mendel is able to explain the purpose of the trains and provide a possible method of escape for his fellow Mahmirim.

Englander depicts the Rebbe as a learned person, whose knowledge is derived from Jewish law and is applicable in any circumstance. By showing the universality of the rabbi's wisdom, the author subtly refutes the implication throughout the story that Jews are materialistic, clumsy, and ignorant.

Annette M. Magid

THE TWENTY-SEVENTH MAN

Author: Nathan Englander (1970-   )
Type of plot: Metafiction, frame story
Time of plot: Between 1949 and 1953
Locale: Prison in Russian village X
First published: 1999

Principal characters:
PINCHAS PELOVITS, an unpublished writer
VASILY KORINSKY, the author of an ode praising Stalin
MOISHE BRETZKY, a Yiddish poet
Y. ZUNSER, a famous, elderly Yiddish writer

The Story

The main action in the "The Twenty-seventh Man" occurs within the Russian village of X and its prison. Orders are issued from Joseph Stalin's country house to arrest twenty-seven writers and take them to the prison on the same day so that they can all be killed by the same burst of gunfire. Pairs of agents are to carry out the arrests simultaneously and in secrecy. Four arrests are explained in detail.

The first capture is of Vasily Korinsky, whose wife causes problems by hitting one of the arresting officers in the head. Korinsky, who would have gone along peacefully, is knocked unconscious and dragged away. The second arrest is of Moishe Bretzky, who is found, passed out, in a whorehouse. Twelve companions, dressed in the frilly boudoir garments of the brothel, help carry Bretzky to the waiting car.

The third arrest is of an eighty-one-year-old writer, Y. Zunser, whose real name is Melman. One arresting agent has had a Jewish literature instructor, so he makes an effort to be respectful. The agents are especially worried about killing him during the arrest, something they had been warned against.

The fourth arrest is of the twenty-seventh man, Pinchas Pelovits, who lives near the prison. Pinchas at first refuses to go with the agents but decides his crime must have been to have read and enjoyed Zunser's book. When Pinchas tries to bring along his notebooks, he is beaten unconscious and rolled, shoeless, into a blanket.

The story continues in the prison. The last four prisoners to arrive—Zunser, Korinsky, Bretzky, and Pinchas—are placed together in the same cell. Zunser, the eldest, expresses hope when he sees the light bulb illuminated. Korinsky complains about his personal comfort, Bretzky attempts to endure the humiliation, and Pinchas quietly works on a piece of writing he is creating while imprisoned.

The prisoners have impassioned discussions regarding writing techniques. The mood of the cell changes during a heated exchange regarding intellectual approaches to the Stalin regime. Korinsky identifies himself as a principal member of the Anti-Fascist Committee and the author of an ode, "Stalin of Silver, Stalin of Gold," a national favorite. Next, Bretzky reveals his anti-Stalin theories and identifies Zunser as a writer whose accomplishments exceeded those of any other living writer in Russia. Even though Pinchas can quote Korinsky's ode, he is elated at the thought that he is in the presence of the famous Zunser.

Another mood shift occurs after Pinchas is beaten. The guards beat Pinchas because he created a loud disturbance when he first learned that Zunser, whom he greatly admires, is imprisoned. Zunser and Bretzky exhibit their compassion when they try to help Pinchas by sharing their water and holding him while he recovers. Only Korinsky is worried that he will miss out on his ration of water.

The prisoners are then exposed to torture, and once again the mood shifts. Zunser and Pinchas hear each other's screams, but Bretzsky and Korinsky react to the torture with silence. The narrator reveals that Bretzsky cries, not from the pain he endures, but because of his realization of the human cruelty involved.

Right before the prisoners are led out to the yard to be executed, Pinchas, the unknown writer, asks if he might share a story he created while he was in the cell. Zunser and Bretzky encourage him to recite it, but Korinsky cannot understand the point of listening to it. Pinchas's gem of a story is highly regarded by Bretzky, Korinsky, and Zunser. All then file outside where the twenty-seven writers are shot simultaneously.

Themes and Meanings

Alienation, a theme in several of Nathan Englander's stories, is also evident in "The Twenty-seventh Man." The title reflects the plight of an individual; however, twenty-six others were also caught up in the Stalinist purge of Jewish writers. Although alienation usually refers to the struggle of an individual against others, the twenty-seven men are emblematic of the alienation of Jewish people in Russian society.

Another theme in this story is the struggle of the individual against society. It is pointed out that Stalin ordered the murder of the Jewish writers not because he hated them but because he questioned their loyalty. Those arrested wrote in the Yiddish language rather than in Russian. The government of a society whose members refer to one another as comrades apparently had difficulty accepting any thoughts that are not the party line.

The twenty-seven Jewish writers are identified as one unit because they are all intellectuals criticizing various issues. Although Korinsky wrote positively about Stalin's government, he was still identified among the Jewish dissident writers. The free, creative thinking of Zunser, Bretzky, and other Jewish writers was threatening to Stalin's government. The influence of the Jewish writers is reflected in Pinchas's reaction at his arrest: He thinks that merely reading Zunser is enough to justify his arrest.

Even in the inhumane setting of the prison cell, the incarcerated individuals are able to exhibit some acts of kindness to one another. Bretzky and Zunser make an effort to cover Pinchas's bare feet with their shoes and socks. They also make an effort to help Pinchas after he is beaten for acknowledging the greatness of Zunser.

Korinsky, the writer who tries to appease the Russian government by writing favorably of it, acts less kindly toward Pinchas. Even though Pinchas is able to quote Korinsky's ode by heart, it is not until they are about to be taken out into the yard to be shot that Korinsky acknowledges the significance of Pinchas's story within the story. Thus Stalin, through his error of including an additional writer in his purge, provides an emerging writer with his own private audience and his moment of recognition.

The story Pinchas tells reinforces the plight of the twenty-seven men who are about to be exterminated. The focus is on death and obedience to the rules of Jewish law. Pinchas's story has two characters, Mendel Muskatev and a rabbi. Mendel, a person in a small community, awakens to find all of his possessions missing and, thinking he has died, says a prayer for the dead. When he discovers that he is alive, he thinks he has committed a sin by saying his own death prayer and seeks his rabbi, a religious sage, to ask if he has sinned. When Mendel arrives at the rabbi's home, he finds all of his possessions in the home of the rabbi. Mendel then asks which of them should say the prayer for the dead. The question becomes: Who will say a prayer for any of them when they are all exterminated?

Style and Technique

In his postmodern rebellion against the traditional surprise endings of many modern short stories, Englander gives his short stories endings that are seemingly weak. In the case of "The Twenty-seventh Man," the story ends simply with Bretzky, one of the writers, shot several times and living long enough to realize that he has heard the guns and is dying.

Englander has been called the heir apparent to Bernard Malamud, who in turn has been called the king of the American Jewish story. Shorter forms of writing have held an important place in the works of Jewish writers such as Malamud, Shmuel Yosef Agnon, and Isaac Bashevis Singer as well as in the Yiddish literature of the nineteenth century. Englander, like Malamud, interweaves traditional and modern elements using characters who struggle in the modern world while carrying the emotional baggage of the old life.

Even though the protagonist, Pinchas, has only a few moments of recognition when he recites the story he creates in the prison cell, he seeks to prove himself worthy of being in the company of such august writers. Writing and recording are the tools of a writer's trade. The twenty-six established authors represent an eminent selection of the surviving Yiddish literary community in Europe. Pinchas represents not only the new generation of Yiddish writers but also the audience necessary to continue the existence of the Yiddish literary community. Stalin's mass execution was an attempt to destroy the future of Yiddish writing in Russia.

The use of the third-person omniscient narrator allows the reader to become a voyeur and witness these individuals' last moments. Englander uses Yiddish words without italics or explanation, as if they were common parlance among his readers. Through this technique, he incorporates Yiddish into the dominant language, ending its life as a unique, separate language, and he thereby emphasizes the deaths and end of the Yiddish writers.

A story within a story is a device that has been used effectively by many writers, including William Shakespeare. Unlike the stories of the other twenty-six writers, Pinchas's masterpiece is created and stored within his mind and is never written down. Through his creation, Pinchas has his moment of fame, which propels him into the spotlight enjoyed by the twenty-six other writers. Although Stalin had stripped everything—pen, paper, readers, publishers, and the next generation—from these writers, they retain their creative minds until their very last breaths.

Annette M. Magid

TWENTY-SIX MEN AND A GIRL

Author: Maxim Gorky (Aleksey Maksimovich Peshkov, 1868-1936)
Type of plot: Social realism
Time of plot: The late 1890's
Locale: Provincial Russian town
First published: "Dvadtsat'shest' i odna," 1899 (English translation, 1902)

Principal characters:
A GROUP OF UNNAMED PRETZEL MAKERS
TANYA, a sixteen-year-old seamstress
A HANDSOME BAKER, a former soldier

The Story

Maxim Gorky begins this first-person narrative with a description of a wretched working environment: a basement-level bakery where twenty-six men, "living machines," as the narrator calls them, work long hours making pretzels. The room is cramped, airless, and stuffy. The huge oven that dominates the room stares pitilessly at the workers like a horrible monster. The workers themselves move and act like automatons, for their vital feelings have been crushed by their ceaseless toil. Only when they begin to sing do they feel a sense of lightness and gain a glimpse of freedom.

In addition to their singing, the twenty-six workers have one other source of consolation. Every morning, a sixteen-year-old seamstress named Tanya stops by the workshop to ask for pretzels. To these grim, coarse men, the cheerful girl seems a precious treasure, and her regular visits gradually make her a sacred being to them. As the narrator notes, all humans need something to worship; Tanya thus has become their idol. Although the men often make rude jokes about women, they never once consider viewing Tanya with anything other than the highest respect.

This situation, however, is not destined to last. A new man, a former soldier, is hired at the bakery next door, and this fellow turns out to be a dashing, bold figure who enjoys regaling the twenty-six pretzel makers with tales of his prowess with women. The pretzel makers find him an engaging individual, but his boasting touches a sensitive nerve. The head baker rashly suggests that not all women would fall prey to the boaster's charms. This assertion pricks the dandy's vanity, and he presses the baker to name the person who could resist his attentions. Angrily, the baker mutters Tanya's name, and the dandy immediately announces that he will seduce the girl within two weeks.

The pretzel makers are highly agitated by the dandy's challenge, and they become obsessed with the question of whether Tanya will indeed be able to spurn the man. Imperceptibly, this new element of curiosity and inquisitiveness creeps into their relationship with Tanya, and on the final day of the two-week period they understand for the first time how much they have put on the line through this foolish rivalry with the dandy. When Tanya makes her regular visit that morning, they greet her with silence, and after an awkward exchange of words, she runs out without her pretzels. Later, the dashing baker enters and instructs the workers to keep their eye on the cellar door across the yard from their building. Horrified, the men watch as Tanya and the baker go into the cellar. After an anxious interval, they see the baker emerge, followed a short time later by Tanya, with eyes shining in joy and happiness.

For the pretzel makers this is unbearable. They rush out of their building, surround Tanya, and begin to abuse her loudly with crude obscenities and insults. As they see it, she has let them down and betrayed them, and they will make her pay for this misdeed. However, after bearing their jeers with astonishment for a few moments, she suddenly flares up in anger herself. Proudly she begins to walk away, breaking through their circle as if they were not even present. Turning toward them, she calls them scum, and then, proud, erect, and beautiful, she leaves them behind forever. The workers must now return to their underground prison to work as before, but they have lost the one precious human element in their otherwise dreary world.

Themes and Meanings

Dominating the first part of the story is Gorky's sympathy for the plight of the downtrodden workers in Russia. His initial description of the bakers accentuates the oppressive effects that a life of relentless toil can have on the human spirit. His pretzel makers seem barely human. Deprived of sunlight and freedom, they have nothing to say to one another, and they do not even have the energy to curse one another. Even their songs, which are the only vehicle of transcendence or release that they possess, are permeated with the sorrow and yearning of slaves.

Complementing Gorky's compassion for the oppressed is his anger toward the oppressor. The pretzel makers' boss is never seen in the story. He seems to exist as an invincible force who has placed numerous restrictions on the workers but who does not deign even to visit them. Instead, the huge stove which looms so large in the bakery stands as a silent emblem for the boss and his rapacious, insatiable appetite. All he cares for is productivity: during the two-week period in which the workers were preoccupied with the dandy's pursuit of Tanya, the boss managed to increase their work by an additional five hundred pounds of flour a day.

Gorky's story offers more than an exposé of difficult working conditions in prerevolutionary Russia. His treatment of the complex emotional attitude demonstrated by the workers toward Tanya reveals a sensitive understanding of human psychology. In the workers' early reverence for Tanya one finds a basic human desire for objects worthy of adoration, and in their willingness to subject their idol to a test one sees a characteristic human weakness: a perverse impulse to submit one's idols to outside challenges. As for the dandy, Gorky indicates that his eagerness to prove his power as a ladies' man belies a deep-rooted sense of insecurity. Many people, the narrator declares, are so needy of having something distinctive in their lives that they will even embrace an illness or a vice rather than risk seeming average or ordinary.

Finally, in the workers' outraged reaction to Tanya's conduct at the end of the story, Gorky reveals the astonishing excesses to which people will go when their cherished assumptions are undermined or overturned. Tanya never asked these men to put her on a pedestal, nor did she ever pledge not to become infatuated with an attractive man. It is they who engineered a shallow test for her, and, as the final scene of the story indicates, it is they who are acting basely, not she. Tanya herself perceives this, and thus she walks away proud and undefiled, while they are left alone, bitter and abandoned. Gorky's story is filled with pathos and irony. Weighed down by the burdens of oppressive labor and confinement, these men make a feeble attempt to demonstrate that they possess something of worth in the midst of their wretched environment. As it turns out, however, this gesture only contributes further to their inescapable misery.

Style and Technique

The emotionally charged style of "Twenty-six Men and a Girl" is characteristic of Gorky's early narrative prose. The writer reveals a predilection for dramatic, bold metaphors and imagery, such as the huge oven, which he compares to the ugly head of a fantastic monster and which stares pitilessly at the workers as if they were slaves. Gorky's descriptions often have a sustained symbolic resonance. At the outset of the story, the narrator notes that the basement windows are covered so that the sunlight cannot reach the workers. Later, he states that Tanya had in some sense taken the place of the sun for them. It is significant, then, that the day on which Tanya consummates her relationship with the dandy turns out to be wet and rainy. On that day, the workers lose their sun, both literally and figuratively.

Gorky's emotional style also manifests itself in the passage about the workers' singing. His prose in that section is extremely lyrical and rhythmic. The Russian lines pulsate with a palpable beat, and one observes a complex interweaving of recurring consonant and vowel sounds. This lyrical, dynamic dimension apparent in Gorky's early prose style had a significant impact on the prose of the subsequent generation of Russian writers.

Julian W. Connolly

TWO BLUE BIRDS

Author: D. H. Lawrence (1885-1930)
Type of plot: Domestic realism
Time of plot: The early twentieth century
Locale: England
First published: 1927

Principal characters:
CAMERON GEE, a novelist and literary journalist
HIS WIFE
MISS WREXALL, his secretary

The Story

Cameron Gee, a modestly successful literary figure, has been married for several years. For the last three or four years, he and his wife have found it impossible to live together for any length of time, so his wife has taken to spending long holidays in a warmer country, where she carries on discreet love affairs. Gee makes no objections, however, and they seem satisfied with their arrangement. They have a strong attachment to each other but simply cannot live together happily. Busy with his literary work, the husband is helped by Miss Wrexall, an efficient and adoring female secretary, and his home is run by her mother and sister. The long absences of his wife seem irrelevant to Gee, both personally and professionally.

The story focuses on an occasion when the wife is home for a short time; she considers Gee's domestic and professional arrangements and finds them disturbing. She suggests that the secretary is making things too easy for her husband and that his work is suffering as a result of the complaisant way in which the secretary and her family make his life too comfortable. She has no wish to participate in the family, however, and finds the tepid, nonsexual nature of the arrangements between the master and his secretary depressing. When she accuses her husband of abusing the loyalty and adoration of his employee, Miss Wrexall becomes alarmed and protests that the arrangements are both acceptable and innocent, and that she is assured by Gee that he, too, finds their unfeeling relation to his liking. Gee's smug acceptance of the situation at the end of the story seems to suggest that his wife may be right to despise him, and that Miss Wrexall is not telling the full truth. Unmoved by his wife's criticism, Gee has no plan to change the way he lives, or the kind of service that he has come to expect from his servants—especially from his young secretary.

Themes and Meanings

D. H. Lawrence was always interested in problems of male-female relationships, not only in terms of their grander, more romantic implications, but also in their often subtler nuances and details. This story is particularly interesting to a late-twentieth century reader because it involves not only the difficulty of men and women learning to live together, but also the nature of the roles that women and men play as individuals, both in and out of matrimony, and the ways in which male-female connections impinge on, and sometimes distort, female aspirations.

In the early years of the twentieth century, Lawrence understood that English middle-class society expected women to be satisfied with the role of patient supporters of their husbands in their public careers. The fact that Mrs. Gee knows she is temperamentally unable to fulfill that role has something to do with her inability to live with her husband. What the story reveals, however, is that she cannot see any role for herself, other than to indulge in idle love affairs. She has, in a sense, no awareness of herself as an independent personality. She has little interest in her husband's career, although she is concerned that it is not quite as good as it ought to be, and she is sensitive to the kind of relationship with which he is most comfortable. One would think, therefore, that she might attempt to terminate this odd and somewhat tasteless arrangement. She is honest enough to know it is not what she wants, but she seems to think that her only alternative is to continue as Gee's wife, if in name only, and expect him to support her, and to accept her superficial dalliances, out of sight, and out of mind. There is something ignoble about the conduct of both parties.

Miss Wrexall, the secretary, is less to blame, if her supine adoration of her employer suggests that she, too, should get out of his employ as quickly as possible. When Lawrence wrote this story the opportunities for women were limited, and the general ideas about females and careers, and about relations between men and women, were considerably narrower than they became late in the twentieth century. Lawrence was notorious for being too frank and imaginative in his exploration of sexual themes, and this simple, seemingly innocent tale of marital pusillanimity is an example of how far he was ahead of his time in dealing with the problem in one of the more banal areas of how people try to live their lives within the confines of social convention when they are obviously unsuited to do so.

Style and Technique

Lawrence uses a disarmingly simple style for this tale of marital discord. It is not only appropriate in terms of allowing for a clearheaded examination of the Gee marriage, but it is also a succinct comment on the emotional tepidity with which the couple deal with their situation. The style reflects the lack of emotional commitment. The Gees are sensible, intelligent, and understanding; what they are not is passionate. Only at the end of the story does Mrs. Gee, for a short time, seem to have her feelings fully engaged, when she rejects the idea of being one of the blue birds fawning at the feet of her husband. The two blue-tits (an English breed of finch) may seem too obtrusively symbolic. The intrusion of battling male birds, with the suggestion of sexual competition, is an obvious symbol, made even more obvious by Mrs. Gee remarking on it in her determination to stop any suspicion that she might want to be part of this unhealthy competition for her husband's attention.

Lawrence is less heavy-handed in his use of luxuriant flowers to suggest a self-indulgent Eden in which Gee lolls about with his adoring secretary at his feet. He is even defter in the way in which he has Miss Wrexall change into a silk dress of a color similar to that of the wife's, when she is invited to take tea with the couple. The secretary's suggestion that her dress is not quite as smart as that worn by Mrs. Gee is a juxtaposed symbol of what the contending women have to offer their lord and master. Mrs. Gee immediately retorts that smart or not, the secretary's dress was, at least, paid for with hard-earned money, while she has done nothing to deserve her own. Lawrence's wittiness, which is often overlooked, appears immediately on this exchange, when Mrs. Gee's question about the tea, "You like it strong?" seems as much a threat as an innocent question as to how the secretary prefers her tea. There is, in fact, a good deal of threatening ambiguity in conversations, particularly in those between the Gees, which suggests that they are a match for each other in cool toughness. There is much left unsaid, which is being implied by these two sophisticated people who well know how to take care of themselves verbally—in ways that anticipate those in which playwright Harold Pinter later saw the middle classes. The Gees use language as a lethal instrument to dominate, irritate, and triumph, however empty a victory may be.

Only for a wry instant does the bird image hold possibilities of romance as Mrs. Gee catches sight of the first blue bird, but the lawn is soon invaded by the second bird, and the aptness of its arrival takes over. It is, in short, a very mean-spirited tale, and it might be suggested that its two birds are not exclusively to be seen as the two women, but sometimes as Mr. and Mrs. Gee.

Structurally, the story has three parts. It begins at a distance in the voice of a third-party narrator, who seems to be socially and morally at one with the Gees. The voice does not judge, nor is it on one side or the other. Then it becomes closely identified with the point of view of the wife, putting her reactions into context in a general consideration of the relationship, but again the tone is cool. Lawrence narrows the field once again, reverting to the third-person narrator relating the quite specific story of the encounter in the garden, with occasional intrusions into the mind of the wife. The voice is restrained, and the action reported with discretion—fastidious, watchful, and nonjudgmental.

The story has something of the shape of a scientific examination of an insect. First on the wing, then in the hand, and finally on the head of a pin—all without feeling, as befits the sour story of the Gee marriage. It is as much an exercise in tone as it is in incident, and its tone is, in part, its meaning.

Charles Pullen

MASTERPLOTS II

SHORT STORY SERIES
REVISED EDITION

TITLE INDEX